Understanding Theories of Religion

To Rebecca Harkin
the best imaginable editor an author could have:
encouraging, critical, and inspiring

Understanding Theories of Religion

An Introduction

SECOND EDITION

Ivan Strenski

WILEY Blackwell

This second edition first published 2015
© 2015 Ivan Strenski

Edition history: Blackwell Publishing Ltd (1e, 2006)

Registered Office
John Wiley & Sons, Ltd, The Atrium, Southern Gate, Chichester, West Sussex, PO19 8SQ, UK

Editorial Offices
350 Main Street, Malden, MA 02148-5020, USA
9600 Garsington Road, Oxford, OX4 2DQ, UK
The Atrium, Southern Gate, Chichester, West Sussex, PO19 8SQ, UK

For details of our global editorial offices, for customer services, and for information about how to apply for permission to reuse the copyright material in this book please see our website at www.wiley.com/wiley-blackwell.

The right of Ivan Strenski to be identified as the author of this work has been asserted in accordance with the UK Copyright, Designs and Patents Act 1988.

Library of Congress Cataloging-in-Publication Data

Strenski, Ivan.
   [Thinking about religion]
   Understanding theories of religion / Ivan Strenski. – Second edition.
      pages   cm
   Revised editon of Thinking about religion / Ivan Strenski. 2006.
   Includes bibliographical references and index.
   ISBN 978-1-4443-3084-7 (pbk.)
   1. Religion–Methodology.   I. Title.
   BL41.S72 2015
   200.7–dc23

                                   2014024544

A catalogue record for this book is available from the British Library.

Cover image: © pashabo / Shutterstock
Cover design by Nicki Averill Design & Illustration

Set in 9.5/11.5pt Minion by SPi Publisher Services, Pondicherry, India

1   2015

Contents

Preface to the Second Edition: Understanding, Instead of Just Thinking   vii

1   Introduction: Understanding Theories of Religion Is Better than Just Being Critical   1

Part I   The Prehistory of the Study of Religion: Responses to an Expanding World   7

2   Jean Bodin and Herbert of Cherbury: True Religion, Essential Religion, and Natural Religion   9

3   Understanding Religion Also Began with Trying to Understand the Bible   19

Part II   Classic Nineteenth-Century Theorists of the Study of Religion: The Quest for the Origins of Religion in History   31

4   Max Müller, the Comparative Study of Religion, and the Search for Other Bibles in India   33

5   The Shock of the "Savage": Edward Burnett Tylor, Evolution, and Spirits   45

6   The Religion of the Bible Evolves: William Robertson Smith   55

7   Setting the Eternal Templates of Salvation: James Frazer   65

Part III   Classic Twentieth-Century Theorists of the Study of Religion: Defending the Inner Sanctum of Religious Experience or Storming It   75

8   Understanding How to Understand Religion: "Phenomenology of Religion"   77

9   How Religious Experience Created Capitalism: Max Weber   93

10   Tales from the Underground: Freud and the Psychoanalytic Origins of Religion   106

11   Bronislaw Malinowski and the "Sublime Folly" of Religion   118

12   Seeing God with the Social Eye: Durkheim's Religious Sociology   129

13   Mircea Eliade: Turning Back the "Worm of Doubt"   142

**Part IV Liberation and Post-Modernism: Race, Gender, Post-Colonialism,
            the Discourse on Power**   **155**

14 From Modernism to Post-Modernism: Mostly Michel Foucault   157

15 Theorizing Religion with Race in Mind: Prophecy or Curiosity?   171

16 Sex/Gender and Women: Feminists Theorizing Religion   189

17 Another "Otherness": Post-Colonial Theories of Religion   216

18 Conclusion: Being "Smart" about Bringing "Religion" Back In   241

Index   254

Preface to the Second Edition: Understanding, Instead of Just Thinking

This is the second edition of *Thinking about Religion*, now retitled *Understanding Theories of Religion*. This new edition slightly trims the original, but adds an entire new part, containing four new chapters and a new conclusion. So, given the substantial extent of these additions, I thought it best retitle the book to bring out better a key aspect of the original. There, I emphasized the remarkable fact that at some time in the history of early modern Europe, a few rare individuals systematically began doing something radically different with what one and all assumed was a special feature of their lives – religion. They could be said to have begun thinking about religion, instead of just believing. This is not to say that those who did such thinking stopped believing, merely that they did more. And this brings me to the reason for the new title. In taking the original, often brave, step of taking religion as an object of human inquiry and curiosity, they wanted to give an account of religion. They wanted to understand it, and often to explain it. Religion became something these pioneers of human consciousness wanted to hold up for thoughtful consideration – and finally, to understand or explain.

At the same time, the founders also assumed a certain identity to this object of their discourse, called "religion." Religion was for them a natural object, like other objects of their world – nature, the economy, arts, music, politics, and other dimensions of human life. That these categories emerged at certain points in history, and in certain places, was something of which, they, on the whole, were unaware. Of course, in our own time, we resist seeing these objects of knowledge as "natural kinds," independent of the way the knowing subject decided to carve up the world of experience. Except for rare cases, it would have been unthinkable to contest the definitions of such categories, such "objects." We, on the other hand, rightly in my view, assume a "critical" attitude to these categories of human experience. We are thus, also, loath to think of them naively as "out there," objective realities unconnected to the way people in a certain part of the world live. The modern critical attitude entails that we believe that categories are historical and geographical – they emerged at a certain time, in a certain place. Religion today is seen in the same way, spawning an entire literature about the precise time and place of its origins as a term or category of thought.

Since this side of the critical study of religion may seem remote and abstruse to many readers, let me suggest an analogy to help convey the point I am making about how the modern critical attitude to categories differs from the point of view of most of the theorists in Parts I–III of this book. Perhaps what I mean by pointing out the emergent character of religion can be seen in the analogy of the category of "gay" to signify a distinctive class of sexuality. Consider alone how in the lifetimes of many readers of this book this category emerged into general usage. For many, to be gay simply names an objective state of a person's sexuality. It is not something, for example, that can be cured or "prayed away." But to these folks one needs to say that the category or term – as currently understood – has not always existed, and that people everywhere and at all times did not have such a notion in mind. As a category of sexuality, it is a distinctly Western notion, whose origin can be traced to no earlier than the end of the nineteenth century. So there's a historical or subjective side to the concept to match the conviction that there really are objectively, and "out there," gay people. "Religion" is just like "gay." Readers need, then, to note this: Today, we and the theorists of Part IV, as we will see, tend to take the subjective, critical and historical character of the term "religion" as decisive, while the thinkers of Parts I–III see "religion" as the name of an objective, natural kind that they discovered.

Thus, although I realize I am running somewhat against the current of the age in celebrating the founders for what some would say was naivety, I continue to have deep appreciation for them. Their efforts were aimed at understanding something they thought was a natural part of their world – religion – rather than either just accepting its practice or even idly thinking about it. And, besides, even those who approach the term "gay" historically surely don't think that real gays don't exist in the world outside our critical efforts. The new title of this volume thus also reflects my admiration for the attempts by the founders to *understand* religion, instead of just adhering to it mindlessly.

The new material in Part IV also prompted me to change the title. This book has never been conceived as an encyclopedia, which partly explains the absence of a number of well-known theorists in the study of religion, such as J.Z. Smith, W.C. Smith, William James, or even Clifford Geertz. I was determined not just to tag on theorists to an ever longer list. I am arguing that a theoretical *trajectory* can be discerned in the study of religion as it has come to be institutionalized in departments of religious studies. The present volume is, then, more like John F. Kennedy's book *Profiles in Courage* than an exhaustive *Who's Who* in the study of religion. I have done some controversial

selection, including some theorists, but also, to the displeasure of some readers, excluding others. But any book such as the present one will perforce do the same, unless it is to result in a massive encyclopedia, which no publisher could afford to sell and few students afford to purchase. I invite those who disagree with my construction of the history of the study of religion to join with me in debate. What I offer, I am prepared to argue, is a possible trajectory. I welcome critics who wish to take issue with my proposals.

For this reason, I decided to mark what I am arguing has been a radical historical shift of register in the theoretical study of religion. This is the shift to "post-modern" styles of inquiry that I argue, again, can best be understood in dialectic tension with the trajectory and character of the theories in the first three parts of this book. Part IV has been added to mark this change of register. Part IV is not about stringing another theory or two along the same thread as the original. Rather, it signals what for many in our field believe to be a Kuhnian paradigm shift. Here readers will find four additional chapters, one each on religion and post-modernism, race, sex/gender and the post-colonial condition, respectively. I have added a new conclusion to round things out.

But Part IV does not, as I have said, stand alone as if it had nothing to do with the classic theorists of the past. Therefore, readers will find that Part IV integrates post-modern theories of religion with those "modern" and "early modern" theories treated in *Thinking about Religion*. Post-modern theorizing of the last quarter of the twentieth century fits into a pattern with the classic "early modern" and "modern" theories of religion, dating from the sixteenth through the mid-twentieth centuries, respectively. Just how they do is something readers will have to find out for themselves. I trust readers will also find the new versions of the original Parts I–III somewhat tighter and more condensed. In the new Part IV, they will find what I hope is a recognizable and welcome extension of the method followed in the original to many of the latest theoretical trends in the study of religion.

A few more words about Part IV. Readers will find the length of the three principal chapters of Part IV – chapters 15–17 – much greater on average than comparable chapters in Parts I–III. Their extensive length reflects the explosion of scholarship in the study of religion in the last third of the twentieth century up to the present. Most chapters in Parts I–III center about the theorizing of single individuals. But, in our day religious studies have arrived, and scholarly production has exploded. There are, without doubt, more scholars studying religion today, and more who explicitly identify with the academic study of religion, than ever before in the history of the West, if not the world. One naturally faces the daunting task of doing justice to the immense quantity that has been written. Similarly, the history of these theories is harder to read, in part because insufficient time has elapsed to assess their overall position in the sweep of theoretical approaches to the study of religion. However, I have still been guided by the key question, "Why did they think they were right?", and shall pursue it throughout as ardently as data will allow. So, too, I will not be shy about arguing why I think a theory is *wrong*, as I have in early discussions. But overall I try to maintain consistency over the course of 200,000 words of text. I look critically at the validity of theories, yet still organize my thinking around the same question that shaped the first edition: "Why did they think they were right?"

IVAN STRENSKI
LOS ANGELES

Introduction: Understanding Theories of Religion Is Better than Just Being Critical

A New Kind of Method and Theory Book

This is not "your mother or father's" method and theory book. Thinkers who made a big difference in the way we study religion today still lead the way, but with a difference. Competent as several other theory books may be, I feel they leave us uniformed about how and why our leading theories came to be. Yes, we all want to know what's *wrong* with a theory. But should we be satisfied with just cutting up a theory? What about how a theory was woven together, built up, brick by brick, and so on? Unless we get deep inside the minds of theorists – unless we really *understand* them – we cannot hope to do them and the high-order act of theorizing justice. I believe that unless we know why they thought they were right we risk making an empty academic game of the study of theories of religion. Finally, the approach I have been trying to teach in this book entails asking why a theorist thought they were right in going down a certain path. Answers to this question may, in turn, arise from considerations internal to a line of thinking, typically to the world of ideas circulating in a certain field of study or academic profession. But the external context of a thinker's life – the political, cultural, social, religious world in which they live – may

also incline a theorist to think they were right to advance a given theoretical idea.

In the preface to this second edition, I also mentioned recognizing major epistemological breaks in theorizing, such as that between modern and post-modern. I shall argue that theories develop dialectically, according to a logic worked out in history. Theories "speak" to other theories in a kind of conversation with one another. In this light, I am arguing that the new chapters of Part IV on race, feminism, and post-colonialism carry on the conversation theorists in the study of religion have been having for the past 400 years. The story of theory in our field is not, then, a piecemeal and unhistorical serialization of theories, as if they pop up one at a time, here and there, and in no particular relation to one another. What makes the history of theories of religion in the West like none other is the existence of this centuries-long conversation. Thus, while it is vital to recognize classic thinkers from Muslim, Indian, or Chinese civilizations who took a critical, and often comparative, look at religion, their efforts did not add up to a *tradition* of critical and comparative study of religion. They shot across a sky of discourse like blazing comets, burning brightly, soon to flame out. They failed to ignite the kind of centuries-long controversies that are

Understanding Theories of Religion: An Introduction, Second Edition. Ivan Strenski.
© 2015 Ivan Strenski. Published 2015 by John Wiley & Sons, Ltd.

the stuff of the study of religion as we have come to know it in the West. I am finally, then, arguing that the key to a good theory book is finding the connecting threads in that long conversation. Both *Thinking about Religion* and, now, *Understanding Theories of Religion* do this by calling attention to the historical dialectic at work shaping the production of theories of religion.

In treating theories of religion, I am convinced that we have an enormous amount to learn, not only about the past, but also about how we should study religion today. By seeing how our field came about from its classic historical beginnings, we situate ourselves within a long, meandering stream of thinking reaching back to the dawn of the modern era. This takes us back to the childhood of religious studies, a time when people were just discovering the different religions for the first time. What was it like in the minds of our field's heroes when they met religions unknown up to that point? What was it like when many heretofore unknown peoples of the world first came to know each other? What was it like at first contact? The original edition, *Thinking about Religion*, told us about these first and subsequent contacts. Working away, mostly in secret, to avoid religious persecution, early modern theorist Jean Bodin put together the first dialogue of religions where the religions spoke to each other as *equals*. Assembling believers of many different sorts – not only Christians and Jews, but Muslims too, Bodin let them challenge the credentials and validity of each other's claims to the truth. Just think what Bodin would have done had he known of the Buddhists, Hindus, Native Americans, and Australian or African native folk, as later modern or post-modern theorists would? But Bodin had had no contact with them. We had not yet introduced ourselves to each other. By the eighteenth century, our theorists represent thinkers who had now had that further contact with the many other peoples of the world. Friedrich Max Müller made the religions of India his specialty, and put forward his broad comparative theory of religion that embraced India and the West under one single rubric. How different then from Bodin's was this new world that Max Müller opened up, when he extended the study of religion to the religions of India? That first contact, as we will see, exploded conventional thinking about the nature of religion in ways we have still perhaps not yet digested. Max Müller spoke of an "Aryan Bible," and threw open questions about the uniqueness of Abrahamic revelation like none before him. Students still query whether Buddhism can be called a religion, because a god does not occupy its center. Another first contact, here with the archeological remains of the Neolithic ancestors of modern peoples, drove the efforts of anthropologists like E. B. Tylor or Sir James Frazer. Not only did they seek to extend the history of humanity far beyond contemporary imaginings, but their progressive evolutionary vision of the human past reacted dialectically to Max Müller's diffusionist story of humanity's decline from a religious golden age.

In this new edition, I update the results of those earlier first contacts and incorporate post-modern approaches – in a broad sense of the term – in Part IV. Doing so permits us to have what we might call dialectical second looks at the entire archive of data of the study of religion given us by the classic modernist theorists, but now through eyes of the post-modern critics of modernist theory. In a way, the entirety of Part IV can be read as a systematic taking apart of the foundations upon which the major theorists of the past have stood – especially the modernists Weber, Freud, Malinowski, Durkheim, and Eliade.

These newly added chapters on post-modern theories of religion showcase a clear and thorough dialectic reaction to the modernist theoretical trends of the past. These primarily deal with religion in terms of issues that particularly vex us in ways ignored by modernist theories. Against modernist claims of scientific objectivity and neutrality, the post-modernists assert a concern for human dignity, social justice, and the victims of a globalized world. Themes such as power, race, sex/gender, and global social justice run through these theories like a bright red thread. Post-modern theorists would, accordingly, be prompted to raise such questions as whether, for example, Tylor would have referred to the folk of traditional societies as "savages" or "primitive" had he not been comfortably ensconced in the seat of imperial power. Or would Eliade have written of "religious *man*" had he been more sensitive to the way classic theorists overlooked sex/gender in the make-up of the religious world? In reaching all the way back to the past and concluding with the present, theorizing about religion shows both longevity and vitality. We own a marvelously rich tradition of scholarship. Like some luxurious oriental carpet, theory in the study of religion has, over many centuries, been woven together out of a dialectical arrangement of contrasting and complementary intellectual threads into something rich.

There is also a second way this method and theory book departs from conventional ways of studying theories. I absolutely *love* theory and theorizing. I think it is one of the finest acts we can perform as thinkers. But it is not a game. Therefore, to me, doing theory is not just the analysis of ideas, or a contest to see who is the sharpest knife in the drawer. It is about showcasing a worldview, telling an important story, engaging an often dramatic clash of ideas. As such, theories have their "internal" and "external" contexts. They are formed within an internal intellectual context of a disciplinary or academic craft, where one member of the craft speaks to another. At some point, musicians or mathematicians can only talk to other musicians or mathematicians, because only a narrow sliver of humanity can master their refined, specialized languages. Nevertheless, musicians *perform* for audiences, often illiterate in their special language: music *connects* because it taps into larger emotional networks, external to the disciplined world of the musician. What makes music work is its ability to connect with the totality of human life external to the special language of music. That is why I also insist upon studying the formation of theories within a wider, external, context defined by the political, religious, sexual, esthetic worlds that we all inhabit.

Beyond saying what a theory is, the study of theories of religion is about accounting for how and why theories actually came to be. Part of my answer to this question of how theories came to be resides in life itself. That is why I have brought in the external context of theorizing – the network of politics, religion, esthetics, etc., – that often weighs on theorists in the formation of their theories. Theories, thus, emerge to some degree from attempts to make sense of the world and our place in it. More than just smart, a good theory also evinces wisdom and wide experience of life in all its diversity. Theories have implications beyond the classroom or seminar, shaping the way we see life overall. Thus, theories and worldviews are often hard to tell apart. Malinowski, for example, wrote some of the first books about sexual practices among faraway tribal folk, but he was also active in the early days of Planned Parenthood. Do we really think we could – or should – separate these "external" interests in sex from his overall "internal" intellectual and professional theoretical perspective on religion? I don't think so. In my chapter on Malinowski, readers will discover why.

Teachers are always pleased if students are smart about theories, and can master their logic. Jumping through the mental hoops of explaining a theory and pointing out its strengths and weaknesses are basic skills. But I look for more than cleverness in a student, more than the ability to rack up good scores in an exam, or even to get the right answer. I look for students ready to study theory in quite another spirit. I look for students moved by real curiosity who try to understand why theorists thought they were right about their theoretical proposals. In brief, I look for students who want to understand theory and theorists! This book will invite students to dive into the lives and times of theorists to see how theories emerged from a picture of why they thought certain ideas were "right." Let's begin.

From Religion to the "Problems of Religion"

Understanding Theories of Religion takes its stand squarely on the importance of understanding how and why people have come to *think* about religion, and how they try variously to understand or explain it. Everybody knows that people can often be passionate, even violently so, about religion, either for or against. Many Christians feel that the imperative to "preach the gospel to all nations" weighs heavily upon them. That is why is, along with Buddhism, Christianity is the most successful of all missionary religions. For these Christians, religion is so charged with emotion that it bubbles over in zealous energy to proselytize. But someone might note that powerful emotions do not accompany the missionizing enterprise of Buddhism, nor is its spread impelled by a strong imperative. Instead, Buddhists get especially emotional when they feel under threat of attack or elimination. Protecting the key

Buddhist institutions, such as the *Sangha*, then becomes an overriding imperative. This book too lives by passion. In the theorists we study, I want to convey their thirst to know and understand, their reckless lust for truth and obsession with curiosity. I want us as well to experience for ourselves something of their relentless impulse to question and doubt.

People may have been believers or just have "lived" their religions from time immemorial. But the characters in this book were the first who subjected religion to questioning and curiosity. They submitted religion to endless systematic interrogation in the quest to understand and explain this seemingly unexplainable and mysterious aspect of life. In a way, they truly made "religion" emerge. What, for example, was the first religion? How does it compare to the religions of our day? Are there religions elsewhere than in the West? Or is religion a univocal, culturally-specific term that cannot be employed outside the West? How has religion been employed as means of resistance to domination? How does a religion articulate with the nation-state"? Does religion change – say, according to any regular principles that we might discover, such as evolution or degeneration? Is religion essentially private or instead essentially social (Strenski 2003)? The attempt to solve these and similar problems marks the beginning of what we call *theories*. This is not to say that in the spotty history of human curiosity these questions never occurred to believers. It is only to say that until fairly recently there were no major books or treatises, no sustaining institutions or "schools," no lasting cultural influences in the forms of lines of inquiry or major questions about religion. And as schools of mathematics and the scientific study of language developed first in ancient India, and not in, say, Frankish Europe, so also was it in the West that the study of religion as we know it came to be. The study of religion came to be because religion itself became the object of questions and problems in some sustained way. That is why this book places so much emphasis on *understanding* theories and theorists: why did they think they were right?"

British cultural critic Terry Eagleton catches the spirit of our book. He explains that the appearance of theories indicates the existence of perceived "*problems*" – that "something is amiss." Problems of religion pop up like those dreaded small bumps on the neck, warning us that all is not well in the religious world (Eagleton 1990). Theories aim to fix these problems by explaining how and why they occur. In the modern West, we have experienced a rash of such questioning and what Eagleton calls "a really virulent outbreak of theory," something indeed "on an epidemic scale" (Eagleton 1990). This epidemic of problems of religion has ignited intense theorizing about religion that has conspicuously engaged practically every major Western thinker of any note since the 1500s – Spinoza, Locke, Hume, Kant, Hegel, Marx, Durkheim, Max Müller, Freud, and, into our own day, figures like Ninian Smart, Charles Long, Caroline Walker Bynum, or Bruce Lincoln. *Understanding Theories of Religion* is about trying to understand and explain this "epidemic" of theorizing about religion. What are the reasons – intellectual, social, and cultural – why the great figures in the study of religion bothered to theorize about religion? Why did these thinkers believe that they were right in giving their particular answers to the many problems of religion?

Like other aspects of life, such as society, culture, art, and economic concerns, religion became the object of a disciplined academic program of self-reflection – what can be called "science." Only in the past century and a half has there been anything called a "science of religion." Although we tend not to use the term these days, it is still the normal way the study of religion is identified, for example in France, where the *sciences religieuses* can claim a solid history of over a century and a half. Likewise, in the German-speaking world under its formidable-sounding title, *Religionswissenschaft* holds sway, as it does in the Netherlands, as we will see, in the title of the Dutch scholar Cornelis P. Tiele's major work, *Elements of the Science of Religion*, itself inspired by Max Müller's project for a "Science of Religion" at Oxford. All these represent major and deliberate efforts to go beyond belief, and even to go beyond everyday curiosity about religion. If this situation were otherwise, we would have to explain why the documentary evidence for a "natural" or much earlier disciplined and systematic study of religion is simply non-existent.

Until the time thinkers started studying religion in order to understand and explain it, studying religion was the main business of the religions themselves. Their intellectual efforts served the special needs of religious communities. Shakers, for example, worried about how they might expand their membership. Muslims meditated about whether their chief leadership should be confined to blood relatives of Muhammad. Roman Catholics disputed among themselves about how to deal with the role of women and the like.

While the problems that the individual religions wrestled with were real problems, they were "in-house" problems. They were not the kind of problems that mattered to any and all religions, or for religion *as religion*. Shakers, Muslims, or Catholics may well have had their problems, but they were those only afflicting Shakers, Muslims, and Catholics, respectively. As such, the answers offered for their problems were not like scientific theories, since they did not need to appeal to the broad range of human belief and experience. Shakers did not have to satisfy Catholics about the answer they gave to their own "in-house" Shaker problems, and vice versa. But the theories we will study did need to speak across sectarian and religious lines. These theories needed to speak about issues of understanding and explaining. They had to appeal to the broadest consensus about the nature of facts, evidence, and such that they could. The new studies of religion had therefore to be in some sense objective and subjective at the same time. *Subjective* states and experiences were part of the data of religion. Visions of Jesus were data as much as a lock of his hair. The study of religion was *objective* in the sense that anyone of any religious persuasion, in principle, could agree on what the data were. Jesus may or many not be Lord, but the date of his birth is a datum. Flowing from this ideal of a common world of data, the study of religion was *comparative* in the sense that no religion could be privileged, and all religious facts mattered equally.

But Why *Did* They Think That They Were Right?

My way of tying the great theorists together is to ask each of them, in effect, *why they thought they were right* about the answers they gave the problems of religion. Why were their theories the right ones? In this way, *Understanding Theories of Religion* differs fundamentally from most other treatments of theories in the study of religion. Most other treatments are obsessed with showing why the great theorists were *wrong*. While this volume is critical about the major theories, it is more than that. I concentrate on why they thought they were right because I think we can learn much more by this approach than by a relentlessly negative one. This does not mean that I am a relativist who believes that all theories and methods are equally true. There are real flaws in any theory. But I have yet to meet the perfect "Prince Charming" of theories that waits to carry us off to some intellectual paradise. In the absence of this charming Prince, and since making the flaws in theories our main preoccupation is sterile, I have opted for another way. Once we get over the idea of a Prince Charming and once we have exposed the weakness or fatal flaws of a theory, what have we finally accomplished? Do we draw the conclusion that theorizing is a relatively worthless activity, since any theory can have holes shot in it? Do we scorn theorizing in the same way biblical Creationists disparage Darwinian evolution, because it is, after all, "only a theory"? Or, if we still think theorizing may be a worthy activity, what have we learnt about how theories actually come to be – and thus perhaps how we ourselves might construct them – merely by shooting holes in them, or by cutting them up? Every course in methods and theories that I know seems to conclude by leaving a trail of wreckage – a littered scene of disabled or terminated theories breathing their last. Is this what we really want as the end result of our critical inquiry into theories of religion? *Understanding Theories of Religion* was written and conceived in the belief that those who value theorizing in the study of religion want *more*.

Leading Questions: On Seeing Both the Forest and the Trees

This "more" is to deepen our understanding of theorizing as an embedded activity. What did the great theorists want to achieve – even when they failed to achieve it? This "more" involves delving into the contexts of the creation and formation of theories, so that we can begin to see what the theorists were really trying to achieve. As such, this effort at understanding theories of religion essentially entails an approach to theorizing about religion as a historical enterprise. The classic thinkers of Part I sought first to uncover by repeated historical searches Natural Religion, conceived as the "first" religion, or the origin of religion. The answers given in the quest for Natural Religion by the first wave of great theorists dominate the polemic of Part I. The second thing the classic thinkers sought to do was to address the central problem of the ultimate nature and status of religious *experience*. Was there some common psychological denominator of all religions, some fundamental human capacity for religiousness, analogous to a moral sensibility or the esthetic sense? Here, the historical quest for an absolute beginning point has been abandoned in favor of attempts to explain what essential religious experience was. Was it some sort of absolute dependence upon a great power, often constituting the essence of the reports of encounters with the sacred by believers, to be taken at face value? Or, as Freud would suggest, are we not rather in the presence of mythologized versions of our childhood memories of parental power? Or again, to follow Durkheim, are we better advised to trace these indubitable feelings to the even more indubitable fact of our absolute dependence upon society? Part II of the present volume seeks to lay out some of the more influential accounts of the real nature of so-called religious experiences. In Part III, the concern lies with the way religion is shaped in and by the realities of diversity – diversity of race or sex/gender, or the differentials of global power. Are there such things as Black theories of religion, or female ones? Does one's race, sex, or relation to the centers of world power change how one would, or should, theorize?

One final suggestion for students as they read through the book. Be alert to three steps I tried to follow as I wrote each chapter. First, each chapter tends to be organized about a basic *problem* of religion emergent at a particular time because of various changes that occur in a society. Such a change might be the discovery of heretofore unknown prehistoric societies of Europe, and the way they put into question the Bible's version of the human past. This, in turn, put into question the account of the world and humanity given in the sacred scripture of the West, and thus of the religious life led in accord with its guidance. Or such a change might be the "discovery" of the Freudian unconscious and the revision this has caused in many quarters of our sense of our own ability to know ourselves – and especially to know if we can trust our religious experiences.

Second, once these shocks to the religious self-consciousness are felt, what reactions by way of new *theories* of religion emerged? What, for example, did Robertson Smith have to say about modern Christianity, with it strong emphasis on *belief* in God, once what he took to be the earliest levels of biblical religion seemed totally devoid of beliefs as such? What was Freud to make of the prevalence of modern Christian religious experience of absolute dependence upon God the Father, when to him it seemed as if this might be based on childhood memories of the power of our own human fathers?

Third, and finally, no matter whether we find that thinkers like Robertson Smith or Freud were wrong or not about their conclusions about religion, the job of understanding these (and all the other) theories is only complete when we have satisfied ourselves that we understand *why the theorists thought that they were right*! How and why, for example, could anyone, like Robertson Smith, to take a case in point, think that there could even be people, much less religious people, who lacked beliefs? Whatever else students take from this book, I hope they will at least feel that they understand how and why some remarkable folk tried to *understand and explain religion*. And that, incidentally, is why I titled this book *Understanding Theories of Religion*.

References

Eagleton, T. 1990. *The Significance of Theory*. Oxford: Blackwell.

Strenski, I. 2003. "Why It Is Better to Have Some of the Questions than All of the Answers." *Method and Theory in the Study of Religion* 15(2): 169–186.

2

Jean Bodin and Herbert of Cherbury: True Religion, Essential Religion, and Natural Religion

Forming a Common Mind about Religion in Early Modern Europe

In sixteenth-century western Europe something unprecedented in human history happened to religion. Radical curiosity was turned upon an aspect of human life generally recognize as "religion." From the beginning, it was just assumed that such cultural phenomena as Judaism, Islam, paganism, Brahminism (what these thinkers called the religion of the Hindus), as well as the cultic systems of the ancient Greeks, Romans, Celts, Germanic tribes, belonged to the same class of human cultural phenomena. They accepted such a designation as surely as they accepted, without any critical questioning, that different peoples had different cuisines, because they cooked and ate differently, that they showed different styles and forms of art, because they fashioned images and plastic forms differently, that they practiced different forms of morality or had different customs, because they ruled certain behaviors in or out.

Yet what marks the historical period in this chapter is that instead of just observing their own forms of religious belief or practice, or indeed those of others, people started asking questions about what they believed and practiced, often doing so in response to the stimulation of their encounter with religions other than their own.

The mid-sixteenth century saw the beginnings of widespread attempts to do what we would recognize as "comparative study of religion." What had seldom or never stood out for attention, gradually did so, and did so in comparison with other like-fashioned religions. Religion began having what we call "salience" – literally something that "leaps out" – from the quotidian background of human affairs. While today this might lead us to think that these thinkers had in fact invented the phenomenon we call religion, for them it was pure discovery. Of course, in some sense the first comparativists of religion did their share of creating as they went about their business. But that was definitely not how they would have seen their work of discovery. Religion, for them, existed as an objective and plural reality. So, in this time when skepticism flourished across the progressive spectrum of European intellectual life, they raised all sorts of questions about religion and the religions as, indeed, they did about all the foundations of their way of life.

But they also sought to transcend mere skepticism, and strove instead to form something of what we can call a "common mind" about religion. The founders took the first steps toward what might be called a science of religion, since they sought to establish consensus about religion so that it could become the object of common

Understanding Theories of Religion: An Introduction, Second Edition. Ivan Strenski.
© 2015 Ivan Strenski. Published 2015 by John Wiley & Sons, Ltd.

discourse and debate. In this, these first thinkers about religion fall into place as paradigm members of their age. We might recall that in this so-called early modern period of European history we also witnessed the rise of the natural sciences, or sciences of nature, such as physics, chemistry, and astronomy. Our founders then were kin to the likes of Newton, Galileo, Kopernick, Descartes, Kepler, and a host of other scientists in their efforts to come to a common mind about the objects they studied.

But religion, of course, differs from the objects of the sciences of nature. Religion involves people in existential life choices and life commitments. So, by *studying* religion, some of the founders felt that they might deepen their own religious life. Others, however, studied religion to free themselves of it. These thinkers "thought they were right" to be curious about religion because the world presented them with real *problems* about religion. Religions claiming the exclusive possession of divine revelation – Judaism, Christianity, and Islam – drew the sharpest questions. This chapter explores how these thinkers both posed and addressed fundamental questions about the very nature of religion itself. To understand these pioneers we will have to take note of some of the social, cultural, and political changes rocking western Europe from the sixteenth century onward.

Here are some of the places curiosity about religion led these first religious studies theorists. Which of the many religions is the true religion? And how can we tell, given that everyone thinks their own religion is the true one? Is it natural for people to be religious, or is religion something imposed? Indeed, is religion a good thing, given the strife it seems to have caused in so many places? If religion is part of our human nature, what do the great teachers or prophets like Moses, Jesus, the Buddha, Confucius, or Muhammad add to it, if anything?

Of course, religious people have always puzzled about their own personal faith. They have had to form a common mind about the meaning of their own personal and collective religious lives. Religious folk have wondered about the nature of their God, about whether it was better to pursue Nirvana, or to follow the Bodhisattva path, whether there be life into eternity, or whether we are doomed to eternal reincarnation, or damned to eternal hell fires, and so on. In different religious traditions, people have had to come to some sort of resolution to these questions because, in varying degrees, their answers shaped their religions. These are "insider" questions – problems one encounters when one tries to form a common mind about one's own religion.

But forming a common mind about one's own religious life is far from forming a common mind about religion, or the religions. Commitment to a particular religion is at issue for the insider. It is not for us, as students of religion. Our questions are not "insider" questions, but problems arising when we try to form a common mind about the basic nature of religion in general – like the question of whether religion is a good thing at all – or about the religions taken comparatively – like which religion is the oldest. These questions assumed that we could (and should) place different religions alongside one another to compare them for different purposes. Which religion is richest in ritual life, in mythology, in the expressive graphic and plastic arts?

Consider again the question of the identity of the true religion. I believe that this is a question that cannot be fruitfully broached from the inside, because everyone will say that their own religion is the true one! That question can only be asked by agreeing to lay the facts about the many religions alongside one another to compare the evidence. It is not a job for insiders. Sometimes this question was answered by equating it with the question of which religion, if any among the many, could claim to be the first or oldest religion. In this way, a common mind could be achieved by agreeing upon rules of evidence – a way we could date the various religions vying for the title of oldest, and thus true. In this chapter, we see how Jean Bodin, for example, takes on this question by appealing to comparative religious evidence, framed in the form of an inter-religious dialogue and debate. Once set on this course, the first, and most important, device the founders created to achieve a common mind about religion was their idea of Natural Religion.

Natural Religion, Naturism, the Religion of Nature, and Revealed Religion

Since terms like "Natural Religion," "religion of nature," "nature religion," and such can cause confusion, let's make some distinctions. Herbert and Jean were, not on the whole, great nature lovers. Centuries later, the Romantics, especially the English and German Romantics, declared their love of nature both as a source of poetic inspiration and, most importantly, as a source of spirituality or contact with divinity. As we will see in Chapter 4, Friedrich Max Müller swam with this cultural tide. And just to make it more confusing, he also coupled his nature religion with a more abstract and philosophical Natural Religion.

Because of cases like Max Müller, I want to distinguish four terms that use "nature" or some derivative of it: the *naturalistic* study of religion, *Natural* Religion, *naturism*, and the *religion of nature*. First, by a naturalistic study of religion, I mean a study of religion that proceeds within the limits of ordinary – "natural" – reason and experience, thus unaided by divine intervention or religious faith. Second, "naturism" and "religion of nature," are synonyms, indicating an actual religion consisting in the worship of "nature." Here "nature" typically refers to violent shows of power, such as thunderstorms, volcanic eruptions, and earthquakes, or to gentler happenings, like the sunrise, sunset, or eclipses. Then again, the "nature" that is worshiped might take the form of great natural phenomena such as the vast oceans, tall mountains, or high heavens, or as well prominent heavenly bodies – the distant sun and moon. Third, and finally, there is "Natural Religion." Here, religion or the religious sensibility are seen as things given the normal course of the formation of human nature. We are not religious because of some miraculous divine intervention but rather because that's the way people were made as a general species. "Natural" Religion, thus, contrasts with "revealed" religion, whereas "naturism" would contrast with other sorts of religion such as animism, the worship of souls, or polytheism, the worship of many gods.

What makes Müller particularly interesting is his fusion of the Natural Religion stream with the religion of nature stream. He is therefore both a naturist, in the modern sophisticated sense typical of the Romantics, and not therefore in the naive sense of nature worshipers described in ethnographic literature, or even perhaps of the Veda; but he is also – without qualification – a devotee of Natural Religion. Part of the puzzle in understanding his thinking about the study of religion is to understand how his religious pursuits – both in regard to nature and in regard to Natural Religion – contributed to the development of a study of religion that he took to be naturalistic at the same time.

Despite what seems in its name, *Natural* Religion is not *nature* worship. That, I will call "naturism" or, straight out, "nature religion." Natural Religion embodies the belief that religion is an innate, built-in "common" feature of being human. It is therefore "natural," because it is a "normal" part of who we are. Natural Religion reflects the belief that all people are born with a capacity or talent for being attracted to the ultimate reality. People are, on this view, religiously "musical" by birth, so to speak. The desire to understand nirvana, to worship ultimate reality or the godhead, is born into every human being just by virtue of who we are. We do not have to be taught Natural Religion since it was, in the words of American revolutionary Tom Paine, the "only religion that has not been invented" (Paine 1794, p. 233). Natural Religion is "natural" as well in the sense that to lack it would be like lacking moral sense or esthetic perception, such as in the cases of sociopaths, psychopaths, or cultural philistines, respectively. The skeptics that brought forth the ideas of Natural Religion felt the same way about the essentially human quality of the religious sense. One could not truly be human if one lacked the natural religious sensibility represented by the idea of Natural Religion.

But, as one might expect, the more religiously orthodox had other attitudes toward Natural Religion. How, they asked, was this Natural Religion related to what is called "revelation"? The champions of revelation insisted that the unaided human mind simply could not reach the heights of spiritual insight given in scripture. Revealed scriptures such as the Quran, the Bible, the Vedas, and so on told people of things they could never have imagined. Could people conceive of the Ten Commandments, just by *thinking*? Could they, as well, deduce the concept of a covenant between humanity and God out of pure reason? Was Krishna's saving power and worshipful reality, likewise, an idea that might just occur to someone? No! Real religion contained ideas that had to be God-given, because they went beyond what mere thinking about religion could conceive. Real religion was marked by its supernatural origins.

On the other hand, partisans of Natural Religion – often called Deists – rejected revelation entirely. They felt revelation was superfluous, and just cluttered up the pure simplicity of Natural Religion. Tom Paine makes such a stance plain in his *The Age of Reason* (1794):

> there is no occasion for such a thing as revealed religion. What is it we want to know? Does not the creation, the universe we behold, preach to us the existence of an Almighty power that governs and regulates the whole? And is not the evidence that this creation holds out to our senses infinitely stronger than anything we can read in a book … [?] (Walters 1992, p. 223)

To these partisans of Natural Religion it was a simplified, "stripped down" religion. Free as it was of elaborate social organization, hierarchy, ritual, or irrational mythologies, Natural Religion presented itself as uncorrupted.

But Natural Religion was more than just religion in its simplicity and purity. It was also conceived as the capacity in humans for being religious in any form whatsoever. Thus, if revelation came to people, it needed some place to "fit" into human nature. To be religious, we needed a *capacity* or *aptitude* for being religious, just as we needed similar aptitudes for being artistic, moral, political, musical, and such – all the aptitudes that marked humans as special. This foundational aspect of Natural Religion gave further strength to the point of view of its partisans, since Natural Religion was, then, a necessary foundation for revealed religion. As such, it embodied the *essentials* of religion. If so why shouldn't we think it the best of the religions? And if that is so, then revelation was not really needed at all. Natural Religion could replace the revealed religion everywhere. Or such, at any rate, were the arguments of the partisans of Natural Religion for doing away with, or at least ignoring, traditional religions of "revelation."

Religious Wars, the New World, and the Concept of Religion

The quest for Natural Religion in the early modern period, and thus the rise of the study of religion, also owed much to two great "shocks" administered to the worldview of sixteenth-century western Europe. We can also look on these shocks as part of what I called the "external" context in which a thinker like Bodin was located. I shall be arguing throughout this book that such an external contexts were among the resources giving theorists of religion reasons to "think they were right" about their views of the nature of religion. First, for example, the Protestant Reformation undid the religious stability of the West. Many of Europe's religious certainties were dashed in the process. I put it to my readers that such instability in the wider (external) political and religious worlds gave some thinkers warrant to "think they were right" to seek Natural Religion as a solution to religious disorder and strife. Second, the European discovery of the New World exploded Western notions of humanity and its history. How do we make sense of the unprecedented alien civilizations of the New World? Were the temples of human sacrifice in Mexico monuments to religion or Satanic enslavement? Taken together, these events placed previous notions of "religion" into question. This unprecedented eruption of religious differences also informed the external context in which thinkers like Bodin found himself. For someone who worried about the truth of religion, as Bodin did, here as well was another reason that he would "think he was right" about his quest for the original religion.

Consider first the shock to conventional thinking about religion in western Europe caused by the Protestant Reformation. Today, we take for granted that Catholicism and Protestantism are really different "religions." In the early days of the Reformation ambiguity ruled. There were arguments, yes, but they were "inside the family," between different shades of Christians. And so long as differences remained blurry, nuanced, and non-confrontational, crisis was averted. But confrontation, radical opposition, and "objectification" of the other soon took hold. The standard facilitating device for "othering" was the "confession" of fundamental doctrines – "The (Catholic) priest has the power to forgive sins." Once confession was made, a dialectic was set into motion, and an opposing one followed – "Only God has the power to forgive sins." In the process, dividing lines between religious factions hardened, and the "religions" became defined much as we know them now. The force and reality of that "othering" upset the earlier, free-flowing worldview, and threw the well-ordered worldview of sixteenth-century western Europe into confusion. Since there is one God, how could there be *two* "true religions"? And, if not, how do we determine which is *the* true religion? And this Catholic–Protestant controversy about the identity and nature of the "true" religion only foreshadowed the questions to come as the West encountered what represented themselves as contenders for the title of *the* true religion, such as Islam and Christianity's old nemesis, Judaism. I am arguing that this sort of disarray set into motion the thinking that eventuated in the formation of the idea of Natural Religion, and along with it the beginnings the modern study of religion. Both cases dramatize the quest for a common mind about religion that escaped the discipline of confessional religious belief.

But opposition between Catholics and Protestants turned from mere theological conflicts to military campaigns and religious warfare that lasted many years. Religious wars brought home the reality of "the simple existence of a plurality of embodied, and embattled, faiths... . Objectification arose, then, out of the need, to describe one's own or other people's way of belief and life, as if from outside" (Bossy 1982, p. 56) Marking this emergence of the concept of many "religions," historian John Bossy notes that thinkers had traditionally referred to religion as "as worship or worshipfulness." But after the Reformation and the religious wars that ensued, writers "ended up by talking about 'religions'" in the plural. These warring entities were "objective ... [and] erected around a set of doctrines or principles and therefore true or not true, but above all different" (Bossy 1982, pp. 5–6).

All of a sudden, religious difference had to be addressed. The realities of religious warfare compelled people, who otherwise had a casual a live-and-let-live attitude about religion, to make up their minds. People had to stand up and be counted. They had to form a common mind about religion with some people, but radically oppose others. "Confessionalism" is the name given to label this phenomenon of feeling the imperative to *declare* – "confess" – differences, oppose them, and to adhere to one's own "confession."

But confessionalism ironically set the conditions for an approach to the religions that was not just that of the true believer – the insider's point of view. This non-confessional viewpoint took all the religions into its purview, and from that point sought to form a common mind about them, so that anyone could join the conversation. The first effort to achieve this common mind was the quest for a Natural Religion. Those embarked on this quest believed that they could move beyond confessional religious differences. Their invention (or discovery) of an objective and general notion of religion – Natural Religion – arose, I am arguing, precisely from the desire to overcome the destructive differences expressed in the Wars of Religion (Bossy 1982, p. 6).

A second shock to conventional thinking about religion came with the discovery of the New World of the Americas. Hernando Cortez had conquered Mexico by 1521 after a two-year campaign that took him through parts of Central America as well. By 1608, the Jesuit order had established a presence in Paraguay. As early as 1584, Sir Walter Raleigh had established a colony in Virginia, and in 1608 the Jamestown settlement was founded there as well. In 1620, the Massachusetts Bay colony was established by the Pilgrim Fathers. Along with colonial enterprise, European expansion into the New World had profound connections with religion and ultimately for the study of religion. This was worked out in two ways.

First, in some ways, the voyages of discovery carried on the Europe-wide warfare between Catholics and Protestants, but also included Islam. The fifteenth-and sixteenth-century Spanish and Portuguese enterprises of discovery and navigation were in part driven by the need to get round a virtual blockade between Europe and India, produced by Islamic dominance of the overland trade routes in the Near East. The colonial efforts of Protestant powers, England and the Netherlands, were often motivated by competition with the Portuguese and Spanish Catholics for religious dominance of the New World. Portuguese and Spanish commercial and colonial activity in the New World sought to do the same over against British and Dutch Protestant efforts in the same areas.

But the discovery of the New World also shocked western European thinking about religion in another way. European encounters with the utterly novel religions of the Americas showed how little Europeans knew of the radically different indigenous cultures of the Americas. The religions of the Native Americans had no precedent. This lack of precedent made it nearly impossible at times for the Europeans to make sense of these new religions. As different as Islam was from Christianity, at least Christians realized that it was part of the Abrahamic tradition. Where, however, did these New World religions come from? Were they newly evolved from a form of humanity close to that of Adam and Eve, and close, therefore, to a "primal" form of religion? Or did they represent a long historical decline or degeneration from more "advanced" forms of religion? Perhaps, they were not *religions* at all – especially those of Mexico, where human sacrifice was commonplace? There was really no end to the speculation about the real identity of these "Others" just as today we would imagine all sorts of scenarios were we to make contact with intelligent creatures from another planet. Is it not easy to see how these first contacts had the potential for throwing conventional attitudes about the nature of religion into confusion? And once conventional thinking was disrupted, is it not just as easy to see how some people would begin trying to sort out the subject of religion?

Taken together, then, both the Reformation and the New World discoveries shook the self-confidence of Western civilization by challenging an endless list of long-standing assumptions about religion. Most, however, were motivated by the desire to dampen the fires of warfare caused by disputes between Catholics and Protestants over the Reformation. How could the differences between Christians be mediated in some fair and peaceful way – a way which did not prejudice the case of one against the other, or provoke any side to violence? Whatever the source for such self-questioning, a movement of creative skepticism gradually took shape in western Europe. Among a select group of courageous thinkers – the "heroes" of the present book – these shocks generated immense intellectual curiosity and energy. Thoughtful people – skeptics – entered a period of healthy questioning about religion. In this way, I believe, religious studies or the study of religion came into being.

A Time of Problems and Creative Ferment Too

Religious studies was born in some illustrious company. Challenges, questioning, and testing the limits of human knowledge seem to bring along

with them great surges of creativity. In England, the late sixteenth to the late seventeenth centuries saw the glorious reigns of the Tudors, Henry VIII (1491–1547), his daughter, Elizabeth I (1533–1603), and James I (Stuart) (1566–1625) and the cultural ferment their reigns produced in the figures of Shakespeare (1564–1616), philosopher Francis Bacon (1561–1626), and political theorist Thomas Hobbes (1588–1679). This period also saw the publication of the celebrated English translation of the Bible, the King James version. On the Continent, an illustrious list of names can be counted, such as Leonardo da Vinci (1452–1519), Niccolò Machiavelli (1469–1527), the humanist Erasmus of Rotterdam (1466–1536), the critical theologians and biblical scholars Laelius (1525–62) and his nephew Faustus (Sozzino) Socinus (1539–1604), the political philosopher and jurist Hugo Grotius (1583–1645), and the Spanish humanists Francisco de Vitoria (ca. 1485–1546) and Bartolomé de las Casas (1484–1576). The beginnings of religious studies belong to this same world of creative intellectual ferment.

What may be distinctive about the religious thinkers of this Age of Discovery was their different attitudes to traditional religion. Many became outspoken enemies of religion, traditional or otherwise. These anti-religious skeptics turned their skepticism against a committed religious life. Yet they were also venturing on a religious quest (Byrne 1989; Preus 1987). These religious skeptics saw no opposition between religion and human knowledge or science. This was in part because they already regarded reason as a God-given endowment to humanity. Their view was that science and religion complemented one another. They felt that embarking on a rational inquiry into religion would liberate them from gross errors, and deepen their understanding of God's reality.

Jean Bodin: Comparing Law Teaches Us How To Compare Religions

Perhaps the earliest recorded figure to try to create a substantial scheme for coming to a common mind about religion was the French Renaissance humanist and Sorbonne professor, Jean Bodin (1530–96). Although he personified the skeptical mind, his rational inquiries were deeply motivated by his own personal religious and ethical commitments. In his public life, Bodin was a prominent jurist and diplomat, an academic historian, and a philosopher.

As a legal professional, Bodin wanted a new – more universal – foundation for the laws of France – much as he wanted some common grounding for the religions. Bodin's approach to law anticipated his way of dealing with religious differences. In legal studies, Bodin was a consistent and inveterate comparativist. He felt that French law could be perfected by taking lessons from the law of other nations. Here, Bodin practiced an elemental cross-cultural comparison for the first time in a systematic way in the West. Bodin felt, for example, that by *comparing* French laws with those from other times and places – by placing French law within a larger *human* context – they could arrive at solutions to specifically French problems that would otherwise be harder to obtain. The French could not ignore the laws and history of other peoples – even the so-called barbarians, such as the Franks, Angles, Saxons, Goths, and so on. Nor did Bodin believe that he could remain ignorant even of the laws and history that lay beyond the boundaries of European Christendom – notably in the Muslim domains of Saracenic or Turkish history (Franklin 1963, p. 45). It is from that same all-inclusive human spirit that Bodin engaged the comparative study of religion, thus potentially giving birth to religious studies as we know it today. He is surely one of our heroes!

The True Religion *Must* Be the Oldest Religion

In his life as a diplomat, Bodin worked tirelessly to mitigate the horrors of the French Wars of Religion. Even at the risk of his own safety, he fought for political solutions to France's civil war (Preus 1987, p. 6). At a time when confessionalism was driving Catholic and Protestant Christians apart into separate religions, Bodin tried to maintain an even hand between the warring factions. Bodin, however, fought a losing battle, which unfortunately only made him suspect to the powerful Catholic faction. When his efforts at mediation failed, defeated and in fear of his life, Bodin withdrew from the public arena into scholarly seclusion. It was from these final years of his retreat from active politics, dreaming

of a world free of religious violence, that Bodin created the first great work in religious studies. This is his deliciously titled dialogue of religions, *Colloquium of the Seven about Secrets of the Sublime* (1587). In it, Bodin argued for a fundamental religion linking all of humanity, and in doing so, sought to overcome religious difference and violence. This spirit of non-partisan inquiry informed Bodin's eventual quest for a what I am calling Natural Religion.

Bodin's *Colloquium* stages an often lively fictional dialogue and debate among representatives of *seven* different religious positions. These seven are: two kinds of Protestants (Lutheran and Calvinist), a Catholic, a Jew, and a Muslim, as well as an anti-religious skeptic and a philosopher. Readers familiar with the manner and procedure of arguments in a court of law will find the same temperament governing the *Colloquium*. Codes of evidence and set procedures maintain an orderly and civil exchange of ideas. Each side make its case. Argument and counter-argument ensue. This civil style of discourse let Bodin give all sides their say.

Bodin shaped the *Colloquium* around the first explicitly stated "problems of religion." He then struggled to arrive at a common mind. His approach was to seek the identity of the best or truest religion, since that would surely compel the loyalty of any person of good will.

But how did Bodin think we could decide this question or come to an answer? He constructs a debate that rages over hundreds of pages, until one participant (standing in for Bodin) argues that the best and truest religion must be the *oldest*. Bodin felt he "was right to think" this in part because it was then commonly accepted that the Genesis story was the true history of human origins. There, the Bible tells us of Adam and Eve's dismissal from Paradise, and of the dispersion of humanity after its failed attempt to build a Tower of Babel to the sky. This commonly accepted biblical perspective on human sin and decline gave Bodin the conviction that, in matters of religion, he could appeal to Genesis, where we also learn that the primordial beginnings of religion, of humanity's peaceful comingling with God in Paradise, must be the best and truest of religions. The oldest religion held sway at the beginnings of things, before humanity had sinned, and spread out over the earth into its different, ultimately feuding, subgroups. That oldest religion *must* be the one, true religion!

But was Bodin able to be more precise, and specify what that oldest religion was? And would his argument persuade Catholics and Protestants, who were warring against each other, to accept his conclusion? Here, again, Bodin resorted to the common mind of his time. Surely, both Catholics and Protestants would accept the Genesis account of world history as a basis for agreement. Accordingly, in Bodin's great debate among religions, he concluded that the oldest (and therefore *true*) religion *must* be the religion of Adam. Since, by biblical (and Quranic standards), Adam was the first human, Adam's religion must also not only be the oldest, but the truest and best. It was the religion that humanity enjoyed before the Fall.

Yet identifying the oldest religion with Adam's religion tells us nothing of its content. What did Adam, for example, believe? Bodin is ready with an answer, however controversial it turned out to be. Not only was Adam's religion the oldest, but it therefore must be monotheistic – much as the religion proclaimed by Moses, for example (Preus 1987, pp. 11–13). Reasoning further, Bodin argued that even if the details of the religion of Adam were not known, the religion of Moses was. We could then reconstruct Adam's religion by taking Moses' religion as our guide. Now, the Bible implies that Moses did not try to create a *new* religion in his day; he merely re-established the religion of Adam. (Of course, unbeknownst to Bodin, Muhammad also argued that he too was only *restoring* original monotheism.) Although Bodin is somewhat coy on this point, some commentators say that Bodin indeed thought that Judaism was the true religion – because it was (at that time) thought to be oldest of all religions.

Quite understandably in this time of religious tensions, Bodin's suggestion led his enemies to charge him with being a secret Jew – a "Judaizer" – and thus an apostate to Christianity. While it is not known whether the charge of "Judaizer" had merit, it is true that Bodin was one of the first students of religion to place Christianity on the same level as its religious rivals, such as Islam or Judaism. Indeed, one of the characters in Bodin's *Colloquium* even explicitly challenges the pre-eminence and universal truth of Christianity (Preus 1987, pp. 12–13). But Bodin's leveling of the religious field proved to be costly. He courted the real possibility of religious persecution for putting Christianity on the same level as other religions.

However agreeable Bodin's approach to religion is, there is one obstacle to embracing him and his *Colloquium* wholeheartedly as the kind of founder of a tradition of the study of religion. Fearing reprisals for the unorthodox views advanced in the *Colloquium*, Bodin held back on publication. Indeed, it only saw the light of day 300 years later. We cannot therefore really determine how influential the *Colloquium* was. From the time of its composition in the sixteenth century, copies circulated clandestinely among a small circle of skeptics. We simply do not know how widely these copies were distributed, nor how significant those who read it thought it to be.

Yet what makes Bodin still relevant was his use of exemplary methodology for resolving the question of the nature of the best or the true religion. Even if we disagree with his conclusions, Bodin asked good questions, and showed how to answer them. These procedures relied on a rational basis. Thus, the *age* of a religion was something that could be determined in the same way as the age of any other feature of the human world. Bodin thus established a common, rational ground for discussion and debate between and among religions. He laid the foundations, suitable for his times, for forming a common mind about religion. Human thinking was by its nature God-given from the start. No improvement upon creation was needed, thank you very much! Appeals to additional supernatural or extrasensory "revelation" or divine authority were unnecessary. Nor, of course, could these appeals to revelation or sacred authority settle these questions of the antiquity of a religion anyway, since those very approaches themselves were part of the dispute. They relied on sources of knowledge that were peculiar to the different religions, such as papal authority, for example, and therefore could not in principle form the basis of a common human mind about what was acceptable evidence (Preus 1987, ch. 1). In this, Bodin shows himself to be a champion of religious studies.

Natural Religion Is the Essence of Religion: Herbert of Cherbury

Some generations later in England, the attempt to achieve a common mind about religion took a different turn. Edward, Lord Herbert of Cherbury

(1583–1648) – often identified as the first Deist – exemplifies this effort. Like Bodin, Edward was another well-rounded, multi-talented "Renaissance man." Like Bodin, Herbert also pursued the career of a professional diplomat, serving the English Crown in France. While in royal service on the Continent, Herbert came to know many of the great philosophical skeptics and freethinking intellectuals of the day, such as Pierre Gassendi and Hugo Grotius. As a thoughtful individual caught in the midst of religious strife between the Puritans and Cavaliers who fought the English Civil War, Herbert felt drawn to work for religious and political peace. Although sympathetic to Puritan theology, Herbert remained neutral between contending parties throughout the disorder of the war. As a member of the landed gentry, he first lined up with the royalist Cavaliers. But later he offered no resistance to the occupation of his estate by Puritan parliamentary forces (Hill 1987, p. 16). Like Bodin, he abhorred confessionalism and the polarization of viewpoints it created. Above all, he resisted taking sides for as long as possible. This earned him the dubious epithet of "ambidexter," from his extremist critics, mostly because he hated confessionalism (Hill 1987, p. 15).

Herbert's views on religious tolerance are recorded principally in his 1633 treatise, *De Veritate*. Its "catholic" scope and ambition revealed an openness to religious pluralism that immediately provoked a reaction. Despite Herbert's rationalist reputation, he conceived his investigations into the origin of religion as an opportunity to deepen his own piety. In creating this world and all it contains, Herbert believed that God the Creator left his image inscribed thereon. Thus, the careful – empirical – study of the world was a religious act, like reading the Bible. This sensibility also inspired scientists and philosophers like Francis Bacon, to bring great confidence to the task of studying nature; Herbert simply applied this confidence to the study of religions. But while Bacon did much to advance empirical and humanistic methods in the natural sciences, he – like Herbert – acknowledged the divine power behind these human investigations. Bacon says that God "gavest the light of vision" to humanity (Bacon 1620, p. 342). Herbert sounds much the same humble note in his autobiography, where he tells us that he appealed to prayer to overcome his reluctance to publish *De Veritate*, "as I knew it would meet with much opposition"

(Herbert of Cherbury 1888, pp. 176–177). This humility led Herbert to oppose claims to a specially revealed religious truth. Such "confessionalist" arrogance only encouraged fierce and intractable religious conflict, such as plagued Herbert's world (Preus 1987, p. 25). To avoid such conflicts, he felt, we needed a rational and neutral way to arrive at a common mind about religion.

Herbert's "Ambidextrous" Theory of Natural Religion

Herbert's project for achieving a common mind about religion was typically double-sided or "ambidextrous." First, he rejected religious exclusivism and confessionalism, such as the Christian claims to being the true religion (Hill 1987, p. 20). Like Bodin, Herbert felt that Christianity was only "one particular religion among many particular religions" (Hill 1987, p. 32). Second, once all religions were given the benefit of the doubt, as it were, he argued that each of them rested upon a universal, innate, shared religious common ground. This is, in effect, what I call Natural Religion (Preus 1987, p. 23).

Herbert's answer to religious conflict was, then, like Bodin's, to posit a universal essential religion in which all the particular historical religions participated. But unlike Bodin, Herbert believed that this common religion was not to be identified as the oldest. Rather, it was something akin to a lowest common denominator of the key shared beliefs of the religions. In Herbert's view, this common denominator consisted of five points: first, belief in God; second, that God should be worshiped; third, that virtue and piety are mutually related; fourth, that our crimes must be repented; and finally, that judgment about good and evil would take place in the afterlife. This universal religion was, in a sense, the true essence of all the religions because all religions shared these beliefs.

Herbert "thought he was right" to arrive at this five-point delineation of the essence of religion simply because he had complete faith in Francis Bacon's experimental method. Herbert thought he had scoured all the *empirical* evidence available. He thought he could come to a common mind about religion by assembling data on the world's religions, and then inductively sift through them back to the elements they held in common – all the while guided by divine light, of course (Byrne 1989, pp. 32–33). Critics like David Hume (see Hume 1963), for example, counter Herbert's empirical approach with a more robust empiricism. They challenge him on the quality of his data. Other critics have rightly noted that Herbert's five points look conveniently like his own form of early modern, reformed Christian beliefs. Belief in one God, obligation to worship God, and an attendant morality, complete with a transcendental reward/punishment system – all these were stock-in-trade for the kind of Christian Herbert was. The picture gathers form and color in Herbert's classic Reformation attacks on priestcraft, ritual, and other features of pre-Reformation Christianity.

Fair as these critical comments are, I would urge us to celebrate Herbert's *method* of empirical research, of amassing data about the religions, of acquainting ourselves with those details, and

seeking correlations. Herbert was, in short, perhaps as good a *student* of religion as there could be at that time. He worked with the data he had access to. Surely, like Herbert, we can be equally good students of religion without necessarily following him to the end. An empirical approach remains part of the methodological equipment of the student of religion, even though we may not arrive at Herbert's particular conclusions. Further, in Herbert's work we can see how the quest for Natural Religion generated one of the first attempts to make sense of the nature of religion in itself. We also see how, together with Bodin, the affairs of the world, such as religious warfare, produced shocks to the thinking of Western people that compelled them to think hard about the nature of religion. The quest for the first religion, for original religion – for Natural Religion – was thus an original spur to thinking about religion as such.

References

Bacon, F. 1620. *The Great Instauration and the Novum Organum*. London: Kessinger Publishing.

Bossy, J. 1982. "Some Elementary Forms of Durkheim." *Past and Present* 95: 3–18.

Byrne, P. 1989. *Natural Religion and the Nature of Religion*. London: Routledge.

Franklin, J.H. 1963. *Jean Bodin and the Sixteenth-Century Revolution and the Methodology of Law and History*. New York: Columbia University Press.

Herbert of Cherbury, E., Lord. 1888. *The Autobiography of Edward, Lord Herbert of Cherbury*. London: Walter Scott.

Hill, E.D. 1987. *Edward, Lord Herbert of Cherbury*. Boston: Twayne.

Hume, D. 1963. "The Natural History of Religion." In R. Wollheim (ed.), *Hume on Religion*. London: Collins.

Paine, T. 1794. *Age of Reason: Being an Investigation of True and Fabulous Theology*. New York: Books, Inc.

Preus, J.S. 1987. *Explaining Religion*. New Haven: Yale University Press.

Walters, K.S. 1992. *The American Deists: Voices of Reason and Dissent in the Early Republic*. Lawrence: University of Kansas.

Further Reading

Locke, J. 1975. *An Essay Concerning Human Understanding*, ed. Peter H. Nidditch. Oxford: Oxford University Press.

McGinnis, P., A. Harrison, and R. Kearney (eds.). 1997. *John Toland's Christianity Not Mysterious*. Dublin: Lilliput Press.

Tindal, M. 1995. *Christianity as Old as the Creation: The Gospel, a Republication of the Religion of Nature*. Chippenham, Wilts.: Thoemmes Press.

Tooley, M.J. 1955. *Jean Bodin, Six Books of the Commonwealth: Introduction*. Oxford: Basil Blackwell.

Tweyman, S. (ed.). 1974. *The Religion of Nature Delineated*. Delmar, NY: Scholars' Facsimiles and Reprints.

PART I

The Prehistory of the Study of Religion: Responses to an Expanding World

3

Understanding Religion Also Began with Trying to Understand the Bible

Since Reverend Doctors now declare
That clerks and people must prepare
To doubt if Adam ever were;
To hold the flood a local scare …
That David was no giant-slayer …
And Joshua's triumphs, Job's despair …
And Daniel and the den affair,
And other stories rich and rare,
Were writ to make old doctrine wear
Something of a romantic air …
Since thus they hint, nor turn a hair,
All churchgoing will I forswear,
And sit on Sundays in my chair,
And read that moderate man Voltaire.

> Thomas Hardy, "The Respectable
> Burgher, on 'The Higher Criticism'"

The Bible's New Readers: Skeptics and Seekers

Jean Bodin and Herbert of Cherbury attempted to respond to the tumultuous political and religious crises of their times by devising a way of arriving at a common mind about religion that offered an alternative to the intransigent, confessional religious exceptionalism. The seventeenth century witnessed the widespread, revolutionary, application of God-given reason to politics, jurisprudence, diplomacy, nature, and many mundane human affairs. The orthodox saw the application of God-given reason as inappropriate to religion! But that is precisely what Bodin and Herbert did in trying to arrive at a common mind about religion. Through their achievements, they showed how a modern study of religion could be intellectually plausible. At a certain point, then, in the intellectual history of the West, at least two thinkers had arrived at, albeit different, ways to form a common mind about religion. Of course, not everyone was interested in forming such a cross-confessional common mind. They continued to prefer to devote themselves to the pastoral needs of their own religious communities. They thus worked to form common "confessional" minds, to sharpen the "voice of the church" – that is, to produce what are called "theologies."

It should be no surprise that the heftiest authority bolstering confessional minds was the Bible. Let us, then, now turn to efforts to form a common mind about the contents of the Bible. The focal question here is the significance of the critical study of the Bible for the more general purposes of the study of religion. (I shall adopt the convention of calling the new methods of criticism of the biblical texts "Higher Criticism," a term that properly came to prominence later,

Understanding Theories of Religion: An Introduction, Second Edition. Ivan Strenski.
© 2015 Ivan Strenski. Published 2015 by John Wiley & Sons, Ltd.

during the last third of the nineteenth century.) Our early modern skeptics contributed to the rise of the historical-critical study of the Bible primarily by submitting it to humanistic and naturalistic methods of study. I am thus arguing that the larger external context of a Europe-wide wave of cultural transformation carried biblical scholars along with it. In the spirit of the new skeptical age, they challenged attempts to form and preserve exclusive confessional minds by submitting the biblical narrative to the sciences of philology, history, and the study of ancient literatures. In addition to their support of these scientific approaches to religion, the Deists also gave impetus to the *art of interpreting* these documents – hermeneutics (Byrne 1989, p. 94).

In theory, therefore, the Deists, skeptics, and the Higher Critics of the Bible all shared the conviction that the Bible *could and should* be scrutinized like any other piece of literature. It is hard to resist the conclusion that being part of such a great cultural revolution helped biblical scholars "think they were right" about the critical path they were to pursue. Furthermore, since critical study of the Bible was open to any and all, it addressed the external context of the scandal of religious divisions in Europe. In the Higher Criticism of the Bible, people across religious confessions should be able to arrive at a common mind about the biblical narrative, because it demanded no commitments of faith. It was those confessional commitments of faith that divided Christian from Christian. Higher Criticism of the Bible required no such confession. Instead, it operated in terms of the normal human rational, empirical, and naturalistic methods of study that brought people together, rather than driving them apart. No wonder the Higher Critics of the Bible "thought they were right"!

Higher biblical criticism met with opposition and controversy from the start. Its opponents "thought they were right" in so doing because of the long tradition of biblical authority in Christendom, both Western and Byzantine. While it is true that critical historical inquiry into the Bible grew out of a pious desire to form the common mind of the faithful, some religious folk could simply not abide permitting the "their" Bible to be the subject of the formation of the common mind about scripture by those who, in some cases, were not believers at all. Even when it

did not immediately upset ordinary expectations about the nature and content of the Bible, higher critical study of the Bible produced results that collided with entrenched views among the faithful. Of this impact of historical critical methods of Bible study, historian Van Harvey notes that the great modern theologian Ernst Troeltsch (1865–1923) "discerned that the development of this method constituted … a revolution in the consciousness of Western man" (Harvey 1966, pp. 3–4). To entrenched defenders of confessional readings of the Bible, the results of historical criticism were nothing short of "traumatic" (Harvey 1966, p. 6). Supernaturalism, miracles, Christian uniqueness, reliance on faith as a fundamental basis for life – all these came into question with the advent of Higher Criticism (Harvey 1966, p. 5). Indeed, often enough the collision between the confessional and non-confessional mind produced casualties. One of the most radical of biblical critics, David Friedrich Strauss (1808–74), slid into heresy. Although Strauss began by promising only strict historical criticism, he ended by abandoning Christianity altogether (Harvey 1966, p. 7).

But cross-confessional critical thinking about the Bible did not inevitably drive out the believers then; nor does it today. The liberal Protestants in the present volume, such as William Robertson Smith, were more typical of the spirit of biblical criticism than the Strausses. They saw the critical historical study of the Bible as a necessary vehicle for a more mature religious conviction. Robertson Smith was a student of Julius Wellhausen, one of the pioneering biblical critics to be discussed later. Smith vigorously affirmed the Christian value in taking the critical scientific and historical path: "The higher criticism does not mean negative criticism. It means … the effort everywhere to reach the real meaning and historical setting, not of individual passages of the Scripture, but of the Scripture Records as a whole" (Smith 1912, p. 233). Robertson Smith was, of course, hardly oblivious to the potentially upsetting impact of the critical work of a Strauss: "The science of Biblical Criticism has not escaped the fate of every science which takes topics of general human interest for its subject matter, and advances theories destructive of current views on things with which everyone is familiar and in which everyone has some practical concern" (Smith 1881, p. 1).

But this shaking of the conventional foundations of religion was no reason for a daring religious soul, like Robertson Smith, to draw back from the challenges of forming a wider cross-confessional or non-confessional mind about the biblical narrative. Again, Robertson Smith lays down a challenge: "We must not be afraid of the human side of Scripture ... the more closely our study fulfills the demands of historical scholarship, the more fully will it correspond with our religious needs" (Smith 1881, p. 27). Speaking in the optimistic, positive voice of a progressive Christian, Robertson Smith resolved the problem of the relation between criticism and biblical piety. The same spirit continues to inform Higher Criticism of the Bible today. But, for the sake of balance, we should also note that skeptics like Ernest Renan felt little desire to celebrate the supernaturalistic elements in biblical narratives. Nor did those like Strauss resist the opportunity critical study of the Bible provided to launch his own post-Christian theological agenda. Each critic will have to be taken on their own terms.

"Frodo Lives!" Myth, History, and Mystery

The late Middle Ages and early modern periods had their pioneers in a Higher Criticism of the Bible. The Italian theologian Fausto Sozzini (1539–1604) resorted to the newly emerging historical disciplines to challenge the credibility of the biblical authors. His major work here is *On the Authority of Holy Scripture* (1570). The French Catholic priest Richard Simon (1638–1712) was also determined to bring historical critique to the Bible. Influenced by Baruch Spinoza, about whom we will read more below, Simon published his ideas in his *Histoire critique du Vieux Testament* (1685). Significantly, both early writers had to evade the fierce state/church censorship of the day, and had to resort to foreign publishers. Altogether different was the situation of the nineteenth-century German Protestants who established Higher Criticism as we know it today and, in general, both freely taught and published their critical works as neither Sozzini nor Simon could. Jesus was the focus of their critical gaze. The Jesus of the gospels became particularly controversial because of the post-Reformation insistence upon literal readings of the Bible. Literal

readings were powerful for their clarity and definitive power. Yet they are also vulnerable in at least two ways. First, literal readings of the Bible might suggest a superficial equation with prestigious modern literary modes, such as history. If the Bible said Jesus rose from the dead, then it was a historical fact! But such literal readings were denied the immunity from criticism enjoyed by allegorical or symbolic readings, which could always claim exemption from close scrutiny. If Jesus' resurrection is taken symbolically, it is exempted from the demand, for example, to produce empirical evidence of its occurrence. After all, it is only a "symbol," not the "real" thing. Literal reading cannot escape from such interrogation so easily.

Second, if one reads the Bible literally, why should we also not read other ancient narratives – what we call "myths" – literally? If Jesus literally rose from the dead, did Attis and Demeter as well? Or if we say that the return to life of Attis and Demeter is only a "myth," does that suggest that Jesus' resurrection story is too?

Reasoning further, some of these Higher Critics of the Bible posed the question whether, despite the "mythical" qualities of the gospel narrative, parts of the gospel might contain *historical* elements nonetheless. Once this move to sift out the historical features concerning Jesus from the mythical ones begins, the quest for a "historical Jesus" was launched. Here we seek information about Jesus, the flesh-and-blood man, who lived during the time of Caesar Augustus in Palestine. We seek to know about Jesus in the same sense as we would seek to know about any other historical personage, such as Socrates, Plato, or Caesar.

Another way of talking about the historical Jesus was by contrasting him with the "mythical" one. The term for this Jesus, friendlier to Christian believers and more current in today's religious discourse, is to refer to the opposition between the "Jesus of history" and the "Jesus of faith." Here, the Jesus whose acts and words can be affirmed by the historical sciences is the "historical Jesus," the Jesus, for example, attested to have existed by the Jewish historian of the first century, Flavius Josephus (37–100). The Jesus of faith would then be that understanding of Jesus affirmed in Christian creedal statements, but including aspects either of a dubious historical nature or statements with no historical basis at all.

Here would be aspects of Jesus' career such as his "sitting at the right hand of the Father" – not the kind of claim put forward as a candidate for "history" since it would be a state of affairs occurring in eternity. But although it is believed by Christians to have occurred in time and space, the resurrection of Jesus would qualify as a state of affairs encompassed by the rubric, the "Jesus of faith," because of its miraculous nature. Indeed, *believing* that the resurrection is a historical fact is for many Christians a defining feature of Christian orthodoxy.

The point to be made here is that the raising of questions or problems has been one of the leading ways that theorists have tried to come to a common mind about religion. Put otherwise, the effort to form a non-confessional common mind about the Bible has forced a whole series of probes into its veracity that would not be appropriate for the formation of such a common mind. For that reason alone, we need to appreciate the vital role in the making of modern-day religious studies played by the Higher Criticism. To do this with the right degree of depth and polish, we need to press on and learn something of the ways that Higher Criticism first challenged received understandings of the Bible. I shall do this, first, by attending to the *methods* employed to form a non-confessional common mind." Second, I shall introduce some of the first *major players* in the Higher Criticism.

Biblical Criticism's New Methods

Whether seeking to destroy faith or deepen it, biblical critics wanted to ask questions, wanted to give their curiosity free creative rein. The biblical critics "thought they were right" to be critical because they, at least, had "internal" reasons for doing so, connected to the new developments in their field as historians and students of language. Recall as well that they also had "external" reasons for developing new methods with which to study the Bible, which spoke to the scandal of Christian disunity. They learned from at least four new disciplines for studying religion. The successes of history, philology, textual criticism, and hermeneutics had all taught them how they could make great strides in knowledge. Unlike Herbert, who knew only philosophy, and Bodin,

who knew only jurisprudence and law, the biblical critics were massively armed with the tools of the new knowledge. Those who wished to study the Bible critically needed to master more than polemics: Higher Criticism of the Bible demanded being a good historian, being adept in the *ancient languages* of the Near East, knowledgeable about how texts were *assembled*, and, finally, adept at *interpreting* them. The biblical scholars combined all these varied skills. More importantly for us, thanks to the biblical critics, these disciplines have been fundamental in the study of religion at large. Scholars of religion are routinely expected to know languages, often exotic ancient ones, to negotiate their way through historical data, to be aware of the existence (or lack thereof) of texts, and to see the interpretation of data as just one of the things we naturally do.

First, *history*. In their commonly held belief in the value of the humanistic and naturalistic treatment of religious texts – especially those of Christianity – Deists, skeptical empiricists, and Higher Critics of the Bible each advanced the humanistic and naturalistic study of religion in their own way. Like the Deists in their quest for what might lie behind or precede revelation, we will see that the Higher Critics sought to uncover the historicity – the actual historical substrata underlying biblical narratives. As skeptical, empirical historians, Higher Critics wondered, for instance, whether there really had been a great *historical* flood as related by Genesis? Did the walls of Jericho, also, *in fact* 'come tumbling down'? Or, at least, is there *empirical* evidence that they did so when and if a *historical* Joshua was *in fact* on hand to expedite their collapse? In this connection, historical approaches to religion raised questions of religious documents, asking whether there was a written record of events said to have occurred in the past, in contrast to events which were only imagined, such as handed-down stories and myths. Likewise, the growing prestige of the historical sciences boosted their confidence that they "thought they were right" about bringing a historical method to the Bible.

The skeptical empiricist, Scots philosopher David Hume (1711–76) set something of an example of the way in which history could be applied to the study of religion. His *Natural History of Religion* provides an object lesson in how one can submit religion to the rigors of historical inquiry and criticism. Hume showed, in effect, that it was not enough just to be clever at dialectic, as he supremely was. Nor was it enough to excel in legal polemics or in working the nuances of concocting diplomatic compromises, as both Bodin and Herbert of Cherbury were. A firmer grasp was needed of "doing history," as well. Thus, Hume challenged Herbert on the identity of Natural Religion by appealing to the new ethnographic data coming in from the contemporary voyages of discovery: on surveying this literature, one failed to find anything like Herbert's Natural Religion with its five characteristics. Indeed, one did not even find belief in one God. Instead, Hume pointed out that all that we could conclude from the data was that the earliest and most widely deployed kind of religion was polytheism – a belief in many spirits.

We will recall as well that, by training and inclination, the Deists tended on the whole to be philosophers. Thus, when Bodin did historical work, as he had in his legal histories, he pursued this discipline in relative isolation rather than in a growing movement with others engaged in a definite kind of special inquiry. The rise of Higher Criticism represents something altogether different – namely the growth of a historical mentality or consciousness.

The Deists, then, had been concerned with comparing religious doctrines and beliefs, or religions as institutions. The Higher Critics, on the other hand, were devoted to the historical study of the religious scriptures common to both Judaism and Christianity, and to the historical contexts in which these documents arose. We will look more closely at the work of critical historians in exploring the contributions of representatives of the influential "Tübingen School" based at the progressive Eberhard Karls University (Tübingen) in the Germany of the early to mid-nineteenth century, F.C. Baur and D.F. Strauss.

Next, *philology*. Once the question of the historicity of religious texts was engaged, the texts had to be read in their own languages and/or translated into modern European languages. Students of religion needed to be trained in *philology* – the serious study of language in all its dimensions. The new biblical scholars had often to determine facts as elementary as the identity of the languages in which the Bible had been originally and subsequently written. They had to check older translations for errors, or construct afresh the grammars of the ancient tongues for the first time. As students of ancient texts and obscure literary forms, these scholars were reconstructing lost cultures and civilizations through the study of ancient languages.

History and philology, in their turn, called forth yet another discipline – *textual criticism*. From the time of the late Middle Ages to the Renaissance, two cultural developments set into motion the need to develop critical methods of reading biblical texts. The first was the discovery of biblical and other religious manuscripts allegedly of great antiquity. The second was the development of printing. Both developments produced a massive number of actual physical texts – copies – in circulation throughout Europe. Some of these copies were authentic, others forgeries (Popkin 2003, p. 219). This inevitably gave rise to questions about how to distinguish the real versions of old texts from false ones. How do we determine authenticity, and find the "best" physical text? The questions the discovery of these actual texts provoked similarly gave these early critics of the Bible confidence – internal reasons for thinking that "they were right" to press on with their critical work.

What applied generally to any ancient text applied to the Bible itself. Such a realization produced a veritable cascade of questions about the Bible. Indeed, critical historical and textual methods produced so many, and so many profound, questions that we have yet to achieve a common mind about many aspects of the Bible. Take this list of preliminary questions to start with. Since different versions of the biblical texts circulated at a particular time, it made sense to ask whether a particular text was authentic or a clever counterfeit, whether one text contained fewer errors than another, whether one was a "better" one than another. Or they might want to know which particular text may have been based or derived from another text. How indeed could we assign dates of composition or of creation to the texts in hand, since most of the texts did not come with such explicit identifying markers, or if they did, how could one be sure these were accurate? Students of the ancient literatures want to know, for instance, whether there might be textual errors in the Bible, mistakes that perhaps had crept in during the course of copying and recopying by medieval and ancient scribes. Were there even deliberate distortions made to the texts by unscrupulous scribes or scheming clerics? And how do we know what the words of these texts meant for the people of the time of their creation? Was the text at hand the product of a single author, and who was that author, if it be only one? Or was the text the edited sum of the works of several authors or voices? Who, indeed, were they? And what have they to do with each other? Are they allies, opponents, or something different yet again?

Jewish philosopher Baruch Spinoza (1634–77) provides a very influential early example of how sacred texts were studied in order to unpack the mysteries of their authorship. But, as we will see, the conservative forces of many religions succeeded in suppressing the rise of Higher Criticism of the Bible until the nineteenth century. Here, it fell to the Tübingen School, especially F.C. Baur, D.F. Strauss, finally to produce a rigorous and durable practice of text criticism of the Bible. Even the renegade Roman Catholic biblical critic Ernest Renan drew inspiration from the Germans, while ignoring his own French precursor, Richard Simon. It is Spinoza, however, who is generally recognized as precursor of the work eventuating in the Tübingen School, because of his querying the Mosaic authorship of the Torah. In its full-blown form, the critical study of texts entailed the systematic and rigorous study of documents for the purpose of determining their actual authenticity, their factual authorship, their true date of creation, the cultural and social circumstances of their origins – what the German Higher Critics called *Sitz im Leben*, their situation in a particular living context.

In their close attention to the empirical details of religious data, then, the Higher Critics fostered a humanistic and naturalistic study of religion that contributed to the formation of a common mind about the Bible. Revelation was not denied because the Bible was now to be studied non-confessionally; confessional commitments just had to be squared with what these investigations of religious texts turned up. Faithful Roman Catholics might, for example, point to Matthew 16: 18's reference to Peter as the "rock" upon which Jesus will build the church. They have formed a common confessional mind around a

reading of this passage that justifies the present institution of the Roman papacy. But what did it mean to be a "rock" or "church" in the time and place of the author of Matthew? Are Protestants obliged to accept the Roman Catholic common mind formed about Matthew 16: 18? They surely do not think so. Thus, in that case, what are those who wish to stand back and encompass both Roman Catholic and Protestant readings of Matthew 16: 18 to do? The Higher Criticism provides one answer to this dilemma – resort to the sciences of textual criticism that are neutral regarding confessional commitments. One great contribution to the humanistic and naturalistic study of religion, made by the Higher Criticism, then, was to approach a sacred text, such as the Bible, as a *human* document that could be pulled apart and held up to the light of critical scrutiny (Harvey 1966, ch. 1).

Finally comes *hermeneutics*. Once these languages had been identified, their grammars mastered, and some notion of the composition of the biblical text achieved, the students of the Bible were faced with the most interesting and intellectually challenging problem of all – interpreting what the biblical texts meant in their original and present form, and how they should be construed in the future. This eventually called forth a general theory of interpretation, *hermeneutics*. How, for example, does the whole of a text shape the way we interpret any given part? How and why can Matthew 16: 18, for example, be pulled out and treated in isolation from everything else, even in Matthew? Can, paradoxically, we even understand any part of a text until we grasp the meaning of the whole? Does the larger context of the composition of the Gospel According to Matthew perhaps help us know how to "read" Matthew 16: 18 better than reading it out of context? Philosopher Friedrich Schleiermacher (1768–1834), who is generally acknowledged as founder of philosophical hermeneutics, put it this way: "The sense of every word in a given location must be determined according to its being-together with those that surround it" (Bowie 1998, pp. 44). To this end, Schleiermacher constructed a system of interpreting texts correctly that modern readers will find more reminiscent of a technical manual on engineering than a treatise on how to read the Holy Book. In this vein, Schleiermacher advanced methodological maxims, arranged in numbered paragraphs, laying out the rules of interpretation. Here are some examples:

> 23. Even within a single text the particular can only be understood from out of the whole, and a cursory reading to get an overview of the whole must therefore precede the more precise explication.
>
> Second Canon: The sense of every word in a given location must be determined according its being-together with those that surround it. (Bowie 1998, pp. 27, 44)

I would be remiss if I did not also mention that Schleiermacher argued that hermeneutics also involved understanding the *subjective* or "psychological" presuppositions and talents of readers (Bowie 1998, p. 12). In this sense, interpretation was more of an "'art', because it cannot be fully carried out in terms of rules" (Bowie 1998, p. xi). For this insight, Schleiermacher may also be seen as a precursor of the phenomenology of religion and its insistence upon empathy: "Before the application of the art one must put oneself in the place of the author on the objective and the subjective side," says Schleiermacher (Bowie 1998, p. 24). Together with history, philology, and textual criticism, hermeneutics comprises a truly impressive repertoire of methods for the study of sacred texts carried on by the present-day Higher Criticism of the Bible.

Higher Criticism: Internal Discrepancies

It is easy to understand pious resistance to the application of such a battery of scholarly methods of inquiry to the Bible. Scholars wanted to form a different kind of common mind from that each religious confession sought to nurture. A confession's sacred scripture should not be analyzed as if it were profane. That would be to locate scripture outside the charmed circle of a religious confession's treasured heritage, and place it, instead, in the public square of debate. Besides, don't such critical studies put into question the Bible as eternal revealed truth? The critical study of the biblical text, therefore, launched a whole raft of questions understandably causing consternation, and often antagonism, among the faithful. I want to divide these into two broad categories. First were questions prompted by an "internal" critique

of the biblical narrative; other problems were generated by what one may call an "external" critique of sacred scripture.

Take internal critique first. Here, one investigates puzzles thrown up by certain oddities and inconsistencies inside the text itself. The most often sited discrepancy occurs in chapter 4 of the book of Genesis where it recounts the story of Cain and Abel, Adam and Eve's only children. As we know, Cain kills his brother Abel. Shortly thereafter, God asks Cain where his brother is, only to receive the now classic retort "Am I my brother's keeper?" Unhappy with this answer, God curses Cain and dooms him to bear the mark of his murder – the infamous "sign of Cain" – and to be forbidden henceforth to settle and practice agriculture. What, however, struck the new critics of the local narratives was the fact that in Genesis 4: 17, the Bible tells us that Cain subsequently went on to marry, produce a son, Enoch, and continue his life as a city dweller. Cain's marriage stood out because the Bible tells us that Adam and Eve only bore two children, both sons. Who produced Cain's wife? How, indeed, could Cain have found a wife to marry, if he and Abel were the only offspring, as the Bible relates, of the first parents of the human race? The Bible is silent on this matter, but the critics of the biblical narrative fell upon this inconsistency as a sign of the human – imperfect – character of the biblical text. In the New Testament we find similar internal discrepancies in the genealogies attached to Jesus. Matthew, chapter 1, traces Jesus' origins to Abraham. Yet in Luke, chapter 3, Jesus' genealogy is traced as far back as Adam. At the Last Supper, Luke records that Jesus used two cups (see Luke 22: 17 and 22: 20), while Matthew 26: 26 and Mark 14: 23 mention only one.

From the viewpoint of the Higher Criticism, these discrepancies did not necessarily invalidate the claims of Christianity or ancient Judaism. They only raised questions about the composition and character of biblical texts. We know, for example, that the early Christian church assembled the Bible in the form in which we now have it. In this sense, the Bible is the daughter of the church. Thus, the church decided which books and which teachings were to be included in the Bible – placed into the canon – and which were not to be included. Recent scholarship into these rejected texts, the so-called Gnostic gospels, not to mention their popularization in Dan Brown's runaway best-seller, *The Da Vinci Code*, conveys some of the excitement and scandal that new readings of the Christian canon can produce (Brown 2003).

As we will learn in greater detail as I explore developments in the study of the Bible by feminists, the scandals keep coming. Princeton biblical scholar Elaine Pagels believes that the study of non-canonical texts, such as the notorious, Gnostic gospels may help us understand the development of Christian attitudes toward women. Why were some gospels included and others (the so-called Gospel of Thomas, for example) excluded from the New Testament canon? It is often asked these why women have traditionally had an inferior role within Christianity. But when one encounters Pagels' Gnostic gospels, women there are often quite prominent. Why were such gospels rejected from the canon? Could the casting of women into inferior roles in the canonical gospels have been more a matter of early Christian misogyny rather than, say, straightforward loyalty to the words and wishes of Jesus? This juxtaposition of canonical and non-canonical gospels thus has the power to make us think anew about commonly accepted assumptions about religious orthodoxy. It creates one of those "problems of religion" that I mentioned in my introduction, and that are so important in the development of critical studies of religion. It also shows how forming a common mind about Christianity that includes women as full participants in religious life can unsettle a confessional mind that rules out the implications of what Pagels claims to have discovered in her Gnostic gospels.

But what of the external criticism of the Bible? Here, critics homed in on the *factual truth* of the biblical narrative. Critics looking for external flaws in the Bible challenged the veracity of certain events, such as the virgin birth and the resurrection of Jesus, the occurrence or performance of miracles, such as the multiplication of the loaves and fishes or the ascension of Jesus into heaven. They bluntly asked whether the events narrated could ever have happened, or whether the beliefs affirmed could be justified by appeals to reason.

One strategy for checking the factual nature of biblical events asks whether these events could be "historical." How do biblical accounts of events square with those of contemporaneous documents of indubitable historical value? Is the Bible good history or is it something else entirely? Do Roman or Jewish records of the time confirm biblical accounts of the same period? Was there really a Roman procurator in Judea named Pontius Pilate, and was he involved in the condemnation of Jesus to death? Indeed, did such a person as Jesus of Nazareth exist? Did his career conform the picture given of him in the Bible? And so on.

A second strategy for checking the factual accuracy of the Bible – especially regarding miracles – is by comparing claims made there to our knowledge the natural world. Is it possible, for example, that Moses could have caused the Red Sea to divide? Is the virgin birth of Jesus or any other human being a biological possibility? When the Bible says that God made the sun stand still at the battle with the five kings of the Amorites, could this really have been the case – especially since we know that relative to the sun it is the earth that moves?

Now, when critics put both internal and external critiques to work, they produced predictably upsetting results for the faithful. Some believers ceased altogether in their observance. Others, like Robertson Smith, as he explained, felt that criticism purified and matured religious belief. Why should a mature Christian fear the discovery of internal discrepancies in the biblical narrative? They revealed the human element in scripture, and thus brought it closer to people. Progressives also dealt out the same contempt to their co-religionists who needed miracles to strengthen their faith. Thus, many progressive Christians welcomed the way Higher Criticism swept away what they took to be peripheral to the true Christian life.

Spinoza

Lest I give the impression that the Higher Criticism was a solely Christian, and Protestant at that, affair, we owe the practice of seeking internal and external discrepancies ultimately to the great Jewish religious thinker, Baruch Spinoza (Simon-Nahum 1991, p. 12). From the start, Spinoza tells us of his desire to study the sacred text free of any confessional connection. He speaks of doing so according to the light of reason – scientifically or naturalistically, following only the light of his God-given faculty of curiosity. Like Bodin and Herbert, Spinoza was determined to form a non-confessional common mind about the Bible. Spinoza wanted to construct this religiously *neutral* common mind for the very same reasons Deists did – to reduce religious violence. In his case, Spinoza tried to defuse conflicts caused by different readings of the Bible within his own Jewish community. "I determined to examine the Bible afresh in a careful, impartial, and unfettered spirit, making no assumptions concerning it, and attributing to it no doctrines, which I do not find clearly therein set down" (Spinoza 1670/1951).

Beyond such sincere scientific resolutions, Spinoza laid out a series of procedures and questions that would inform the future Higher Criticism. His "method of Scriptural interpretation" could be used to guide critical or humanistic and naturalistic inquiry into the biblical narrative: "What is prophecy? In what sense did God reveal Himself to the prophets, and why were these particular men chosen by Him? Was it on account of the sublimity of their thoughts about the Deity and nature, or was it solely on account of their piety?" (Spinoza 1670/1951, p. 8). Like the Deists, Spinoza understood that the study of religion begins with asking questions, with identifying problems, with seeing what God-given curiosity and imagination use to challenge us before coming to a common mind about religion.

In Part IV of our book, we will also see how feminist and African American scholars exploit the methods of Higher Criticism to justify why they "think they are right" about their new theoretical programs. Outside Western civilization, as well, our own day has seen scholars from religious traditions like Islam trying to apply the same kinds of critical tools to the analysis of their sacred texts as Christian and Jews had from the early nineteenth century. A Muslim scholar in Germany writing under the pseudonym Christophe Luxenberg has argued that the Quran has been misread and badly translated for centuries. Luxenberg's scholarship concerns itself with the earliest extant copies of the Quran, and argues that parts of Islam's sacred scripture are derived from pre-existing Christian literature, later misinterpreted by Islamic scholars preparing editions of the Quran that are still read today (Stille 2002: p. A1).

Major Protestant Players: Ferdinand Christian Baur and the Tübingen School

Despite the brilliant beginnings made by Spinoza, it took nearly 150 years before his theoretical insights bore fruit. German Protestant historian and philosopher Ferdinand Christian Baur (1792–1860) first fully articulated and extensively practiced the approach adumbrated by Spinoza. As Spinoza challenged the Mosaic authorship of the Torah, Baur made an even more general critique of traditional readings of scripture. They should not be tolerated. Instead, the critic should apply the methods of interpretation sufficient to attain a historically defensible understanding of the text. The Bible reflects human authorship, as Spinoza, too, had argued. The Bible in its entirety did not fall whole and supernaturally formed from the hands of God, even if it remains divinely inspired. Biblical criticism should then be directed at understanding the human processes that went into the formation of the Bible.

For Baur, a principal influence for understanding human historical processes was Georg Wilhelm Friedrich Hegel's (1770–1831) philosophy of history. Hegel taught Baur to discern the logic of historical change as a dynamic interaction between "thesis" and its opposite, "antithesis," which subsequently resolved into a "synthesis." Hegel made Baur sensitive to patterns of opposed tensions and struggles, which issued in resolutions that shaped both profane and sacred history. In the Bible, Baur discerned how opposed theological parties contended for dominance in resolving religious history into some sort of synthesis. It is easy to see how Baur's stress on opposition, contest, and struggle in the Bible offended many of the faithful, who wished only to see a simple, uncomplicated revelation of a pre-formed divine plan.

For Baur, an excellent example of this pattern of Hegelian dialectic tension was to be found in the Pauline letters. When read through Hegelian eyes, the letters of Paul reveal a theological battle between two opposed factions of early Christians – the party of Jewish Christians associated with the apostle Peter on one side (Petrine), and, on the other, the new Gentile Christians recently evangelized by Paul (Pauline). Baur argued that the Petrine party lined up with those still clinging to their Jewish identities, while the other fell in with the more radical universalizing line taken by the "new apostle to the Gentiles" – Paul of Tarsus. Baur saw nothing less than a dynamic logic of Hegelian opposition pitting Petrine thesis against Pauline antithesis. The resolution of this opposition in a new synthesis would define the nature of early Christianity and, in effect, how the church would evolve from that point forward. The synthesis achieved between the confrontation of these two factions, Baur argued, was summed up in the Gospel of Matthew. Despite such a seemingly innocent resolution to the struggles that Baur saw in the New Testament, his entire approach was so profoundly disturbing to the received wisdom of traditional believers that Baur was severely attacked over the years, and finally isolated from his colleagues.

The Quest for the Historical Jesus: David Friedrich Strauss

Beyond the critical studies of the Bible by Baur and others in the early nineteenth century, one major question has dominated the fortunes of historical criticism right up to our day. This is the so-called "quest for the historical Jesus." Although more than just a single quest, this was an attempt to sort through the traditional narrative representations of Jesus in order to provide a historically reliable biography of Jesus (Harvey 1966, p. 9). It was this quest that attracted some of the most prominent figures of nineteenth-century biblical criticism, such as a one-time student of Baur's, David Friedrich Strauss.

Strauss well deserves the reputation for being his generation's chief protagonist in pressing the critical historical examination of the life of Jesus. His *Life of Jesus* (*Leben Jesu*, 1834) – marked a major event in the progress of critical study of the Bible. Although it was not the rationalist skeptical and demythologizing biography of Jesus that Renan achieved, its theological assaults on received conceptions about the character of Christianity created scandal enough in its time. Strauss challenged a host of traditional beliefs about Jesus in his great work – the historical

accuracy of the birth stories, the narratives of Jesus' temptation by Satan, his baptism by John, the many reported occasions of miraculous healing performed by him, and, of course, Jesus' transfiguration, resurrection, and ascension (Harvey 1966, p. 11). But Strauss went beyond naturalist skepticism and sought to build on the ruins of the biblical narrative a new religious vision entirely – religious humanism (Harvey 1966, p. 7).

With Strauss, we find at first the same skeptical attitude to miracles so well worked out in the writing of David Hume, Baur, and others. But we are also introduced to Strauss' technical conception of "myth." Thus, while Strauss argued that any biblical passage containing a reference to the occurrence of miracles could not, *ipso facto*, be considered "historical," he wanted instead to reflect upon the religious consciousness that took miracles to be real. It was true for Strauss that Christians, for example, proclaimed Jesus' resurrection, and equally true that Jesus really did not come back to life – in a *historical* sense. Yet Strauss did not believe that the evangelists or early Christians were lying, mistaken, or holding back what they knew to be true. Instead, Strauss felt that in calling attention to the miraculous and "mythical" character of parts of the biblical narrative, he was saying that the people of biblical times thought about the world differently than modern folk. We thought "historically"; they thought about the world "mythically." We and they had different minds. In biblical times, human mental development simply had not evolved a historical consciousness. Thus, there was no question of biblical authors deliberately fabricating false stories – "myths" – about Jesus. Instead, they rather naively and sincerely saw the world in an unpremeditated "mythical" way. They were only expressing themselves in a way appropriate to their level of mental development. People of today, informed as they were by a historical and scientific consciousness, could no longer see the world in this "primitive" way.

Taken together, then, the combined influence of the representatives of Higher Criticism of the Bible – from Spinoza through Baur to Strauss – for the general study of religion would be to put into question the status of any sacred scripture. In bringing to bear questions about the historicity of the Bible, in querying the character of the versions of the Bible in circulation, in raising the matter of the historicity and authenticity of the authorship of various sacred books, in interrogating sacred scripture about its internal discrepancies, the Higher Criticism has helped religious studies immensely in forming a common mind about something thought to be totally taboo to critical thinking.

What E.B. Tylor and Max Müller Learned from the Biblical Critics

As we will see with Friedrich Max Müller in the next chapter, the method of the Higher Criticism was combined with a cross-cultural *comparative* method, and extended in principle to *all* religious texts from *all* traditions. Applying these methods of the Higher Criticism to the study of ancient Indian texts, Max Müller too sought to identify and to reconstruct the character of the different historical strata of Indian religion in a humanistic and naturalistic way from evidence provided by the systematic study of language. Are the Vedas as primitive as the Hindus of today claim? If so, does linguistic evidence indicate this? Or are such claims theological and political? Does the study of the Vedic language point to the existence of a religion that historically preceded and materially contributed to the character of the Vedas? From linguistic evidence, such as comparative phonology, can we deduce that the Vedas have precedents, near relatives and such among other religious traditions outside India, such as other scriptures composed in Indo-European languages

like the Avestan of Iran? Why are so many of the features of Vedic religion like those found in *comparison* with ancient Iranian, Greek, and Roman religion, and so on? These kinds of questions asked by Max Müller of ancient India were typical of the same kinds of questions critical textual scholars and historians had been asking about the Bible for well over a generation.

Now while Max Müller was no anthropologist, since he limited himself to the study of written texts, the advent of the historical linguistic study that he practiced bore on the work of future anthropologists of religion such as Tylor and Frazer. I argue that we cannot really understand the context of Tylor's work, the "father of anthropology," without taking into consideration the relation of his thinking to the theories of Max Müller, his great Oxford colleague, rival, and critic, as well as the leading critical philologist and historian of (Indian) religions of his time. Both thought they had been able, in their related but different ways, to uncover the nature of the origins of religion – and certainly the methods by which one could do so. Yet they disagreed about both their methods and results. Second, the historical critical method of the study of the biblical texts, as developed in Germany under Paul Lagarde and Julius Wellhausen, made direct methodological contributions to the development of the anthropology of religion associated with William Robertson Smith, Durkheim, and the Durkheimian school. For these and many other reasons, the rise of the critical study of the Bible made a massive contribution to the emergence of the study of religion in general.

References

Bowie, A. (ed.). 1998. *Schleiermacher, Hermeneutics and Criticism and Other Writings*. Cambridge: Cambridge University Press.

Brown, D. 2003. *The Da Vinci Code*. New York: Doubleday.

Byrne, P. 1989. *Natural Religion and the Nature of Religion*. London: Routledge.

Harvey, V.A. 1966. *The Historian and the Believer*. New York: Macmillan.

Popkin, R. 2003. *The History of Skepticism*. New York: Oxford University Press.

Simon-Nahum, P. 1991. *La Cité investie: La "Science du Judaïsme" français et la République*. Paris: Cerf.

Smith, W.R. 1881. *The Old Testament in the Jewish Church*. New York: D. Appleton & Co.

Smith, W.R. 1912. "What History Teaches Us to Seek in the Bible." In J.S. Black and G. Chrystal (eds.), *Lectures and Essays of William Robertson Smith*. London: Adam & Charles Black.

Spinoza, B. de. 1670/1951. *A Theologico-Political Treatise and a Political Treatise*, trans. R.H.M. Elwes. New York: Dover.

Stille, Alexander. 2002. "Scholars Are Quietly Offering New Theories of the Koran." *New York Times*, 2 March: A1.

Further Reading

Albert, P.C. 1977. *The Modernization of French Jewry: Consistory and Community in the Nineteenth Century*. Hanover, NH: Brandeis University Press.

Bultmann, R. 1957. *History and Eschatology: The Presence of Eternity*. New York: Harper & Row.

Carbonell, C.-O. 1979. "Les historiens protestants dans le renouveau de l'historiographie française." In A. Encreve and M. Richard (eds.), *Les Protestants dans les débuts de la Troisième République (1871–1885). Actes du colloque de Paris, 3–6 octobre 1978*. Paris: Presses Universitaires de France.

Chadbourne, R.M. 1968. *Ernest Renan*. New York: Twayne.

Chadwick, O. 1975. *The Secularization of the European Mind in the Nineteenth Century*. Cambridge: Cambridge University Press.

Ermarth, M. 1978. *Wilhelm Dilthey: The Critique of Historical Reason*. Chicago: University of Chicago Press.

Evans, D. 1963. *The Logic of Self-Involvement*. London: SCM Press.

Fiske, J. 1876. "The Jesus of History." In J. Fiske (ed.), *The Unseen World and Other Essays*. Boston: Houghton Mifflin.

Frazer, J.G. 1923. "Ernest Renan et la méthode de l'histoire des religions" (1920). In *Sur Ernest Renan*. Paris: Claude Aveline.

Harrison, P. 1998. *The Bible, Protestantism and the Rise of Natural Science*. Cambridge: Cambridge University Press.

Houtin, A., and F. Sartiaux. 1960. *Alfred Loisy: Sa vie, son oeuvre*. Paris: Éditions du CNRS.

Neusner, J. 2000. "Conservative Judaism." In J. Neusner, A.J. Avery-Peck, and W.S. Green (eds.), *The Encyclopaedia of Judaism*, vol. 1. Leiden: E.J. Brill.

Pelikan, J. 1974. *The Spirit of Eastern Christendom (600–1700)*. Chicago: University of Chicago Press.

Renan, E. 1861. *The History of the Origins of Christianity*, Book 1: *Life of Jesus*. London: Mathieson & Co.

Wolf, I. 1980. "On the Concept of a Science of Judaism." In P.R. Mendes-Flohr and J. Reinharz (eds.), *The Jew in the Modern World*. New York: Oxford University Press.

PART II

Classic Nineteenth-Century Theorists of the Study of Religion: The Quest for the Origins of Religion in History

4

Max Müller, the Comparative Study of Religion, and the Search for Other Bibles in India

Max Müller in the Center of a Whirlwind

The present chapter takes its inception from a single question, answered, as it happens, by Friedrich Max Müller (1823–1900). If the Bible can be looked upon as a *historical* document, fit to be judged by normal historical and empirical standards of scholarship and knowledge – and not faith or supernormal cognition – then why cannot *any* religious scripture be seen in its human, historical aspect? Why, therefore, should not all the texts of all the religious traditions of the world be subject to critical textual and historical examination for the purpose of understanding the ways that they have changed over the eons? Despite their claims to supernatural, divine, or trans-historical origins, are not all religious scriptures *at least at some level* documents owned by human beings and transmitted by human beings to their descendants? To all these questions, Max Müller gave a rousing positive answer.

Straight off, I must alert students that Max Müller's theoretical thinking is perhaps more complex and contorted than that of any other thinker in this book. He lived at the center of a confluence of world-shaking trends of thinking, many pulling him in opposite directions. Romanticism, Protestant theological liberalism and hyper-orthodoxy, German nationalism, the European discovery of the languages and literatures of India, British and western European imperialism and colonialism, and rising industrialism name only some of the more salient cultural forces surging round Max Müller. Added to these, external forces, Müller cannot be understood without taking seriously his own sincere, mystical piety. What then makes him so hard to understand is that he tried to reconcile all these forces and his own personal spiritual yearnings together in one seamless theory. In my discussion, I shall also argue that in some sense the story of the study of religion Müller produced can only be understood by seeing how his internal piety played against and along with these exciting cultural forces. That, at any rate, is what I am arguing, and what I hope will give students a rich understanding of arguably the very first religious studies scholar who "looks" like us.

The Bible and Beyond

In the last chapter, I argued how Higher Criticism of the Bible succeeded famously in complicating the reading of at least one cardinal religious text. In doing so, it changed the face of religion, and the study of religion in the Atlantic world. Although the original biblical critics never

Understanding Theories of Religion: An Introduction, Second Edition. Ivan Strenski.
© 2015 Ivan Strenski. Published 2015 by John Wiley & Sons, Ltd.

intended to reach beyond the Jewish and Christian religious worlds, their success made possible the application of the same techniques to any and all religious texts. Religious texts now could be appreciated as human creations, shaped by historical processes, rather than solely as visitations from eternity. Religious texts continued to be inspiring, and even inspired. But words of the spirit often rode the broad backs of rambunctious political, moral, theological, or psychological "tigers" as well. Texts came to life; and life came to texts.

Now, what brings us to the business of the present chapter is that Friedrich Max Müller was among first to act on the conviction that the critical tools of the Higher Criticism of the Bible could and should be applied to all the world's religious scriptures (van den Bosch 2002, p. 517). "I had been at a German university, and the historical study of Christianity was to me as familiar as the study of Roman history... . [It] left me with the firm conviction that the Old and New Testament were historical books, and to be treated according to the same critical principles as any ancient book" (Müller 2002a, pp. 191–192). For that one fact alone, we should be eternally grateful to the life and work of Max Müller. But I get ahead of myself. Müller's link to the biblical critics was solid. He even learned the techniques of Higher Criticism from those close to its founding generation in Germany. Unlike most biblical critics, however, Müller looked on all the world's religious texts as equally sacred, as "revelations." For him, the Bible was a most excellent example of a sacred text, but there were others as well that he revered. He thus approached all the sacred books in a spirit of scientific historical curiosity and discovery. His goal was to help form a nonconfessional common mind about the sacred texts of all the world's religions, and thus a common mind about religion. It is thus easy to see why we should revere Müller as one of the founders of the study of religion. His open, critical approach to religious scripture remains a lasting legacy of his work in the study of religion.

While his stance left Müller open to the charge of agnosticism, he, nevertheless, accepted it in good cheer because it gave him an opportunity to declare his allegiance to a broadly scientific approach to the subject of religion. "In one sense I hope I am, and always have been, an Agnostic," because, as Müller defined the term, an agnostic is someone "relying on nothing but historical facts and in following reason as far as it will take us ... and in never pretending that conclusions are certain which are not demonstrated or demonstrable" (Müller 1901, pp. 355–356). Committed to the full exercise of his God-given curiosity, he lets nothing but loyalty to the evidence stand in the way of his pursuit of truth.

We should, then, think about Müller as joined in spirit not only to the efforts of the Higher Criticism, but also to Bodin, Herbert of Cherbury, and, as we will see later, William Robertson Smith. He was one of those thinkers I call a "positive skeptic." He used curiosity and questioning to deepen his own spirituality. He did not, for example, engage in destructive debunking or demythologizing of sacred texts for its own sake. Müller shared the view of liberal Christians of his day in believing that the Higher Criticism would bring out the "original Christian message by undoing it from the accretions of supernatural and superstitious beliefs" (van den Bosch 2002, p. 78). That ultimately may be why Müller "thought he was right" to pursue his special approach to the study of religion.

Müller's Theological Liberalism and Comparison of Religions

As a typical theological liberal, Max Müller felt that "orthodox" Christianity was a cramped Christianity. He wanted to expand it, as we will discover, by cross-fertilizing Christianity with the wisdom to be gleaned from the world's religions. He was not shy about borrowing ideas from other religions to adapt to his own religious practice. Theological liberals like Müller thus typically rejected biblical literalism, saying that a "belief that these books had been verbally communicated by the Deity, simply because it was recorded in these sacred books, was to me a standpoint long left behind" (Müller 2002a, p. 192). Müller proudly chose the path of progressive religion. But, unlike most theological liberals, he felt that things were in a long, slow spiritual decline. Civilization was not advancing forward as the more Protestant progressive evolutionists thought. The advance of industry and technology crushed the human spirit. Social forces like secularism took people further from a religious sensibility, a reverence for nature, or a hunger for the divine. Technology and industrial development despoiled the natural environment.

Yet Müller thought there was hope for the human spirit in retrieving the sublime glories of ancient religion of the deep past. At the beginning of things shone the spiritual light of a Natural Religion that would magnetize people into its contemplation. He felt that the new techniques and scholarship only recently available to him and his generation would make the best case possible for this earliest and truest Natural Religion. In his deep religious orientation, Müller again shows how traditions of sound scientific scholarship have sometimes been driven by deep religious motivations. In this, he is in the good company of his forebears in the study of religion, Herbert of Cherbury and Jean Bodin.

Despite these progressive values, however, Müller was reluctant to promote them as an alien in his adopted country. He certainly never *confronted* his theological enemies. So, he avoided confrontation with the established church and "stood aloof from the conflict of parties, whether academic, theological or political." As he tells it, "I had my own work to do, and it did not seem to me good taste to obtrude my opinions, which naturally were different from those prevalent at Oxford" (Müller 2002a, p. 156). But in actuality Müller's "own work" turned out to spark a consequential controversy. He went public with his plan of a universal *comparative study of religions* emergent in the publication of his great collection of the religious scriptures of the world, *The Sacred Books of the East*. The Anglican ecclesiastical establishment that dominated the academic and religious scene in Oxford in the latter half of the nineteenth century was, however, alert to the slightest signs of non-conformity. Anything which suggested, as Müller's collection did, that the religions of the world ought to be regarded as equals alongside one another was taboo! And so, despite his precautions, the Church of England establishment finally threatened to censor Müller's work and, effectively, end his career.

The details of this brewing crisis are now well known. In his introduction to the *Sacred Books of the East*, Müller seemed to throw down a gauntlet to the church. "The time has come," said Müller,

"when the study of the ancient religions of mankind must be approached in a different, less enthusiastic, more discriminating, in fact, in a more scholar-like spirit" (Chauduri 1974, p. 352). Part of Müller's meaning here came in the form of proposing to publish the Hebrew Bible and New Testament in the *Sacred Books of the East* alongside all the other scriptures of the world. Like Bodin, Müller treated Christianity as an equal among the world's religions. And however he might have tried, he could not avoid giving offense to Oxford's conservative theological establishment. In the end, the establishment won, and successfully blocked the inclusion of the Bible in the collection (Chauduri 1974, pp. 355–356). The established church felt that it could not abide having incomparable Christianity *compared* with "pagan" (*sic*) cults. Müller had to settle for a compromise. He was able to publish his "Bibles of humanity," the *Sacred Books of the East*, but without the Bible.

Müller's plans for the study of religion were essentially a response to the discovery of massive stores of the literatures of many long-lived religious traditions theretofore unknown in the West. His approach, the "science of religion," was one of the first disciplines successfully to exploit these new facts. His idea in establishing a "science" was, at the very least, to form a common mind about religion, so that scholars and other thinkers could engage the facts of religious difference and similarity. No one was barred from this discourse because of confessional commitment.

A good example of how Müller imagined this new discourse of religion would go might be found in his reaction to the critical writing of David Hume. Recall that Hume had challenged Herbert of Cherbury's idea of monotheism, integral to his concept of Natural Religion. Hume appealed to some of the same new data, available to Müller, and concluded that it showed polytheism to be the oldest known religion. Answering Hume's attacks, Müller argued that the texts of the most ancient of the religions of India supported a position more like Herbert's. On the surface, they did, in fact, evidence a kind of polytheism, as Hume had claimed. Yet Müller argued that a more profound look at the data revealed something like the Natural Religion of Herbert and Jean Bodin lurking *behind* Hume's polytheism. Müller insisted that the best historical and scientific evidence we have pointed to a mystical religion of transcendent and infinite oneness. (We might look on this as Müller's version of Natural Religion.) Hints of this straining for mystical unity showed through the religion of Vedic nature worship, said Müller. Those texts themselves seemed to esteem a oneness, analogous to the monotheisms both Bodin and Herbert proclaimed! The matter would not rest there, of course, because Tylor was determined to vindicate Hume against Müller, here by arguing that animism, a belief in plural spirits – and thus polytheism of a sort – was the universal and oldest religion.

A final word: as we can see by the doggedness of this argument and its attendant emotional tone, pure science was not in play. Hume and Tylor were enemies of religion; Müller was a devotee. While Müller may be accused of theological intentions, Hume and Tylor are no better. They too play the theological game of requiring ultimate commitment to a particular worldview. In a sense, they simply play the role of atheistic theologians to Müller's mystical theism. I conclude here that Müller's intense persistence in pressing his case arose from a genuine conviction of the actual reality of the Infinite in his own life. He had reasons "internal" to his life – his own religious experiences – that gave him another reason to "think he was right" to form a common mind about his approach to the study of religion. We will see in our study of Tylor that his motivations were diametrically opposed. He held a life-long grudge against religion, or at the very least established religion of England. He intended his so-called "scientific" theory of religion to do nothing less than destroy the Church of England.

The Discovery of the East–West Link in Sanskrit

Now, how was Max Müller to justify seeing profound unity behind radically empirical plurality? How was he able to defend his view that a deep mystical unity in the divinity hid itself behind the wild and unpredictable polytheism of the ancient religions of India, and their Indo-European cousins, the religions of Greece, Rome, and the Germanic and Celtic worlds? To answer these questions, we need to follow Müller down the

path he blazed in using the *historical* study of languages to ground his approach to religion. And as we should be prepared to expect, for Müller the starting point for all such inquiries was the languages of India and their historical relation to the West.

The growing European consciousness about ancient India was a principal part of the nineteenth-century European effort to learn about the civilizations of the ancient world through language. As we have seen, with the biblical critics, the critical study of languages was fundamental to humanistic studies. So it was also with India, and her relation to the West. The West's new knowledge of India came at first primarily through the recovery of ancient manuscripts collected by Sir William Jones, a British jurist posted to India in the late eighteenth century. Jones was also the first person systematically to argue that the ancient sacred language of India, Sanskrit, was a close relative to Latin, Greek, and even English. Sanskrit words such as *pitar, matar,* and *bhartr* were simply too close to their Latin counterparts, *pater, mater,* and *frater,* and to the English *father, mother, brother,* Jones argued, for it to be a mere accident. There had to be some kind of – yet unknown – historical link between East and West. In short, our Western languages had Eastern origins! Müller joined these efforts to master ancient languages such as Sanskrit. And since the British kept the only complete set of Sanskrit manuscripts of the Rig Veda in Oxford, Müller abandoned the Continent for England.

Müller succeeded famously in making a new life in Oxford, largely through his own courage and effort, but also though the timely aid and assistance of the sponsorship of extraordinary patrons. He exploited Jones' work on the Vedic texts. And, as a comparativist, he went even further to parlay that into the claim that ancient tongues of Rome and Greece, indeed most of the modern languages of western Europe, constituted a "family" related to the family of Indic languages related to Sanskrit.

But just what followed from the fact of such linguistic affinities between East and West? And how did this help Müller show that Hume was wrong about polytheism being the oldest and most fundamental form of religion? Let me briefly show how Müller worked toward his desired conclusions. First step: he sought to delve as deeply as possible into the meanings of our modern European words. Consider his example of the English noun, "divinity" and its verbal relative, "to divine." We all know what divinity means in common parlance. The dictionary states: "the state or quality of being divine; especially, the state of being a deity." When we begin with a simple comparison with a sister language such as French, a near-perfect cognate occurs – *divinité* – meaning deity or god. Likewise, Spanish yields the abstract noun *divinidad* of the same meaning. How do we account for these similarities, at least from the point of view of English? Either "divinity" originated in one of these tongues, and then passed to the others, or they are all derived as equals from a third source. And if all these words for divinity stemmed from a common third source, it must indicate that something important is being retained across all the linguistic differences of Indo-European.

Next step: what else do these relationships tell us about the original meanings of such words? What did "divine" mean originally, especially since it does not come from Hebrew biblical sources? If, for example, one of our English words for God is derived from the Latin, is it not possible that our very idea of God might also be derived to some degree from Roman ideas of the gods? Müller answers first by noting that when we trace such words as "divine" to their Latin origins, we find that they come from *divinus*. Now, in the Roman world *divus* is a soothsayer, and a veritable god! So, these relations suggest that a "diviner," for example, may be one who manipulates godly – "divine" – powers. Here, we might just recall how someone being inspired by a god (*divus*) carries over into our conceptions of, say, a "water diviner," someone who finds water with a "*divining* rod."

Next step: Müller was not satisfied only to trace modern European languages to their Latin roots. He wanted to trace their origins back into what he believed to be the ancient source of modern Western languages, their ultimate Indo-European roots, by way of Sanskrit, because he thought this told us about ourselves. What, therefore, are the root Indo-European meanings of, say, "divinity" and its relatives, "divine," "diviner," and so on? Müller answered with a remarkable series of replies. For starters, the Sanskrit word for "god" was *deva* – virtually the same word for "god" as the

Latin *divus*. At the very least, comparison implied that classic European and Indian language about deity may well be at root a *common* set of concepts, shared all across the 6,000-mile distance and 5,000-year-long history of the Indo-European crescent, extending from Sri Lanka to Ireland, or even across the Americas to Australasia. We are still digesting the implications of such facts today. So, when Müller delved into the root meaning of words like "divinity," *divus*, and *deva*, he concluded that even before Latin and Sanskrit, another language, Indo-European, must lie beneath. This root language was the root, mother tongue of this great "Aryan" (or, now, Indo-European) language family. And when he searched for the root meaning of all these various forms for "god," he found the little word, "div." From this little particle, "divinity", *deva*, and such derived. But what did "div" mean? "Div" just meant "to shine" – a radiant, high god was what the Indo-Europeans worshiped, and passed on to us!

So, where then does this leave us? Here, it suggests why so many myths of the Vedas are addressed to the sun. And since the Indo-Europeans conceived the sun as male, that most radiant of all shining objects, received their worship, rather than, say, the earth, our life-giving home. Müller accepted the patriarchal values both of his own age and of the Indo-Europeans. Both held that worship of the sun was the highest form of nature religion. As Rig Veda X: 1 says:

High has the Mighty risen before the dawning,
and come to us with light from out the darkness.
The glooms of night you, Brilliant Babe,
    subduest, and art come forth,
loud roaring, from your Mothers.

Müller's joy increased, as we will see shortly, when he also realized that there was a convergence of this Indo-European solar religious imagery with motifs in the German Idealist philosophy in which he had been educated (Voigt 1967, p. 32). In both of them, the sun was the leading emblem of an original transcendental, yet natural, unity of the philosophical ultimate, the Absolute (Mosse 1964, pp. 70–72, 89). Everything was beginning to fall nicely into place for Max Müller and his increasingly sophisticated worldview. Müller, then, felt he had established that an Indo-European *mentality*, detectable and transmitted in language, lived on in the present in us. In particular, basic Indo-European ways of thinking held sway over Western thinking about the divine. Since our modern languages are rooted in Indo-European ones, this linguistic link explained, in part, why we think about religion as we do. That is why we in the modern West continue to think about God as "divinity" analogously to the way the Indo-Europeans of millennia past did. They thought their *devas* were high, often father-gods, radiant and, as we will see, typically male. Rather pleased with himself for concluding this deep link between East and West, Müller asks rhetorically, "And are we so different from them?" (Müller 1881a, p. 451). Another of Müller's contributions to the study of religion, then, was the idea that it should be studied historically and through language for traces of its ancient formation.

But is Müller right that our thinking owes such a debt to the ancient roots of our language in Indo-European ones? The point remains disputed. But, at least, he has forced us to consider how language shapes our thinking, and how it does so across great historical spans of time. In chapter 16, we will see how today's feminist critics and theorists of religion take very seriously the propositions embedded in Müller's great project. Feminist critics of "patriarchal" religion challenge our modern Western notion of a father-god and blame that inscription of patriarchy on our language. Feminist theorists, like Marija Gimbutas, explicitly blame Indo-European male linguistic formations of *deva* for patriarchy. The feminist critics charge that our Indo-European "daughter" languages retain an ancient male-dominated Indo-European/ Aryan conception of divine male power and violence, of a high father-god, such as we see in the Vedas. Its high god, Indra, lives above in a heavenly abode, and is at the same time a warrior god. Given what we know of the structure of Indo-European ideas of gods/*devas*, the feminist critics have a point. Along with them, why should we allow our conceptions of divinity to continue to be so limited by their Indic origins? Why not break out of the straitjacket of language that shapes how we see the divine? In chapter 16, we will see how the feminists argue we can escape the confines of the patriarchal Indo-European ways of imaging the divine. We will see how they urge adoption of the goddess, a figure who exemplifies feminine-gendered qualities of cooperation and love, and who is resident

immanently in the earth, our home, rather than the violence and domination of the Indic high gods.

Max Müller therefore cherished the belief that the lessons learned from seeking the Indo-European roots of our language could reveal the roots of our religions as well. While Müller honored the Bible and revelation, like Herbert of Cherbury, he felt that the human mind possessed a natural aptitude for religion, preparing it to receive biblical or Vedic or Quranic revelation. This ultimate root of religion was Müller's version of Natural Religion. By the painstaking use of a comparative method of the study of languages he thought he could make his case for what he thought Natural Religion was.

Max Müller's "Romantic" Comparativism and Western Imperialism

It is worth noting at this point how Müller, Bodin, and Herbert of Cherbury all thought they were right to study religion in a very special way – *comparatively* and cross-culturally. But the different times in which they lived pressed them to do so for different reasons. By Müller's time, the age of religious warfare among European Christians had long passed. Comparing Protestantism and Catholicism was neither particularly controversial nor really much called for in the mid-nineteenth century. Instead, cross-cultural and comparative study honed a new edge as a result of European colonial expansion. Western imperial intrusions into territories populated by peoples of other religions sparked feelings of Christian exceptionalism among the Westerners. British imperialists tacitly thought that Christianity must be better than the religions of India or the Near East because Western powers dominated India and the Near East economically and militarily. Also reinforcing Western imperial exceptionalism was the rising prowess of Western science and technology. Dynamic modern industrialism seemed, as well, another sign of Western prowess. That the industrial state itself fed on the resources extracted from the colonies simply reinforced a sense of Western, and thus Christian, superiority. "We" were "winners"; "they," the "losers." In chapter 17, we will see how these Western colonial attitudes of the nineteenth century become the basis for contemporary post-colonial theories of the religions of the colonized "Other."

Müller was prominent in his time because he swam against the stream of the pervasive Christian and Western religious exceptionalism. These religious exceptionalists refused to compare Christianity with other religions in any way. For them, the two were as distinct as apples and oranges. Christianity was the exception to the rule, so to speak, since it was a "revealed" religion, while the others were simply human creations. Christianity was, therefore, privileged or incomparable. Now while it is also true that Max Müller took pride in his own German Christian background, he did a great deal to promote the dignity of the religions of the world, beginning with the religions of India. A look into Müller's world might help us see how this attitude partook of larger changes in the mentality of the nineteenth-century German world. Why, for example, was Müller open and generous to religious difference, when all about him raged the forces of imperial domination and Christian religious exceptionalism?

Müller's immersion in the German Romantic movement made exotic cultures like India's and its religions attractive to him. But what was Romanticism, and how did Müller's approach to the study of religion participate in it? Romanticism was a complex and many-sided cultural movement. When we think of Romanticism, we should think of the "natural" look in fashion. Think women in free-flowing, gauzy gowns instead of stiff, corseted dresses. Imagine men in elegant frock coats and big, floppy hats. Recall both men and women sporting carelessly combed, even slightly disheveled hairstyles rather than the formal powdered wigs of the previous generation. Romanticism, thus, not only encompassed literature, such as the poetry we all read in school, but it also marked all the domains of life – the arts, such as painting, sculpture, architecture, and music, but philosophical, political, and religious thinking as well. Müller's remarks on the new valuation of nature encouraged by poets such as Walter Scott and Wordsworth reveal how deeply he was involved in the new Romantic sensibility. He observes their novelty: they "discovered the beauties of their native land." In what others only saw as "bare and wearisome hills, they saw the battle-fields and burial places" of gods – "the primeval Titan struggles of nature" (Müller 1858, pp. 114–115).

We can call Müller's method for studying religion "Romantic" because it shared common values with the ideals of the Romantic movement. That massive cultural wave brought with it a host of external reasons for Müller to "think he was right" about the way to study religion. First, Romanticism placed a high value on nature. Müller's horror at heavy industry's destruction of nature and urbanization's eradication of intimate village life conditioned him to yearn for the lost world of simple piety and the bucolic life. His nostalgia for the natural environment encouraged him to "think he was right" about celebrating those aspects of the religions of India that reflected that same affection. In an autobiographical reflection upon his youth, Müller yearns for the small town of Dessau in which he grew up: "I was born and brought up in Dessau, a small German town, an oasis of oak trees ... a town then overflowing with music. Such towns no longer exist" (Müller 1898, pp. 4–5). Years later, reflecting on the harshness and depersonalization brought by the industrial age, he observed with sadness: "All this is changed now; few people remember the old streets, with distant lamps swinging across to make darkness more visible at night" (Müller 1898, pp. 5–6).

In the imagined world of the ancient religions of India, Müller rediscovered a distant echo of the bucolic world of his youth. The Vedas revel in nature, and imbue it with religious radiance. Fire is no mere flash of flame. He is Agni, the lord god of fire. Dawn is no bland description of the time of day. She is Ushas, the gracious goddess of the new day, and so on. Second, Romantic sensibility exalted the non-Western "other." The Romantics declared that foreign – "other" – cultures, especially ancient India and its religions – were the equals of the West. Indian civilization rivaled those of Greece, Rome, or the Near East. All were "great" civilizations. Indeed, a veritable "Indomania" raged across early nineteenth-century Europe. We should, therefore, see Müller as part of this great cultural vogue, just as we saw Bodin and Herbert as part of larger European skeptical movements (Trautmann 1997, pp. 138–140).

Third, the Romantics preferred a mystical, monistic sort of spirituality, rather than the personalized monotheism of the Abrahamic tradition. They often spoke of desiring to be one with nature, to lose their individuality in some metaphysical "All." When the West discovered Hindu texts celebrating these ideas, say in the Atman-Brahman principle of the Upanishads, the Romantics took special note. Müller's celebration of the Infinite as the pinnacle of religious life, is of a piece with the Upanishadic mysticism broadly embraced by the Romantics.

Fourth, the Romantics made nationalism a potent "external" cultural force. To them, nationalism affirmed the local and the rooted. It affirmed "natural" affinities of common blood and history, over against the ideal of an abstract humanity of the Enlightenment. In large part, Müller's personal spiritual quest was also enriched and complicated at the same time by being bound up with emergent search for a German national soul. This Romantic theme merged not only with the theme of the "natural," but also with others we have already reviewed. For example, while Müller's nationalism was German, it took what seemed a sharp detour through India. German nationalists felt that they carried on a common cultural legacy traceable to ancient India – thus the vogue for Indology in Romantic Germany. Müller was caught up in this bizarre, but potent, enthusiasm for a rooted sense of natural belonging that caused German nationalists to embrace faraway India!

The Search for Germany's National Soul in India ... of All Places

Max Müller's interest in India cannot completely be understood unless we tie his Indian work to his nationalist feelings for his native Germany. Nor can his approach to religion be best understood apart from his engagement in the "German problem." German intellectuals, especially the Romantics, were consumed by the quest for German national unity and deep identity. Despite what one may think, Germany is actually a young nation that only attained unity in 1871. England, France, Spain, Poland, and even the much smaller Portugal or the Netherlands were centuries ahead of Germany in achieving *national* unity. This is so because, before the late nineteenth century, what we today understand as "Germany" was no single polity. Rather, the name "Germany" covered a loose array of scores of fiercely independent city-states, duchies, principalities, and kingdoms of various sizes, sometimes bound together in confederation, but at other times not. The German Romantics, like Max Müller, felt the pain of such political disunity, especially in the face of the general linguistic unity of German-speakers: how would they deal with it? Müller's somewhat alienated existence in England might also be factored into the formation of his mentality.

It may not seem so strange that Romantics like Müller appealed to India to help remedy the problem of German national inferiority, since we already know about Müller's theories of the Indo-European origins of European languages, German, of course, included. National pride demanded a strong national identity. But what could the quest for German national identity possibly have to do with India? Language already united the disparate German states. Did spoken German have a noble, root identity that might speak to the national identity crisis? The Italians or Spanish could trace their historical origins to their Latin heritage, linked as it was to the glories of ancient Rome. But the Germans seemed thwarted from following that route because their linguistic roots and historical ancestry lay with the barbarians that invaded and then destroyed Rome. Where were the Germans to find an equivalent classic high-culture ancestor? This is where the work of Romantics and Indo-Europeanists came in handy. For them, the link would be direct. By leapfrogging both the Greco-Roman and Jewish sources of Western cultural identity, the German Aryanists felt that they could tap the roots of ancient India and its Aryan past. Best of all, the linguistic scholarship of the Indo-Europeanists gave German Aryan identity a scientific basis. Müller filled out these links in terms of cultural – in particular, religious – links between Germany and ancient India.

German Unity via Hindu Myth

German nationalists, like Müller, felt that the Germans had finally found the ancient forebears they sought for yet another reason: not only was German *language* derived from original Indo-European root stock, where Sanskrit occupied a privileged position, but the very spirituality of the earliest strata of Sanskrit religion and literature – the Vedas – conformed with the Romantic, monistic sensibility of advanced German thought! The Vedas spoke to Müller's own heart. They lent themselves to being read as the perfect expression of a religion of nature. In Rig Veda I: 113, the Vedic goddess Ushas – Dawn – is celebrated in rich metaphors worthy of Müller's Romantic contemporaries:

This light has come, of all the lights the fairest:
The brilliant brightness has been born effulgent... .
Daughter of Heaven, she has appeared before us,
A maiden shining in resplendent raiment.
Thou sovereign lady of all earthly treasure,
Auspicious Dawn, shine here today upon us.

But there is more. Indian scriptures pointed to the monism at the center of German Idealist philosophical spirituality. Müller believed that some of the natural world so transcends human abilities to encompass it, that it generated in early people the very idea of a realm radically beyond our own, where the gods dwelt. For instance, Müller suggests how early ideas of the transcendent arose in the Vedic contemplation of objects of great power and immensity, like the sun, ocean, or great mountains. Many other peoples knew what the Vedic sages knew – "unknown ... infinite beings ... *Devas* ... the same word which, after passing through many changes, still breathes in our own word, *Divinity*" (Müller 1892, p. 218). Müller reveals himself in speaking in mystical tones, saying that in contemplating nature, "do we not feel the overwhelming pressure of the Infinite ... from which no one can escape who has eyes to see and ears to hear?" (Voigt 1967, p. 32).

These ideas of cosmic oneness seemed to gain support from the Vedas as much as did the more straightforward naturism that they seemed to confirm. Thus in Rig Veda I: 1, a hymn to the Vedic god of fire, Agni, the sacrificial fire, is addressed first of all as a person, then addressed directly as the personification of the god Agni himself along with the priest offering the sacrifice.

I extol Agni, the household priest, the divine
    minister of sacrifice, the chief priest, the
    bestower of blessings ...
O Agni, the sacrifice and ritual which you
    encompass on every side, that indeed goes
    to the gods.
May Agni, the chief priest, who possesses the insight
    of a sage, who is truthful, widely renowned,
    and divine, come here with the gods.

Typical of the idealism and Romanticism of his generation of young German intellectuals, Müller's own religion tended in the same way toward pantheism. He, like others of his class, much admired the later Vedanta philosophy of India, where the unity of all things was not merely suggested in poetic metaphor, as in the Vedas, but asserted outright. Müller's religious sensibilities were accordingly cast in terms of a Romantic nature mysticism to which the Vedas might be said to point, married all the while to the constant philosophical bent of his mind. In one of his last essays, he rejects with vigor the notion that he is an agnostic in the vulgar sense of the term. Müller feels he knows, indeed feels, more of what the truth of things may be ever to accept that epithet: "If Agnosticism excludes a recognition of an eternal reason pervading the natural and the moral world ... then I am a Gnostic, and a humble follower of the greatest thinkers of our race, from Plato and the author of the Fourth Gospel to Kant and Hegel" (Müller 1901, p. 356). Müller is a self-declared monist.

Giving the lie, then, to Hume's belief in the archaic status of polytheism, Müller is convinced that humans at their earliest stages of development were not polytheists, but devotees of a mystical, monistic unity. "To men who lived on an island," says Müller, "the ocean was the Unknown, the Infinite, and became in the end their God." For this reason, Müller could declare the Vedas the equivalent of the (Hebrew) Bible. Indeed, he called it the "Aryan Bible." In Müller's view, ancient Aryan myths, such as the Vedas, were a repository of the ancient wisdom of the Aryans. In some real sense, then, the deepest content of the Vedas lay at the root of Western culture, and thus German national identity. "We are by nature Aryan, not Semitic," said Müller proudly in 1865.

I cannot leave the matter of the racist history connected with Aryanism without comment. While Müller was an Aryanist, and not free of anti-Semitism, he distanced himself from explicitly racist/biological interpretations of Aryanist discourse. He never felt that Indo-European philology had anything to do with race as a biological category, as it was for the nationalist Aryanists. There are, for Müller, no Aryan skulls. Yet with the genie out of the bottle, not even he could control "Maxmüllerism." It took on a life of its own and influenced the racism of such disciples of

Müller's as the American, John Fiske (Poliakov 1974, p. 214).

This quick tour through the political and cultural thought-world of Müller's formative years should give readers some idea of the significance of the Vedas for him. Müller was primed to see many things in the Vedas that his position at the heart of the German Romantic and nationalist movements favored. Both expressed love of nature and the native land, the prestige of mystical religion and spirituality, and so on. Because they seemed to be truly archaic, and thus closer to the natural religion of the dawn of humanity, the Vedas held pride of place for Müller. As such, he believed that they should be recognized as co-equal in cultural stature with the biblical traditions and literature of the ancient Hebrews – but now most importantly as the source of properly European, read "Aryan," cultural heritage. In the Vedas, Müller saw a record of the religion of a pre-European golden age. They provided a direct route into a profound philosophy, the primordial wisdom of the human race, and in particular into what he believed to be the mother race of the West – the Aryans.

By way of conclusion, we should now better be able to see how and why Müller "thought he was right" about the complex details of his theory and methods for the study of religion. For example, his regard for Natural Religion remained central. Despite his respect and affection for mythology and nature, Müller thought that religions rich in concrete, material imagery, such as the Vedas, could not be considered to represent religion at its best. He "thought he was right" that something serious was lacking in them, because he took it for granted that religion must be spiritual. It had to be something like the abstract religion of the Deists – Natural Religion. Thus, he inevitably came to "think he was right" to believe that mythologically informed, personified religions were inferior forms of religion. The term of choice used to name these sorts of religions was "Physical Religions." In Müller's scheme of religions, he ranked these lower than the lofty, abstract and *impersonal* "Philosophical Religions" of his own preference. Thus, he could "think he was right" in charging the Vedas with being "childish" in depicting jealousies among the gods. This meant that he had to press on beyond Humean polytheism or Tylorean animism to deeper levels

of religious unity to fulfill his comparative program's goals.

At the same time, however, Müller did not totally dismiss Vedic religion, because he "thought he was right" that religions like the Vedic could still point to an impersonal absolute. In Müller's view, the Vedas and certain polytheistic religions then had *relative* value. They marked progress along the way to a more abstract monotheism or impersonal monism – a religion of the Infinite. The Vedas, for example, did, after all, admit that the universal powers were governed by a kind of unifying law – *rita* or dharma. In bringing the host of the gods under such law-like regulation, Müller saw a unity being imposed upon the otherwise chaotic *devas*. They acted in concert with one another. This was far from the riotous polytheism of Hume, and, as we will see, the similarly unstructured animisms of Tylor. Vedic polytheism was, rather, a "henotheism" – a system in which many gods congregated and cooperated under law-like *unifying* principles, within an impersonal system. Müller believed that the henotheism of the Veda was thus a way-station on the road to an abstract monotheism or impersonal monism. And that is why he "thought he was right" about the value and ultimate meaning of Vedic religion and myth. For the ecumenical but pious Müller, this evidence of ancient wisdom reaffirmed his belief in a divine plan by which all human beings would be led to the truth, despite appearances to the contrary. Thus, the "real history of man is the history of religions: the wonderful ways by which the different families of the human race advanced toward a truer knowledge and a deeper love of God" (Müller 1882, p. 129). Making that history evident was Max Müller's goal for the study of religion.

What Max Müller Can Teach Us about Studying Religion

Taking together the work of these many potent "external" cultural forces – Romanticism, nationalism, anti-imperialism, the discovery of Indo-European sources, and so on – should help us see why Max Müller "thought he was right" about how to study religion as he did. In our world, we might not choose to study religion as he did, or for the reasons he did. But, what matters for our understanding of Max Müller is that *he* did! As it happens, the methods he applied to the study of religion have outlived the political and cultural factors that inspired them. We can "think we are right" to study religion in many of the ways Max Müller did – comparatively, historically, linguistically – without accepting with his rationales for doing so. I would list three of these separable methodological achievements.

First, religions can be studied is by tracing their *diffusion* and distribution across the globe, by seeking their historical origins. Along with Müller, we can seek aspects of the religion of our own times in what was carried over from ancient, even Indo-European, times. But, we don't need to get all misty-eyed about the glories of the Aryan heritage – which is, in any event, linguistic and not racial. In the twentieth century, Georges Dumézil, the great French Indo-Europeanist, established an illustrious scholarly reputation on the basis of his arguments that there was an original Indo-European ideology, and that it entailed a tripartite organization of society – the king, the warrior, and the priest (Littleton 1982).

Second, we owe to Müller the development of the notion that there are *families*, *types*, or *styles of religions* – for example, Abrahamic, Indic, Semitic, Greco-Roman, Sino-Tibetan, and such. Just as there are families of languages – Indo-European, Altaic, Semitic, and such – there are families of religions. This makes Müller something of a proto-phenomenologist of religion. In our day, Ninian Smart, for one, has used this sort of scheme to bring out comparisons and contrasts between Christianity and Buddhism with great skill.

Third, we owe Müller a huge debt for his practice and promotion of *comparative studies of religion*. Based again on his experience of the comparative study of languages, he was the first scholar prominently to show how useful it would be to study religions in relation to one another. He put the proposition paradoxically, saying that a person who knows only one religion, knows none (Müller 2002b, p. 113). A person who knows about only one religion can never be sure that they know more than just what may be peculiar to that particular religion, rather than something fundamental about religions. Ever the scientist, Müller insisted that comparison was absolutely necessary for the study of religion to be scientific. "There is no science of single things, and all progress in human knowledge is achieved through comparison," he added (Müller 1892, pp. 417–418). Comparison, in particular, is so vital to the very identity of the study of religion that it is worth dwelling on this point of Müller's legacy. Comparison makes us *think*, by suggesting analogies, similarities, and differences we might not have entertained before. It stirs up our curiosity, and gives us a method for addressing our need to explain things.

References

Chauduri, N. 1974. *Scholar Extraordinary*. London: Chatto & Windus.

Littleton, C.S. 1982. *The New Comparative Mythology: An Anthropological Assessment of the Theories of Georges Dumézil*. Berkeley: University of California Press.

Mosse, G. 1964. *The Crisis of German Ideology*. New York City: Grosset & Dunlap.

Müller, F.M. 1858. *Wilhelm Müller*. London.

Müller, M. 1879–1910. *Sacred Books of the East*, 50 vols. Oxford: Oxford University Press.

Müller, F.M. 1881a. "Comparative Mythology" (1856). In *Selected Essays on Language, Mythology and Religion*, vol. 1. London: Longmans, Green & Co.

Müller, F.M. 1881b. "On the Philosophy of Mythology." In F.M. Müller (ed.), *Chips from a German Woodshop*, vol. 5. London: Longmans, Green & Co.

Müller, F.M. 1882. "On the Vedas or the Sacred Books of the Brahmans" [1865]." In *Selected Essays on Language, Mythology and Religion*, vol. 2. London: Longmans, Green & Co.

Müller, F.M. 1892. *Natural Religion*. London: Longmans, Green & Co.

Müller, F.M. 1898. "Musical Recollections." In F.M. Müller (ed.), *Auld Lang Syne*. New York City: Charles Scribner's Sons.

Müller, F.M. 1901. "Why I Am Not an Agnostic." In F.M. Müller (ed.), *Last Essays: Second Series*. New York: Longmans, Green & Co.

Müller, F.M. 2002a. *My Autobiography*. New Delhi: Rupa & Co.

Müller, F.M. 2002b. "On the Science of Religion, Lecture One" (1870). In J.R. Stone (ed.), *The Essential Max Müller: On Language, Mythology and Religion*. New York: Palgrave Macmillan.

Poliakov, L. 1974. *The Aryan Myth*. New York: New American Library.

Trautmann, T.R. 1997. *Aryans and British India.* Berkeley: University of California Press.

van den Bosch, L.P. 2002. *Friedrich Max Müller: A Life Devoted to the Humanities.* Leiden: E.J. Brill.

Voigt, J. 1967. *Max Müller: The Man and His Ideas.* Calcutta: Firma K.L. Mukhopadhyay.

Further Reading

Müller, F.M. 1891. *Physical Religion.* New York: Longmans, Green & Co.

Müller, F.M. 1986a. *Anthropological Religion.* New Delhi: Asian Educational Services.

Müller, F.M. 1986b. *Theosophy or Psychological Religion.* New Delhi: Asian Educational Services.

Sharpe, E.J. 1986. *Comparative Religion: A History.* La Salle, IL: Open Court.

Stone, J.R. (ed.). 2002. *The Essential Max Müller: On Language, Mythology, and Religion.* New York City: Palgrave Macmillan.

Strenski, I. 1996. "The Rise of Ritual and the Hegemony of Myth: Sylvain Lévi, the Durkheimians and Max Müller." In W. Doniger and L. Patton (eds.), *Myth and Method.* Charlottesville: University of Virginia Press.

Tylor, E.B. 1958. *Primitive* Culture (I). New York City: Harper & Row.

5

The Shock of the "Savage": Edward Burnett Tylor, Evolution, and Spirits

---

Mr. Tylor and His Science

It was Max Müller who dubbed anthropology "Mr. Tylor's science." At least since then Edward Burnett Tylor (1832–1917) has been seen as the first anthropologist. Like Muller, Tylor held academic posts at Oxford. But unlike Max Müller, Tylor spent some time visiting traditional societies, such as on his trip to Mexico in 1856. Pairing up with a fellow Englishman Henry Christy (1810–65) of the science-minded Ethnological Society of London, Tylor recorded his adventures in his first book, *Anahuac* (1861) (Stocking 1987, p. 195; 2001, p. 107). Also unlike Max Müller, Tylor therefore pushed for a direct, face-to-face study of religion rather than a close study of scriptures. He encouraged others to try to understand traditional or "primitive" peoples alive and rather than through a literature.

Tylor scarcely mentioned the term Natural Religion, yet he sought the first religion or the origins of religion. Here, he reasserted Hume's challenge to Herbert of Cherbury to provide empirical examples of Natural Religion. This quest eventuated in *Religion in Primitive Culture*, his greatest book, and one in which 70 percent dealt with religion, much of that with animism. Tylor argued that animism was, in effect, the first and most fundamental religion, not Max Müller's

elevated idea of Natural Religion as the contemplation of the Infinite, for example. Both Tylor and Hume saw the first religion – animism or polytheism – as a kind of rational projection of the ordinary experience of powerful people onto a supernatural realm. The theory of animism shows the "universal tendency among mankind to conceive all beings like themselves … in order to bring them nearer to a resemblance with ourselves" (Tylor 1873, p. 61). For Tylor animism was both historically the oldest and structurally the most fundamental of all religions. Thus, he packaged a historical thesis – which religion was first in time – along with a logical one – which religion was most basic, fundamental in form. This was his way of replacing all other proposals pretending to discover either the first or most fundamental religion. In this chapter we will explore why Tylor "thought he was right."

Animism as the True Natural Religion and First Attempts at Science

Tylor assumed that religion was really about giving an objective account of, or *explanation* of, the world. It was, thus, attempting what our science does – to explain things. This meant that Tylor looked at religious claims as if they were

Understanding Theories of Religion: An Introduction, Second Edition. Ivan Strenski.
© 2015 Ivan Strenski. Published 2015 by John Wiley & Sons, Ltd.

scientific hypotheses. They could fail or succeed according to how they squared with objective reality. Did Muhammad ascend into heaven? Were Adam and Eve the first humans? Does the accumulation of karma really determine one's chances of rebirth or reincarnation? All such religious claims were to be measured against empirical evidence. And in doing so, Tylor believed we would learn that Muhammad could not have ridden his horse into heaven. Nor could we test the theory of karma and rebirth empirically; and so on. Given this literal-minded way of reading religious claims, it is easy to see why Tylor "thought he was right" to presume that the religions tried to explain things – that they were about explanation.

But Tylor had so many reasons for thinking he was right that it is hard to decide which one mattered most to him. There were first the "internal" reasons for thinking he was right – the reports from people about the conceptions they had about things like dreams, the mysteries of death and dying, or even the movements of heavenly bodies. To Tylor, the evidence for his theory must have seemed overwhelming. It was ubiquitous, and thus relatively easy to find testimonies supporting his theory. That the existence of spirits, souls, gods, and so on explained events in the world was something many cultures believed, both past and present, near and far. The theory of animism, then, seemed to Tylor, rather obvious.

Consider first the experience of our dreams. In dreams, many feel that we ourselves were moving about in space without the resistance that our material bodies cause us. Now one can fly, now battle great beasts, now pass through walls, now run effortlessly across broad landscapes! Many cultures have naturally interpreted dreams as being real experiences of things that happen to us once our true spiritual natures are liberated from the shackles of the body. In the Upanishads, we are warned never to wake someone suddenly for fear that their spirit will not have sufficient time to return to the body once awake. Thus, when we dream, our spiritual selves actually move about in an ether, in a spiritual space where bodies are not needed. Evidence like that gave Tylor confidence that he was right.

Observation of the process of death and dying provoked similar conclusions. Here, the relation of breath to life is the key. In his article "The Religion of the Savages," Tylor explains why he thinks some so-called "primitive" peoples might have thought that the life-force inside us is somehow related to breath. Again, it is obvious that all living animals breathe, and once they stop breathing, we can assume they are dead. Perhaps it is the breath that determines life: "The act of breathing, so characteristic of the higher animals during life, and coinciding so closely with life in its departure, has naturally been often identified with the life itself" (Tylor 1866b, pp. 72–73). The ordinary experience of death – the cessation of that mysterious, invisible "something" (breath) – also might make animists think they are right about the way the world is. Tylor thinks this experience is why many cultures have identified with breath as a source of life, and thus as the essence of the soul or spirit. Does not the Bible say that "the spirit blows where it will"? Early medical experiments in Europe proceeded on the assumption of the reality of breath. Some tests were even proposed to try to detect the absence of this life principle in a dead body. The experiment consisted of placing a body that was about to die on the scales and waiting for death. Once the animal or person had died, their weight was registered once again in an effort to detect the difference in weight between the living and dead body. That difference the investigators thought would be accounted for by the absence of the soul or spirit in the body. The soul as breath was, then, thought to be real.

Max Müller even inadvertently adds weight to Tylor's theory. Recall some of what he told us about Vedic religion. Fire is not a mere thing; it is the *personal* god/spirit Agni present on earth. Fire glows red because the god of fire, present *as* flame, expresses "heated" emotions or shows off his splendor. Likewise, the sun – the personal fire/Agni in the sky – gives heat because it is the same "Agni" of the fire smiling at, and hence warming, those under the sun or gathered round the hearth. Stars, as well, are not mere dead matter. They live and move across the heavens because they *are* personal spiritual beings directing their course. Does not the god Phaeton make the day pass by driving his chariot across the heavens just as a human charioteer does his earthly vehicle? And, yes, there really is a "man" in the moon! Or, as the Buddhist Jatakas tales tell us, those same marks indicate the presence of a rabbit on the lunar surface. Even in our own time, some religious people sometimes resort to animistic explanations of "natural" events, such as 9/11 or Hurricane Sandy. They were acts of divine judgment by a personal agent – God – upon the sinful. The ubiquity of animism, and its apparently "natural" form, may be reasons even some prominent students of religion of our own day, like the cognitive scientists, "think they are right" to reprise a broadly Tylorian theory of religion. Thus, Tylor's theory of religion involving a belief in spirits and spirit agency encompasses all levels of religious belief, from local to universal, from the so-called "primitive" to the modern.

Now, while Tylor thinks such attributions of personal agency to inanimate things are "naturally" understandable, it doesn't mean that such attributions are true to reality. Animism may be natural, but that doesn't mean that it conforms to reality, Tylor would say. People in traditional societies (or modern theists!) mistake the true causes of things because they project everyday social experience onto nature. The creation of the world (by the gods or God), for example, is built upon the analogy of people making something. If we explain why and how houses exist by pointing to the carpenters who constructed them, then we can explain why and how the whole world exists by pointing to the Great Carpenter, to a spiritual carpenter, so to speak. But however widespread this way of thinking, Tylor thinks such a projection of the personal is a mistake. The universe is inanimate and impersonal. Personal models have no place in science. People just need to accept facts.

When I said that Tylor had perhaps *too many* reasons for thinking he was right about animism, I was also thinking of the larger, external context of his theorizing. The theory of animism was particularly agreeable to religions similar to those of Tylor's own upbringing. First, Tylor had been raised in a religious tradition – the Society of Friends (Quakers). Central to Quaker worship meetings was a "waiting for the *spirit* to move one to speak." Thus, the assembled worshipers remained in a state of silence, until one of their number felt that they had been urged to speak – by a *spiritual* force. So moved, the individual would rise and address the meeting confident that the spirit was at work. Thus, Tylor's own religious socialization might have given him ample

reason to "think he was right" about religion having to do with spirits. Second, the England of Tylor's time found Spiritualism enjoying a cultural vogue. Spiritualism was, in effect, a kind of animism because it held that the disembodied souls of the deceased could make contact with the living. Séances, consultations with spirit mediums, ouija boards, and such were popular (Stocking 1994, p. xvii). Thus, perhaps the "external" context of the religious fashion of Spiritualism gave Tylor a further reason for thinking that the belief in the existence of spirits was important to religion.

But there is a third, stubbornly negative, reason that Tylor thought he was right about the animistic nature of religion. Here, we see him responding to the external context of his situation in Oxford. Tylor deeply hated religion, especially the Church of England. Roman Catholics came in a close second as a target of Tylor's wrath. The intellectual and social world dominated by the Anglican Church formed a kind of external context against which Tylor rebelled. A moment's reflection should make this clear. If the theory of animism is true, then all beliefs in a spirit or god are essentially the same. After all, is not the belief in one God, so to speak, only "animism" (lowercase) writ large as Animism (upper-case)? When all is said and done, Christianity, like primitive animism, has always preached the existence of a great soul who cares for, acts in, and governs the world that, in fact, God has created. We can see some of the conclusions of such thinking in Tylor's contempt for the Mexican Catholics recorded in his first book, *Anahuac*. Referring to the elaborate ritual life of Mexican Catholicism, Tylor said: " There is not much difference between the old heathenism and the new Christianity … the real essence of both religions is the same to them." He could make such a claim because he believed that Mexican Catholicism looked liked so many "primitive" religions. They too had gods that "might be favourable to them, and give them good crops and success in their enterprises. This is pretty much what their present Christianity consists of" (Tylor 1861, p. 289). These words, dripping with sarcasm, should signal how deep and abiding Tylor's lofty contempt for religion was. Arrayed around him, manipulating affairs in Oxford, was the Church of England – a powerful external reality that gave Tylor all the reasons he needed to press on with the theory of animism as the basis of a universal theory of religion.

But there was a hitch in Tylor's project. While examples of traditional or so-called "primitive" societies might well be expected, in Tylor's view, to imagine that spirits or souls inhabit everything, they do not explain why *contemporary* religious folk should continue to think the same. Modern religious folk know about science, for example, and therefore should have beliefs that conform with the discoveries of science. But they don't! That modern religious folk continued to believe in spirits, such as God, Allah, Vishnu, and so on, presented a problem for Tylor. How was it that these "modern" folk were in fact no "smarter" in this respect than people from "pre-modern," ancient or small-scale traditional societies? Did modern religious believers simply not know their science? Tylor was unwilling to give up his evolutionary theory of human culture, so he had to explain data pointing to the lack of evolution.

Tylor's famous "theory of survivals" was supposed to deal with this annoying problem. Tylor thought he had disposed of the problem of the persistence of things that confounded evolutionary progress simply by concluding that some things simply hung on. Like bits of flotsam and jetsam, some stuff did not get carried along on the waves of historical development. Thus, modern religious believers simply had got stalled at a lower stage of mental evolution, in much the same way that some people fail to develop emotionally beyond adolescence. Their belief in God is a survival of "primitive" ignorance, not unlike the immature behavior that survives in people we think have not grown up emotionally. That was the best Tylor could do to explain religion's continued vitality. He was unwilling to give up the idea of progressive evolution. It meant everything to him.

1859 and All That: The Discovery of the European "Primitive"

Now behind why Tylor assigned religion to the dustbin of history was his incorrigible commitment to a theory of progressive evolution. Both the idea of survival and the idea of animism belong to Tylor's basic – and, for him, unchangeable – original theoretical developmental framework.

Everything Tylor wrote depended upon that assumption. Undermine his developmentalism, and the whole of his anthropology crumbles, as indeed it later did. So, we are then left to try to understand why Tylor might have "thought he was right" to be so incorrigibly – religiously – committed to his version of evolutionism.

Recall how Max Müller was stimulated to think anew about religion by his discovery of the scriptures of ancient Indian civilization. How could we encompass the religious import of these documents? How could we do so without rejecting them for confessional reasons? How could we see other religions within a new, expanded common mind that did not prejudice one over the other? In Tylor's case, inspiration for evolutionism came from closer to home. Dramatic eruptions of Europe's own local prehistory unsettled the cozy world of mid-nineteenth-century England. Such new historical data challenged Tylor to arrive at a common mind about religion that took these new facts into consideration. I refer to the series of spectacular archeological discoveries that totally revolutionized the European sense of history and the place of religion in it. People had existed tens of thousands of years ago, but had been utterly forgotten by their modern European heirs.

What *problems of religion* did these discoveries of the prehistoric human past create for Tylor and those like him? How did Tylor try to convey a sense of the meaning of these discoveries? Especially unsettling was the greatly extended sense of the human past far beyond anything suggested by the Bible. This realization only multiplied the effect of the blows to a biblical authority already reeling under the impact of Higher Criticism. These events demanded new theories to encompass the new knowledge only lately appearing on the European intellectual scene. They demanded the formation of a new common mind free of the constraints imposed by confessional religion. How would Tylor go about this?

As if religious consciousness had not been shocked enough by this new understanding of world history, Charles Darwin's *On the Origin of Species* (1859) only deepened the crisis of Western self-understanding. Darwin's naturalistic account of the development of all living forms, moving slowly but inexorably in geological time, made no mention of a divine creative initiative. For many, this explosion in the sense of the scope of the recoverable past presented yet another challenge to the intellectual foundations of religious belief in the West. If our own conflicts between religion and science are any guide, Darwin's challenge continues to excite controversy. What would Tylor make of Darwin? Would he adapt Darwin's evolutionary theory to his own? Or would he compartmentalize Darwin's views and go on, in effect, as if Darwin had not written at all?

The Caves and Their Religion

Now, although Darwin's revolution figures in any story of evolutionism, Tylor's attitude to religion may have been more shaped by the revelations of European prehistory unearthed in the caves of England and France. In 1859, a notable excavation at Brixham cave on the south coast of England shocked scientific and popular opinion. A local builder was digging the foundation for a row of terraced houses when he broke through into a subterranean cavern (Gruber 1965). There, the bones of animals, long since extinct in England, such as rhinoceri, lions, and elephants, were found. Adding fuel to the imagination of the late nineteenth century, some bone pieces showed signs of human fashioning.

Darwin happened to be particularly impressed by these discoveries. He felt that they "established the great antiquity of man." For many Europeans, it slowly became clear that literally right beneath their feet lay buried an entire prehistoric world of forgotten European ancestors. Tylor picked up on this link and developed ideas about present-day people into a total system. He looked for a link "to some antecedent primate form," and went on to translate this idea "into a systematic investigation of human sociocultural origins" – which is precisely what his anthropology would be (Stocking 1987, p. 172). Tylor's long-standing adherence to the pre-Darwinian developmentalist thinkers made it easy for him to imagine humanity to have grown up through many long stages of development (Stocking 1987, p. 178). In this sense, we might say that Tylor welcomed the problems created for religion by the discoveries at Brixham cave – especially the problems they made for the biblical literalists and theologians who made his life (and Max Müller's as

well!) so difficult in Oxford. But, in terms of the larger picture, what did Tylor think that these discoveries of the prehistoric world taught about religion?

On the one hand, one might argue that there is something decidedly "primitive" about these societies marked by the levels of technology found at Brixham cave. These societies lived by hunting and gathering, and thus had not yet developed agriculture or settled life in cities. Archeological evidence also indicates that these folk hunted and worked with stone tools rather than with technologies involving metal-working. Data such as these, therefore, led thinkers of Tylor's ilk to regard our ancient prehistoric ancestors as lower in their development than we. They were, to him, "primitive." But Tylor seemed blind to the sophisticated artistic quality of the wall painting found in the caves. Of the four chapters of his *Anthropology* entitled "The Arts of Life," he writes only about utilitarian material culture – technologies, tools, and implements (Tylor 1881). There is nothing on the esthetics or beauty of so-called "primitive" material culture. On the other hand, R.R. Marett, Tylor's biographer and an anthropologist in his own right, saw the cave paintings as unmistakably indicating esthetic refinement and even intellectual command. Philosopher Georges Bataille suggests as well that with the appearance of cave art humans moved out of the grim world of the workaday into a richer, and in a sense more human, domain of creative freedom (Bataille 1955). They were "primitive" no more! But Tylor had no taste for the cave paintings that so impressed Marett as fine art. He literally and figuratively never *saw* sophistication and high culture in the caves. He saw only what he wanted to see – the "primitive."

Does Religious or Cultural Evolution Make Sense?

The key to answering this question lies in understanding how and why Tylor, as well other cultural evolutionists, such as Frazer and Robertson Smith, whom we will meet shortly, thought they were right to think that human culture and the human mind evolve. All of them thought that some cultures were simply better or more advanced than others. Some cultures were like children or teenagers, while others were adult and mature. Nor was this belief restricted to scientists. Liberal Protestants, in particular, embraced radical progressive religious and social evolution as a "quasi-certitude," as one of their number asserted in the 1880s (Goblet d'Alviella 1885, p. 173). They all believed that humans evolved in terms of their kindness or trustworthiness, in their success at achieving happiness, in their native intelligence or honesty, in their range of emotional responses or abilities to sympathize with others, and so on. But we no longer agree. We no longer think that it is really progress to diminish the role of myth, and thus imagination, from religion in order to replace it with doctrines. Nor do we take for granted that it really is progress in religion to ignore the body, and thus ritual, and replace it with a series of ethical dos and don'ts. But if we were nineteenth-century folk in Britain or the USA, we would!

These questions are not at all easy to answer, and thankfully we do not have to solve these problems here. The point to be made is that it is not at all clear that it makes sense to speak about cultural institutions like religion, art, politics, and such as evolving at all, but Tylor and his generation had none of our scruples and doubts. The thinkers of the late nineteenth century, however, thought they knew quite well what it meant to speak of "progress" in religion. It meant the movement from polytheism to monotheism, from priesthood and sacrifice to prophecy and ethical purity of heart, from hieratic and hierarchic religious structures to a godly egalitarianism, from ritual to morality, from myths to beliefs, from superstitions to rational beliefs, and so on. In short, in the nineteenth century and earlier, the religious program of the Protestant Reformation of evolution and progress in religion was simply assumed as given as a "quasi-certitude" (Goblet d'Alviella 1885, p. 173). And because this mentality had sunk into that of the times, many secular thinkers felt the same way. Tylor's confidence that progress could be tracked in the human mental and cultural realm came from the same sources.

Yet beyond the spirit of the age, there is one more source for Tylor's belief in cultural evolution that we need to recognize . The answer we would like to develop here gives Tylor and the other evolutionists the great benefit of the doubt and cuts loose for the moment from any of these "external" influences bearing upon him. The very logic of evolutionary thinking itself explains much of why Tylor and others found evolutionism so compelling. Evolution possesses a powerful core insight. It holds that a given state of affairs – say, our possession of material technology like an iPod – requires previous facilitating stages of material and social technology – say, the device that reads the data, the electronics, a supply of electricity, the technologies of metallurgy, plastics, and so on – without which an iPod, for example, would not have been possible. Technology does not leap from stone wheels or chunks of unworked wood to an iPod. It relies on a long series of steps, one laid upon the other, and mounting steadily to places others would take them – even to have the thought of an iPod. These lay the successive stages of development that culminate in the products that populate our world.

Now, Tylor in effect asked himself what *enabling steps* or *stages* had to be presumed in order for the mental and moral cultural things in our world to have come to be in the first place, and to have survived over the course of so many years. How did modern-day Protestant ethical and rational monotheism, for example, come to be, when we know that people had been religious for ages in a riotously different series of ways? How could Tylor form a common mind about how we got from Brixham cave's religion to the Church of England or to Tylor's own Quakerism – presuming that we do not get there by way of supernatural intervention into our world?

That is the problem of religious evolution that Tylor sets for us. It is therefore why he deserves to be taken seriously. He and other evolutionary anthropologists started with common data we all can agree upon – the material data of the ancient technologies found in places like Brixham cave. He then proceeds to ask us how we got from stone implements and bone tools to hair dryers, record players, and all the other products that are so characteristic of our world. Thus, in this study of how problems of religion generate theories of religion, Tylor in effect asks us how we got the religion we have today from the religion of our prehistoric ancestors, or, as we will see later, by analogy with the "primitive" folk of our own time. Tylor seeks to put this question forward knowing full well that modern-day religious believers will not fare well in the bargain. Either modern-day religious belief in one God – monotheism – will turn out to be only trivially evolved from the belief in many gods or spirits – animism – of the "savages," or modern-day religion will be seen as a fusty survival of old, obsolete, and fundamentally ignorant ways of thinking about how to explain the world. So it is evolutionary thinking in terms of the necessity of facilitating stages of development that helped Tylor form a common mind about the origins and nature of religion.

We Have Met the Primitives, and "They" Are "Us"

A second great jolt to European religious consciousness was now set to double the impact of the discovery of prehistoric Europe. We will recall how in the sixteenth century the first encounters between Europeans and the so-called "primitives" provoked problems of religion for pious Christians, in particular about the status of the religions of the peoples of the New World. We will also recall how those problems stimulated the early Deists to imagine an ideal Natural Religion that formed a common human basis or capacity for religion. In this way, the Deists were able to absorb the strange religions of the New World under the same umbrella that included Christianity, Judaism, and other religions familiar to them. All the religions of the world were for them at the very least local manifestations or variants of Natural Religion. The task before the study of religion was, then, to mark how far from or near to a given historical religion was the ideal of Natural Religion. Hume, Darwin, and the rise of natural history, however, changed all this.

Just as Max Müller had sought, in effect, to answer Hume's challenge for *empirical and historical* examples of such a Natural Religion by producing a detailed picture of what was at that time regarded as the oldest of all religions – Vedic religion – Tylor gave the wheel of the dialectic another turn and, in effect, challenged Müller about the identity of the oldest and most fundamental religion. With the discoveries of human prehistory, geology, and evolutionary biology, a new developmental historical landscape, with new its scientific investigative

criteria, lay before anyone seeking to make claims about Natural Religion. And now, with the new discoveries of ethnography, Tylor was ready to advance the case against Müller even further. From these new data and theories, Tylor felt that he had found in the belief in spirits – in animism – the very essence of religion. Here was the most ancient of religions, one that survived with only the most trivial of changes wrought by evolutionary development, and which had now lodged itself in place in modern times cloaked in the sophisticated jargon of theology. The trick, however, was to link to two sorts of inquiries so that Tylor could show that he was right about animism being the first and essential religion. This meant joining the discourse of the prehistory of the folk of Europe with the ethnographic researches on contemporary "primitives." Tylor's way of making this all-important link lay in the proper application of developmentalist and evolutionist theory.

We owe this new vision of the equivalence of prehistoric folk to our "primitive" contemporaries to the developmental thinker and geologist Charles Lyell. Although everyone in the human sciences at this time bore something of the mark of the influence of Darwin, Lyell arguably made more of a specific impact upon Tylor. Tylor's evolutionism was thus pre-Darwinian and more generic in style than anything that conformed to Darwinian orthodoxy. Tylor never applied a strict Darwinian principle such as "survival of the fittest" to his analyses of culture, for example – even though Max Müller had done so in arguing how Indo-European languages showed how certain synonyms were "eliminated" by virtue of just such a Darwinian struggle (Leopold 1980, p. 31). Indeed, the problem standing in the way of a Darwinian outlook for Tylor is that quite often the *unfit* survived! Tylor's "survivals" were just this sort of useless fossil washed up on the shores of the present.

Anthropology was nonetheless for Tylor, as it was for Darwin, a branch of natural history, thus making Tylor a Darwinian in the relatively weak sense that he felt that human cultural evolution proceeded in a lawful and natural way. Adopting nature as a whole, instead of local cultures, as his strategic level of inquiry provided Tylor with a powerful comparative tool. It meant that he could aim at human species universals and pass over the endless oddities of individual cultures. Human nature was something thus fundamentally universal, constant, and invariant. All humans shared a common psychic unity much as they did a common physical anatomy (Stocking 1994, p. xx).

Nowhere did Tylor's commitment to the universal and constant species nature of humans have more impact than on his approach to religion. Religion for Tylor was to be studied just like any other feature of the natural world.

To fall back once again on the analogy of natural history: "the time may soon come when it will be thought as unreasonable for a scientific student of theology not to have a competent acquaintance with the principles of the religions of the lower races as for a physiologist to look with the contempt of past centuries on evidence derived from the lower forms of life, deeming the structure of mere invertebrate creatures matter unworthy of his philosophic study" (Tylor 1958, p. 24).

Implied in this association of natural history and religion was the further association, owed to Lyell, of the studies of European prehistory with the results of anthropological fieldwork among "the primitive." Notably, Tylor faithfully followed a program of identifying the prehistoric Europeans with the "primitives" of today, anticipating the arguments of Darwin's *The Descent of Man* (1871).

> The main conclusion arrived at in this work, namely, that man is descended from some lowly organized form, will, I regret to think, be highly distasteful to many. But there can hardly be a doubt that we are descended from barbarians. I will never forget the astonishment I felt on first seeing a party of Fuegans on a wild and broken shore, for the reflection at once rushed into my mind – such were our ancestors. (Darwin 1970, p. 276)

And so it was that Tylor "thought he was right" to identify the religion of the folk of prehistoric Europe with the religion he met on the ethnographic field: both were examples of "primitive" religion in the loose Darwinian sense of the term as the first and least developed of the human species (Stocking 1994, p. xvi). Without "their" efforts in the dim past of prehistory, "we" could not have mounted the heights of progress that Tylor felt the nineteenth century had achieved – even if

in religious terms this progress would be relatively slight. "They" provided the enabling first stages of animism upon which all later religious developmental steps of human religious progress were painfully constructed over many eons. By thus bringing religion into the sphere of disciplines such as natural history, Tylor hoped to revolutionize the religious world of his day.

From the point of view of providing a tool for explaining religion, Tylor's theoretical approach had manifest obvious and ominous – for religious believers – power. With the merger of the study of prehistoric societies with those encountered on the ethnographic field, both could be explained at one go, without the bothersome details of local histories. Both were for Tylor (and Darwin) "primitives" or "savages" in the identical sense of occupying a common place in the trajectory of human cultural evolution. Tylor believed that the prehistoric, proto-European folk whose remains we find in places like Brixham cave are at an equivalent level of species maturity as the modern-day primitive "other" we meet on the ethnographic field, and close as well to the peasant folk of the Europe of Tylor's day. As Tylor colorfully put it, "the European may find among the Greenlanders or Maoris many a trait for reconstructing the picture of his own primitive ancestors" (Tylor 1958, p. 21). They can be compared, because they are comparable sorts of people in terms of their technologies, social patterns, and, most pointedly, their religion.

Thus, we would expect to find many parallel religious beliefs and practices between these far-flung folk and ourselves. We should be able to fill in details missing from one set of folk by matching them with the other. If we find a belief in many spirits in "primitive" societies, we can expect to find (slightly) "higher" forms of such beliefs – monotheism – in more "advanced" societies. If we find human sacrifice in today's ethnographic contexts, we would do well to look for it in the historic domain: if today's Yanomami tribal folk carry out human sacrifice, we might expect those proto-Europeans inhabiting the caves of Lascaux tens of thousands of years ago to have done the same. The inferences flow in the opposite direction as well – from what the paleolithic folk did, such as fashioning stone axes, to what we might expect among the Yanomami in terms of their technology of axe-making.

Whether it be ultimately valid or not, such examples show how powerful Tylor's evolutionist style of comparison could be. In *Anahuac*, Tylor remarks on the similarities of stone axes:

The family-likeness that exists among the stone tools and weapons found in so many parts of the world is very remarkable. The flint-arrows of North America, such as Mr. Longfellow's arrow maker used to work at in the land of the Dacotahs, and which, in the wild northern states of Mexico, the Apaches and Comanches use to this day, might be easily mistaken for the weapons of our British ancestors, dug up on the banks of the Thames.

With diffusionists like Müller no doubt, in mind, Tylor is also quick to head off any explanation of the similarities between cultural traits that might be attributable to cultural borrowing or transfer:

The wonderful similarity of character among the stone weapons found in different parts of the world has often been used by ethnologists as a means of supporting the theory that this and other arts were carried over the world by tribes migrating from one common centre of creation of the human species. The argument has not much weight, and a larger view of the subject quite supersedes it. (Tylor 1861, pp. 101–102)

With this encompassing vision, Tylor moved ahead confidently to become the English-speaking world's leading proponent of anthropology – a universal science of humanity, a science that encompassed all of human history from its rudest beginnings to the modern day.

Max Müller argued that the study of religion must be historical (chiefly philological), but unlike Tylor, Müller saw religion on the whole in a state of degeneration. Every religion of which we have any direct evidence signaled to Müller that it was somehow defective, showing a kind degeneration from a better state, after a kind of 'Fall.' Thus, to study religion through comparison with Tylor's present-day or past "savages" was to err, because one was trying to understand one degenerate form of religion by comparing it with another degenerate form of religion. Such comparisons were likely to be unfruitful because they had little "traction," so to speak. That is to say, they did not supply us with any perspective, since they consisted in comparisons between essentially the same kinds of thing.

The problem for the student of religion was both to chart and to explain why and how things had declined. This presumption of decline, rather than development, in turn called for comparison between later degenerate forms with earlier lofty forms of religion. Müller felt that historical comparison was best undertaken within the context of "developed" (rather than "savage" or "primitive") societies. In many ways, he translated the spirit and some of the techniques of the new critical attitude to the Bible to his own studies of Vedic religion and the religions of ancient India. What Max Müller was doing was thus one thing – a "science of religion" to employ his own language; Tylor, on the other hand, in his ambitions to found a "science of man," was certainly doing anthropology of religion. His not-so-secret desire "all theologians to expose," thus shaped his research program for religion in ways which would present even modern-day religion as a survival of long since outmoded ways of thinking, or at the very best, a trivial development of "savage" animistic beliefs. In these respects, then, the two men could not have differed more in their approaches to the problems of religion that their age presented to them.

References

Bataille, G. 1955. *Lascaux*. Lausanne: Skira.

Darwin, C. 1970. "The Descent of Man." In P. Appleman (ed.), *Darwin: A Norton Critical Reader*. New York: W.W. Norton.

Goblet d'Alviella, C.E. 1885. "Maurice Vernes et la méthode comparative." *Revue de l'histoire des religions* 12: 170–178.

Gruber, J.W. 1965. "Brixham Cave and the Antiquity of Man." In M.E. Spiro (ed.), *Context and Meaning in Cultural Anthropology*. New York: Free Press.

Leopold, J. 1980. *Culture in Comparative and Evolutionary Perspective: E.B. Tylor and the Making of Primitive Culture*. Berlin: Dietrich Reimer Verlag.

Marett, R.R. 1914. *The Threshold of Religion*. New York: Macmillan.

Marett, R.R. 1936. *Tylor*. London: Chapman & Hall.

McCutcheon, R.T. 2001. *Critics Not Caretakers: Redescribing the Public Study of Religion*. Albany: SUNY.

Stocking, G.W. 1987. *Victorian Anthropology*. New York: Free Press.

Stocking, G.W. 1994. "Introduction." In G.W. Stocking (ed.), *The Collected Works of Edward Burnett Tylor: Anahuac: Or Mexico and the Mexicans, Ancient and Modern*, vol. 1. London: Routledge/Thoemmes Press.

Stocking, G.W. 2001. "Edward Burnett Tylor and the Mission of Primitive Man." In G.W. Stocking (ed.), *Delimiting Anthropology*. Madison: University of Wisconsin Press.

Tylor, E.B. 1861. *Anahuac: Or Mexico and the Mexicans, Ancient and Modern*. London: Reader & Dyer.

Tylor, E.B. 1866a. "On the Origin of Language." *Fortnightly Review*: 544–559.

Tylor, E.B. 1866b. "The Religion of Savages." *Fortnightly Review*: 71–86.

Tylor, E.B. 1873. *Religion in Primitive Culture*. New York: Harper.

Tylor, E.B. 1881. *Anthropology*. Ann Arbor: University of Michigan.

Tylor, E.B. 1958. *Primitive Culture*, vol. 1. New York: Harper & Row.

Further Reading

Durkheim, É. 1995. *The Elementary Forms of the Religious Life*, trans. K.E. Fields. New York: Free Press.

Frankenberry, N.K. (ed.). 2002. *Radical Interpretation in Religion*. Cambridge: Cambridge University Press.

Lévi-Strauss, C. 1966. *The Savage Mind*. London: Weidenfeld & Nicolson.

Lévi-Strauss, C. 1968. "The Structural Study of Myth." In C. Lévi-Strauss (ed.), *Structural Anthropology*, vol. 1. London: Allen Lane.

Lévi-Strauss, C. 1976. "Race and History." In In C. Lévi-Strauss (ed.), *Structural Anthropology*, vol. 2. New York City: Basic Books.

Lyell, C. 1863. *The Geological Evidence of the Antiquity of Man*. London: John Murray.

Müller, F.M. 1886. "On Manners and Customs." In *Chips from a German Workshop*, vol. 2. London: Longmans, Green & Co.

Müller, F.M. 1891. *Physical Religion*. New York: Longmans, Green & Co.

Müller, F.M. 1892. *Natural Religion*. London: Longmans, Green & Co.

Réville, A. 1883. *Les Religions des peuples non-civilisés*, vol. 1. Paris: Fischbacher.

Stocking, G.W. 2001. "Books Unwritten, Turning Points Unmarked: Notes for an Anti-History of Anthropology." In G.W. Stocking (ed.), *Delimiting Anthropology*. Madison: University of Wisconsin Press.

Strenski, I. 1985. "Comparative Study of Religions: A Theological Necessity." *Christian Century*: 126–129.

Strenski, I. 1985/1996. "Misreading Max Müller." *Method and Theory in the Study of Religion* 8: 291–296.

Strenski, I. 1985/1996. "The Rise of Ritual and the Hegemony of Myth: Sylvain Lévi, the Durkheimians and Max Müller." In W. Doniger and L. Patton (eds.), *Myth and Method*. Charlottesville: University of Virginia.

Tylor, E.B. 1880. "The President's Address." *Journal of the Anthropological Institute* 9: 443–458.

Tylor, E.B. 1888. "On a Method of Investigating the Development of Institutions." *Journal of the Anthropological Institute* 18: 245–272.

6

The Religion of the Bible Evolves: William Robertson Smith

Dear, dear! So Moses did not write the books of Moses! (As if anybody ever believed he did.) If you republish, read (unless you have read) Spinoza, who proves the late date philologically. (Sir Richard Burton to William Robertson Smith, 1880 [Black and Chrystal 1912b, pp. 406–407])

The Religion of the Bible and Its Problems

A consistent theme in this book has been that much of the progress in the study of religion is tied directly to the study of the Bible. For this reason I have tried to throw more light on Higher Criticism of the Bible than is usually done in trying to comprehend the rise of religious studies. Of course, once given a moment's thought, the biblical studies–religious studies connection makes perfect intuitive sense. The Bible is and remains the focus of passionate religiosity in the West. Changing attitudes to the status of the Bible had to have had consequences for the way religion was to be studied. At the present moment, analogous movements in the critical study of the Quran, Adhi Granth, and other traditional scriptures are moving ahead. They will doubtless provoke as much religious turmoil in these traditions as Higher Criticism has produced over the past two centuries in the West. Accordingly, this chapter will focus on the work of the polymath biblical scholar William Robertson Smith – notable as "the first person in Britain to apply the comparative evolutionary anthropological approach to the study of an entire family of religions, the Semitic" (Ackerman 1987, p. 58). Hailed (and cursed) in his own time for joining an evolutionism like Tylor's to the critical techniques of Higher Criticism, Robertson Smith soon became a world famous (or infamous) figure in the study of religion as a whole (Bediako 1995). In Robertson Smith's hands, as well, the Bible and its religion became an episode in the *general history of religion*, and not just a document reflecting a particular people and the local peculiarities of their religion (Smith 1912c, pp. 229–233).

Robertson Smith shows us how attempts to deal with problems arising in the study of the Bible have made significant contributions to the overall study of religion. This happened in two steps. First, he integrated the new ethnographic insights and fieldwork research practices urged by John F. McLennan and E.B. Tylor for the study of the Bible. For Robertson Smith, the Bible was no longer seen only as a *text*, as literature, but as rich in data about the religious *life* of biblical folk.

Understanding Theories of Religion: An Introduction, Second Edition. Ivan Strenski.
© 2015 Ivan Strenski. Published 2015 by John Wiley & Sons, Ltd.

More than just studying the Bible, Robertson Smith studied the *religion of the Bible*. He devised a method by which we could engage the rituals, customs, myths, social institutions, and such of biblical times. To do his part in the ethnographic dimension of his work, he traveled among the Semitic tribes of Arabia of his own day. Just as had been done by Tylor, Robertson Smith appealed to direct, empirical observation – to on-the-ground ethnography – in the interests of forming a common mind about biblical religion. Surely no one could doubt his results if they were based upon such common elements of human knowledge.

Second, Robertson Smith studied the Bible for the sake of studying the *religion of the Bible* or pre-biblical times. He was only remotely interested, for example, in the internal or external discrepancies that troubled the first generation of biblical critics. His interest in miracles was slight, if not nonexistent. Instead, Robertson Smith asked the evolutionist's question: What was the religion of the Bible at various stages of its development? We in modern times may assign our own meanings to priesthood, prophecy, sacrifice, ritual, purity, the sacred, totemism, and other religious institutions. But what meaning have they in their original, historical context in the religion of the ancient Hebrews? Robertson Smith asked these questions in pursuit of a larger context of purposes external to his professional academic pursuits. He wanted to reform the Christianity of his day by isolating the "primitive" elements still lodged there. In purging them from the body of Christian belief and practice, Robertson Smith could envision a path to Christian renewal.

In our own times, Robertson Smith's greatness has only been amplified. Anthropologists like Mary Douglas have demonstrated how fruitful his marriage of biblical studies, ethnography, and the comparative study of religions has been. In her classic, *Purity and Danger*, Douglas shows how the sometimes opaque features of biblical religion – proscriptions against eating certain animals, for example – can be understood in terms of more general features of religious life. She also shows biblical scholars how to problematize biblical religion by comparative analysis with other religions (Douglas 1970). The apparently trivial proscriptions of the Hebrew Bible against eating certain animals lay bare the religious vision of ancient Israel, and by analogy the religious practices studied by anthropologists, such as taboo. Who, then, was this man, William Robertson Smith? What does he have to say about how we should study religion? And why did "he think he was right" about that?

The Great Renown and Short Heretical Life of William Robertson Smith

William Robertson Smith (1846–94) hailed from a religiously conservative clerical family that belonged to a small offshoot of mainstream Calvinism – the Scottish Free Church. A precocious young man, he began his university education at 15 in Aberdeen, where he studied classical languages and theology. Early in his career, from 1869 to 1873, Robertson Smith even published a series of technical academic papers dealing with such rarefied issues as the theory of geometry, fluxional calculus, electricity, and the metaphysics of the sciences (Black and Chrystal 1912a, p. xi). As Robertson Smith matured, he shifted his academic venue to Edinburgh and focused increasingly on biblical studies and theology, the interests that would prove to become dominant in his intellectual life.

Despite his strict Calvinist upbringing, Robertson Smith was attracted to the liberal Protestant theology, then in vogue in Germany – the same movement Max Müller found so hospitable. The Higher Criticism of the Bible practiced by Julius Wellhausen (1844–1918) and Paul Lagarde (1827–1891) appealed to him. In 1869, Robertson Smith decided to study Arabic and advanced biblical studies with Wellhausen and Lagarde. Wellhausen and Smith went on to become lifelong friends. Despite the suspicions that these relationships and Smith's orientation to German liberal theology created among the theological conservatives in Scotland, Smith at first overcame local suspicions. In 1870, he took ordination in the Free Church, and immediately won appointment as Professor of Hebrew and Old Testament at the Free Church College in Edinburgh.

Smith's troubles with his conservative church were soon to begin when he was attacked for teaching Higher Criticism (Beidelman 1974, p. 7).

In his heart, Robertson Smith never felt that free inquiry into the biblical narrative militated against his own profound religious faith. To him, the Bible was "the story of God's saving self-manifestation," pure and simple. Thus, in 1870, he wrote passionately in defense of Higher Criticism from a strictly *progressive* religious point of view: "higher criticism does not mean negative criticism. It means the fair and honest looking at the Bible as a historical record, and the effort everywhere to reach the real meaning and historical setting, Scripture Records as a whole." Robertson Smith argued for grasping the larger context of sacred scriptures. Christians must speak "from a historical study of the books themselves" and not rely upon "vain traditions" (Smith 1912c, p. 233). Like Max Müller, Robertson Smith pursued scientific studies of the Bible and biblical religion in the spirit of progressive religious faith. Knowledge only deepened faith, even if, in the short run, it stirred doubts. The more that he learned about the world, he believed, the closer he came to God.

Nevertheless Robertson Smith was branded a heretic by his theological enemies. The charges against him wounded his pious heart. He could not understand how pursuing historical scholarship could do anything but deepen faith. He felt that the spiritual inner core of revelation lay hidden beneath the outer, corrupting layers of scribal composition and redaction (Smith 1912c, p. 224). He likened himself to the Reformation fathers, who sought "the *real meaning* of every heart-spoken word" of the Bible. He saw himself as a mature reader of the Bible who "pierces through the expression and sees in the words this and this alone." Mature readers grasp "the personality of God's word" because the Bible is "the direct personal message of God's love to me" (Smith 1912c, pp. 225–226). It is small wonder he found the charges of heresy both deeply galling and dispiriting.

However inspiring his theological vision was, Robertson Smith's conservative opponents pressed on to destroy him professionally. By 1876, the church fathers successfully brought Smith to trial for heresy for denying the divine inspiration of the Hebrew Bible. Like Baruch Spinoza centuries before, they accused Smith of questioning whether Moses had written the book of Deuteronomy and whether the sacred authors were free from all error in terms of factual statements, and of challenging the idea that no part of the Bible was fiction, such as the love poem the Song of Solomon. In a surprise verdict, Smith was cleared of all charges, except his rejection of Mosaic authorship of the book of Deuteronomy. Convicted in 1881 of this single charge, he was deprived of his livelihood as professor at the Free Church College in Edinburgh.

Abdullah Effendi Smith of Arabia

While awaiting the verdict of his heresy trial, Robertson Smith wintered over for six months in Egypt, Libya, Palestine, Syria, and Arabia. This was more than a holiday from the bitter theological disputes in the cold, dark north. Nor was it some gentleman's tour of exotic sites, like Tylor's stint of tourism in Mexico. In the Libyan desert, Robertson Smith reports traveling for 20 hours by camel and spending two nights with the local Bedouins (Black and Chrystal 1912b, p. 333). But he also kept company with the controversial explorer and orientalist Sir Richard Burton. It was during this visit to Arabia that Robertson Smith moved about the peninsula on an expedition into what was, for his orientalist mind, a secret world of alluring exotica. While in Arabia, Smith even assumed the alias Abdullah Effendi, and traveled about the region near Mecca by permission of its emir. Donning local garb at the "serious" urgings of his Arab guides, but also in order "to avoid intrusive curiosity," Smith successfully disguised himself for the duration of his visit (Smith 1880, p. 497). But in Arabia he diligently pursued a program of self-education about the world of the Arabs, interviewing various local religious and political leaders. Like anthropologists among their "primitives," Robertson Smith believed he had happened upon nothing less than a "primitive" Semitic religious world, close to the vanished world of the Bible.

Smith betrayed the mindset of late nineteenth-century European high culture in his unflattering orientalist descriptions of the local populations. He opines, for example, that Arabs as well as Hebrews are of the "sensuous Oriental nature." People like this, says Smith, are somewhat

> pitiful in that they cannot help but respond to physical stimuli with a readiness foreign to our more sluggish temperament; to the Arab it is

an excitement and a delight of the highest order merely to have flesh to eat. From the earliest times, therefore, the religious practice of the Semites tended to assume an orgiastic character and become a sort of intoxication of the senses, in which anxiety and sorrow were drowned for the moment. (Smith 1923, p. 261)

Confident, then, in his lofty position atop the ladder of human development, like Tylor regarding Mexican Catholics, Robertson Smith often looked down with contempt on cultures and religions that he perceived as differing significantly from his own – like the Catholics and modern Jews, as we will see. Difficult as it may be to abide Robertson Smith's biases, we must not be as summary in rejecting what he has to say about religion. He was very important in stimulating interest in tribal religion with his serious first-hand ethnographic field observations of the religious and social lives of the tribal folk of Arabia. His book *Kinship and Marriage in Early Arabia* (1885), as well as articles such as "Animal Worship and Animal Tribes among the Arabs and in the Old Testament" (1912a) are cases in point. By contrast, the so-called father of anthropology, E.B. Tylor never equaled the serious fieldwork of the biblical scholar William Robertson Smith!

Robertson Smith's "Arabian Revolution" in the Study of Religion

Robertson Smith's experiences among the nomadic tribes in Arabia convinced him of an idea that would revolutionize the study of the religion of the Bible. His revolution proceeded in two steps. First, like the good historian he was, he agreed that to understand the present, we must understand the past. He believed that this past would include, as it did for Bodin, Herbert, and Max Müller, recognition of a "natural" religious basis for all revealed, or so-called "positive" religions. He believed this because he shared the theological inclinations of the liberal Protestants – German Lutherans – under whom he studied, Julius Wellhausen and Paul Lagarde. Thus, he says that beneath "Judaism, Christianity and Islam lies the old unconscious religious tradition." This is nothing less than "the body of religious usage and belief which … formed part of that inheritance

from the past into which successive generations of the Semitic race grew up" (Smith 1923, pp. 1–2). Far then from being a Christian exclusivist, Robertson Smith taught an orthodox liberal Protestantism. He felt that the religion of the Bible owed much to the "natural" religious or "pagan" template upon which it rests. Historical events abhor a vacuum, and always lean on the stages in history that enabled them to come forth.

Robertson Smith embraced the idea of religious evolution, analogous to that of Tylor and McLennan. This also meant that he believed that his ethnographic observations in Arabia were like snapshots of the past. "The religion of heathen Arabia … displays an extremely primitive type, corresponding to the primitive and unchanging character of nomadic life," Smith tells us (1923, p. 14). Therefore, we could study the past by observing the present, since the past survived in the living institutions and practices of the present. Historical figures who had long since disappeared could, as it were, be *directly observed* in the present, because there were identical living equivalents of things and institutions of the past (Bediako 1995, p. 121).

Despite the brevity of Robertson Smith's stay in the Muslim lands, his experience of Arabian nomadic folk convinced him that what he saw there with his own eyes were living survivals of the kind of religion practiced by the Hebrews in the days of their desert wanderings thousands of years earlier. The nomadic tribal Arab peoples and the ancient Hebrews, while differing in various respects, were actual kin. A stunning realization this, since it reinforced Robertson Smith's belief that he could better understand ancient Jewish religion not only from the Higher Criticism, but in his fieldwork. He could actually *observe* something very close to ancient Hebrew religion being lived among the nomadic tribes of Arabia at the end of the nineteenth century! "The defects of historical tradition must therefore," says Robertson Smith, "be supplied by observation" (1923, p. 6). Evolutionary theory and ethnographic observation had fitted Robertson Smith out with a kind of time machine for traveling far back into remote prehistoric times in order to encounter face-to-face the religious life of the people who wrote the Bible itself – the ancient Hebrews.

Upon returning in 1881 from his Middle Eastern travels to find himself stripped of his teaching position, Robertson Smith bounced back. He was fortunate enough rapidly to regain employment when invited to serve first as co-editor and principal contributor to the ninth edition of the prestigious *Encyclopedia Britannica*, then subsequently as its editor in chief. In that influential position, he was able to maintain and expand his contacts in the academic world, and eventually move on to a professorship in Arabic at Cambridge a mere two years later in 1883. As the *Britannica's* editor in chief, Smith enlisted distinguished Continental authors to write for the encyclopedia, but he also discovered, and thus patronized such future luminaries in the study of religion as James Frazer. In the following chapter, we will see how Frazer, then a classicist at Cambridge, continued many of the enterprises that Robertson Smith had begun, especially the attempt to interpret Christianity and other modern religions in terms of their supposed "primitive" roots.

Robertson Smith and Higher Criticism: Wellhausen, Comparison, and Context

Much of what made Robertson Smith's revolution in the study of biblical religion heretical can be traced to liberal Protestantism as conveyed by the approach to the Bible of Julius Wellhausen, Robertson Smith's German mentor in the Higher Criticism. Wellhausen also taught that religions should never be approached in splendid isolation. Instead, they should be studied in their various contexts – their "physical surroundings, material culture, manner of life, social and political organization, and relations with neighboring peoples" (Frazer 1927, p. 286). The *methodological* result for Smith? The Hebrews belonged "to the whole circle of nations of which they formed a part" (Smith 1923, p. 3). In the opening pages of his *Lectures on the Religion of Semites*, Robertson Smith tells us how he "take[s] it for granted" that "when we go back to the most ancient religious conceptions and usages of the Hebrews, we shall find them to be the common property of kindred peoples, and not the exclusive possession of the tribes of Israel" (Smith 1923, pp. 3–4). Unless we let the Bible, here, speak in this way, we risked projecting the prejudices of our own time and place, and thus reading scripture through our own eyes only, and thus not really attending to the

word of God. It is this sort of rationale, "internal" to Robertson Smith's discipline that gave him the assurance that he was "right" to press on with a contextual approach in his *Lectures on the Religion of the Semites*.

Wellhausen, like Max Müller, also encouraged the comparative study of religion. While Wellhausen does not consider comparing the religion of Israel with Islam, or for that matter with the religions of ancient Romans and Greeks, Polynesians and Native Americans, Robertson Smith did. He, like Max Müller, believed that all aspects of culture, religion included, should be studied *comparatively*. Again like Müller, Robertson Smith fostered the formation of a common mind about religion, free of confessional limitations. His comparisons were open to anyone willing to use the common capacity of humans to ask questions. This spirit made him one of the great founders of the comparative study of religions.

Wellhausen marked Robertson Smith's method for the study of religion in a second way. Jewish religious history should be divided into periods of *evolving* religious quality, some good, some not so good, and some indeed even bad. The ethical religion of reform of the prophetic age stood at the developmental pinnacle of the religion of the Hebrew Bible (Anon. 1960). At the correspondingly "lower" end of Israel's religious evolution stood the "corrupting" priestly strand, with its lavish rituals, sacrifice chief among them. Like Tylor, too, Wellhausen's critique of ritual and priestly religion scooped up Roman Catholicism along with modern Judaism in the same liberal Protestant polemic. For Wellhausen, ritualism spelt trouble for any real religion, because it exposed a tendency for Israel to lapse back into the idolatrous "crude nature religion" so hated by the prophets (Hubert 1901, p. 218). Robertson Smith bought into this view completely. Let's now see how he brought Wellhausen's methodological guidelines to his major work, his *Lectures on the Religion of the Semites*.

Smith's *Lectures on the Religion of the Semites*

Robertson Smith's classic offers yet another answer to that great fundamental question, posed by the earliest founders of the humanistic study of religion: What was primal Natural Religion? How could we form a common mind about the identity of the origins of religion, one that did not assume allegiance to a confessional faith? Müller argued that the methods of the science of language could be applied to this problem, such that we were led inexorably to the religions of India. Robertson Smith did the same, but through the religion of the Semites. For reasons like Bodin's, Robertson Smith felt that the religion of the ancient Hebrews had a reasonable claim for being one of the older, if not the oldest, known religion. Like the religion of the ancient Hebrews, the kindred religion of the Arabian nomads, whom he had observed, "displays an extremely primitive type, corresponding to the primitive and unchanging character of nomadic life" (Smith 1923, p. 14). The empirical results of Robertson Smith's on-the-scene scholarly observation about the religion of the nomadic Arabian tribes provided him with at least one "internal" reason why he "thought he was right" about the problem of the nature of the original religion.

The *Lectures on the Religion of the Semites* is a great book because it tries to deal with a number of big issues at the same time. First, in terms of theoretical advances in the study of "primitive" religion, the *Lectures* provide a theory about the original nature of sacrificial rites; they introduce perhaps the most influential thesis on the meaning and function of totemism, thought at the time by some to be the first religion. Second, the *Lectures* also offer a universal explanation of the origins of morality and the development and growth of religion. As an evolutionist, Robertson Smith believed that our own institutions grew out of older ones. "Primitive" institutions set the conditions and provided the necessary facilitating stages to insure that future "modern" institutions came into being. Human inventions such as DVDs or iPods did not leap from stone wheels or chunks of unworked stone at one go. And as a *religious* evolutionist, Robertson Smith believed that religion evolved similarly: it went through stages of *growth*. Unlike Tylor, who saw religion as animism, as something basically unchanging from the beginning, Robertson Smith thought religion itself could change in significant ways. Both sacrifice and totemism were, for example, coarse "primitive" rites that subsequently, over time, developed into higher,

healthier, "modern" forms of spiritual religion. Sacrifice, for example, rested on the arrogant idea that humans could put "the deity under a social obligation," or "buy the favor of the gods." But this "primitive" rite could grow up, so to speak. In Robertson Smith's words, sacrificial giving would – given the right conditions – develop into the lofty ethical ideal of altruism, a pure, uncalculating giving of the self for others (Smith 1923, p. 434). What had been a badly misguided ritual practice would, *evolving* over time, be transformed into the highest human ideal – altruism or selfless charity.

In Robertson Smith's view – a rather thinly disguised claim of liberal Protestant theology – just such a progressive evolution *away* from ritual *toward* morality characterized the history of the Protestant West. In Israel, what had been a gross and material kind of ritualism would gradually over time, and thanks to divine intervention, become the high-minded and purified spiritual morality of the prophets, Jesus, the Reformation fathers, and their liberal Protestant heirs.

Robertson Smith felt he was right that original religion was devoid of any doctrines or ethical vision because there were few traces of them – no "primitive" books or other written records. He also thought he was right because, like many evolutionists, he presumed that the "primitives" did not think reflectively like "moderns" did. They primarily just *acted*. As we will see in our discussion of post-colonial theory, the external context of the British imperialism of Robertson Smith's day cannot be discounted as a factor that enabled such reasons. By casting the "natives" as their inferiors, Western colonial or imperial agents could justify moving into their territory and establishing Western authority. We may be familiar with the idea of assuming paternalistic custodial responsibility for "them" in title of Rudyard Kipling's poem, "The White Man's Burden." Because Robertson Smith bought into such assumptions of superiority, he felt he was right to think, for example, that in "ancient religions all the ordinary functions of worship are summed up in the sacrificial meal, and that the ordinary intercourse between gods and men has no other form" (Smith 1923, p. 265). Unlike Max Müller's pessimistic view of religious decline, Robertson Smith's argued that religion evolved, casting off the dullness of material forms of worship such as sacrifice. In time, it took on the luminosity of pure spirit: he felt this would be the result of his attempts to reform Protestantism along the liberal lines thriving in Germany. Robertson Smith felt he was living in the latter days of a magnificent religious evolution culminating in a reformed liberal Protestantism, what he called a higher form of spiritualized religion.

The sacrificial conception of the Roman Catholic Eucharist, for example, shows this evolution, but it also shows how it stalled without reaching the pinnacle of religious perfection. Among the "primitives," such as he had observed in Arabia, interaction between humanity and divinity requires nothing less than sacrifice: "sacrifice is the typical form of all complete acts of worship in the antique religions" (Smith 1923, p. 214). But as a sacramental sacrifice, the Catholic Eucharist showed how modern religion had evolved a stage beyond actual blood sacrifice. There, the body and blood of the sacrificed god-man would be eaten – *sacramentally* – by the faithful in communion. But for the hyper-liberal Protestant Robertson Smith, references to blood and sacrificial killing still clung to ritualism. Under the right circumstances – such as the Protestant Reformation's conception of Communion – the Roman Catholic Eucharist would evolve out of its ritualistic talk of sacrifice into higher spiritual forms. There, stripped of externals like the Mass and its imagery of bloody, expiatory sacrificial killing, Reformed Protestants see Jesus' altruistic giving up of himself to the Father as a pure, unsullied symbolic model of perfected human morality.

But brilliant as Robertson Smith's evolutionary interpretation of the course of religious growth and development was, he still had to prove it. Part of his problem was that religious people differed – often significantly – about what sacrifice was. For Jews, at a certain later period in their history, Robertson Smith believed, sacrifice was a "gloomy" affair, "filled in times of distress with the cowardly lamentations of worshipers, who to save their own lives were ready to give up all they held dear, even to the sacrifice of a firstborn or only child" (Smith 1923, p. 415). How did it come to be that way, he puzzled, since biblical evidence pointed to an earlier joyous festival, replete with a sacrificial banquet among the Israelites (1923, p. 254)?

Significantly, the Roman Catholics of Smith's own day repeated all the theological errors of Israel, not to mention those of the "heathen" (Smith 1923, p. 439). Since the Catholic Eucharist reasserted the passionate sacrificial death and immolation of Jesus as an atonement, Roman Catholics fell back into the primitive practice of seeing this bloody ritual as a way of insuring their own salvation. Where was the sense of communion with the divine or the sublime joy of kinship that spoke to the religious heart of Robertson Smith? Catholic eucharistic expiatory sacrifice was a dreary affair, dominated by conniving priests, and dependent upon memories of a bloody, mechanical ritual. To Robertson Smith, it was "materialistic." He thus endeavored to uncover a purer conception of sacrifice rooted in the biblical tradition itself, more in line with his Reformed theological orientation (Smith 1923, pp. 439–440).

Robertson Smith felt history, harnessed to ethnography vindicated his Reformation theology. Like earlier theorists, he felt he could achieve a common mind about his view of the evolution of religion by appealing to the historical sciences. The Catholic conceptions of sacrifice as atonement could be shown to be *historically later* than the kind of lively sacrificial feast he felt was primitive in the "purest" levels of biblical religion. Robertson Smith felt that the more one went back to the earlier stages of the history of Israelite religion, the purer this religion would be. Indeed, he believed it to be the "dominant type of Hebrew worship" for the Israelites of that early time (Smith 1923, p. 254). Sacrifice as a joyous *communal banquet* of sharing in a meal of the sacrificial victim must be, for him, an early conception of sacrifice. Proof of this comes from the fact that this banquet knew nothing of cosmic bribery – a corrupt *later* form of worship. Smith's thinking relied upon his conviction that people became cynical and began to think that they could buy off the gods with sacrificial offerings. But in the beginning they dined together at the same table, and enjoyed their kinship with each other. Says Robertson Smith,

When men meet their god, they feast and are glad together, and whenever they feast and are glad they desire that the god should be of the party. This view is proper to religions in which the habitual temper of the worshippers is one of joyous confidence in their god, untroubled by any habitual sense of human guilt, and resting on the firm conviction that they and the deity they adore are good friends, who understand each other perfectly and are united by bonds not easily broken. (Smith 1923, p. 255)

In the beginning, then, sacrifice was a festive, high-spirited, and joyful marking of kinship of people with their deity – an occasion "full of mirth" (Smith 1923, p. 414). Robertson Smith felt he was getting close to clinching his case about the evolution of religion from ritual to morality.

But, first, how does Robertson Smith "know that he was right" about this *historical* ordering of ideas of sacrifice? How did he know that the "jolly feast" was really *earlier* than sacrifice as bribe? Some scriptural support showed that he might be right. A very old biblical text helps. The book of Samuel (Smith 1923, p. 254, nn.1–6), for example, speaks of such a "merry sacrificial feast" (1923, p. 257). But I think such evidence was really less potent than Robertson Smith's liberal Protestant evolutionary theological prejudices. Protestant liberalism dictates that the human race is moving upward and onward. As Robertson Smith explains, "The communities of ancient civilisation were formed by the survival of the fittest." And "they had all the self-confidence and elasticity that are engendered by success in the struggle for life" (1923, p. 260). These societies were successful ones, and had no need to bribe their deity. Indeed, a mood of celebration dominated their optimistic outlook on life (Smith 1880, p. 532). Sad to say, however, the innocent happiness of the youth of humanity had to give way, eventually, to the sobriety of adulthood. A rosy picture of early humanity *must* be immature, because it corresponds to the early history of individual human beings – the bliss of childhood. People at this early stage of human development, said Robertson Smith, exhibit a measure of "*insouci-ance*, a power of casting off the past and, living in the impression of the moment, which belongs to the childhood of humanity, and can exist only along with a childish unconsciousness of the inexorable laws that connect the present and the future with the past" (1923, p. 257).

But childhood cannot last, as any adult can testify from their own individual experience of growing up to face the hard facts of life. So, as time goes on, an inevitable change begins to occur as "the more developed nations" emerge from "national childhood": they soon "find the old religious forms inadequate … and are driven to look on the anger of the gods as much more frequent and permanent than their fathers had supposed." They thus begin thinking about their relation with God in terms of fear and the need for divine "bribery" – atoning rites to make up for transgressions. They "substitute for the old joyous confidence a painful and scrupulous anxiety in all approach to the gods (Smith 1923, pp. 258–259). Humanity follows this ineluctable course everywhere.

Robertson Smith also had religious reasons for wanting to emphasize this particular reading of the scriptures of the West. This belief required him to make implicit appeal to the external forces of great movements of historical change, such as the Protestant Reformation. For Robertson Smith, the Reformation marked real progress in the course of religious evolution. He had thoroughly internalized a liberal Calvinism that he felt stood at the pinnacle of religious progress. This liberal Protestantism taught that the prophets, and Jesus among them, were both *new* and a *restoration* of original piety. This was really Wellhausen's idea. For him, the Jewish prophets returned Israel to a lost level of communion with God. Robertson Smith bought into Wellhausen's vision that the prophets represented revolutionary *evolution* beyond the immediately previous historical stages of priestly ritualism. The religion of Israel is raised up again by divine revelation through the prophets. The prophets were called to restore what had been lost. In Robertson Smith's view, the Reformation does the work of the prophets as well, in re-establishing the primal unity enjoyed between divinity and humanity.

One final point ought to be made here in relation to how Robertson Smith's religious motivations gave him external reasons for being confident in "thinking he was right" about his scientific conclusions. While Robertson Smith was thus a great "critic" of the religion of his day, and indeed one of our greatest classic theorists, he was also someone who saw himself as a caretaker – someone who felt he was also advancing a religious agenda at the same time. Like Max Müller, Robertson Smith saw science (here, the historical sciences) and religion as compatible, and mutually reinforcing (Bediako 1995, p. 118). Thus, far from the dichotomy some authors would have us draw between critics and caretakers, we have seen how two of the most seminal classic theorists in the study of religion, Max Müller and Robertson Smith, are both critics and caretakers at the same time.

Robertson Smith Can Still Teach Us a Lot

Whether or not his views of the earliest religions are true or not, the study of religion has benefited a great deal from Robertson Smith's conception of the earliest religion, namely that religion "in primitive times was not a system of belief with practical applications; it was a body of fixed traditional practices, to which every member of society conformed as a matter of course." For him, "the sum-total of ancient religions" was "ritual and practical usage" (Smith 1923, p. 20). While, in reality, Smith overstates the case that intellectual reflectiveness is not to be found among the adherents of ancient religions, it is useful to begin thinking about religion as rooted in other aspects of human life than just the cognitive or intellectual. Religion is more than what people think; it is also what people do. Religion is more than doctrine, beliefs, or even myths; it is also ritual and moral practice. Robertson Smith greatly enhanced our appreciation of the multidimensional character of human religiosity by affirming that religion has to do with establishing networks of relationships – both the divine and with other humans. Similarly, Smith may be correct that, religion has less to do with *thinking* about things than with *behaving* properly, as ritual directs. After all, there is more to human life than making theories or explaining the world. There is worship itself – a doing, an action, a performance directed at the divine, that is not in itself a piece of theoretical thinking. Finally, does not the gospel tell Christians that acts of faithfulness matter more than words (Matthew 7: 21)? Perhaps that is why Robertson Smith ultimately "thought he was right" about the precedence of acts to words true religion?

References

Ackerman, R. 1987. *J.G. Frazer: His Life and Work.* Cambridge: Cambridge University Press.

Anon. 1960. "Wellhausen, Julius." In *The Jewish Encyclopedia* (12). New York City: KTAV.

Bediako, G.M. 1995. "'To Capture the Modern Universe of Thought': *Religion of the Semites* as an Attempt at a Christian Comparative Religion." In W. Johnstone (ed.), *William Robertson Smith Essays in Reassessment.* Journal for the Study of the Old Testament Supplement Series 189. Sheffield: Sheffield Academic Press.

Beidelman, T.O. 1974. *W. Robertson Smith and the Sociology Study of Religion.* Chicago: University of Chicago Press.

Black, J.S., and G. Chrystal (eds.). 1912a. *Lectures and Essays of William Robertson Smith.* London: Adam and Charles Black.

Black, J.S., and G. Chrystal. 1912b. *The Life of William Robertson Smith.* London: Adam and Charles Black.

Douglas, M. 1970. *Purity and Danger.* London: Penguin.

Frazer, J.G. 1927. "William Robertson Smith." In J.G. Frazer (ed.), *Gorgon's Head.* London: Macmillan.

Hubert, H. 1901. Review of Wellhausen, *Prolegomena zur Geschichte Israels. L'Année sociologique* 4: 218.

Smith, W.R. 1880. "A Journey in the Hejaz". *The Scotsman.*

Smith, W.R. 1885. *Kinship and Marriage in Early Arabia.* Cambridge: Cambridge University Press.

Smith, W.R. 1912a. "Animal Worship and Animal Tribes among the Arabs and in the Old Testament" (1880). In J.S. Black and G. Chrystal (eds.), *Lectures and Essays of William Robertson Smith.* London: Adam and Charles Black.

Smith, W.R. 1912b. "The Place of Theology in the Work and Growth of the Church." In J.S. Black and G. Chrystal (eds.), *Lectures and Essays of William Robertson Smith.* London: Adam and Charles Black.

Smith, W.R. 1912c. "What History Teaches Us to Seek in the Bible." In J.S. Black and G. Chrystal (eds.), *Lectures and Essays of William Robertson Smith.* London: Adam and Charles Black.

Smith, W.R. 1923. *Lectures on the Religion of the Semites.* London: Adam and Charles Black.

Further Reading

Douglas, M. 1993. *In the Wilderness: The Doctrine of Defilement in the Book of Numbers* Journal for the Study of the Old Testament Supplement Series 158. Sheffield: JSOT Press.

Kristof, N.D. 2004. "Martyrs, Virgins and Grapes." *New York Times*.

McCutcheon, R.T. 2001. *Critics Not Caretakers: Redescribing the Public Study of Religion*. Albany: SUNY.

Reif, S.C. 1995. "William Robertson Smith in Relation to Hebraists and Jews at Christ's College, Cambridge." In W. Johnstone (ed.), *William Robertson Smith: Essays in Reassessment*. Journal for the Study of the Old Testament Supplement Series 189. Sheffield: Sheffield Academic Press.

Reinach, S. 1922. "La Théorie du sacrifice." In S. Reinach (ed.), *Cultes, mythes et religions*, vol. 1. Paris: Leroux.

Sharpe, E.J. 1986. *Comparative Religion: A History*. La Salle, IL: Open Court.

Stocking, G.W. 1995. *After Tylor: British Social Anthropology, 1888–1951*. Madison: University of Wisconsin Press.

Toy, C.H. 1895. Review of William Robertson Smith, *Lectures on the Religion of the Semites*. First Series, 1894. *The New World* 4: 386–390.

7

Setting the Eternal Templates of Salvation: James Frazer

Le roi est mort; vive le roi! Ave Maria!
The king is dead; long live the king! Hail
Mary!

(James Frazer, *The Golden Bough*)

The Long Life and Great Renown of Sir James Frazer

An embarrassment in the eyes of many anthropology professionals today, the work of Sir James Frazer (1854–1941) did much to establish the discipline of social and cultural anthropology. In this chapter I shall show how Frazer contributed to the creation of the study of religion. Frazer hailed from the same strict Calvinist world as William Robertson Smith. Like Robertson Smith, he studied classics and philosophy, and like Tylor he became enamored of the skeptical, empiricist philosopher David Hume. His prize research dissertation at Cambridge earned him a research fellowship. And he essentially never left, except to travel and undertake the amateur exploration of ancient archeological sites in the sunnier Mediterranean world. The ancient pre-Christian town of Nemi, Italy, situated alongside its picturesque lake, became the site of the speculations enshrined in Frazer's great work, *The Golden Bough*. But Frazer was shaken out of this leisurely

tourist's approach to traditional cultures by reading Tylor's *Primitive Culture* (Fraser n.d.). This put Frazer so much into the Tylorian camp that almost anything Frazer wrote about evolutionist ideas can be traced to Tylor. It was that conviction of the truth of Tylor's overall thought that made it easy for Frazer to "think he was right" about human culture, especially religion. We can then safely revert to the internal context: Tylor's theory of survivals; his method of comparison; his general evolutionist conception of the step-wise growth of cultures; his preference for independent origination over diffusionist transmission as the explanation for similarities among cultures; his association of the primitives and ancients; his conception of anthropology as a "reforming science," aimed fundamentally at discrediting religion in modern society. All form the "internal" Tylorian context of the reasons why Frazer "thought he was right" about so much. Frazer was perhaps Tylor's most loyal student.

Apart from reading Tylor, Frazer was also fortunate to have been tutored at Cambridge by Robertson Smith. But Robertson Smith's call to ethnography couldn't budge Frazer out of his study. In 1898, he refused an invitation to join the pioneering Torres Straits expedition (Fraser n.d.). Ever the bookish scholar, he satisfied himself with working out the implications of Tylor's evolutionism

Understanding Theories of Religion: An Introduction, Second Edition. Ivan Strenski.
© 2015 Ivan Strenski. Published 2015 by John Wiley & Sons, Ltd.

(Ackerman 1987, pp. 58–59). Unlike his tutor Robertson Smith, Frazer focused on the Greek and Roman worlds, especially as revealed in Pausanias' detailed descriptions of rural Greek culture. Despite Frazer's bookish habits, his influence on theories of religion has been both widespread and substantial. Bronislaw Malinowski (1884–1942) declared that "anthropology, as presented by Sir James Frazer, is a great science, worthy of as much devotion as any of her elder and more exact sister studies" (Malinowski 1992, p. 94). Malinowski had in mind here the influence of Frazer's mammoth twelve-volume *The Golden Bough*. That work proposed an all-encompassing cross-cultural theory of the evolution of religion which, like Tylor, undercut Christian claims to uniqueness. Frazer argued that Christianity was actually formed from a pagan religious template, and thus actually prolonged pagan religious notions.

Unlike his progressive Christian friend Robertson Smith, Frazer rejected Christianity quite early. He joined the camp of Hume and Tylor, over against Max Müller, Herbert of Cherbury, Jean Bodin, and, significantly, Robertson Smith. Frazer was thus no caretaker of religion – even a liberal one. He became a kind of undertaker of religion, someone who wanted to bury Christianity, saying, "'I am not a Christian … [On] the contrary I reject the Christian religion as utterly false'" (Stocking 1995, p. 128, quoting Frazer 1935, p. 132). Tylor's idea of anthropology as a "reforming science" – a device useful for the destruction of established religion – suited Frazer's tastes.

How Did We Get from "There" to "Here" … Again?

It may be difficult for us to realize in our own high-tech times just how impressive late nineteenth-century Westerners regarded their own scientific and technological achievements as being. Frazer was particularly impressed with progress, especially by human control over the environment (Ratnikas n.d.). The last two decades of the nineteenth century saw a tremendous burst of technological innovation made widely available to ordinary people. In 1879, the first hearing aid came onto the market, and Thomas Edison demonstrated the first incandescent light. In 1880, the world's first electric streetcar made its inaugural run near Berlin, and news of the Afghan war was received by telegram dispatch in London. In 1882, Edison illuminated a square-mile area of New York City by electricity. By 1885, most people in the urban areas of the Western world could expect home delivery of newspapers. In 1886, the first typewriter ribbon was patented. The first Kodak box camera (100 exposures) could be had for $25 in 1888. In 1891, the first telephone connection between Paris and London was established, followed in 1896 by the first use of the X-ray machine, and in 1897 by Marconi's first radio communication. One year earlier, Frazer published the first volume of *The Golden Bough*. As we will see shortly, it is small wonder that Frazer "thought he was right" about the superiority of science and technology – certainly over religious means of knowledge and their ability to enhance human life by controlling nature.

Just as important, the last two decades of the nineteenth century marked a great burst of colonization by the major European powers. Now, not only were older colonial powers like France, the Netherlands, and Great Britain busy locking up vast areas of the globe, but newly formed nations, such as Max Müller's Germany, as well as tiny Belgium, got into the colonialism business. This expansion of Western power served the needs of the late nineteenth-century industrial economies for the raw materials needed to produce the very technologies of which Frazer and his ilk were so proud. But it would also shape the way Westerners looked on technologically less well developed peoples. The technological disadvantages of the newly colonized folk made it easy for Frazer and others "moderns" to "think they were right" to call them "primitive"

This juxtaposition of the power of the industrialized nations over the newly the colonized folk puzzled those who pondered large civilizational questions. Why, indeed, are "we" *here*, and "they" *there*? Why are they still "primitive" and we now "modern"? One answer ascribed to Tylor, but accepted by Frazer and Robertson Smith, assumed that the "primitives" were developmental survivals of people who were in most respects just like our own prehistoric ancestors (Stocking 1995, p. 131). What they are, we once were. After all, had not the archeological finds of the mid-nineteenth century shown that our pre-historic technology was identical to that of today's "primitives," and thus by extrapolation, that many of the other institutions of our own prehistoric past were as well? So, once more the original question came back at European thinkers like Frazer in an especially salient form. How did we get from *there* (and the way today's "primitive" people were) to *here* – to the level of sophisticated science and technology that made "modern" Westerners who they were?

For Frazer, the spectacular rise of technology taught him how much the ability of moderns to control nature had been enhanced. "They" had no medical technology adequate to prevent the scourge of infectious diseases, to remedy some of the ravages of old age, and so on. This raised the inevitable question of the ways that "primitive" humanity had attempted to do the same as our technology. How did they try to control nature so that they could enhance life (Stocking 1995, p. 131)? Here, however, Frazer broke with Tylor. "Primitive" folk were not the primitive scientists or philosophers of Tylor's imagination. They were not primarily interested in *explaining* how nature worked in and for itself. Instead, they were engineers in the making. They wanted to devise techniques by which they could enhance and protect their health, and extend their lives. As we will see, Frazer "thought he was right" about this desire to live, in part, because of a larger external cultural trend which swept him up, along with others of his time and later, such as Malinowski. This was called vitalism. The great influence of this larger external cultural trend of thinking also enabled him to believe he had arrived at a common mind about the nature of religion that surely anyone of good faith would accept. If the popularity of *The Golden Bough* is any indication, Frazer had good reason to think he had succeeded.

From Magic to Religion to Technology, Not Science

But if "primitives" were really driven by a pragmatic need to enhance life, how did religion make sense? Did religion prepare the way for the stunning, life-enhancing technologies of Frazer's time? Religion and technology hardly seemed like the same or even analogous things. But since Frazer believed that civilization evolved, religion had to be involved in some way as part of one of those necessary steps that the human species used to advance into the modern world.

Frazer's answer to this question was given in his argument for the evolution of what he inaptly called "science." His idea was that modern technology – not science – evolved from magic, but also passed as well through a religious evolutionary stage. Frazer relied on his common sense in concluding he was "right to think" that most early human beings lived in terror of death, famine, and disease. To Frazer, it was just natural that when ordinary means of protection failed our ancestors, they would have resorted to a special sort of primitive technology to master nature. Frazer calls this "magic." "In magic man depends on his own strength," says Frazer, "to meet the difficulties and dangers that beset him on every side. He believes in a certain established order of nature ... which he can manipulate for his own ends" (Frazer 1958, p. 824). Just where this power comes from is either unclear or at least contested. Nonetheless, it is a power some specially gifted or designated humans can control for their own purposes. These are our "magicians."

Sooner or later, however, Frazer thought that common sense would dictate that our ancestors would realize that magic was unreliable. In their obsession with survival, their passion for life, the "primitives" had little alternative but to resort to powers higher than those under the control of humans. People called these powers their gods or spirits. "Religion," then, for Frazer, is simply the name people give to the way they negotiate with the gods to obtain what they need to enhance their lives. Thus, Frazer contradicts Robertson Smith and claims that religion begins in sacrifice as a bribe. The institution of sacrifice shows how people seek to supplicate the gods by making gifts to them in order to win their aid. Nowhere to be seen is Robertson Smith's "jolly feast": the sacrificial communion meal.

Finally, Frazer resorts again to common sense to explain why and how religion failed human beings at their hour of need. Many prayers went unanswered; sacrificial gifts won no reciprocal favors from the gods. Desperate once more to secure their survival, people now began to act rationally: they began to rely upon themselves and thus created technology. Human effort, taken to higher levels of sophistication, is the only real source of power and productivity. Thus, Frazer's belief in humanity's eventual common-sense realization that only technology could address their needs, plus his infatuation with it, seemed to give him the confidence that he was "right to think" that his story of human progress was true. Technology succeeded religion and magic because Frazer's time was the "century of progress."

The Golden Bough: From Norseland to Nemi

Many of Frazer's contemporaries proposed their own "just so" stories of the course of human evolution. But they languish in obscurity, while Frazer's has had great success. I would suggest this might be because he packaged his evolutionist ideas in an immensely popular literary work, *The Golden Bough*. In some degree, the status of *The Golden Bough* as an accessible literary piece made its ideas penetrate the common mind of Frazer's time. *The Golden Bough* took on the character of an encyclopedia, a reference book, simply displaying objective facts about the world's mythologies. Therefore what strikes a reader first about it is not its philosophical or theoretical content, but rather the engaging collection of myths, relations of exotic customs and bizarre rites – all packaged as a kind of multivolume detective story. Here is where the very literary and material form of a theory-laden work aided its common acceptance, and thus its success as a medium for the formation of a common mind about ancient religion and myth for people in the early part of the twentieth century.

If we are to believe Frazer's own words, the puzzling records of a strange ancient Roman rite set him on a quest that would culminate in the publication in various editions, stretching from 1890 to 1915, of his ultimately twelve-volume classic study of religion, myth, and folklore. But his abstract plan of the evolution of human consciousness from magic through religion to science had to be packaged inside an enticing story. That overall storyline holds *The Golden Bough* together. Since the larger story told by *The Golden Bough* conditions Frazer's methodological ideas for studying religion, we need to get a feel for the theme contained in that larger package. Let's start at the beginning. What story does *The Golden Bough* finally want to tell?

The bough of the book's title refers to mistletoe. In winter, Frazer tells us, when the host oak tree has lost its leaves and seems drained of all life, the "golden" mistletoe bursts forth from the trunk and upper branches of the dormant oak. It promises the return of new life by embodying the very life of the oak itself. Without following Frazer down every turn along this rather long corridor, we can trace two major comparisons that give some of the winning flavor of the work, all the while illustrating his method. These concern puzzles he tries to solve involving the sacrificial death of the god and the promise of new life in the process, all with the help of a sprig of mistletoe!

Balder, Death, and Life-Giving Mistletoe

First, consider a myth figuring prominently in the book – the myth of Balder, the Norse hero and son of the father-god Odin. Traditionally, Balder and the mistletoe are symbolically identified. Balder's "existence is inseparably bound up" in the mistletoe. Yet, tragically, "his own death is the result of it" (Frazer 1958, p. 812).

The gods intend to make Balder invulnerable to attack by getting all the material gods to agree never to harm him. They agree. But other kinds of gods decide to test Balder's resistance, attacking with all the weapons of warfare – axes, swords, arrows, and such. Protected as he is by the material gods, nothing fazes Balder. The god Loki changes strategies and decides to attack Balder with a mere twig – of mistletoe. As soon as this mere "golden bough" struck Balder, he was "pierced ... through and through, and he fell down dead" (Frazer 1958, p. 704). Triumphant, the non-material gods cremate Balder's body upon an immense funeral pyre.

This myth, like so many others, leaves most modern readers scratching their heads in puzzlement. Why? How? Frazer seizes the moment to play detective. Now, Frazer knew many myths relate how something tragic lurks at the center of the relationship between life and death. A seed must die so that new life can come forth. The rhythms of seasonal change rehearse the same cycle of new life springing from the death of the old. Frazer notes, for example, that, in the northern reaches of Europe, people celebrated the death and cremation of Balder by sacrificing human Balders in fire festivals at critical times in the growing season. Says Frazer: "we may reasonably infer that in the Balder myth on the one hand, and the fire-festivals and custom of gathering mistletoe on the other hand, we have, as it were, the two broken and dissevered halves of an original whole."

What seemed unconnected – Balder's protection from death and his death from the glancing blow of a twig of mistletoe – is actually held together by reference to a deeper lust for life, symbolized in the blazing fires of sacrificial immolation. Like the mistletoe in the dead of winter, bouquets of those mysterious new growths spring from otherwise barren-looking oaks. We may thus assume that the myth of Balder's death was not a *mere* tale; it was an important story that people told themselves about the mysteries of life and death.

The Lessons Balder Taught Frazer: The Power of Comparative Method

What lessons did Frazer take from this sort of analysis? In true evolutionist style, he knew – among other things – that all cultures passed through identical stages of development and that the human mind was everywhere essentially the same. Thus, even though the old Norse culture of the Balder myth is a long way in time and place from, say, ancient Rome, Frazer was confident in the explanatory power of the *comparative* method. Thus, he believed that he could move by various leaps and bounds to connect what he knew (or did not know) about Balder and mistletoe to what he did not know (or what he knew) about other accounts of a hero or god being killed, and in which mistletoe was involved. Frazer found an analogous case to that of Balder's slaying in the rite of the murder of the priest at the shrine of Diana along the shores of the lake at Nemi: mistletoe figures in both places! By this kind of comparison, Frazer felt that he could get at something deeply human, given that historical borrowing between the stories seemed out of the question.

Murder Feeds the Life-Cycle

Let us, then, look at Frazer's dramatic account of the murderous goings on at Nemi. Frazer's narrative begins with the myth of the god-priest of the sacred grove there. In a nostalgia-infused scene set on the shores of the lake at Nemi, Frazer begins to cast his spell:

> Who does not know Turner's picture of the Golden Bough? The scene, suffused with the golden glow of imagination ... is a dream-like vision of the little woodland lake of Nemi – "Diana's Mirror" ... Diana herself might still linger by this lonely shore, still haunt these woodlands wild. (Frazer 1958, p. 1)

With writing as lush and romantic as this, it is easy to see how and why *The Golden Bough* was such a popular success among the reading public of the early twentieth century.

But Frazer soon breaks the spell of his pastoral, since he has to relate a grisly tale of murder, set on the shore of that same arcadian Lake Nemi of *The Golden Bough*'s opening lines. "In antiquity this sylvan landscape was the scene of a strange and recurring tragedy," says Frazer, setting the scene. "In the northern shore of the lake, right under the precipitous cliffs on which the modern village of Nemi is perched, stood the sacred grove and sanctuary of Diana ... or Diana of the Wood." Enter the criminal: "a grim figure might be seen to prowl. In his hand he carried a drawn sword, and he kept peering warily about him as if at every instant he expected to be set upon by an enemy." This "grim figure," armed and ready for his deadly deed, is no common homicidal thug, but a holy man. "He was a priest and a murderer," charged with the brutal and paradoxical commission of that holy site. But for whom does he lie in wait? He came to murder a man, Frazer says, who "sooner or later [was] to murder him and hold the priesthood in his stead." Horrific tale, indeed, and one deliberately set into motion, since such "was the rule of the sanctuary. A candidate for the priesthood could only succeed to office by slaying the priest, and having slain him, he retained the office till he was himself slain by a stronger or a craftier." Frazer tells us more about the holy stalker. This murderous stalker-priest is likewise a "king," but a king who would also become the target for the next killer-priest, his successor. The king is dead; long live the king (Frazer 1958, pp. 1–2)!

Frazer's little crime thriller may finally may make us want to ask, "*Why* dunnit?" instead of "*Who* dunnit?" No mystery surrounds the whodunit, since Frazer tells us so from the start that a different priest-king serves each time in the role of hunter and hunted. The mystery of the killing of the priest-king by his successor, the next priest-king to be, lies in the rationale for such an apparently irrational custom. "*Why* dunnit?"

Frazer is ready with a beginning of an answer. "The strange rule of this priesthood has no parallel in classical antiquity, and cannot be explained from it. To find an explanation we must go farther afield," such as to the myth of Balder (Frazer 1958, p. 2). We must become *comparativists* in the style of Frazer, Tylor, and others, and make significant links with such examples "farther afield."

A Textbook Case of Frazer's Use of Comparison

Without going into all the details that Frazer loads into *The Golden Bough*, let me show how Frazer's comparative method operates here. The method is based upon *analogous* facts: it seeks "likes." Thus, both in the case of Balder and the priest-king of Nemi, for example, a sacred personage is killed by other sacred personages – whether this be the gods in Balder's case or the priest-king to be in the case of Nemi. Also, associated with both is the change of seasons and the return of new life corresponding to them. The midsummer fires lit in honor of Balder and the ancient custom of annual human sacrifice in connection with these "Balder fires" parallel the high-summer fire worship of Diana, the huntress and fertility goddess to nubile and expectant women at Nemi; they also parallel the hunting down and killing – the death and resurrection, as it were – of the priest-king by his successor. *Le roi est mort; vive le roi! Ave Maria!* – "The king is dead; long live the king! Hail Mary!" (Frazer 1958, p. 827). Virbius, god of the hunt, too, is worshiped at Nemi along with Diana, as a kind of male counterpart to the goddess, reminiscent of the way Attis, for example, is linked with Cybele. Like the near-invincible Balder, Frazer suggests, Virbius too is characterized by a tremendous ability to resist death, and is therefore a powerful

emblem of ever-renewed life (Frazer 1958, pp. 4–6). But Frazer is not satisfied just to marshal similarities between superficially different cases. He seeks to deepen the implications of the analogy.

What would seem to clinch the analogy for Frazer are two additional details. First, Virbius is acknowledged as the "mythical predecessor or archetype of the line of priests who served Diana under the title of Kings of the Wood, and who came, like him, one after the other, to a violent end" (Frazer 1958, p. 9). He then shares the fecundating nature of Diana, now linked with the hunting/killing and renewal of the life of the priest-king of the wood. Second, the priest-king of Nemi, like Balder, is identified with mistletoe. He personifies the oak tree upon which the golden bough of mistletoe grows. And, like Balder again, as embodying the spirit of the oak, he can only be killed when a sprig – of mistletoe, in this case – is broken from the sacred oak itself. When the Balder fires are lit at midsummer, this also signals the gathering of mistletoe in the northern woodlands (Frazer 1958, p. 769). So while the comparison between Balder and Nemi seemed far-fetched, in fact, beneath the superficial details is a deeper unity.

But what of our original question about the overall meaning of the larger story told by *The Golden Bough*, and its relation to Frazer's evolutionary vision of the origins (and death) of religion? What *The Golden Bough* finally teaches through a patient use of comparative analysis is the ceaseless rhythm of life, death, and rebirth, and the human desire to see *life* triumphant. It is that story that lies at the heart of the strange rites of the sacrifice of the god, and the kernel message of *The Golden Bough*.

The Hidden Paganism of Christianity Revealed

Now, if we can make one further link to Frazer's evolutionary sensibilities, his strategies for undoing Christian exclusivism, even, like Tylor, for undoing Christianity itself, I think we can grasp Frazer's ultimate purpose in *The Golden Bough*. "The resemblance of many of the savage customs and ideas" – such as those having to do with the death and resurrection of gods like

Balder or Virbius – "to the fundamental doctrines of Christianity is striking," Frazer says coyly. Frazer quickly follows up this potentially explosive remark by stepping back. "'I make no reference to this parallelism, leaving my readers to draw their own conclusions, one way or the other'" (quoted in Ackerman 1987, p. 95). Can anyone take Frazer at his word – that he hasn't aimed his comparative method at showing how Christianity seems to preserve pagan models, even be based upon pagan mythical archetypes? Following the adage that "whatever can be insinuated can be stated," I shall herewith say flat out what I think what Frazer means, but has not got the nerve to say, about the ultimate intentions behind *The Golden Bough* and its comparisons.

It is no accident that Frazer dwells on religious ideas, motifs, myths, and rituals that *deliberately* echo Christian ones. The death and return to life of both Balder and Virbius, their connection with the enhancement of life, all have recognizable Christian parallels. Christian apologists have long claimed that these parallels show that Providence created these pagan simulacra of Christianity to prepare humanity for the Gospel. This not only anticipates the ideas of Natural Religion, but also presumes that religions evolve! Of course, just because religions parallel each other in various ways, we cannot conclude that one side of the parallel is theologically prior to the other. But since Christianity is *later* than the pagan religions mentioned, we can say the pagan religions are *prior* historically. Christianity then might have *built on* pagan models, or could be said to have *evolved* beyond the pagan models in question.

For other Christians, these ancient pagan religions were more akin to ancient Judaism in establishing what Christian apologists would call certain preparatory religious models or *templates* in their myths, rites, images, and so on. These pre-Christian religions were thought to have got people ready for Christianity, so that when the missionaries came with the Gospel, Christianity would fit with their religious sensibilities and not seem alien. In our survey of theories of religion, we will recall that the devotees of Natural Religion often felt the same way. They felt that our aptitude or capacity for religion was built into human nature, and was part of a divine plan for laying the foundations of what would be revealed to Jews and Christians in the fullness of time. Christianity

was still unique, but its outlines had been imprinted on the human religious mind millennia before the coming of Christ. When Christianity appeared, it was then by definition, for Christians, a more highly *evolved* form of religion.

Frazer was repelled by these self-serving Christian views. Contrary to what the Christian apologists argue, pagan analogies to Christian motifs showed that he was "right to think" that Christianity just mimicked old pagan forms. Instead, Frazer thought he was right that Christianity *was to be explained* by reference to its membership in a larger class of religions, within the global history of religion. Christianity was not unique. Contrary to the views of Christian apologists, the pagan religions did not prepare the Mediterranean Basin for Christianity. That was not why Christianity and the pagan religions of the Mediterranean looked alike. These comparisons showed *not* how the pagan religions were really Christian beneath the surface, but rather how pagan, primitive, and savage Christianity actually was (Stocking 1995, p. 131). Frazer's comparative method was his way of undermining Christianity and fulfilling his career as an "undertaker of religion."

Frazer Finds Other Christs

The power of Frazer's attack can perhaps be most strongly felt by considering the supposedly unique Christian idea of Jesus as an incarnate god. Frazer attacks this belief in a series of ways. In Frazer's view, Christians had become comfortable in thinking that the idea of the god-man comes late in the history of religions. After all, the well-known, and earlier, Jewish background out of which Christianity grew lacks this idea. But Frazer "thought he was right" that if we looked beyond the narrow purview of the ancient Hebrew world we could find parallels to Jesus. Frazer could say this with confidence because his classical studies informed him that the idea of a god-man abounds in ancient mythologies.

Christian apologists need, therefore, to take note of India, and the god-man Krishna. Says Frazer, "perhaps no country in the world has been so prolific of human gods as India; nowhere has the divine grace been poured out in a more liberal measure on all classes of society from kings down to milkmen" (Frazer 1958, p. 115). Christianity, thus, fails the first test for establishing uniqueness. As Frazer will endlessly argue, many religions can lay claim to worship incarnate deities similar to Jesus.

A Christian critic might reply that, indeed, there may be vague and general similarities between Jesus and other deities. That proves little or nothing. Frazer would need to show that other features essential to the basic template or structure of Christianity can be found elsewhere before Christian uniqueness is troubled. Are the crucifixion, the savior's atoning, self-giving sacrificial death, and miraculous resurrection not just too specifically Christian to have their uniqueness diluted by comparison with other religions? Or is the poignant figure of Jesus' mother, at once a virgin, miraculously preserved from sin, and at the same time mother, again too uniquely Christian to yield to the corrosive effects of Frazer's comparative method?

But Frazer had internal reasons for thinking that he was right from his vast erudition in his field of study. Deliberately contrived to undermine the uniqueness of such standard Christian beliefs, Frazer details comparisons with non-Christian religions that mimic all the major *specific* Christian images and ideas. He shows how early Christian evangelists modeled Christian symbols on pagan ones in order to compete with pagans. These early Christian evangelists, in effect, stole pagan symbols outright. The appropriation of 25 December as Jesus' birthday is just one such example. The gospels make no mention of the nativity's date. Moreover, Christians previously had celebrated it on 6 January. So, why is it that ever since 375 CE, 25 December has been designated as the true date of the birth of Jesus? Supported even by Christian documents of the time, Frazer shows how rivalry with devotion to the Mediterranean sun-god, the "Sun of Righteousness," Mithras, decided the issue of fixing the birthday of Jesus. Mithras' birthday was 25 December (Frazer 1958, p. 417)! In addition, the link between Christmas and the birthday of Mithras on 25 December makes a neat link to Frazer's belief that religion was really about fertility and increase of life. In the northern hemisphere, 25 December marks the beginning of the return of the sun, and thus the beginning of the new growing season. What Frazer tried to show was that a Christian pattern of baptizing pagan beliefs and practices was not exceptional. Early Christians were doing it all the time as a way of dealing with pagan rivalry in the early centuries. It became the rule for the Christian missionizing of pagan Europe, with broad and profound implications for the missionizing of the New World. No wonder Frazer thought he was right!

The Holy Families and Other Christs

Perhaps the crowning touch in Frazer's attempt to undermine Christian uniqueness was his comparison of Christ and the Virgin Mary with Attis and his mother, the goddess Cybele. First, Frazer argues that the Christian images both of Jesus' life, death, and resurrection along with his miraculous birth to the Virgin Mary reprise rather detailed correspondences with the myths of ancient pagan dying gods and their Great Mothers. In the story of Cybele and Attis, like Jesus, the Good Shepherd, "Attis was said to have been a fair young shepherd or herdsman." Then, echoing the Christian belief in Jesus' virgin birth, Frazer reports that Attis' "birth, like that of many other heroes, is said to have been miraculous. His mother, Nana, was a virgin." Frazer implies, then, that Cybele, "mother of the gods" and goddess who brings life and fertility, corresponds exactly to Mary, virgin mother of Jesus, known by many Christians as "Holy Mary, Mother of God … full of grace." Then, Frazer finds the pagan precursor to the cross upon which Jesus is crucified in Attis' death, hung from a tree. In one version of this myth, Attis dies at the foot of a pine tree after having bled to death from a self-inflicted castration (Frazer 1958, p. 407). In another version of the Attis myth, he is tied to a tree and killed (Fraser 1994, p. 355). So convinced is Frazer of the internal connection between the Christ and Attis myths that he undertakes to show that Catholic Lenten Passion pageants, for example, repeated old pagan rites widely celebrated to remember Attis' bloody death and fixing upon a tree. On the appointed day at the spring equinox, "a pine-tree was cut in the woods and brought into the sanctuary of Cybele, where it was treated as a great divinity," Frazer relates. Then, Christ-image upon

Christ-image tumbles out: "The trunk was swathed like a corpse with woolen bands and decked with wreaths of violets ... and the effigy of a young man, doubtless Attis himself, was tied to the middle of the stem" (Frazer 1958, p. 405). Like Jesus as well after his death, the body of Attis is "laid in the sepulcher," and just as in the Christ story, his resurrection follows straight on:

> The resurrection of the god was hailed by his disciples as a promise that they too would issue triumphant from the corruption of the grave. On the morrow, the twenty-fifth day of March, which was reckoned the vernal equinox, the divine resurrection was celebrated with a wild outburst of glee. (Frazer 1958, p. 407)

Finally, in commemoration of the death and resurrection of Attis, a sacramental meal and communion – what Frazer calls a "blessed sacrament" – are celebrated. Thus, not only do the Christ and Attis myths respectively mirror one another, but so also do the rituals attending them.

"It is at the very least a remarkable coincidence, if it is nothing more," says Frazer, "that the Christian and the heathen festivals of the divine death and resurrection should have been solemnized at the same season and in the same places" (Frazer 1958, p. 407). Ever attentive for evidence of vitalism, such as the rhythms of seasonal vegetative death and rebirth, Frazer notes how the mystical new lives of the twin savior gods cohered with the new life of nature's spring season of rebirth.

But most radical of all, Frazer suggests that the parallels between old paganism and Christianity itself go well beyond abstract structural similarities. These comparisons carry with them a load of common religious *meaning*, that applied to *all* religions. Every religion – like the Attis and Christ cults – wants people to "have life and have it more abundantly." All religions are vitalist at their core. It was this virtual obsession with enhancing life, and perhaps his own in the bargain, that grasped Frazer's whole being, and seemed, in the process, to dictate the many choices he made in trying to understand and explain religion.

References

Ackerman, R. 1987. *J.G. Frazer: His Life and Work.* Cambridge: Cambridge University Press.

Frazer, J.G. 1935. *Creation and Evolution in Primitive Cosmogonies and Other Pieces.* London: Macmillan.

Frazer, J.G. 1958. *The Golden Bough.* New York: Macmillan.

Malinowski, B. 1992. "Myth in Primitive Psychology" (1925). In R. Redfield (ed.), *Magic, Science and Religion and Other Essays.* Prospect Heights, IL: Waveland Press.

Ratnikas, A. n.d. *Timeline Technology.* http://timelines.ws/20thcent/1988.html.

Stocking, G.W. 1995. *After Tylor: British Social Anthropology, 1888–1951.* Madison: University of Wisconsin Press.

Further Reading

Douglas, M. 1978. "Introduction." In S. McCormack (ed.), *Sir James Frazer, The Illustrated Golden Bough.* London: George Rainbird.

Duffy, M. 1923. *Source Records of the Great War*, vol. 1. http://www.firstworldwar.com.

Eliot, T.S. 1922. *The Waste Land.* London: Faber & Faber.

Fraser, R. 1890. *Frazer, Sir James (1854–1941).* Milton Keynes: Open University.

Fraser, R. (ed.). 1994. *James George Frazer, The Golden Bough: A New Abridgement.* Oxford: Oxford University Press.

Frazer, J.G. 1926. Letter to Bronislaw Malinowski, 14 February 1926, ed. B. Malinowski. Bronislaw Malinowski Papers: Manuscripts and Archives: Yale University Library.

Frazer, J.G. 1927a. "For a Scrap of Paper (from the French of Paul Hyacinthe Loyson)." In J.G. Frazer (ed.), *Gorgon's Head.* Freeport, NY: Books for Libraries Press.

Frazer, J.G. 1927b. "William Robertson Smith." In J.G. Frazer (ed.), *Gorgon's Head.* London: Macmillan.

Hume, D. 1963. "The Natural History of Religion." In R. Wollheim (ed.), *Hume on Religion.* London: Collins.

Jarvie, I.C. 1964. *The Revolution in Anthropology.* London: Routledge & Kegan Paul.

Lord, S.J., and A. Daniel. 1912. "The Christianity of George Bernard Shaw." *America* 16.

Lord, S.J., and A. Daniel. 1916. *The Christianity of George Bernard Shaw*. New York: America.

Malinowski, B. 1962. "On Sir James Frazer." In B. Malinowski (ed.), *Sex, Culture and Myth*. New York City: Harcourt Brace.

Parker, R.A. 1997–2002. "Exploring the *Waste Land*." http://world.std.com/~raparker/exploring/thewasteland/explore.html.

Shaw, G.B. 1912. "Preface to *Androcles and the Lion*: On the Prospects of Christianity." A Penn State Electronic Classics Series Publication (ed.) J. Manis. Pennsylvania University.

Strenski, I. 1987. *Four Theories of Myth in Twentieth-Century History*. London and Iowa City: Macmillan/Iowa University Press.

8

Understanding How to Understand Religion: "Phenomenology of Religion"

Religion – It's So Very Simple

The classic nineteenth-century founders of the study of religion, such as Friedrich Max Müller, James Frazer, or Edward Burnett Tylor, presumed (at least) three things about religion:

- First, they presumed that religion had "no moving parts" – that it was a *simple* thing, and therefore that it only required simple explanations. Religion, therefore, required minimal description, virtually no account of its constitution, and virtually nothing about how its constituent parts might articulate into a whole.
- Second, in terms of *explaining* religion, the nineteenth-century founders simply took for granted that the only questions worth asking, and thus the only explanations worth having, were historical, typically developmental or evolutionist, ones. "History" was, typically, understood in the rather narrow sense of chronology. What institutions came first and gave rise to succeeding ones? Or what historical stages laid the necessary facilitating conditions for the evolution or "devolution" of stages of religion to follow? The extent to which evolution was simply taken for granted can be judged by the comment of Belgian historian of religion Comte Eugène Goblet d'Alviella in 1885, that the evolution of religion seemed not even to be a theory, but rather a "quasi-certitude" (Goblet d'Alviella 1885, p. 173).
- Third, the nineteenth-century founders of religious studies were consumed by the question of where to assign data to the evolutionary schemes that they had constructed. Tylor's doctrine of "survivals" essentially let him dismiss the integrity of data that he could not (or would not) include within his evolutionary scheme. Religion in modern Europe? A survival of something that science had long since made obsolete. Religion in modern Europe? Something to be dismissed as peripheral to the moving train of historical development, despite its ubiquity.

Even for someone like the devout Max Müller, religion needed no explanation, much less critical conceptual scrutiny. He already knew all he needed to know about what religion was: the contemplation of the Infinite. What required explanation was how and why so much of what passed as religion failed to live up to its "real" essence. Why rituals, why childish myths, why the production and veneration of florid iconography, why sectarian clinging to separateness

Understanding Theories of Religion: An Introduction, Second Edition. Ivan Strenski.
© 2015 Ivan Strenski. Published 2015 by John Wiley & Sons, Ltd.

caused by affirmation of dogmas? Max Müller responded with a master-narrative of the decline or devolution of "essential religion" into the corrupted religions of history. Humanity had suffered a kind of second Fall. It had simply strayed from an aboriginal blessedness where humanity and divinity were at one, and the lion lay down with the lamb. Significantly, Müller never set foot in India, nor did he immerse himself in the social life of emigrant Indian communities, such as they were, in Europe. For him, further empirical studies of lived Indian religion would have taught him nothing: texts were sufficient for his work (Van den Bosch 2002, p. 137).

For his part, Frazer sized up religion as just an attempt by "primitive" peoples (and Catholics, most of all) to control their environment by supplicating the deity. On Frazer's scale of progress, religion was a developmental prelude to technology, and itself successor to exotic human attempts to manage reality by magic, so-called. We had learned that magic did not work, so we resorted to petitioning the deity. When humanity finally understood that religion failed as well, we once more took matters into our own hands and developed technologies. But while Frazer was an avid traveler throughout the Mediterranean world about which he wrote so much, the facts he met there only seemed to confirm what he already believed. We do not have robust evidence of Frazer making efforts to check his evolutionary scheme. Again, like other evolutionists, his priorities were to preserve whatever evolutionary scheme happened to fit his needs.

Religion: Simple? Not So Much

Would that the story of religion were as simple as the evolutionists and devolutionists thought! While it remains a matter of dispute how disenchantment with evolutionism arose, I shall argue that the movement we have called "phenomenology of religion" arose, in part, as a result of internal – purely intellectual – criticisms of evolutionism. Structurally, phenomenology of religion inverts everything for which religious evolutionism stands. It is synchronic, while evolutionism is diachronic; it eschews theory and explanation for empathetic understanding grounded in human subjectivity, while evolutionism

confidently seeks to construct theories to "explain" religion in an "objective" way; it asserts the autonomy of religion and, thus how religion helps us understand things in the world, while evolutionism is reductionist in that it seeks to explain away religion in terms of non-religious factors.

These differences mean we should look briefly at why the thinkers of the day "thought they were right" for being critical of evolutionism, reasons that were internal to the arguments and theories themselves. One reason often given for shifting away from evolutionism, for example, was the arrival of new facts about other societies that greatly exceeded what was known before. Cornelis P. Tiele, a precursor of phenomenology of religion, came round to this view slowly but surely. An American reviewer of Tiele's *History of the Egyptian Religion* (1882) reported in *The Nation* that the "author … saw that the attempt to construct a general history of religion was premature until the particular religions had been worked out in detail" (Anon. 1882, p. 361). Thus, whatever else may be true, the massive overload of new religious data seems to have intellectually strained evolutionary or devolutionary schemes beyond their breaking point.

Other internal factors intensified the strain upon these progressivist growth stories. In France, for example, Christian theologians were beginning to pick apart the pretensions of cultural evolutionism by noting internal *contradictions*. Paris' Maurice Vernes concluded that if religions really did develop progressively, as the evolutionists said, why were cultural traits considered "primitive" found in supposedly higher stages of development? Merely coining the word "survival" could not cover up such embarrassing counterfactuals. Were progressive developmentalism true, how was it possible that, say, the ("primitive") Roman Catholic cult of the saints comfortably existed alongside a "higher" monotheism? How could one consider, say, Mexican Roman Catholicism a "primitive" polytheism, as Tylor implied, given its highly developed legal and philosophical nature? And why should one assume that polytheism was "primitive"? In their heart, does not every polytheist enter the spiritual mindset of a monotheist when they focus on their particular deity (Goblet d'Alviella 1885, p. 173)?

These arguments against evolutionism, deployed within the internal intellectual world of these professional scholars of religion, played their part in causing thinkers simply to abandon a whole series of questions or problems of religion, and to shift to others associated with what can be grouped under the rubric "phenomenology of religion." In a way, we could say that the first conversations about religion were about the nature of true religion, or the identity of a Natural Religion. The problems associated with this quest were, as we will recall, first articulated in the sixteenth and seventeenth centuries by Jean Bodin and Herbert of Cherbury. Down to the late nineteenth century, the problematic of Natural Religion had become the axis round which the study of religion turned (Byrne 1989). Thus, for the Frazers, Tylors, Robertson Smiths, and Max Müllers of the day, the "problems of religion" focused on issues like identifying the chronologically first or true religion, or discovering the historical origins of religion in time and place. How had religion grown out of (or declined from) a particular historically comprehended stage of primitive human development or fallen from a pristine archaic stage of spiritual perfection before the onset of human decline?

Nothing, however, guaranteed that these questions would retain their interest for scholars. And, sure enough, by the late nineteenth century, the topic of the conversation about religion shifted. Old topics of conversation about religion ceased being interesting or compelling partly for reasons already discussed. Part of the reason these older topics lost their interest ought to be understood, I am suggesting, in terms of many external factors – generational changes, and religious, esthetic, and political revolutions.

What the Phenomenology of Religion Owes to the Dutch Higher Education Act 1876

That a new approach to the study of religion should have emerged was remarkable, given the intellectual and institutional character of late nineteenth- and early twentieth-century Europe. The entrenched theological ethos of European universities bent thinkers toward confessional treatments of religion, and the evolutionist biases

supporting them. Like many other Christians, even liberals shared the view that divine direction lay behind a movement of history which marched in their favor. Providence dictated that Christianity represented the highest, or most highly evolved, form of religion. In the late nineteenth and early twentieth century, even liberal Christians felt that Christianity was the epitome of religious development, growth, and evolution. This period was, accordingly, an intense period of Christian missionizing and European imperial activity. Yet it was among liberal Protestants that the swing away from evolutionism began. It began with reconceptions of what a "science of religion" really needed to be, and eventuated in the creation of the special professionalized discipline that can be roughly gathered under the rubric "phenomenology of religion."

How, then, did it happen that the break with evolutionary thinking about religion – phenomenology of religion in the *specific sense* – was not only led by liberal Christians, but by ordained ministers of a particular liberal Christian church? There are many candidate answers, since this break occurred in different places at about the same time. But I want to pick up the arguments of a Dutch colleague, Arie Molendijk, to emphasize the need to consider the Netherlands, and the external institutional and political factors active in this change (Molendijk 2005). Molendijk argues that what is *specifically* called "phenomenology of religion" was made possible only by the direct action of the government of the Netherlands. It was only by virtue of such legislative acts as the Higher Education Act of 1876 that departments were formed, faculty appointed, and their salaries paid – something those who tend to ignore institutional realities should heed. But there also needed to be a fit between institutional bases and fundamental conceptualizations; in the Netherlands this was furnished by Protestant theologians in a position to make decisions about the shape of university curricula. That is to say that the new externally constructed governmental arrangements needed to fit the facts of the internal intellectual context of the academic profession in the Netherlands.

Once again, we see that liberal Protestants led the shift in such fundamental theological orientations that bore on the study of religion. And the more liberal liberals, so to speak, the Arminians or

Remonstrants, were most prominent. They believed that knowledge of the world was good in itself. It deepened religious commitment and insight because it deepened knowledge of God's creation. Two theology professors at the University of Leiden, Jan Hendrik Scholten and Abraham Kuenen, led the modern theology movement in Holland. Like Müller and Robertson Smith, they believed that thinking about religion in a critical way promoted a more mature religious commitment. Like the Natural Religion theorists, Scholten taught that human beings contained within themselves "the germ of a spiritual development, the objective ideal of which is God Himself" (Réville 1864, p. 283). Studying nature brings people closer to the God, who expresses himself in and through his creation. Because they studied nature and religion as part of nature, Scholten called his study of religion "science of religion," just as liberal Protestants Robertson Smith and Müller had, and for pretty much the same religious reasons.

A New Kind of Science

But how does one exploit one's external context, one's institutional setting, in order to convert theological attitudes into a science – especially a science of religion – at one go? How, in effect, did the Dutch liberal Protestants use the conditions of their external political and institutional context to shape ideas within the internal context of professional talk about religion? Evolutionist models had dominated the internal context of older science of religion, and in doing so gave the old science of religion its scientific integrity. But once the phenomenologists abandoned evolutionism they risked losing any scientific rationale for their work. In the absence of an evolutionist theoretical framework, how, then, could they defend the *scientific* status of their new studies of religion to their colleagues in the study of religion with intellectual arguments?

Luckily, in the Netherlands an alternative model of science was available. It was called morphology, and was found in the burgeoning biological sciences. Doing morphology required rigorous, rational sorting of data into classes or kinds, and then further classification of these kinds into more general species and so on until the "tree of life" had fully branched out. All this

surely constituted scientific activity for those practicing the life sciences. Cornelis P. Tiele's "morphologies of religion," for example, exemplify this commitment to a science of religion, based upon the practice of the life sciences. Tiele sorted out different kinds of religions, for example, into respective classes and subclasses until he had filled out the tree of world religions.

However, Tiele's new scientific methods needed to satisfy those who populated his internal context – the powerful Dutch theological establishment – as well as those further out in the external direction. Otherwise, without real institutional research and teaching units with their paid employees and a professorate, who would know of the phenomenology of religion? And without the economic support of presses that published books and periodicals, Tiele's religious morphology would have been confined to his study. Further, without theological support, or at least without a muted theological opposition, Tiele's phenomenological program would never have been certified for inclusion in any university curriculum. All these considerations are what make up the external context of the conditions that make the spread of knowledge possible. Luckily, this early iteration of the phenomenology of religion got an institutional foothold in the Netherlands state educational system. By a series of remarkable accidents, governmental intervention produced the radical unintended consequence of founding a new secular, discipline – the phenomenology of religion. Here's how.

The Higher Education Act of 1876 laid the legal and institutional foundations for a new discipline of the science of religion (Molendijk 2005, ch. 3). The act, first, sought to guarantee neutrality in teaching about religion – a scientific approach, it said. Tiele's history, and later his morphology, passed muster as "scientific." Second, perhaps unwittingly, the government apparently contradicted its own purposes in founding a science of religion by fostering Christian theologizing in the same bill. Parliament, however, did not feel these goals were in conflict with each other, because they tacitly accepted the liberal theological proposition that the more one knew about religion, the more Christianity would show itself to be the best and truest religion. As a liberal Calvinist, an Arminian, or a Remonstrant, Tiele benefited from this concept. He was thus confident that if he studied religion scientifically, he would naturally and without coercion come to the conclusion that Christianity was the one true religion. The scientific cross-cultural comparison of religions of the world, for example, would lead one by the natural light of reason – objectively – to conclude that Christianity was superior to all other religions. The data of the study of religion were thought to be so powerful and compelling that the Remonstrants were sure of their beliefs. The establishment of the so-called "science of religion" by the government, then, gave the liberal Protestants a franchise to put their theology into practice. This combination of the scientific and theological made the careers of the leading lights of phenomenology of religion – Cornelis P. Tiele, William Brede Kristensen, and Gerardus van der Leeuw – possible. For this complex of internal and external reasons and causes, they felt that "they were right" in doing the science of religion, in the form of phenomenology of religion. All the major founding figures in the phenomenology of religion in the Netherlands (save Chantepie de la Saussaye) – Tiele, Kristensen, Van der Leeuw – not only emerged from this Remonstrant theological formation, they never really left it. Here's how Cornelis P. Tiele tried to do both science and theology at the same time.

Phenomenology's Liberal Christian Beginnings: Tiele and Kristensen

Like many thinkers at the threshold of change, Tiele only tentatively stepped into the morphology of religion. A full reorientation of thought into phenomenology would only come with Tiele's successor in the chair at Leiden, William Brede Kristensen (1867–1953). Kristensen was never in the grip of the evolutionism that Tiele could not shake off. So Kristensen really laid the foundations for what today has come to be known as the phenomenology of religion, even down to establishing the current usage of the term itself (Molendijk 2000a, p. 24). Kristensen also trained Gerardus van der Leeuw (1890–1950), the individual who, if anyone, can certainly be credited with being the first undisputed phenomenologist of religion

(Molendijk 2000a, p. 35). But how did Tiele's break with evolutionism occur? Why did he "think he was right" to take such a radical turn in thinking?

Tiele called his strategy for revealing the nature of this deeper level of religion "morphology." He laid out that program in his two-volume *Elements of the Science of Religion* (1896). Volume 1 was subtitled *Morphological*, volume 2, *Ontological*. Tiele's morphology, modeled as we know on the biological sciences, encompassed both the descriptive categorization of organic life forms and the rules of their development. Tiele's morphology, then, sorted out both the different kinds of religions as well as a chronicle of their growth (Tiele 1896, p. 17). Ahistorical, structural, or synchronic kinds of studies must, at least, complement whatever history had to offer. Thus, by the nineteenth century's end, Tiele had in effect mounted an argument for, at a minimum, the coexistence of the *history* of religion with the newer *phenomenological* style of studying of religion.

In these works, Tiele also was among the first to assert three other features of what would become identified with the modern phenomenology of religion. First was the practice of *detached* study, of what has also been called "bracketing" one's beliefs, or *epochē*. In Tiele's words, the study of religion required a "calm impartiality" (Tiele 1896, p. 8). A true scientific study of religion will, therefore, study all religions without prejudice, just as a biologist would study the forms of living things without prejudice. Second, Tiele's morphology of religion suggested that the study of religion should start by sorting out or *classifying* religions according to their different kinds – "careful classification" (Tiele 1896, p. 6). Thus, Tiele discussed the differences between various *kinds* of "gods" (p. 35ff), or between religions having founders versus those arising by "unconscious growth" (p. 42f), or religions of "world-negation" contrasted with those of "world-affirmation" (p. 62f), or "ethical" religions over against "nature" religions (pp. 63–68), or "Spiritism" versus "Animism" (pp. 72–83), and so on. For Tiele, then, religion was anything but *simple*, as those like Tylor or Frazer thought. Third and finally, Tiele promoted the doctrine of the *autonomy* of religion. This doctrine was organically part of Tiele's liberal Protestant Remonstrant or Arminian faith. Recall Hendrik

Scholten's view that people contained within themselves "the germ of a spiritual development, the objective ideal of which is God Himself" (Réville 1864, p. 283). Virtually committed to the Natural Religion of a Bodin, Herbert, or Max Müller, Tiele believed that all people had a unique and innate capacity for religiousness. All humanity was blessed in equal proportions with a pure primordial monotheistic revelation. Later, this liberal Protestant idea of the innate nature of the religious capacity would be expressed by the Dutch phenomenologists of religion, like Kristensen or Van der Leeuw and, spectacularly, by Otto and Eliade, as the doctrine of the autonomy of religion. This doctrine, which came to be identified with the phenomenology of religion, taught that religion existed in a splendid isolation from all things profane, and in its most extreme iteration, could only be studied in and for itself. Therefore, religious *experience* must be some unique form of consciousness, safely secured from the enemies of the faith, within the walls the doctrine of autonomy constructed.

Tiele did not use the language of autonomy, although his practice of the science of religion presumed as much. I say this because Tiele's idea of the purpose of the science of religion was to track the ways that Natural Religion – the ultimate root of all religion – was lurking within the many religions of the world. Tiele presumed a two-level view of the world of religion, much as had the earlier proponents of Natural Religion. At the superficial level were the many different religions, but at a fundamental level, was the one essential religion. At the superficial level were the many conflicting *forms* of religions of revelation. But at the profound level was the one Natural Religion, the knowledge of which was open to all people of good faith. Declaring a doctrine of the autonomy of religion in so many words Tiele said that "religion itself is entirely independent of such forms; that forms may change and vary without sacrificing the eternal ideas and the immortal aspirations which constitute the essence of religion" (Tiele 1896, p. 222). Once Tiele entered the domain of speaking of religion as "entirely independent," in his heart he was declaring the same doctrine of autonomy that started as the liberal Protestant dogma of a Kristensen, Van der Leeuw, or Otto, and which would later be loudly proclaimed by Eliade and others of his ilk.

In sum, Tiele got the phenomenology of religion started, but his doctrine of autonomy also made from it a way to shore up his own faith. Tiele remained a Remonstrant theologian. He really wanted to channel the truth of the one religion more than he wanted to stimulate curiosity about religion. He also never totally abandoned historical explanatory strategies, directed at seeking to establish the historical existence and character of Natural Religion (Molendijk 2000b, p. 92). In the end, Tiele left us a confused legacy – one part a devotion to the ideal of a science of religion, but the other part a sophisticated apologetic theology, aided and abetted by the doctrine of the autonomy of religion. As for the tradition that came to be known as phenomenology of religion, Tiele's successor in the chair at Leiden, William Brede Kristensen, made a clean break with evolutionism. But Kristensen also continued to promote liberal Protestant devotion to Natural Religion under the guise of the doctrine of the autonomy of religion.

William Brede Kristensen: The First "Phenomenologist" of Religion

While the Netherlands was the true home of the phenomenological study of religion, the Norwegian William Brede Kristensen was perhaps its first real exponent. Kristensen fell into line with the *general* approach of the phenomenologists. Most importantly, he dismissed the idea of the progressive evolution of religion. It was to be only one of many ways of interpreting the data of religion. It was hardly the "quasi-certitude" his contemporary, the Belgian historian of religion Goblet d'Alviella, declared that it was (Goblet d'Alviella 1885, p. 173; Molendijk 2000a, p. 32). Moreover, the evolutionists had not really penetrated religion, nor indeed plumbed the insides of the minds of religious people. They neither interrogated the way a religion was put together nor did they even attempt to see religion from the "native's point of view." How, then, could the evolutionists pretend to understand what any religion, much less religion in itself, really was (Kraemer 1960, p. xxiii)?

But Kristensen made some lasting contributions to the way many of us study religion as well. He staked out two – albeit extreme – methodological positions defining the phenomenology of religion as we know it today. First, Kristensen recognized *the religious insider's point of view* – but to the extreme extent of granting it privileged primacy. Second, he asserted the *distinctiveness* of religion – but, again, in the unnecessarily extreme form of asserting the absolute *autonomy of religion*. Let me take these in order.

Phenomenologists of religion have sought to establish the value of the religious insider's point of view by adopting what they called an *empathetic* approach to the religious beliefs and practices of those they studied. This insider's viewpoint might prove to be wrong, but it was, at least, a place to start making sense of religion. As the saying goes, scholars at least had to walk a mile in the moccasins of religious folk before they *interpreted* religion, or certainly before they tried to explain religious behavior (Geertz 1973, 1983).

Another way of expressing this subjective side of phenomenological method is by linking it to *interpretive* or hermeneutic ways of studying. The hermeneutic method, in turn, implied the primacy of an empathetic understanding of human action, and the preference for *understanding* religion over *explaining* it. Thus, unlike the evolutionists, the phenomenologists of religion did not seek to theorize about religion, and therefore did not try to explain what may have caused it. They tried instead to take religion as a phenomenon – as it was presented to them. With these data in hand, they then tried to make sense of it by seeing how the various parts of a religion fit together to make a whole. For them, this constituted *understanding* religion. Unlike an *explanation* of religion, understanding sought connections among religious data, not the *causes* of religion or religious institutions. Bronislaw Malinowski captured the spirit of this interpretive or *empathetic* approach in a classic statement of the method: "the final goal, of which an Ethnographer should never lose sight … is to grasp the native's point of view, *his* relation to life, to realise *his* vision of *his* world" (Malinowski 1961, p. 25).

But Kristensen goes further even than many phenomenologists of religion: he granted a privileged position to the believer's viewpoint. He, in effect, insulated religion from criticism, and thus took on the role of a "caretaker" of religion – a kind of theologian in disguise: "there is no religious reality other than the faith of the believers." For example, Kristensen says that "If

the historian tries to understand the religion from a different viewpoint than that of the believers, he negates the religious reality" (Kristensen 1960, p. 13). "Negates" is strong language indeed. Kristensen has thus elevated the insider's point of view out of range of critical inquiry. What the "natives" say goes. They cannot be contradicted. Religious folk always know best. The investigator becomes a mere reporter of religions, a scribe taking dictation from religious folk. Critics, dissidents, just shut up! Not a very scientific way to study religion.

Do the "Insiders" Really Know Best?

But why does Kristensen "thinks he is right" in taking such an extreme position in making the believer's point of view absolute? Why does he "think he is right" in saying that insiders or believers must know best? Of course, it is always possible that Kristensen's claims could, on occasion, be right. But the *general sweeping* claim that the "believers always know best" is just as dogmatic as the claims of the reductionists that "doctor knows best." Both are extreme methodological principles that are not subject to real challenge or correction. I would hope that readers would agree that the issue of just who does "know best" should be left to the actual process of argument – not to some dogma. Do believers, we or anyone else, really have perfect knowledge of their own religions and inner religious commitments? Can't believers make mistakes about their own religion as easily as any reductionist? Freud will have a few choice things to say about these assertions. Nevertheless, despite these problems, Kristensen does move the methodology of the study of religion further along.

One item of lasting value that we can take from Kristensen might be to establish a minimum requirement that the claims of the investigators should, at least, have to touch base with the believers. A believer should at the very least be able to *recognize* themselves in the picture that an investigator presents of them. Thus, countering an evolutionist reference to a religion as "primitive," Kristensen says: "No believer considers his own faith to be somewhat primitive, and the moment we begin so to think of it, we have actually lost touch with it … Do 'infidels' really think of themselves as 'unfaithful'?" (Kristensen 1960, p. 13). Maybe the so-called "infidels'" judge those so accusing them to be the real infidels? Do fetishists really worship things? Do naturists really worship rocks and trees? And how would we know if they did? As long as I am forbidding anyone in the process of explanation from playing doctor, we would need to be open to the possibility that either both investigator and believer were wrong or that neither was. No one gets an automatic free pass. Kristensen, therefore, is arguing, in effect, that the proposals of scholars about religious people need to be governed by some kind of scheme of checks and balances, some way of correcting or revising their ideas against the data of religion. To do otherwise would really be bad scientific practice, since it could invite dogmatism. Even the ideas of scientists – indeed especially their ideas – need to be open to correction or refutation, as philosophers of science like Karl Popper have argued (Popper 1963, pp. 33–39). But by the same token, sometimes an outsider can see more about what goes on in a group than members inside the group. Esthetic distance or a fresh perspective often bring new insights invisible to insiders. But sometimes the opposite may be true, too. The insiders might have better information than the outside investigator. They know the secrets, the subtle codes ruling behavior, and so on. Regrettably, Kristensen does not leave things methodological at that. He in effect becomes dogmatic by making the religious insider "doctor," by making the insider's point of view absolute and incorrigible. "For the historian only one evaluation is possible: 'the believers were completely right.' Only after we have grasped this can we understand these people and their religion" (Kristensen 1960, p. 14).

This dogmatic assertion of the insider's point of view sets the stage for Kristensen's insistence upon the equally absolute ideal of the *autonomy* of religion. One can imagine Kristensen thinking about theorists, like Tylor or Frazer, who explain religion away, that religion is *just* belief in spirits, religion is *just* third-rate technology, and so on. This reductionist way of thinking does not allow that people really do things for religious reasons or purposes. For reductionists, there are always other hidden – non-religious – reasons for or causes why people do things. The hunger for power or riches (not reducible!) is cited. One reviewer of Tylor's *Anthropology* (1881) picked up on the reductionism in Tylor's work on religion, by noting that, for Tylor, "compared with a philosophy, a religion is something posterior and derived" (Anon. 1881, p. 181). Kristensen, on the other hand, knows nothing of religion as "derived" or caused by non-religious factors. Kristensen feels that religious people always had distinctive, religious, reasons for what they did. Thus, in asserting that "there is no religious reality other than the faith of the believers" Kristensen affirms religion as an *autonomous* domain of human life – religion is its own reality, so to speak. Is takes little reflection to appreciate how extreme a position this is. Are reasons for doing things, religious or otherwise, so discrete – so clearly and cleanly separable from other sorts of reasons? Don't we act typically for mixed motives, since life is itself a complex mélange of many different levels and components? But, for Kristensen, bringing up the complexity of human life would be unwelcome. Now, it is "Doctor" Kristensen who knows best.

Understanding Why Most Christians Pray on Bended Knee with Folded Hands

As evolutionism waned in certain circles, entirely new sets of puzzles and problems about religion came forward. These new problems were spawned in part by Kristensen's desire to recognize the *interpretive* character of religious data. Kristensen stood for the ideal of trying to understand religion solely by trying to grasp the viewpoint of religious believers. His desire to be faithful to the insider's point of view of a religion – even if *too* faithful – at least put the matter of understanding on the table alongside the ideal of explanation. But Kristensen's conflation of understanding with simple empathy muddies the waters. One way empathy and understanding differ is that an understanding of religious action should make things clearer to a religious actor and/or investigator than they were before. Empathy does not necessarily achieve that. We can ask why Christians often pray with folded hands, and in doing so learn what they think. But empathy alone is not enough for us to be able to say that we can *understand* why Christians *as a group* pray with hands folded instead of in any number of other ways. So just relying on the insider's point of view of what believers say about themselves and their religious situation may not suffice even to understand them. And we have not even broached the far more serious matter of *explaining* what they do. We need to move to a higher level of knowledge – to *understanding* in the strong sense of that word.

See if the following example helps you *understand* the point I am trying to make. The great historian of feudal Europe Marc Bloch (1886–1944) tells us about the style of a certain focal rite performed in the courts of medieval Europe *before* people generally prayed with hands folded (Bloch 1961, pp. 145–147). This was the court ritual of the making of a vassal to a feudal lord, the acceptance into fealty. The ceremony is well documented as moving through the following steps: the new vassal first kneels before the lord; then, he folds his hands together with fingers pointed toward the lord; finally, the vassal places his folded hands between the encompassing hands of the lord who at this point secures the union between himself and the new vassal.

Bloch argues that today's praying on bended knees with folded hands was influenced by that feudal model of acknowledging fealty to a lord, and the lord's reciprocal pledge to save the supplicant from danger. Significantly, the relation of vassal to lord was more important than any other in the medieval world, more important than relations of blood or marriage. About the only relation like it in our world is that between TV Mafia *capos*, like Tony Soprano and their henchmen. Nothing is more sacred in that Mafia world, or in the medieval feudal world, than these relations of protection/subordination and the acknowledgment of leadership. In the case of prayer, of course, the "lord" in question is God almighty. As the extreme violence ensuing upon violation of these codes in the Mafia case implies, nothing is more sacred than these bonds. Nothing. The style in which many Christians pray, then, quite appropriately mimics the way that medieval vassals literally pledged their lives in service to a feudal lord, and their lord pledged to protect them. The medieval feudal world was, in a way, held together by this bond, and no other.

Now, recognizing the sacred power and influence of this rite, and knowing as well that this bended knee/folded hands style of prayer dates from the same period, surely helps us understand this particular religious behavior. For now we know why this style of prayer could well have become general, rather than just something individual. Bloch is, in fact, arguing that the most sacred social bonds of the medieval feudal world set a style for society at large, shaping the way people prayed and, I would add, how they *imagined* the world of God. Empathy alone tells us nothing about this possibility. So, I am using the word "understand" to indicate the higher quality of knowledge we have about, say, a style of prayer, than we would simply by asking believers what they were really doing – empathy.

One small point. Of course, you might accept all I have said about "understanding" why we pray with hands folded on bended knee, but object that I still have not "explained" why Christians pray at all! I would have to admit that you are right. That is because understanding is like knowing the rules of the game – here the deep historical roots, as I have argued from the work of Marc Bloch. Explaining why people pray with folded hands, or indeed *why* people pray at all, is like knowing what "causes" people to pray in the first place, or why people bother playing the prayer "game" at all, rather than some other, or none. "Explanation," as I am using it, refers to a much more ambitious project of knowing than "understanding." So, back to conclude my discussion of Brede Kristensen.

Despite Kristensen's slide back into the role of a "caretaker of religion," he nonetheless created conceptual space for new and interesting problems of religion. Once we recognize the "native's point of view," so to speak, new questions arise. How, for example, do the various religions hang together, knowing now what we do about their great variety and diversity? What are the key elements that go to making up what a given religion is? What elements of religion are the most important for sustaining a religion – its myths, rituals, doctrines, or some other dimension of religion's constitution? How do we reconcile disparities between what believers say about their religion and what outside observers say? What are the deep, say historical or cultural, reasons – not "causes" – why people act religiously? Is religion utterly unique and independent of them, or does it fall into line along a spectrum of cultural entities, such as morals, the arts, or politics? Once evolutionism had been thrown off, a host of such questions arose as if suppressed by hidden forces. These puzzles are analogous to questions we might have about a particular game – the "religion" game – and the moves that could be made within it.

Rudolf Otto and the Autonomy of Religious Experience

Thus far, I have tried to make sense of the emergence of the phenomenology of religion by setting it over against evolutionism. But the phenomenology of religion can also be comprehended from another, complementary, angle. Here, we pay special heed to the subjective, emotional, experiential sides of religion, rather than the way it has worked out "objective" or structured schemes to define itself. Exemplifying these two complementary sides of the phenomenology of religion are Rudolf Otto (1869–1937) and Gerardus van der Leeuw, respectively. Otto was a German Lutheran historian of religion and a theologian who flourished during the years on either side of World War I. Gerardus van der Leeuw was another Dutch phenomenologist of religion, Kristensen's own student, who lived to the mid-twentieth century. Let me begin with Otto.

Otto's great classic, *The Idea of the Holy* (1917), made a strong case for the *autonomy* of religion. Although some might not want to classify Otto among the phenomenologists of religion because of his remoteness from the Dutch scene, it is useful to employ him to illustrate at least the strong *subjective* element in the change of theoretical register effected by the phenomenologists. So at the risk of inciting a quarrel over how to classify Otto, let me show how he can be seen to have modeled religious phenomenology in three ways. First, Otto elaborated the case for religion's *autonomy*. Second, he did so by bringing out what he believed to be the single, central, constituent *category* of religion – the notion of the numinous, or the holy third: he elaborated this category by describing what he took to be a distinctive class of subjective religious *experience*. For Otto, it was the "internal" context of the religious life that gave him the confidence to declare his famous theory. This shows how Otto went right to what he regarded the very heart of religion. He sought to understand the experiences he felt made religion distinctive, and in the process autonomous and thus irreducible. That there may be good "external" reasons for Otto's doing so cannot be ruled out. But thus far evidence of them seems scarce. He seems to have been well wrapped up in the intellectual academic world, and the world of religious experience. As far as the "internal" theological and philosophical context of Otto's approach goes he was deeply involved in overturning prevailing nineteenth-century liberal Protestant conceptions of religion, such as Robertson Smith's – namely that religion was really morality. But Robertson Smith was not alone among our classic theorists in making this identification of religion and morality. Weber, Freud, and Durkheim too held this position at one time or another. Otto, however, felt this rather "domesticated" religion by making it altogether too social and rational. Put otherwise, the identification of religion with morality *reduced* religion to something other than it was. But just what was this essence of religion?

Otto thought religion was categorically different from other parts of culture. It was quite, even absolutely, distinctive. Religion's essential distinctiveness rested on the distinctiveness of a particular kind of experience – the feeling of holiness. For Otto, reductionists were those who, "with a resolution and cunning which one can hardly help admiring … shut their eyes to that which is quite unique in the religious experience" (Otto 1958, p. 4). Religion was something in and for itself – *sui generis*. Says Otto, "if there be any single domain of human experience that presents us with something unmistakably specific and unique, peculiar to itself, assuredly [it] is that of the religious life" (Otto 1958, p. 4). In this distinctiveness, religion was rather like music. Trading upon this analogy, Otto says pointedly:

> "Musical feeling is … something 'wholly other', which, while it affords analogies and here and there will run parallel to the ordinary emotions of life, cannot be made to coincide with them by a detailed point-to-point correspondence". (Otto 1958, p. 49)

Music and such similar things were thus worth considering in themselves – as *phenomena* meriting serious attempts at understanding. So why not religion, too?

Otto argued, accordingly, that religion arose from what seemed like a unique kind of subjective *psychological* datum. He called it a "numinous" experience. The term is derived from the Latin word *numen*, which is the term for a deity that presides over a particular place, such as Diana or Virbius did over the sacred grove at Nemi, and about whom Frazer wrote in *The Golden Bough*. This numinous experience is what we feel when we encounter what is holy or sacred – an experience that for Otto was an experience of something that was "wholly other." The numinous experience was, thus, a feeling of being in the presence of a "*mysterium tremendum et fascinans*" – a tremendously powerful, yet magnetizing, fascinating mystery. Such feelings arose in people because in it they sensed their dependence upon that all-powerful mystery. Indeed more than this, people sensed their absolute and utter dependence upon this power, a feeling totally appropriate for a creature to have regarding their creator (Otto 1958, chs. ii–v). To Otto, it was therefore an experience that transcended all others, as the terms applied to it imply. Consider this classic example.

In the book of Isaiah, a powerful religious experience erupts in the temple as the prophet lies there immobilized. Isaiah chapter 6 says:

In the year that King Uzziah died, I saw the Lord.
He was sitting on his throne, high and exalted,
and his robe filled the whole temple.
Around him flaming creatures were standing,
    each of which had six wings.
Each creature covered its face with two wings,
and its body with two and used the other
    two for flying.
They were calling out to each other:
"Holy, holy, holy!
The Lord Almighty is holy!
His glory fills the world."
The sound of their voices made the foundation
    of the temple shake and the temple itself
    became filled with smoke.
I said, "There is no hope for me!
I am doomed because every word passes my lips
    is sinful,
and I live among the people whose every word is
    sinful.
And yet, with my own eyes.
I have seen the King, the Lord Almighty."
    (Isaiah 6: 1–5)

Again, this passage from Isaiah relates an experience combining divine energy, overpowering force, and the densest mystery that results in the poor prophet being forced to the ground. There, he trembles in awe and quickly becomes aware of his abject creaturehood and utter dependence upon that transcendent, "wholly other" God. In light of what we read here, is it hard to see this as an experience of divinity of obvious religious dimensions? Understanding it as such, instead of as an attack of moral scruples or a spell of fey esthetic pleasure surely seems the most obvious of ways to make sense of what we read in this extraordinary document of the religious consciousness. It is the creature, profane, powerless, and utterly dependent, brought low by the sacred.

Not only were such experiences found in the traditions of Judaism and Christianity: they were universal. As such, Otto's approach invited a broad cross-cultural grasp of this *sui generis* religious experience as the experience of the numinous. An oft-cited case comes to us from the Hindu scripture, the Bhagavad Gita. Here again the essence of the divinity bursts forth into the cozy human world, blowing apart attempts to domesticate the divine. The scene is set on the field of battle central to the civil war dominating the great Hindu epic, the Mahabharata, of which the Bhagavad Gita is a part. In a chariot on the front lines of the forces of one side are Prince Arjuna and his noble charioteer, the god Krishna disguised in human form. Arjuna is demoralized by doubts about the value of taking up arms against his own kin. He has lost the will to win – the will to fight and kill – and confesses this to Krishna, who nevertheless urges him to do his duty and press on with the battle. First, Krishna shows Arjuna the real divine – numinous – form that lies hidden beneath his human bodily form:

Having spoken thus, O king, Krishna, the great lord of the possessors of mystic power, then showed to the son of Pritha [Arjuna] his supreme divine form – having many mouths and eyes, having within it many wonderful sights, having many celestial ornaments, having many celestial weapons held erect, wearing celestial flowers and vestments, anointed with celestial perfumes, full of every wonder, the infinite deity with faces in all directions

And when he had once done that, Krishna showed him the tremendous power of his divinity that inspires Arjuna to bow down in profound and humble worship:

> If in the heavens, the brightness of a thousand suns burst forth all at once, that would be like the brightness of that mighty one. There the son of Pandu [Arjuna] then observed in the body of the god of gods the whole universe all in one, and divided into numerous divisions. Then Arjuna was filled with amazement, and with hair standing on end, bowed his head before the god, and spoke with joined hands.

Tremendous fear seizes Arjuna as he comes face to face with the otherworldly reality of the numinous, as he realizes his utter and absolute dependence upon the lord of all the worlds:

> Seeing your mighty form, with many mouths and eyes, with many arms, thighs, and feet, with many stomachs, and fearful with many jaws, all people, and I likewise, are much alarmed, O you of mighty arms! Seeing you, O Vishnu, touching the skies, radiant, possessed of many hues, with a gaping mouth, and with large blazing eyes, I am much alarmed in my inmost self, and feel no courage, no tranquility. And seeing your mouths terrible by the jaws, and resembling the fire of destruction, I cannot recognize the various directions, I feel no comfort. Be gracious, O lord of gods, who pervades the universe!

With data like this, anyone would understand how Otto could "think he was right" in seeing religion as autonomous and grounded in such "numinous" experiences. Such reports of dramatic eruptions of the holy into the world of the everyday had no parallel in other modes of life, certainly not morality, for instance. The "King, the Lord Almighty" of Isaiah 6 has no scruples about plunging his loyal prophet into an abyss of despair. The God of the Hindus even demands that Arjuna kill his own kin; in the form of Krishna, he reveals himself as well as a violent slayer of the innocent, ruthlessly chewing human victims in his great grinding jaws. Compassion, mercy, fairness, justice, and other sweet *moral* values are conspicuously absent on the horizon of a landscape defined by the holy. It must be so, on Otto's view, since the numinous

(and all forms of experience of the numinous) is autonomous, independent of all forms of human life and activity – just as is our experience of it, and religion too – the *sui generis* human response to such singular subjective states of consciousness. To Otto, morality could not therefore be the essence of religion, since religion trafficked in the "wholly other," in the transcendent. Religion was not, therefore, to be *reduced* to morality – to human conceptions of obligation and duty. Religion was autonomous, independent of morality, and of every other thing as well. It was humanity's relation to the numinous. Or, at the very least, this is what we grasp when we seek empathetically to understand the religious experience of pious peoples.

From the position Otto has staked out about the essence of religion, it is easy to see how he rebelled against Frazer or Tylor. Religion was neither the result of a primitive scientific instinct (animism) nor did it arise from the desire of "savages" for a technology to control nature through the aid of higher powers. For Otto, religion did not result from reasoning or thinking at all. It was instead a visceral reaction to an encounter with the "Other." Most of all, religion did not originate from something ordinary. It was convictions such as these that led Otto to "think he was right" to approach religion from the inside, in and for itself. Given Otto's perspective, there was no "explaining" religion at all, since whatever *causes* there might be of this perplexing and amazing behavior lay well beyond human comprehension.

Anatomy of Religion: Van der Leeuw's Phenomenology

If Otto can be cast as making the most dramatic case for an elaborate exploration and exposition of *sui generis* religious *subjectivity* – experience – then Gerardus van der Leeuw shows us the phenomenology of religion as an exercise in laying out the anatomy or structure of religion – its *objective* aspect. One might say that Van der Leeuw takes the original morphological approach, attempted cautiously by Tiele, to its logical extreme. Van der Leeuw thus benefited hugely from the professionalization and institutional establishment of the phenomenology of religion begun with the Dutch Higher Education Act of

1876, that established an "external" context in which the study of religion became actually and institutionally possible in the Netherlands. The Act gave him both the intellectual license to practice phenomenology of religion and it also allowed him the academic freedom to specialize to a high degree. Van der Leeuw can be said to have *professionalized* the phenomenology of religion, but in doing so, I believe, he rendered it perhaps too abstract for wide use. Van der Leeuw might then be a model of the over-professionalized academic – someone too isolated by state institutionalization to exploit the external forces raging in the world about him, to leave behind a vital study of religion. In the end, he may have brought the phenomenology of religion to a rather static and even sterile end.

Gerardus van der Leeuw was Professor of the History of Religions and Theology at the University of Groningen from the tender age of 28 until his death in 1950. Like other Dutch phenomenologists of religion, Van der Leeuw was a pious Christian, an ordained minister and parish pastor in the Dutch Reformed Church. Accordingly, it is no surprise that he describes his academic work as a "handmaiden" to Christian theology (Sharpe 1986, pp. 232–233). Van der Leeuw divided his writing between theology and phenomenological treatments of the arts in religion and the religion of small-scale societies (Van der Leeuw 1948, 1949, 1952, 1963, 1964). Van der Leeuw's emphasis on hermeneutics, interpretation, empathy, and understanding can be said to come directly from Wilhelm Dilthey (1833–1911), one of the chief thinkers in the "hermeneutic" tradition we first met in our discussion of biblical criticism (Van der Leeuw 1964, pp. 671, 676). Van der Leeuw's phenomenology of religion generally rehearses all the main features of the phenomenology of religion of Tiele, Kristensen, and Otto. As a self-styled "scientific" methodologist, Van der Leeuw set out a relentless, scheme of objective or structural classification of religion that echoes all the way back to the beginnings of this tradition with Tiele's morphology. Van der Leeuw's classic of the phenomenology of religion, *Religion in Essence and Manifestation* (1938), fell somewhere between being a catalogue or encyclopedia of religious *variae* and a handbook of methods for the study of religion. It assembled long lists of basic categories or structural pieces of

what made up *religion*. Thus, terms like prophet, priest, sacrament, sacred, taboo, and savior, along with a host of others, clearly fell into the class of distinctively religious notions. A glance through the table of contents of *Religion in Essence and Manifestation* lists four pages – of chapters alone – in which such categories are explored. Moreover, when one unpacks these chapters in the list of topics in the index one is struck by the myriad phenomena contained there – about 700 terms in all.

Like Kristensen before him, Van der Leeuw married these objective elements of the phenomenology of religion with subjective features, such as empathy and understanding. As for the subjective features of Van der Leeuw's phenomenology of religion, one point is original. This is a special subjective attitude recommended to the prospective phenomenologist of religion – the mental act of *epochē*. This notion means a "bracketing" of what is experienced or derived from our empathetic understanding of the other so as to exclude judgments of truth or value regarding the phenomenon. The phenomenologist takes a "step back," so to speak, and withholds judgment until finished with the job of *understanding* what has been presented by means of *empathy*. Van der Leeuw wants us to "bracket" religious data so that we regard it in a neutral and detached way, and do not therefore lapse into an all too easy partisan attitude to religious data.

Thus, what Van der Leeuw means by *epochē* can be seen if we take up a Hindu example, where devotees call Krishna, "lord," and believe him to be sovereign in their lives today. But the phenomenologist is only required to note or record that this is so *for Hindus*. They employ *epochē* and thus "bracket" out *truth* claims about Krishna's lordship. Adherence to *epochē* means a phenomenologist cannot go beyond phenomena. Believers may say that "Krishna is lord" signals the underlying reality of his actual divine lordship. But phenomenological method, as Van der Leeuw expounds it, "brackets" out such claims about the *noumenal* level of things. Phenomenology deals only in *phenomena*. It leaves the level of the ultimate truth or explanation of the status of Krishna to philosophers or scientists ready to reduce religious phenomena to something of another sort. They concentrate, instead, upon getting the belief in Krishna's lordship as a phenomenological category right, and leave things at that level of understanding.

What Can We Learn from the Phenomenology of Religion?

Not enough scholars pursue the phenomenology of religion, and certainly not in the way Van der Leeuw painstakingly did. While a scheme like Van der Leeuw's may be impressive for how it multiplies items in the vocabulary of religion, his phenomenology never really gained a wide following. The pursuit of finer and finer-grained analyses for its own sake seems to need a justification that Van der Leeuw does not provide. Instead, we might continue to work in his spirit by practicing a more thoroughgoing program of a *critique of key categories*. What differences, if any, should we suggest for the definition of "sect," "cult," "spirituality," or indeed "religion"? These terms keep coming up in public discourse and continue to lead it into confusion. Those of us with a flair for the critique of categories can continue the legacy of the phenomenology of religion by rolling up our sleeves and doing some hard work out there in the world in trying to shed light on public discourse about religion.

Another way to continue the work of the founders of the phenomenology of religion is to take up the suggestion of Ninian Smart to add "dynamism" to the classification process. Van der Leeuw's approach was too *static* to do justice to such a lively and contested reality as religion. Smart wants us, instead, to understand religion as "alive" – as an organic, internally interactive whole. This is work that has hardly begun. Van der Leeuw tried to put religion back onto the stage, so to speak, but failed to supply the stage directions to get it into action. His phenomenology is like a set of snapshots, with appropriate commentary to distinguish one from the other. Smart argued that we needed, instead, something more of a moving picture of religion, where actors interact, scenes change, and real drama is played out. Like them or not, evolutionist approaches to religion placed the dramas of change in the course of human history. Van der Leeuw's rather static phenomenology of religion, on the other hand, tells us no story at all.

But Smart's accusation of the sterility of Van der Leeuw's phenomenology of religion only captures part of the reason it has failed to bear fruit. I think two interconnected reasons may account for its failure to gain wide acceptance – at least in the current epistemological mood of our times.

First is Van der Leeuw's fundamental rejection of theorizing and explanation. And even though Van der Leeuw championed something akin to explanation – *Verstehen* or understanding – we see virtually none of it done in his work. This is to say that he avoids the *Why?* question. But many people think the *Why?* is irresistible. People want accounts, explanations, reasons, causes, and such for what happens – in religion as in every other domain of life. This wish for something more than extensive classification was felt by thinkers we will meet in the coming chapters. The theories of Freud, Malinowski, and Durkheim, as well as historian of religion Mircea Eliade, represent attempts to speak to the desire for theorizing. As we will see, unlike Van der Leeuw, these theorists won huge popularity among both everyday readers and the university community of scholars and students.

The second reason for Van der Leeuw's failure to catch on is what could be called his epistemological naivety. He presumed that the names of religious "things" are written on them, so to speak – that the naming process is really unproblematic, and in a way, automatic. He supposed that the cultural world is composed of natural kinds, rather than that human beings do an immense amount of contestable sorting and classifying themselves. Just *who* says X is a cult or sect? These are key terms in the study of religion about which we debate and quarrel. Van der Leeuw thought that he could just avoid contestation by proceeding as if everyone agrees with the names he gives things. But classifying and categorizing religious things will always remain a problematic matter, because they reflect our basic cosmologies, our basic way of seeing the world. Naming and classifying things in religion is not, then, a simple operation.

The Durkheimians are to be commended because they believed that even seemingly simple acts of naming, sorting, or classifying were ineluctably bound up in the ecologies of theoretical and conceptual networks. Little consensus formed round what, totemism was (or even if it existed).

Accordingly, arguments raged as well as about what was really sacrifice or magic, or even religion. Could the practices of so-called "primitives" really be dignified with the name "religion"? Heaven forbid! So, in reality, things were hardly as simple as the phenomenologists of religion would have us believe.

As it happens, the Durkheimian scholars, Émile Durkheim, Henri Hubert, and Marcel Mauss, knew and studied the Dutch phenomenology of religion. They concluded that the Dutch had not gone far enough in establishing the credentials of our categories. So when the Durkheimians came to write about magic, charity, gift, *mana*, totems, sacrifice, the sacred, and even religion itself, they felt they had to defend and argue about their meanings. Durkheim's "Concerning the Definition of Religious Phenomena," Henri Hubert and Marcel Mauss' books on magic, gift and sacrifice, all presumed – unlike Van der Leeuw – that the definition and understanding of the main categories of religion

must be open to contest – to theoretical debate (Durkheim 1899 74–99; Hubert and Mauss 1904, 1964; Mauss 1967, p. 66). The ground must be prepared for *thinking with* our key categories, such as sacrifice, magic, sacred, religion, and so on. And that ground must be readied in order that we can understand and explain religion. In order to think *with* certain categories, we need to think hard *about* them as need requires. Durkheimian theory of religion, in fact, learned much from Dutch phenomenology of religion. But they also learned that they needed to improve upon it.

In the following chapters, we will see how this appetite for explanation and conceptual critique is reawakened in the works of Weber, Freud, Malinowski, Durkheim, and Eliade. While each of these thinkers can be seen to owe debts to the general phenomenological movement, they try to move beyond a merely phenomenological approach to religion to engage in intense theorizing about its nature and causes.

References

Anon. 1881. "Tylor's Anthropology." *The Nation* 33/844 (1 September): 181.

Anon. 1882. "Tiele's Egyptian Religion." *The Nation* 35/904 (26 October): 361–362.

Bloch, M. 1961. *Feudal Society: The Growth of Ties of Dependence*, vol. 1, trans. L.A. Manyon. Chicago: University of Chicago Press.

Byrne, P. 1989. *Natural Religion and the Nature of Religion*. London: Routledge.

Durkheim, É. 1899. "Concerning the Definition of Religious Phenomena." In W.S.F. Pickering (ed.), *Durkheim on Religion*. London: Routledge.

Geertz, C. 1973. *The Interpretation of Cultures*. New York: Basic Books.

Geertz, C. 1983. *Local Knowledge: Further Essays in Interpretive Anthropology*. New York: Harper & Row.

Goblet d'Alviella, C.E. 1885. "Maurice Vernes et la méthode comparative." *Revue de l'histoire des religions*, 12: 170–178.

Hubert, H., and M. Mauss. 1904. *A General Theory of Magic*, trans. R. Brain. London: Routledge.

Hubert, H., and M. Mauss. 1964. *Sacrifice: Its Nature and Functions*. Chicago: University of Chicago Press.

Kraemer, H. 1960. "Introduction." In J.B. Carman (ed.), *W. Brede Kristensen, The Meaning of Religion*. The Hague: Martinus Nijhoff.

Kristensen, W.B. 1960. *The Meaning of Religion: Lectures in the Phenomenology of Religion*, trans. J.B. Carman. The Hague: Martinus Nijhoff.

Malinowski, B. 1961. *Argonauts of the Western Pacific*. New York: E.P. Dutton.

Mauss, M. 1967. *The Gift: The Form and Functions of Exchange in Archaic Societies*, trans. I. Cunnison. New York: W.W. Norton.

Molendijk, A.L. 2000a. "At the Cross-Roads: Early Dutch Science of Religion in International Perspective." In S. Hjelde (ed.), *Man, Meaning and Mystery*. Leiden: E.J. Brill.

Molendijk, A.L. 2000b. "The Heritage of Cornelis P. Tiele." *Nederlands Archief voor Kerkgeschiednis* 80: 78–114.

Molendijk, A.L. 2005. *The Emergence of the Science of Religion in the Netherlands*. Leiden: E.J. Brill.

Otto, R. 1958. *The Idea of the Holy*, trans. J.W. Harvey. New York: Oxford University Press.

Popper, K.R. 1963. "Science: Conjectures and Refutations." In K.R. Popper (ed.), *Conjectures and Refutations*. London: Routledge.

Réville, A. 1864. "Dutch Theology: Its Past and Present State." *Theological Review* 3: 275–277.

Réville, A. 1875. "Evolution in Religion, and Its Results." *Theological Review* 12: 230–248.

Sharpe, E.J. 1986. *Comparative Religion: A History*. La Salle, IL: Open Court.

Tiele, C.P. 1896. *Elements of the Science of Religion*, vol. 1: *Morphological*. Edinburgh and London: W. Blackwood & Sons.

Tylor, E.B. 1881. *Anthropology*. Ann Arbor: University of Michigan.

Van den Bosch, L.P. 2002. *Friedrich Max Müller: A Life Devoted to the Humanities*. Leiden: E.J. Brill.

Van der Leeuw, G. 1948. *Inleiding tot de theologie*. Amsterdam: H.J. Paris.

Van der Leeuw, G. 1949. *Sacramentstheologie*. Nijkerk: G.F. Callenbach.

Van der Leeuw, G. 1952. *De primitieve mensch en de religie: Anthropologische studie*. Groningen: J.B. Wolters.

Van der Leeuw, G. 1963. *Sacred and Profane Beauty: The Holy in Art*, trans. D.E. Green. New York: Holt, Rinehart & Winston.

Van der Leeuw, G. 1964. *Religion in Essence and Manifestation*, trans. J.E. Turner. London: George Allen & Unwin.

Further Reading

Bossy, J. 1991. "Unrethinking the Sixteenth-Century Wars of Religion." In T. Kselman (ed.), *Belief in History: Innovative Approaches to European and American Religion*. Notre Dame: Notre Dame University Press.

Jastrow, J., Morris. 1981. *The Study of Religion*. Chico, CA: Scholars Press.

McCutcheon, R.T. 1997. *Manufacturing Religion: The Discourse on Sui Generis Religion and the Politics of Nostalgia*. New York: Oxford University Press.

Penner, H.H. 1970. "Phenomenology, a Method for the Study of Religion?" *Bucknell Review* 18/3 (Winter): 29–54.

Réville, J. 1903. "Leçon d'ouverture de M. Maurice Vernes." *Revue de l'histoire des religions* 47: 430–432.

Spiegelberg, H. 1969. *The Phenomenological Movement: A Historical Introduction*, vol. 1. The Hague: Martinus Nijhoff.

Tiele, C.P. 1877. *Outlines of the History of Religion to the Spread of the Universal Religions*, trans. J.E. Carpenter. Boston: James R. Osgood.

Young, M.W. 2004. *Malinowski: Odyssey of an Anthropologist, 1884-1920*. New Haven: Yale University Press.

PART III

Classic Twentieth-Century Theorists of the Study of Religion: Defending the Inner Sanctum of Religious Experience or Storming It

9

How Religious Experience Created Capitalism: Max Weber

"We must exhort all Christians to gain all they can, and to save all they can; that is, in effect, to grow rich." (John Wesley, quoted in *The Protestant Ethic and the Spirit of Capitalism*)

Weber and the Problems of Understanding and Explaining Capitalism

While it may seem flat-footed to begin a chapter on Max Weber with his life story, his biography reads like an irresistible extended metaphor, reprising essential tensions in his approach to religion. It also reveals part of what made him "think he was right" about his views of the nature of capitalism, and about religion's role in giving it birth. It exposes an external context from which Weber drew moral and intellectual lessons that shaped his thinking. His tormented relations with his parents are of a piece with the same dilemmas that afflicted religion in the rise of a capitalist economy. His thinking about them paralleled his thinking about economic matters. Weber's struggles with his parents dramatize the struggles he felt within himself about the demise of a gentle, but inefficient, economic system and its replacement with a fiercely competitive capitalist

system. On the one side was Weber's sweet, perhaps impractical, mother, and on the other side, his sometimes brutish worldly father. Feminist theorists may also see, or at least feel justified in investigating, how deeply influential sex/gender cosmologies are in Weber's theorizing. Is the capitalism Weber defined "gendered" masculine, not only because Weber's father lived it, but also because it embodied essentially patriarchal values? An intriguing question, but one I shall leave for another publication!

Weber's view of the transition to capitalism was literally tragic, both as a matter of economic history but also because it touched something eating at the core of his personality. While he loved his mother and her values, he ultimately came to "think he was right" that only his father's values guaranteed success in the world. I want us, therefore, to see Weber's view of the economic transition to capitalism as internally conflicted between a nostalgia for a hopeless past and a loathing for a stampeding future. So although it may be conventional to begin discussing Weber's ideas by reciting his life story, the results of doing so should, I hope, be anything but conventional.

Born into the middle class during the better days of Bismarck's German Empire, Max Weber (1864–1920) had a good start in life. However, the otherwise unruffled exterior of late Victorian

Understanding Theories of Religion: An Introduction, Second Edition. Ivan Strenski.
© 2015 Ivan Strenski. Published 2015 by John Wiley & Sons, Ltd.

bourgeois life concealed a deep disquiet. The family of his mother, Helene, had been genteel schoolteachers for generations; the family of his father, Max Senior, by contrast, were fixtures in the tough world of business. Despite modest origins, Weber's mother's family had amassed considerable wealth and prestige, placing them above Weber's father with his coarse commercial manners (Mitzman 1969, p. 44). Weber thus emerged split over his emotional bonds with his mother and the dutiful pursuit of his worldly father's severe life.

Religion was an area of conflict within the Weber household. Weber's father was neither a practicing nor a believing Christian; Helene Weber was a pious liberal Protestant – in fact, a Lutheran. Weber resolved this parental conflict creatively. Thus, despite the power of the male role model, Weber was always intellectually engaged by religion throughout his life. Even though a non-believer, Weber was quite literate in the theological controversies of the times. He was also a great admirer of major figures in the Higher Criticism of the Bible, such as David Friedrich Strauss and Ferdinand Christian Baur (Honigsheim 2003, pp. 229–230).

Despite seeming to follow his father's secular ways, Weber had a passion for the moral issues arising out of religion. He was vexed by the relations between individual believer and collectivities such as the church. His liberal ideas reflected those of his liberal Protestant mother and her concern for social justice. Gradually, however, Weber came round to his father's harder ways of looking at political and economic matters (Diggins 1996, pp. 87–88). Weber's relation to religion gets even more complicated by the emotional interplay within the Weber nuclear family, so that the bitterness between mother and father shaped his professional attitudes to religion. Max Senior would routinely belittle his wife for her adherence to the softer liberal Christian notions of compassion and charity toward the poor, while young Max Junior looked on helplessly.

If we turn from religion to Weber's educational career, by all accounts we find further evidence of deep divisions within his personality. Like his pious and abstemious mother, Weber played the role of a disciplined and serious student at Heidelberg – at least for a while. Yet, more like his aggressive father, he followed the conventionally rowdy life of bellicose male bonding. Dueling for sport and honor, boozing in the local beer halls, and carousing with his loutish (male) contemporaries dominated Weber's leisure hours. No matter how he may or may not have tried to mediate the tensions within his personality between ascetic discipline and spontaneous pleasure-seeking, this opposition would remain central, as we will see, to his tragic sense of the gains and losses of embracing the worldly asceticism that defined the central values of the new capitalist order.

Weber's indifference to conventional religious practice and his orientation to a secular professional life more in keeping with his father's ideals of success never diminished his emotional affinities with his mother. Indeed, his affection for and emotional identification with her only increased as he recalled the ill-treatment meted out to her by her abusive father. Incapable of fighting her husband, Helene "poured out her grief" to Weber, putting him thereby in the most profound opposition to the harsh master of the house (Mitzman 1969, p. 45). All these tensions would come to a boil when one day, Weber's parents arrived to visit their son to celebrate his success at winning a university professorship at Heidelberg. Weber chose that precise moment to exact revenge upon his father for Max Senior's abuse of his wife. Weber himself, now master in his own house – located significantly in his mother's home city – angrily refused his own father entry, literally driving the old man from his door. His father died only a few weeks later. Shortly thereafter, Weber suffered a nervous breakdown, resulting in years of mental disability (Mitzman 1969, p. 150f).

I dwell upon Weber's tortured relations with his parents because I believe they were illustrative of theoretical tensions within his thought about religion. In a way, Weber could not live with religion, nor could he live without it. He might well have liked to avoid considering religion as active and important in the world, but his conscientious scholarship simply prevented him from denying what he came to learn. Indeed, his great classic, *The Protestant Ethic and the Spirit of Capitalism*, which appeared in 1905, emerged out of this period of emotional turmoil. From 1915 to 1920, it was followed by studies of India (Buddhism and Hinduism), China (Confucianism and Taoism), and ancient Israel. By any standard, these books are models of the comparative study of religions in the way they both reflect encyclopedic knowledge of many different religious faiths and do so in a rich comparative context. Witnessing to the wealth and suggestiveness of Weber's books on the relation of religion to economic values, they are still read with admiration in our own time. Indeed, they have inspired many imitators as well, even giving birth to a distinctly "Weberian" approach to the explanation of the rise and shape of economic systems the world over (Bellah 1957; Singer 1972).

In this review of Weber's life, I think we can begin to anticipate some of the key issues that he would investigate and try to resolve. Some of them will draw us into concerns about how both individuals and societies should balance such perennial poles of human life as pleasure and restraint. Some will place us face to face with the consequences of opting for a particular style of economic life that, while producing many benefits, also seems to kill something of the human spirit. What makes Weber, however, so important for the study of religion is that for him these great human dilemmas all point back to even more fundamental religious foundations. Let me then move from putting Max Weber into the perspective that his life story provides to the way his work fits with and differs from the approaches to religion that we have lately been considering.

Max Weber Turns the Tables: Religion "Explains" Things, Too

Classic theorists like Tylor, Frazer, Robertson Smith, Herbert of Cherbury, Bodin, and Max Müller all tried to *explain* religion, or track down the first religion. Whether that be the Deist idea of a divinely implanted Natural Religion or something arising from secular interests – Tylor's idea of religion as proto-science or Frazer's understanding of the essence of religion as our need to control nature – all tried to *explain* religion. The phenomenologists, on the other hand, avoided all talk and action about *explanation*, and sought to *describe* religion and *catalogue* its parts. Weber arrives fully armed with a mediating methodological position: he uses religion to *explain* secular realities. But, like a phenomenologist, he first employs classic *phenomenological* methods of empathy, understanding, classification, and a good deal of *epoché* to identify what he explains.

Weber's use of religion to explain things puts him at odds with Karl Marx. Addressing himself to economistic or materialist attempts to explain the Protestant Reformation, Weber tries to explain why he "thinks he was right" about Marx: "We must free ourselves from the idea that it is possible to deduce the Reformation, as a historically necessary result, from certain economic changes." The historical details of a world-historical event like the Protestant Reformation simply make it too complex to yield to straightforward causal accounts. In particular, an economic determinism like Marx's fails, since "countless historical circumstances … cannot be reduced to any economic law, and are not susceptible of economic explanation of any sort" (Weber 1976, pp. 90–91).

Even if Weber doubts a law-like relationship can describe the rise of capitalism, he does seek to introduce religion into the *causal* chain eventuating in capitalism: "we are merely attempting to clarify the part which religious forces have played in forming the developing web of our specifically worldly modern culture" (Weber 1976, p. 90). For Weber, human life is an arena of competing powers, "forces," or "causes." Religion is, in a way, nothing special, just another of these "forces." As a social scientist, Weber felt that religion was a robust, powerful reality that took part in the "rough and tumble" of human life. Oddly enough, it may well have been Weber's relation with his maternal uncle, Hermann Baumgarten, a man of liberal religious and political views, that made him take seriously the role that religion could play in the secular world. Thus, in the spirit of Baumgarten, Weber saw religion as mattering in the political world. His view of religion in society was thus a realistic, dynamic, and unsentimental one, informed by a man of the world, his uncle. It has set a fruitful course in religious studies that has had many followers ever since.

But having said that Weber embraces causal explanation in human affairs, we must understand that he believed these social causes are *immaterial*. He believed that ideas, experiences, visions, beliefs, values, justifications, and legitimations could be *causes* of human action. Philosophers often refer to these kinds of causes as "ideal." American philosopher Sidney Hook characterized Weber fairly enough as holding that "ideas make history." And Weber himself said of his great classic, "The following study may thus perhaps in a modest way form a contribution to the understanding of the manner in which ideas become effective forces in history" (Hook 1930, p. 478; Weber 1976, p. 90). The "ideas" he will bring to the fore are religious "ideas."

Weber's Synthesis of Phenomenology and Causal Explanation

Together with his commitment to causal explanations, Weber is methodologically interesting for synthesizing causal explanations with phenomenology. Anthropologist of religion Clifford Geertz even argues that Weber was deeply influenced by Wilhelm Dilthey, one of the seminal thinkers of the phenomenological movement (Geertz 1983, pp. 5, 7, 16, 21–22, 51, 69, 121). While Weber objected to Dilthey's conception of empathy as verging on mind-reading, he used empathy as a normal attitude toward beginning the understanding of other persons (Ermarth 1978, p. 377n11). As his commitment to causal explanation would lead one to think, Weber also believed that social science needed more than to "understand" the human world (Ringer 2004, p. 18). That is why Weber situated his "understandings" within a causal historical process that could be known objectively. Still, in all, despite Weber's careful qualifications of phenomenological methods, he nonetheless represents an attempt to synthesize, at the very least, the spirit of phenomenology's interpretive and hermeneutic methods of understanding into causal explanations (Käsler 1988, p. 178). Why do I say that Weber really has a phenomenological side?

Three features of Weber's method make it look like phenomenology has taught him a thing or two. Weber, first, seeks to know what things meant to the insiders. This means employing the method of *understanding* to capitalism. This also means that he has assigned religious *feelings or experiences* a prominent place in the nexus of social causes acting upon capitalism to inform his grasp of the capitalist's way of looking at the world. Second, Weber does what the phenomenologists called "naming" and "classifying" phenomena. He scrupulously attends to the need to *define and classify* "capitalism." Such a term is what Weber calls an "ideal type," and is roughly equivalent to classes of phenomena the likes of Tiele or van der Leeuw busily assembled. Third, Weber takes an active theoretical stance toward

his category by arguing, often implicitly as the phenomenologists themselves do, that the definition he has made up is the "best" or most "fruitful." His definition is the one we *should* use. In a way, the test of the value of Weber's definition of religion is whether the overall argument of the book itself persuades us, its readers.

One last point on these conceptual and methodological matters. Oddly enough, Weber only applies phenomenology's critical approach to "capitalism," not to "religion." This should puzzle readers of today. We have lately been in the habit of being critical of terms, like "religion," in part because of public controversies over so-called "cults" and "sects." Many religious folk resist calling certain religious bodies, often classified as "new religious movements," – NRMs – "religions." We should note with interest that Weber accepts definitions of religion uncritically, off the shelf, so to speak. He is completely unreflective about what we should mean by "religion." He "knows" what religion is by just looking around. Buddhism, Roman Catholicism, Lutheranism, Anabaptism, Hinduism, Judaism, Pietism, Confucianism, Calvinism – all "have their names written on them." There is no need to reflect upon what makes them all religion. Weber just takes it for granted that they are. But not so for capitalism. He needs to define capitalism in a certain way because it is intimately tied up in his entire project.

The old problems of religion – the old quest for original religion, Natural Religion – are now put aside. Weber accepts the everyday things labeled "religion" at face value, and cites them as causes of capitalism. Calvinism, for example, is simply accepted as a given religious institution and tradition. No questions asked. Weber just "plugs in" Calvinism or Lutheranism or Roman Catholicism as needed. Natural Religion might just as well not exist for all that Weber cared! And, for Weber, it doesn't. He has shifted register to another kind of problem altogether – how religion helped the West get rich by embracing capitalism.

Profit, More Profit, and the Rational Outlook

Here's how Weber did his work of defining the category "capitalism." For starters, although people disagreed about what a capitalist really was, most could agree about who were typical capitalists. Weber is here appealing to nothing less than what we have considered as a common mind – a set of mutually, if unconsciously, agreed-upon views about the ways things are. What kinds of people actually created the modern conception of the edifice we all recognize as capitalism? Who's behind Mercedes-Benz, Microsoft, Samsung, Lenovo, IBM, Apple, and such? Of what sort of "stuff" were the persons behind these paradigmatically capitalist enterprises? We all know their names, Bill Gates, Steve Jobs, Henry Ford, Andrew Carnegie, the "robber baron" industrialists of the late nineteenth century, and, reaching into literature, Scrooge in Dickens' *Christmas Carol*. Weber's personal favorite "ideal type" of the early capitalist was the eighteenth-century inventor and entrepreneur, Benjamin Franklin. These men differ in many ways, but they all seemed cut from the same mold.

But Weber wanted to dig deeper into the rationale behind our common mind about the nature of capitalism. At the very least, we could agree on some descriptive features. They were all, for example, what Weber called "worldly." By "worldly," Weber means that capitalists directed their behavior at this world, not the next. They wanted to make money, start businesses, run corporations, and such. Diametrically opposed to them, Weber argued, in respect of worldliness would be the "contemplatives," such as Buddhist or Christian monks. We wouldn't call such folk "worldly." By contrast, monks and such are par-adigmatically "other-worldly," since their lives are focused on a heavenly or nirvanic realm beyond or outside of this world. Those who seek escape from the everyday into trances or extra-sensory states or sites also fit this description. So Weber believed we could all agree to form a common mind about a definition of a capitalist as at the very least someone pursuing a worldly occupation.

What else can we agree on? Well, capitalists seem like people who work hard. They may take pleasure in their work, but we wouldn't call them people who valued simple (or sometimes exotic) pleasure for its own sake. Weber categorized those who did just live for pleasure "hedonists." Such folks surely could not be part of our common mind about what capitalists were. By contrast, that made capitalists anti-hedonists, what he termed, "ascetics." They would be too preoccu-pied with their work to devote their lives simply to the pursuit of pleasure. They'd go broke if they did, for one thing. Further, they worked in a kind of systematic way. That is to say, they sought to rationalize their labor in order to get the highest yield for their efforts. This attitude of rationaliza-tion led to what we call "efficiencies" in produc-tion. For example, Henry Ford's assembly line of production tried to make most efficient use of the labor of each employee. Each worker did only a single task, so they became expert in it, and thus better able to maximize the utilities of their labor. Weber appeals to the model of modesty, sobriety, industry, and self-discipline from American his-tory, everyone from Benjamin Franklin to Henry Ford, to exemplify the ideal type or personality of the capitalist. Franklin's adages betray that right subjective attitude of the capitalist to a T. Dickens' Scrooge also fits this pattern, but at the extreme of rationalizing his resources to the point of stingi-ness. On the other hand, Franklin's adages con-jure up the image of a watchful, cautious, (literally) calculating pursuer of wealth.

> Remember, that *credit* is money. If a man lets his money lie in my hands after it is due, he gives me the interest, or so much as I can make of it during that time.

> He that loses five shillings, not only loses that sum, but all the advantage that might be made by turning it in dealing, which by the time that a young man becomes old, will amount to a con-siderable sum of money.

> Remember, that time is money .... He that idly loses five shillings' worth of time, loses five shil-lings, and might as prudently throw five shillings into the sea. (Weber 1976, pp. 48–50)

Now, if the word, "ascetic" calls forth the image of Buddhist and Christian monks or Hindu sages, then we have fallen into a little trap of Weber's. He meant to suggest that a devotion to ascetic values typified both these religious contemplatives *and*, paradoxically, capitalists. Weber felt that a study of the personality profiles of capitalists of the time showed he was right. Both monk and capitalist chose the path of self-control, denial, limiting or restraining pleasure – all for the sake of goals dependent upon delayed gratification. If either stopped to indulge themselves in pleasure, they would risk damaging the attainment of their goals. Were a monk to indulge in orgies of sex and drinking, that monk would surely derail himself from the pursuit of purity and the spirit. Similarly, were a capitalist to relax and do likewise, they might risk losing their "competitive edge," and be overwhelmed by their rivals in business. Essential to both styles of life was the ascetic spirit, not the path of the self-indulgent hedonist. But again, we wouldn't call monks capitalists just because they were ascetic in behavior.

Now, let us put these value orientations together. When we do, we see that Weber argued that the ideal capitalist ought to be seen as someone who was both "worldly" and "ascetic." Weber describes what may seem the unlikely combination of focus upon goals in *this* world, but inspired and guided by a near-religious ethic of self-denial, discipline, restraint and so on, usually connected with "other-worldly" occupations, such as the monkhood. The classic capitalists, like Henry Ford or Andrew Carnegie, were more than just rich. They displayed a distinctive *rational calculating* attitude about getting rich that differed from just *being* rich. Thus, paradoxically, it could be easier for someone not yet rich to qualify as a "capitalist" in Weber's sense than a rich person. Think of a small businessperson just scraping by, yet working with capitalist principles. Capitalism should mean, for Weber, an objectively distinct method of trying to get rich along with a distinctive value attitude toward doing so.

But why should these values of a kind of disciplined life in the world be internally fitting to the "spirit of capitalism," as Weber argues? Weber notes that people, for example, have always *wanted* to be rich, and tried many methods to achieve wealth. But a desire for wealth does not sufficiently define the capitalist. Lots of other different sorts of folk have wanted to be rich. "Adventurers" – pirates, warring plunderers, brigands, thieves, treasure finders, gamblers, and such – have both sought wealth and often succeeded. But we would not call them "capitalists" (Weber 1976, p. 17). Why? Thieves and plundering armies are clearly "worldly," since their activity was directed at this world. But significantly, unlike capitalists, their days of wealth were fleeting and occasional. Something about the values of capitalists kept them rich for long periods of time. Ford Motors was not made to last for a day!

What all these adventurers seeking wealth lacked was the *discipline of a rationally calculating* sort. Like the spendthrift grasshopper of the children's tale, they made no provision for the future, unlike the hardworking, calculating ants. They squandered their plunder in great gushes of showy expenditure. "Adventurers" did not plan or "save for a rainy day." So that too ruled them out of our common mind about the nature of capitalism.

To illustrate, typical nineteenth-century industrial magnates like Henry E. Huntington, Henry Ford, or Andrew Carnegie came by their riches by disciplined and calculated manipulation of the institutions of wealth creation. Although labeled "robber barons" for their voracious appetite for wealth, they were neither *literally* "robbers," such as the local burglar, nor men of noble "baronial" lineages. Instead, they distinguished themselves by establishing highly rationalized, systematic, bureaucratic systems for producing wealth that would even survive their demise. They were, in short, the very picture of what a capitalist should be in Weber's eyes. He even described them in terms that suggest monastic discipline, "ascetic."

Weber further doubted that layabout heirs of great wealth, perhaps scions of capitalists like Andrew Carnegie or Henry Ford, should be called capitalists. Whether the young Fords or Carnegies were capitalists depended on what values governed the *use* of their inherited wealth. What if they were content to simply spend away what they had, and not add to their fortune by doing business? Weber wouldn't call these rich heirs capitalists. Rich folk have always existed, even long before anything one might call "capitalism" existed. So, therefore, Weber drives his argument to force us to focus upon the qualities of capitalism that make it a distinctive category worthy as a tool of research and study. If he is right, we need to look to the source of the values of "worldly asceticism" and to the kind of style of life it made legitimate. Weber also thought that *structures* too, along with *attitudes*, distinguished this new breed of economic system and the people adapted to it. Distinctively new *objective* changes to economic practice came about. Capitalist enterprises operated by radically new and different procedures than those governing earlier forms of manufacture, service, and other forms of business. Weber's words are very precise about the guiding practice of capitalism: "*capitalism is identical with the pursuit of profit, and forever renewed profit, by means of conscious, rational, capitalistic enterprise*" (Weber 1976, p. 17; my emphasis).

Moreover, the capitalist typically establishes an institution such as a company, firm, or business, so that profit-making can continue even after the founder's death. As such Weber believes we must not obsess about the capitalist hero, the "entrepreneur." The real test of the capitalist is whether a lasting capitalist institutional change persists in society. Excessive attention to the heroic figure of the entrepreneur can reduce capitalism to the kind of pre-capitalist "adventurist" freebooting enterprises that Weber felt did not get to the heart of what made capitalism distinctive. The entrepreneur can indeed kick off a capitalist enterprise, but what distinguishes at least mature capitalism is its persistence over time by means of a rational organizational structure, such as a bureaucracy. As we will recall, for Weber "*capitalism is identical with the pursuit of profit, and forever renewed profit, by means of conscious, rational, capitalistic enterprise.*" The capitalist measures the output of workers over against the productivity of their work. Labor is measured out in precise packets of time. Hours worked are measured by the ubiquitous time clock. Efficiency of labor is likewise measured by time and motion studies that determine how actual work matches up to its results. All these go to making up the "rational" character that defines capitalism in Weber's sense as a profit-driven enterprise of gaining wealth. If this is not the picture of Weber's overbearing father, what is? Is this affinity of personality with economic structure a mere coincidence? I am arguing for the interconnection between socioeconomic realities and the kinds of people they produce. Weber (and his sainted mother) lived the consequences of the creation of this new personality type in his own life.

How the West Got Rich: The Basic Values of Capitalism

As a methodological idealist, Weber wanted to explain how this modern capitalist economy arose out of the cultural conditions of the West, such as its religious make-up. He had no interest in discovering the "first" or "universal" religion, nor even, despite his German nationalist feelings, the original religion of the Germans, Aryans, and such that so fascinated another patriotic German scholar, Friedrich Max Müller. He was not interested in how religion evolved, but rather in how religion made secular institutions, such as the economy, evolve! How, in particular, did religion account for the West's getting rich?

Unlike the evolutionists, Weber did not hold to some belief in the *biological* or racial superiority of the West over others. Why resort to these far-fetched possibilities when we had not even considered cultural or historical differences? Weber was similarly unimpressed by discoveries such as those at Brixham cave that inspired Tylor and other evolutionists. Prehistory taught us relatively little about today, certainly compared with the richly documented history of the recent past. But capitalism, as he understood it in terms of the emergence of a "worldly ascetic" mentality and its accompanying structures of work and industry, had only come about in the past several centuries. The answer to its existence then seemed, at first glance, to lie in tracking the history of its rise.

The notion that Protestant values had something to do with the rise of capitalism was batted around in the early twentieth century, when Weber was trying to formulate his ideas. He was the first, however, to make "an empirical proof of concrete historical connections" (Kippenberg 2002, p. 158). But what gave Weber the confidence that following this lead could bring results were some statistical studies linking religious affiliation and economic behavior. These studies pointed to something important. In the Germany of Weber's time, Protestant and Catholic populations mixed together; there was nonetheless strong tendency for the two populations to disaggregate in terms of economic status and occupation. The Catholics, on the whole, gravitated to the more comfortable, traditional, humanistic professions of law and medicine, while the Protestants were disproportionately found among the new, riskier, managerial, commercial, technical, and business classes. And among Protestants, Calvinists, rather than Lutherans, led the way in the new economic order (Weber 1976, p. 35). Calvinists "naturally" oriented themselves to capitalist careers. This anomaly set Weber thinking about the possible role Calvinist religious affiliation, especially, had in shaping economic behavior. Why these correlations?

In sum, here is Weber's answer. The economic system of capitalism required a certain "work ethic" to motivate the efforts of those working within it. The origins of the capitalist work ethic are to be found in the justifications that people need to have for their participation in capitalist enterprise. Weber believed that these justifications or legitimations were ultimately to be found in Calvinist theology. Religion, therefore, in the form of theological legitimation causes or explains the rise and persistence of the great economic system of our own time. But what was it about Calvinism that enabled it to serve this function? Why not Lutheranism or Roman Catholicism?

Traditionalism and Catholicism

Let's follow Weber's thinking about why Catholicism could not do the job of launching capitalism. We can expect him to point to the prominent role that monastic contemplative life of "otherworldly asceticism" played in Roman Catholic culture. For the Roman Catholics of Weber's Germany, the monastic life modeled the heights of Christian perfection. Monks were the equivalent of religious "royalty" – remote, but adored and exemplary. As one might expect, this otherworldly spiritual perfection was attainable only by an elite. For the masses of the Roman Catholic faithful, another kind of spirituality prevailed, one that accepted the limitations of ordinary folk. Thus, when Weber takes sharpest aim at Roman Catholicism, he focuses on the vast majority of the Catholic community, those who formed the laity. This takes us to his critique of "traditionalism."

As Weber describes it, capitalism puts a lot of pressure on someone running a business along capitalist lines. Self-sacrifice and discipline take their toll. Applying "rational" means of organization entails additional burdens of needing to adhere to exact methods of book-keeping and allocation of capital. Yes, capitalism promises wealth and riches. But if there were an easier, risk-free way of making wealth, would anyone voluntarily choose the capitalist route of "worldly asceticism"? Why would anyone choose such an ascetically rigorous and rationalized style of life?

Recent anthropological studies have focused on certain small-scale societies that have become "affluent," but without the need to pursue capitalism's disciplined, rationalized, profit-maximizing economic style of life. These societies do not accumulate surpluses, either of goods or capital, in part because their environments make accumulation and storage unnecessary. What they cherish is leisure time. They know how to work in a disciplined way, but only enough to meet immediate needs. Nevertheless, they achieve "an affluent society … one in which all the people's material wants are easily satisfied" not by "producing much, but by desiring little." They do not need to maximize profits and compete because they restrain their needs and desires. They have adopted the "Zen strategy," as anthropologist Marshall Sahlins calls it (Sahlins 1972, pp. 1–40). Some of the first Western sailors who encountered these societies on the early European voyages of discovery in the South Pacific fell utterly in love with this low-pressure way of living. Many jumped ship rather than return to the then "modern," world of capitalist calculating, rationalized, disciplined striving for wealth and ever more wealth.

But Sahlins' "Zen strategy" is not unique to some South Pacific paradise. In many respects, the South Seas paradises resembled the pre-capitalist world of western Europe. Weber characterized the values of such societies as "traditionalist." To him, the most significant impediment to the rise of capitalism was this traditionalist way of life. In traditionalist Europe, there were no time clocks to punch, no hourly calculations of wages, no precise piecework quotas of production to meet; the pace of life and work was slow and regular; and the rewards were proportionately moderate. Businesses avoided the fiercest competition with one another and preferred instead to find a comfortable niche and guaranteed markets in the local economy with a regular circle of loyal clients and customers. As Weber describes the traditionalist business world, where the "number of business hours was very moderate, perhaps five to six a day, sometimes considerably less," one detects a telling note of nostalgia for the loss of what he calls an "idyllic state" (Weber 1976, p. 68). At the end of the work day, things even got better, when a "long daily visit to the tavern, with often plenty to drink, and a congenial circle of friends, made life comfortable and leisurely" (Weber 1976, pp. 66–67).

But why link traditionalism with Catholicism, especially the Catholicism of the early modern period? While Catholicism valued ascetic practice and monasticism, it also offered the assurance of an elaborate system of mediating structures that eased transactions with the divine. Cycles of holy days and ritual observances, a rich sacramental life, a system of indulgences, and a universe of mediating holy folk – the saints – plus holy places, such as shrines, cathedrals, holy springs, wells, and so on – all functioned to channel holiness to the faithful. Believers inhabited an "enchanted" world of religious meanings and occasions for access to the holy. This Catholicism placed few restrictions on the easy-going traditional life of modest pleasure-taking.

Catholic moral teaching helped prop up traditionalist work and business, but was particularly hard on the intense acquisition and enjoyment of wealth. Pursuing wealth for its own sake put one in danger of sinning by *turpitudo* (feeling good about even justly won wealth) or *avarice* (the desire for gain) (Weber 1976, p. 73). Traditionalism meant approval of *modest* levels of pleasure and wealth. But taking pleasure in wealth in itself, or seeking to amass ever more wealth, seemed to exceed the norm of modesty. Traditionalism's core value could be said, then, to be a modest "worldly hedonism," which opposed capitalism's core value of "worldly *asceticism*." By this time, with the mention of the South Pacific "Zen" societies and now early modern European traditionalism, many readers may be wondering why anyone would *prefer* to be a capitalist, in the sense Weber has constructed. Weber asks himself the same question. Most people would prefer the easier life offered by traditionalism over against the rigors of capitalism. How, then, was traditionalism overcome? How, indeed, did capitalism ever succeed against such odds?

How Capitalism Killed Traditionalism

To explain how traditionalism fell, Weber offered a stunning historical example that captures how a revolution in values spelt the end of traditionalism and ushered in the new world of capitalism. He begins by showing us what the new capitalists faced when their labor force was dominated by traditionalist values. During harvest season, crop loss threatened certain agricultural enterprises. So employers tried to speed up the rate of labor in order to protect against crop loss. Employers would offer workers a higher piece rate in the expectation that this would provide an incentive for higher production. But this policy often had a surprising result: workers produced *less* than they did at the lower piece-work rate! Why? As Weber nicely sums up:

> The opportunity of earning more was less attractive than that of working less. He did not ask: how much can I earn in a day if I do as much work as possible? But: how much must I work in order to earn the wage … which I earned before and which takes care of my traditional needs? (Weber 1976, p. 60)

Nor did the employers succeed in raising the level of output when they tried to "get tough" and reduce wages. Laborers worked just as long, but less hard. In the end, they produced correspondingly less, and hurt the profits of the business (Weber 1976, p. 61). Nothing seemed to be able to bring down traditionalism's "stone wall of habit" (Weber 1976, p. 62). Other observations about the traditionalist workforce should be noted. The workers showed no *dedication* to their work. For them, their work at any given time was irrelevant. What mattered was attaining a certain level of life, and no more. Labor was a means, never an end. Their lives revolved around family and friends, religious sodalities and social clubs, the cycle of liturgical religious rituals that marked births, baptisms, marriages, and deaths in the community, or that sanctified other moments in the religious calendar. How, then, were traditionalism's formidable moral structures and rich religious sanctions overcome? "The spirit of capitalism … had to fight its way to supremacy," says Weber, "against a whole world of hostile forces" (Weber 1976, p. 56).

But surely someone must have found traditionalism stultifying. Someone must have wanted change. Weber finds such a community that, in effect, become the "foot in the door," the "thin edge of the wedge," an unwitting vanguard of the new capitalist system that begins the unraveling of traditionalism. Among the employees we recently discussed for their resistance to change, Weber found one community of employees who – unlike most – did respond to the incentives offered in the form of higher pay rates for piece-work. Unlike their traditionalist co-workers, these others willingly worked harder when given higher wages for so doing.

What explains this out-of-step community? When Weber scoured the data, he discovered that these workers differed from their traditionalist co-workers only in one respect: they were all affiliated with a Protestant sect called Pietism. Unlike their traditionalist co-workers, they displayed a sense of obligation to their work, a sense of the value of labor as an end in itself, a guiltless desire for gain along with the self-discipline and deferral of gratification needed for preserving and consolidating one's gains, and so on – in short all the traits that set traditionalism on its head. Employers duly took note of the more desirable work habits of groups like the Pietists. They began hiring workers with Pietist or similar religious affiliation in preference to their Roman Catholic traditionalist neighbors – with predictable results.

Cases like this must have multiplied until, as Weber notes, "at some time this leisureliness" of traditionalism "was suddenly destroyed." First, objective practices changed. In the textile business, a model entrepreneur – "some young man" – decides not to maintain the family tradition of patronizing certain suppliers. Instead, he goes out and gets a better price for his raw materials from someone outside the familiar circle of vendors from his own region. This "young man" – an early capitalist, in effect – ventured forth and *rationally* chose new weavers, with one eye on the lookout for their religious affiliation.

At the same time, he also further *rationalized* his supervision of their work. As competition for jobs increased, he may even have succeeded in turning traditionalist Roman Catholic peasants into pliable laborers like the Pietists. The Catholics were formed anew inside a capitalist scheme of production. Further, in order to increase his profits, he might also market directly to the consumer, cutting out entire levels of "middle men" who may have depended upon his patronage for generations. This process of economic rationalization was repeated everywhere, and resulted in a competitive marketplace. Those who could not keep up fell by the wayside,

and went out of business. For Weber, this shift to an entrepreneurial, profit-driven, competitive, rationalized economy spelt doom for traditionalism. "The idyllic state collapsed under the pressure of a bitter competitive struggle ... The old leisurely and comfortable attitude toward life gave way to a hard frugality" (Weber 1976, pp. 67–68). The values and ways of Weber's father won out over his mother's.

Religion Rushes in to Justify the New Capitalist System

Changes of objective conditions alone were not enough to secure the new system. The novel capitalist way of doing things required elaborate justification or legitimation. The sudden break with traditional ways of doing business provoked demands to explain *why* they should be. Why was competition such a good thing if it meant that, for example, long-established traditional firms went out of business, and their employees were deprived of their livelihoods? Somebody would have to do some explaining. How could the capitalists do this? What could they say to defend their new, frankly rather cruel and unfeeling system, with no respect for tradition? Why was it good, for example, that some became wealthier while others became poor because they lost out to capitalist competition? Why were the new capitalist values of "creative destruction" better than the old traditionalist values of stability? And it was clear that the new capitalists had to do more than just *declare on their own terms* that, say, that freedom to be ambitious and dynamic was a good, even a better, value than those they hoped to supplant. But why was freedom a better value, say, than stability, security, and so on? Says who?

Now considering that traditionalism was so deeply rooted, and as we recall, capitalism presented a system of hard, disciplined ascetic attitudes toward work, the justifications to change must have had to be powerful. Momentous changes in economic values required equally robust legitimations. Weber reasoned that this fact alone strongly suggested that the justifications must be religious. It was religion alone that wielded the power to invoke ultimate sanctions capable of revolutionizing the morality of making a livelihood. What could be more powerful than that?

To be precise, Weber, in effect, joins forces with Otto in arguing for the importance of the psychological part of religion – religious *experience*. Experiences of tremendous, other-worldly power, analogous to Otto's "numinous" experience filled the new capitalists with confidence. One common way this experience was described was as a "calling." God was literally "calling" the new capitalists to initiate their novel economic endeavors, giving them a feeling of absolute confidence that they were doing God's will. First introduced by the German, Martin Luther (1483–1546), the first great Protestant reformer, this appeal to a "calling" had explosive consequences. Primarily, it gave license to the individual conscience to challenge the Roman Catholic Church, or indeed any church, on the principle of the supremacy of the conscience. "Calling" also dramatized Luther's ideal of a one-to-one relationship between God and each believer. Religion was suffused with the sense of standing alone before a fierce power, naked of excuses or supporting structures. Only by heeding God's "call" and placing total confidence in it could one hope for salvation. The ability of the capitalists to explain and justify their confident radical behavior took its strength from the same divine source – being "called" to a certain course in life. Only new *divine* duties could supplant the older ones of the traditionalist era.

But as a perfect fit for the new capitalist order, Lutheranism had one tragic flaw. Yes, Luther linked "calling" to a worldly engagement in the economic realm, but the faithful were only "called" into "worldly activity within the limits imposed by his established station in life" – specific pre-formed, traditional professions (Weber 1976, p. 85). "The individual should remain once and for all in the station and calling in which God had placed him," observes Weber of Luther. Dutiful Lutheran sons and daughters were, for example, "called" to follow in the footsteps of their fathers and mothers.

By contrast, the new capitalism knew no such conventional limits or restrictions on the kind of business or profession to be pursued. The world was wide open for possibilities of gaining wealth, limited only by the ability and imagination of the individual. So if Lutheran teaching fell short of providing the rationale the new capitalists needed to feel justified in what they undertook in the spirit of "worldly asceticism," what religion did?

For Calvin, "Calling" Overcomes All Obstacles

The Protestant Reformation provided a host of candidates, but by this time Weber had focused his aim on Calvinism. Swiss theologian, Jean Calvin (1509–64), Luther's co-equal as a mainstay of the Protestant Reformation, broke even further away from the lingering traditionalism of Luther. It was Jean Calvin's theology that Weber believed ultimately provided the theological justification, or "ethical" basis for the values that we have come to know as capitalist values – or the capitalist "spirit" of the title of Weber's classic. Indeed, it might have been more accurate for Weber to have entitled his masterpiece "The *Calvinist* Ethic and the Spirit of Capitalism." Calvin differed from Luther significantly on the critical idea of "calling." Calvin's "calling" was a harsh and unpredictable thing – "predestination."

By this, we usually think that Calvin only meant each human being had been determined by God either for salvation or damnation. But actually, the doctrine of predestination meant even more explicitly that we are predestined to some role, profession, occupation, and such in life in the world. While this seems unfair, and even to justify the charge of "extreme inhumanity" against Calvinism, the doctrine of predestination also displays a "magnificent consistency" (Weber 1976, p. 104). An all-knowing, perfect God not only must know the fate of each creature, but also must will that fate. Now, while Calvinist predestination seemed cruel and unfair to those selected for damnation, it was an iron-clad guarantee of eternal happiness for "the Elect." In religious terms, this assurance of salvation could give the Elect enormous levels of self-confidence. If they knew they were fated for heaven, then life offered no real problems. For the Damned – the hapless Charlie Browns, the "losers" of today – not so much.

One little problem clouds this clear blue sky of theological consistency. Dispelling it was critical in letting Calvinism play its part as the "spirit" of capitalism – capitalism's moral legitimation. How does a person know whether they are among the Damned or the Elect? This uncertainty became a huge source of anxiety for Calvinists. Critics called it their "salvation panic" (Ringer 2004, p. 119). There then was immense pressure to resolve anxiety among the faithful. The theological solution devised to satisfy the religious needs of the faithful played right into the hands of the new capitalist need for divine sanction for their new enterprises. The Calvinist theologians resolved this problem by flipping things around, so to speak. Instead of preaching that election *caused* a feeling of confidence in the faithful, they preached that a sure *sign* of election was a *feeling* of confidence in one's being saved. The really Elect person had a duty to dismiss all doubts that they were not among the blessed (Weber 1976, p. 111). Further, a really confident person – someone who felt the "call" of salvation, would necessarily thrust themselves into worldly activity. Better yet, the more one engaged in "intense worldly activity," the more confident one became in one's salvation (Weber 1976, p. 112). "If that God, whose hand the Puritan sees in all the occurrences of life, shows one of His elect a chance of profit, he must do it with a purpose. Hence the faithful Christian must follow the call by taking advantage of the opportunity" (Weber 1976, p. 162). Problem solved.

We would not be far from the mark to see in this desire for success and continuous success the source of what Weber identified as one of the marks of capitalism – "the pursuit of profit, and forever *renewed* profit" (Weber 1976, p. 17; my emphasis). Appearances had to be maintained, because appearances marked one as saved. Indeed on the Calvinist view, anyone who voluntarily wished to be poor, such as those in the Catholic monastic and mendicant orders, were wishing to be "unhealthy" (Weber 1976, p. 163). In its present form in our capitalist world, the ugly attitudes of certain insolent rich toward the poor recall their original Calvinist roots. These poor somehow *deserve* to be poor, just as being among the "winners" is thought to be both earned and deserved. In this way, Calvinism and its "worldly ascetic" values overturned the Catholic world both of traditionalist "worldly hedonism" and the monastic life of "otherworldly asceticism." Painting a dynamic picture of how the hard value of asceticism, fled the monastery and marched confidently forward into everyday life, where, thanks to Calvin, it conquered the world of work and industry by submitting it to the rigors of the monastic life, Weber says:

> Christian asceticism, at first fleeing from the world to solitude, had already ruled the world which it had renounced from the monastery, and through the Church. But it had, on the whole, left the naturally spontaneous character of daily life in the world untouched. Now, it strode into the marketplace of life, slammed the door of the monastery behind it, and undertook to penetrate just that daily routine of life with its methodicalness, to fashion it into a life in the world, but neither of nor for this world. (Weber 1976, p. 154)

I have tried to show how Weber's historical analysis of the rise of capitalism not only reflected his impressive grasp of historical realities, but also was congruent with the personal tensions afflicting him. I have not delved deeply into these matters of personal psychology, but only noted how they seem to have been a factor in the way Weber saw the world. In turning now to the monumental work of Sigmund Freud, we will be able to see how at least one great genius tried to solve the mysteries of the psychological life, some perhaps like Weber's themselves, and in doing so how the phenomenon of religion can itself be explained.

References

Bellah, R.N. 1957. *Tokugawa Religion*. Boston: Beacon Press.

Diggins, J.P. 1996. *Max Weber: Politics and the Spirit of Tragedy*. New York: Basic Books.

Ermarth, M. 1978. *Wilhelm Dilthey: The Critique of Historical Reason*. Chicago: University of Chicago Press.

Geertz, C. 1983. *Local Knowledge: Further Essays in Interpretive Anthropology*. New York: Harper & Row.

Honigsheim, P. 2003. *The Unknown Max Weber*. New Brunswick: Transaction Publishers.

Hook, S. 1930. "Capitalism and Protestantism." *The Nation* 131: 476–478.

Käsler, D. 1988. *Max Weber: An Introduction to His Life and Work*, trans. P. Hurd. Chicago: University of Chicago Press.

Kippenberg, H.G. 2002. *Discovering Religious History in the Modern Age*, trans. B. Harshav. Princeton: Princeton University Press.

Mitzman, A. 1969. *The Iron Cage*. New York City: Grosset & Dunlap.

Ringer, F. 2004. *Max Weber: An Intellectual Biography*. Chicago: University of Chicago Press.

Sahlins, M. 1972. *Stone Age Economics*. Chicago: University of Chicago Press.

Singer, M. 1972. "Industrial Leadership, the Hindu Ethic, and the Spirit of Socialism." In M. Singer (ed.), *When a Great Tradition Modernizes*. London: Pall Mall Press.

Weber, M. 1976. *The Protestant Ethic and the Spirit of Capitalism*, trans. T. Parsons. New York: Charles Scribners' Sons.

Further Reading

Defoe, D. 1948. *Robinson Crusoe*. New York: Modern Library.

Gerth, H.H., and C.W. Mills (eds.). 1946. *From Max Weber: Essays in Sociology*. New York: Oxford University Press.

Suttner, B.V. April 18, 1906. "The Evolution of the Peace Movement: The Nobel Lecture." Stockholm.

Taylor, C. 1985. "Understanding and Ethnocentricity." In C. Taylor (ed.), *Philosophical Papers: Philosophy and the Human Sciences*, vol. 2. Cambridge: Cambridge University Press.

Weber, M. 1975. *Max Weber: A Biography*, trans. H. Zohn. New York: John Wiley & Sons.

10

Tales from the Underground: Freud and the Psychoanalytic Origins of Religion

---

In the slow ample beauty of the world,
And the unutterable glad release
Within the temple of the holy night.
O Atthis, how I loved thee long ago
In that fair perished summer by the sea!
(Bliss Carman,
"I Loved Thee, Atthis")

The Freudian Moment

In playing up the emotionally charged relations of Weber to his parents in the last chapter, I had two intentions in mind, only one of which I revealed at the time. I wanted readers to consider that Weber's personal tensions corresponded to analogous dilemmas he observed in society's choices of economic systems. In a gentle anticipation of my treatment of feminist theories of religion, I deliberately posed the "softer" side of Weber's mother's charitable, but unrealistic, nature mirrored as analogous to the gentler, "feminine" world of easy-going traditionalism. The "harder" side of his father's disciplined, workaholic, "masculine" bourgeois worldview would then reflect the harsh, but realistic, perhaps even "patriarchal," Calvinist work ethic. Weber seems torn between these extremes both in his family life and in his analyses of the relations between religion and economic systems. By enlarging our conception of Weberian thought to include his own personal torments, I also wanted readers to think about the opposed horns of the perennial dilemmas across which much of human life is poised. Desire and its denial, most notably sexual, caused Weber his gravest anxieties. His diffidence about Calvinist worldly asceticism as a necessary ingredient in making the modern world of rational capitalist enterprise reflected similar unresolved tensions in his own psyche.

But at the same time as I explored this set of tensions, I hoped that my focus on Weber's relations with his parents would ease the transition to this chapter on Freudian psychology of religion. The influence of Weber's childhood nurture, the agonies of sexual desire, their realization or frustration, anticipate great Freudian themes such as "civilization and its discontents." Freud meditated on the same contradictory demands of rationality and restraint over against the desire for sexual gratification that so consumed Weber. About Weber, I pose the proposition that those deep and troubled relations with his parents formed a personality that may have made it "natural" for him to "think he was right" about religion in analogous ways. We know Weber failed to consummate his own marriage, yet he had numerous extra-

Understanding Theories of Religion: An Introduction, Second Edition. Ivan Strenski.
© 2015 Ivan Strenski. Published 2015 by John Wiley & Sons, Ltd.

marital affairs. We know as well of Weber's fascination with Protestant worldly asceticism while at other times he evinced a hearty desire for a carefree worldly hedonism, and cherished a nostalgia for the lost world of traditionalism. We know too of his movements back and forth between the "softer" interpretive modes of understanding and "harder" causal ones of explanation. I cannot imagine why these tensions would not be reflected in how he thought about religion.

The biographical material on Weber offers an open invitation to Freud (1856–1939). In a way, the "only" thing Freud does is tell us persuasive stories about the deeper levels of the human mind that we have explored in Weber. In this chapter, we will see how Freud deliberately explains religion – specifically, religious experience – in terms of the dynamics of the human mind. Freud makes problems for religion by arguing that religious experiences are to be explained in terms of mental causes that are themselves not religious. For example, Freud could accept that the religious experience of being "called" motivated early capitalists to undertake economic endeavors. But he pushes things a step further, and asks what explains – short of actual divine intervention – the experience of being "called". As a classic *reductionist*, Freud stands starkly opposed to the phenomenologists of religion and, especially, their assertion of the autonomy of religion. These experiences have to do basically with relations between children and parents, not between people and God. The main lines of Freud's approach come into focus when we look at how he treats great religious personages, such as Moses. Heeding feminist trends in religion, we will also look at how a contemporary Freudian, Michael Carroll, has tried to explain the origins of the cult of the Virgin Mary.

Mentalism and the Two Psychologies

When speaking of the psychology of religion, we do need to be aware of at least a few broad distinctions between kinds of psychologies. Broadly speaking, psychologies are either "mentalist" or "behaviorist." Freudian psychology is generally seen as a paradigm of a mentalist approach to

explaining human behavior. For mentalists, psychology is about the mind, or mental states. Freudian psychology thus takes the term "psychology" literally. It is the scientific study of the *psyche* – the Greek word for "soul" or "spirit," and by extension, mind.

How would such a science look? First, Freud deals empirically with the intentions, motives, feelings, experiences, drives, needs, desires, wishes, and so on of people who typically came to him for medical treatment. People talked; Freud listened. He then tried to see if he could make any sense of – construct a *theory about* – what people said. Did their reports tell a story, hang together, point in some direction? Freud even believed that someday scientists would show that mental states corresponded, one for one, with the way physical states of the brain fit together in a causal pattern.

As if addressing Otto, Freud rejected the ideas of his mystically minded friend, the French philosopher Romain Rolland. The Frenchman shared with Freud his experiences of what he called an "oceanic feeling." Reminiscent in ways of Otto's "numinous" experience, although not identically described, Rolland spoke of a sense of "eternity, a feeling as of something limitless, unbounded … the source of the religious energy" (Freud 1961, p. 11). Like Otto, Rolland implied that such experiences came from an overpowering transcendent source, and thus that they were "the *fons et origo* of the whole need for religion" (Freud 1961, p. 12).

However much Freud sympathized with Rolland's appetite for the irrational, he would have none of Rolland's theologizing. More than anything else, Freud wanted to ground religion and religious experience firmly in the earth-bound human realm. Religious experiences were expressions of wholly human determinants of human thought and action. Religion, as believers consciously understand it, is an illusion. They do not really experience a supernatural object, only a natural one, masquerading as supernatural. "There is no distinctively religious need – only psychological need" (Rieff 1979, p. 271). And although these needs are beyond the powers of ordinary reason to control, they are nonetheless part of our (mysterious) human nature. Freud, then, stands diametrically opposed to Kristensen's view that the believer's point of view is final and incorrigible. To Freud, the reports of religious believers are just the raw material for his explanations.

The Behaviorist Revolution

Freudian psychology, like all "mentalisms," holds to the existence of immaterial realities, such as mental states. This has provoked another class of psychologists, known as behaviorists, to label Freudians superstitious. Behaviorists reject all talk of mental states or mind to focus exclusively on individual human *behavior*. If we could imagine a behaviorist studying Isaiah's vision in the temple (see chapter 8 above), the behaviorist would focus on observable *behavior* such as the prophet's manifest excitement, his terror and sweating, and so on. But no unobservable interior states of mind, such as motives, intentions, etc., would be allowed to enter the causal chain of explanation. How can we tell objectively that Isaiah saw what he tells us he did? The insides of Isaiah's mind are private, and thus closed off from the observable public realm that science requires. All we can explore is public and observable behavior. We will see how Malinowski tries to harmonize his own Freudian beliefs with newly acquired interests in behaviorism in his approach to religion (Malinowski 1948, pp. 47–54).

A good case in point is how Malinowski treats the public mortuary rites for the deceased in the Trobriand Islands. First, he dutifully records overt actions or behaviors, such as weeping, expressions of horror, etc., into his notebooks. Then, he notices that some – ritual – behaviors can be connected with others. Following upon the performance of some ritual grieving, for example, a series of manifestations of equilibrium, joy, gladness, relief, and so on can be detected. In behaviorist style, Malinowski concludes that somehow, then, the mortuary ritual behavior might have acted as a *stimulus* (cause) to induce the *response* (effect) of emotional equilibrium. If so, then, we can explain the emotional reaction of participants in terms of the causal action of the ritual behavior! Case closed. Before dismissing behaviorism, it would be well to recall the success of the wide use of "behavior modification" therapy in helping people overcome bad habits, like overeating or smoking.

Part of the power of the behaviorist approach is its comfortable, commonsense nature. We have all had experiences such as chronic procrastination. We have all also had experiences in which such a behavior was altered by an external stimulus. As children, we may feel rebellious or experience antagonism to our parents. But although it does not work in all cases, that feeling of rebellion or antagonistic motivation – indeed all mental states – can be sometimes be "broken" or changed by the application of the right sort of external stimulus. All I am saying is that in many cases, people do "change their minds" by having their behavior altered or affected. In those cases, they do not change because their mental states have been addressed, but because their behavior has been.

Freudian Psychoanalysis: Pseudo-Science and/or Therapy?

Freud's approach is diametrically opposed to behaviorism. His psychology was and is, above all, a theory of practical healing – *therapy*. It took mind seriously; it took what people said seriously. Freud brought all the skill and humanity of his practice as a common medical doctor to the task of doctoring the mind. He became an ordinary physician in part because of the rampant anti-Semitism in the sciences and professions. He had been blocked from pursuing his desired career in chemistry, zoology, or brain anatomy by the race haters of his time (Rieff 1979, pp. 5–7). Freud was, however, able to aspire to the practical craft of family medicine. Perhaps feeling his genius stifled, he departed from the standard practice of his peers in the medical profession: he actually talked with his patients! He looked at (and talked with) the whole patient, not merely focusing upon the results of tests or on something called a "disease," as his more professionalized peers did. In large part, because Freud began to *listen* to his patients, the classic techniques of psychoanalysis took their distinctive shape (Rieff 1979, p. 12).

By characterizing Freudian psychotherapy in this humanistic way, some critics have argued that it is not the stuff of science. Others, however, reply: So much the worse for science! Why should we diminish Freudian practice just because it employed of the art of interpretive decoding – of seeing things as signs of other things? After all, are not doctors supposed to be especially skilled at reading the body as offering symptoms? And is not "symptom" just another word for "sign" or "symbol" – a thing that points to something else? The work of psychoanalysts is to *read* what they see as signs, indicators, effects, or symptoms of certain underlying mental structures, and then to address those structures so that patients can be relieved of their suffering. As early as his first great publication, *The Interpretation of Dreams* (1900), Freud saw dreams, for example, as symbols (Rieff 1979, p. 7). While Freud did think his work would eventuate in a "hard" science, he also embraced interpretation. He listened to what people said, dreamt, fantasized, etc., and applied *hermeneutics* to it – not unlike interpreting Bible verses. He approached dreams exactly "like a sacred text" (Preus 1987, p. 185). On the interpretive – hermeneutic – view of Freudian method, then, the psychoanalyst is more like Sherlock Holmes, a genius, an automechanic, or the trusted family doctor, than a chemist, physicist, or, even less, an engineer. The impact of Freud upon the study of religion arises from the creativity and suggestiveness of his *interpretations* of religion. Freud creates "problems of religion." He is one of those theorists who plant that gnawing worm of doubt into the minds of religious folk, especially those who center their religion around a powerful god or other mighty sacred being, such as the Virgin Mary, the "mother of God."

What Lies Beneath: Freud's Idea of the Unconscious

Since Freud wanted to shed light into what he took to be the dark internal mechanisms conditioning human behavior, was there some kind of inner dynamic that produced behavioral facts? If so, what was it? The Freudian "unconscious" is name of the mechanism he believed lay beneath public, behavioral facts. Four features are salient in Freud's idea of the unconscious.

First, Freud's unconscious is an *absolute* unconscious. The Freudian unconscious is unknown and unknowable to us by introspection. Individuals need to rely on the clinical therapeutic help of an expert investigator of the unconscious – the Freudian psychoanalyst.

The Freudian unconscious is new kind of mental "space." Freud bifurcates mental space into separate, watertight compartments – unconscious and conscious – such that the unconscious is opaque to introspection. The contents of the unconscious mind are latent or hidden, not manifest like the conscious mind (Freud 1938, p. 238). Freud's unconscious thus differs from his idea of the "preconscious." The unconscious is not composed of those trivial things that we happen from time to time not to remember, or of which we are not conscious, as Dan Pals amusingly notes, "things like the ages of our parents, what was served for dinner yesterday, or where we intend to go on the weekend" (Freud 1938, pp. 491, 518, 544–545; Pals 1996, p. 58).

Second, the Freudian unconscious is a repository of deeply and actively suppressed *memories*. The unconscious memories have been buried because to admit them to consciousness would threaten our sanity. Freud believes repression functions to retain sanity (Preus 1987, pp. 179–180).

Freud felt that classic repression occurred in early childhood, not in adulthood. But we can get a sense of the power of his viewpoint by extrapolating to a perhaps more accessible example of the psychological mysteries of a certain kind of jealous murderer – a stock figure in fiction but also one found in many real-life cases: the man who kills his wife and the man he thinks is her lover, but who is also by all accounts a loving husband and father. The typical narrative is that he denies having committed the murder of his wife and her companion. But let us complicate matters psychologically, and assume that he is "telling the truth" in asserting his innocence. I say "truth" because it is quite possible he may not be able to remember having committed the crime. He is thus being "true" to his self-knowledge – as far as that goes. How could this be, if he did the murders? Consider the following scenario. On this view, this otherwise normal man murdered his wife and her friend in a blind emotional rage. This might incidentally be precisely what the prosecution argues in the trial, as evidence of his culpability. Yet consider how the performance of the gruesome deed might have affected its perpetrator. Imagine the trauma and horror impressed upon him by its ghastly results, being the murderer of both his once treasured wife and the mother of their children. Freud might suggest that the murder was so fraught with emotion that it could well have triggered the classic repressions typical of early childhood. These repressed feelings thus become *constitutive* of the murderer's sense of himself. He cannot both *admit* his guilt to himself and simultaneously maintain an image of himself consistent with the retention of his sanity. He has to repress consciousness of his guilt, and sink it deeply into an absolute unconscious. He needs to slip into a state of denial, in which he so deeply buries the conscious memory of his deed that he may truly no longer be able to remember it. Thus, his protestations of innocence, while actually false, may be true *to him*, "true" in *his own conscious mind*, and thus honest and sincere protestations of his own innocence. That, at any rate, is what might follow if Freud were right about the ability of people to repress formative early childhood memories and to seal them away in the "hurt locker" of our unconscious.

Third, in Freud's view, the unconscious controls us, not, as is commonly thought, our conscious mind. Freud overturns the classic humanist view of human nature, prevalent since at least the Renaissance. Human beings are neither significantly self-aware nor free. Instead, we are blind to our deep inner nature, and subject to our darker side. And even though we are unaware of its action upon us, the unconscious nevertheless works from great depths to cause us to behave in certain ways – and ways over which we have virtually no control of our own. Think, for example, of the way some people obsess about things. Why does murderous Lady Macbeth obsessively scrub her hands long after any signs of Duncan's blood have faded, unless her unconscious knowledge of her crime continues to haunt her? She may declare as loudly as she will "Out, damned spot! Out, I say" (*Macbeth* V.i.38). But if Freud is right, it is to no avail, because the unconscious rules.

Fourth, Freud further thinks that the unconscious is the most powerful force constituting how we act. This is why we repress those unconscious matters vital to self-preservation. They made us who we are. To release repressed materials, and to disrupt this part of our identity, would shatter our emotional stability. Thus, if indeed a man murdered his wife, the chief reason that he might persist in repressing his memories would be that admitting them would destroy his sanity.

The Structure of the Self: Ego, Superego, and Id

Freud's originality extends beyond his theory of repression and the unconscious. The human self, already a mixture of conscious and unconscious, now is revealed as a dynamic, dramatic system of pressures and drives, made up of three components – ego, superego, and id. At the most basic level – the id – people are still beasts, driven by coarse biological needs, by primal survival instincts. When we are hungry, we want to eat; when our lives are threatened, we fight to resist our attackers; when we are sexually stimulated, we want to achieve gratification. The id's deep origins in our animal natures are unconscious to us, although we have all felt and recognized the powerful compulsions associated with the id and its cravings for satisfaction.

In Freud's view, were we left to ourselves as id-driven beasts, we would never have evolved into a species that could be called human. We would simply be raging appetites seeking satisfaction. Luckily for the survival of a human species, the energy of the id is restrained. The superego, as Freud calls it, restrains the surging energies of the id. Morality is a manifestation of superego, replete with its disciplining norms and values. Max Weber's "worldly ascetic" values that guided capitalist enterprise come to mind.

Both Weber and Freud believed that however unpleasant it might be to discipline our urges, without restraint we could not have civilization. We could not have truly *human* life. That is to say, without the superego restraining the id, that distinctive mark of human individuality – the ego – could not emerge. A true "self," then, is only possible because we learn to balance our id energies against our superego limitations. Freud quickly attacks conventional thinking about the human individual. "This ego appears to us as something autonomous and unitary, marked off distinctly from everything else" (Freud 1961, pp. 12–13). But it is not – because it is the product of the intersection of two more primal forces. Further, the ego pays a price in the uneasy "discontents" it suffers for the "civilization" achieved. Freud wrote about these in his classic on the subject, *Civilization and Its Discontents* (1930). Balancing id's insatiable desires with superego's restraints is unstable at best. We seem to lurch to one side or the other, but never attain a perfect mean. As if confirming Freud's insights, the dramas of Weber's attempts to balance the values of his mother against those of his father, or of traditionalism's "worldly hedonism" over capitalism's "worldly asceticism," tell the same story. Now our question becomes: How can Freud's creative theoretical machinery be wheeled in to explain and understand religion?

Totemism, Taboo, and Sacrifice: A Father's Burden to Bear

One way that we could bring out Freud's distinctiveness is by comparing him with some of the earlier figures we have met in the field of religious studies. We should exploit the fact, for example, that Freud read William Robertson Smith and James Frazer. Indeed, he relied heavily upon them in two of his four main writings on religion, *Totem and Taboo* (1913) and *Moses and Monotheism* (1939). Yet, however highly Freud esteemed the work of Robertson Smith and Frazer, Freud was not their slavish imitator. Robert Ackerman speaks ominously of Freud going "beyond Frazer in his investigations into the volcano" (Ackerman 1987, p. 213). I should like to conclude this chapter by showing precisely how Freud established an entirely new style of approach to the study of religion by standing on the shoulders, as it were, of his two great predecessors, Robertson Smith and Frazer.

Freud found three great themes from Robertson Smith and Frazer irresistible: totemism, taboo, and sacrifice. Freud appropriated these themes into a psychodynamic and psychoanalytic interpretation of the formation of the human self. With Freud, then, we get a psychological *explanation* of why these institutions took the social and historical form that they did. For example, let us recall Frazer's interest in the sacrificial death of the priest at Nemi. Why, Freud asks, is it necessary that the younger

slay the older? Why could it not be the other way round, so that the new priest is older than the former? Are generational jealousies at play here? Or, with Robertson Smith, what motives lie behind rendering totemic sacrifice as a *joyous* communal event? Whose interests are being served thereby?

Let us look at Robertson Smith first. He saw the ideas of totem, taboo, and sacrifice as intimately related to one another. Freud did as well. While he accepted all of Robertson Smith's general conclusions, Freud added something new. Freud believed that he had discovered something with *universal* psychological implications in Robertson Smith's work. Freud believed that all animal sacrifices actually symbolically replayed the earlier religious practices that Robertson Smith found among the Semites. Freud thought the main victim in all sacrificial killing was actually a human being, even if this was not manifest. Freud believed that the victim of the sacrifice was someone who fulfilled the role of father for those who originally did the rite. Like Darwin, Freud actually thought the earliest forms of human society were literally small bands. But Freud went considerably further. He also argued that these primeval bands were mainly composed of desperate young males, deprived of wives, and descended from a common, once powerful and dominant, father. Because the father had monopolized sexual access over the females in the band, the brothers were effectively locked out from realizing their maturity. So resentful and blindly angry did the brothers become that they rebelled *en masse*, and murdered their own father. At last they were able to realize full manhood by taking wives, even if that meant murdering their tyrannical father.

Freud "thought he was right" about the father–son antagonism at the root of the primal human condition for at least two reasons, if not more. The clinical evidence of his individual patients pointed to a primal psychological situation that seems to replay the logic of the primal band's parricide. In the clinical situation, the male child especially suffers deep ambivalence toward his parents. He feels overpowered by them, especially the father. But the male child feels the additional attraction to the nurturing mother's breast. This desire to possess the mother seems to lead to hatred of the father for monopolizing the mother.

When the parental bedroom door closes, the male child is left out, and resents the father's exclusive access to the mother. So the male child is caught between the parents, all the while recognizing his dependence upon them. The male child loves the mother, perhaps too much, but tends to fear the father, even while benefiting from dependence upon him.

Freud also felt he was on to something about the male child–father antagonism because ancient myths confirmed it. The ancient Greek myth of Oedipus tells the tragic story of a boy born of royal parents, who eventually kills his own father and marries his mother. The tale begins with warnings from a soothsayer that Oedipus' birth is inauspicious, because Oedipus is fated to kill his father, the king, and marry his mother. To evade fate, the king abandons the infant to sure death in the wilderness. But as fate would have it, a shepherd happens upon the child, and raises it as his own son into adulthood. One day the king is abroad and meets the adult Oedipus at an impasse on the highway. Neither the king nor Oedipus will yield right of way. A struggle ensues, and Oedipus slays the king who, unbeknownst to him, is his own father. Proceeding to the royal city some time later, Oedipus meets the widowed queen, Jocasta. Mutually attracted to one another, they marry, and produce children of their own. Throughout, neither knows the identity of the other or Oedipus' role in the death of the former king. Once these secrets are revealed, however, the horror of the situation drives Oedipus and his wife-mother into emotional ruin. The queen commits suicide; Oedipus inflicts blindness upon himself in a vain attempt to alleviate his guilt. For Freud, this drama holds many powerful lessons. The most germane for us is its indirect psychodynamic lesson: male children secretly desire to possess their mothers entirely and eliminate their fathers. This is Freud's famous "Oedipus Complex." Let us link the Oedipus story to the dilemma faced by the parricide band of brothers.

Oedipal Consequences

Although the brothers initially rejoiced in their victory over their overbearing father, the deed had unforeseen consequences. Whatever the circumstance, the act of murder, and especially that of one's own parent, cannot lightly be tossed off. On the one hand, at some point, the brothers realized that they had, after, murdered their own father. A father, even an unjust one, is still a father. The brothers responded to their complex feelings of joy and guilt by inaugurating a series of actions designed to embrace both aspects of their ambivalent feelings. These reactions to the primeval parricide set the template for religion today the world over. Responding, first, to their feelings of guilt – of sin – the brothers *repressed* the actual nature of what they did. In an *unconscious* attempt to distract themselves from coming to terms with their egregious act, and as well to make up for their misdeed, they began to revere and honor, and eventually to worship, their dead father – who though now dead was conceived to exist in a heavenly realm above this world. The brothers, in effect, invented *religion* by projecting the image of the dead father into the heavens. Thus were the gods born – in mixed feelings of guilt and shame.

To keep alive the sacred memory of the father, periodic animal sacrifice was inaugurated, later to be identified by Robertson Smith and Frazer as totemism. Since the father had been the head of the band, the totem animal now was also seen as the main symbol of the community. The sacrifice also served some welcome functions. Because sacrifice demanded the giving up of something that was precious to the sacrificers, it functioned to propitiate the guilt of the brothers, and to mitigate their original sin of murder. It was common as well for the successors of the murderous brothers likewise to inflict pain upon themselves in an effort to atone for their crime. This was, from Freud's point of view, how all religions really began, with their nexus of the feeling of guild and sinfulness, the worship of heavenly father gods, bloody sacrifice to them in expiation for sin, and so on.

Freud thought his theory of the primal parricide gave him an answer to why the early sacrifices were jolly communal feasts, as Robertson Smith thought. Since ambivalence reigned over the killing of the father, elements of joy would persist as well as sorrow and guilt. After all, the brothers were now liberated from the demeaning tyranny of the father and free to become fathers and adults themselves. Joy arose partly because in the communal eating of the sacrificial victim, the entire community felt that it had regained union with the father, but on terms more in keeping with their own sense of self-respect and adulthood. It also explained why, at the same time, the totemic sacrificing community would also weep over the animal that they had just killed sacrificially. Ambivalence reigns. While religious devotees surely feel the sense of dependence on and submission to the will of the father characterizing religious attitudes – in Freud's view at least – they feel an abiding sense of joy in communion with the father along with a peace of mind that comes with the acknowledgment of unwavering divine authority.

Mighty Mothers and Their Dying, Risen Sons

Whatever else one may think of Freud's contributions to understanding religion, the extravagant creativity and originality of his interpretations are wonders of the human imagination. Let me add a second example that demonstrates how Freudians can raise interesting questions about the nature of religion. If, for example, we alter the sex/gender identity from male god to female goddess, can Freudian analysis still bring interesting results? Michael Carroll's account of the psychoanalytic origins of the cults of the Great Mother, Cybele, and the Virgin Mary, respectively, is just such an example of a contemporary adaptation of Freudian ideas across the sex/gender line (Carroll 1992). Since Carroll also deals with the same data as Frazer, he also lets us compare two different approaches to religion.

Frazer was always seeking to undermine Christian uniqueness by claiming that early Christians took over – "baptized" – pre-Christian customs, beliefs and practices and simply replaced them with Christian ones. Thus, Frazer tried to show that many of the Catholic saints have an uncanny resemblance to older, pre-Christian – pagan – gods and goddesses, or that the Jesus story of resurrection, say, was patterned on old pre-Christian fertility cults. Perhaps the more poisonous consequence of Frazer's work was how he implicitly argued that pre-Christian religion changed early Christianity as much as Christianity had transformed paganism. As a case in point, Frazer claims that the myth of the god-hero Attis provided just such a prototype for gospel lives of

Jesus. But more than this, Frazer suggests that the content of the Attis myth informed the believing Christian concept of Jesus! Attis and Jesus really meant the same thing – they were both bringers of new life. Carroll argues in like fashion that the Mediterranean image of the Great Mother informed the image of Mary. Was she not Cybele, Attis' mother, mother of god, echoed in the Christian salutation, "Holy Mary, mother of God"?

It is in Frazer's *The Golden Bough* where the story of Cybele and Attis gets considerable attention, because Frazer was so sure that it vividly foreshadowed that of Mary and Jesus. Attis is, like Jesus, the Good Shepherd or herdsman. Like Jesus again, Attis was born to a virgin, or in some other miraculous way. For her part, Cybele is celebrated like Mary as "mother of the gods" and depicted as the Great Mother, a kind of earth mother. As a goddess, she brings life to the land. Mary is correspondingly "full of grace," and God's chosen vehicle for conveying Christ, the giver of divine life, to the world. Pressing the analogies further, Frazer relates that a reasonable consensus of accounts of Attis describe his death in terms of hanging from a tree, his burial as being laid in a sepulcher, and most stunning of all, his *resurrection* shortly thereafter on or about the date of Easter – the vernal equinox! Finally, harking back to Robertson Smith's and Freud's totemic communion notions, the devotees of Attis celebrate and commemorate his death and resurrection with a sacramental meal and communion that Frazer called, in full awareness of the blasphemous implications of the term, a "blessed sacrament." For Frazer, such parallels afforded lavish occasions to indict Christianity, especially Roman Catholicism, as resting – unawares, *unconsciously* – on a template of "primitive" religious practices and beliefs. Despite arrogant claims of Christian uniqueness, both pagan and Christian mythologies fundamentally concern the mysteries and value of life.

The Psychodynamic Origins of the Cult of the Virgin Mary

Unlike Frazer, Carroll's book deals more narrowly on the godly qualities attributed to Mary. He begins with a puzzle. Why is there a cult of the Virgin Mary in Catholic and Orthodox circles at all? For both Catholics and Orthodox, for instance, theology provides an obvious and complete answer. God preserved Mary from carnal "knowledge" of any mere man, and insured that she would remain virgin and sinless, even though she gave birth to Jesus. In a final statement of her quasi-divine status, she did not die a normal death, but was, instead, taken up directly into heaven. There, in heaven, she serves as primary spiritual intercessor between Jesus and humanity, and receives the devotion of the faithful. But Carroll thinks that the theologians have some questions to answer first. Why did these beliefs about Mary, and her "cult" – her worthiness for devotion – only appear 400 years or so *after* the time of Mary and Jesus? No cult of Mary existed until somewhere in the fourth century CE, and then not necessarily for her virginity, or for her being the mother of Jesus. And why, as well, did it arise in particular areas of the southern Mediterranean basin?

Carroll concludes that since the Marian cult thus seems particular to the Roman Empire in the fourth century, as a local historical phenomenon, it calls out for particular causes. Did the cult arise in a particular locale, perhaps? Did it recruit only people of the same sex? In reply, Carroll says that the first devotees of the Marian cult were recruited from populations of rootless young men, typically displaced to Rome for employment from their home provinces in north Africa, Spain, and southern Europe. Strangely enough, it was here that the exuberant and emotional Marian cults first arose as lower-class religious – male – phenomena.

Given their rambunctious and déclassé nature, these new "Marian" Christians didn't always get along with the Christians of fourth-century Rome. For, contrary to conventional thinking, fourth-century Christians tended to be dignified aristocrats, not the "poor of the earth." While the newer Marian forms of religion seemed coarse and overly emotional to the established urban Christians, gradually they welcomed the Marian Christians into the mainstream of Christian life in Rome. After a period of internal struggle for recognition of the Marian cult, the church devised a way to include the new spirituality, as it had so many others – especially if we believe Frazer.

The official triumph of this new Marian spirituality can in fact be dated to two great church councils – Ephesus (431) and Chalcedon (451). Ephesus declared that Mary was what the Greeks called the *theotokos* – the God-bearer. In our parlance, this would be the "mother of God." For Carroll, Mary's elevation to this level in effect made her a kind of goddess. For its part, Chalcedon only accentuated this deification of Mary by promulgating the doctrine that she was eternally a virgin, even after having given birth to Jesus. Mary had thus been miraculously conditioned, and could no longer be regarded as just another person or even just another saint. She was very special. These conciliar declarations marked a kind of legitimation of the Marian cult by, in effect, imbuing her with divine qualities. They marked the triumph of a new spirituality that had swept in from the outer reaches of the empire into the metropole.

At the same time as this legitimation of the Marian cult was under way, Carroll notes that the fourth century also marked the rise of what appear at first glance to be other distinct new religious developments. In fact, Carroll claims, they are intricately linked to the theological and institutional implications of the Marian cult's prominence. For example, the origins of today's controversies over an exclusively male priesthood can be dated to the fourth century in Rome. The exclusion of women from the priesthood was codified in this era. Further, the drive to require male celibacy in the Roman priesthood culminated in the fourth century with its official approval and canonical enforcement. In the fourth century as well, for the first time, the image of the suffering, dying, tortured, crucified Jesus gradually came into prominence. Likewise, sacrificial language increasingly came to be used about the Eucharist. Carroll believes these collateral changes are not at all distinct from the dynamics that gave rise to the Marian cult. For Carroll, their rise and the rise of the Marian cult are one and the same. Well and good, but, how is Carroll going to bring us back to the main point, namely how Freudian theory explains the Marian cult?

The nurture and family situations of these young male devotees of Mary have much to tell any Freudian analyst. Because of economic and political instability in the southern Roman provinces, families were thrown into disarray. Fathers were often absent for significant lengths of time, leaving the women of the household in charge.

And even when the fathers would return periodically from abroad, they found it next to impossible to re-establish male authority in households now accustomed to strong female leadership. Growing up in these conditions of strong, assertive mothers and weak or remote fathers disturbed typical patterns of male socialization. From their earliest years, the young men identified with their mothers, not with their fathers. The mothers were the only available adults to offer these children admirable, constant role models of adulthood. But danger lay in this psychodynamic arrangement for the young men. For example, given the incessant power of the id, they fantasized wishes to possess their mothers sexually, and to monopolize their love exclusively. Their inconstant and bothersome fathers were a sort of irritation. Although seldom home to assert leadership, upon returning home, they stepped back into their roles as lovers of the beloved mothers, now also beloved of these young men. Small wonder that the young men secretly wished to eliminate their interloper fathers altogether, perhaps by murdering them, as the band of brothers in Freud's account of the origins of religion argues.

But of course, in Freud's psychodynamic vision of the mind, an action by the id to seek to possess the mother provokes an equal and opposite reaction by the countervailing forces of the superego. These young men recognized that they could not murder their fathers. The superego excludes this possibility, no matter how jealous they felt toward them. Overcome with guilt for contemplating horrendous parricide, they *suppressed* it deep into their unconscious. With the onset of puberty, these feelings became even more agitated. Deeply embarrassed, they realized how identification with their mothers confused their sexual identities. No young man just coming into his manhood wants to be tagged as a "momma's boy." Indeed, they acted out against being effeminate to the point of developing exaggerated male – "machismo" – personalities. Haunted by internalized female images of perfect adulthood from their pre-pubescent days, they did all they could to tell themselves that they were *real* men. Economic conditions then intervened to force many of these young men into migration to Rome or other large cities, to seek employment. But however much they moved from countryside to town, they could not escape their own minds. They retained the complex of deeply repressed feelings now lodged in the darkest recesses of their unconscious. It was in this dynamic mix of economic and psychological factors that Carroll believed the Marian cult was to find the kind of soil in which it could grow.

On the face of it, Carroll's case differs radically from classic Freudian father-killing and its compensating feelings of guilt. In the Marian case, we have something at least phenomenologically defined as goddess worship, yet without expressions of guilt for having "killed" any mother. Yet Carroll is not deterred. For one thing, we have the Freudian Oedipal desire to kill the father who competes for the mother. For another, we have good psychoanalytic reasons for the young men's deifying the (strong) mother by transferring their worshipful feelings toward her in the form of a goddess. They maintain their admiration for their mothers, but now safely free of incest and real conflict with the father, by projecting their adoration for her to a goddess. Instead, then, of simply adoration of their actual mothers, or seeking union with them, the young men now *projected* their feelings for their earthly mothers onto a supernatural object – a mother goddess. Projection affords them freedom to seek unlimited union with their heavenly mother in a way impossible with their earthly one. Freud might smile on Carroll's theory, so well does it show how deeply suppressed wishes find realization in religion.

Carroll in fact suggests as much. These young men projected their conflicted feelings about their own mothers onto the convenient objects of the goddesses of religion. Among them was Mary, who although theologically not a goddess, nevertheless is one from a purely phenomenological point of view. Like any conventional goddess, she is worshiped, adored, the object of a cult, and can intercede with higher beings. For these mother-identified, father-ineffectual men, Mary, became a safe object of their desired maternal union. Safely preserved beyond access to their sexual advances, in heaven, all the demons of hypersexuality could be kept safely confined. But there were costs, as we will see.

What makes Carroll's analysis of these young Christian devotees of Mary especially powerful is that they were not alone. Nor were Mary, and the

Marian cult, alone among goddesses popularly worshiped in fourth-century Rome. Something universal seems to be at work. In other parts of the empire, a similar psychodynamic was working itself out with other similarly constituted male youths from other parts of the empire's Mediterranean territories – but now in relation to non-Christian mother goddesses, mostly notably in cults devoted to Cybele that Frazer had found intriguing in *The Golden Bough*! Like Mary, non-Christian goddesses were explicitly available for worship, and indeed were so conspicuously to young men with the same psychological profiles as the early devotees of Mary, and as we will also see, worshiped in analogous style. It is in the "style" of the worship engaged in by these youthful male worshipers of the goddess that certain "costs" accrued.

The religious identification of the young men with Mary and other mother goddesses entailed not only fierce, self-administered ascetic behavior, but also extreme forms of self-abuse and masochism. Frazer described in detail, if somewhat prudishly, the spectacular features of this new religion of the goddess. Frazer reports that these devotees to the Great Mother – all men – voluntarily mutilated themselves to the point of self-castration. Frazer reports that "it was on the same Day of Blood and for the same purpose that the novices sacrificed their virility ... they dashed the severed portions of themselves against the image of the cruel goddess" (Frazer 1958, p. 405). Spelling out the gory details, Frazer tells us that these ascetic rites honoring the Great Mother, Cybele, took on a male negating form that would be bound to draw the attention of a Freudian like Carroll: "man after man ... flung his garments from him, leaped forth with a shout, and seizing one of the swords which stood ready for the purpose, castrated himself on the spot." After having done the unmanning deed, the devotee put on "a suit of female attire and female ornaments, which he wore for the rest of his life" (Frazer 1958, p. 406).

These young men had, in effect, become women, and as such constituted orders of eunuch priests, that were well known across the southern portions of the Mediterranean basin and further to the east. We should recall these rites of unmanning when feminists discuss the issue of whether transgendered men ought to be received as women by natural women. Feminist philosopher Mary Daly's comment might be particularly apt in light of the work of Carroll and Frazer: transsexuality is a *male* problem.

The grotesque character of these rites drew the interest of Carroll, and they paint for us a vivid, if gruesome, picture of ways that Freudians think that religion can embody the dark secrets of the unconscious. Romans tell us about the Galli, the emasculated priests of Attis, who seemed commonplace before the end of the republic. These unsexed beings, in their oriental costume appear to have been a familiar sight in the streets of Rome, which they publicly traversed in open procession (Frazer 1958, pp. 404–405).

As Frazer is wont to do, he deliberately suggests that these pagan rites survived in Christianity. Why else would both Christians and pagans celebrated similar festivals on approximately the same dates? The pagan rite was a fertility ritual, occurring on the date of Easter. And is not Easter really a kind of Christian fertility festival, the celebration of the coming of the new life inaugurated by Jesus's resurrection?

Carroll notes that among these devotees of Mary and other goddesses, such as Cybele, we should delve into a correlation that, at first glance, will surprise us. These young men, so eager now to negate their own male sexuality in religious rituals, were the same young males who had displayed their characteristic southern European machismo. The exaggerated form of male assertion had now literally flipped into its opposite – the ascetic and male negation of the devotees of the goddess. For Carroll, this is an invitation to wheel out the Freudian interpretive machinery. To wit, in their particular psychological condition, the young men have repressed their desire to be one with their mothers. First, this is expressed by exaggerated, and doubtless defensive, male behavior. But repressed though their deep desire to be like their mother is, given the right conditions it will emerge. And emerge it does in the gory rites of the mother goddess. Instead of uniting sexually or otherwise with their real mothers, they project that image onto the heavens by worshiping a goddess, like Cybele, or of course, Mary. In order to perfect this ritual identification with the mother some devotees even go so far as to alter their physical bodies to be like women – they remove the marker of the male gender;

they dress in women's clothing, as Frazer notes, and so on.

One last point remains. Although the new Christians may have devoted themselves to and identified themselves with Mary, they certainly do not seem to have engaged in the same self-mutilating, or even sex-denying behavior. Carroll agrees. But this does not mean that Christianity escapes the psychodynamic logic worked out in the fiercer ascetic practices of the Cybele devotees. Indeed, as we know from Max Weber, Christianity does so in many different forms. The other-worldly asceticism of the Catholic monastic tradition, notable for its suppression of sexual activity, as well as the worldly asceticism of Weber's "Protestant ethic," with its strong puritan militancy against sex, are but two cases in point. In both cases, male sexuality is put under wraps and restrained. For Carroll and his kind of Freudian, psychodynamic reasons cause religious experiences, not because of an actual divine calling – either to the contemplative life or to the life of worldly asceticism outside the monastery in capitalist enterprise. Freud, like Carroll, seeks to make an end to religion by discrediting religious experience.

References

Ackerman, R. 1987. *J.G. Frazer: His Life and Work*. Cambridge: Cambridge University Press.

Carroll, M.P. 1992. *The Cult of the Virgin Mary: Psychological Origins*. Princeton: Princeton University Press.

Frazer, J.G. 1958. *The Golden Bough*. New York: Macmillan.

Freud, S. 1938. "The Interpretation of Dreams." In A.A. Brill (ed.), *The Basic Writings of Sigmund Freud*. New York: Modern Library.

Freud, S. 1961. *Civilization and Its Discontents*, trans. J. Strachey. New York: W.W. Norton.

Malinowski, B. 1948. "Magic, Science and Religion." In R. Redfield (ed.), *Magic, Science and Religion*. New York: Doubleday.

Pals, D.L. 1996. *Seven Theories of Religion*. New York: Oxford University Press.

Preus, J.S. 1987. *Explaining Religion*. New Haven: Yale University Press.

Rieff, P. 1979. *Freud: The Mind of a Moralist*. Chicago: University of Chicago Press.

Further Reading

Cioffi, F. 1970. "Freud and the Idea of a Pseudo-Science." In R. Borger and F. Cioffi (eds.), *Explanation in the Social Sciences: Confrontations*. Cambridge: Cambridge University Press.

Fulton, P. (ed.). 2005. *Mindfulness and Psychotherapy*. New York: Guilford Press.

Lévi-Strauss, C. 1968. "The Sorcerer and His Magic." In C. Lévi-Strauss (ed.), *Structural Anthropology*. London: Allen Lane.

Otto, R. 1958. *The Idea of the Holy*, trans. J.W. Harvey. New York: Oxford University Press.

Ricoeur, P. 1970. *Freud and Philosophy: An Essay in Interpretation*. New Haven: Yale University Press.

Skinner, B.F. 1999. "From *About Behaviorism*." In J.S. Crumley (ed.), *Problems in Mind: Readings in Contemporary Philosophy of Mind (I)*. New York: McGraw Hill.

11

Bronislaw Malinowski and the "Sublime Folly" of Religion

Anthropology's Pragmatist

The gnawing effect of the "worm of doubt" that Freud dropped into the midst of religious life is hard to overestimate, since it threatens to eat away at what seems the last solid place of security for religious consciousness – the autonomy of religious experience. If we begin to doubt the integrity of our own inner religious feelings and thoughts, just what safe harbor remains for the pious soul? If even our inmost religious experiences can no longer be trusted, many believers will have come up hard against a very substantial problem of religion indeed. And here I do not single out Christians. The problem of religion provoked by Freudian undermining of confidence in our own introspective powers is perhaps gravest of all for those religious traditions centered about mental cultivation, such as the varieties of Daoism, Buddhism, and Hinduism. Part of the Buddha's claim to authority is to have given us a reliable "map" of the pathways of mind, along with an accurate escape strategy out of suffering and life's dead ends (Strenski 1992). But when the map can no longer be trusted, can the Buddha's exit strategy be?

As I hope we have learned throughout this volume, the story of the impact of problems of religion, such as those thrown up by Freudian ideas and clinical practice, is not, of course, the whole story. In the case of a Freudian critique of Buddhist religious experience, for example, we find clever adaptations of Freudian theory that bolster Buddhist conceptions of how the mind really works, and how Buddhist religious experience fits in (De Silva 1973, 1974). Or there may even be other – non-supernatural – sources of the numinous experience of absolute dependence than Freud's. He saw the source of religious experience in the infant experiences of parental power. But maybe the religious experience of dependence and numinous power arose out of our experience of collective life? Or if Freud can show that religious experiences are really just disguised experiences of a powerful father or mother, does this open the door for Eliade to show that experiences of parental power only hide a transcendent revelation of the sacred?

In the theories of social anthropologist Bronislaw Kaspar Malinowski (1884–1942), Freud's legacy continues. Malinowski was one of the earlier enthusiasts for the psychoanalytic movement within the social science community. He regarded Freud's genius so highly that he sought to have Freud nominated for a 1938 Nobel Prize (Ellis 1936). Despite Malinowski's admiration for Freudian ideas, he never really followed Freud blindly.

Understanding Theories of Religion: An Introduction, Second Edition. Ivan Strenski.
© 2015 Ivan Strenski. Published 2015 by John Wiley & Sons, Ltd.

Malinowski's greatest claim to fame as a Freudian may, ironically, be his criticism of the universality of the Oedipus complex (Stocking 1986, p. 42). Nonetheless, Malinowski believed that the theory of mental operations offered by Freud generally created real and insurmountable problems of religion that he, as a critic of religion, welcomed.

Malinowski also figures in the overall story of the present volume for several other reasons. First, he was an active participant in many of the major theoretical arguments about religion in the late nineteenth and early twentieth centuries. he enthusiastically embraced the phenomenological method of empathy. Indeed, his conception of the empathetic, participant observer grounded his concept of fieldwork based on "participant observation." Malinowski also links us directly to the first generation of anthropologists, such as Frazer, whom he knew personally, but also to the ethnographic traditions of empirical studies of small-scale societies popularized by Tylor and Robertson Smith. In addition to the "English School" of anthropologists, Malinowski embraced the sociologist Émile Durkheim and his school. Malinowski's *Argonauts of the Western Pacific* (1922), for example, left a clear mark on the Durkheimian scholarship, in particular upon Marcel Mauss' classic, *The Gift* (1925). Finally, as major theorist of myth, Malinowski advanced a radical pragmatist view on the nature of myth, engaging familiar figures like Max Müller, Tylor, and others in vigorous debate.

Second, Malinowski is perhaps distinctive in adding an original pragmatist theoretical element. He wants to know how religion does things, how it "works." Taken together with Freudian ideas, Malinowski produces what can be called a pragmatist, pragmatic, or functionalist critique of religious experience. In Malinowski's hands, pragmatism becomes a powerful weapon forcing religion to square its ultimate and transcendent purposes with the observable and measurable results of being religious. Religious people may say all sorts of thing about the transcendent goals of being religious. But what about those we can see, feel, and hear? What are the observable effects, functions, consequences –

intended or unintended – of religion? How do they figure as being the underlying reality of the religious life?

No matter what religious people may *say*, for example, about the other-worldly realities revealed in religious myths and scriptures, Malinowski sees something else entirely. Malinowski, for example, sees myth to be a *practical* tool functioning to enhance real flesh-and-blood human survival. Myths do not really map the transcendent world or offer an escape strategy for eluding eternal death. Myth, in Malinowski's words, is "indispensable" and "vital"– something a society needs – the proverbial crutch without which people cannot materially persist (Malinowski 1992b, p. 82). Myth is thus not really about the other world, but is instead a "hard-worked active force," covering the "whole pragmatic reaction of man towards disease and death" and expressing "his emotions, his forebodings." As such, for Malinowski, myth is practically linked with our basic biological needs (1992b, p. 105). After years of avoiding a frank statement of his beliefs, he finally said, in the 1931 Riddell Lectures, that a "rationalist and agnostic" such as himself, "must admit that even if he himself cannot accept these truths [of religion], he must at least admit them as indispensable pragmatic figments without which civilization cannot exist" (Malinowski 1936, p. 62).

This attitude makes Malinowski a bit of a snob. Malinowski does not believe religion to be literally true. Otto's realm of the numinous, Max Müller's "Infinite" and so on, are false. But these religious images and concepts are much needed for most people to maintain order and a sense of meaning in their lives. Religion thus provides indispensable crutches. And since religion functions to maintain social coherence, we need to keep it to hand – if only for the pragmatic purposes it serves in keeping society from disintegration. As a species, we humans simply cannot do without the fantasies of life after death, personal immortality, divine justice, or eternal blessedness that religion creates for us. As a practical man, despite his own private contempt for human weakness as revealed in religion, Malinowski is determined to conspire in maintaining religion in place. For the sake of social order and stability, after all, it is the only practical thing to do!

Bipolarity in Life and Letters

Knowing where Malinowski's complex thinking comes to rest may not, however, be enough for those who want to understand the madness in his methods. Why did he "think he was right" to interpret religion *functionally* or *pragmatically*? Many critics of Malinowski overlook his move to a hard, pragmatic functionalism from a "softer" humanistic position where empathy was central. Why did he change his theoretical thinking? Understanding why demands that we look at the man within a wider context than simply that of the ideas he advances. Seeing how Malinowski shifted his theoretical ground can, I believe, give us an even greater insight into the heart of his thinking about religion, and perhaps explain what he does. A closer, somewhat Freudian, look into Malinowski's life reveals evidence of what seems an almost clinical bipolarity that is mirrored in both thought and biography. Can we perhaps learn how to fill in the gaps in understanding his bipolar theoretical thinking about religion by seeing it in the context of his personal bipolar turmoil? I shall test this hypothesis in the pages to follow.

Before doing that, however, let me say what I mean by Malinowski's bipolarities. To begin, these are oppositions in his life and work such as those surrounding his upbringing. Beginning in orthodox Freudian fashion with his parental situation, Malinowski was virtually raised in the absence of his father by his mother and her family. Yet, although his mother was his closest companion in his first twenty years, he never shared his most intimate thoughts with her. One is reminded of the young men from father-ineffective families described by Carroll (1992). First, Malinowski does identify with his mother early on, but then as he comes to manhood he seems to suppress this identification. He withdraws emotionally from his mother, and identifies with his remote father's scientific career in folklore studies. Underlining this theme of bipolarity, Malinowski's first avocational calling was to the arts – what some might cast as a career gendered feminine. This is especially so when contrasted to his final decision to seek rigorous training in the more disciplined masculine-gendered fields of philosophy of science, mathematics, and physics at the Jagiellonian University in Cracow. The theme of

bipolar tension between rebellion and conformity repeats itself at yet another level as well: Malinowski fashioned himself into a sober scientist, on the one hand, yet engaged the Young Poland avant-garde movement of the *fin de siècle*. This esthetic and political avant-garde called Malinowski to the satisfaction of his own heightened erotic appetites, which however, he – again – opposed by resisting the total embrace of their debaucheries. Instead, he fixed on a path of strict discipline and a self-imposed regime of ascetic chastisement and purification. Does this choice too reflect a feminine/masculine gender opposition? In religion too, Malinowski engaged an atheistic humanism from an early age, but ironically one that nevertheless taught the identical puritan morality of the Catholic upbringing he sought to escape. And the oppositions do not stop there. Although as urbane and cosmopolitan as any other member of his well-established social class as a member of the gentry, he sought out a career of relative deprivation in a remote anthropological field; while always attached to the ideal of Polish nationality, he wanted above all to be like his acquaintance and compatriot Joseph Conrad, a "British" Pole. Are these data not sufficient to persuade us that some peculiar psychodynamics might have shaped Malinowski's being – including his theorizing about religion?

Perhaps less susceptible to obvious Freudian readings, we can round out our considerations of Malinowski's polarities by noting these others. On the one hand, Malinowski was the consummate professional academic – a teacher of legendary repute at the London School of Economics from 1910 to 1939, the author of a dozen or so books and about fifty or so articles and book reviews, he held forth on subjects as varied as economics, gift exchange, the family, myth, ritual, religion, language, totemism, sexual life and marriage, crime, and magic, all the while being one of the earliest thinkers to engage the problems thrown up by the implications of Freudian thought for social science. Much of his fame derived from promoting his own reputation as founder of the intense and systematic methods of fieldwork that he practiced in his six years of on-and-off study of the native folk of the Massim peninsula of eastern Papua, and in the some of the island groups off the east coast of Papua New Guinea – Mailu Island, the Amphletts, and the Trobriands. On the other hand, there was the active public intellectual of his

London years. Beyond his writing and training in ethnology, he wrote for the wider general reading public on folklore, literary criticism, linguistics, philosophy, psychology, psychoanalysis, religion and, as I have noted, sexuality. He was thus an exciting and provocative thinker – one who tried to combine scientific styles of thinking with the big issues of life and death, and our so-called existential human problems. Such an interesting set of inner contradictions literally calls out for a deeper explanation that I do not pretend to be qualified to offer. But at least, with this in mind, the readers of this book might be enticed to think harder than they might otherwise have been about the deeper meanings of Malinowski's work.

Bringing his professional academic and social activist sides together was Malinowski the teacher and mentor. After his studies at LSE, he put in six years or so of fieldwork despite wartime restrictions upon his travel in New Guinea and Australia. He would return to London in 1920 to begin what would be a two-decade-long association with the LSE. In 1939, while visiting the United States, he had already been entertaining plans to emigrate to America. The advent of World War II forced his hand. During the early 1940s, he lived in New York City, often making trips up to New Haven to give seminars at Yale, while teaching at the New School. He had also begun to do field studies of traditional economies in Mexico. In the year of his death, 1942, Malinowski accepted Yale's offer of an appointment to a permanent professorship there. He was, however, never to assume this post, since he died suddenly of a heart attack in May of that year.

It was in those two decades at the London School of Economics that Malinowski made trend-breaking contributions to women's professional training and advancement at the LSE. So marked is this effort at advancing women in the scientific field of anthropology, and so marked, as we have seen, are the other gender-charged "psychodramas" of Malinowski's life, that one cannot but wonder what a good psychoanalyst would think. Malinowski's youngest daughter, Helena Wayne, noted that her father's efforts in behalf of the dignity of women in the profession of anthropology grew out of a genuine sympathy with his fellow "outsiders" on the opposite side of the gender divide. Malinowski's women students, notes Mrs. Wayne,

had great affection for him not just because he was attractive as a man, as his detractors have said, but because, in England at least, women were not really accepted in academic life, it was still cranky to go to university, and the middle-class woman was expected to be cultured but not really efficient at anything. As Audrey [Richards] put it, there was a horror of the clever woman, but [Malinowski] … didn't have it at all, and women blossomed in this atmosphere of being taken completely seriously. (Wayne 1985, p. 537)

But perhaps Mrs. Wayne just demonstrates the natural tendencies of a loving daughter to enhance the reputation of her father? Did Malinowski's behavior to women perhaps rather underline other paternalistic qualities of his character, so much easier to deploy over a more dependent audience? Or does it represent, perhaps, the avant-garde nurture of his youth, with its egalitarian ethos that became so apparent in his being comfortable in the company of accomplished women – especially when this would have been so unusual in the patriarchal British academic world of those days? But amidst all this celebration of Malinowski's relations with women must come recently revealed accounts of moral callousness in his relations with his own wife and family. First, his moral reputation takes a hammering with his record of incessant philandering. Then, his desertion of his wife and family in the hour of his wife's greatest need, when paralyzed with multiple sclerosis, leave us with the image of moral monstrosity. Such heartless and narcissistic behavior only makes the mystery of Malinowski's fiercely bifurcated personality all the deeper.

Malinowski nevertheless helped the women students in his charge overcome one of the chief internal obstacles working against women in their time – the particularly debilitating self-limiting feeling of which feminist historian of science Evelyn Fox Keller, has written so eloquently – the hard time women in professions had of "taking themselves seriously, being professional" (Keller 1997, p. 25). Perhaps it was because he, like Max Müller, never forgot the wounds inflicted on an outsider in Britain like himself that Malinowski well understood the pain of his women students, and thus did a great deal to lift its burden? Perhaps sympathy for the plight of the outsider explains the marked character of his relations with his women students, although given all the other unusual features of his relation to gendered relationships, one would still like to know what a Freudian and feminist psychoanalysis would turn up.

I note these matters not just for their obvious salience but, as I shall argue in concluding this chapter, also because they fit into the larger pattern of the overall shape of Malinowski's thinking about religion. To venture to interpret or explain them in themselves would take us too far afield. The list of women anthropologists trained and formed by Malinowski includes the likes of Hilda Beemer Kuper, Phyllis Kaberry, Rosemary Firth, Lucy Mair, Monica Wilson, Elsie Clews Parsons, Camilla Wedgwood, Hortense Powdermaker, Margaret Read, and Audrey Richards. What leaps out at us is this: Malinowski was, far more than anyone in his time, the leading scholar-teacher to take a direct, forceful hand in promoting the careers of the entire first generation of women anthropologists. Again, this is a datum that just stands out. I suggest, therefore, that it must be noted.

A Biology of Religion: Survival Fits

Ever the synthesizer, Malinowski made perhaps the first major attempt to integrate Durkheim's functionalist analyses of religion into both Freudian and behaviorist psychologies. In the end, this would produce Malinowski's trademark social psychology of religion. In his 1935 *Coral Gardens and Their Magic*, Malinowski lays out his plans for "reducing Durkheimian theory to the terms of Behavioristic psychology" (Malinowski 1935, p. 236). Of religion, therefore, Malinowski makes a clear and explicit declaration of its practical function in society: "religious faith establishes, fixes, and enhances all valuable mental attitudes." And what does he believe drives this need to establish such an effort to solidify a life? Above all, it is "the prospect of death" that moves people to religious faith and practice. Religion, then, has what Malinowski calls "immense biological value" (Malinowski 1992a, p. 89). Profound denial, driven by a pragmatic obsession about human survival, thus were the secrets of religion's origin and persistence.

Malinowski reaches these conclusion by a series of well-thought-out steps. First, he argued that societies were systematic wholes. As such, they cohered by the cooperation of mutually functioning subsystems, such as magic, myth, politics, religion, and economy. As wonderful as this effort to maintain the integrity of societies was, Malinowski was haunted by the fragility of social arrangements. For him, social wholes were constantly at risk of dissolution, because every social system depended on supporting subsystems that might conceivably fail to do the work required of them (Malinowski 1948, pp. 39–41, 46). Pragmatic or utilitarian as Malinowski's functionalism was, though, it was also haunted by the specter of catastrophe and impending danger. *Every*thing in culture serves – *must* serve – a pragmatic, workaday, or practical function. *Every*thing in culture serves – *must* serve – a useful or utilitarian purpose. Social wholes as organisms teetered on the edge of crisis. Disrupting them in any way risked destroying these cultures, because their sustaining practical or utilitarian functions might be disrupted in the process.

Second, Malinowski linked cultural functions to definite biological needs. No matter what else we may be, Malinowski wanted to impress us with the fact that humans are essentially material, organic beings. As such, our biological needs trump all others. Cultural things, such as religion, were practical, useful, or worked – functioned – *because* somehow they directly corresponded to biological needs. They fulfilled certain organic needs of the human biological unit. As such, so-called religious experiences were no more than expressions of the biological conditions of human beings in crisis, impelled, as it were, by our drive to survive (Malinowski 1948, pp. 51–53). Along with all other life forms, as organisms, we seek to enhance life and to insure our own survival. Our natural, in-born biological natures impel us do those things that will function for our survival. Plants exhibit phototropism – a tendency to grow in the direction of life-giving light to enable their photosynthetic processes. Why, then, should not an intellectually endowed species like *Homo sapiens* exhibit its own "vivo-tropism" – a drive for survival, for enhancing life?

Malinowski seems especially impressed with the incredible intelligence of our species' understanding of biological systems. Together with Freud, Malinowski felt that we fundamentally understand what we need to survive. We do what is right for our survival. We instinctively take appropriate action to protect ourselves from harm and to enhance our lives. We, of course, take simple everyday precautions against danger and risk. But we also minimize the chance of wounds being inflicted upon us. The psychological practice of "denial," for example, would be one way we try to protect ourselves. Freud also wrote of "wish-fulfillment" in the same way. Things may not turn out as we wish, but we cling to the hope that our wishes may be fulfilled. Or we may even deceive ourselves into believing that they are fulfilled in order to overcome the depression of lost hopes. Wish-fulfillment has been so powerful in human history that it has taken the form of the belief that life goes on after death. The idea of a spiritual human soul realizes one of our "wishes" for life eternal. Religions fulfill this wish to transcend death in the face of the counter-evidence. Unless we are deranged in some way, or called to some higher conception of survival, we therefore work for survival. We maximize those behaviors and states of mind that function for our survival, and minimize those that do not. Religion is a principal weapon in the human armory of survival.

Malinowski's originality can be appreciated by the contrast of his approach with what were, at the time, conventionally accepted attitudes toward traditional cultures. His pragmatic functionalism, for example, spelled an end to Tylor's theory of "survivals." Unlike Tylor, Malinowski doubted that institutions, traits, and so could survive their own impracticality, their own irrelevance. If something does not perform its function in society, it will simply not survive – and, thus, it will not turn up as a Tylorian "survival." What Tylor labeled as a survival must, therefore, actually be serving some kind of function. It was the job of the anthropologist to discover what that, perhaps hidden, function was. If put to the test, and challenged by Tylor, Malinowski would try to demonstrate that a function was being performed for the sake of the integrity of a society. Men's neckties might, for example, be seen as Tylorian "survivals." Once they functioned like scarves to keep the neck warm in cool weather, or simply to fasten the collar of a shirt. Now, they are mere ornament, a functionless bit of material culture that has survived, like something washed up on the beach. In that case, Malinowski might retort: Yes, the necktie no longer functions as it did originally to close up the top of men's shirts. But today, even as an ornament, it may serve a social function to assert, and thus to

secure, one's social rank, identity in a certain social circle, membership in an exclusive club, or as a measure of financial position. The "school tie" has a long tradition of doing precisely this. It is no survival, but very much alive as a useful way to do the work of leveraging social position for personal gain. It "functions"!

Death: It All Ends Badly

Often, a telling example can drive home an abstract theoretical point. Malinowski believed his theory of religion could be demonstrated by the example of a funeral rite in a small-scale traditional society (Malinowski 1948, pp. 47–53). The forebodings around death and immortality formed the "very nucleus of all religious belief and practice," claimed Malinowski (Malinowski 1992a, p. 48). So, if we can understand the death–immortality nexus, we can understand religion itself. And what better method to test this thesis empirically or scientifically than by means of close observation (of behavior)? Malinowski's method of intense fieldwork paid attention to what we can see happening in a society. Faced with death, close observation tells us that the survivors fear death. Indeed, in a small society, every death threatens the survival of the entire group. Individual members of the group accordingly suffer palpable stress in the face of such loss. Thus, death is a serious matter that needs to be managed. Otherwise, the psychological – and ultimately physiological – equilibrium of the group is endangered. Malinowski argues that rituals function to manage the stress brought on by the death of one of society's members.

Step by step, here is what Malinowski sees. First, he sees that the death of a lone individual is actually a *social* event: "As death approaches, the nearest relatives in any case, sometimes the whole community, foregather by the dying man, and dying, the most private act which a man can perform, is transformed into a tribal event" (Malinowski 1992a, p. 48).

Second, as "soon as death has occurred," Malinowski sees – observes – the high emotional states of those preparing the corpse. Once exposed to view, "the immediate mourning, begins ... [with] more or less conventionalized outbursts of grief and wailing in sorrow ... The body is sometimes kept on the knees of seated persons, stroked and embraced" (Malinowski 1992a, pp. 48–49).

Third, when the group must part with the corpse, their mood must change, painful as it must be. Malinowski observes a "two-fold contradictory tendency," among the survivors. They do not want to part with their fellow, so they seek ways to "preserve the body, to keep its form intact, or to retain parts of it." But this runs into psychological limits, because it reminds the survivors of death itself. Thus, the folk "desire to be done with it, to put it out of its way; to annihilate it completely," as well (Malinowski 1992a, pp. 49–50).

Four, the desire both to be rid of the deceased and that the deceased remain produces a most remarkable outcome. The belief in the survival of the deceased in *spiritual* form arises. Malinowski believes he has discovered the true origins of the belief in the "soul" or spirit that Tylor's theory of animism attributed to the "savage" need for explanations. Instead, Malinowski claims that powerful, even contradictory, emotions manufacture the belief in spirits or immortal souls. The "mortuary ritual *compels* man to overcome the repugnance, to conquer his fears" of death and the dead. Instead of clinging to the material body, the folk innovate by creating a "belief in a future life, in the survival of the spirit."

Malinowski thinks that emotional compulsion, doubtless rooted in our physical natures, determines that we imagine a life beyond the grave. Humans are "hard-wired," so to speak, to push the idea of oblivion out of their minds, and instead create the belief in personal immortality. In the mortuary rite, says Malinowski, "*direct emotional forces* [are] created by contact with death and with the corpse." In turn, these emotions "function" or, do their own work, to manufacture "the idea of the spirit, the belief in the new life into which the departed has entered" (Malinowski 1992a, p. 50; my emphases). Malinowski concludes his behaviorist account of the origin of the belief in immortality in the oddest kind of way – in pure Freudian style. He states that our *desires or wishes* for immortality produce our belief in an afterlife. Wish-fulfillment emerges out of the deep unconscious to be fulfilled in reality.

Fifth, and finally, when Malinowski asks why all this should be as he has seen, or observed it, his answer is again Freud merged with an appeal to a surging wave of the biological drives. Describing the pathetic attempt to deny humanity's dark fate, Malinowski sets the scene. "Grasping at it, man reaches the comforting belief in spiritual continuity and in the life after death." So we are back once more with Freud seeing in religion the pathetic expression of an immature desire to have our fantasies fulfilled. "Thus the belief in immortality is the result of a deep emotional revelation, standardized by religion, rather than a primitive philosophic doctrine" (Malinowski 1992a, p. 51).

In sum, then, Malinowski believed religious behavior could be explained by the inability of humans – simply as biological systems – to accept death. Our innate biological will to live resists dwelling upon the certainty of our end. We *must* deny the reality of death. Denial therefore generates – as a biological reflex alone – both the *belief* in immortality and the concomitant religious *experiences* that confirm this belief (Malinowski 1948, p. 51). Religious doctrines and experiences mask the inevitability of this grim reality. In religion, we find "the embodiment of the *sublime folly* of hope, which has yet been the best school of man's character!" (Malinowski 1948, p. 90; my emphasis). From his superior position, Malinowski "knew" that ordinary folk could not face the finality of death. They therefore needed religion. They cooperated in their own self-deception by being religious. Common folk fulfilled their fondest wishes in their religious beliefs and practices. In his 1931 Riddell Lectures, Malinowski made all this blatant: religious beliefs, such as belief in immortality, are "indispensable pragmatic figments without which civilization cannot exist" (Malinowski 1936, p. 62).

Malinowski Thinks He Knows All This because of Freud

But why does Malinowski "think he is right" to believe that religion reflects wish-fulfillment for an endless life, for immortality? I think we need to acknowledge both Freud's intellectual and his existential impact on Malinowski. The power of the Freudian id was felt palpably by Malinowski, because he *lived* it (Young 2004, p. 124). From an intellectual point of view, Malinowski's familiarity with the leaders of avant-garde movements sympathetic to Freudian ideas about sex is well established. Malinowski befriended sex theorists like Henry Havelock Ellis, and acknowledged him in his book, *The Sexual Life of Savages*. This was followed by books echoing Freudian notions, such as *Sex and Repression in Savage Society* (1927). Freud's daring and wide-open explorations of the dynamics and dilemmas of sexual life compared favorably with those of Ellis for their frankness about this taboo subject.

Yet Malinowski rebelled from a strict Freudianism by denying the universality of the Oedipus complex. Malinowski's fieldwork taught him that Freud went wrong in his *Totem and Taboo*, where he "assumes the existence, at the outset of human development, of a patriarchal family with a tyrannical and ferocious father who repressed all the claims of the younger men" (Malinowski 1992c, p. 56). Malinowski's field studies in Melanesia revealed that families do not conform to Freud's patriarchal model. In eastern New Guinea, for example, Malinowski shows how different things can be, when "the mother and her brother possess ... all the legal *potestas*" – *not* the father. Instead, it is the "mother's brother [who] is the ferocious matriarch." The father, on the other hand, "is the affectionate friend and helper of his children." Malinowski thus concludes authoritatively that "none of the domestic conditions required for the sociological fulfillment of the Oedipus complex ... exist in the Melanesian family of Eastern New Guinea" (Malinowski 1992c, p. 56).

The undertones of these words hint at the troubled nature of Malinowski's relation with his own father, and thus at his receptivity to Freud and special sensitivity to the Oedipus complex. A recent biographer states that "Malinowski was inclined to see his own father ... [as] pompous, wooden, tactless" (Young 2004, p. 19). Add to Malinowski's estrangement from his father that he was especially close to his mother and his many doting maternal aunts, and the deeper reasons for his attraction to Freud are obvious. Malinowski remained so closely attached to his mother that even in his thirties he vacationed alone with her for months at a time. By contrast, as a youth, Malinowski had little to do with his father practically, and even less to do with him emotionally. The Oedipal circumstances of Malinowski's own youth are not the only factors that help us understand his attraction to Freudian theory. His sex life seemed troubled to the point

of disaster. His positioning between his very different parents may account for his bipolarity. He seemed tormented, but nonetheless thrilled, by his adventures with the unruly power of the libido. At once riding its wild energies and, at other times, trying to wrestle it into submission, his infatuation with libido and his attempts to repress it are perennial themes in his personal diaries. It is no wonder, then, that he was magnetized by Freudian ideas – and here for their existential, not intellectual, value. Freud offered Malinowski mature meditations on the causes of wild oscillations between libidinal desire and asceticism that tormented him throughout his life. Thus, although Malinowski often gave free rein to his id, he swung strongly in the direction of asceticism. He had officially rejected his ascetic Roman Catholicism at an early age, but he perhaps never totally freed himself from its imperatives. Recall that Freud, too, admired asceticism for it contributions to "civilization," as did Max Weber for its creation and maintenance of capitalist economic structures. Malinowski was as torn as these two in his own way. He believed, along with his mentors in the science of sex, that indulgence in his insatiable id would cause his career to suffer. Here, reflecting the same values his ascetic father manifested, Malinowski scorned being an indulgent wastrel of no particular intellectual achievements. His ego needed to learn the lessons of self-restraint and to redirect his sexual energies toward his career. In the suppression of his wilder eros-driven nature, Malinowski was able to create – at least for stretches of time – a successful professional scientific identity and a conventional married family life, complete with house and children. He became his father's child.

The "Phenomenological" Malinowski?

What I have outlined so far are the main elements of Malinowski's better-known or what we might call his "mature" theory of religion. But returning to the theme of bipolarity once more, this would be a good time to note that Malinowski's behaviorism (and, perhaps, even his Freudianism) marked changes from an earlier, more humanistic theoretical position, closer to our phenomenologists of religion. At one point early in his career, Malinowski articulated a nice statement of the interpretive, saying that what he seeks in facts is *the insider's point of view, the "native" meaning and understanding* of their situation, not causal explanations delivered from on high:

> details and technicalities acquire their meaning in so far only as they express some central attitude of mind of the natives …
>
> What interests me really in the study of the native is his outlook on things, his *Weltanschauung*, the breath of life and reality which he breathes and by which he lives … a definite vision of the world, a definite zest of life. (Malinowski 1961)

In this, Malinowski seeks nothing less than access to the subjectivity of the natives. He seeks "to grasp the native's point of view, *his* relation to life, to realize his vision of his world … We must study what concerns *him* most, ultimately, that is, the hold which life has on him" (Malinowski 1961, p. 25). Statements such as these seem to echo the work of late nineteenth-/early twentieth-century anti-positivist philosopher, Wilhelm Dilthey. He articulated central features of phenomenology – empathy, understanding, and such. This "echo" seems to be a true one, since Malinowski is reported to have read and absorbed the works of Dilthey directly from his writings. Malinowski was also exposed to Dilthey indirectly from studies with Leipzig experimental psychologist and budding social psychologist Wilhelm Wundt.

The humanist episode in Malinowski's theoretical career was not to last, as we know from his later embrace of scientist behaviorism. In his last book, he consigns empathy to the methodological trash heap as "dangerous guesswork," in what must be one of the wildest swings of the intellectual pendulum even for so "bipolar" as personality as we have seen Malinowski to have been (Malinowski 1944, p. 23). Upon assuming a position in the British intellectual world at the LSE, Malinowski had to adapt to its norms. The British social scientific establishment was generally inhospitable to talk of "empathy" and other such Continental concoctions. Therefore, Malinowski seems to have adapted the justification of intense fieldwork to the British empiricist tradition. Now, instead of appealing to the intellectual authority of Dilthey's humanism, he appealed to the behaviorism that flattered British empiricist traditions. In coming to London, Malinowski, in effect, adapted his theoretical style to the empiricism of Hume and Tylor.

Malinowski, Sex/Gendered?

Partly to conclude this discussion of Malinowski, but also to anticipate my discussion of feminist theories of religion, I wish to probe the issues of sex/gender salience in Malinowski's methodological approaches. What I mean is that some philosophers of science argue that the interpretive method, as Malinowski expounded it in his phenomenological moments, reflects a "feminine" approach to knowledge. By contrast, a causal or behaviorist approach, boasting its "objectivity," is a "masculine" approach.

Historian of science Evelyn Fox Keller tries to link sex/gendered methodologies in science with a sex/gendered life. For example, Keller suggests that an interpretive approach *may* indicate a "feminine" gendering of explanatory styles, while a behaviorist one, the opposite. This is not to fall into the trap of saying that women are creatures of feeling and intuition, and thus "naturally" favor empathetic or interpretive modes of human inquiry. Nor does she accept that men are objectifying and "scientific," and thus "naturally" favor "hard," "masculine" modes of inquiry such as behaviorism or "linear" cause–effect explanations. Instead, we can make such links only in certain contexts.

For example, it would be significant if a male were to champion those methods of inquiry conventionally marked as "feminine." Malinowski did this in promoting his empathetic interpretive method of understanding other cultures in a context where a causal, positivistic model was the norm. He ran counter to the stereotype of the way a *male should do science*. That may be why his first book, *Argonauts of the Western Pacific*, was rejected by some thirty publishers before finding a home. Another example comes from Fox Keller's book on the great American biologist Barbara McClintock. Keller shows how hard it was for McClintock to buck the male-dominated profession's ideas of the "right" kind of methodology. She wanted to sell an "empathetic" approach to life forms to her profession, dominated by males. Were their different approaches only products of the pure scientific mind at work, or were sex/gender factors at work in the culture of the life sciences dictating positivist, objectivist models of scientific objectivity (Keller 1983)? McClintock's proposals were dismissed as "soft" and "feminine" because they didn't conform to the model selected by the male culture of the biological sciences as the right one.

In suffering an analogous fate to McClintock, the Malinowski of *Argonauts*, with its empathetic methods, was scorned by the empiricists, positivists, or behaviorists in charge. Thus, Keller is right to be skeptical of those who would say that their approach is "scientific" and "objective" because subjectivity is ruled out. Ironically, the later Malinowski contradicted his earlier self and treated people without considering their "subjectivity" – without considering the meaning their acts had for them. Behaviorists and the later Malinowski suffer from what Keller calls "the *objectivist illusion*" (Keller 1996, p. 30). By contrast, the earlier Malinowski and McClintock attempted to "question the very assumptions of objectivity and rationality that underlie the scientific enterprise" (Keller 1996, p. 30). In doing so, they seek to "legitimate those elements of scientific culture that have been denied precisely because they are defined as female" (Keller 1996, pp. 32, 35).

I am, then, suggesting that Malinowski might have "thought" about society in the way he "lived" the differences between what his mother and father meant to him. Along with Evelyn Fox Keller I am placing gender squarely within the cultural and social domains – and thus within the ambit of the familial socialization of both men and women. This would include not only Malinowski's relations with his parents and his unusual (but apparently above-board) relations with his women students, but also his maneuverings to install himself in the foreign world of British academe. Given the severity of these primarily intellectual oppositions that I have called Malinowski's "bipolarities," Malinowski seems to have given us an open invitation to treat him to some of the same psychoanalyzing that he freely dispensed to his native subjects. This, in part, is the approach I have taken in looking at his study of religion.

References

Carroll, M.P. 1992. *The Cult of the Virgin Mary: Psychological Origins*. Princeton: Princeton University Press.

De Silva, P. 1973. *Buddhist and Freudian Psychology*. Colombo: Lake House Investments.

De Silva, P. 1974. *Tangle and Webs: Comparative Studies in Existentialism, Psychoanalysis, and Buddhism*. Kandy, Sri Lanka: T.B.S. Godemunne & Sons.

Ellis, H. 1936. Letter to Malinowski, 1936. Bronislaw Malinowski Papers, Manuscripts and Archives, Yale University Library.

Keller, E.F. 1983. *A Feeling for the Organism: The Life and Work of Barbara McClintock*. San Francisco: W.H. Freeman.

Keller, E.F. 1996. "Feminism and Science." In E.F. Keller and H.E. Longino (eds.), *Feminism and Science*. New York: Oxford University Press.

Keller, E.F. 1997. "Developmental Biology as a Feminist Cause?" *Osiris*, 2nd series 12: 16–28.

Malinowski, B. 1927. *Sex and Repression in Savage Society*. London: Routledge.

Malinowski, B. 1935. *Coral Gardens and Their Magic*, vol. 2. London: Allen & Unwin.

Malinowski, B. 1936. "The Foundation of Faith and Morals." In B. Malinowski (ed.), *Sex, Culture and Myth*. New York: Harcourt, Brace & World.

Malinowski, B. 1944. *A Scientific Theory of Culture and Other Essays*. Oxford: Oxford University Press.

Malinowski, B. 1948. "Magic, Science and Religion." In R. Redfield (ed.), *Magic, Science and Religion*. New York: Doubleday.

Malinowski, B. 1961. *Argonauts of the Western Pacific*. New York: E.P. Dutton.

Malinowski, B. 1962. "On Sir James Frazer." In B. Malinowski (ed.), *Sex, Culture and Myth*. New York: Harcourt, Brace & World.

Malinowski, B. 1992a. "Magic, Science and Religion" (1925). In R. Redfield (ed.), *Magic, Science and Religion and Other Essays*. Prospect Heights, IL: Waveland Press.

Malinowski, B. 1992b. "Myth in Primitive Psychology" (1925). In R. Redfield (ed.), *Magic, Science and Religion and Other Essays*. Prospect Heights, IL: Waveland Press.

Malinowski, B. 1992c. "Psychoanalysis and Anthropology" (1923). In I. Strenski (ed.), *Malinowski and the Work of Myth*. Princeton: Princeton University Press.

Stocking, G.W. 1986. "Anthropology and the Science of the Irrational: Malinowski's Encounter with Freudian Psychoanalysis." In G.W. Stocking (ed.), *Malinowski, Rivers, Benedict and Others: Essays on Culture and Personality*. Madison: University of Wisconsin Press.

Strenski, I. 1992. "Gradual Enlightenment, Sudden Enlightenment and Empiricism." In I. Strenski (ed.), *Religion in Relation: Method, Application and Moral Location*. London and Columbia: Macmillan/University of South Carolina Press.

Wayne, H. 1985. "Bronislaw Malinowski: The Influence of Various Women on His Life and Works." *American Ethnologist* 12: 529–540.

Young, M.W. 2004. *Malinowski: Odyssey of an Anthropologist, 1884–1920*. New Haven: Yale University Press.

Further Reading

Frazer, J.G. 1926. Letter to Bronislaw Malinowski, 14 February 1926. Bronislaw Malinowski Papers, Manuscripts and Archives, Yale University Library.

Frazer, J.G. 1936. Letter to Bronislaw Malinowski, 13 August 1936. Bronislaw Malinowski Papers, Manuscripts and Archives, Yale University Library.

Keller, E.F. 1989. "Just What Is So Difficult about the Concept of Gender as a Social Category? (Response to Richards and Schuster)." *Social Studies of Science* 19: 721–724.

Keller, E.F. 1996. Excerpts from Two Lectures on Human Biology. Sydney, Australia.

Lévi-Strauss, C. 1942. "Souvenir of Malinowsky." *VVV* 1: 45.

Sarzin, A. 1996. "Evelyn Fox Keller: Templeton Lecturer." http://archive.today/soQqm.

Stocking, G.W. 1995. *After Tylor: British Social Anthropology, 1888–1951*. Madison: University of Wisconsin Press.

Strenski, I. 1982. "Malinowski: Second Positivism, Second Romanticism." *Man* 17: 766–771.

12

Seeing God with the Social Eye: Durkheim's Religious Sociology

Think Group!

Whether it be Freud, the Freudian Malinowski, or the behaviorist Malinowski of chapters 10 and 11, each has tried to explain religious experience, and hence, religion, solely in terms of the individual. To that extent, it does not matter that the focus of Freud and the Freudian Malinowski rests on internal unconscious psychological dynamics. Nor does it matter that the gaze of the behaviorist Malinowski falls upon the logic of stimulus and response fundamental to the mechanics of all organisms. These explanations of religious experience focus solely upon the hard reality of the individual human person.

From the concrete individual, Freud and Malinowski feel that they can explain groups. To explain religious *institutions*, such as sacrifice, guru-ship, temple prostitution, sacred times and spaces, initiations, prophecy, sacraments, rituals, sin and expiation, and so on, we need only understand the individuals participating in them. Or to explain religious collectivities, such as churches, movements, *ummas*, Chosen People, totemic clans, brotherhoods, sodalities, *sanghas*, covens, cults, sects, priesthoods, religious orders, *varnas*, and such, we need only study their individual members. The dynamics of a group is just a multiple of the experience of a sufficient number of individuals. That is why psychologist Michael Carroll "thinks he is right" that he can make sense of the entire Marian cult simply by reference to the psychological dynamics of individuals. Malinowski likewise "thinks he is right" about the belief in immortality emerging from funeral rites the world over because he knows individuals fear death.

Émile Durkheim (1858–1917) thinks that the best strategic level to access religion is through the group, since the group makes the individual, not the other way round. Durkheim looks at religion with a social eye, and contributes a sociological apperception to our academic, non-theological, and "scientific" study of religion. He wants to explain religion as much as Freud or Malinowski, and not just understand it. However, he does so by seeking the sociological determinants of religious behavior. Durkheim is, if not the first, then one of the most powerful proponents of a holistic, social, sociological, or collective way of explaining the religious world.

How would the Durkheimian social causality of religious experience look? Think of the immersion of a believer in a religious group – say at a revival meeting – and how it shapes the consciousness of the believer. The Durkheimians believe that we experience an Otto-like mysterious power because of the feelings generated by being in a group. Think of how being at an electrifying concert, or

Understanding Theories of Religion: An Introduction, Second Edition. Ivan Strenski.
© 2015 Ivan Strenski. Published 2015 by John Wiley & Sons, Ltd.

a thrilling football game in a vast stadium, can make us feel connected to a source of energy superior to the everyday. "Under the influence of collective enthusiasm," says Durkheim, people "are sometimes seized by a positive delirium which compels them to actions in which even they do not recognize themselves." In addition, even in more mundane circumstances, he adds, when people "live a communal life, the very fact of their coming together, causes exceptionally intense forces to arise which dominate them exalt them, give them a quality of life to a degree unknown to them as individuals" (Durkheim 1975a, p. 183). Durkheim thus reverses the causal priorities of the Freudians and Malinowski by saying that what we experience or feel going on "in our heads" – especially, religious experience – comes from our participation in groups.

Contrary to conventional views, Durkheim was far more than a sociologist. His conception of sociology actually merged history and philosophy. He was also a leading pedagogical and moral theorist. He owed a lot to ethnography, too. Together with Malinowski, Tylor, Frazer, and Robertson Smith, he studied small-scale societies largely for what they could tell us about ourselves. Durkheim also led an active public life, writing patriotic tracts during World War I and championing charitable relief efforts for Jews fleeing the Russian pogroms of the early twentieth century. As a leading defender of Captain Alfred Dreyfus, the Jewish artillery officer falsely accused of treason, Durkheim championed human rights. For these reasons, and because he felt that the study of religion was central to his own career, there is hardly another theorist to match his importance for us.

One of Durkheim's earliest books, *Suicide* (1897), shows us how his sociological approach made religion pivotal. There, he argued that the frequency of suicides was not just because individual people arbitrarily happened to take their lives. Individual psychology did not give him an answer as to why some people committed suicide and others did not. Although the suicide at first seems "to express only … personal temperament," this is an illusion. Suicides "are really the supplement and prolongation of a social condition" (Durkheim 1951, p. 299). Therefore, Durkheim looked to available social causes. Rich people seemed as prone to suicide as the poor. So

poverty seemed to have nothing to do with the occurrence of suicide. Further, people of both sexes committed suicide at the same rate. So Durkheim turned to religion as a factor. There, something interesting turned up. It seemed that we could correlate suicide rates with membership in certain religious social groups. Durkheim discovered that something about the collective conditions of being a member in certain religious groups caused or discouraged suicides. "The conclusion from all these facts is that the social suicide-rate can be explained only sociologically," concludes Durkheim.

Based on rigorous statistical surveys that made allowances for other variants, Durkheim discovered that the more collectively minded Catholics and Jews of his own day suffered much lower rates of suicide than their Protestant peers. Why should this be so? Durkheim reasoned that the collective character of Catholic and Jewish life was the key variable in accounting for these differences in suicide rates. There seem to have been emotional costs inherent in the life that French Protestantism – mostly Calvinist – created. Catholics and Jews were somehow inoculated against the scourge of suicide suffered by French Protestants. That lonely, heroic individualism of the Calvinist/ capitalist entrepreneur, struggling to overturn traditionalism, of whom Weber wrote, apparently paid a price for material success. Because the capitalist often disrupted comfortable social conventions, the entrepreneur would also make enemies, and lose both friends and social support. Weber mostly talks about the confidence and revolutionary energies of the Calvinist capitalist. He says little about the darker side of this new life of worldly asceticism. It was left to Durkheim to bring out how the loneliness of individual capitalists might well make them vulnerable to the psychological preconditions of depression that lead to suicide. So convincing were Durkheim's results that he set out on course that would lead him to take religion seriously, and in doing so, become one of the giants in our field.

Life and Times

Born *David* Émile at Épinal in Lorraine in 1858, Durkheim was descended from a long line of rabbis. Yet the teenage Durkheim abandoned

Jewish religious practice shortly after completing primary school. Under the influence of his secular education and the rising patriotism of the period just following the 1871 loss in the war against Prussia, he made French nationalism into a kind of personal religion. He revered the ideals of the French Revolution and its Declaration of the Rights of Man and of the Citizen so much so that they seem to have eclipsed his sense of distinct Jewish identity. He was thus repelled by the notion of the Jews as "a people apart" (Lukes 1972, p. 627), and avoided being seen as Jewish, even if that meant to be singled out as a Jewish success story.

These feelings of Durkheim's did not, however, mean that he hated his Jewish roots, or that he shunned the companionship of Jews. Like other dissident Jews of his day, Durkheim distanced himself from Jewish practice and belief yet maintained solid relations with prominent Jewish academics, as well as with much of the spirit of the liberal Judaism of his day. Of those Jewish scholars who enjoyed his respect, the chief talmudic scholar of his age, Rabbi Israel Lévi, stands out. Of liberal French Jewish scholarship, the "Science du Judaïsme" (Scientific Study of Judaism) also bears mention. Science du Judaïsme was for French Jews what the Higher Criticism of the Bible was for Christians. Indeed, the Science du Judaïsme recognized our old friend, Baruch Spinoza, as a forebear. It advanced the same ideals of scientific scholarship that animated Durkheim and his team of sociological co-workers (Strenski 1997, ch. 4).

Durkheim was like a significant number of liberal French Jewish intellectuals in another way as well. His reverence for the French Enlightenment's universal values of social justice rang true to traditional liberal Jewish piety of the day. In the minds of liberal French Jews, the prophets of the Hebrew Bible preached the same lofty ethical values. In the most important learned journal of Jewish studies in France, the editors in fact defined French Judaism as showing a native "Jewish universalism" that bore the "imprint of the French spirit" (*Revue des études juives* 1880, p. vii). James Darmesteter, the principal proponent of the liberal universalist Judaism of Durkheim's era, went further. He felt that the central values of Judaism and the Enlightenment were identical. This should remind us of Robertson Smith, who,

like Darmesteter, declared the epitome of Judaism to be the so-called "prophetic faith." In doing so, Darmesteter, like Smith, celebrated the Jewish prophets as idealist ethical reformers over against the "primitive" and "materialistic" ritualistic religion of the ancient Semites. To Darmesteter, then, this liberal modern Judaism could lay a valid claim to being the religion of a modern France (Réville 1892, p. 256). Touches of this religious liberalism, characteristic of many French Jewish scholars, may have helped Durkheim "think he was right" in attacking religious literalism in his address to the Free Thinkers and Free Believers, as we will see later.

Like many a talented provincial youth, Durkheim left home to pursue further studies in Paris. In doing so, he became socialized into an entirely new life. There, he attended most prestigious schools and elite institutions of higher learning in the Third Republic. In Durkheim's case, he would advance to the illustrious École Normale Supérieure, where the instructors (*instituteurs*) staffing the nation's secondary schools (*lycées*) were trained – this was no mere institution of practical pedagogy. Durkheim excelled in philosophy and history, elite subjects which he would later teach in French secondary schools.

Durkheim's years at the École Normale Supérieure (1879–82) fitted him for the new life he would lead among France's intellectual and cultural elites. Among his classmates were future luminaries such as the philosopher Henri Bergson and the great statesman, the socialist Jean Jaurès. Academically, Durkheim was greatly influenced by the "scientific" history of Gabriel Monod and even more perhaps by the historian of Roman religion and domestic rituals, Numa Denis Fustel de Coulanges. Among philosophers, Durkheim favored the neo-Kantianism of Émile Boutroux. He also followed Alfred Espinas, who along with Boutroux taught the independence of different levels of being. These thinkers constituted the internal context of Durkheim's thinking, that helped him "think he was right" about the primacy of the social over the psychological. This internal context of intellectual influences made it easier for Durkheim to share the idea of the existence of independent – irreducible – realms of human reality with the Dutch phenomenologists of religion, to which he was somewhat attracted. Durkheim "thought he was right" to argue that society could not be explained in terms of either biology or psychology, much less economics, in part because he had been socialized in an intellectual context in which such notions were dogma.

Another vital part of the internal context of Durkheim's formation was the philosopher Charles Renouvier. The leading disciple of Immanuel Kant in France. Renouvier preached the Kantian ideal of the sacredness of the human individual. For Durkheim as for the Kantians, the human individual could not be used as a means to an end. The individual was a sacred being, and as such was always an end, and never a means. People could not, therefore, be sacrificed, say, to "save face" for the state, as Durkheim's enemies argued in the Dreyfus case. Alfred Dreyfus was a captain in the French army who was accused of passing secrets to the German enemy. Wrongly convicted, he was sentenced to a horrid exile on Devil's Island in the Caribbean.

The case came to a head when the army refused to absolve Dreyfus of guilt, even after he was proven innocent. The army argued that Dreyfus must be sacrificed so that the nation could save face. The greater common good surely took precedence over the fate of a single lone individual, like Dreyfus. There could be no greater offense against Durkheim's Kantian ethic of commitment to the human individual, so he and others came to the defense of Dreyfus. Durkheim in particular argued publicly that the French nation risked contradicting its own historic commitment to human rights by refusing to admit its error in convicting Dreyfus. It was wrong that this individual man should die for the sake of the nation. France stood for the sacred value of the human individual, as did Kant and Durkheim's great teacher, Charles Renouvier.

Durkheim's involvement in philosophy had its practical side too. Following the normal practice for graduates of the École Normale Supérieure, his first job was teaching philosophy for several years a number of provincial secondary schools, interrupted by a short state-sponsored study tour of German universities (1885–86). In 1887, his growing acclaim enabled him to be appointed to the faculty of the University of Bordeaux in a position, created especially for him, in social science and pedagogy. In Bordeaux, Durkheim began to develop an interest in ethnological topics, such as totemism, and also religion.

In 1902, Durkheim moved to the University of Paris, as Professor of the Science of Education. There, he organized his famous team of young thinkers, who were to become the troops in Durkheim's battle for a revolution in sociology. Together, they worked to produce the famous review annual, L'Année sociologique. Two of Durkheim's closest co-workers were his nephew, the Indologist Marcel Mauss, and the historian of ancient European religions, Henri Hubert. Durkheim's location in Paris placed him in the thick of the struggles over the future of the Third Republic against its Catholic adversaries. In the capital, he also produced the work for which he is justly most famous, The Elementary Forms of the Religious Life (1912). He died on the eve of the end of World War I, considerably wounded in spirit by the death of his son, André, on the field of battle, but writing what he considered would be his masterpiece, a book to have been entitled La Morale.

Durkheim's Theory Begins with Problems

More than any other factor, I shall argue, Durkheim's passionate, indeed religious, devotion to and love of the French nation and its special values accounts for much of why he "thought he was right" to address religious questions. For most of his formative years, France was in the throes of a national depression. The Prussians had soundly routed the armies of Napoleon III in 1871, and had taken as their prize the cherished eastern départements of Alsace and Lorraine. A mood of national humiliation and desire for revenge plagued the nation. The young Durkheim grew up in this French eastern territory. As an early teen, he felt the shame of national defeat when he witnessed the forces of the Kaiser marching in triumph through his hometown. These events seemed to have magnetized him into a certain religious devotion to France. His loyalties to the Judaism of his own family and to his upbringing took a back seat to this patriotic enthusiasm. This theme of nationalism as a religious phenomenon recurs in Durkheim's writings, and is one of the lasting contributions of his thinking to the study of religion.

Love of country also may have motivated his first book, *Suicide*. Recall that the problem of establishing a secure and viable social order in modern France troubled Durkheim. The rash of suicides in this period indicated that society was falling apart. How could France hope to maintain social cohesion so that it could continue the fight against an enemy as strong as Germany? However, at the same time, how could France preserve its dedication to the rights of the individual? Could the energy of often divisive French individualism be channeled into preserving a cohesive society where individual liberty flourished? I am saying that Durkheim's concern for well-being of his country explains in substantial part why he "thought he was right" to assert the value of sociability, but in a special way that also affirmed individualism.

As for French sociality, the Catholic appetite for collective duty and the need to overcome selfishness in the face of national need impressed Durkheim. However, the Roman Catholic tendency toward authoritarianism ruled out going along with the Catholics. Closer to Durkheim were the republican liberals. They defined France as embodying the ideals of the Enlightenment and the French Revolution. They proposed a France consisting of a freedom-loving people, individualistic, and thus in politics republican, democratic and devoted to the Declaration of the Rights of Man and of the Citizen. In economics, the liberals were also pledged to capitalist or market economics, because they gave freest reign to the initiative of the individual entrepreneur. Despite its economic individualism, the republican tradition was nevertheless intensely *nationalistic*, deeply patriotic and, thus, devoted to a national social life. But while Durkheim favored the liberal love of individualism, he could not abide their giving unfettered freedom to the individual in all domains of life. He preferred to create an ethic of social responsibility by persuading the leading *liberal* professional classes to wield their power for the good of the whole society (Durkheim 1957, 1962) He believed that France needed some sort of reconciliation between the values of community and of the individual.

Durkheim worked out his middle way between the extremes in a remarkable intervention into the Dreyfus Affair, his essay, "Individualism and the Intellectuals" (Durkheim 1898). His involvement in that crisis seemed to give him the confidence that he was right in proposing a kind of social individualism. In this essay, Durkheim wound up celebrating the sacredness of the individual, but as a social value knitting together French society; and he supported the human rights of Dreyfus against the attacks of radical right-wing Roman Catholics. Significantly, Durkheim does not – rightly or wrongly – defend Dreyfus on the basis of his being a Jew. Rather, he argues that Dreyfus' being a human individual grants him a dignity that transcends political purposes. Indeed, all citizens of France shared in that common dignity. After all, the defenders of Dreyfus, like himself, were the kind of individualists who actually strengthened national solidarity, since their individualism was entirely French – given its origins in the Enlightenment and the French Revolution. "Thus the individualist, who defends the rights of the individual," says Durkheim, "defends at the same time the vital interests of society" (Durkheim 1975b, p. 69). Indeed, Durkheim argued, the core value of respecting the integrity of individual differences was perhaps the *only* national collective value imaginable in a divided nation like France.

> There is one country among all others in which the individualist cause is truly national, it is our own; for there is no other whose fate has been so closely bound up with the fate of these ideas … We cannot therefore renounce it today, without renouncing ourselves, without diminishing ourselves in the eyes of the world, without committing real moral suicide. (Durkheim 1975b, p. 69)

Durkheim thus argued that the proposed right-wing and Catholic policy that would sacrifice Dreyfus might save face for the army, but it would also violate the national values of the dignity of the human individual as a sacred being. If Dreyfus were proven guilty, let him suffer the consequences. But if, as now appeared to be the case, Dreyfus was innocent, then let him enjoy the freedom due to any individual of a republic like France. Sacred in his capacity as an individual Dreyfus had an absolute right to justice. However, the sacrality of the individual did not appear out of thin air. The human person was sacred because the French *believed* it to be so. Individualism was an entirely social value. Durkheim's rhetorical defense of individualism as a religion at the height of the Dreyfus case not only affirms the generally positive place that religion has in his worldview, but also shows how cleverly he tried to balance the social and individual sides of life.

However, what of the larger question mark that usually hangs over the head of Durkheim – the relation of society to God (or religion)? We might well see Durkheim's point of view that French social values invest belief in the integrity and sacredness of the individual with authority. However, we then might naturally want to ask whether he felt that all religions were likewise indebted fundamentally to society. The standard story is that Durkheim is a simple sociological reductionist, who believes that all references to God or other sacred beings are only mistaken references to society. However, I think this is a crude caricature. Durkheim has been misjudged about his supposed sociological reductionism of religion as badly as he was about his supposedly collectivist suppression of the individual.

God Is Really Society, but Society Is Really Godly

Durkheim's thinking about the relation of religion and society presents us with an intriguing ambiguity. He can be read *both* as reducing God to society, and as asserting that society had an essentially religious – "godly" – core. Durkheim's was a far more creative mind than the standard reductionist interpretation suggests. Here is why. First, I will outline the reductionist reading. In *Elementary Forms of the Religious Life*, Durkheim says quite explicitly that "society has all that is necessary to arouse the sensation of the divine in minds" (Durkheim 1915, p. 236). Reminding us of Otto, Durkheim claims that "society also gives us the sensation of a perpetual dependence" (1915, p. 237). Society indeed has a special "aptitude … for setting itself up as a god or for creating gods" (1915, p. 244). More eloquently even, in 1914, Durkheim used the occasion of a meeting of French thinkers from opposite sides of the religious divide – the agnostic or atheist Union of Free Thinkers, and a corresponding liberal, mostly Protestant, body of traditionally

religious folk, the Union of Free Believers – to engage the relation between religion and society. To the Free Believers, Durkheim seemed at first to offer cold comfort for their faith. He seemed to assert an uncompromising sociological atheism in these words: "above and beyond all the dogmas and all the denominations, there exists a source of religious life as old as humanity." In addition, that is social life, or as Durkheim spells it out, "the fusion of consciences, of their communion in a common set of ideas, of their co-operation in one work." However, anticipating the objections of the pious believers, Durkheim tries to allay their fears: "You may think, no doubt, that this religious life is not enough," namely that society does not suffice to satisfy human religious longing. Believers may think "that there is another one, which is higher, which springs from an altogether different origin." However, Durkheim counters that society can be a sufficient object of our religious inclinations. In addition, its powerful presence can be experienced in the here and now: "there exists in us, outside us, religious forces which … [exist] by the mere fact of coming together, thinking together, feeling together, acting together" (Durkheim 1975a, pp. 185–186). For Durkheim, therefore, experiences of a transcendent God can be doubted. But we can achieve a common mind about the social nature of religion because we have direct experiences of society that *feel* like an experience of God. Society "gives us the sensation of a perpetual dependence," says Durkheim. It overwhelms us, commands us, creates in us a feeling of obligation and sacrality for its holy objects, such as the human individual (Durkheim 1915, p. 237).

Expressed as a relation of identity, the society–God identity can be represented as "God ≡ society" – God is (really) society. I will call this D1 (Durkheim #1). It stands for a first – sociological reductionist – reading of Durkheim's view of the relation between religion and society. "God ≡ society" means that the underlying reality of an experience of God – religious experience – is really society! Methodologically, this implies that we can study religion by studying its social causes.

However, consider another – *non-reductionist* – reading of the God–society identity. Remember, Durkheim deliberately created ambiguity by referring to his sociology of religion as a *sociologie religieuse* – a *religious* sociology! As an identity relation, the God–society identity would be read as "society ≡ God" – society is really God, or godly. This relation is D2 (Durkheim #2). This identity expresses nothing less than that society has a religious – *godly* – nature! What could this mean?

Let's return to the meeting of the Free Thinkers and Free Believers. Remember that, there, Durkheim challenged the atheists of the Union of Free Thinkers as vigorously as he had earlier confronted the Free Believers. First, he dispels charges that religion is a mere illusion, such as we might associate with Freud (*The Future of an Illusion*) or Marx. Religion, Durkheim asserts, "has been too widespread throughout humanity and is too established to be illusory. An illusion does not last in this way for centuries" (Durkheim 1975a, p. 183). Why does Durkheim "think he is right" about this? He thinks that religion is not an illusion, at least because he thinks that "religion is not only a system of ideas, it is above all a *system of forces*." Durkheim's idealism, his spiritualism, dictates that religion is not just a scheme of abstractions. Says Durkheim, "The man who lives according to religion is not only one who visualizes the world in a certain way." Instead, the religious person "is above all a man who feels within himself a *power* of which he is not normally conscious, a *power* which is absent when he is not in the religious state." Religion is a felt reality, immaterial, yet nevertheless real because people *feel* it – live it in their *experiences*: "these forces must be *real*; they must *really be there* inside me" (Durkheim 1975a, pp. 182–183; my emphases). I cannot leave Durkheim's engagement with the Free Thinkers and Free Believers without at least calling attention to his appeal there to part of the program of the phenomenology of religion – empathy. He tells, indeed lectures, his agnostic audience: "what I ask of the free thinker is that he should confront religion in the same mental state as the believer." Presto, empathy! Durkheim urges empathy for purely scientific reasons: "it is only by doing this" – empathizing – "that he can hope to understand" religion. "Let [the unbeliever]) feel it as the believer feels it." For unless one does so, one "cannot speak about it! He is like a blind man trying to talk about colour" (Durkheim 1975a, p. 184). I would submit that these are not the words of a crude reductionist. They may be those of a shrewd and sophisticated (somewhat confused) one, of course. And if so, they capture something elemental in Durkheim's approach to religion.

The Spirit Is Willing

In contrast to Malinowski, for instance, Durkheim sees society as something of its own – a collectivity constituted and directed by "spiritual" – immaterial – forces. No society can exist without such immaterial, spiritual forces to maintain it and the psychological health and integrity of individuals. Reading the society–religion identity as D2, then, means that, unlike Malinowski, Durkheim was no materialist. His outlook is profoundly spiritual – although not at all theistic. Accordingly, Durkheim says: "Nothing is wider of the mark than the mistaken accusation of materialism which has been leveled against us." Instead, he says, "social life is defined by its hyperspirituality." By "spiritual," he does not mean Tylor's animism. He is instead saying that society is like our mental life, our consciousness, "but elevated to a very much higher power, and in such a manner as to constitute something entirely new" (Durkheim 1974, p. 34). Society is like a group mind, like the feeling of unity experienced in moments of ecstatic community, such as at concerts, sporting events, with ones we love, and so on. Does not the phenomenon of sports fans, sitting comfortably before their TV sets screaming that "*We* won!" – when they are miles from the game – tell us something about the magical nature of social identification discovered by Durkheim? The fans and the team become *one*. The fans have achieved what can well be called a *spiritual* unity with the team. Readers will not be surprised that, in reviewing *Elementary Forms*, Malinowski accused Durkheim of bringing in non-scientific ideas. To the materialist, behaviorist Malinowski, Durkheim's "society" was something "metaphysical" that lacked "any empirical meaning" (Malinowski 1962, p. 287). Malinowski was right. But at the same time, that means that branding Durkheim a crass reductionist, or materialist, falls short of the mark.

As a bonus, Durkheim's spiritualist outlook offers an alternative to Tylor's animist concept of soul. Durkheim said that the human soul, for example, could not be reduced to matter, or to innate psychological endowments. Tylor, Freud, and Malinowski, take note! On Durkheim's view, the human soul was simply the presence of society in us. Doesn't the experience of guilt and conscience just reflect internalized social norms that dominate us? The notion that we had souls was not a brute or primary psychological fact of life for Durkheim, as it was for Tylor. For Durkheim, people felt that they had souls because being human meant living in groups, and living in groups meant having norms imposed upon the members. Thus, Durkheim shared with Weber the view that what moved the human world were our common consensus *norms* and *values*.

Durkheim's *Sociologie Religieuse* Explains Religion in General

Just from the foregoing conclusions one can get some idea of the vast scope and sophistication of Durkheim's thinking about religion. Let me, nevertheless, venture an interpretation of what makes his theory of religion tick. Again, whether or not Durkheim is correct in his thinking about religion, as I interpret him, we need to keep sight of our goal of asking *why he thought his theory of religion was right*. How was it, then, that Durkheim imagined that he could say with equal conviction that "God is really society" and that "society is really godly"?

First, Durkheim believed he could make sense of religion in modern, complex urban societies studying small-scale, so-called "primitive" societies. His focus on modern urban society might confuse some, since his great masterpiece, *The Elementary Forms of the Religious Life*, is ostensibly about the small-scale, totemic religious life of aboriginal Australian folk. Underlining the message of the title, Durkheim says, "In this book we propose to study the most primitive and simple religion which is actually known, to make an analysis of it, and to attempt an explanation of it" (Durkheim 1915, p. 13). Yet if readers proceed to the bottom of the same page, Durkheim seems to reverse himself: "The man of to-day ... There is nothing which we are more interested in knowing." Quickly reassuring his readers that he has not strayed off into the world of exotic primitivism, Durkheim says, "we are not going to study

a very archaic religion simply for the pleasure of describing its peculiarities and its singularities." Rather, he promises to keep faith with his interest in the big sociological issues. He sought "an understanding of the religious nature of man, to show us an essential and permanent aspect of humanity" (1915, p. 13). This grand universal aim of his scholarship proceeds, however, by Durkheim's "method of elementary forms." Understanding this conception of the study of religion is essential to understanding what Durkheim has to say about the nature of religion, and why he feels he is right to say it.

The Durkheim of *Elementary Forms* was convinced that cultural and social things grew or developed out of previous stages of growth and development. Recalling Tylor, Robertson Smith, or Frazer, he too believed that every cultural phenomenon relied on an enabling level of cultural development. Durkheim felt that we owed a debt to the past. For him, the past acts by creating the present. In one of his more beautiful moments of reflection on human life, Durkheim asks rhetorically: "Indeed what do we even mean when we talk of contemporary man, the man of our times?" Are we only talking about "today's Frenchman" as "distinguished from the Frenchman of former times"? Not so, say Durkheim: focusing only on the present "cannot really give us a picture of the whole of modern man." Beyond and behind this surface man lies another: "for in each one of us, in differing degrees, is contained the person we were yesterday." And, further, those "past personae predominate, since the present is necessarily insignificant when compared with the long period of the past" (Durkheim 1977, p. 11).

This existence of the past in the present has certain consequences for how we should study religion. "How can we fail to realize," Durkheim asks in a somewhat mystical moment, reminiscent of Freud on the "primal horde," "that we contain within us hidden depths where unknown powers slumber but which from time to time may be aroused according to the demands of circumstances?" Such an intimation has *methodological* consequences. Beyond the study of the present done solely in terms of the present, we need to adopt a *historical* point of view. The proper study of the present-day "us" requires taking account of the historical "them" of the past.

Like the other evolutionists, Durkheim too embraced the view that our actual historical ancestors led lives analogous to those of the peoples of present-day small-scale societies. Both occupied the same evolutionary level of development. Thus, both in the conditions of our ancient ancestors and in the modern-day "primitives," we could discern cultural traits of religion, for instance, of an *elemental* or *simpler* sort. What Durkheim therefore learned from Australia could, he reasoned, be *analogously* applied to our own cultural ancestors. "We" were only more complex, more developed or built-up versions of the elemental "them" – whether "they" be the folk from old Brixham cave or the Australian outback. Durkheim felt that he could thus understand and explain the complicated "us" – as he and his contemporaries assumed we were – better by looking at the "simpler" "them." In reports of aboriginal religion in the Australian outback, Durkheim therefore thought he had data about the conditions of all humankind, since he believed that in Australia he had found the most "primitive" of all religions.

"Their" Secret Is Sacrifice

However, how is this method of "elementary forms" brought to bear on Durkheim's theory of religion? The approach I have been trying to teach in this book entails asking why a theorist "thought they were right" in going down a certain path. Answers to this question may, in turn, arise from considerations internal to a line of thinking, typically to the world of ideas circulating in a certain field of study or academic profession. But the external context of a thinker's life – the political, cultural, social, religious world in which they live – may also incline a theorist to "think they were right" to advance a given theoretical idea. In Durkheim's case, the external social and political problems afflicting the France of his day would carry significant weight. Threats to national integrity presented by Germany, the twin, but opposed, dangers posed by right-wing Catholic attacks upon individualism and the threat of reckless individualism in the form of anarchism and social unrest, not to mention the social malignancy of suicide – all these informed the context defining the prime of Durkheim's life.

I suggest that he "thought he was right" about religion because his thinking about religion was worked out in relation to this complex of social and political issues. The method of "elementary forms" gave Durkheim a device for thinking through these interconnected problems. In a nutshell, Durkheim thought that simpler – "primitive" or "elementary" – societies might have had ways of managing problems analogous to our own. If so, then, we might try adapting some of the solutions to our own time. So, for example, if, as was the case, France suffered from an epidemic of suicides, perhaps we could learn the secret of preventing suicides from those societies which lacked them?

Despite his evolutionist tendencies, Durkheim thought that the so-called primitive, or small-scale, societies surpassed modern societies in achieving a high degree of social cohesion. He thought that if he could identify the "elementary" institutions small-scale societies used to secure coherence, then perhaps modern folk could adapt "primitive" social technologies for their own use. *The Elementary Forms* is the book he wrote in order to show how aboriginal Australian society achieved a degree of social cohesion that might serve as a model for modern France. If *Suicide* taught us that anomie and lack of social cohesion could *cause* suicide, then what could Australian aboriginal society teach us about how to prevent it?

Durkheim would argue that the social cohesion of aboriginal society somehow seemed to be a function of the elaborate sacrificial ritual and religious life of these people. However, why should this be so? It had always been clear to Durkheim that religion was a unifying force within society. It embodied the common values to which all members of society subscribed. However, how did sacrifice fit into this picture? Durkheim had, for example, studied Robertson Smith's *Lectures on the Religion of the Semites* carefully. Smith's book seems to have lent Durkheim an especially helpful hand in conceiving the nature of so-called "primitive" religion in such a way that some of Durkheim's questions were beginning to get answered. Smith impressed upon Durkheim the idea of the religions of small-scale societies as consisting in ritual practices, rather than systems of beliefs or moral norms. Perhaps, Durkheim reasoned, social cohesion was more a matter of achieving a kind of consensus of practice or morality, rather than risking the danger of trying to find uniformity in beliefs. Durkheim's admiration for Smith may have been one reason he "thought he was right" to doubt the long-term value of being literal-minded about religious beliefs or scriptures. In the modern world, it was very difficult to achieve the necessary consensus about religious beliefs, if we took them literally rather than symbolically. Regarding religious dogma, Durkheim queried, "why should we be confined to its literal expression? Words have no meaning in themselves ... and even the most sacred texts need interpretation" (Durkheim 1975c, pp. 27–28). For this reason, Durkheim welcomed those Free Thinkers and Free Believers who were "willing to interpret dogmas more symbolically," those for whom the "essential thing is not the letter of these formulae but rather the reality they hide and which they all express inexactly to a greater or lesser degree." With them, "there is hope of conversation across the gulf separating believer and skeptic." There is the prospect of real religious dialogue (Durkheim 1975a, pp. 184–185).

As a consequence of his critique of belief-based religion, Durkheim became open to the non-cognitive parts of religion, of which Robertson Smith had written. In turn, he became open as well to non-cognitive means of attaining social solidarity. This move to grasp the power of non-cognitive – in fact, ritual – means of creating social solidarity offered an answer the questions left hanging from Durkheim's early book, *Suicide*. People who *lived* together in groups, as Catholicism and Judaism encouraged, rather than as lone individuals, as Protestantism favored, inoculated themselves from suicide.

It was then only a small step for Durkheim to take in the direction of Robertson Smith's view that small-scale societies and their religions were constituted by *ritual actions*. Smith singles out two: totemic worship and sacrifice. In Smith's mind – and thus in Durkheim's – these rituals constituted the bulk, if not the totality, of religion at this "primitive" stage of religious evolution. Governed as well by elaborate systems of taboo and the sacred, and marked by concerns about physical matters, such as purity and pollution, these religions seem to have assembled an armory of weapons to ensure social solidarity. Robert Alun Jones has even suggested that Durkheim's

idea of religion as a locus of forces is owing to the influence of Robertson Smith (Jones and Vogt 1984, pp. 47f, 55).

But this then just pushes the inquiry along another step. Why should *sacrificial* ritual actions be so potent in achieving social solidarity in small-scale societies such as those of aboriginal Australia? Much of Durkheim's gravitation to sacrifice and an appreciation of its social power had to do with Robertson Smith too. We might recall that Smith argued that in the earliest phases of Semitic religion, sacrifice *celebrated* community and kinship between humanity and the gods. "When men meet their god, they feast and are glad together, and whenever they feast and are glad they desire that the god should be of the party." Smith argued, as well, that the oldest Semitic sacrifice was far from any bribe of the deity or palliation of the gods out of fear. "This view is proper to religions in which the habitual temper of the worshippers is one of joyous confidence in their god, untroubled by any habitual sense of human guilt" (Smith 1923, p. 255). Sacrifices marked a special, pre-eminently *social* time when gods and their devotees enjoyed kinship with each other. There is little need to wonder why Durkheim would not find such a sketch of human society attractive. Perhaps modern society should adapt similar festivals to promote social solidarity? Durkheim says as much when he reflects upon the wondrous unity of spirit that prevailed, say, in the French Revolution:

> This aptitude of society for setting itself up as a god or for creating gods was never more apparent than during the first rears of the French Revolution. At this time, in fact, under the influence of the general enthusiasm, things purely laical by nature were transformed by public opinion into sacred beings: these were the Fatherland, Liberty, and Reason. A religion tended to become established which had its dogmas, symbols, altars, and feasts. It was to these spontaneous aspirations that the cult of Reason and the Supreme Being attempted to give a sort of official satisfaction. (Durkheim 1915, pp. 244–245)

But how precisely was modern France, or indeed any so-called "modern" society, to recapture the methods of achieving social unity described by Robertson Smith in aboriginal Australia and which manifested themselves for a time in the French Revolution? Did modern society need to revive ritual sacrifices? One of Durkheim's wilder intellectual offspring, Georges Bataille, for example, planned to institute human sacrifices in the Place de la Concorde in the heart of Paris. Bataille reported that there was no shortage of willing volunteers for these sacrificial spectacles! Bataille's extremism raises the question of how close the analogy between sacrificial ritual and its modern adaptation need to be. Durkheim adapted ritual sacrifice to modern circumstances. This required the reinterpretation of sacrifice into a qualitatively modern cosmology. For Durkheim, the appropriate modern-day analogy to some ritual sacrifice like the *Intichiuma* would lie in the domain of morals and public ethics – not in the kind of Surrealist neo-primitivism of the likes of Bataille (Strenski 2002).

But there is more. Sacrifice was as well a joyous alimentary sacrament of communion linked to totemism. It was what Durkheim called the "positive cult," similar the "merry sacrificial feast" of Robertson Smith's Semites (Smith 1923, p. 257). In *Elementary Forms*, Durkheim appealed to the *Intichiuma* rite to demonstrate this "positive" cultic pattern of sacrificing the totem-god, followed by a totemic clan communion meal. The *Intichiuma* offered aboriginal Australians renewal and revival of their cherished values. However, notably, this revival of society was not achieved by sermons full of words or allegiance to creeds. Durkheim – like Smith – believed ritual acts, not doctrines or beliefs, fulfilled these purposes in a way appropriate to their "primitive" status. The "negative cult" was, by contrast, one that focused on interdictions or taboos, upon asceticism and a kind of dreary self-denial. They were not aimed specifically at facilitating kinship or communion – society – between gods and humans, but at keeping sacred and profane separate from each other, and in this way protecting the sacred from dangerous pollution. Summing up, Durkheim declares his preference for the positive priorities of the religious life: "Whatever the importance of the negative cult may be, and though it may indirectly have positive effects, it does not contain its reason for existence in itself ... it supposes this

more than it constitutes it." He asserted a positive view of the way religion and sociability reinforce once another:

> Men have never thought that their duties towards religious forces might be reduced to a simple abstinence from all commerce; they have always believed that they upheld positive and bilateral relations with them, whose regulation and organization is the function of a group of ritual practices. To this special system of rites we give the name of *positive* cult. (Durkheim 1915, p. 366)

But one feature of Durkheim's attitude to sacrifice is often overlooked. In Durkheim's view, sacrifices, such as the *Intichiuma*, were made to *pre-existing* deities. In sacrificing – killing and eating – the totemic animal, the devotees connect with a "sacred principle residing [already] in it" (Durkheim 1915, p. 378). Durkheim, however, changed his mind about the relation of the ritual to the deity (Jones 1981, pp. 191–196). In *The Elementary Forms of the Religious Life* Durkheim also offered a *second* theory of sacrifice, borrowed from Hubert and Mauss. The new theory trumped the first, and became Durkheim's mature view of sacrifice's relation to the gods. There, Durkheim turns Smith's view that sacrifice is offered to a pre-existing god or gods on its head. Sacrifice creates and sustains the gods! Sacrifice is "independent of the varying forms in which religious forces are conceived" (Durkheim 1915, p. 385). This makes the gods dependent upon humans, since, for example, the gods are often conceived as being fed by people with food offerings in sacrifice. Thus, Durkheim tells us that the gods cannot do without worshipers any more than society cannot do without individuals (Durkheim 1915, pp. 388–389).

One huge consequence of this reorientation takes us to the heart of Durkheim's theory of religion. Since sacrifice literally makes the gods, sacrificial ritual, in effect, *produces* the sacred. Accordingly, the sacred is not a natural and pre-existent condition of certain things, which, for example, sacrifice only stirs up or revives (Durkheim 1915, pp. 378–381). With the *Intichiuma* in mind, Durkheim tellingly adds that the animal sacrificed "*ordinarily acquires this [sacred] character artificially in the course of sacrifice*" (Durkheim 1915, p. 378; my emphasis). Similarly, not only does ritual make the gods, but so also does belief. Gods are gods because we *believe* them so to be (Durkheim 1915, p. 386). Do Apollo or Zeus still live? Would Yahweh or Allah continue to exist, if they were forgotten by people, and not worshiped? We will see shortly how some seek to restore the goddess to her proper place in the heavens. But doing so, demands she be worshiped, not just made part of an intellectual argument! And that is what some of our feminists, like Carol Christ, will do.

Thus, when we read closely the crucial second chapter of the third book of *The Elementary Forms*, we see that it must be read as a treatise on the sacred. *The Elementary Forms* is at once a treatise on the social aspect of religion as well as on the religious aspects of society. There is no religiousness – no sacredness, no sense of obligation, no respect, no authority, no energizing force moving human beings to concerted action – outside the force field generated by society. So also there is no society without a sense of sacredness: there are no boundaries, moral forces, proscriptions, inspiring ideals, respect, and so on outside the domain of sacredness. This interest in the social and sacred is why, I submit, Durkheim devoted the core of his great book to what he called the "positive cult."

Tying together some loose ends, we can now see how *The Elementary Forms* shows not only how a traditional Australian aboriginal society was welded into a coherent whole, but also how its modern analog – civic sacrifice or duty – might insure France's integrity. In virtually his last work, then, Durkheim completed the answer to the question he had raised at the start of his career in *Suicide*. How can our modern, complex, and largely secular societies attain analogous levels of social solidarity to that enjoyed by small-scale Australian aboriginal societies, sufficient to prevent their self-destructive malaises? The answer to Durkheim's question comes from all the way down under in the Australian outback: *sacrifice!* Not only is sacrifice a "giving of the self," and by virtue of that, a counter-agent to the modern egoism that lay at the root of suicide, but it is also a powerful rite that creates, at the same time, the sacred. This, in its turn, puts the spiritual back at the center of social life as well. The meaning of the word "sacrifice," we will recall, is rooted in its Latin form – *sacra-ficium* – a "making holy." If we want to restore a measure of wholeness to our society, we need, says Durkheim, to restore some sense of rising above our own individualities to embrace common values that we hold sacred – that form the consensus that binds us together. We need a way to protect against *desecration* – our *sacred*. We need, in effect, a "religious" core at the center of our lives.

References

Durkheim, É. 1915. *The Elementary Forms of the Religious Life*, trans. J.W. Swain. New York: Free Press.

Durkheim, É. 1951. *Suicide*, trans. J.A. Spaulding and G. Simpson. New York: Free Press.

Durkheim, É. 1957. *Professional Ethics and Civic Morals*, trans. C. Brookfield. Westport, CT: Greenwood Press.

Durkheim, É. 1962. *Socialism*, trans. C. Sattler. New York: Collier Books.

Durkheim, É. 1974. "Individual and Collective Representations." In *Sociology and Philosophy*. New York: Free Press.

Durkheim, É. 1975a. "Contribution to Discussion 'Religious Sentiment at the Present Time.'" In W.S.F. Pickering (ed.), *Durkheim on Religion*. London: Routledge & Kegan Paul.

Durkheim, É. 1975b. "Individualism and Intellectuals." In W.S.F. Pickering (ed.), *Durkheim on Religion*. London: Routledge & Kegan Paul.

Durkheim, É.1975c. Review of Guyau, *L'Irreligion de l'avenir* (1887). In W.S.F. Pickering (ed.), *Durkheim on Religion*. London: Routledge & Kegan Paul.

Durkheim, É. 1977. *The Evolution of Educational Thought: Lectures on the Formation and Secondary Education in France*, trans. P. Collins. London: Routledge & Kegan Paul.

Jones, R.A. 1981. "Robertson Smith, Durkheim and Sacrifice: An Historical Context for *The Elementary Forms*." *Journal of the History of the Behavioral Sciences* 17: 184–205.

Jones, R.A., and P.W. Vogt. 1984. "Durkheim's Defence of *Les Formes élémentaires de la vie religieuse*." In H. Kuklick (ed.), *Knowledge and Society: Studies in the Sociology of Culture. Past and Present*, vol. 5. Greenwich, CT: JAI Press.

Lukes, S. 1972. *Émile Durkheim*. New York: Harper & Row.

Malinowski, B. 1962. Review of *Elementary Forms of the Religious Life*. In B. Malinowski (ed.), *Sex, Culture and Myth*. New York: Harcourt Brace.

Réville, J. 1892. Review of Darmesteter's *Les Prophètes d'Israël*. *Revue d'histoire des religions* 25: 253–256.

Revue des études juives. 1880. "A nos lecteurs." *REJ* 1: vii.

Smith, W.R. 1923. *Lectures on the Religion of the Semites*. London: A. & C. Black.

Strenski, I. 1997. *Durkheim and the Jews of France*. Chicago: University of Chicago Press.

Strenski, I. 2002. *Contesting Sacrifice: Religion, Nationalism and Social Thought in France*. Chicago: University of Chicago Press.

Further Reading

Bossy, J. 1982. "Some Elementary Forms of Durkheim." *Past and Present* 95: 3–18.

Chantepie de la Saussaye, P.D. 1904. *Manuel d'histoire des religions*, trans. H. Hubert and I. Lévy. Paris: Armand Colin.

Filloux, J.-C. (ed.). 1970. *Émile Durkheim: La Science sociale et l'action*. Paris: Presses Universitaires de France.

Jones, R.A., and N. Gross (eds.). 2004. *Durkheim's Philosophy Lectures: Notes from the Lycée de Sens Course, 1883–1884*. Cambridge: Cambridge University Press.

Mauss, M. 1967. *The Gift: The Form and Functions of Exchange in Archaic Societies*, trans. I. Cunnison. New York: W.W. Norton.

Strenski, I. 2003. *Theology and the First Theory of Sacrifice*. Leiden: Brill.

Weber, E. 1959. *The Nationalist Revival in France, 1905–1914*. University of California Publications in History 60. Berkeley: University of California.

13

Mircea Eliade: Turning Back the "Worm of Doubt"

A Real Religious Radical

Mircea Eliade (1907–86) was the most influential comparativist and interpreter of religion of the modern day. Almost singlehandedly, he established the study of religions in North America. And if any theorist in this book is radically religious, Eliade is. The depth of Eliade's religiosity perhaps played a role in making it natural for him to "think he was right" about resorting to modes of argument for studying of religion that approach the religious in nature. I would even suggest that he sincerely believed that he could achieve a common mind about religion by proceeding from points of view and styles of argument that seem, as we will see, typically religious.

Someone classically trained in mystical traditions, Eliade recalls Max Müller's affection for "The Infinite" and "The Unknown." For his part, yoga and tantra, rather than German Romanticism, informed Eliade's mystical vision. Venturing to India to sit with gurus in the foothills of the Himalayas when few Westerners did, Eliade seems never to have abandoned his youthful metaphysical spirituality. Hindu monism, especially *Advaita Vedānta*, guided much of Eliade's philosophical orientation. His tutor in Calcutta from 1928 to 1931, the great Surendranath Dasgupta, taught that the only true reality is the one underlying

holy power, *brahman*. The everyday world is a mere illusion – *māyā*. From the point of view of the internal context of Eliade's thought, this neo-Hindu religious orientation seems to hold a key to understanding much of what makes his theory of religion cohere. For Eliade, achieving a common mind about religion will depend a good deal upon the ability of readers to buy into the assumptions underlying his religious orientation.

The religious structure of Eliade's thinking clashes radically and systematically with the empirical epistemological and ontological foundations of the modern secular world. And this accounts for the difficulties certain so-called "secular" thinkers (I include myself here) have with Eliade's theory of religion. For Eliade, ordinary means of knowledge and experience are not only flawed, but really spread a veil of *māyā* over reality. Eliade's life-long commitment to a radical form of "new religious consciousness," moreover, laid the foundation for his study of religion. As Robert Bellah and Walter Capps, respectively, noted, Eliade's approach to the study of religion was motivated by the desire to play a key role in "stimulating new religion" (Bellah 1978, p. 111; Capps 1978, p. 103). Eliade is perhaps, then, the most radical student of religion we have met because he is an earnest "maker" of religion. For this reason, as the title of this chapter indicates,

Understanding Theories of Religion: An Introduction, Second Edition. Ivan Strenski.
© 2015 Ivan Strenski. Published 2015 by John Wiley & Sons, Ltd.

I allude to the image of the "worm of doubt' – that metaphor signaling the slow gnawing away of religious vision and faith brought on by modern trends of secularization. One way to look at Eliade's approach to the study of religion is, then, as a deliberately (and contrary) religious assault on secularity – a turning of doubts about religion into doubts about secularity at its very roots. I therefore devote this chapter to addressing how Eliade approaches religion from this radically – for him – religious perspective, and why he "thinks that he is right" in doing so. Not surprisingly, my story of Eliade's revolutionary "History of Religions" begins with his paradoxical assault on the historical study of religion.

An "Antihistorian of Religion"

During the course of this book, I have underlined the immense contribution made to the study of religion by the historical disciplines. Historical criticism of the Bible, Max Müller's historical philology of Indo-European languages, myths, and religions, Max Weber's "religious history" of modern capitalism, all speak loudly of these benefits. Eliade, too, seems to want to join in this common mind about how to study religion by referring to his approach as *history* of religion. The "historian of religions *sensu stricto* can never ignore that which is historically concrete," says Eliade, and adds that "religious documents are at the same time historical documents" (Eliade 1959, p. 88). Fine. But as I shall show briefly, he really doesn't mean to be a historian. Thus, having tipped his hat to history, Eliade wags his finger at "historical" methods of treating religion. He "thinks he is right" so to do, because he believes religion itself transcends the plane of everyday – historical – being. For Eliade, the object of the study of religion lies beyond historical reality. Therefore, the student of religion must reflect that transcendence by adopting a method that also transcends history – an *a-historical* method: "What distinguishes the historian of religion from the historian … is that he is dealing with facts which, although historical, reveal a behaviour that goes beyond the historical involvement of the human being" (Eliade 1961, p. 32f). This attitude effectively undermines Eliade's assertions of loyalty to the historical method. The

common mind he hopes to achieve about religion will not, then, be grounded in a common acceptance of historical data. Instead, Eliade celebrates his own "history of religions" as dealing in "higher," "deeper," "primary," or "original" meanings – whatever these may be (Eliade 1959, p. 94; 1964b, p. xiii; 1965, p. 210). Eliade, therefore, wants to go well beyond what the historical disciplines have to offer to some other remote and mysterious place. His true methodological loyalties lie with a kind of psychological study of religion that he calls "creative hermeneutics." He is no historian.

Eliade as Psychologist of Religion

Eliade thinks he is right to toss history aside because he has a far better method of getting at the fundamentals of religion. He calls for "a total hermeneutics, being called to decipher and explicate every kind of encounter of man with the sacred, from prehistory to our day" (Eliade 1969b, p. 58). This "total hermeneutics" interprets religion by employing empathy, but of a mysterious kind. When asked how he did his "scientific" writing, Eliade is reported to have replied: "by intuition, the same as when I write my novels." Eliade also calls this method of high-order intuition, "creative hermeneutics." Taking his lead from Freud's student, Carl Gustav Jung, Eliade sought to decode data, seeing them as signs of other hidden causes. These observable data became symptoms of what lay beneath.

At one level, then, Freud, Jung, and Eliade work like detectives, reading what they see as indicators of certain underlying mental structures. The task is then to address those underlying meanings so that patients can be healed by reference to the hidden condition behind the particular set of symptoms.

Like a depth psychologist, Eliade applies models to his data in an attempt to make sense of them. In an odd way, even though he disdains the scientism of Freud and others, his conception of a "total hermeneutics" is remarkably scientistic. For Eliade, depth psychology actually discovers new facts about religion. Like Jung, Eliade believes that these facts consist in real structural elements that shape religious experience. They are the "archetypes." Jung believed that they accumulated in the mind over the long history of humanity (Dry 1961, p. 92). As Eliade himself puts it, "Every historical man carries on, within himself, a great deal of prehistoric humanity" (Eliade 1961, p. 12). These "archaic modes of psychic life are 'living fossils' buried in the darkness of the unconscious, which now become accessible to study through the techniques developed by depth psychologists" (Eliade 1960, p. xix). Eliade seeks to lay out those "archaic" elements of the human mind.

As the depth psychologist theorizes about the way the psyche works, say, in terms of Freud's theory of ego, id, and superego, Eliade applies his own theory of the deep mind. For Eliade, religion works because, like Jung, certain *archetypes* in the deep mind shape religious data in certain ways. As depth psychology attributes certain experiences of an individual's history to the working out of the psychic archetypes, so similarly does Eliade interpret religious data from what he calls a "more spiritual standpoint" (Eliade 1961, p. 31). Religious experience is really formed by these deep archetypes in the mind itself! Eliade believes he is right in this quest because of "immediate intuition" (Eliade 1959, p. 95). This intuitive power lets him see into "the mental universe of archaic man." These archetypes are "preserved in myths, symbols, and customs which still, in spite of every corruption, show clearly what they meant when they began" (Eliade 1958, p. 10). He thus challenges the empiricist and relativistic idea that the symbols are confined to the meanings of which people are conscious. Symbols have far deeper meanings than this. Depth psychology has taught Eliade that the symbol delivers its message and fulfills its function even when its meaning escapes awareness – even when we are unconscious of the workings of symbols (Eliade 1959, p. 106). So, together with Freud and others like him, Eliade thinks that "doctor knows best."

The "Worm of Doubt" Turns: Eliade's Creative Hermeneutics

Eliade's creative hermeneutics is designed to rally scholars of religion to a bold, revolutionary approach to their subject (Eliade 1969b, p. 62). Those in the field have "sinned" "through an excessive timidity and leave to others the task of interpreting … spiritual universes" (Eliade 1969b, p. 71). He challenges religious studies scholars to regain their "nerve." To be "creative" here means to produce revolutionary effects in today's secular society. Eliade is by no means just a run-of-the-mill academic scholar. He is a revolutionary of the religious kind. The whole purpose of Eliade's intellectual career and all his many publications is directed at this active "creative" goal: "the history of religions envisages, in the end, cultural *creation* and the *modification* of man" by our becoming aware of the religious archetypes that shape our behavior from deep in the deep mind (Eliade 1969b, p. 67). For this reason, Eliade appeals to the analogy between his methods and movements in culture, like Freudian psychoanalysis, or in the arts, such as surrealism. Eliade's project marks nothing less than an insurgency against the secular scientific (and "scientistic") establishment. He praises surrealists for their "attacks on bourgeois society and morality," and the way they "elaborated a revolutionary aesthetic." They "also formulated a technique by which they hoped to *change* the human condition" (Eliade 1969b, p. 65) – even to the extent that surrealism contributed to the "destruction of the official cultural world" (Eliade 1969b, p. 4).

However, Eliade also wants to use Freudian-style techniques to turn the tables on the likes of Freud. If Freud's "scientistic" approach destroyed the "official religious world," why should not creative hermeneutics engineer a religious "destruction" of secular consciousness? Thus, for Eliade, creative hermeneutics "is more than instruction, it is also a spiritual technique susceptible of modifying the quality of existence itself" – again meaning an existence which is not religious.

How does Eliade's creative hermeneutics propose to bring off this turning of the tables? How does he propose to turn the consciousness of the secular world upside-down? Eliade does not imagine that he can convert people to a *new* religious point of view; instead, he thinks he can convince secular people that they are *already* religious! The secular worldview, then, is a kind of *māyā*, an illusion that Eliade wants to discredit and dispel. He believes – like Freud and Jung – that buried in the deep unconscious mind of modern people are powerful meanings that only wait to be released into the consciousness. Eliade's job is to reveal these. He believes that he can snap modern secular people out of their dogmatically anti-religious "slumbers" by showing how our basic orientations in time and space reveal our dependence upon religious archetypes and models. We can no more evade experiencing the world religiously than we can evade living in time/space. Here is how Eliade believes the arrangement of time/space conveys religious meanings.

Time and Space of the Creative Center

For Eliade, all religious experience rests upon a template of the two most basic conditions of experience itself – time and space. This generates two of the most common themes in his work: sacred space and sacred time. Like Immanuel Kant, whose approach Eliade's faintly echoes, his model of religious experience in time and space is universal. It applies to all members of the species, *Homo religiosus*, male or female, black or white, etc. Thus, Eliade argues, first, of sacred space, that it "is structured hierarchically and formed according to a definite set of values." Sacred space it is not the formlessness of "homogeneity and relativity" that characterizes "profane space" (Eliade 1957, pp. 20–22). *Homo religiosus* marks a definite place or orientation in space (1957, p. 65). Some spaces and places matter more than others. The world experienced in terms of sacred space is hierarchical and diverse, not flat and uniform. Consider the example of the church (or the mosque). It "shares a different space from the street in which it stands ... The threshold that separates the two spaces ... indicates the distance between two modes of being, the profane and the religious" (1957, p. 25). *Homo religiosus* thus separates the world into domains, and reserves what is special or sacred as its treasure.

In the hierarchy of sacred space, the experience of one place stands out above all others – the place whence creation emanated. Eliade believes that centers best express sacrality. The hierarchy *Homo religiosus* experiences of the sacred world is that of a *centered world*, oriented about a focal point. In creating the world, the divine therefore orients life around a central core of values. In the religious world, nothing is meaningless, because everything is experienced as existing hierarchically in subordination to a center from which

creation emanates. The place of creation constitutes the most fundamental fixed point that there can be. It is the central axis for all future orientation. When the sacred manifests itself at such points of creation, "worlds" come into being (Eliade 1957, pp. 20–21). The place of absolute beginnings is the home of absolute reality.

Can we get more down-to-earth about what Eliade says? He might offer that we should meditate on the power of centers. Eliade's "centered" way of experiencing the spatial dimension as sacred accounts for the remarkable number of instances in which religious sites are organized about concrete centers (Eliade 1957, pp. 36–47). Whether this be the Ka'aba at Mecca as the focal point of all Muslim devotion, the conception of Jerusalem, the holy city, as the "navel" or center of the world, the location of the capital of the Chinese king at the center of the world, or Mount Meru of South Asian Hindu and Buddhist religious mythology being likewise thought to be the focal point of earthly space, the same idea seems apparent. Similarly, symbols such as the cosmic tree, totem pole, church steeple, minaret, and so on confirm Eliade's insight.

Here's a good sample of how Eliade treats the relation of a particular tree and the archetypal tree of sacred space to creation. "It is because the Cosmic Tree symbolizes the mystery of the world in perpetual regeneration" – continuous *creation*. As such, this archetypal tree "can symbolize ... the pillar of the world and the cradle of the human race" – in short, any and all centers. "Each one of these *new* valorizations is possible," Eliade goes on, "because from the beginning, the symbol of the Cosmic Tree reveals itself as a 'cipher' of the world grasped as a living reality, sacred and inexhaustible" (Eliade 1959, p. 194). So, the particular and local sacred tree cults take their holiness from a model, universal one – Eliade's archetype of the Cosmic Tree of the original Creation. They participate in the absolute sacredness of the primal archetype of the "Cosmic Tree."

For Eliade, then, all of physical space radiates these powerful universal meanings. The external world lives with significance that can engineer mental attitudes in religion. Thus the *mandalas* of Buddhist and Hindu meditational practice or the mazes and labyrinths of medieval Christianity not only passively *reflect* the idea of the prestige of the center, they also *shape* and *inform* experiences to mold them to religious purposes. By drawing the viewer ever more inward to their sacred centers, these devices for centering consciousness function to *condition* human consciousness for centering values throughout the world. As physical space is arranged, so also the mind follows, and as the mind is shaped, so the experience of the world follows as well.

Eliade's method of creative hermeneutics supplies these *religious* interpretations of things because it brings out their centering, orienting, focusing aspects. That is its job. Thus, Eliade wants to persuade modern secular folk, first, to value their own mundane centering, orienting, or organizing activities. Then, he wants them to appreciate the analogy of these mundane attempts to center life and space with classic religious expressions of sacred space. Finally, if successful thus far, Eliade hopes that ordinary folk will see their mundane acts of orientation as internally linked to classic religious ones. Indeed, our appetite for order may induce religious nostalgia for the freshness and purity of the absolute divine beginnings of things. For Eliade, achieving this level of self-consciousness would be at least the beginning of transforming secular consciousness into sacred. Like the post-Freudian who cannot any longer innocently see the proverbial cigar as a cigar, Eliade hopes his hermeneutics can make it impossible for post-Eliadeans to see everyday centers, foci, and other similar configurations of space as the mere mundane features of life that they seem to be on the surface. He believes that he can plant the "worm of doubt" among the doubters. He believes he can "re-enchant" the secular world by pointing out their unconscious nostalgia for centering, and thus for the divine creation of the world. Indeed, how could it be any other way, Eliade pleads? "The creation of the World being *the* pre-eminent instance of creation" thus "becomes the exemplary model for 'creation' of every kind" (Eliade 1964a, p. 21).

Myth Tells Us of the Eternal Time of Origins

What, however, of time? How is our experience of time rendered as sacred over against profane temporal consciousness? Eliade thinks that space as centered recalls the ordering, constructive quality of an archetypal divine creation over against chaos. But what qualities of time recall the same archetypal creative moment when all things came to be "by the grace of God'? Knowing what we already know about Eliade, some answers readily present themselves. If the *first* divine act – creation – remains the commanding archetypal religious event, so to speak, then the *first* time – the time of *origins* – must define sacred time for him. And indeed it is. The data for sacred time come from "myth."

I have put quotes around the word, "myth," because Eliade thinks that only *creation stories* are worthy of the name, "myth." A "myth", says Eliade, "is always related to a 'creation,' it tells us how something came into existence, or how a pattern of behaviour, an institution, a manner of working were established" (Eliade 1964a, p. 18). So, for Eliade, myth too harks back to the creation: "In general, one can say that any myth tells how something came into being, the world, or man, or an animal species, or a social institution" (Eliade 1969a, p. 75). Put otherwise, Eliade asserts that every myth is an "account of what came to pass in the holy era of the Beginning." Myths are the "archetypal history: how the world came to be" (Eliade 1968, p. 15).

I emphasize Eliade's definitional *Diktat* to warn readers who may find this definition disagreeable. I, for one, don't think Eliade is right to legislate the way we use the word, "myth" as creation stories, or even as stories of existential centering. Some myths, if by "myths" we mean folk stories and such, doubtless are. But all (Strenski 1987)? But with this duly noted, let me return to the problem how and why Eliade "thought he was right" to think myths are both creation stories and the key to understanding sacred time. If getting secular people to open their minds to the possibility that their orientations to centers and creativity reflect a deep nostalgia for "the Center" and thus the Creation, how does Eliade's idea of "myth" introduce the "worm of doubt" into secular consciousness about time? How does he think "myth" stimulates a sense of sacred time for people who know only the mundane time of the everyday?

The answers to these questions are several, and all intriguing. First, if we agree that "eternity" is a good benchmark instance of sacred time, we can see how and why Eliade finds the Creation such a suitable point of reference. Would not the moment just before Creation – or Big Bang – be a time without temporal duration, a "time" without time, so to speak, or the "time of God"? And is not that what we ordinarily mean by "eternity"? From the Creation onward, mundane time unrolls, and the essentially sacred "time" of eternity is left behind. Thus, the question becomes how myths awaken people to an experience of eternity, in particular to that blissful "time" before time. How do myths begin the work of re-enchanting the temporal consciousness of secular folk?

Eliade then asks is it not this same – phenomenologically – "timeless time" we experience when we immerse ourselves fully in writing, or in some narrative – in some myth? Are not these moments of escape from the consciousness of mundane time a taste of – the bliss of – eternity? Narrative carries us off to a dream world where we escape ordinary life. That, says Eliade, is the special task of myths. In hearing them, we enter another state of consciousness before temporal duration began – we enter the time of creation. Believers, says Eliade, "emerge from their historical time – that is, from … profane personal and intrapersonal events – and recover primordial time … eternity … an eternal present" (Eliade 1957, p. 88). This means that *consciously* secular folk, pursuing their otherwise secular activities have religious experiences! In attending the cinema or reading a good book, they attain the same spiritual "transport" out of mundane time into timelessness. That's why the cinema got the name "dream factory." That's why cinema steals countless mythical motifs – fights between hero and monster, initiatory combats and ordeals, road movies as quests. Do not modern media replace "the recitation of myths in archaic societies and the oral literature"? Reading, too, works the same magic as cinema: "through reading, the modern man succeeds in obtaining an 'escape from time' comparable to the 'emergence from time' effected by myths" (Eliade 1957, p. 205). The pity of it is that most modern secular folk do not realize the deeper meaning of their yearnings to "escape from time" to the sacred "timeless time" of eternity. Eliade's creative hermeneutics seeks nothing less than to confront secular folk with – to wake them up to – their own mundane appetites and desires as religious in their ultimate nature.

Even as these insights about film and narrative give one pause, I have been troubled by Eliade's reliance on "creative intuition" and, especially, its stipulations about the meaning of symbols and myths – stipulations that in a way seem like words from a guru or an authoritarian. Yes, critics of Freudian or Jungian psychologies raise the same objections. But just how do we *know* that the meanings of symbols declared by an Eliade, Freud, or Jung are what those symbols mean, and to whom? Does it even make sense to talk about "the" meaning of a symbol or myth? What do we make of Eliade's outrageous statement – with his own emphasis added – that those practicing creative hermeneutics ought to seek meanings *"even if they aren't there"* (Eliade 1977, p. 85)? Really? Clearly, for good or for ill, Eliade strays far from the ideal of the naturalistic or humanistic study of religion in development since Jean Bodin and Herbert of Cherbury. Eliade reveals himself to be another one of those doctors – like Freud, Jung, and Malinowski – who know best. We will see in the next chapter how such an epistemological stance draws fire from the post-modernists.

It is also ironic that Eliade's modernist claim to be the doctor who knows best conflicts with the classic phenomenology of religion. I say "ironic" because Eliade routinely claims to be doing phenomenology of religion himself. To be fair, he does keep faith with several of phenomenology's principles. First, he asserts the absolute *autonomy* of religion. Thus, he scolds his colleagues for surrendering to "reductionists" – to "the audacious and irrelevant interpretations of religious realities made by psychologists, sociologists, or devotees of various reductionist ideologies" – to wit, Freud, Malinowski, Durkheim, Frazer, Tylor, and other pillars of the study of religion (Eliade 1969b, p. 70). Secondly, Eliade, at least pays lip service to the phenomenological methods of *Verstehen* and empathetic understanding in the interests of grasping the religious perspective they embody. It is surely laudable, as Eliade in part argues, that those who study religion should at least approach cultural facts to see to what extent we can call them "religious." But Eliade goes overboard in the authoritarian/guru direction again, saying that unless we approach these religious-looking cultural facts "in the perspective of the history of religions, they will disappear as spiritual universes; they will be reduced to facts about social organizations, economic regimes, epochs of pre-colonial and colonial history, etc. In other words, they will not be grasped as spiritual creations; they will not enrich Western and world culture" (Eliade 1969b, p. 70). Well, yes, but I don't think we can *presume* that anything that "looks" religious really is. And that is what Eliade means since he just asserts that all "spiritual universes have a religious origin and structure." How do we know unless we look, and look/feel, inside the point of view of the folk?

The phenomenologists still best Eliade in meeting the "other," because they give the "other" at least some chance to speak. Eliade seems already, like Freud and Jung, to have decided matters in advance. In this way, he shows himself to be a classic modernist theorist. He, and "doctors" Freud, Malinowski, Jung, and other modernists, assume themselves to be personal authorities: they *know best*! We will explore the significance of the modernist designation further when we meet modernism's contemporary theoretical rival, post-modernism, in the next chapter.

Another Life: Eliade's "Ficciones"

Now, given such a radical and unprecedented approach to the study of religion, we might ask Eliade a question running through this entire book. Why would he think such things? Why would he believe "that he was right" to propose an anti-historical, anti-scientific, creative hermeneutic study of religion? Does Eliade's life story help us to understand whether there are external reasons why his study of religion takes this shape? I have already linked Eliade to the internal context of traditions of early twentieth-century depth psychology. But without going too far with the idea, I have also hinted at contexts external to his intellectual tradition. Eliade's experiences in India in yoga training and in working under a traditional guru were formative. Is it possible that he would have fashioned his view of religion and the study of religion with no reference to that external context? Let me now devote the remainder of this chapter to exploring the external context or contexts of the situation of Eliade's ideas. In this way, I believe I can aid understanding his theory – especially its revolutionary and authoritarian aspects. I think that the strength of Eliade's

commitment to both these features of his theory of religion cannot adequately be explained in terms of the force of ideas. Life also stands behind them.

Let me begin, first, by locating Eliade's theories of religion in that part of his "other life" – an external context – as a writer of objective fantasy or magical realist fiction. Eliade himself assigns great importance to his life as a writer, so we should at least see where that takes us. Although conventional wisdom dictates separating a scholar's scientific work from any artistic interests, Eliade himself does not. I claim that Eliade's history of religion and his literary efforts are actually not two things at all, but part of a single whole. Many of the same motives, revealing many of the same thematic interests, and expressing much the same worldview, drive both. Eliade's mind did not compartmentalize scholarship and fiction writing. His mind was much larger than our conventional professional attitudes allow.

In literary circles, Eliade is best known for the massive work he most loved – *The Forbidden Forest*. Its appearance in an English translation in 1978 (it was first published in France in 1955) triggered a new appreciation for Eliade. Instead of the short stories and tales that had announced his literary ambitions, here was a tome of epic sweep. In *The Forbidden Forest* dreamy narratives waft along, sustained for nearly 600 pages, broken by the staccato, machine-gun-like reports of civil anarchy in wartime Romania. People are shot without pity to bleed their lives away on some anonymous pavement; political foes assassinate one another in rapid, efficient, but unending succession. But Eliade makes these hard, horrid *historical* events fade into the insignificance of the "white noise" of mindless, and thus *meaningless*, chatter. In the face of massive, ceaseless, and banal violence, any opposition would only add to the horror. The only sane alternative is retreat into another world, free of history. Fleeing in this way from the "terror of history," both the novel's main characters and the reader are drawn into that world of an eternal, blissful, dreamy, non-historical reality. For Eliade, the heart of that blessed dream world of retreat from the terror of Romania's violent history is love itself. In the midst of the horrors of death and chaos that surround events and persons in novel, Eliade carves out a place of refuge constituted by the precious love affairs he recounts there, and that he counterposes to the terrors of their historical moments. Loves are won, but lost again, as historical events trample them under. But significantly, some lost loves are restored, often in magical ways as the dead seem to rise again – we are never quite sure what is real and what is imagined – to embrace the living left behind. *The Forbidden Forest* accordingly concludes with its leading character, Stefan (Eliade himself?), reuniting with his lost love. But even then, Eliade never lets us rest confident of certainties, in the assurance of a clear and distinct cleavage between life and death. Is this reunion of Stefan and Ileana a "real" one in "historical time," is it a waking dream or hallucination of a broken mind, or does Eliade offer a mystic vision of a magical reunion in death itself of these two? We do not know, and Eliade is surely not about to tell us, as the final words of the novel suggest:

> That moment – unique, infinite – revealed to him the total beatitude he had yearned for, for so many years. It was there in the glance she bestowed on him, bathed in tears. He had known from the beginning this was the way it would be. He had known that, feeling him very near her, she would turn her head and look at him. He had known that this last moment without end, would suffice. (Eliade 1978, p. 596)

Whatever the "truth" of Ileana's existence, Eliade shows us a person for whom "history" has become catastrophic. In *The Forbidden Forest*, Eliade echoes the distaste for historical reality and thus for the "science" of history, and his love of "timeless time" and eternity that we saw at work earlier in this chapter. About history, he says, "we're slaves of History. The terror of events is not only humiliating to each of us as human beings, but in the long run it's sterile … what does this struggle reveal to us? Only terror." And about the remedy for the terror of history, Eliade reminds us of his love of mysticism and eternity: "Against the terror of History there are only two possibilities of defense: action or contemplation … Our only solution is to contemplate, that is to escape from historic Time, to find again another Time" (Eliade 1978, p. 250). Doesn't Eliade suggest we too escape history and plunge into the sacred world of eternity, using whatever devices are to hand?

It seems obvious that Eliade's judgment against ordinary historical existence might well give him reasons to "think he is right" to be preoccupied with the idea of erasing hard and fast boundaries between dream and waking state, fantasy and reality, between *māyā* and *sat* (Being). Indeed, this theme marks much of Eliade's literary output. Here is the same mind at work in Eliade's fiction writing as in his history of religion. This selfsame mind sees the everyday world – the world of historical events – as ultimately unreal when compared to the world of the sacred and transcendent. I am arguing that this helps us further understand why Eliade "thinks he is right" to make the methodological choices about sacred space and time etc. that we have already glimpsed – all ones that seek to negate temporal duration.

The appeal of the trans-historical over the historical was thus deep and broad in Eliade's worldview. To boot, the fantastic or magical realist trend in Eliade's fiction – the 1930s – arrived in the narrow time-span when he was forming his thinking about religion (Calinescu 1978). In his *Mademoiselle Christina* (1936), Eliade accepts the reality of ghosts, as Stefan seems to do of the dead Ileana. In *The Serpent* (1937), Eliade introduces a strong theme that would dominate his literary thinking – "'the unrecognizability of miracle,'" or the concealment of the sacred in the profane (Ierunca 1969, p. 352). The theme of the "camouflage of the fantastic (and the absurd)" in the everyday, mundane event frames Eliade's whole epistemology of the sacred. As we might recall, he wants to awaken us to the way experiences of the sacred are symbolized in the world (Perry 1975, p. 49). For Eliade, what matters is not to be fooled by the many disguises assumed by the sacred as it sojourns in "history." The point is to realize eternal, timeless Being, and to dispel the *māyā* of illusion that is "history."

I have, first, argued, then, that we can draw one circle around Eliade's thinking by situating it in an external context of the literary world of objective fantasy or magical realism. Next, I shall recommend situating Eliade's thinking in a second external context – the politics of the Romania of the first several decades of the twentieth century. I do so not because of a subjective impression about some phantom spirit of the times. No; Eliade's early formative life was one of intense, active engagement in that external political and religious context. Thus located, I think I can make the case that Eliade "thought he was right" to have written his history of religion in its history-negating and "doctor-knows-best" style in large part because of his external Romanian political situation. He certainly was as much involved in the politics of Romania through the first half of the twentieth century as he was in objective fantasy literature. Eliade's approach to religion ought, accordingly, to be seen as externally situated within a particular politics, but also in his attempts to escape from it as revealed in his fictions.

In and Out of Romania's "Hooliganized" History

As the Ottoman Empire collapsed, Romania regained historically Romanian provinces, and greatly enlarged both her territory and population. A movement of "young generation" intellectuals stood hopeful and ready to lead a revival of her national fortunes. Eliade played a significant role in this Romanian national drama, which at once birthed the man he was to become, and almost killed him in the process. Born in 1907 in Bucharest, Eliade studied philosophy and religions at the university there. Some months abroad in Rome to study Renaissance hermeticism led to his spending three years studying philosophy and training as a yogin in India (1928–31). When he returned to his native Romania he took up a post in the Philosophy Department at Bucharest, then headed by the right-wing intellectual, Nae Ionescu. The year 1932 marked the beginning of a period of intense turmoil as the fascist right, communist left, conservatives, and liberals battled to determine the shape of the century. Right-wing Romanian author Emil Cioran proudly recalled the Eliade of those days as a leading ideological combatant against the traditional conservatives and liberals of the "old generation." "We scorned the 'old duffers' and 'doters' – anyone over thirty, that is," Cioran reports. "Our mentor [Eliade] was waging war against them; he would take aim and fell them one by one. Rarely did he fire wild," Cioran relates with relish. The intergenerational struggle Eliade led, Cioran concludes, "seemed to us the key to all conflicts, the explanatory formula of every event. Being young was, in our eyes, a certificate of genius" (Cioran

1969, p. 407). Eliade, Cioran, and the "new generation" believed confidently that they had a positive vision of what the new Romania could be. Cioran further recalled the days when Eliade would publish regular opinion pieces for Nae Ionescu's newspaper, *Cuvântul.* With some embarrassment at his youthful zeal, Eliade, too, recalled one of his first publications. His incendiary article, "Apologia pro causa sua," notes Eliade, was lobbed, Molotov cocktail style, "right into the middle of the polemics about the young generation … And I shut up the 'old fellows' once and for all" (Eliade 1977, p. 19).

Those bothersome "old duffers" represented the secular, liberal, individualist camp that idolized the same French Republic we have just seen Durkheim defend for its elevation of individualism to the level of a religion. The freedom of the individual, Durkheim tells us, was a sacred value for France because it elevated human conscience, formed within society, above all. But Eliade and his upstart comrades hated individualism. They hated the liberal West, especially a vision of Romania modeled on France and Western cosmopolitanism. Eliade and his friends hewed to radical "traditionalists." To them, the cosmopolitan program of Western liberal freedom smothered the growth of a specifically Romanian national folk-spirit, which yearned to burst forth and express itself (Hitchins 1978, pp. 142–144). At best, "liberals" only offered "negative" liberty to the Romanian masses. Liberalism only offered freedom *from* whatever restrictions people felt. It failed miserably – indeed deliberately – to provide a positive picture of the liberated society. "Positive" liberty was truly liberation, because it articulated a clear vision of a "freedom *to*" shape the nation over and above what the chaos of individual wills desired. The "new generation" was thus a "liberationist" movement, not a "liberal" one – a distinction which will feature prominently in the coming chapters.

Eliade's cherished mentor and life-long friend, the philosopher Nae Ionescu, intellectually shaped the vision of the "positive" liberation of the Romanian folk embodied in the "traditionalist" movement, especially its "irrationalist" wing. Western secular, liberal democracy could not accommodate Romania's pious Orthodox peasant masses. Indeed, as secular rationalists and modernists, the French liberals were eager to eliminate religion. In political terms, this was fatal. Secular liberals could not connect with the passionate mythological and symbolic religio-political nationalism of Romania's masses. Rooted in the intellectualism and anti-clericalism of the French Enlightenment, Romanian liberals were unable to tap the "irrational" mythico-religious forces of Romanian identity that moved the masses. But Eliade's traditionalists knew how to exploit these irrational forces and techniques – even if later these traditionalist forces swept the Eliades and Ciorans "out to sea," engulfing Romania in the process (Gentile 1996)!

A provisional "bottom line"? Eliade's "new generation" political vision seems homologous in form and meaning to his attitudes as expressed in his creative hermeneutics. Both visions show contempt for reason, science, and thus critical historical thinking. Both visions promise radical liberation from the limits of the mundane world and access into a vivid transcendent one. The "new generation" embraced Ionescu's relativism and mystical transcendentalism, where he claimed to have "rediscovered security, authority and discipline in God and religion" (Weber 1965, p. 535). Only if individuals surrendered their curiosity, freedom of inquiry, and skepticism upon the altar of traditional religious faith could they be "saved." It was precisely the values of individual liberty and integrity that Durkheim celebrated that Ionescu found antipathetic to the spirit of the so-called wisdom of Romanian peasant folk religion, as rendered by his philosophy. "'I believe because it is absurd'" was how Ionescu encapsulated his attitudes to the skeptical and critical thinking fundamental to individualism (Hitchins 1978, p. 145f). Eliade's disdain for the historical sciences and the critical reason is embodied in his glorification of intuition as *the* method for doing history of religion. Ionescu's irrationalist epistemology is, then, a center in the internal context of influences feeding Eliade's young mind. Furthermore, this philosophical center nestles cozily within the external context of Ionescu's equally irrationalist, traditionalist Romanian politics.

Swept Away

To complete my story of what the politics of the "new generation" and traditionalism meant to Eliade, let me pick up my reference his having been "swept away" by the radical political forces Ionescu and he had nurtured. Many of those moved by Eliade or Ionescu went further than the intellectual engagement that seemed to define Eliade's role in the politics of radicalized Romania: many of the "new generation" took to the streets, and rallied round the banner of a messianic politico-religious organization called the Legion of the Archangel Michael. Better known was the Legion's militant wing, the *Garda Fer* or Iron Guard. Corneliu Codreanu (1899–1938), their charismatic founder, led both organizations. Accounts of Codreanu's campaigns echo Ionescu and Eliade's infatuation with the Romanian peasantry, their native symbolism and traditional religious affiliations both with Romanian Orthodoxy and a perhaps pre-Christian folk religion. On a splendid white charger, done up in lavish peasant costume, Codreanu celebrated a kind of mythic identification between his modern political movement and the nativist archaic "soul" of an imagined indigenous Romanian people. Merging religion and politics, he led his green-shirted Legionaries in rowdy, often violent, demonstrations of bully-boy political power, yet all the while bearing lighted candles and holy icons, against the forces of a corrupt secular liberalism (Wiles 1969, p. 176). Inevitably, the nativist and traditionalist ideology of a Codreanu and his Legion would become practical, and take active form. The Legion led many violent and murderous political attacks against Jews and their other perceived enemies in their quest to liberate Romanians into the "positive" liberty of a pure (*sic*) Romanianism.

I know of no evidence that Eliade took to the streets with the Legion. But we do know he was a well-known sympathetic, ideological apologist for Codreanu. Moreover, he never distanced himself from the Legion or disavowed his association with it (Eliade 1981, pp. 280–281; Wasserstrom 1999, pp. 131–132). Worse yet, Nae Ionescu linked his Legionary philosophy directly with Hitler's revolution in Germany. In volume 1 of his *Autobiography*, Eliade suggests that he was aware of the fascist character of Ionescu's political thought. In 1933, Eliade noted that Ionescu spoke of being "very impressed" with the "revolution" taking place in Nazi Germany. "A similar revolution would have to take place some day in Romania," said Ionescu (Eliade 1981, p. 263).

Eliade's sympathies for the political analysis of the European right – "what we young people were thinking ... between 1925 and 1933" is, therefore, in large part clearly identifiable (Eliade 1977, p. 197). It may be called by many names, such as "fascist," "rightist," and so on, and even as displaying a rightist "Catholic sensibility," as the late Susan Sontag labeled both Cioran and Eliade (Sontag 1966, p. 88). In the end, labels matter little compared with the reality of Eliade's true political and ideological worldview in the late 1920s through the end of World War II.

Now, for getting "swept away." Eliade's ideological fellow-travelers intensified their opposition to other kindred groups in the early 1930s. Civil conflict erupted with as much fury between different "fascist" groups as between left and right. Worse yet, Romania's internal anarchy sent ripples out beyond her borders. Both Western and Nazi governments urged the Romanian government to liquidate the troublesome Legion, in the way Hitler's Nazi Party (of order) liquidated the adventurist Nazi Party (of disorder), the "Brown Shirts." At this point, the Romanian king, Carol II, staged a royal coup, dissolved parliament, and manufactured his own version of the Legion. Moving swiftly, Carol had Codreanu imprisoned and secretly executed in 1938. The adventurist and idealistic wing of the Legion fell victim to its own success. The king's counter-revolution, however, failed, and whatever anarchy there had been before his royal coup paled in comparison with that which followed. In 1940, with Codreanu's "spiritual" revolutionaries losing the battle, Eliade fled Romania, never to return. Eliade and all for which he worked had been swept away by the changing tides of history. Speaking perhaps of himself and the catastrophes that rained down upon him and the political enthusiasms of his youth, in *The Forbidden Forest*, Biris describes Stefan (Eliade?) in words that might well indicate Eliade's own desperate and defeated internal condition at the time:

> He suffered a nervous shock, that's all ... History has taken revenge on him. He has a phobia against History. He has a horror of events. He'd like things to stand still the way they seemed in the paradise of his childhood. So History takes revenge and buries him as often as it can. It

throws him into the detention camp by mistake. It kills men in his place, always by mistake ... (Eliade 1978, p. 214)

Is it any wonder, again, that Eliade thinks that "he is right" to presume that "history" only brings on "terror," and that his creative hermeneutics should, therefore, aim at releasing us from this mundane historical time into a timeless time of eternity?

Luckily for Eliade, the intervention of influential individuals permitted him to escape his own premature death, not to mention the further disintegration of his country. He waited out the war as Romanian cultural attaché in Portugal (1940–45), where he continued writing, notably a commentary on the rightist revolution of the Portuguese dictator António de Oliveira Salazar, *Salazar și Revoluția în Portugalia* (Eliade 1942; 2000, p. 30). In an interview that Eliade was able to obtain with the dictator in 1942, Salazar expressed interest in the existence of a "common front" – *espíritu de frente* – in Romania as a force for making modern-day social revolutions. Salazar clearly had Eliade's Legion in mind, or at least recognized in Eliade – and rightly so – someone of authority and influence in these matters (Eliade 2000, p. 39). Eliade then began a series of migrations that marked the next decade or so of his life. By various routes and turns of good fortune, he taught for a brief time in Paris at the École Pratique des Hautes Études (1950–55), and from there he moved to the post at the Divinity School in the University of Chicago that he held from 1956 until his death in 1986.

Eliade had thus literally experienced the "terror" of the failure of "historical" plans for which he and his generation had worked. It seems a modest and reasonable interpretation of his orientation regarding "history" in the study of religion to suggest that Romania's historical catastrophes might well have given him reasons to "think he was right" about the study of religion and religion itself. What I think emerges is that a person who lived through political and historical disasters as Eliade did would tend to "think they were right" to look on political and historical ambitions with a peculiar tragic sense, even to the extent of expressing scorn for the often cruel vicissitudes of history and politics. History in Romania had been for Eliade literally a terrible, murderous disaster, not only for him, but for every political and social value to which he had adhered since returning from India. It is for reasons such as these that I have tried to suggest that Eliade was motivated to "think he was right" to declare history the source of terror, rather than an arena of salvation and happiness, and therefore to think he was right to turn his mind to places beyond those that history could reach – to blissful realms of transcendence – where no historian had any business to be. Salvation, or at least personal mental survival, can be found by escaping into a world stabilized by transcendent unmovable centers and heavenly archetypes that exist in the unchanging, but creative and life-affirming, "timeless time" of eternity, of mythical time.

From this new set of priorities, it may also be easier to see that Eliade might want to have recourse to the methods of superior knowledge that likewise condition his approach to the study of religion. Eliade the yogin, the would-be guru, lived on in his intuitive approach to understanding religion. With history a wreckage, would not someone like Eliade, who had imbibed both yogic methods of attaining higher knowledge as well as Nae Ionescu's irrationalist contempt for ordinary means of attaining knowledge, feel that he could access higher (or deeper) ways of understanding religious data? Did not Eliade think he was right precisely because he felt that he *knew* he was right at the deepest core of his being?

References

Bellah, R.N. 1978. "Religious Studies as "New Religion."" In G. Baker and J. Needleman (eds.), *Understanding the New Religions*. New York: Seabury Press.

Calinescu, M. 1978. "The Disguises of Miracle: Notes on Mircea Eliade's Fiction." *World Literature Today*: 558–564.

Capps, W.H. (ed.). 1978. *The Interpenetration of New Religion and Religious Studies*. Understanding the New Religions. New York: Seabury Press.

Cioran, E. 1969. "Beginnings of a Friendship." In J.M. Kitagawa and C.H. Long (eds.), *Myths and Symbols: Studies in Honor of Mircea Eliade*. Chicago: University of Chicago Press.

Dry, A. 1961. *The Psychology of Jung*. London: Allen & Unwin.

Eliade, M. 1942. *Salazar și Revoluția în Portugalia*. Bucharest: Gorjan.

Eliade, M. 1957. *The Sacred and the Profane*. New York: Harcourt, Brace & World.

Eliade, M. 1958. *Patterns in Comparative Religion*, trans. R. Sheed. London: Sheed & Ward.

Eliade, M. 1959. "Methodological Remarks on Religious Symbolism." In M. Eliade and J. Kitagawa (eds.), *The History of Religions: Essays in Methodology*. Chicago: University of Chicago Press.

Eliade, M. 1960. "Encounters at Ascona." In J. Campbell (ed.), *Man and Time: Papers from the Eranos Yearbooks*, Bollingen Series 4. London: Routledge & Kegan Paul.

Eliade, M. 1961. *Images and Symbols*. London: Harvill.

Eliade, M. 1964a. *Myth and Reality*. London: Allen & Unwin.

Eliade, M. 1964b. *Shamanism*. New York: Bollingen.

Eliade, M. 1965. *The Two and the One*. London: Harvill.

Eliade, M. 1968. *Myths, Dreams and Mysteries*. London: Harvill.

Eliade, M. 1969a. "Cosmogonic Myth and "Sacred History."" In *The Quest*. Chicago: University of Chicago Press.

Eliade, M. 1969b. "Crisis and Renewal." In *The Quest*. Chicago: University of Chicago Press.

Eliade, M. 1977. *No Souvenirs*. New York: Harper & Row.

Eliade, M. 1978. *The Forbidden Forest*. South Bend, IN: Notre Dame University Press.

Eliade, M. 1981. *Autobiography*, vol. 1: *1907–1937. Journey East, Journey West*, trans. M.L. Ricketts. New York: Harper & Row.

Eliade, M. 2000. *Diario Portugués*, trans. J. Gariggós. Barcelona: Kairós.

Gentile, E. 1996. *The Sacralization of Politics in Fascist Italy*, trans. K. Botsford. Cambridge, MA: Harvard University Press.

Hitchins, K. 1978. "Gindirea: Nationalism in Spiritual Guise." In K. Jowitt (ed.), *Social Change in Romania, 1860–1940*. Research Series 36. Berkeley: Institute of International Studies.

Ierunca, V. 1969. "The Literary Work of Mircea Eliade." In J.M. Kitagawa and C.H. Long (eds.), *Myths and Symbols: Studies in Honor of Mircea Eliade*. Chicago: University of Chicago Press.

Perry, T. 1975. "The American and Romanian Literature." *Cahiers roumains d'études littéraires* 3: 40–50.

Sontag, S. 1966. *Styles of Radical Will*. New York: Noonday.

Strenski, I. 1987. *Four Theories of Myth in Twentieth-Century History*. London and Iowa City: Macmillan/Iowa University Press.

Wasserstrom, S.M. 1999. *Religion After Religion: Gershom Scholem, Mircea Eliade, and Henry Corbin at Eranos*. Princeton: Princeton University Press.

Weber, E. 1965. "Romania." In H. Rogger and E. Weber (eds.), *The European Right: A Historical Profile*. Berkeley: University of California Press.

Wiles, P. 1969. "A Syndrome, Not a Doctrine." In G. Ionescu and E. Gellner (eds.), *Populism*. London: Macmillan.

Further Reading

Borges, J.L. 1998. "Fictions: The Garden of Forking Paths." In A. Hurley (ed.), *Jorge Luis Borges: Collected Fictions*. New York: Penguin.

Calinescu, M. 1982. "The Function of the Unreal: Reflections on Mircea Eliade's Short Fiction." In N.J. Girardot and M.L. Ricketts (eds.), *Imagination and Meaning: The Scholarly and Literary Worlds of Mircea Eliade*. New York: Seabury Press.

Cioran, E. 1956. "Thinking Against Oneself." In S. Sontag (ed.), *E.M. Cioran: The Temptation to Exist*. New York: Quadrangle.

Dudley, G. 1977. *Religion on Trial: Mircea Eliade and His Critics*. Philadelphia: Temple University Press.

Eliade, M. 1972. "The Clairvoyant Lamb." In *Zalmoxis: The Vanishing God*. Chicago: University of Chicago Press.

Eliade, M. 1982. *Ordeal by Labyrinth: Conversations with Claude-Henri Rocquet*. Chicago: University of Chicago Press.

Nagy-Talavera, N.M. 1970. *The Green Shirts and Others*. Stanford: Hoover Institution.

Preus, J.S. 1987. *Explaining Religion*. New Haven: Yale University Press.

Skinner, Q. 1969. *Meaning and Understanding in the History of Ideas*. Middletown, CT: Wesleyan University Press; repr. from *History and Theory* 8(1).

Todorov, T. 1989. *The Deflection of the Enlightenment*. Stanford: Stanford Humanities Center.

Trautmann, T.R. 1997. *Aryans and British India*. Berkeley: University of California Press.

Voigt, J. 1967. *Max-Müller: The Man and His Ideas*. Calcutta: Firma K.L. Mukhopadhyay.

PART IV

Liberation and Post-Modernism: Race, Gender, Post-Colonialism, the Discourse on Power

14

From Modernism to Post-Modernism: Mostly Michel Foucault

A New "New Generation" Takes on Eliade

For Eliade, religion or religious experience essentially involved existential escape from the "terror of history," a withdrawal into a world of transcendental "timeless time" of the Creation. This religious realm was independent of any worldly taint. The study of religion pioneered by Eliade was, thus, proclaimed by him to be an autonomous discipline dealing with an autonomous and unique subject. By its very nature, then, Eliade's study of religion had nothing essentially to learn from other disciplines, and the major tropes of other disciplines had virtually nothing to do with informing his "history of religion." Further, Eliade's history of religion really had no place for political power or politics in the study of religion. As Eliade himself clearly puts it, "religious forms are nontemporal; they are not necessarily bound to time … religious reality … transcends the plane of history" (Eliade 1968, pp. 79–80).

In singling out Eliade, I do not concede the entire field of religious studies to him and the many fine scholars produced by the History of Religions program at the Divinity School of the University of Chicago. Yet Eliade's popularity as a religious studies scholar was without parallel. The key assumptions guiding his approach to the study of religion became part of the discipline's credo more than those of any other leading theorist. Russell McCutcheon, among others, caught hold of the way Eliade's theoretical nostrums, especially autonomy, dominated the religious studies community from the middle of the twentieth century (McCutcheon 1997; Strenski 1973). McCutcheon's reaction is to indict the entire religious studies community of buying into Eliade's idea of the autonomy of religion. While McCutcheon's jabs at Eliade land serious blows, his attempt to knock out the modern study of religion is well wide of the mark. Is McCutcheon accusing historian J.Z. Smith of selling wares out of the Eliade shop? Neither should those trained at Harvard by Wilfrid Cantwell Smith be lumped with Eliade. And even less should the many scholars from Great Britain, the Commonwealth, and the Americas, produced by Ninian Smart at Lancaster and the University of California, Santa Barbara be grouped with the Eliadeans. While McCutcheon does not seem to realize that the assumption of the autonomy of religion dates from the century-old influence of liberal Protestantism, he is right on the mark as

Understanding Theories of Religion: An Introduction, Second Edition. Ivan Strenski.
© 2015 Ivan Strenski. Published 2015 by John Wiley & Sons, Ltd.

far as Eliade and the great number who invoke his authority in matters of theory are concerned (Strenski 1998, 2002). Eliade did spread an imprecise presumption that religion was an autonomous reality, splendidly isolated from other academic disciplines and the rough and tumble of the rest of life.

I am claiming that one way to understand the new generation of theorists discussed here in Part IV is to see them as pushing back, consciously or not, against the Eliade tradition and the older, underlying, givens inherited from the nineteenth- and early twentieth-century liberal Protestant pioneers in the study of religion. Here I have specifically in mind Otto, and the liberal Calvinists, who created the phenomenology of religion. In place of the older priorities, the new generation featured the historicity of religion, its cultural, racial, and gender diversity, its intimate involvement in the machinations of power and politics, and they exhibited a readiness to engage other disciplines. I am suggesting that we can at the very least look at this new generation of thinkers, featured here in Part IV, as united in an informal, but nonetheless common, effort to overturn much of what typified Eliade's project in the study of religion.

Just for the sake of convenient labeling, if we can refer to the thinkers in Parts II and III as founders of the "modern" study of religion, then those in Part IV might – at least broadly – be called theorists in a "post-modern" mode. At bottom, the modern attitude assumed a certain theory about *knowledge*, including thinking or knowing about religion. Modernists believed, first, that religion could be known *objectively*, or at the very least neutrally, that is to say free of any particular religious bias. Second, modernists also believed that the investigator made no significant contribution to the knowledge thus supposedly acquired objectively.

These beliefs about knowledge and the knowing subject often led the theorists in Parts II and III to assume that they stood over religious subjects as the "doctor" over against the "patient." At it most extreme, the modernist attitude of objectivity can perhaps best be summed up as "doctor knows best." Indeed, Freud, an actual practicing medical doctor, consciously applied the attitude proper to aches, pains, fractures, and such to the "soul" or psyche of his patients. Indeed, one sometimes refers informally to professional psychoanalysts as "doctors of the soul." The second assumption about the act of knowing by modernist theorists implied that the subjective conditions of the investigators thinking about religion could be discounted from any conclusions they reached about religion. No need to situate the knower in the act of knowing, because the investigator does not shape what they investigate. No need, either, for theorists to confess their ideological biases and situate themselves in the act of theorizing (Hackney 1998, p. 145).

We don't need to buy everything the post-modernists want to sell us. Rather, we can pick and choose what works. For example, post-modernists say that objectivity is impossible – never asking, though, how one could know this fact objectively! But putting aside their own confusions, we can get something valuable out of what the post-modernists say. They seek to encourage understanding and explaining of religion by attending to the *subjectivity* of religious people in constructing the world. The post-modern theorists in Part IV see themselves as neither objective scientists nor historians – least of all "scientific" historians. They are also skeptical about hermeneutic claims to "interpret" the "meaning" of religious beliefs and practices, because of a lingering essentialism – the idea that there is just *one meaning* in play. "Meaning for whom?" they ask. The new post-modern buzz words are "deconstruction," not "science," "genealogy," not "history," and "reading" instead of "interpretation," "explanation," or even "understanding." Students need to learn them, but without being bewitched by them. Don't surrender your critical intelligence to anyone. Among other things, then, these are some of the distinctive features of the new generation of theorists in Part IV, the "post-modernists."

Foucault's Radiance: A Usable Theory of Power and Liberation

Although the landscape of the latest theorists in the study of religion is well populated, one figure stands out, Michel Foucault (1926–84). When Foucault's work was first received by religious studies scholars, most had already been formed by the classic theorists of Parts I–III. This led to attempts to add Foucault to what they had learned from Eliade, Weber, Freud, Durkheim, and others. At other times, Foucault, or some other "hot" theorist of the day – Derrida, Lyotard, Baudrillard, Lévi-Strauss, and so on – simply displaced the classic theorists. As one may imagine, the resultant permutations and combinations of such attempts are far too numerous and complex to render here. Suffice it to say that the new generation theorists of Part IV all assume some level of acquaintance with the classic theorists. It is no longer controversial, therefore, to say that psychological, depth psychological, or social factors shape religion. Neither can meaning and interpretation be entirely ignored. This is to say that leading proponents of hermeneutics, Freud and his ilk, or Durkheim and other sociological theorists, have been "domesticated" by present-day religious studies scholars, even if they may not be slavish devotees of any one of them. Only Eliade and the phenomenologists seem particularly indigestible, with their weakness for quasi-theological notions of religion as autonomous. Nevertheless, the appearance of this new crop of theorists at least sets the stage for unavoidable tensions with the theorists discussed in Part III (West 1989, p. 236). I focus on Foucault in Part IV because I believe readers will find that his obsession with power, as I shall explain, provides a particularly salient thread linking discussions of theories of religion and race, sex/gender, and the post-colonial situation. So who was Foucault and why did he attract such devotion?

Michel Foucault was yet another brilliant product of the elite system of French education. His achievements raised him to the very summit of the French academic world, a chair at the Collège de France. For many years, he also taught on an annual basis at the University of California, Berkeley. His teaching abroad afforded him escape from what he felt to be the oppressive French atmosphere against his open homosexuality. In order to maintain the life he and his partner of twenty years had created, Foucault taught in Tunisia when his partner was posted in the military there.

Foucault's sexuality seems to have attuned him to the destructive power of social conformity. Returning to France in 1960 at the beginning of the vogue for the insurgent structuralism of ethnologist Claude Lévi-Strauss, Foucault was often seen as an ally. Both often cast themselves as critics of what they took to be a bloated and self-important Western individualism, a trait they also shared with their Marxist compatriots. For a time, Foucault even was a formal member of the Stalinist-leaning French Communist Party. But he became alienated from the party after the Soviets crushed the Hungarian revolt of 1956. Perhaps these repeated episodes of alienation, sexual, political, or intellectual, fed his creativity?

Speaking of "alienation," Foucault's time as a visiting professor in Berkeley, 5,000 miles from Paris, fit the pattern. Whatever else Berkeley may have done for Foucault's creativity, San Francisco's flourishing gay scene laid a banquet table of sexual delights for anyone coming from the more closeted world of Europe. The new freedom Foucault found there, in turn, set off a rush of creativity, including the initiation of his unprecedented, and unfinished, multi-volume work, *The History of Sexuality*. There, Foucault not only showed mastery of the literatures of ancient Greece and Rome, but also celebrated that once shunned "self" in his development of the Greek theme, "care of the self." With *The History of Sexuality*, he also turned from an exclusively negative focus on power as oppressive domination over personal freedom to a conception of power as the freedom of an agent creatively to make a self. His sex life in the Bay Area held the key to this realization, because in it he experienced both the freedom *from* the repression of the old world and the freedom *to* shape himself in the new world. Sadly, the HIV-AIDs plague threw a chill over the exuberant gay culture of San Francisco in the 1970s, and Foucault along with it. The joyous risk-taking often casually assumed at the height of the fervor of San Francisco bath-house and gay culture proved fatal. He died in Paris in 1984, from what is widely assumed were complications related to HIV-AIDS.

Power, Power, Power

Foucault's explorations of power centered his thinking. He raised questions about how power, in its various fine-grained forms and intimate context, determines relations among and within persons. How, for example, is power over others achieved through language, or just through our normal human interest in classifying others? How does the intellectual confinement of some people within certain categories contribute to their physical confinement in real-life institutions such as prisons, asylums, or even convents and monasteries? He wrote influential books devoted to exposing the meanness of seemingly innocent institutions, such as the asylum or clinic. He was particularly interested in exposing the means by which avowedly benign institutions, such as mental hospitals, asylums, or "enlightened" products of prison reform, actually dehumanized the persons caught within their networks of power.

Foucault's critique of institutional prisons – *Discipline and Punish* (1977) – also attests to his horror of the depersonalizing power of even the most seemingly humane forms of imprisonment – new "model" prison structures, or even the most seemingly subtle forms of containment – within the "gaze" of their captors. Notorious here is Foucault's analysis of the Panopticon, the central feature of a reformed prison, designed by the English Utilitarian and social reformer, Jeremy Bentham. No longer would prisoners be crowded into dark dungeons or left to rot in solitary confinement. No longer would they be "punished"; society would seek to "reform" them. Bentham proposed a devilish device for such character reformation, designed in the spirit of the Enlightenment. In new model prisons, inmates would be provided open, well-lit, clean, and orderly cells of their own. But these cells would he built round a central courtyard in which a warden or prison guard would be housed in what Bentham called the Panopticon. From this central vantage point, prison guards could maintain constant surveillance of their charges in their exposed cells. Inmates would be constantly fixed by the gaze of their keepers so that their reformation could be scrupulously supervised.

Of course, constant surveillance dehumanized the prisoners, something Foucault suggests the authorities may secretly have wished. Books such as *Discipline and Punish* brought out the negative power of containment and denial, emphasizing the intense cruelty of seemingly enlightened practices. Foucault subsequently put this knowledge gleaned from his historical studies of prisons to work as a leader in prison reform in France. But just as well, as we will see, later in life Foucault wrote about the positive creative power that persons deployed in making their "selves," such as in

the acceptance of one's sexuality and the development of it in the form of an empowered self. Sensitive as he was to the imprisoning capacity of language and conceptualization – "knowledge" – Foucault was particularly allergic to any sort of labeling of his thought. He successively refused the labels that sprouted up in the modish, hothouse intellectual environment of Paris, such as post-structuralist, post-modernist, or even Marxist.

But some would rightly argue that Foucault's analyses of the subtle, and often unintentional and well-meaning, means by which power was deployed have even more sinister implications. Otherwise well-meaning institutions, such as hospitals and asylums, worked their will to power over their inmates by means of the attendant sciences that facilitated their establishment. The behavioral and social scientists classified people under their care, physically immured in mental hospitals and prisons as deviants, neurotics, psychotics, recidivists, repeat offenders, and such. In "knowing" them in this way, they submitted their inmates and patients to regimes of knowledge as restrictive as the physical walls of the institutions containing them. *Madness and Civilization* (1960), for example, developed just such themes of control of individuals by "knowledge" in mental institutions. Along the way, Foucault showed how the history of insanity in the West revealed attitudes to the so-called "insane" radically different from what such modern institutionalized treatments presume. In pre-modern times, the so-called "mad" might be seen as especially gifted, inspired, and such, rather than deviants to be housed away behind the walls of asylums. Foucault's critique of the behavioral sciences showed that power could be deployed, and people subjected to domination, even through mental constructs, such as everyday and scientific knowledge.

Politics Is Everywhere

Foucault's name, then, is synonymous with the central trope around which the new generation's theorizing about religion revolves – power. "Power" in this discourse primarily means *political* power. This power is not that which ranges from the flutterings of the Holy Spirit through the intoxication of people "empowered" by religion noted by Durkheim, all the way to the terrifying explosions of energy felt by Arjuna's vision of Krishna's revelation of his divine inner nature. Foucault contributed a particular notion of power to post-modern theorists – a "pervasive dynamism or tension existing in a particular network of social relations … a complex network of forces, tensions and energy that constitute a political systems." What we should note is that instead of power being something focused on the state, "power is a dynamic energy that infuses a social system" (Chidester 1988, p. 8). Foucault believed that if we think about power only in terms of "legislation and constitution, in terms solely of the state, and the state apparatus," we will fatally impoverish "the question of power" (Foucault 1977b, p. 158). Instead, Foucault wants totally to overhaul our ideas of power and "the political" by extending them in the broadest possible way. For Foucault, then, politics is not what happens during elections or parliamentary sessions, but a general "strategy for co-ordinating and directing" relations of power. As such,

> Every relation of force implies at each moment a relation of power … and every power relation makes a reference, as its effect, but also as its condition of possibility, to a political field of which it forms a part. To say that "everything is political" is to affirm this ubiquity of relations of force and their immanence in a political field. (Foucault 1977a, p. 189)

For Foucault, politics is ultimately about the "micro-fascisms of everyday life" – all the perverse little ways we maneuver to dominate each other. Therefore all agency collapses into politics, and ultimately, into war. When Foucault and his followers among post-modern thinkers claim that "everything is political," they should be taken at their word.

Liberationism and Foucault's Discourse on Power

It is easy to understand why good-hearted folk would be moved by Foucault's relentless analysis of ubiquitous power. To the extent that such good-hearted folk migrate to areas of study like religion, it is again no surprise that our new generation of religion theorists should be so deeply

influenced by him. If we are to believe Tom Tweed, the view of religion of the liberal Protestants and Eliade precluded having the ambition to "negotiate power as well as meaning" (Tweed 2006, pp. 112–113). Eliade opted for meaning. A new, good-hearted, generation seized upon power, typically in the interests of defending victims of power and domination. Whether it be black liberation theology, women's liberation, or third world liberation, Foucault's articulation of the logic of domination at the root of racism, sexism, and such has been seminal to the thinkers of Part IV. I shall label that broad category of religious studies scholars eager to negotiate power in the interests of human liberation, "liberationists."

Many liberationists ask questions about how the power of religion encourages or inhibits human liberation. Indeed, for some, the essence of religion itself seems to be nothing more than power. Post-modernist anthropologist Talal Asad thus asks, "How does power create religion?" (Asad 1993, p. 45). Others focus more locally and demand interrogations of the possible role that religion plays in the origins and persistence of domination. For liberationists, the study of religion should concentrate upon how religion's power has harmed (or helped) the interests of people marginalized by the powerful – the poor, racial minorities, women, and former subjects of European colonial domination. *Liberationism*, as theoretically informed by Foucault among others, turns a generational page in the study of religion.

Foucault, Japanese Women Shamans, and the Power of the Male Gaze

In his study of Japanese women shamans, Allan Grapard offers just such an illustrative display of Foucault's liberating methods, wrapped into a critique of Eliade's conception of the autonomy of religious experience. Grapard's use of Foucault brings out the many subtle ways that the shamanic religion of certain Japanese women seems to owe its existence to the power of social domination so profoundly criticized by Foucault. And since shamanism was the subject of one of Eliade's first books (Eliade 1964), one must imagine Grapard deliberately selecting shamanism as a test case of Eliade's theory against Foucault's. Grapard aims to show that Foucault exposes the profound knowledge–power relationships that actually produce the mystical or otherworldly shamanic "knowledges" that Eliade attributes to sacred archetypes. Let us follow Grapard's thinking as he lays it out.

Grapard asks, first, why most shamans in a certain Japanese locale are women. A trifling few shamans are men. Grapard immediately attacks the idea that women shamans possess some special power – some special connection to the sacred – as Eliade and his devotees would hold. Grapard refuses to accept that these women shamans are imbued with a pre-existing "sacred" talent for the ways of god-given religious clairvoyance (Grapard 1991, p. 20). Whether or not they are so endowed, Grapard asks how the network of power relations confining these women shamans can be ignored. Is it possible or plausible that their situation of powerlessness makes no difference to who and what they are and experience? Grapard argues that they are, in effect, prisoners within their social networks by virtue of male domination. Their only outlet from such cultural confinement is to imagine some kind of magical – shamanic – escape into a transcendent realm. The otherwise lofty spiritual claims of these poor women to possess the "ability to communicate with the realms beyond" are false. Instead, their desire for escape into the spirit world "appears to be related to pathological disorders that are related to modalities of knowledge and to strategies of power" (Grapard 1991, p. 20). How does Grapard make his case?

Grapard notes that this particular society seems consumed by the idea of the magic of *seeing*. But seeing – and therefore "looking" or "gazing" – are not what women do to men, but only what men do to women. Men can "check out" women; women cannot do likewise to men. Grapard believes that this produces a harsh society in which women are imprisoned by the all-encircling male gaze. Women are powerless to do anything about this, and in this way, men routinely master the bodies of women merely by the power of the "gaze."

As we might expect, given this society's obsession with the value of seeing, Grapard realizes that women will want to do some seeing as well. Prevented from being able to gaze at men in everyday life, these women engaged in controlled opportunities to see in ways that did not threaten the male monopoly. Grapard believes that men connived to let women be "seers" into the "other world," while they cheerfully kept a tight rein on their power over seeing in the everyday world. In effect, the "voyeuristic intrusions of males," say Grapard, "have caused women to be clairvoyant" – to claim to be empowered to see into another world beyond ours. Women get "to see what nobody else can." Male power over women thus coerces them to "see" in the only way permitted by the men who dominate society. The women shamans dream their religious ecstatic dreams; they have what Eliade and others would call "religious experiences." But, in truth, no secret inner talents hide undetected within these encircled Japanese women (Grapard 1991, p. 20). Their attempt to escape cultural imprisonment only represents "an attempt on the part of women, to delineate an area of expertise through which they might exercise some kind of control" (Grapard 1991, p. 20). Men are still in control over women, but let women imagine that they are free.

Foucault's Liberalism Meets Post-Modern Liberationism

Grapard shows us how Foucault can explain how and why a particular religious experience of freedom is shaped by power. Since the theorists of Part IV use very different concepts of freedom, liberty, and liberation, a few distinctions are in order. What Foucault urges can be described as a program of "*negative* liberty" – a program for freeing the dominated *from* their oppression. Black American liberationist intellectual Cornel West laments that Foucault stopped at "negative" liberty. For West, this reduces actual revolution to a mere "Great Refusal addressed to the dominant powers that be." West thinks that Foucault stops short of promoting *radical* liberation, what would be comprehended in the idea of "positive" liberty. Says West, Foucault fails "to articulate and elaborate ideals of democracy, equality, and freedom," and in failing so to do, only "provides merely negative conceptions of critique and resistance" (West 1989, p. 226). Foucault adds nothing to the articulation of a vision of *positive freedom* that would succeed regimes of domination.

The reason Foucault does not lay out a plan of positive freedom touches on something in his soul. He thinks every social arrangement will breed domination. The birth and rebirth of "new modes of subjection and disciplinary control" knows no end (West 1989, p. 226). We don't know what happened to the women shamans, once Grapard left and once they had attained their liberation. Did they perhaps exploit their devotees and clients? Did they devolve into "designing women," using their spiritual prestige for material gain? Foucault thinks tragedy is our lot. Unlike West and other religious liberationists, as we will see, Foucault's fatalism causes him to reject "all forms of ends and aims for political struggle" (West 1989, pp. 225, 226). So, in the case of Grapard's newly liberated women shamans, Foucault expects the worst. They too will turn into oppressors as soon as they become powerful.

But Cornel West, for one, thinks Foucault has sunk too far into a "fervent anti-utopianism" (West 1989, p. 226). Many religious studies liberationists in effect agree. They typically promote some positive picture of what they think their efforts at liberation should achieve. We will see in the coming chapters of Part IV how they craft programs of "positive liberty" about racial justice, sex/gender equality, and such. Thus, even while drawing general moral inspiration from Foucault's war against domination, religious studies liberationists want to go further and articulate visions of positive freedom. Often assuming the title of "social critic," the liberationists among the new generation advocate pursuing "engaged" scholarship. Indeed, some even go so far as to see engagement as the chief aim of scholarship. Cornel West declares that the "major priority of the black intellectual should be the creation or reactivation of institutional networks that promote high-quality critical habits primarily for the purpose of black insurgency" (West 1985, p. 122). That sounds like a pretty clear call to campus activism.

Liberalism and Liberationism, Negative and Positive Liberty

During the course of Part IV, I shall be appealing to the distinction, explained in brief already, between the "liberals" and the "liberationists," and between their correspondingly different concepts of liberty, negative and positive. I believe that we can make a great deal of sense out of different theories of knowledge, "modernism" over against

"post-modernism," by recognizing that they parallel the liberal/liberationist opposition. On this view, a liberal notion of freedom generally maps onto modernism, while a liberationist point of view corresponds to post-modernist theoretical perspectives. If I am right, we cannot, therefore, understand the post-modernist theories of Part IV without understanding them as wedded to liberationist orientations. I think many of the theoretical positions staked out in Part IV can be better understood as shaped by these oppositions.

Another reason to dwell on the liberal/liberationist distinction is that it governs what happens in the classroom. At the top of any list of differences is that newly arrived post-modernism challenges the "old" (modernist!) ideal of objective knowledge. Knowledge, say the post-modernists, is so shot through with subjectivity that talk of objectivity is invalid. We tend to be sensitive to sex/gender differences, for example, in selecting which authors to place on a syllabus. Men may tend to overlook women authors, while women would tend to be more sensitive to the historical exclusion of women from the academic world. Their subjectivity will shape such decisions, say post-modernists. There is not likely to be some "objective" set of authors all will agree deserve inclusion on a syllabus. Taking such positioning seriously could free those teachers from the anxiety that they must attain some – unattainable – ideal of objectivity or neutrality. Given the fact that all thinkers are "situated," it is simply impossible to speak from an objective or neutral point of view. Further, we no longer need to keep our values or interests hidden behind a veil of pretended neutrality. We should confess our value orientations. Indeed, it has become commonplace to hear that we should say "where we are coming from." Speaking from a self-confessed "situated", "positioned" subjectivity can even become a sign of virtue, a brave act of candor.

Two features of this new epistemology might be briefly queried here. First, has not Freud taught us that we should be suspicious of claiming authority about knowing ourselves? A little more humility might be in order before post-modernists assert so confidently that *the* "situation" or "position" of a person, even oneself, can be known with certainty. Do all black folk, for example, speak from their "situation" as African Americans? Do any of us, even, always know why we say or do things? Second, no one wants to return to the days of "doctor knows best," and the problems afflicting claims to objective knowledge. But does that mean there are no rules of fairness in describing what we teach? Does that mean we can only teach material from a "subjective" perspective, and therefore that we are free to teach ("preach") from our own particular political preferences? Since these issues bear directly on what happens in the classroom, students will have to ponder the choices the new attitudes toward knowledge present to them, as we move into Part IV.

Let me illustrate what I have in mind by recent developments in the study of religion, inspired by the desire to defeat social evils such as racism, sex/gender inequality, or the iniquities and inequities of Western imperialism. On the one hand, we do not want to strike a false pose of moral or political neutrality or detachment when it comes to matters of manifest evil. When subjects like the Holocaust, apartheid in South Africa, or female genital mutilation arise in the classroom, how should teachers react? In many cases, these subjects are so obviously morally condemnable that nothing needs be said. And even if the desire to preach is irresistible, preaching to the converted generally irritates its intended audience. The evil nature of such subjects is taken for granted. Dealing with such great moral matters differs from decisions about teaching klezmer music, Afrikaans grammar, or women's Olympic beach volleyball. But what about cases where other important social values are at stake? How should social values, and especially those about which there may be little consensus, be treated? Affirmative action in race or sex/gender hiring or admissions, for example, remains hotly contested. Or what about gun ownership or legalization of recreational drugs? Is it enough to follow the ideas of negative liberty, and join the struggle *against* the factors of social life that oppress folks of various races? Or are teachers supposed to go further and promote and articulate practical visions of positive liberty, which might include affirmative action? Is it, then, enough only to prevent race hatred, or should we also further concrete policies designed for racial uplift, such as affirmative action? Should teachers "preach" affirmative action? Or, are they only permitted to "preach" against racial hatred? Should teachers be agents of positive liberty, or are they restricted to being negative liberators?

Let me extend this discussion of negative/ positive liberty into religion. Anyone who knows religion will know that there is great scope for *freeing people from* ignorance and prejudice about religion. Take *freeing* students *from* prejudices against so-called "primitive" or traditional religions. Robert Orsi, for example, has written widely against the prejudices applied to what he calls "religions of presence," prominent among urban Italian American Catholics. Rather than centering religious life on affirmations of belief in doctrines, this Catholicism offers "opportunities to form deep ties with saints, ancestors, demons, gods, ghosts and other special beings in whose company humans work on the world and themselves" (Orsi 2005, p. 2). Freeing students from prejudices against such a religion of presence – because it smacks of "superstition" – would fit into the liberal project of enabling negative liberty. It frees students from the belief that there is an absolute scale of religions, ranked according to their relative intellectuality, say.

However, unlike liberationists, in striking a pose of neutrality between the religions of modernity and those of presence, liberals take no position on the value of either. Nor do they buy into any deeper commitment to the status of these religions. The matter of religious commitment, the pursuit of a *freedom to* develop their religiosity in one way or another, is left to the conscience of the student. Liberals offer no positive vision of religion here that might provide students with positive direction about realizing a "true (religious) self."

Interestingly, though, Orsi also serves to illustrate what the post-modern liberationist option looks like in the case of his work on the religion of presence. Orsi is not satisfied with negative liberty – merely with *liberating people from* prejudices against the religion of presence. He wants to do more. He actively promotes the religion of presence – positively – as *superior* to more modern forms of Catholicism that had been conventionally thought to have "progressed" beyond the religion of presence. A liberationist "prophetic" imperative seems to inspire Orsi, since he is armed with a positive program of change. It is not enough (negatively) to "liberate" people from their ignorant prejudices about the religion of presence. It is not enough achieve the negative liberating task of creating doubts about so-called "modern" religion. Orsi seeks more. He paints what he believes is a liberating positive picture of what real religion is – namely the religion of presence. Modern, post-Reformation religion represents a degradation, a desiccation, of religious life. The religion of presence is the real thing!

Post-Modernism after Post-Modernism: Four Key Points

As the name implies, *post*-modernism suggests an evolution from the "modern" to something succeeding it – "post." Using such language implies objective historical facts reminiscent of nineteenth-century cultural evolutionists like Tylor or Frazer. Post-modernists present their theory as if it belonged to a different, new epoch from that which modernist theories inhabited. For example, post-modernist theologian Carl Raschke speaks confidently about the post-modern as a historical category. The "post-modern era," says Raschke marks "the unveiling of a new epoch in the historicality of Being" (Raschke 1990, p. 685). Raschke even sets a firm date to its beginnings – September 11, 2001 (Raschke 2008, p. 102). As such, terms like "modern" or "post-modern" play in the same league as terms we met in our discussions of evolutionist theories of religion – primitive/modern, undeveloped/developed, unevolved/evolved, savage/civilized, and so on. "Modern" and "post-modern" go together logically in the same way as up/down, left/right, sacred/profane, and so on. This sort of talk of historical epochs leads Johannes Wolfart to conclude that "post-modernists … posit the progression of the ages in linear, teleological, or even eschatological terms" (Wolfart 2000, p. 382).

But other post-modern theorists, reject "post-modern" as referring to objective historical *epochs*. Instead, they prefer to define the post-modern condition *epistemologically* – in terms of the *rules of discourse* – even if they still think in terms of *progress* over modernism. The title of the book authored by the leader of the post-modern movement, Jean-François Lyotard, *The Postmodern Condition: A Report on Knowledge* (1984), tells us a great deal in this respect. Thus, what people accepted as "given" or "taken for granted" about thinking at one time, no longer prevailed at another. The rules of governing the way we talk have changed. We have already seen similar ruptures in the rules of discourse, going all the way back to the shift in styles of inquiry about Natural Religion. For Bodin or Herbert, the pursuit of Natural Religion was a pursuit of origins, largely in the *historical* sense. However, to Malinowski, Durkheim, Freud, and others, the pursuit for the *natural* origins of religion became one of a pursuit for the *experiential* or psychological bases of religion. The ways we once talked – "discoursed" – no longer worked. New styles of discourse and inquiry took their place.

Let us then put aside the idea of the post-modern condition as a historical era. We don't want to repeat all the errors of nineteenth-century evolutionist talk about "primitive" and "modern." People who assert that history falls into objective periods, especially in a way that implies progress from one period to another, predictably place themselves at the top of the heap! Instead, I wish to concentrate on the far more fruitful line of appreciation of the post-modern, that is, as designating a mode of discourse, a way of thinking, a set of rules governing the way we should talk, and so on. Let me try to recapitulate some of the points we have in part already seen that post-modernists believe happened to our way of talking and thinking.

First, as I have already mentioned, post-modernists think that we are not allowed to speak about of "objective" knowledge. Modernist theorists, like Freud, Malinowski, Durkheim, Eliade, and so on, took it for granted that "doctor knows best," *and* that they were the doctor! Freud, for example, believed that his interpretations of religion were "objective" facts. Likewise, Durkheim believed that he produced a *scientific* study of objective "things." Malinowski never doubted that a "scientific theory of culture" – religion included – was possible and well within his grasp (Malinowski 1944). However, post-modernists query the idea that "objective" knowledge is even possible at all. Is not the very claim to have such knowledge a matter of one's own subjective judgment? Other psychologists disagreed with Freud about the nature of the allegedly "objective" facts about the mind. Does not disagreement mean that Freud thought about the mind in *his own* way, just as his opponents have? And does that not mean that he and they therefore "constructed" the mind according to their own perspectives? In addition, if so, has not "objectivity" gone out the window? Has not the claim to objective knowledge been exposed as the height of arrogance, nicely captured in the phrase, "doctor knows best"? Ought we not to explore how and why theorists see the world, or how and why they think that they believe religion is explainable by appeals to certain objective workings? (Personal disclaimer: I share much of this view.)

Secondly, post-modernism would eliminate all talk of "science," and even more a "scientific study of religion." On this view, despite their respective claims to be doing a "science of religion," neither Max Müller nor Durkheim can be said so to be doing. Since objective knowledge is no more, so too is science. All discourse rests on presuppositions which themselves are axiomatic, or taken without question. All discourse is socially constructed, science as well. The task of a study of religion is, then, to "deconstruct" the way the data have been put together.

The mention of deconstruction gives me an opportunity to credit the French philosopher Jacques Derrida (1930–2004) for his contribution to some of the principles of a post-modern study of religion. Given the immense complexity of Derrida's thought and the massive extent of his oeuvre, it would be hopeless to try here either to summarize it or to expound it at length. Regrettably, therefore, my recognition of Derrida's contributions to the post-modern moment in theorizing about religion will be scanty at best. Underlining the difficulty in presenting Derrida's thinking, one could add that it is actually more accurate to call it "post-structuralism," rather than "post-modernism," even though a kinship of spirit exists between the two.

Returning to the post-modern rejection of a scientific study of religion, I must point out that an unwelcome consequence has been the return of a theologized religious studies. Theologian Garrett Green, accordingly, welcomes the "post-modern turn," because it asserts that "'all data are theory-laden' – theological, religious or indeed, so-called 'scientific' data" (Green 1995, p. 473). All such views "are socially and historically located and necessarily implicated in paradigmatic commitments to certain values, concepts, and methods" (Green 1995, p. 473). Theology, then, stands on the same relativistic ground as any allegedly "scientific" study of religion. With Durkheim in particular in mind, Cambridge

theologian John Milbank adds to this position and rather baldly asserts that "theology encounters, in effect, in sociology only a theology, and indeed a church in disguise, but a theology and a church dedicated to promoting a certain secular consensus" (Milbank 1990, p. 4). If Milbank and Green – and post-modernism – are right, there is no justification for restricting theological teaching in the university, or for preferring a scientific study of religion over a theological one. We will see how key theorists in the coming chapters put these post-modern methodological and theoretical principles into practice by attempting to re-theologize the study of religion.

Third, post-modernists believe we can better study religion by *engaged commitment* in a religion. They see no need to distinguish between *engaging* in religion and *studying* religion. Not only do the two not mutually exclude one another, they reinforce one another! Sometimes, this amounts to the good-sense recognition of the value of a religious insider's point of view. We can better understand religion if, at least at one time, we were or are religious. As such, the commonsense version of this post-modernist position reflects a healthy skepticism about the modernist claims of "outsiders" to understand a religion better than "insiders." Post-modernists refuse to submit to the modernist view that "doctor knows best." Readers of Parts II and III will recognize glaring examples of the "doctor knows best" position, already mentioned, perhaps most obviously in Malinowski's embrace of behaviorism. For this later, hyper-scientific Malinowski what the "natives" think or what the "insiders" say was irrelevant to understanding and explaining their religious life. All that counts is observable religious "behavior." And since religious "behavior" is overt and public, the "doctor" can observe and diagnose – understand and explain – it *objectively*. Post-modernists not only argue that objectivity is impossible, but that we better understand and explain religion if we attend to the subjectivity of religious people.

But lately, however, full-scale, if non-confessional, theologizing has appeared in the study of religion, marching under the flag of a new generation of post-modern theorizing. These scholars deny the distinction between confessional theology – teaching *of* religion – and the scientific study of religion – teaching *about* religion. They do so because, as Chicago historian of religions Martin

Marty says, science as well as theology makes "its own kind of quasi-creedal commitment" (Marty 1985, p. 8; Wiebe 2000, p. 352). Both science and religion, in effect, rest on acts of *faith*. As such, what is called "teaching about religion" has actually always been a "teaching of religion" because putatively detached, neutral, or objective methods of teaching religious studies themselves rest on unacknowledged absolute faith commitments too. Is not the value and validity of the pursuit of scientific knowledge itself accepted on "faith" (Wiebe 2000, p. 352)? We are all engaged; we are all subjective. All the efforts made by the founders of the study of religion to keep religious and scientific enterprises distinct from one another were, then, the mistakes of a now superseded and naive "modernist" project. There are, of course, dissenters from the post-modern agenda, such as Toronto's Donald Wiebe. He claims that, if applied to the study of religion, post-modernism would actually promote reversion to pre-modern – theological – forms of inquiry (Wiebe 2000, p. 364).

Fourth, post-modernists deny the *universal* pretensions of any putative scientific study of religion. As Catherine Bell has argued, "neither religion nor science is exempt from socio-cultural influence." All knowledge is "local" – including knowledge about religion, such as would be produced by some putative scientific study of religion. All our ideas, theories, and terms are "embedded in particular experiences and 'conventional perspectives'" (Bell 1996, p. 185; Wiebe, 2000, p. 353). These should be embraced. As we will see, this perspective gives warrant to the feminist theoretical claim that Eliade's universal idea of *Homo religiosus* ought not to be the basis of a study of religion. There is no such universal, gender-neutral style of religiousness. Rather, all human beings are "gendered," and thus no scholar studying religion, no participant in ritual, is ever "neuter" (Bynum 1986, p. 2). Thus, the ambitions of the founders of the study of religion to do general cross-cultural comparison should be abandoned. No further sweeping generalizations about people would be allowed, such as Freudian Michael Carroll made about the impact of father-ineffective families on the psyches of young men. Nor would the efforts of Malinowski or Durkheim to argue for a universal function of religion be likely to produce good results. Their sweep was just too

broad. "What is needed," Wiebe reports of Bell's view, "is a view of science that does not simply reflect the ideology of science but instead allows for a study of religion 'that is not universal or hegemonic'" (Bell 1996, p. 188; Wiebe 2000, p. 353).

So, in summary, post-modernist approaches to religion will, first, resurrect subjectivity and do away with the "doctor knows best" style of the modernists. Second, post-modernism brings a critical eye to all discourse, especially to ideas taken for granted. If all discourse is "constructed" with some human purpose in mind, the job of the religious studies scholar is to "deconstruct" theoretical discourse to get behind the agendas lurking there. The idea of a "science of religion" seems incoherent from the start. Third, the post-modern scholar declares commitment to liberating human values. As a scholar, one should also be engaged in realizing the positive liberation of those populations suffering under the oppression of unjust powers. The negative liberation of liberalism is not enough. Fourth, and finally, post-modern religious studies scholars should immerse themselves in local scenes, and avoid making pretentious universal claims about religion as such.

Questions

Resistance to post-modern styles of inquiry springs from reservations about the substance of post-modern theory itself. First, critics question whether an actual "rupture" in discourse exists (Wolfart 2000, p. 381). Villanova University religion theorist Gustavo Benavides has argued that the term "post-modern," may be part of a politics – ironically, in Foucault's sense of a player in the "micro-fascism of everyday life." It plays a tactical role in *creating* – rather than just naively *reflecting* – new ways of talking. As such, post-modern styles of talking just don't "happen": they deliberately set out to oppose the idea of the "modern": it is "self-conscious distancing" (Benavides 1998, p. 187). But why put such a marked gap between the modern and the post-modern? Johannes Wolfart again fixes on the possible politics behind such talk. Even when the talk is about new styles of *discourse* rather than historical *epochs*, Wolfart believes the subtext of post-modern theory is *progress* beyond whatever lingers in the "modern" condition. "You" are not like "us": we are "post-modern"; you are "modern" – and it is best to be post-modern.

The question is, of course, whether the gap between modernity and post-modernity, like that between the primitive and the modern, marks a real difference in value, and if so, what is this difference? Is the gap presumed to exist between modern and post-modern really so "linear, teleo-logical or even eschatological" as post-modern theorists would have us believe? In addition, if gap there is, does it justify claims to post-modern uniqueness? Gustavo Benavides challenges the entire premise of the uniqueness of post-modernity. Benavides thinks one way to look at the post-modern is as an intense self-examination of the notion of modernity. However, this "unavoid-able exercise in self-examination," says Benavides, is what modernism does all the time. Thus, post-modernity is best understood as an "intensification of modernity" itself (Benavides 1998, p. 200). Post-modernity is just another turn in the ratcheting up of the intellectual tensions provoked by modernity itself. Students should note these criticisms so that they do not become victims of faddish thinking. In the chapters in Part IV, I shall begin by taking at face value the ways that post-modern theorists "think they are right" in believing their theories are uniquely different from modernist theories of reli-gion. After that, you, the reader, and I, can argue among ourselves (at least virtually) about if and why post-modern theories are right!

Post-Modern Studies of Religion Focus on Race, Gender, and Post-Colonialism

In asking post-modernists why they "thought they were right" I start with what I take to be their stronger proposals for the study of religion. The post-modern change of sensibility suggests the elaboration of three broad, but interrelated, new theoretical tropes in the study of religion: race, gender, and post-colonialism. In the process, this reaction to what Eliade represents takes us to meet theorists of religion and race, such as W.E.B. Du Bois and Cornel West, theorists of gender and religion, such as Rosemary Radnor Reuther, Karen McCarthy Brown, and, derivatively, Judith Butler, and theorists of post-colonialism and religion, such as Talal Asad and Edward Said.

Behind each of these three movements in the post-modern theorizing of religion are, as well, the shadows of commanding "master theorists" who, in effect, made the focus on race, gender, and post-colonialism theoretically possible. I have argued that the master theorist of the new sensibility is Michel Foucault, mostly for his bringing of power to the fore. Of course, theorists like Jean-François Lyotard, who coined the term "post-modernism," and post-structuralist Jacques Derrida, father of "deconstructionism," cast long shadows over the origins of this new sensibility. However, Foucault, with his passion for liberation and sympathy for the oppressed, stands out as the real spiritual progenitor of the post-modern sensibility – at least in the study of religion.

One final point. I have emphasized theories and theorists of religion just as I have in Parts II and III of this book. This is not a general book about theoretical writing or discourse, although I have tried to be alert even to indirect or derived theorizing about religion. This book is about the-ories of religion. For that reason, someone like Judith Butler, a renowned feminist theorist, will get only brief attention in this book because she has not dealt in any sustained way with religion. This promised to change when Butler was recen-tly engaged to take religion seriously by feminist scholars of religion such as are found in Armour and St. Ville's *Bodily Citations: Religion and Judith Butler* (2006). There, the editors note that while "Butler's writings have been crucial and often controversial in the development of feminist and queer theory, *Bodily Citations* is the first anthology centered on applying her theories to religion." Yet despite these valiant efforts to draw Butler into dialogue, critics of this anthology note how little concern Butler evinces for religion in her replies to contributors to this volume. In the prestigious H-Net review of this collection, the reviewer refers to Butler's "afterword" as "truly disappoint-ing." One problem is that although Butler "recog-nizes that 'resistance' does not get at the complexity of agency, there is little evidence that she recog-nizes the challenge that truly taking account of religious bodies, practices, and histories poses to her analyses." In the end, Butler remains, "paro-chially secular." If this review is accurate, one will not expect much from her, as indeed, the balance of her oeuvre would already suggest. Specifically *religious* identity does not particularly interest

Butler. Identity as such does. Accordingly, Butler does not qualify as a major religious studies theorist. This is not to say that she might not well do so in the future, in the same way Foucault originally did not, but later came to be (Pritchard 2007).

Liberationist approaches to the study of religion take aid and comfort from these post-modern views about human knowledge. Liberationism exploits post-modernism's critiques of "objectivity" and "neutrality." Most importantly, it blurs the difference between religious studies and theology. Post-modernism smooths the way for the characteristic liberationist affirmation of "prophecy" or engagement in the university. As we will see in the coming discussions of theories of religion and race, sex, or post-colonialism, post-modern theorists ultimately seek to justify liberationist political goals by appealing to tenets of post-modern theory. The immediate aim of the theorists of Part IV is radically to revolutionize thinking about the relation of religion to racial, sexual and post-colonial "Others" (Wolfart 2000, p. 390). This new generation of theorizing religion will occupy us in the succeeding chapters.

References

Armour, E.T., and S.M. St. Ville (eds.). 2006. *Bodily Citations: Religion and Judith Butler. Gender, Theory, and Religion*. New York: Columbia University Press,

Asad, T. 1993. *Genealogies of Religion: Discipline and Reasons of Power in Christianity and Islam*. Baltimore: Johns Hopkins University Press.

Bell, C.M. 1996. "Modernism and Postmodernism in the Study of Religion." *Religious Studies Review* 22(3): 179–190.

Benavides, G. 1998. "Modernity." In M.C. Taylor (ed.), *Critical Terms for Religious Studies*. Chicago: University of Chicago Press.

Bynum, C.W. 1986. "Introduction: The Complexity of Symbols." In C.W. Bynum, S. Harrell, and P. Richman (eds.), *Gender and Religion*. Boston: Beacon Press.

Chidester, D. 1988. *Patterns of Power: Religion and Politics in American Culture*. Englewood Cliffs: Prentice Hall.

Eliade, M. 1964. *Shamanism*. New York: Bollingen.

Eliade, M. 1968. *Myths, Dreams and Mysteries*. London: Harvill.

Foucault, M. 1977a. "The Eye of Power." In C. Gordon (ed.), *Power/Knowledge: Selected Interviews and Other Writings, 1972–1977*. New York: Pantheon, pp. 146–165

Foucault, M. 1977b. "The History of Sexuality." In C. Gordon (ed.), *Power/Knowledge: Selected Interviews and Other Writings, 1972–1977*. New York: Pantheon.

Grapard, A. 1991. "Visions of Excess and Excesses of Vision: Women and Transgression in Japanese Myth." *Japanese Journal of Religious Studies* 18(1): 3–22.

Green, G. 1995. "Challenging the Religious Studies Canon: Karl Barth's Theory of Religion." *The Journal of Religion* 75: 473–486.

Hackney, J.R. 1998. "Derrick Bell's Re-soundings: W.E.B. Du Bois, Modernism and Critical Race Theory." *Law and Society Inquiry* 23(1) (Winter): 141–164.

Lyotard, J.-F. 1984. *The Postmodern Condition: A Report on Knowledge*. Minneapolis: University of Minnesota Press.

Malinowski, B. 1944. *A Scientific Theory of Culture and Other Essays*. Oxford: Oxford University Press.

Marty, M. 1985. *What Is Modern about the Modern Study of Religion?* The University Lecture in Religion at Arizona State University. Tempe: Department of Religious Studies, Arizona State University.

McCutcheon, R.T. 1997. *Manufacturing Religion: The Discourse on Sui Generis Religion and the Politics of Nostalgia*. New York: Oxford University Press.

Milbank, J. 1990. *Theology and Social Theory: Beyond Secular Reason*. Oxford: Blackwell.

Orsi, R.A. 2005. *Between Heaven and Earth: The Religious Worlds People Make and the Scholars Who Study Them*. Princeton: Princeton University Press.

Pritchard, E. 2007. "Religions That Matter." Review of Ellen T. Armour and Susan M. St. Ville (eds.), *Bodily Citations: Religion and Judith Butler. H-Net* (April).

Raschke, C.A. 1990. "Fire and Roses: Toward Authentic Post-Modern Religious Thinking." *Journal of the American Academy of Religion* 58(4): 671–689.

Raschke, C. 2008. "The Religion of Politics." *Journal for Cultural and Religious Theory* 9(1) (Winter): 101–111.

Strenski, I. 1973. "Mircea Eliade: Some Theoretical Problems." In A. Cunningham (ed.), *Theory of Myth*. London: Sheed & Ward.

Strenski, I. 1998. "On 'Religion' and Its Despisers." In T.A. Idinopulos and B.C. Wilson (eds.), *What Is Religion?* Leiden: E.J. Brill.

Strenski, I. 2002. Review of Russell T. McCutcheon, *Critics, Not Caretakers: Redescribing the Public Study of Religion. JAAR* 70: 427–430.

Tweed, T.A. 2006. *Crossings and Dwellings: A Theory of Religion*. Cambridge, MA: Harvard University Press.

West, C. 1985. "The Dilemma of the Black Intellectual." *Cultural Critique* 1 (Autumn): 109–124.

West, C. 1989. *The American Evasion of Philosophy: A Genealogy of Pragmatism*. Madison: University of Wisconsin Press.

Wiebe, D. 2000. "Modernism." In W. Braun and R.T. McCutcheon (eds.), *Guide to the Study of Religion*. London: Cassell.

Wolfart, J.C. 2000. "Postmodernism." In W. Braun and R.T. McCutcheon (eds.), *Guide to the Study of Religion*. London: Cassell.

Further Reading

Asad, T. 2001. "Reading a Modern Classic: W.C. Smith's *The Meaning and End of Religion*." *History of Religions* 40(3): 205–222.

Bellah, R.N. 1978. "Religious Studies as 'New Religion.'" In G. Baker and J. Needleman (eds.), *Understanding the New Religion*. New York: Seabury Press.

Berlin, I. 1958. *Two Concepts of Liberty*. Oxford: Oxford University Press.

Capps, W.H. (ed.). 1978. *The Interpenetration of New Religion and Religious Studies*. Understanding the New Religions. New York: Seabury Press,

Chidester, D. 1996. *Savage Systems: Colonialism and Comparative Religion in Southern Africa*. Bloomington: Indiana University Press.

Cone, J.H. 1970. *A Black Theology of Liberation*. Philadelphia: J.B. Lippincott.

Durkheim, É. 1975. "Contribution to Discussion 'Religious Sentiment at the Present Time.'" In W.S.F. Pickering (ed.), *Durkheim on Religion*. London: Routledge.

Eliade, M. 1959. "Methodological Remarks on Religious Symbolism." In M. Eliade and J. Kitagawa (eds.), *The*

History of Religions: Essays in Methodology. Chicago: University of Chicago Press.

Eliade, M. 1965. *The Two and the One*. London: Harvill.

Eliade, M. 1969. "Crisis and Renewal." In *The Quest*. Chicago: University of Chicago Press.

Eliade, M. 1977. *No Souvenirs*. New York: Harper & Row.

Foucault, M. 1977. "Two Lectures." In C. Gordon (ed.), *Power/Knowledge: Selected Interviews and Other Writings, 1972–1977*. New York: Pantheon.

Jaeger, H. 1985. "Generations in History: Reflections on a Controversial Concept." *History and Theory* 24(3): 273–292.

Kirkpatrick, F.G. 1999. "Review of Mark C. Taylor, *Critical Terms for Religious Studies*." *Journal for the Scientific Study of Religion* 38(2): 320–321.

Long, C.H. 1986. *Significations*. Aurora, CO: Davies Group.

Taylor, M.C. 1984. *Erring: A Postmodern A/theology*. Chicago: University of Chicago Press.

15

Theorizing Religion with Race in Mind: Prophecy or Curiosity?

What "Color" – Race – Is Your Theory?

The classic theorists would have considered the question of the "color" (race) of their theories an absurd one.[1] For the classic theorists, theorizing occurred outside positions of differential agency of social or political position, outside of space and time – somewhat like mathematics. Theorists simply theorized, or thought, with no consideration for matters extrinsic to the theorizing in question. For that reason, it made no sense to them to think that people of different races might theorize in different ways. Theorizing, like thinking, was a universal human act, common to all members of our species.

Up to a point, I think this view of shared humanity is worth embracing – as long as it respects what I call the "local" differences of race, sex/gender, differential agency, and so on. Indeed, this chapter is devoted to grasping the ways in which race makes a difference to the ways we theorize. I shall do so without accepting what would be, in effect, an "apartheid" theory of humanity – one which would deny our essential common humanity. Yet before saying why I think we need to think more carefully about what would "color" our theories, we need frankly to admit that a number of social theories, generated and deployed by the West, Japan, and other imperial

powers, were *deliberately* "*colored*" – in the sense that they were put to use to justify a color-conscious racism. Until quite recently, such theories of racial – White – superiority, for instance, held sway in South Africa with its apartheid policies. But even more insidious were nineteenth-century evolutionist theorists, who may have lacked explicit racist intentions in their theorizing, but who nevertheless could be indicted as "colored" White and racist. Much, if not all of the talk of "primitives" was a form of "colored" – in this case "White" – theorizing. At best, the discourse on primitives might not have been deliberately "colored," although this is cold comfort to those folk so classified.

But granted, then, that E.B. Tylor's evolutionist theorizing, for instance, constituted colored (racist) theorizing, would that imply that all evolutionist theories of human development are? It's not so easy to tell. To be sure, an evolutionist theory which placed Japanese atop the developmental scale above, say, the Chinese and European, would be just as "colored" – except in another way – as Tylor's. But could we not imagine an evolutionist social theory which did not use "race" or "color" as a marker of value, either superior or inferior? An evolutionist theory might be based on differentials of intelligence, wealth, physical attractiveness, and so on. We

Understanding Theories of Religion: An Introduction, Second Edition. Ivan Strenski.
© 2015 Ivan Strenski. Published 2015 by John Wiley & Sons, Ltd.

might find reasons to object to such a theory, but it would not be because it was a colored (racist) theory.

The theorists I bring to the table in this chapter all, however, think that something is lacking in the way religion has been theorized by the classical mainstream of the field, all of whom, incidentally, happen to be White men. They thought about religion as a human universal. For them, religion had no color, for one thing. They hardly imagined that their racial position in the world, seated in the capitals of the great imperial empires, left any significant marks on their theorizing. That meant a number of things. When the religions of non-Whites were studied, they were regarded in ways that typically disadvantaged them or overlooked entirely matters salient to the folk studied. Whites set the intellectual agenda for non-Whites, because they owned the disciplines studying others. Consider alone the evolutionists.

What then does it mean to "color" one's theorizing, given that we know in general now what the grievances against classic theorists on this score are? I want to suggest that a "colored" theory would address these grievances in two ways. First, it would change the *subjects* and *objects* to which we address questions; second, it would change the kinds of *questions* we ask about religion. A "Black" theory of religion, for example, would both address different subjects and objects, as well as pose different questions. It would have its own intellectual agenda of questions. Quite simply, a theory of religion "colored" Black might well turn its attention to the religions of Black people, and quite probably in a different way than the nineteenth-century evolutionists. As we will see in the following chapter, Karen McCarthy Brown devoted her celebrated book, *Mama Lola*, to a Black Haitian Vodou priestess, in and for herself. Not to essentialize Blacks or anyone else, similarly, a Black theory of religion might be expected to address certain issues of historical concern to Black folk. Again at the risk of essentializing Black or any other folk, perhaps the racially situated point of view of Black scholars might generate its own distinctive interests?

Again, we would want to bear in mind throughout that we do not want to reinstate some sort of apartheid theory of knowledge, such that

only Black folk could see things from a Black point of view. After all, one of the big breakthrough books exposing the hypocrisies of slavery was *The Peculiar Institution*, written by White historian Kenneth M. Stampp (Stampp 1956). Nevertheless, we would not be surprised to see that a Black historian of religion, Anthony Pinn, pioneered the study of slave auctions, here as religious rituals of subjugation. Or could not membership in the African American community have pressed Black historian of religion Albert Raboteau, likewise, to study the entire sweep of what he calls "slave religion"? Do we really imagine that these intellectual agendas are accidental?

But beyond addressing Black religion as a subject or object of study with what might be called a particularly racially inflected point of view, I would argue that we really only get to the theoretical level of the study of Black religion when we begin asking critical questions about categories. And this is precisely what Black scholars like Pinn and William Hart do. They raise critical theoretical questions naturally imaginable in a "colored" theory of religion, even if it would certainly have been open to non-Blacks to raise the same questions. Therefore, I am arguing that a theory is "colored" to the extent that its central questions are conditioned by location within a certain racial community. For example, what do we mean when we speak of "Black" religion? Is there, even, such a thing? Here, Raboteau shows how such a "colored" theory, in the sense of being self-critical about concepts, can enrich the study of religion as a whole. He gives us a totally new concept of a kind of religion that he calls "slave religion." Raboteau's work sends ripples out into the larger pool of the study of religions. How does Raboteau's "slave religion" measure up comparatively to other "religions of the oppressed"? Is there something distinctive about the religion of Black American slaves when compared with them? How does "slave religion" compare with what we might call the "serf religion" of the Russian Empire? These are the kinds of questions we would ask if we thought that race mattered in theorizing religion – if we thought our theories were "colored." In sum, nothing decides the question of the "color" of one's theory more than the questions we want to ask. The "color" of one's theories is a simple function of the kinds of questions we ask. Theories are "colored" if the questions they pose embrace matters of race or color.

Let me then turn to the way Black scholars have approached Black religion such that their racially located point of view may have developed in them certain sensitivities to the subject and objects to be studied, as well as the critical questions of be posed.

As we will see, the imperatives to speak to the place of Black folk in the United States will generate two different styles of inquiry, fundamentally in conflict with each other. I shall call them "prophecy" and "curiosity," respectively. Prophets want to change the world. They are an impatient lot, and have little time to quibble about the meanings of words. When it comes to Black religion, for example, the prophet assumes they know what it is, thus freeing the prophet to act upon that knowledge. The person of curiosity wants to ask a lot of questions about so-called Black religion. They want to understand what it is, and even if it is something unique or distinctive. I want to suggest that, as much as the moral power and actual achievements of the prophet are to be praised, our chief job in the university is to do our utmost to *understand* things. That does not mean we could not or should not want to go on and become "prophets" in our own time, but only that the two acts differ. Our job is to be critical, to ask questions – especially the ones no one else has the courage to ask. That often means taking our time before acting. If so, so be it.

Social Research and History: The Two Cardinal Methods

Before recommending certain methods and theories, let us see just what methods and theories Black scholars in the study of race and religion actually used. In this way, we can shift to the point of view of Black scholars to see what they thought was important. Take *method* first. Two methods for the study of religion seemed compelling – social research and historical writing or "history." In social research, or sociology, the great W.E.B. Du Bois led the way. Over a hundred years ago, he applied the methods of the scientific study of society, learned at the University of Berlin, to produce mainline demographic and statistical studies

of the Black community. As for historians, they are too numerous to single out any one at this point, although we will soon review some of the major players.

Du Bois and His Modernist Program of Social Research

Let me introduce the method of social research as it was pioneered by Black scholar W.E.B. Dubois to see what lessons we can draw from it. The career of Du Bois falls into two radically different phases that have been emblematic for Black scholars. While he began as a paradigm modernist, he concluded as a post-modernist *avant la lettre*. Du Bois' first works are standard-issue modernist efforts in scientific studies of religion in Black America; Du Bois changed radically, however, into a great activist and advocate for the rights of Black Americans. He totally abandoned the path he had laboriously taken in his Harvard doctorate and in his studies in Germany – sociology. Well in advance of his time, he also worked for women's liberation. The radical quality of these changes can hardly be exaggerated. As an activist publicist, he shed his modernist faith in science decisively, never again to resume scientific work. While Du Bois' achievements in the sociology of the Black American church are rightly praised, his lasting legacy for Black scholars remains his "prophetic" stance.

I would never presume to opine whether Du Bois was right to give up science for the sake of activism. That is a question only my Black colleagues and fellow-citizens can answer from the depths of their consciences. My question, rather, concerns the *study of religion* in a university. What place, if any, does the kind of activism Du Bois practiced have in the university? Further, is Du Bois' conception and practice of a "scientific" study of religion the only, or even the best, model available to Black scholars of religion? In order to respond to such questions, we need to pay close attention to the way Du Bois traversed both sides of the science/prophecy opposition. His journey is, furthermore, emblematic of theoretical debates that have vexed the study of Black religion until the present day, and the dilemmas he faced will show themselves to be the very same ones our Black colleagues today face. In this way, understanding Du Bois helps us understand at least one perennial dilemma: defining Black studies in religion.

Why did Du Bois "think he was right" first to take up the path of science and then to forsake it for that of prophecy? The story begins in his early life in western Massachusetts, passes through his years as a student at Fisk, Harvard, and Berlin, and culminates with his reactions to the hard facts of racism in the United States. I suggest that Du Bois' years in Germany the late 1890s were decisive. Those years dramatized the choice between social research and social activism in the university, because that choice was vexing a whole generation of students in the German universities of the time. On the modernist/scientific side, Du Bois was drawn to the leading social scientists in the German Empire. Here we include Berlin economist Adolf Wagner (1835–1917) and economic historian Gustav von Schmoller (1838–1917). From them, Du Bois learned how to transform his native talent for insight into social situations into rigorous and pioneering social research. He thus felt himself equipped with the prestige of high-powered science that he would later use in his studies of the religion of Black Americans. The clout science gave his work would alone make Whites listen to the case he would make in behalf of Black folk, or at least so Du Bois thought. On the activist/(pre-)post-modernist side, were very different sorts of role models. These were the influential radical social and political activists, *Kathedersozialisten* – the Socialists of the (Professorial) Chair. A major figure here was philosopher and historian Heinrich von Treitschke. In him and his ilk, Du Bois found models of how social and political activism could be brought to the classroom. Du Bois' German experience thus presented him with sharply opposed life and career alternatives that would be the same for subsequent generations of justice-minded African American religious studies scholars in our own time.

Let's back up slightly to delve into Du Bois' state of mind upon arriving in Berlin. In the years before studying in Germany, Du Bois, who was descended from an ancient line of mixed-race ancestors, resident in the Hudson Valley since its Dutch settlement (Aptheker 1968, p. 104), gradually accumulated lessons on the meaning of racial identity and racism in America. Germany

provided him a set of clear-cut options for what his reaction to the plight of Blacks in America would be. Surprising though it may be, Du Bois tells us that at first he experienced little or no racial discrimination, and certainly vastly less than did the newly arrived Irish immigrants (Aptheker 1968, pp. 82, 94). Second, along with little or no experience of racism, he knew next to nothing about the lives of most Black folk in America. He knew nothing, for example, of the Black church for the greater portion of his youth. When some newly freed slaves from the South appeared in Great Barrington, and rallied together in a church of their own – a Negro Methodist Zion church – Du Bois saw them as exotic. He could not understand why these Black folk separated themselves from the rest of Great Barrington. Great Barrington's Black folk "were not set aside … [They] were a part of the community of long-standing" (Aptheker 1968, p. 83).

In time, Du Bois was to feel the sting of the subtle form of racism against Blacks in Great Barrington. Although shows of overt hatred toward Blacks was not part of his youthful experience in western Massachusetts, Blacks were stereotyped as suitable for only certain types of careers, and these did not include the university, to which Du Bois aspired (Aptheker 1968, p. 106). Gradually, this soft racism hardened into something that frustrated Du Bois' scholarly and intellectual ambitions. A "veil of color," as he famously put it, fell over him. As he grew into full adulthood, "intermingling with my white fellows would grow more restricted. Friendships would become a matter of explanation or even embarrassment to my schoolmates." The "spiritual isolation" that Du Bois had begun to feel even in his hometown would only become greater, perhaps unbearable. That grim "veil of color" was going to fall upon him, no matter what he did or became (Aptheker 1968, p. 83). Therefore by the time he set off for Berlin, he had caught up on the experience of racism felt by America's Blacks.

This growing racial conscious matured further after his decision to "go south" to attend the historically Black Fisk University in Nashville. A rejection by Harvard effectively also cut off that path for the time being. Undeterred, he pursued his intense curiosity about the heartland of Black America. In addition, there he confronted his own African American racial identity: "Above all

I was going to meet colored people of my own age and education of my own ambitions," he wrote (Aptheker 1968, p. 105). These first contacts stirred inchoate but powerful emotions in Du Bois. About hearing Black spirituals for the first time, he tells us: "I was thrilled and moved to tears and seemed to recognize something inherently and deeply my own in that music" (Aptheker 1968, p. 106). He also recalled how during his summers, free of classes and lectures, he taught Black children in the rural South. In a way that his own Black "blood" had not taught him, he was "learning to become Black." Du Bois had, in a way, joined his "race." He had associated himself and the African blood flowing in his veins with the history and culture of Black America. Like Barack Obama, Du Bois was an African American who had to learn *about* being Black, and then learn *to be* Black.

The Making and Breaking of a Scholar-Activist

Du Bois went on from Fisk to become the first African American to win admission to the Harvard doctoral program. His program at Harvard included two years (1892–94) abroad studying at the University of Berlin with the world's masters of social research. There, he befriended Max Weber, as well as economist Adolf Wagner, economic historian Gustav von Schmoller, and philosopher and historian Heinrich von Treitschke, mentioned earlier. Although Du Bois maintained a long professional relationship with Weber, it was, rather, Wagner, Schmoller, and Treitschke who seemed to have made the biggest impression on him.

Schmoller supplied Du Bois with a scientific strategy that Du Bois used to attack the color bar in the United States (Barkin 2000, p. 89). But, science aside, he apparently made the longest-lasting impact upon Du Bois in his role as "prophet" or social critic. Schmoller, along with Wagner, often took their politics into the lecture hall as key members of a political movement thriving among the university set, the *Kathedersozialisten*. These "Socialists of the Chair" merged the careers of the academic professor and activist political "prophet" into one. They felt a duty as teachers of the youth to support a progressive national

politics. Treitschke, on the other hand, made no effort to distinguish academic and political identities: he preached his own political doctrines directly from the podium. Du Bois tells us how much he admired their being passionately concerned about contemporary issues (Barkin 2000, p. 92). Doubtless, the example of the *Kathedersozialisten* helped Du Bois "think he was right" to inform his own sociological researches with the high-minded moral purposes of progressive social reform in behalf of Black America. He thus returned from Germany convinced that he was "right to think" that science could be infused with political values. He was "exhilarated by the belief that he could have an impact on racial discrimination in America."

The first intellectual fruits of this strategy of trying to rally White America to the Black cause were the first two books he would produce – *The Philadelphia Negro* (1899) and *The Negro Church* (1903). *The Philadelphia Negro* is a rigorous, empirical work of social research in the Berlin tradition of massive statistical and documentary scholarship. "I was going to study the facts, any and all facts, concerning the American Negro and his plight, work up to any valid generalizations which I could," declared Du Bois (Aptheker 1968, p. 206). The pages and pages of statistics, charts, maps, and tables Du Bois and his team assembled remind one of nothing so much as the classics in sociology already known to readers of this book, such as Durkheim's *Suicide*. He tells us, for example, that he gathered all the data for *The Philadelphia Negro* "from the streets – empirically," using questionnaires administered by a team of his own researchers in Philadelphia's African American neighborhoods. The book tells of the "social behavior, social networks, social organizations and social institutions" of the Black church as rigorously as any work of social science of the day did.

We will miss the thrust of these two early works of Du Bois if we imagine that he wrote them with no social or moral purpose in mind. We know that in addition to their being impeccable works of mainline social *science*, he wanted these works to serve the cause of reform, much as some of the *Kathedersozialisten* had urged. Du Bois naturally took on American racism. However, he ruffled the feathers of the Black church as well. With shades of Max Weber's affirmation of the "this-worldly" values of Calvinism, Du Bois complained of the "otherworldliness" of the Black churches. They had systematically resisted political engagement in behalf of Black liberation (Zuckerman 2002, p. 248).

However, things did not go well for Du Bois professionally. Despite everything he had done to adhere meticulously to the canons of mainstream sociology of religion, despite his Harvard and Continental credentials, his books were virtually ignored. The prevailing racist ideology among mainstream sociologists, such as the social Darwinism we have met in Tylor, Frazer, and others, blinded them from recognizing Du Bois as "one of their own." Mainstream sociology had no interest in Du Bois' Philadelphia Blacks amid its absorption in the concerns of White immigration to America. "So far as the American world of science and letters was concerned," Du Bois lamented, "we never 'belonged'; we remain unrecognized in learned societies and academic groups. We rated merely as Negroes studying Negroes, and after all what had Negroes to do with America or science?" (Aptheker 1968, p. 278). After all Du Bois' efforts to establish his legitimacy among White social scientists, these were bitter pills to swallow.

Added to the dismal reception of his first books, Du Bois had hoped that the power of "objective" science might have at least dented White America's racism. "I could not persuade myself," wrote Du Bois, full of modernist optimism, "that my program of solving the Negro problem by scientific investigation was wrong, or that I could possibly fail of eventual support when once it was undertaken" (Aptheker 1968, p. 225). America's racist hatred of Blacks was so transparently "based on widespread ignorance," that Du Bois expected (scientific) truth to win out (Aptheker 1968, p. 228). However, his experience of being ignored professionally forced him reluctantly to conclude that race hatred was stronger than objective facts. Racism was somehow too deeply rooted in the darker, inaccessible, irrational side of the American psyche to yield to rational arguments, however well made (Barkin 2000, p. 92). White America's social science establishment thus gave Du Bois abundant reasons to "think he was right" to change the entire course of his career, and alter the tactics employed in his fight against racism. Science had rejected him, so he rejected science. Instead of science, Du Bois made "prophetic," moral or political activism his career. "My career as a scientist," he tells us, "was to be swallowed up in my role as master of propaganda" (Aptheker 1968, p. 253). And so it was.

Events in the wider world of American racial relations also sped Du Bois' turn from science to activism. A spectacular rash of vicious lynchings and race riots of the "Red Summer" of 1919 drove Du Bois down a proverbial "road of no return" toward his mature career as a prophet. The new prophet filled lecture halls across the nation; he founded the landmark monthly magazine *The Crisis*, a hugely successful national forum for discussions of race; he wrote for all sorts of national publications; he played a major role in the creation of such organizations as the National Association for the Advancement of Colored People (NAACP). Even when Du Bois turned to writing novels and short stories, he regarded literary creative solely for its use in the cause of Black liberation. "All art is propaganda," he stated provocatively, "and ever must be, despite the wailing of purists." Du Bois "did not care a damn for any art that is not used for propaganda" (Lemons 2001, p. 185).

Du Bois: A Prophet of Positive Liberty

Du Bois' life not only records a luminous moment in Black history, it also models what seems a perennial dilemma facing Black scholars in religious studies: science or prophecy? Du Bois' sociological work may remain a monument in the study of Black religion, but his conversion to an *activist* agenda always stands ready to eclipse it. The reasons are not hard to determine. Like Du Bois then, nowadays both Black Americans and Black religious studies scholars still face racism in American society that seems to resist science. Further, post-modern discourse welcomes liberationist and prophetic styles in the classroom. They carry the message of antipathy to science as well as Foucault's call to resistance. What impresses me as I have surveyed the literature of Black religious studies is the struggle to find the "sweet spot" between prophecy and curiosity, between modernist and post-modernist styles. I shall appeal to no less an example than the celebrated Black intellectual Cornel West to show

how a major contemporary Black scholar tried to negotiate the same academic/prophetic, modernism/post-modernism divide. I shall ask whether West was any more successful than Du Bois in negotiating this treacherous divide. But, more to the point, I want to ask whether there might be common ground for the study of religion between prophetic and post-modern styles of inquiry, on the one hand, and academic ones celebrating critical, skeptical, and modernist styles on the other? If so, what would West's idea of such a new religious studies be? But we get ahead of ourselves.

Du Bois' experiments in using sociology to study Black folk failed to move White America to revisit its attitudes to Black folk. Racism is a deep thing, garbed in myth and resistant to argument. One might well conclude, were one a Black scholar, that it would be far better to reverse the attention of the Black gaze from trying to convert White America to trying to delve into what made Black folks who and what they are. For this task, social research and sociology are little use. History, on the other hand, spoke directly to the needs of Black folk to enhance their own view of themselves.

History's Radical Legacy for Black America

So while no one should diminish the achievements of Du Bois' social research, no method for studying Black religion can really compare for existential impact with *history*. Black scholars seemed to have decided that knowledge of their own past was critical for establishing the self-esteem of Black folk. No surprise, then, the application of *historical method* to the Black experience has been perhaps the single-most important means by which Black Americans have approached Black religion. The theory supporting the correctness of this choice would seem to be a psycho-social one, namely that a people needs to know who they are. And knowing who we are depends upon knowing where we came from. The list of names of historians providing this collective grounding of a folk identity is long and illustrious. Henry Levering Lewis, Albert J. Raboteau, Joseph Washington, and sociologist and historian C. Eric Lincoln are only a few of the

authors to have become leaders in the writing of histories of African Americans and their religion. Intriguing as well is the fictionalized history/historicized fiction of Alex Haley's immensely popular book and TV series, *Roots*. Haley tapped into the intense hunger for historical knowledge about African Americans, especially among Black Americans themselves. My former colleague, feminist author Karen McCarthy Brown, was more than a little fascinated with Haley's genius. I believe it motivated her to attempt, as we will see in the next chapter, something of the same "genre-bending" *Roots* did so effectively. Returning to the academic camp, an Afro-American Religious History Group holds sessions at the annual meetings of the American Academy of Religion. Witness, as well, the vitality and clout of a truly monumental historical enterprise such as the African-American Religion: A Documentary History Project, under the general editorship of Professor David W. Wills. This comprehensive archive seeks to gather information about African American religion in its widest senses. From a *methodological* point of view, Willis' project should recall the comparable passion for historical knowledge about the Bible that we read about in chapter 3 on the rise of the (primarily) historical criticism of the Bible. Some Black historians of religion have even tried to join African American perspectives and the Higher Criticism of the Bible. Claremont's Vincent L. Wimbush leads in trying to bring Higher Criticism into the Black church. But he has had to swim against the current of the conservative kind of Bible study prevalent in Black seminaries and theological colleges, much as Robertson Smith had to do a century ago in Scotland (Wimbush 1989).

Of interest to the theoretically inclined are the unique topics these historians of Black history select, and as well the questions they seek to pose. Often, these questions betray a "demythologizing" project, designed to upset pious views of Black religion's past, just as Spinoza, say, offended local Jewish authorities by demythologizing their uncritical acceptance of the Mosaic authorship of the Torah. Did Africans readily embrace Christianity, or were they compelled to convert? Was Christianity a constructive or destructive force in the history of Black Americans? Did it primarily teach meekness and subservience or dignity and equality, as well as the value of righteous rebellion? Such questions, and many, many more, seek "inconvenient truths" that historians and church folk might prefer to overlook, deny, or simply just not *see*.

What Black Post-Modernism Owes Foucault

Chief among the themes uncovered by Black historical work are power, domination, and hegemony. Not surprisingly the work of Michel Foucault found a warm welcome among Black historians. But even before Foucault, historical method played a powerful role in writing liberating histories of Black Americans. For example, in 1952 White Berkeley historian Kenneth Stampp wrote a landmark, radical unmasking of slavery in the American South, *The Peculiar Institution* (Stampp 1956). It blew away the myths and falsehoods about slavery that had dominated the conventional wisdom of Southern slavery being a benign institution.

But while modernist, demythologizing histories like Stampp's have done their share in sweeping away destructive stereotypes about Blacks, post-modern Black historians want to do more. For a while, Foucault's radical program seemed full of promise, even if, in the end, it did not prove adequate to the task. The radical historians wanted Blacks to achieve more than just negative liberty – "freedom from" – they sought to articulate images of *positive Black liberation*. In a post-modern vein, they aimed at articulating novel images of being Black, and where possible, to effect social change through activism. The Black post-modern scholar seeks to be an agent shaping history. These critics of modernist history offer a foretaste of what will become a post-modern style of theorizing in the hands of theologian Cornel West. Historian Gayraud S. Wilmore shows how post-modernism makes its mark. He dedicates an entire section to "Historical Studies" in his useful volume, *African American Religious Studies: An Interdisciplinary Anthology*. There, he showcases a new generation of post-modern historians informed in part by Foucault's critiques of power differentials. Yet Manning Marble and his *Blackwater: Historical Studies in Race, Class Consciousness and Revolution* (1981) may even have gone beyond Foucault. Set in a post-modern template, Marble's book not only debunks myths

about Black submissiveness to the slavers but also articulates a view of positive liberty in approving the role played the Black church in defeating oppression. Similarly, C. Eric Lincoln's work on Black Muslims in America offers an admiring vision of the positive liberty attained in a "new religion" such as the Nation of Islam (Wilmore 1989, p. 268). Maulana Karenga, the founder of *Kwanzaa*, elaborates a radical "positive" liberationist vision of a Black religious future. Karenga writes of an "ontological blackness" that is violated by the imposition of Christianity upon Black folks (Karenga 1989, p. 271).

These samples of post-modern trends among Black historians should give us some idea, then, of how the certainties of modernism have been systematically assailed. In this assault on modernism not even a Black icon like W.E.B. Du Bois is spared. Notably Cornel West stands as one of Black America's most severe critics of Du Bois. West does not do so by practicing a new kind of post-modern history but by assuming the role of prophet and engaging in a theologically inflected polemic. West takes leave of Du Bois' modernist world of social research and sociology, and enters straightaway into theological/ideological polemic, articulated in the latest post-modern style of discourse.

Cornel West: A Black Scholar's Post-Modern Dilemma

Descended from preachers himself, and socialized into the politically savvy Black church of the civil rights movement, Cornel West stands as a dynamic and influential Black presence in the study of religion. Where race and social justice are concerned, West steps in as a "prophetic" public intellectual. Although West has not written extensively on religion, his advocacy of a prophetic liberationist stance for African American intellectuals has shaped an entire generation. Among his more than a score of books is such varied fare as *Black Theology and Marxist Thought* (1979), *Prophesy Deliverance! An Afro-American Revolutionary Christianity* (1982), and *Breaking Bread: Insurgent Black Intellectual Life* (1991). West is the most influential Black American public intellectual of the past two decades, and for that reason alone we need to pay heed to what he says about the study of religion.

First and foremost, West embraces the career of a self-styled "freedom fighter." Even while teaching at Harvard, he would not suppress his fighting nature:

> "The life of the mind was just unbelievable; it was emancipating in a lot of ways, but it didn't change my calling, my vocation, at all. It's been the same all the way through. And that's been a blessing, actually, because I can't conceive of a life of more joy that fighting for freedom." (Goodman 2003)

West thus represents a paradigm figure asserting a strong program in "positive liberty." His is not the diffident liberal ideal of "negative liberty." West does not just want to free Black folk *from* hindrances, but rather to go further and free Black folk *to* some certain positive end. This is only one reason that radical Black liberationist theologian James B. Cone serves as West's personal guide, rather than the more ambivalent Du Bois. Indeed, West has deliberately opposed himself to the liberal (early) Du Bois: "he and I are birds of very different feathers" (West 1999a, p. 87). Yet West enthusiastically embraces the Du Bois of social criticism, prophecy, and activism. Like American pragmatist philosophers such as John Dewey, West seeks to "understand pragmatism as a political form of cultural criticism" (West 1999c, p. 151). If there is a distant echo of the politically engaged scholarship, espoused by Du Bois' *Kathedersozialisten,* this may be it.

West also find post-modernism's program congenial insofar as it rejects the relentless optimism so conspicuous in the failed efforts of the early, modernist, Du Bois to get American racists to respond to his scientific work on Black America. In West's view Du Bois clung to modernist optimism, even after his turn from science – for West a tragic display of naivety (West 1999a, p. 89). West feels that racism is deeper and more resistant to reasoned argument than Du Bois learned only too late (West 1999a, p. 97). The differentials of power between Blacks and Whites are simply too deeply embedded in the American corporate state for racism to be overcome – and unquestionably not by Du Bois' naive use of social science!

Black religious studies scholars must above all, then, as Foucault taught, be sensitive to the role of power. Well-born elitists, like Du Bois, could afford to be oblivious to power, largely because they never needed to fight as much to sustain their status. People at the grassroots, such as the bulk of Black America, could not indulge such fantasies. Since West sees himself as just this sort of grassroots "fighter," engaged in the activist church, he might well "think he is right" in advocating liberationist approaches to the study of religion. Because power holds center stage for West, Michel Foucault claims a place in West's heart.

However, West's critiques and resistance, unlike Foucault's, are unashamedly guided by religion – by Christian moral ideals (West 1989, p. 226). Hope seems to infuse everything he says; a grim sort of tragic vision, on the other hand, casts long shadows over Foucault's attitude to the future. West continues to live the Black church's vision of apocalyptic optimism. He is eager to lay plans for a better future. Stirred by the eschatological spirit of the Black church and the successes of the civil rights movement, West finds Foucault's "fervent anti-utopianism" unpersuasive (West 1989, p. 226). Grassroots Black civic associations have done an enormous amount over the years for lasting Black emancipation (West 1999a, p. 95). West "believes he is right," then, that this spirit is to be carried into the university, into the study of religion for example. Foucault fails "to articulate and elaborate ideals of democracy, equality, and freedom" – of "positive liberty." In addition, in failing so to do, Foucault is no better than a garden-variety bourgeois liberal. He only "provides merely negative conceptions of critique and resistance" – a human ideal of mere "negative liberty" (West 1989, p. 226). Foucault's atheistic worldview, tinged with the nihilism of hard-core French secularism, dominates his purview. West will have none of that. So, despite their post-modern liberationist kinship of spirit, West just doesn't mimic Foucault. He wants to transcend Foucault's secularism by assuming the mantle of the liberationist prophet.

An Irresistible Prophetic Urge? Theory, Religion, and Race

As far as the study of religion goes, West claims to be as committed to the academic world as to the world of prophetic liberationist activism. He respects the independence of the conscience of his students. He says that the classroom is a very special place: "It's the place ... where the art of dialogue is cultivated" (Goodman 2003). To his credit, West doesn't hide his prophetic intentions in academe: "I have never aspired to be a professional academic or scholar. Instead I have tried to be a man of letters in love with ideas in order to be a wiser and more loving person, hoping to leave the world just a little better than I found it" (West 1999b, p. 19) The question is, however, what do West's ideas mean on the ground, in the classroom? What specifically does a West-inspired "prophetic" liberationist study of religion look like?

For those who wish to see religious studies free itself from its theological past, and to assume instead its place among the humanities and human sciences, West disqualifies himself from being our guide. This is because his "prophetic pragmatism" is really just a theological operation. Coming to this conclusion requires a little detective work and close reading. It is true that in the introduction of a 2003 anthology edited with Eddie S. Glaude, Jr. – *African American Religious Thought* – West maps out what seems at first a humanistic – not theological – future for Black studies of religion (West and Glaude 2003). There, West says that Black studies of religion have reached a "crossroads." Raising hopes for humanists, he argues that Black studies of religion need to change "direction" and cast off domination by "theology." Indeed, notably, he would seem to be striking out on a new path from that of his old mentor, liberation theologian James H. Cone (West 2003, p. xi). But, in fact, West doesn't mean this at all. He wants a new sort of theologized study of Black religion, and in effect returns to Cone's fold. We will recall Cone's celebration of the Black prophetic tradition, the ideal of "Black Power" and the Black church, in his *A Black Theology of Liberation* (Cone 1970). Cone labored specifically at the practical theological task of *soul-making*. Black studies of religion were supposed to fulfill the pastoral role of "enriching personal faith" and "preparing clergy and laity for ministry" (West 2003, p. xi). In a similar vein, Cone ally Gayraud Wilmore disdained any "dispassionate treatment of religion" as "an object of inquiry" – in effect, anything we could call a humanistic study of Black religion. Wilmore does nothing less than

repudiate the whole of the modern study of religion as we have seen it develop since the days of Jean Bodin! This is doubtless why Wilmore declares – with West's approval – that the "best" religious scholarship in the Black academy is, perforce, "believing scholarship" (West 2003, p. xii; Wilmore 1989, p. xii). Says West in addition, White supremacy makes the "armchair theorizing" that he imagines the humanistic study of religion to be, impossible for Blacks. Black scholars of religion have no other choice but to affirm that "theological commitments and practical relevance are central to what African-American scholars do" (West 2003, p. xii). So, West's so-called "new direction" for religious studies isn't "new" at all (West 2003, p. xiii). It simply reinstalls the old confessional theologizing with which West has been comfortable since his childhood: "the discursive practice of black theology ... produces meaning about what constitute African American religious studies" (West 2003, pp. xvii–xviii). West may, thus, be setting forth a Black agenda of questions and such for Black scholars, as I celebrated in the beginning of this chapter. The problem is that West's is a *theological* agenda, better fitted to the seminary, and not to a humanistic discipline like religious studies.

But I would argue that West and his fellow theologizers are not the only voices seeking to articulate a Black agenda of questions for the study of religion. A Black religious studies exists that is really "new," because it tries to liberate us from ignorance about Blacks and religion. This new Black religious studies promises, in its own way, to "offer solutions to urgent problems besetting African-Americans," that West so urgently seeks to discover (West 2003, p. xviii), by satisfying *curiosity* about what solutions make best sense. It offers a venue where we go to debate, sort out, or contest the many solutions proposed to the urgent problems besetting Black Americans. The university and departments of religious studies we go to satisfy our *curiosity* about history, society, or, indeed, Black religion. They provide the venues where we go when we want to *learn* and *ask questions* about the nature of history, society, and Black religion as well. As we will now see, we have many examples of Black religious studies that resist the regressive liberationist move back into theology that West advocates. It is to these that we now turn.

Black Religious Studies in a New Key

West's celebrity voice about the future of study of religion is not the only one worth hearing. Other Black voices reject the need to "believe" Black – or any other – religion in order to teach Black religious studies. They are not prophets or preachers of a "believing scholarship," but inquisitive people like each of us, formulating critical questions about religion. They are committed to knowing and understanding how race and religion articulate rather than to preaching a new theology of post-modern liberation. Here we will find attempts to carry forward the modernisms of Eliade's approach by Charles H. Long, as well as the work of younger scholars setting out on new courses.

At one end of this range of theorizing is Anthony B. Pinn's appropriation of the Eliade school, as it is mediated by Charles H. Long. I need to say a few words about Long because of his unique intergenerational mediating position as scholar of religion. Paradoxically, I would identify Long as a Black *scholar*, but not so much a *Black* scholar. Like his longtime colleague at the Divinity School of the University of Chicago, Wendy Doniger, Long has resisted classification as a *Black* scholar, seeking instead to be a scholar in his own right. As I shall acknowledge in the following chapter, Doniger is one of the leading women scholars of religion in the modern era. She is indeed a feminist who is a scholar, but she has also firmly resisted being categorized as a *feminist* scholar. Doniger has guarded her reputation as a scholar in the universal, modernist sense. Likewise Long has resisted principal identification is as a "Black" scholar of religion, although he has, on occasion, advised Black theologians about their jobs. He has always aimed to speak as a scholar in his own right. For that reason, his work tends to address a general audience, and not one formed by the agendas of Black studies of religion. Long has stood shoulder to shoulder alongside Eliade, Wach, and others, as a master of general method and theory in the history of religions, as developed in Chicago under Eliade. That may be why Long

enters debates about the nature of studies of Black religion principally from his long-time prestigious perch among the senior faculty of the Divinity School of the University of Chicago, and not, I would argue, from the position of a specialist in the study of Black religion. Long might even be better classified as a post-colonial scholar of religion, given his extensive theoretical work on cross-cultural hermeneutics, influencing figures like David Chidester (Chidester 1996). I call Long a mediating figure, however, because lately he has exploited his situation as "other" by virtue of his being a Black scholar. American Blacks open American scholarship in religion to new resources, providing American scholars with opportunities to encounter the "other." Blacks are "Westerners," but of a different sort, different enough to afford other Western scholars an instructive sense of perspective (Long 1986, p. 152). But most of all, Long's prestige as a core member of the Chicago's History of Religions program has played an influential role for younger Black scholars of religion. I shall explore but three: first, and most directly, Anthony Pinn. Then philosopher of religion William D. Hart, one of Pinn's chief interlocutors, merits mention, as does Princeton historian Albert Raboteau.

The question driving the work of these scholars is the nature of Black religion in all its parts. "Black religion" is not a "given"; rather, it is a question. Prophetic pragmatists or Black liberationists may feel that they know enough about what Black religion is, but these younger scholars want to rethink the assumptions made about Black religion. They want to tear the concept down to the ground, and get at what it is. Is it a unique and autonomous religion? Then does the study of Black religion afford us access to a new phenomenological category, such as "slave religion"? To what extent, for example, is the religion of African Americans a "slave" religion? Alternatively, are we, perhaps, looking at Black religion parochially, and failing to recognize kinship with the religion of poor Whites? In addition, if we are looking at Black religion too narrowly, might this not be something even liberationists want to know before they begin to act, given the opportunity for alliances across racial lines made possible by religious affinities?

Pinn and "Rituals of Reference": A Theory of How Black Religion Came To Be

I begin with Pinn. Some readers may know Pinn from his earlier theological career. What makes him interesting for religious studies, however, are his attempts to go beyond his "believing" theological roots toward a non-confessional, critical study of religion. In his first – theological – book, *Why Lord? Suffering and Evil in Black Theology* (1995), Pinn posed the standard questions of philosophical theology or theodicy. Why do the innocent suffer? How does one justify the "ways of God to men" as the old theology textbooks put it? Theology is a *pragmatic* enterprise, because it seeks to offer practical guidance to the faithful, to aid their liberation in times of trial. Pinn's theology book served an activist, pastoral function, not unlike the function that West's "prophetic pragmatist" program would serve.

However, Pinn turns from theology to religious studies, and new questions surface. He is, for example, no longer interested in entertaining and answering the *practical* question why the innocent suffer. What troubles Pinn is the exact nature of this so-called "religion of suffering." Theologians and others simply take for granted such a category. However, is it a special *kind* of religion, a unique *category* or class of religion? And, if so, what makes it special? Such inquiry has many uses, even beyond that of filling out our repertoire of the kinds of religions that there are. It may even be useful to theologians like West, to religious folk with pastoral concerns. How, for example, does a religion of suffering do its practical work? How does it, in fact, address the needs of the faithful, even when their suffering continues unabated? Do these religions of suffering produce a distinct *style* of religion? Do they produce particular doctrines? Does it generate its own ritual expressions, such as the world famous, mournful Black Spirituals? Do they create some distinct, even autonomous, *phenomenological kind* or *class* of religion that might, say, be called "Black religion"?

Unlike his theological treatment of evil, Pinn's *Terror and Triumph: The Nature of Black Religion* (2003) addresses precisely these kinds of "problems of religion." Better yet, Pinn believes he has discovered something new. From his interrogations of so-called "Black religion," he believes that he has discovered a distinct, indeed autonomous, kind of religion. So unique is it, says Pinn, that it is worthy of its own name, "Black religion." It has specific *origins* in the centuries-long experience of suffering of African Americans under regimes of slavery. Pinn's job is to bring out what makes Black religion special.

Attentive readers may recognize much of Eliade's theoretical ideas in Pinn's work – especially his appeal to "autonomy." They would not be wrong. Pinn even follows Eliade, mediated through the work of Charles H. Long, in arguing that religion originates as a response to the terror of history. In particular, the "racial terror" of slave culture was the equivalent of Eliade's idea of the "terror of history." Appealing to this idea of actual historical forms of terror helps us understand or explain the emergence of Black religion and special character (Hart 2004, p. 796; Pinn 2003, p. 99). Pressing his critical, theoretical inquiry further, Pinn even locates the origins of the distinctive terror producing Black religion – namely, what amounts to formative rituals, such as the slave auction and the threat of lynching.

The slave masters not only had to destroy the old African tribal identities of their captives, they needed to create new, pliable identities for them. To do so, the slavers used what Pinn calls "rituals of reference." One such ritual was that of the "ritual terror" of being on the auction block, stripped of human dignity, reduced to a mere commodity. The other, equally terrifying, "ritual of reference" was the horrifying threat, replete with standardized methods of inducing fear, such as perfected by the Ku Klux Klan, of lynching (Pinn 2003, p. 49). Black religion is distinctive, Pinn argues, because White folk employed a malignant genius in creating ritualized means of destroying any sense of security or safety in the Black community. And it is only by reference to these ritualized practices to which Black slaves were submitted that we can understand the expressions and institutions of Black religion. How else to grasp the meaning and deep purpose of the high-powered, emotional expressions of a thirst for liberation and dignity, found, for example, in the spirituals, than against the backdrop of these hideous "rituals of reference"?

William D. Hart's Doubts about Pinn's Theory of Black Religion

Now, like any good theory, Pinn's has drawn critics. Some feel that he should have gone further and radically confronted the *phenomenological* question of what makes Black religion really "Black." James Anthony Noel even feels that Pinn clings to a theological agenda because he presupposes "that black religion always concerns itself with liberation" (Noel 2004, p. 156). Pinn, in effect, Noel charges, is still under the apologetic sway of the idea that religion is necessarily good. William D. Hart, too, objects strenuously to Pinn's view that Black religion exhibits an Eliade-like "autonomy." Hart, in fact, challenges Pinn about the very existence of such a thing as "Black religion" (Hart 2008). Moreover, Pinn has committed that greatest of post-modern sins – he attributes an "essence" to Black religion. As Hart explains, "Essentialism is the claim that there is some significant characteristic common to all members of a class that make them who they are. Blood, genetics, spirit, soul, language, and expressive culture have all been proposed as essence-bearers" (Hart 2008, p. x). Pinn reduces the many and particular to a homogenized one, much as we would expect Eliade's universalizing tendencies to do. In addition, even if we could allow Pinn to claim that Black religion was autonomous, Hart doubts that Pinn has really shown that it is. Hart thinks that Pinn falls into line as a good disciple of Eliade, and simply assumes the autonomy of Black religion.

Hart, however, is not finished with Pinn. He challenges Pinn's theory of the formative role of "rituals of reference" in shaping the Black slave mentality. Indentured Whites were also sold at auction, says Hart, and not only Blacks. Indeed, enslaved Whites got lynched at a higher rate and number – at least before the Civil War – than Blacks (Hart 2004 p. 795). Yet if we examine the religion of indentured Whites, we do not find something analogous to Black religion as Pinn's theory would have us expect. If Hart is right, then, Pinn has misidentified the origins of Black religion. In addition, if Hart is right, Pinn's case for the autonomy of Black religion remains weak.

In the end, Hart is hardest on Pinn because he maintains an innocence of power. He withdraws religion into the pure center of the human heart and its experiences of terror. Pinn needs to take Foucault, in particular, much more seriously, if he is to persuade Hart. Like those benighted Enlightenment social reformers who saw only a reflection of their good intentions in creating what Foucault exposed as institutions of systematic dehumanization, Pinn reveals the same naivety about religion. Hart feels that the Black church has too long been exempted from criticism. Hart, for example, suspects the "neo-Pentecostal" style dominating the Black church of concealing abusive exercises of power. "Neo-Pentecostal" religious style makes "the loudness of one's celebration, and the ostentation of one's gestures an index of authentic Christianity" (Hart 2008, p. 198). The "charismatic authority of the preacher" is manipulative because it is "resistant to reason." In its very structure, the Black church exemplifies the full panoply of social controls: it is "monarchic and anti-republican, antidemocratic … and too often operates, as kings do, by decree and acclamation." In a clear liberationist voice, Hart concludes: "I despise the very idea of royalty," and the position of the preacher in the Black church as a kind of monarch is one of "royalty" *par excellence* (Hart 2008, p. 198). For Hart, the Black church is not anything, therefore, that can be uncritically celebrated as good. As an engine of power and domination, it merits all the critique that a Foucault, for one, can bring. Pinn misses all this.

For the purpose of the argument of the present chapter, books like Pinn's and critiques like Hart's show us how a theoretical study of religion, with race in mind, can also assume its place in the long tradition of *theoretical thinking about religion* that has been the focus of this book. Notice, neither Pinn nor Hart is intending to *make religion* – even if Hart, in effect, accuses Pinn of doing so. Nor are either Pinn or Hart set upon the path of making the study of Black religion an exercise in liberationist activism exemplified by the later Du Bois and Cornel West. They are nevertheless intending to try to *understand religion*, even to the extent of trying to understand if there is such a thing as Black religion. Pinn and Hart, thus, try to understand religion from a *theoretical* point of view just as surely as did Freud, Durkheim, Tylor, Frazer, and other theorists. In particular, Pinn wants his voice to be phenomenological and comparative in the tradition of Eliade and, lately, Charles H. Long. In both Pinn and Hart we can see what *theorizing religion*, with race in mind, means.

Raboteau's "Slave Religion"

In the spirit of Pinn's and Hart's, respectively, wider theorizing, let me conclude by pointing to a possible future contribution that Black studies of religion can make to the more general field of a cross-cultural and comparative study of religion. I should like to illustrate how at least one of the more celebrated recent works in the Black history of religion – Albert Raboteau's *Slave Religion* – provides an example of how intense studies in Black religion can further theorizing in the cross-culturally comparative field of religious studies (Raboteau 2004).

Raboteau sees *Slave Religion* as an effort at retrieval of the "invisible" histories of Black folk under conditions of slavery in North America. Thus, Raboteau tells us, "I have tried to investigate slave narratives, Black autobiographies, and Black folklore in order to gather, literally out of the mouths of former slaves, the story of their religious experiences during slavery" (Raboteau 2004, p. x). As such, the methodological identity of Raboteau's book as *history* places it alongside all those scholars we have come to know in this volume who thought about religion according to the rules of *critical history*. Like the critical biblical scholars of chapter 3, Raboteau looks past the "myths" about Black folk and their religion to the hard historical facts of slave religion that his tremendous work has uncovered. Many questions peculiar to Black American slave religion guide his inquiry: Raboteau's leading questions then would be those such as: What were the origins of Black religion in America? What aspects of African religions were retained by the slaves? How did the evangelization and conversion of African slaves to Christianity take place? What was the nature of the religion to which the slave was converted? What, if anything, was distinctive about religion in the slave quarters? (Raboteau 2004, p. xi).

Raboteau comes up with some surprising results. Contrary to prevailing opinion, he showed that some slaves were, for example, Muslims. Some remnants of African religious practice survived the attempts by plantation culture to efface it. Slaves developed their own institutions of religious practice, such as the secret nighttime religious meetings, the world-renowned spirituals of African American religious life, and so on.

In this way, Raboteau's history is essentially a descriptive and "liberal" modernist work. Raboteau seeks to *liberate* readers from the prevailing misconceptions about the religion of Black slaves. In doing so, he seeks to liberate African Americans from their own conceptions of their past. As such, *Slave Religion* is an effort in realizing "negative liberty." It is stoutly modernist in that Raboteau feels that the story he tells about the religion of slaves is privileged. It is *true*, and as such should demythologize a host of misconceptions about the pasts of African Americans. Notably, the book is not itself a comparative or theoretical one, even if it has theoretical implications, as I shall show. Raboteau simply takes the category "slave religion" off the (descriptive) shelf, and fills it with an impressive mass of detailed information. Critical self-reflection about the precise meaning of the term is not his concern. Doing a history is. Telling the liberating truth about the past of former slaves is.

I want now to argue, however, that although *Slave Religion* obviously tells the story of the *religion practiced by slaves*, it is more, or could be more. I think it could be more if we bring out its theoretical potential. Thus, placed into the hands of the cross-cultural comparative study of religion, Raboteau's book prompts a whole barrage of theoretical questioning. The very success of Raboteau's effort at critical historical retrieval creates the basis for *theoretical* questions perhaps not even anticipated by its author. Raboteau's use of the rubric "slave religion" prompts questions about whether this might be a category of wider application than the American South.

One big question would be whether "slave religion" makes a good cross-cultural comparative category. Are there other "slave religions" than those Raboteau describes? Can they be usefully likened or contrasted to Raboteau's? If there are, I believe this facilitates theorizing about religion because it takes us beyond local studies of slave *religions* to ponder the possibility of different classes of slave religion. Political scientists do this all the time in comparing and contrasting different kinds of "democracy" or "monarchy" or "empire" and so on. After a certain amount of close local study has been done, the larger comparative questions naturally arise. I, again, think Raboteau's book forces us to begin doing some comparative thinking about slave religion.

For the sake of introducing comparison, I shall enlist my "Russian" – Ruthenian –grandmother's support. Serafima Strenski was a stoical yet cheerful peasant woman, illiterate, uneducated, but deeply pious in the traditions of her Eastern Rite Greek Catholic church. Born shortly after the emancipation of the serfs in the Russian Empire (1861), her parents undoubtedly had been "owned" by some Russian "master." I am surely not the first to suggest comparison between the religion that attended serfdom under the tsars with the religion that attended slavery under the White masters of the American South. Why should not we, then, think of them as members of the same class or species of religion – "serf/slave" religion? Might it not be possible, therefore, to understand my grandmother's Eastern Rite Catholic religion as a "slave religion" too? Maybe I could understand my grandmother's religion as analogous to the "slave religion" Raboteau develops for the more limited context of the American South? After all, both serfs and slaves were "owned," confined to estates or plantations, corporally disciplined to behave in certain acceptable ways, dedicated to agrarian labor, and, most important of all, and regarded as sub-human. Might it not, reciprocally, serve to help us understand African American "slave religion" better as well if we could put it up for comparison with the serf religion of Russia?

Raboteau's work even suggests some specific lines of cross-cultural comparison between eastern European "serf religion" and Black American "slave religion." Was Russian "serf religion," for example, as specialized in "orality" as Raboteau's Black American "slave religion" (Raboteau 2004, p. 163)? What are we to make, for example, of the conspicuous eschatological spirit that pervades the mood of the religion of both enslaved peoples? Did not the thirst for Christ's *Parousia*, the central place of the resurrection theology of Easter over against Christmas good cheer, parallel the calls in Black American churches for "hebben," for paradise, for release from earthly

suffering that infuse Black spirituals (Raboteau 2004, pp. 243–266)? Was serf religion also just as conflicted between being a religion of submission and one of rebellion as was African American slave religion? How did it, or did it not, mediate and interpret the master–serf/slave relation? Alternatively, did it inspire the love of freedom that sent my grandparents and their kind to the New World, as surely as Raboteau's Black American slave religion kept the yearning for emancipation alive in the hearts of African Americans (Raboteau 2004, p. 168)? Despite its outward and official institutional form, did my grandmothers' "serf church," like Raboteau's slave churches, also provide cover for "invisible" religious practices, privy to serfs alone and shielded from the prying eyes of the lords of the manor (Raboteau 2004, p. 210)? Such a list of questions could go on for some time.

Shortly after I had written an early draft of this comparison of "slave" and "serf" religions, I was referred to a set of lectures by a Black author, entitled *Sorrowful Joy*. This little book turned out to be a stunning confirmation of my hypothesis that the "serf" religion of my Russian grandmother and the "slave religion" described by Raboteau might belong to the same family of religions! In his own words, the author tells us of his dawning realization: "I was overwhelmed by the spiritual power of the Divine Liturgy, as the Orthodox call their service. I was moved especially by the hymns. They had that same sadly joyful tone which I associated with down home and with slave spirituals." On top of that, the book's author, himself a leading African American religious studies scholar, had recognized the same identity between Orthodoxy and "African American spirituality." In response, he *converted* to Russian Orthodoxy. His name? Albert Raboteau (Raboteau 2002)!

One rarely has such confirmations of theoretical ideas. I not only cherish it for the argument this chapter, but also for the overall argument of this entire book. Questions about religion such as these, that link different cultures, have been the traditional stuff of theoretical thinking about religion from Bodin to Eliade. They simply take for granted that the study of religion is focused upon problems of more universal scope such as these. As I have noted from the work of a Raboteau or a Hart, or even Pinn and Long, these scholars point toward the same kinds of cross-cultural comparison of religion. In them is the beginning of a new Black American attempt to *understand religion*, replete with an entire syllabus of *theoretical* questions arising from the African American religious experience. The classic theoretical thinkers of the study of religion from Bodin to Eliade would well recognize these questions as part of a common project with theirs. It is such studies of Black American religion, which open the way for cross-cultural comparison, that I believe are in the best interests of the study of religion. It is *not*, then, the liberationist efforts of a James H. Cone, Cornel West, or the later Du Bois and their work on Black American religion that best serve the modern study of religion. While admirable in themselves, their liberationist efforts are directed at inspiring action and conviction, not at stimulating curiosity and skepticism. They are a

preaching not a teaching; they easily merge with ideology or creative theology, not with the patient quest for understanding proper the "science of religion" of years past; they are the soul of a dynamic prophecy not the heart of an inquisitive scholarship. In this sense, liberationist studies of religion *narrow* our purview because they insist upon creating a positive "freedom to" articulate a particular vision of the future. I prefer the more modest aim of achieving for us "freedom from" ignorance in part because it stipulates no particular end in sight. Instead, the academic approach of skepticism and questioning leaves the religious world open to the human imagination and to genuine intellectual surprises. We have seen one such surprise in Albert Raboteau's conclusion that categories of Black religion, like "slave religion," were even more capacious than might be imagined. What others might there yet be to be discovered?

Note

1   In this short chapter I cannot hope to sort through the entire matter of the definition of "race." "Race" is far too complex a concept to take on here. In the modern period, it has become the name of a certain way many have chosen to distinguish different classes of humanity, expressed in terms of markers such as pigmentation, physiognomy, and geographical origins. Let me be clear that I understand "race" to be a socio-cultural category that is imagined, by many, to be a biological one. But "race" itself has virtually no biological basis, despite the popular belief to the contrary. Rather, at most, it names communities and cultures, not autonomous species of humans. In reality, "race" has to do with how we decide to "see" people, once

we have "looked at" them, and with how those so viewed likewise see themselves.

For the purpose of this discussion of theory of religion and race, I have necessarily limited myself to the work by and about African American religion. Even then, I soon realized that the quantity of production in this field strained my abilities to do justice to the tremendous scholarly output in this area. Thus, in this chapter, I have had to be ruthlessly selective in dealing with theoretical matters about theory and Black religion. I quickly dismissed, therefore, any notion of writing a single chapter of roughly 12,000 words on theoretical work having to do with religion and all other races! There is work in that for a library of volumes, not a single chapter among many.

References

Aptheker, H. (ed.). 1968. *The Autobiography of W.E.B. Du Bois: A Soliloquy on Viewing My Life from the Last Decade of Its First Century*. New York: International Publishers.

Barkin, K. 2000. "'Berlin Days,' 1892–1894: W.E.B. Du Bois and German Political Economy." *boundaries 2* 27(3): 79–101.

Chidester, D. 1996. *Savage Systems: Colonialism and Comparative Religion in Southern Africa*. Bloomington: Indiana University Press.

Cone, J.H. 1970. *A Black Theology of Liberation*. Philadelphia: J.B. Lippincott.

Goodman, A. 2003. "An Hour with Scholar, Philosopher and Theologian Dr. Cornel West." July 21. www.democracynow.org/2003/7/21/an_hour_with_scholar_philosopher_and.

Hart, W.D. 2004. Review of Anthony B. Pinn, *Terror and Triumph: The Nature of Black Religion*. *Journal of the American Academy of Religion* 72 (3): 795–797.

Hart, W.D. 2008. *Black Religion, Malcolm X, Julius Lester, and Jan Willis*. New York: Palgrave Macmillan.

Karenga, M. 1989. "Black Religion." In G. Wilmore (ed.), *African American Religious History: An Interdisciplinary Anthology*. Durham, NC: Duke University Press.

Lemons, G.L. 2001. "Womanism in the Name of the 'Father': W.E.B. Du Bois and the Problematics of Race, Patriarchy and Art." *Phylon* 49(3–4): 185–202.

Long, C.H. 1986. *Significations*. Aurora, CO: Davies Group.

Marble, M. 1981. *Blackwater: Historical Studies in Race, Class Consciousness and Revolution*. Boulder: University of Colorado.

Noel, J.A. 2004. Review of Anthony B. Pinn, *Terror and Triumph: The Nature of Black Religion*. *Journal of the American Academy of Religion* 84(1): 155–157.

Pinn, A.B. 1995. *Why Lord? Suffering and Evil in Black Theology*. New York: Continuum.

Pinn, A.B. 2003. *Terror and Triumph: The Nature of Black Religion*. Minneapolis: Fortress Press.

Raboteau, Albert J., 2002. *Sorrowful Joy*. New York: Paulist Press.

Raboteau, Albert J. 2004. *Slave Religion: The "Invisible Institution" in the Antebellum South*. New York: Oxford University Press.

Stampp, Kenneth M. 1956. *The Peculiar Institution: Slavery in the Ante-Bellum South*. New York: Vintage Books.

West, C. 1989. *The American Evasion of Philosophy: A Genealogy of Pragmatism*. Madison: University of Wisconsin Press.

West, C. 1999a. "Black Strivings in a Twilight Civilization." In C. West (ed.), *The Cornel West Reader*. New York: Basic Civitas Books.

West, C. 1999b. "On My Intellectual Vocation." In C. West (ed.), *The Cornel West Reader*. New York: Basic Civitas Books.

West, C. 1999c. "On Prophetic Pragmatism." In C. West (ed.), *The Cornel West Reader*. New York: Basic Civitas Books.

West, C. and E.S. Glaude, Jr. (eds.). 2003. *African American Religious Thought: An Anthology*. Louisville, KY: John Knox Press.

Wilmore, G. (ed.). 1989. *African American Religious Studies: An Interdisciplinary Anthology*. Durham, NC: Duke University Press.

Wimbush, V.L. 1989. "Biblical Historical Study as Liberation: Toward an Afro-Christian Hermeneutic ". In G. Wilmore (ed.), *African American Religious Studies: An Interdisciplinary Anthology*. Durham, NC: Duke University Press.

Zuckerman, P. 2002. "The Sociology of Religion of W.E.B. Du Bois." *Sociology of Religion* 63(2): 239–253.

Further Reading

Anderson, V. 1995. *Beyond Ontological Blackness: An Essay on African American Religious and Cultural Criticism*. New York: Continuum.

Berlin, I. 1958. *Two Concepts of Liberty*. Oxford: Oxford University Press.

Bynum, C.W. 1986. "Introduction: The Complexity of Symbols ". In C.W. Bynum, S. Harrell, and P. Richman (eds.), *Gender and Religion*. Boston: Beacon Press.

Crouch, S., and P. Benjamin. 2002. *Reconsidering the Souls of Black Folk*. Philadelphia: Running Press.

Fox-Genovese, E., and E.D. Genovese. 2005. *The Mind of the Master Class History and Faith in the Southern Slaveholders' Worldview*. Cambridge: Cambridge University Press.

Frosh, S. 2005. *Hate and the Jewish Science: Anti-Semitism, Nazism and Psychoanalysis*. London: Palgrave Macmillan.

Gordon, L.R. 1999. "Pan-Africanism and African-American Liberation in a Postmodern World: A Review Essay." *The Journal of Religious Ethics* 27(2): 331–358.

Hackney, J.R. 1998. "Derrick Bell's Re-soundings: W.E.B. Du Bois, Modernism and Critical Race Theory." *Law and Society Inquiry* 23(1) (Winter): 141–164.

Haizlip, S.T. 1999. "Living in Black History Today (Sigh)." *Los Angeles Times*, February 21.

Haskell, T.L. 1998. *Objectivity Is Not Neutrality: Explanation Schemes in History*. Baltimore: Johns Hopkins University Press.

Holt, T.C. 1998. "W.E.B. DuBois's Archaeology of Race: Re-reading 'The Conservation of Races.'" In M.B. Katz and T.J. Sugrue (eds.), *W.E.B. Du Bois, Race, and the City: The Philadelphia Negro and Its Legacy*. Philadelphia: University of Pennsylvania Press.

Lefkowitz, M. 1996. *Not Out of Africa*. New York City: Basic Books.

Lewis, D.L. 1993. *W.E.B. Du Bois: Biography of Race, 1868–1919*. New York: Henry Holt.

Lewis, D.L. 2001. *W.E.B. Du Bois: The Fight for Equality and the American Century*. New York: Henry Holt.

Lincoln, C.E. 1967. "Color and Group Identity in the United States." *Daedalus* 96(2) (Spring): 527–541.

Lodge, H.C. 1909. "The Restriction of Immigration: Speech in the Senate, March 16, 1896." In *Speeches and Addresses: 1884–1909*. Boston: Houghton Mifflin.

Mommsen, W.J. 1984. *Max Weber and German Politics 1890–1920*, trans. M.S. Steinberg. Chicago: University of Chicago Press.

Pinn, A.B. 1997. Review of Victor Anderson, *Beyond Categorical Blackness*. *African American Review* 31(2): 320–323.

Roberts, J.D. 1998. Review of Victor Anderson, *Beyond Ontological Blackness*. *Journal of Religion* 78(2): 279–280.

Stampp, Kenneth M. 1952. "The Historian and Southern Negro Slavery". *American Historical Review* 57(3): 613–624.

Stocking, J.G.W. 2001. *Delimiting Anthropology: Occasional Inquiries and Reflections*. Madison: University of Wisconsin Press.

Strenski, I. 1997. *Durkheim and the Jews of France*. Chicago: University of Chicago Press.

Weber, Marianne. 1975. *Max Weber: A Biography*, trans. H. Zohn. New York: John Wiley & Sons.

Weber, Max. 1918. "Science as a Vocation." Lecture delivered November 17, 1917.

Wellington, D.L. 2002–03. "A Biased Critique of Du Bois' Seminal Work." *The Journal of Blacks in Higher Education* 38 (Winter): 131–133.

West, C. 1999. "Race and Modernity." In C. West (ed.), *The Cornel West Reader*. New York: Basic Civitas Books.

West, C. 2003. "Introduction: Towards New Visions and New Approaches in African American Religious Studies." In C. West and E.S. Glaude, Jr. (eds.), *African American Religious Thought: An Anthology*. Louisville, KY: John Knox Press.

Winant, H. 2000. "Race and Race Theory." *Annual Review of Sociology* 26: 169–185.

16

Sex/Gender and Women: Feminists Theorizing Religion

It's About Women

How is it that men seem to occupy the key positions of power in the world's religions? Popes, cardinals, gurus, sadhus, druids, buddhas, patriarchs, abbots, lamas, bishops, and priests (for the most part), mullahs, imams, khalifs, ayatollahs, and so on. All men. Even God is more often "Father," whether as head of the Christian Trinity or the Sky God of the Indian tradition, Dyaus-Pitr. Why do some Muslims insist upon veiling women, but never their men? Why do Orthodox Jewish men thank God each day in their prayers that they were not born women? What's behind confining women to the gallery, but leaving the main precinct of Orthodox synagogues to men? How was it decided that Christian women needed to be "churched" after childbirth, or that the mikva bath was required of all Orthodox Jewish women? Why did Adam blame Eve for the Fall, and more or less get away with it? We know how important women were to the functioning of early Christianity, so how is it that Paul has the nerve to tell them to be quiet? Where do Southern Baptists get the authority to tell women to be "submissive" to their husbands? What do the Roman Catholics and Orthodox have against ordaining women to the priesthood? Why does the Buddha always need to be born male? And why are Buddhist monks so deathly afraid of women that they dare not even look at the women feeding them on their begging rounds?

In this chapter, I want to explore how feminist theorists – almost all of them women – have confronted the sex and gender biases that give rise to these attitudes in the religions, and hence to theories of religion. Feminist thinkers claim not only that the study of religion *must* take note of these inequalities, but further that they need to get well behind the deep reasons for the pervasiveness of them in religion. The entire study of religion needs to be theorized anew in light of these facts. Feminist thinkers in the study of religion not only, therefore, demand attention to the religious experiences and lives of women, they also believe that we need to understand how and why their experiences have been virtually invisible in the study of religion.

The sheer quantity of work and the massive productivity of the workers in feminist studies of religion makes being comprehensive beyond the ambitions of a single chapter. History, anthropology, biblical studies and philosophy have given us many landmark studies of women and religion. These, in turn, have shaped the major theories used by women scholars in religious studies. Historian Caroline Walker Bynum stands out among their number. Senior

Understanding Theories of Religion: An Introduction, Second Edition. Ivan Strenski.
© 2015 Ivan Strenski. Published 2015 by John Wiley & Sons, Ltd.

anthropologists, such as Margaret Mead, have made the anthropological studies of religion of a Karen McCarthy Brown possible. Women who straddle the line between Christian theology and Higher Criticism of the Bible, such as Mary Daly, Rosemary Radford Ruether, and Elisabeth Schüssler-Fiorenza, enrich both the field of biblical studies and the more general study of religion. Finally, no treatment of the discourse of the goddess can go without mention of Indo-Europeanist Marija Gimbutas, and a theologian like Carol P. Christ. Regrettably absent are many other otherwise worthy entries to this list of dedicatedly feminist scholars, such as Cynthia Eller, Nancy Falk, Naomi Goldenberg, Rita Gross, Darlene M. Juschka, Morny Joy, Sylvia Marcos, Karen Jo Torjesen, Randi R. Warne, and many, many others. In an effort to try to identify cardinal figures, I have had to pass over the vast area of those feminists inspired by them, and the theoretical variety that informs the scholarship of our feminist colleagues. My apologies for not giving so many their due.

But making up for the past neglect to study the female *sex* is only the beginning. Feminist thinkers have also devised strategies for bringing the subtler notion of *gender* to the fore. Feminists have provoked appreciation of gender – for those culturally diverse ideas of what constitute appropriate properties for men and women, respectively. How would our theorizing religion differ once we take how we construct ideals of "real" men and "real" women into consideration? We need to understand why the divine needs often to be conceived as male, but also why "he" is seen as warrior, all-powerful, wrathful, shepherd, leader, wise – all (gender) traits typically classed as masculine. Here, presuming that sex and gender stand in one-for-one correspondence with each other plays a powerful role. Further, it unconsciously and insidiously is presumed that life's rewards will fall disproportionately to men as a "sex," and that the masculine "gender" traits enjoy priority over the feminine. Being strong, competitive, and tough *in our culture*, dominated as it is by patriarchy's views of gender and the sex–gender relation, has consequences. On the other hand, a goodly proportion of life's disabilities fall to women, and feminine gender traits are regarded as naming characteristics of human society that we value less because connected to

the "weaker" sex. The question is, however, how theorizing religion factors in such deep and complex prejudices about women in religion? What intellectual moves would be necessary to reflect awareness of *both* sex *and* gender inequity in religion? What moves would equally well correct sex *and* gender inequities in theorizing religion?

A complex of beliefs unites feminist scholars of religion in a common effort to change religious studies. Feminists suspect that our methods and theories of religion subtly privilege males. Here are three such ways that they do this, turning on different readings of the central, but slippery, Eliadean concept, *Homo religiosus*. First, in using the term "religious *man*" specifically, as opposed to saying "religious women" or "religious persons," feminists think that speakers mean to speak *only* of the religion of men. Women's religion is not important enough for scholarly attention. Second example: When "religious man" is used *generically*, rather than "religious humanity," some feminists suspect that the speaker excludes women in another way. The speaker assumes that male religion *stands for* religion universally, so why bother to distinguish male and female religions? Third, a speaker uses the term "religious man" believing there is religious territory that is *neutral* as to sex and gender. Here the use of the term "religious man" is thought *innocent* of sex and/or gender differences. Let me expand these ideas about the nature of feminist grievances.

First, feminists believe that religious men (the male "sex") get too much attention in our studies of religion. When we look into the religion of a certain people, feminists charge that men's religion and religious experiences immediately take center stage. Women's religion is consider peripheral, or simply not worth studying. Men are where the action is. Gautama, Confucius, Muhammad, Dogen, Ignatius Loyola, Luther, etc. Feminists want this presumption of male-centeredness to end. Women's religion and religious experience should get their share of attention. What of Mary, Rabia, Juana de la Cruz, Aimee Sempel McPherson, Tara? Indeed, the feminist grievance claims that scholars of religion have paid practically exclusive attention to the religion of males. When we say we want to study "religious man" feminists hear this as wanting to study religious *men* – males only. Both usages make them bristle.

Part of the blame for this bias has been laid at the feet of Mircea Eliade. His dominance over the field has promoted the idea of a universal *Homo religiosus*, charges feminist Carol P. Christ. But Eliade's universalism is bogus, because hiding behind it is a patriarchal vision. For Christ, there is no way to get round the "androcentric assumptions ... deeply structured into Eliade's conceptions of the nature and origin of religion" (Christ 2001, p. 574). Such conceptions, in effect, have excluded full recognition of women's religion. Feminists must, therefore, thoroughly root out Eliade's idea of a universal religion with a radically sex/gendered program, that would revolutionize the language and research goals of religious studies.

Homo religiosus also offends female dignity by depriving women of their unique sex specificity. Therefore, insofar as Eliade and the classic theorists mean the term to be neutral with respect to sex – to apply equally to all people in equal measure – feminists find it colorless and uninformative. Caroline Walker Bynum puts the point categorically, if confusedly: "all human beings are 'gendered'. No scholar studying religion, no participant in ritual, is ever neuter. Religious experience is the experience of men and women, and in no known society is this experience the same" (Bynum 1986, p. 2). When Bynum says that "all human beings are gendered" she does nothing short of putting the color back into talk of religion by declaring that there can be no sex- and gender-neutral or universal theories of religion, only sexed or gendered ones.

What are the general remedies that feminists want, then, to apply to a study of religion, for so long a sex- and gender-insensitive enterprise? On the negative side, revolutionary feminists attack any study of religion blatantly dominated by "patriarchy" or "androcentrism" or "kyriarchy," or some other term presuming natural male superiority over women. After having set patriarchal biases aside, feminist theorists have the positive duty to produce theoretical approaches to religion that set matters aright. How do they produce theories that incorporate the validity and importance of the religious lives and perspectives of women? I shall be asking precisely that question throughout this chapter.

How will feminist thinkers in religious studies, therefore, theorize religion anew, giving pride of place to notions like sex and gender? That, as well, will be something to watch. Feminist theories presume that religion *must*, at a minimum, be theorized with attention to differences made by the existence of women – their institutions, their histories, their cultures, their biology, their ways of thinking and points of view and so on – in the history of religion. But do they? I hope to deal adequately with that critical question as well. In sum, my task in this chapter will be adequately to represent what these intentions have realized in terms of theoretical thinking about religion, attempts to construct ways to *understand* religion from feminist points of view.

Let me warn students right off the bat that this discussion will necessarily be complex. It will make intellectual demands of you as well as demands of patience. Modern feminism, and thus modern feminist theories of religion, continue to be in a state of conceptual turmoil, with new theorizations proceeding apace (Maynard 2001, p. 294). Some critics have even called the movement "fragmented" (Castelli 1995, p. 78). As a movement, feminist studies of religion are barely a generation – forty years – old. By contrast, the Higher Criticism of the Bible has been honed for nearly two hundred years. A symptom of this state of flux is how many challenges to fundamental concepts we find in the literature of feminist studies of religion. This means that students may not be able to rely on the everyday conventional meanings of words they encounter in these feminist theories of religion. Feminists argue energetically, extensively, and often inconclusively about the meaning of basic terms like "woman," "sex," "gender," and even "feminism" itself (Juschka 2001b, p. 30f; Walters 2005, p. 1). New "conventions" are being hammered out; new consensuses are being formed. This unsettled condition injects excitement into the feminist enterprise in religious studies, as well as difficulty. By appreciating that we are dealing here with an ongoing, tumultuous uprising representing half of humanity, we can calibrate our expectations accordingly. If such considerations still do not make the reading in the coming pages easier, they might, at least, make readers more forgiving, and thus more patient. In addition, feminist thinkers in religious studies have been exceedingly industrious and productive. The quantity of work to encompass is truly vast. Because of the complexity and sheer volume of theoretical work on sex and gender, I shall devote the first part of this chapter to teasing apart some of the conceptual tangles that I find most salient in theoretical approaches to sex, gender, and religion. Then I shall show how these theoretical threads are woven into the concerns of some of our leading feminist theoretical thinkers.

Six Principles

I try to use six principles to frame my thinking in this chapter. Here they are.

First, this is a chapter about some key *feminist theoretical and methodological ideas about religion*. It is the *methodological* and *theoretical ideas* with a feminist edge that concern me, not the impossibly vast universe of feminist studies of religion.

Second, this chapter cannot, and should not, hope to address all the wonderful descriptive work done on women. That task would not only be impossible to complete here, it would be inappropriate. *Theories* and *methods* remain our foci, not just any study.

Third, the sex/gender theories of religion in this chapter will be those concerning the *female* sex and *feminine* gender. As much as one might wish, this is not a chapter about sex and gender generally, and thus about both (or all) sexes and genders. Ideally, one day, we will have theories that focus as much on masculinity as on femininity. But we simply do not have these yet in sufficient numbers or influence. After all, to be either a man or a woman is to be "sexed"; likewise, both sexes have "gender" qualities attributed to them by cultural convention. Thus, the intellectual process of "gendering" applies to both sexes. But for the time being almost all the work has been done on the cultural conventions that have framed members of the "female" sex – women – in certain ways thought particularly "feminine" – gendering. "All the men are strong, and all the women are good-looking," as it is said of the residents of the mythical Lake Woebegone of Minnesota Public Radio's *Prairie Home Companion*. As it happens, I believe we will find

that most of the work has been done on rectifying the imbalance in the area of sex, with relatively less on the far more elusive logic of gendering.

Fourth, even though I believe men can be "feminist" theorists, this chapter deals only with *women* feminist theorists of religion. I consider my colleague in the University of California, the biblical critic Scott Bartchy, as a scholar not only influenced by feminist theorists but also someone whose work is identifiably feminist (Bartchy 1999). While I am at it, let us not forget our old friends Weber and Malinowski. I deliberately argued how their theoretical thinking may have been deeply shaped by the women in their lives. At least aspects of their work could be called "feminist." Nevertheless, in order to compensate for the lack of women theorists in the first edition of the present text, I shall focus only on feminist theorists of religion who happen to be women.

Fifth, not all female scholars are "feminists," nor do they invariably approach religion in any distinguishably "feminine" (gender) way or from an identifiably "feminist" theoretical or methodological point of view. Females – women – who study religion do not necessarily produce feminine-"gendered" or feminist studies of religion. Something extra is required. Consider a racial parallel. Have all Jewish theorists, such as Durkheim, necessarily produced "Jewish" theories of religion? Have all Black theorists necessarily produced "Black" theories of religion? Why should membership in a given sex, in effect, guarantee an analogously "gendered" cast to the theory produced? Why does being a woman guarantee that one has developed a specifically "feminine" point of view – if indeed there be such an essentialized kind of "women's experience," to trade on Carol Gilligan's term? Many of the most avowedly feminist of thinkers are deeply indebted to male theorists anyway, such as Marx, Foucault, Lacan, Derrida, and so on. Further, religious studies can boast strong, theoretically sophisticated, ideologically and practically "liberated" women, such as Eileen Barker, Mary Douglas, Wendy Doniger, Kathryn McClymond, or Tomoko Masuzawa. But they would not necessarily identify themselves as feminist *theorists* of religion, even though they are well aware of the feminist issues and feminist theory. Nor do I know of arguments that these women approach religion in a feminine-"gendered" way!

A good example of a woman religious studies scholar independent of feminist theoretical trends would be Wendy Doniger. In this, Doniger reflects the approach of her University of Chicago colleague, the Black scholar Charles Long. He, as I noted in the previous chapter, resists being identified solely as a "Black" scholar. For her part, Doniger, has published widely about women and erotic sex in many of its delicious permutations and combinations, rather than about sex in the sense often confused with gender. Moreover, despite her great influence on a generation of women scholars of religion for her independent and fertile mind, she does not consider her work informed by "feminist" theory at all (Doniger 1982, 2006, 2007). Such women scholars as Wendy Doniger can hardly be labeled biased against women, and for that reason a scholar who fell victim to genderless talk about religion because of gender biases. We need to remain open to the possibility of there being aspects of religion where sex and gender difference is simply not salient. The critical thing for those bringing sex and gender to bear on religion is, of course, to identify those aspects, subjects, domains, questions, and such of religion where sex and gender do make a difference.

Sixth, I give special attention to feminist theorists who take seriously the idea of gender as *untethered* to a particular sex. They reject the idea of a naturally fixed "dualistic" and one-for-one correspondence conception of sex and gender relations. They reject the assumption that the sex of a person determines the gender traits of their work. They question nostrums such as those originating in mythical Lake Woebegone, where "All the men are strong, and all the women good-looking." By contrast, feminists generally seek to open us to the possibility that sometimes it may be the men who are good-looking, and the women strong, or where neither (or both) are strong and good-looking. Peacocks, take note! Keeping these questions open respects the complexity and cultural variation in sexual identity and gender ascription. Questioning the fixed or conventional ways of looking at sex and gender also gives feminist theorizing a stimulating edge.

Let's jump right into one of those areas of contest and theoretical turmoil that I said seemed characteristic of debates in feminist studies of religion – that concerning the meaning of fundamental terms like sex, gender, and sexuality (Simmons 2010). Since these terms set the groundwork for everything else that can be said about feminist theories of religion, they make a good starting point for us.

Why the Fuss about Sex and Gender?

A major conceptual question before feminist theorists of religion or of any other subject is how to think coherently about terms like "sex," "gender," and "sexuality." For example, ought they to be seen as basically identical, synonymous, or radically different? One might have dealt with similar difficulties in defining what "race" really was, or indeed, whether it was something "real" at all, in the previous chapter. Similar problems vex modern feminist theory (Castelli 1995, pp. 76–79). What then is an author to do in a book like ours when no consensus seems to exist about how to use key terms? We need to touch base with the usages of prominent feminist thinkers. Taking due note of this, I am going to try, at least, to say how I am using these terms.

Since talk of "sex" and "gender" can be confused, it might help clarity if we accepted that the terms *refer to* or *point to* different aspects of human life. Therefore, we need to bear in mind just what a feminist author seeks to highlight – is it sex or gender, or both? Does she want to study a concrete referent, females or women – the "sex" – say in order to rectify their being ignored by past scholars? Or does she want to study *qualities* thought to be tethered to concrete referents like real women of the female sex? What gender conceptions – of femininity or masculinity, say – do they import into their work? I do not want to limit these choices to the conventional sex/gender binary, but does our feminist scholar, thus, want to study "gender" or "gendering," instead of "sex," or "sex" rather than "gendering," or some combination of the two?

I know that this distinction may be controversial. But I have adopted it for a good (feminist) reason. "Sex" has a certain stubbornness to it, rooted in objective *natural* biology. Women are still commonly treated inequitably because of their sex, and what is *presumed* about the objective, unchangeable nature of their sex ("gender"). Biological nature and a history of being of a biological kind are at least two reasons why feminists balk at allowing a post-operative transsexual (now legally or officially a "woman") into the women's dressing room or "ladies' room." Supporting this implicit acknowledgment of the priority of *natural sexual origins*, radical feminist philosopher Mary Daly, says that physical changes undergone in transsexual surgery "cannot be expected to bring about profound psychic or social changes" that are more fundamental (Daly 1973, p. xviii). This is also why Mary Daly reportedly observed about post-operative transsexuals that theirs is a "man's problem." At some point, therefore, biology, along with a previous life of socialization as male, really matter. And in matters of sex, rather than gender, as we will see, it matters enormously. Sex matters. It matters because it reflects a degree of deep biological and psychic coding in all of us.

Many, if not most, of the problems we meet in thinking about sex and gender arise because of the prevailing belief that gender assignment is fixed in the same way as one's sex. It is commonplace to hear people conflate gender and sex – as if all masculine gender qualities belong naturally and essentially to men, and all feminine gender qualities belong likewise uniquely to women. Thus, men naturally display the "masculine" gender traits of aggressiveness and competitiveness, while women manifest the "feminine" gender qualities of nurture-giving and cooperativeness and so on. Many human societies thus apply certain "gender" characteristics to human beings of different "sexes" in a typically essential and stereotyped way. Indeed, in some cultures sex and gender are not distinguished at all. In Chinese, a word for "gender" did not enter the language until the nineteenth century. For these "essentialists," sex and gender are coterminous realities. Men are men and women are women – and never the twain shall meet! Sex/gender essentialism, in turn, also goes by the name of sex/gender stereotyping: real men don't cook, only (*real*) women do; real men don't cry, (real) women are expected "naturally" so to do; real men don't share in childcare, (real) women are designed for the purpose. Essentialists tend – stereotypically – to gender men as competitive, hard, and tough, but women as cooperative, soft, and nurturing. A male who showed tendencies toward traits such

as emotional sensitivity or vulnerability, who cooked and so on, might well be designated – gendered – as "effeminate," and thus not a "real" man. We need to be aware then of the tendency to think sex/gender properties map onto one another in a one-for-one and essential way.

On the other hand, "gender" has come to be a name for *cultural* or *social* referents – not biological or natural ones. "Gender" involves imagined categories applied to the different sexes, not biological ones *inhering in* the sexes. Thus, masculinity and femininity are "gender" traits, conventionally thought to belong invariably and naturally to men and women, respectively. Androcentrism, patriarchy, kyriarchy, dualism, male or female dominance are all clusters of "gender" beliefs. They are not objective biological qualities inhering necessarily in specific sexes, but rather traits clustered round the sexes on the basis of conventional human beliefs about what make "real" men and "real" women. Therefore, we should underline feminist Darlene Juschka's view that "gender is the social and cultural conception of the roles developed in relation to the sexed bodies of the male and female" (Juschka 2001c, pp. 285–286).

What is interesting is that gender ideology even determines "sex." It teaches people what it is to be a "real" man or "real" woman. People may think of the different "sexes" as biologically based. But what they take to be a sex is often a product of gender *beliefs* – what constitutes "real" men and women. On this point, Mary Daly argues that Genesis is so dominated by an androcentric ideology, that "real" women are seen as being indelibly marked with the sign of the eternal temptress: Eve. After all, it was Eve who led Adam to eat of the forbidden fruit. Further, Genesis also casts the creator in the role of Father-God – male in sex – thus, telling females that they should *believe* they are "subordinate" to men. In human societies then, "real" men need to conform to the role of "man" according to Genesis – which puts them at the head of the family, and "real" women at their feet. Lake Woebegone again (Daly 1973). In other words, Genesis and its Father-God preach the ideology of androcentrism, patriarchy, and all other related ideological *gender* constructs. In practice, what a "real" woman is as a "sex" is defined mostly by a cluster of gender traits reflecting her subordinate inferiority to "real" men. Indeed, says feminist theorist, historian of science, and biologist Evelyn Fox Keller, "the single most important contribution of contemporary feminist theory ... [is] its recognition of gender as a cultural rather than biological category" (Keller 1989, p. 721).

Once gender comes into focus as something usefully distinguished from sex, two closely related and fundamental issues arise. First, are the genders of people, like their sexes, dual, and cleanly opposed to one another? Second, do these polarized gender characteristics (receptivity, aggression, submissiveness, care and nurturing, and so on) belong *necessarily and properly* to one sex, and not the other? Is "gender-bending" out? Or, is the application of gender traits less fixed than many assume? The accomplished French feminist Christine Delphy argues trenchantly against this idea that certain gender roles apply "naturally" to a given sex. For her, there is no one-for-one correspondence between sex and gender. Instead, Delphy seeks to break open our imaginations so that we might conceive of a radically variable relation between sex and gender beyond the dull limits of Lake Woebegone where "All the men are strong, and all the women good-looking" (Delphy 2001, pp. 411–426).

Putting Concepts of Sex and Gender to a Test: Women's Ordination

Are we now at least equipped with some useful tools for thinking about gender/sex and religion? What of the question of the ordination of women into the clergy, especially the Roman Catholic and Eastern Orthodox communions? As recently as summer 2010, the *New York Times* reported that the Vatican decreed that "ordaining women as priests was as grave an offense as pedophilia" (Donadio 2010, p. A1). Quite a claim. I believe that this case shows us a number of things. First, it brings out the salience of the church's position as a focus on "sex." Second, at the same time it demonstrates what has provoked some of the revolutionary feminist theological and theoretical thinking featured in this chapter to do likewise. Using the distinctions developed between sex and gender, I read the church to be asserting that sex trumps gender in the matter of candidates for the priesthood: only males can be

priests. Why? In Catholic eyes, the priest must model Jesus, the first priest. Since Jesus was of the male sex, all priests must be male as well. The Roman Catholic tradition even claims deeper roots in the Jewish temple priesthood, where, as well, only men could be priests. Since this line of priests is hard-wired as male, all subsequent priests must be so as well.

When this sex-based argument is challenged, it is often defended by appealing to the idea of a one-for-one correspondence between sex and certain desirable priestly traits. Thus, the church and its faithful rightly expect their priests to possess qualities of moral and spiritual maturity, leadership, expertise in pastoral care, nurturing, and other Christ-like virtues. What excludes women from the Roman Catholic priesthood is not only their sexual differences, but also the presumption that these priestly moral qualities are *gendered* – tied specifically to the male sex. Small wonder today's women feel hurt and insulted. They argue that this correspondence between male sex and priestly virtues is arbitrary. It represents at best a conventional gendering of a social religious institution. Women can as surely own the requisite priestly qualities as men. The virtues requisite to lead, nurture, model Christ's moral virtues, and so on do not belong to men alone. Indeed, why could it not be argued that woman priests might presumably perform the "shepherd of the flock" role, the nurturing or caring roles, even better than a male? Wouldn't women, who have often been pressed into service as heads of families, likewise make just as capable heads of congregations as males? The gender qualities that one may identify with the priesthood, then, might belong to women as easily as to men. Thus, since they possess the same gender-misidentified virtues as men, they should be allowed ordination. They can do the job, because male biology is not required for the performance of priestly virtues.

As for the study of religion itself, raising such questions can be looked upon as symptomatic of the entire re-examination of conventional (and official) wisdom having to do with the relation of the sexes to religion. One small, but nonetheless startling, example of this potential to upset widely accepted assumptions about the role of the sexes in religion comes from feminist historians of Christianity. Their research has established that Jesus was frequently seen to be *female* and, thus, to possess the corresponding *feminine* gender traits! For example, some medieval devotional literature refers to the nurturing image of a "mother Jesus" (McLaughlin 1979, pp. 101–103). For those seeking ordination of women into the priesthood, an appeal to such an image as "Jesus mother" would strengthen their case that the priest's modeling Jesus amounts to much more than sharing hard-wired sex traits. Developing this insight along theological lines, the "mother Jesus" image suggests that biological men may also perform well in areas supposedly reserved for women, such as nurturing and caring. And why not, *a fortiori*, allow that biological women may not only fulfill the needs of the priesthood in traditionally feminine ways – for instance, as nurturing and caring – but also in ways thought to be reserved for men, such as leadership and protection? Why not see that the biology – the sex – of a priest need not be critical to the performance of the wide range of gender roles demanded of the priest?

Feminist Theory of Religion and Its Moral Bases

Moral impulses for equity drive feminist studies of religion. These impulses also encourage feminist theorists to "think they are right" in taking their chosen routes of study. As I noted at the outset, virtually all the great figures in religion – popes, mullahs, gurus, druids, buddhas, and even sacrificial victims – have been men! Yes, there have been goddesses, Vestal Virgins, sorceresses, sibyls, abbesses, madonnas, female bodhisattvas, tantrikas, and various prophetesses. But even where women had a presence, men have tended to monopolize positions of authority and power within religions, thus exposing the pervasiveness of patriarchy in religion. Or consider what thinkers no less distinguished than Aristotle have done in setting the terms of our thinking about sex/gender. In the first book of *Generation of Animals*, he argues that women are incomplete; women are really diminished men. Only men, therefore, can represent the entire human species, because men are more fully human, more naturally and biologically perfect specimens of our species. Aristotle also abetted thinking that sex/gender

traits are essentialized, and in one-for-one correspondence with each other. The first "Lake Woebegone"? When Aristotle was rediscovered in the West, the most important theologian in the Roman Catholic world, Thomas Aquinas, simply accepted Aristotle's view of women. In his great work, the *Summa Theologica* (1265–74, Part I, questions 90–92), Aquinas explains that women cannot be priests because they are inherently deficient or incomplete when compared to men (shades of Aristotle). Up against such an eminent authority, Roman Catholic women stood little chance of offering theological justification for serving as (priestly) mediators between God and humanity. They could neither model Christ, since they were not male, nor could they model humanity, because as Aquinas taught, they were really, in essence, defective men. Patriarchy again gets inscribed into religious language and thought.

Feminist Strategies for Studying Religion

But how do these and other realizations of inequity shape what feminists do in the study of religion? First, feminists do the obvious: they *redress* the imbalance in treatment of the female sex in the study of religion. The study of religion should at the very least *begin* studying religious *women* – religious "females." A key working hypothesis would be to ask whether sexual difference does make a difference. Is a goddess religion different than a god-worship religion? Does worshiping a male/god makes a religion more warlike than one worshiping a female/goddess? In place of an Eliadean neutrality, dictated by the key idea of a universal *Homo religiosus*, feminists prefer to take the hypothesis that "difference makes a difference" as a point of departure. That is to say, they will seek to test the idea that sex/gender differences in religion have consequences. They matter.

Second, awareness of sexual difference also involves certain implications about gender in the study of religion. Since gender is *conventionally* thought to be derived directly from sex, the two are not often distinguished. Gender traits are thought to be in essential, immutable, one-for-one correspondence with sex, and thus also not conventionally thought different. Thus, women act in a feminine way; males act in a masculine manner. In ancient Israel, for example, "prophetic" gender behavior is what one might expect only from certain gifted males; in Islam, caliph-like warrior leadership qualities belong solely to men. According to script, two women, Martha and Mary, exhibit characteristic feminine gender behavior, such as attending to Jesus, while he himself displays correspondingly masculine leadership traits typical of a Jewish male of his time. But this conflation of gender and sex just perpetuates conceptual errors in thinking about women and religion. Feminists try to "deconstruct" this conflation of sex and gender by attacking the stereotyping conventions of a one-for-one correspondence between sex and gender. Feminist Karen McCarthy Brown, in *Mama Lola*, for example, does so by focusing her entire book on a woman in the (conventionally masculine-gendered) role of religious leadership. Are there some common strategies of inquiry for redressing imbalances in the study of religion, such as Brown has used?

First are simple "retrieval efforts." These are attempts to reclaim lost, obscured, or ignored knowledge about women as a sex, but also to examine the gendered properties that different religions, in their different ways, have considered belong to women as a sex. We will look more closely at examples of such retrieval efforts in the work of Karen McCarthy Brown and Caroline Walker Bynum. While Brown takes a second look at the traditions of Haitian Vodou to retrieve evidence of the leadership roles of women, Bynum reads historical documents for evidence of the active, but overlooked, roles played by women in the history of Christianity.

Second, once evidence of the importance of women in religion has been retrieved, our view of the past will have changed. We are, then, led naturally to *reconceiving* the history of the religious movements, institutions, and such where women played a previously unrecognized role. In the historical dimension, the conventional narrative about the past gets a thorough re-reading. Does the history of Christianity "read" the same way once we learn that women influenced important movements of spirituality? In her studies of Haitian Vodou, Karen Brown, in effect, brings both the "gender" question as well as the "sex" perspective into play in order to reconceive how the entire tradition hangs together. How is it that

a woman could assume the conventionally masculine-gendered role of leader in the Haitian Vodou tradition? Or do Haitians simply not replicate a whole host of mainline Lake Woebegone genderings? What if Brown is right about both the "sex" angle – the real prominence of women leaders in Haitian Vodou – *and* the "gender" angle – Haitian gendering leadership as feminine? What does this say about the mainline, if Brown is right? Might we find similar hidden leadership conditions for women in other religions, as well? From this small example I hope readers can see how rich a trove of questions – "problems of religion" – the new feminist point of view can provoke, and add to those around which religious studies is focused.

Yet even "rectifying" a historical imbalance does not satisfy the ambitions of some feminist scholars. Mere "negative freedom," freeing women *from* the burden of historical misperceptions, is not enough for them. These feminists have goals of realizing "positive freedom" for women. They tend to be theologians, and thus in the liberationist or "prophetic" camp, like Cornel West. As such, they are in the business of "making religion," instead of just studying it, or even re-imagining it in new ways. Among the new ways of imagining religion along these radical feminist lines is advocating for goddess religion. Some women, seeking to institute goddess religion, and insist on the name "thealogian" to replace the patriarchally inflected word, "theologian." Carol Christ is one such "thealogian" whose work we will meet in the following pages. Other radical feminist theologians, like Rosemary Radford Ruether and Mary Daly, also try to defeat the patriarchy in Christianity, and perhaps Christianity too. As such, those founding a new goddess religion exemplify the perennial process of making a religion itself. Similarly, those who imagine only that they are *renewing* a goddess religious tradition may actually be inventing it afresh without knowing it. They are finally not best appreciated as religious studies scholars, or seeking to write studies *of* religion. As such, like Cornel West's "prophetic pragmatist" plan for the study of religion, they represent a recrudescence of theology within the university. Readers who have objections to a re-theologizing of the study of religion – however good for religious traditions themselves – may want to take note of the fact. In some sense, then, "thealogians" *are* religion, rather than the *study* of religion.

Historian Caroline Walker Bynum: What Gain from Such Pain?

We will see more of the re-theologizing efforts as we move on. Feminists like Caroline Walker Bynum actively seek to rectify the sexual imbalances legion in history of Christianity. Bynum's works in the history of medieval Christianity raise fascinating questions about the way religion has shaped attitudes to bodily health and sickness (Bynum 1987, 1995). Bynum picks up themes of body techniques that run through feminist literature, derived in part from Foucault's work on disciplining the body. These include religious practices like fasting or feasting, ideals of health/virtue and illness/sin, and so on. These investigations into pre-modern religion suggest that modernity, specifically scientifico-technological modes of thought and capitalist modes of economic production, may have imposed the rigid dualisms of Lake Woebegone on men and women. That is to say, pre-modern women seem to have been as "strong" as the men, and clearly not as "good-looking" as women in that mythical vale of bland perfection are, either. Bynum argues that medieval religious women are not to be typecast according to the dualistic assumptions we "moderns" make about sex and gender relations. Unlock those tight one-for-one correspondences between sex and gender traits. But Bynum has her limits. Unlike the prophetic voices in religious studies, she refuses to apply the lessons learnt in the medieval period to modern times. Says Bynum: "My approach clearly assumes that the practices and symbols of any culture are … inseparable from it … So I would argue that medieval symbols, behaviors, and doctrines have no direct lessons for the 1980s. They were products of a world that has vanished" (Bynum 1987, pp. 298–299). For good or for ill, this leaves those hungry for "theory," theology or goddess religion's "thealogy" short of the existential lift Brown or Christ offer. But the lack of relevance and existential payoff are hardly the largest of Bynum's problems.

Bynum knows few moderns sympathize with her medieval European world. Her medieval women undergo grotesque agonies, seemingly masochistic spiritual exercises, or excursions into self-hatred – all in the name of Christianity. Why would Bynum, in what has been hailed a feminist project, dwell on this sordid material, much less urge us, or even women in particular, to try to empathize with and understand it? Why would we even want to understand such self-destructive practices? Why should we want to retrieve a past for women that seems to confirm the worst stereotypes of female self-loathing? "What part of self-mutilation don't we understand," one might say? How else should we understand these religious practices than as horrid acts of self-hatred? How else should we understand Bynum's women than as further victims of male power?

If nothing else, Bynum's book provides an acid test of the principles of inquiry introduced by the phenomenologists – empathy and understanding – as well as of the value of reclaiming the lost past of religious women. All are challenging questions for the feminist historian seeking to retrieve a lost world of seemingly hideous women's religious practices. But how can Bynum be hailed a *feminist* author, lionized by many women scholars, for putting them to their present use?

Bynum answers in classic historicist style by appealing to "context." First, echoing phenomenology, she insists upon attention to the "insider's" point of view. What do these women have say about their own condition? And here is where Bynum, the everyday working historian/archivist, makes her appearance. Until Bynum came along, we simply did not know what the women's point of view was! Salvaging ignored, suppressed, or mislaid women's history is precisely the point of a retrieval operation – no matter how ugly. Luckily for the long-term feminist aim of ennobling women by writing women's history, Bynum's salvage job turns up unexpected results. Once Bynum reclaims enough data to grasp these women's points of view, Bynum tells us they ought not to be stereotyped as self-hating submissives at all. On the contrary, these medieval women are not "best understood as creatures constrained or impelled by society's notion of females as inferior" (Bynum 1987, p. 295). Somehow, they have escaped what Foucault might regard as a regime of socially constructed domination. How and why is such a remarkable result possible? How is it that we might be incredulous?

First of all, *our* amazement can easily be explained. We only had certain classes of documents available to us. Those were composed by men. Thanks to Bynum, we now have the women's side of the picture. Bynum's feminist claim is that the *sexes* "constructed" their relation to one another in different ways. In this case, the *sexes* of their authors made a decisive difference. Bynum uncovers the novel fact, for example, that these women never regarded themselves as inferiors – even to their higher-ups in the Roman Catholic ecclesiastical hierarchy! It was the *male* authorities who imposed the classification of "inferior" upon the women ascetics. Until Bynum's painstaking archival digging, we only knew the male story.

But Bynum's greatest discovery may perhaps be that the women did not share the male view at all. They resisted conventional sex and gender stereotyping, and in doing so resisted conventional attitudes about suffering and pain. It was as if they had read Foucault before he had written, and had been inspired by the notion of resistance, of freedom *from* domination. Bynum rescued the voices of resistance of some brave women ascetics, voices that had been easily drowned out in the flood of literature constructed to stereotype them as self-hating submissives.

All very well and good. It helps to know that the women felt they enhanced their dignity, and resisted demeaning male classifications. Fine. But how did Bynum's ascetics escape with dignity in hand? Can Bynum help us digest the ascetic practices of the women any more easily, so that we might better appreciate her work as a *feminist* project? Once we gain the viewpoint of women ascetics, we see that they "gendered" their corporeal travails differently than the way the dominant contemporary literature – all written by men – did. The men abstractly spiritualized suffering; the women "saw themselves as human beings – fully spirit and fully flesh." Further, they expanded their vision well beyond their lone endurance of pain: "they saw all humanity as created in God's image, as capable of *imitatio Christi* through body as well as soul." By embracing the humanity of their vulnerable corporeality, they raised their spirits above the solitary gloom darkening male reports of the same religious phenomena: "Thus, they gloried in the pain, the exudings, the somatic distortions that made their bodies parallel to the consecrated wafer on the altar and the man on the cross" (Bynum 1987, p. 296). They did so because it bonded them to the tragic condition of human corruptibility. They raised themselves above male self-absorption in their own pain, and transformed it into a vehicle traveling the pageant of creation.

If Bynum's interpretation helps make it easier to stomach the embrace of suffering displayed by these women, it will have helped us see how much her work has meant to feminists. Simply picturing medieval women ascetics as empowered recovers a world where the "holy women" of the period revealed themselves as leaders of communities and religious networks. These holy women were not the second-class religious citizens of Christendom as conventional wisdom has cast them. They were strong, independent, and noble (Bynum 1987, ch. 1).

Despite her influence upon liberationist feminists, Bynum refuses the activist, "prophetic" cloak. She won't put this "retrieved" knowledge about women to aid practical ambitions to reform the church, or to fashion a new theology of women's role in the church, and so on. By contrast, these ambitions are very much part of the activist prophetic roles of other feminist religious studies scholars we will take up. Bynum typifies a kind of liberal feminist scholarship that rests with helping women toward some "negative freedom *from*," not the articulation of a vision of positive "freedom *to*" create some social goal for women.

Karen Brown's *Mama Lola*: A Woman at the Center

More ambitious, and certainly activist, is the work of anthropologist of religion Karen McCarthy Brown. Feminists welcome Bynum's "freeing of women *from*" histories that diminish or overlook their roles in the creative religious imaginary. However, Brown seeks more. She wants to imagine a "freedom *to*" a new *feminist* religious consciousness. What makes this radical is her willingness to experiment upon herself as a subject of this new women's religious imaginary.

Putting Brown into the larger context of women ethnologists should help us trace the trajectory of her path. Feminists who work in and through anthropology of religion not only read ethnographic literature, but some even venture into the field to study religion as it is "lived." This line of inquiry first got going with the pioneer sex and gender scholar, American anthropologist Margaret Mead. Widely known for her controversial work on sex in Samoa, Papua New Guinea, and other south Pacific islands, Mead argued for the cultural relativity of gender roles. Much as I have assumed in this chapter, Mead argued that "gender" names a cultural category of human life, not a natural one. Put otherwise, Mead's work argues that, in effect, the sage of Lake Woebegone was mistaken: being "strong" doesn't belong exclusively to men, any more than being "good-looking" naturally applies to women. "Sex" and "gender" name two different things. Depending upon the culture in question, men and women will exhibit properties that, in other cultures, will be applied to the opposite sex. While Mead represents a tradition that many contemporary feminist thinkers still admire for its breakthrough efforts in the first third of the twentieth century, others think Mead's notions need considerable updating (Delphy 2001; Mead 1935). Brown's radical work should give readers a taste of one of the most prominent examples of new feminist thinking in the anthropology of religion.

At first blush, Karen McCarthy Brown might simply be seen as re-reading a religious tradition – that of Haitian Vodou. Describing her celebrated book, *Mama Lola*, in modest terms, Brown calls it an "intimate spiritual biography of a Vodou priestess and her family" (Brown 1991, p. ix). But I would offer that the book's celebrity among feminists and people from professional societies lies less in what we may learn of Haitian Vodou or Alourdes, the "Mama Lola" of the title, and rather in an interest in Brown's explicitly feminist methods and theorizing. Brown does more than practice routine feminist retrieving of Haitian Vodou from sex/gender distortions. She systematically attacks what she labels patriarchal methods of (modernist) scientific neutrality and objectivity. And she crowns that attack by claiming that the feminist way of understanding Vodou is by oneself converting to it, by radically subjectivizing the study of Haitian religion. Brown becomes both the object and subject of an experiment in becoming the Other. This, Brown suggests, is feminist theory's ultimate challenge to the study of religion.

In making a woman the center of the *Mama Lola* story, Brown establishes her own minimal feminist *bona fides*. She shows how Haitian Vodou excels at creating prominent leadership roles for women. Brown wants to put her own spin on the "retrieval" project of women's religious experience by making women "visible" in this way. She shows how female leadership in Vodou defeats the attempts by men to coopt female religious figures, such as goddesses, for their own purposes. "When women's religious leadership is unfettered by male control … religion begins to take account of the circumstances of women's lives." For Brown, this means that what was hidden, overlooked, or downgraded finally gets some attention: "Women become visible. In Vodou, the female spirits have begun to tell the stories of women's lives from their point of view, in striking contrast to religious systems in which goddess figures function largely as the carriers of male projections about women" (Brown 1991, p. 255).

And what do we "see," what is made "visible," when Brown assembles her portrait of Alourdes? Brown shows us a complex woman. For example, since Brown herself is much the same, conflicts will be inevitably become visible. Sometimes, Alourdes guides Brown, then in moments of intimacy, she cossets Brown like the wise, loving mother we should all be blessed to have had. But at other times, despite her best efforts to "undercut the colonial mind set of much anthropological writing," Brown becomes the "professor," the "anthropologist." Alourdes retreats to the level of ethnographic subject, the paid informant (Brown 1992, A56). On a taxi trip with Alourdes in Haiti, Brown recounts how their complex relation was thrown into confusion:

> Usually I am content to treat Alourdes as my Vodou "mother," defer to her wishes, and let her be in charge. But sometimes we have trouble keeping our roles straight… . I had thrown our carefully constructed roles into confusion by reminding the driver that I was the one paying his salary. After that, neither Alourdes nor I knew how to act. (Brown 1991, p. 196)

No mention of this telling vignette would be complete without adding that Brown assigned all the royalties from the sales of *Mama Lola* to Alourdes. Some feminists would note that this remarkable act demonstrates – more than anything Brown might write – a practical faithfulness to the egalitarian and liberationist values at the core of feminism. Brown "walks the talk," so to speak, of negating culturally imposed inequities.

At the same time, however, Brown surrenders her professorial authority. Alourdes' authority grows in word and deed. She retains her position as a woman at the center of a world of multifaceted religious power. She is supreme servant of the spirits, and a wife of one – Danbala, a woman talented in guiding others into receiving possession by them. She reads the dreams of others, and is a vigorous dreamer herself. She heals. She conducts the power of the spirits to those she desires to bring within their orbit. And, as we will shortly see, Brown herself will become one such person empowered through the priestly agency of Alourdes.

Feminists Should Resist Abstraction and Objectification

Brown's writes of Alourdes in vividly detailed literary style, less for esthetic reasons than for methodological ones. She believes there is a feminist-gendered method of accounting for her subject. And that that demands both a literary, narrative style of presentation and an attention to the quotidian details of everyday life. The two are connected, of course. By contrast, masculine-gendered writing will be modernist in tone. It will be abstract and objectivist, and principally pay attention to "important" matters. That, at any rate, is what Brown and a sizable consensus of feminist women theorists claim (Brown 1991, p. 12f; Warne 2000, p. 252). This methodological decision dictates that Brown will celebrate the quotidian and mundane, incidentally those domains typically marked as feminine in gender. She believes the tendency to dismiss the everyday and mundane subjects is another example of gender bias favoring those "important" things men do over against what women do. She claims that male scholars discount "women's work" as "uninteresting." Not so, says Brown. "Our friendship grew through intimacies shared in the midst of a shared in the midst of routine work as well as through stronger bonds forged in the midst of life crises" (Brown 1992, A56).

Brown may even push this methodological line of attention to the quotidian over the edge. Brown disagrees. The feminist-gendered way to see a Haitian woman like Alourdes requires attention to the minutiae of the everyday details of what real Haitian women do. We accompany Brown and Alourdes on their constant shopping trips to gather the paraphernalia for the rituals to be performed that day, or just to get the proper items for the family meal. "I ran errands, helped to cook the ritual meal, and lent a hand constructing the altar that is the focal point of each Vodou ceremony," Brown tells us. We likewise enter the world of family gossip surrounding Alourdes' marriage, or her difficulties with a Haitian community, "where male dominance is both traditional and ideal" (Brown 1991, p. 157). We get a "feel" for her own immigrant life and its trials. Brown likewise casts light on the Foucauldian micro-politics of the religious sphere. The pay-off for this fine-grained focus? Beyond some blind methodological commitment to the everyday, Brown believes that this immersion and recognition of the role of the quotidian yielded insights that could only be obtainable in this way.

A *Mama Lola* Theory of Knowledge?

Behind Brown's attention to the quotidian is a feminist elevation of subjectivity. Feminists need to study the details of the everyday life of women like Alourdes, as Brown recommends, but they need to do so from a "subjective" point of view. This is the feminist-gendered way to attain knowledge. To Brown, conventional "objectivist" theories of knowledge are the result of gender-biased "masculine" ways of thinking. Objectivism reflects the same affection for abstraction and distance that Brown indicted in estrangement from everyday concreteness. Both, Brown claims, are facets of masculinist gender ideology. Men believe they need to objectify things in order to know them. Feminists like Brown think entering into the subjectivity of religious folk is the only way to understand, and thus to know, them.

Just how this bit of gender ideology emerges out of the sexual identity or power situation of men, Brown does not say. To understand why Brown "thinks she is right," we need to remember Brown's indictment of the view that we can know other people "objectively" – without involving ourselves in their lives. As a view of how scientific knowledge about people goes, Brown and others believe it has been foisted on us by the raw power embodied in and deployed by patriarchy. The objectivist view of knowing other people is not necessarily the best; it is just the one that has "won out" in the battle of the sexes. At the very least, it is what men, who have ruled the sciences, *tell* us is the right way to look at things. But Brown and others refuse to accept defeat.

Brown rejects what she takes to be the patriarchal biases behind objectivism, and goes further, indeed much further, in at least two ways. We already know that she, first, has aligned herself with the ideal of the subjectivity of knowledge in affirming the privileged status of the so-called "native's point of view." It is not the academic scholar – the "doctor" – who "knows best." It is the natives, according to Brown who, in direct opposition to modernist epistemology, "know best." When we study the religion of another society, even another society within the larger mainstream society in which we live, we must give priority to what insiders – believers – say about their religion. This takes us back to what phenomenologist Kristensen declared as the proper method for studying religion: "For the historian only one evaluation is possible: "the believers were completely right." Only after we have grasped this can we understand these people and their religion" (Kristensen 1960, p. 14). Brown, in effect, concurs with the spirit and letter of Kristensen's protective attitude to religion by saying: "the people who are being studied should be allowed to speak for themselves whenever possible, for they are the only true experts on themselves." As the only true experts, believers avoid any criticism of their precious religious situation (Brown 1991, p. 14).

How might we understand why Brown "thinks she is right" to assert an authority of believers that seems rather absolute? Brown just seems to turn the tables, and contradicts modernism, in effect aligning herself with post-modernism, even though she denies it (Brown 1992, A56). Hers might be a natural feminist reaction to the extreme "doctor knows best" objectivism of modernist thinkers – the huge majority of whom were males. In the eyes of theorists like Brown, the modernist assurance of a Malinowski, Freud, Tylor, Frazer, and so on that only "doctor" knows best amounts to colossal (male) arrogance. Who would not be offended by such high-handedness? Another reason Brown thinks she may be right comes from her actual experience in the field, immersed in the detailed life of Alourdes. Because modernists don't "listen" and observe believers like this, they guarantee that they will never really *know* or *understand* religious people in any depth.

Without doubt, however, the method Brown pursued in *Mama Lola* brought her and the book national celebrity and acclaim. Brown intensified her already radical *theory* of knowledge with an even more radical *method*. Already dedicated to the privileged status of the insider's point of view, Brown pursued a method of investigation that put that theory into practice. Given her theory of knowledge of the incorrigibility and incommunicability of the religious believer's inside point of view, Brown follows through in practicing a method consistent with that theory. She would do far more than just privileging what the "natives" said to her and others about Vodou. She felt that she had herself to *become* a "native," so to speak! *Mama Lola* records her attempts to abolish the distinction between researcher and object of research by a total conversion to Vodou. Indeed, to speak of "conversion" is not to do justice to Brown's relation to Vodou and its godly powers. She in fact "marries" a Vodou god, and in doing so is assumed into the community.

I learned of Brown's new life quite by accident one day when I asked her about the golden wedding band that I noticed that she had begun to wear. Wearing a wedding band was especially odd, since I knew – or thought I knew – that she had not remarried since her divorce some years earlier. Well, so much for what I thought! The ring, as I learned, marked her as married to Ogou, as Brown told me rather matter-of-factly. As readers of *Mama Lola* will know, that marriage was as real for Karen Brown as that solid band of gleaming gold. This marriage was not make-believe or play-acting. It was a "real" marriage – and one Brown chose with all her heart. At a minimum, the ring showed that Brown had "crossed over" into a new life – that she had made a choice to embrace a new identity and a new reality.

"This spontaneous decision," said Brown – now from "inside" Vodou – "marked a new stage in my relation to Haitian Vodou." And through her Vodou marriage and initiation Brown felt she had attained a "new and deeper understanding of how Vodou actually works in the lives of individuals." Far, then, from being some modernist objective onlooker, or far even from being the "participant observer" of classic ethnographic method, Brown claims to have erased the difference between "us" and "them." She has become one of "them," and she herself has become the object of her own subjective focus.

> When I began to bring my own life to the system for healing, I began to understand more of what it meant for Haitians to do that. In a way, I was setting out to do fieldwork on my own psyche. I remain convinced that this was the best and perhaps the only way for me to move my understanding of Vodou beyond external description into the deep places where it takes up the dreams and fears, hope and pain of an actual life. (Brown 1991, p. 134)

A more self-conscious and sincere statement of a radically subjectivist position one could hardly imagine. Nor can one imagine any more total plunge into the Other than that which Brown records of her own Vodou marriage.

Led by Alourdes, Brown commits to a marriage with one of the lordliest of Vodou lords, Ogou. In a luminous moment of fierce decision, Brown consummates her union with the Vodou god in an intense public Vodou community ceremony. Sincere empathy or even sympathy for such a "marriage" are apparently not sufficient for Brown. She needs to go all the way, because she wants to claim that only an insider really understands what it means to marry a Vodou god like Ogou. Without making an argument for this position, Brown insinuates that as long as one remains outside the community of committed believers, one remains outside the veil of deep understanding. In order to break through our patriarchal Western protective shell Brown claims that one must become a Vodou devotee oneself! And that is precisely what she does.

Critical Remarks

Sincerity and self-awareness aside, Brown's methods and theory raise many questions. First, the book records what we might call an "experiment," although I do not think it really was. It could be read as a test – had Brown chosen to make it such. Whether Brown understands Haitian Vodou better than an outsider, however sympathetic or empathetic, is actually never "put to the test." So, we really don't know if she's right. I say this because there is nothing in the book even to hint that Brown intends it to be a test of her methodological beliefs. I think this avoidance of a test of Brown's method weakens the methodological side of *Mama Lola* because it leaves itself vulnerable to attack. Critics might ask how Brown knows her entry into Vodou gives her greater insights if she has not compared what she learns in this way to another approach that does not require membership. How does Brown know her method is better?

Second, claims about knowledge, such as Brown makes, are no different than claims to have found gold. You can "stake your claim," but that doesn't mean you will actually find gold. As such, claims have no truth value. We need some more arguments. For instance, some questions arise simply at the level of Brown's assumptions in beginning her "experiment." Does Brown's doing "fieldwork on my own psyche" contradict her ambitions to interpret and represent a Haitian "Other"? Can her explorations of her own self and her attempts at interpreting the worldview of Haitian Vodou really be the same thing? Is not Brown just fashioning Haitian Vodou into something of her own – creating her own, perhaps original, version of that religion? How can we be sure her psyche and the Haitian social and psychic realities are the same, especially when Brown herself seems to efface the difference? I could imagine her "trans-culturalism" as subject to the same suspicions that Mary Daly leveled against post-operative transgendered "women" being "real" women. Are Brown's hopes, dreams, problems, and so on really the problems of born Haitian Vodouists? Despite years of intense fieldwork and participant observation, Brown was neither born nor reared in Haitian society. Despite her sincere efforts to empathize with Alourdes and Haitian culture, is she not limited by her own past history as a middle-class, white American? These, at any rate, are some thoughts one might bear in mind in thinking about Brown's claims and actions.

Readers should note that Brown's book brought her great notoriety and popularity, but also inspired envy. Many flocked to her public lectures and bought her book. Others questioned her surrender of neutrality. Brown's account of her possession by a Vodou *Lola* (god) thus created a scandal for many in the academic study of religion. Others, nonetheless, welcomed Brown's challenge to modernist epistemological reserve. By her personal bravery and dedication alone, she had won sufficient respect to gain an initial hearing and a considerable following. "My academic colleagues have raised questions," Brown readily admits:

> Have I lost my objectivity? Has my friendship with Alourdes biased my account of her family history, her daily life, and her spirituality? Has my participation in Vodou colored the way in which I present the religion? The answer to all these questions is a qualified Yes, although that doesn't disturb me as much as some of my colleagues wish that it did. (Brown 1992, A56)

Thus, confident in her approach to Vodou, Brown stakes out a position that divides religious studies to this day. *Mama Lola* remains an object lesson of at least one way that post-modernist feminist methodology in the study of religion earns the name "radical."

Feminist Biblical "Higher Criticism" and Christian Origins

Karen McCarthy Brown's *Mama Lola* has been especially influential in feminist circles in the study of religion. But it is still hard to outdo the impact that feminist critiques of the Bible and Christian origins regularly achieve. This work strikes immediately at the sources of Western religious consciousness in a way even the most fascinating ethnography cannot. So with this potential for unsettling mainline Christian belief and practice in mind, let me now turn to just such a cluster of radical feminist theoreticians of religion – Mary Daly, Elisabeth Schüssler-Fiorenza, and Rosemary Radford Ruether. These feminists work out of the related disciplines of philosophical and biblical theology, as well as a new feminist iteration of the Higher Criticism of the Bible. I treat them together even though they divide by disciplinary affiliation: Daly, philosophy, Schüssler-Fiorenza, biblical criticism, and Ruether, Christian theology. Yet despite these differences of discipline these women show how a common commitment to a "positive liberationist" agenda of Christian women unites them in a remarkably inter-disciplinary effort. I regret that I am limited by space in dealing with the parallel work among feminist theologians such as Rita Gross (Hinduism) or Judith Plaskow (Judaism). Let me at least recognize their efforts as well as feminist theological movements among Sikhs, Muslims, Buddhists, Hindus, or New Age (Juschka 2001a).

Consider at least seven general points of agreement shared by feminist philosophers, biblical critics, Christian theologians, and Christian origins historians:

First, they agree that the entire history of Christianity needs to be looked at anew and reconceived for the many roles women played, and were prevented from playing. Are there, for example, signs that women did function as priests in early Christianity? If so, when were they later prevented from so doing?

Second, all assume that a feminist reading of the history of Christianity, and of human civilization at large, will reveal the outlines of a "battle of the sexes" in a sense.

Third, all agree that men have won this struggle between the sexes, and established patriarchy. What forces within the church caused such changes? And why?

Fourth, in consequence of the victory of patriarchy, men and women are set off against each other. Sex and gender, Lake Woebegone "dualism," are inscribed into the conception of the nature of the relation of the sexes and genders. They all query whether this opposition necessary, and if not, how it can be undermined.

Fifth, patriarchy may have achieved hegemony for the moment, but that ascendancy is contingent upon history. The subordination of women to men, therefore, might have been otherwise, had the epic "battle" turned out differently. And it could be otherwise in the future, should social conditions change sufficiently.

Sixth, all find that the ascendance of patriarchy has shaped a vast array of beliefs, attitudes, and institutions. Many commonplaces of everyday life are rooted in patriarchy – everything from the forms of our language ("man" as the default for "people"), to artistic ideals of beauty (the male figure as perfection), competitive economic systems (capitalism over socialism), or political systems (hierarchies over egalitarianism).

Seventh, feminists believe that the Father-God's theological supremacy marks the ascendancy of patriarchy's cultural hegemony. Feminists must do what they can either to reform their view of divinity that partakes equally of *both* sexual and gender properties, or that *transcends* sex and gender totally. Either would deprive patriarchy of one of its strongest ideological props.

The feminist Christian theologians treated here are not, in one sense, committed to religious studies scholarship as an academic discipline. They are not committed to the formation of a common mind about religion in the way the modern study of religion is. They seek their own particular Christian *communities* to form a common mind around the new theological principles and programs they develop in their theological work. That is what theology is and does: it is the intellectual side of a religious community; it is the voice of the church. But religious studies seeks to speak in a different voice. It is a voice *neutral* to the truth and commitment claims of any religion, or of religion in general. Our feminist Christian theologians do not have to be – indeed perhaps cannot be – neutral to the truth of Christianity. They work within the context of Christian institutions and communities they believe serve a certain set of religious truths. While religious studies students should remember that the feminist Christian theologians are not intended here to be models of scholarship in the study of religion, they should realize that these theologians have left their mark on scholars in the study of religion. Indeed, there is every reason they should be read and studied in religious studies. They are makers of religion itself. It is for that reason that we should study them, and for the way they have influenced how feminists have theorized religion.

The vogue for post-modernism also becomes relevant at this point. Many religious studies scholars embrace the relativism of post-modern principles, and often tack too close to the line between the study of religion and theology. The "gold standard" of such a practical application of post-modern theoretical ideas is Karen Brown's radical methodology. We have seen how she not only voices the post-modern principles of opposition to the subject/object distinction in knowledge, but indeed *lives* them in a most spectacular way. As we have also seen in our discussion of Black prophetic approaches to religion, their positive liberationist values take comfort from Foucault's post-modern emphasis upon the role of power in religion. Here, biblical critic and theologian Elisabeth Schüssler-Fiorenza speaks in a distinctive Foucauldian idiom:

> I seek to utilize rhetorical analysis not as one more method of literary or structural analysis, but rather to analyze how biblical texts and interpretations create or sustain oppressive or liberating theoretical values, sociopolitical practices, and worlds of vision. (Schüssler-Fiorenza 1984, p. 46)

Scholarship here does not, then, dwell on merely esthetic or literary facets of the biblical narrative, but rather on political ones. It seeks to expose the ways biblical texts play to areas of life where power is paramount. In this sense, feminists of Schüssler-Fiorenza's persuasion don't really care about "merely" academic pursuits such as method and theory in the study of religion. Nor does "literary or structural analysis" interest Schüssler-Fiorenza. Instead, what matters is that host of issues bearing on positive human liberation. Now despite the indifference of these scholars to method and theory in the study of religion, their work has had a great impact in the academic culture of religious studies since the advent of "second wave" feminism beginning in the late 1960s. Perhaps emblematic of this influence is historian of American religion Ann Taves. She recalls how the writings of radical feminist philosopher Mary Daly changed her life. "I did various things for a while – worked for the Lutheran Student Movement, enrolled in a seminary-based MA program and considered becoming a minister," Taves tells us. But "then I read Mary Daly, got really angry, and that plan collapsed." So powerful was Daly's impact that after having been "Fired up by questions that a seminary didn't seem suited to answer," Taves found her "way into another life" – this time, into a "theory of religion" course(!) (Taves 2010).

Taves' choice words bring out both the existential power of the impact of these cross-disciplinary Christian feminists but also the irony of that impact. I understand why a woman in the study of religion talking to other women about the hidden prejudices against women in religion would arouse one's ire. But why should getting "really angry" because of the writings of a philosopher and theologian incite Taves to abandon theology? Why not fight it from within? The answer, as we will see, is to be found in the dawning awareness of the profundity, and perceived incorrigibility by many feminists, of the sexism pervading Christianity and its institutions. While some feminist Christians stayed and fought, others fled. They felt that Christianity's structures were deeply anti-feminine, and could not be reformed. These structures must be demolished, Christianity along with them. These are the women we will see questing for the goddess.

Other women scholars from outside the fields of biblical criticism or theology have told similar stories. While many may not have been directly influenced by radical feminist theologians like Mary Daly or reformers like Elisabeth Schüssler-Fiorenza, they were certainly aware of their work. The example of these disruptive women made a difference. In terms of broad appeal, many will recall Daly's appearances at the annual meetings of the American Academy of Religion, always to a packed house, hailing from every sector of the study of religion. While both men and women were drawn to hear Daly, the women were markedly moved. Daly, and others, were talking to *them*. Daly's 1992 plenary address in San Francisco, "Metapatriarchal Adventures and Ecstatic Travels," was such an electric event. Standing room only gave way to overflow audiences in the corridors, to gatherings in separate rooms to watch the live video feed of Daly's plenary. Of course, many of Daly's Christian peers cite her work frequently (Ruether 1993). And, outside the Christian tradition, Jewish feminist Judith Plaskow pays Daly tribute, even while parting ways on certain issues (Plaskow 1992, p. 200). Voices like Daly's have, thus, been heard according to the needs of the women hearing them.

It is some kind of tribute to what these feminist theologians have to say that they have won hearings on both sides of the line dividing theological and academic constituencies, and across the boundaries often dividing religious communities. It is worth bearing in mind, nonetheless, that as "theologians," they are articulating a "common mind" for a particular religious community, and not one across communities as religious studies seeks to do. In this sense, these women *are* religion – religion in its intellectual aspect. And while religious studies is not about doing any church's or religion's "business," but about understanding and explaining religion, churches included, it would be artificial to ignore the influence of cultural movements, epitomized by the Dalys, Ruethers, and Schüssler-Fiorenzas. I shall try to bring out the broader cultural points that transcend any religious confession and its parochial concerns. As we will see, there is a good deal that a Schüssler-Fiorenza or a Daly argue that can easily be translated into the vocabularies of other religious traditions, or none at all.

Schüssler-Fiorenza's Critique of New Testament "Kyriarchy"

Elisabeth Schüssler-Fiorenza's *In Memory of Her* (1983) is another feminist work that goes well beyond merely retrieving data about women. Here, Schüssler-Fiorenza conceives the roles of women in early Christianity anew, specifically by exposing a New Testament ideology of male supremacy. Were her radical view of Christian origins to gain acceptance, it would turn Christianity upside-down.

In what can only be called an ingenious piece of interpretation, Schüssler-Fiorenza accuses the New Testament narrative of deliberately devaluing women in order to legitimize a patriarchal system of hierarchic domination. In effect, recalling a standard theme articulated by Michel Foucault, Schüssler-Fiorenza exposes the way institutions are structured to enable both the empowerment of some and the disempowerment of others. At the heart of Schüssler-Fiorenza's vision is the reality of a "politics," however distant from modern party or parliamentary politics. She is magnetized by her perception of the reality of the power of men over women in all its subtle forms.

But by the same token, Schüssler-Fiorenza is no fatalist. Things might have been otherwise, and they might yet be. The situation of women in the New Testament reflects the realities of power and politics in the early church. It is the result of "social construction," and not a hard fact of brute nature. The situation of women in the New Testament can then be deconstructed to reveal its oppressive forces. It would be news to many Christian women that they do not have to be – by nature (biology) – the way the New Testament says that they are! But casting women into a subordinate position, the Bible imposes a view of what women supposedly "really" are. It specifically "constructs" women according to a set of patriarchal beliefs about them – in sum, that women are the inferiors of men. Schüssler-Fiorenza believe that these rhetorical and conceptual moves reflect an actual power struggle in the early church. They record ideological disputes that really happened between men and women there. For Schüssler-Fiorenza the New Testament is not, then, a pure, ahistorical rolling out of the word of God, free of views about the power relation between the sexes. Power considerations thoroughly inform the New Testament. In fact, it teaches an "explicitly partisan" and dogmatic sex/gender ideology of male hegemonic power over women – whether or not men were the superiors of women in actual fact in early Christianity.

In the New Testament, we again meet the assumption of a one-for-one and essential correspondence between certain male *sexual* traits and certain conventional masculine *gender* characteristics. Assuming as much permits New Testament patriarchal powers to "think they are right" in depicting women as locked into similarly essential sex/gender relationships. These ideologues of New Testament patriarchy sought to engineer the perpetual subordination of women by defining the essential *gender* properties every "real" Christian woman should possess (Schüssler-Fiorenza 1983, p. xiv). From their patriarchal point of view, women should display the submissive, subordinate, and silent *gender* roles felt to be appropriate to members of the female *sex*. To do otherwise, would be to behave unnaturally and thus in violation of the order of divine creation. Christian women must not, therefore, manifest conventionally masculine gender qualities, such as leadership. Nor, should they aspire to priestly/sacrificial roles, since these religious occupations are gendered "masculine" by the patriarchal ideologues, and thus reserved exclusively for the male *sex*.

Yet the actual assignment of roles in the early church was not in practice as patriarchal as the ideology would have it. Women did perform roles considered masculine in gender at the time. What outraged feminists who first discovered this discrepancy was how attempts had been made to suppress the record of women playing masculine leadership roles, for example, in the early church. The patriarchal ideologues had distorted the church's history. The revered authors (or redactors) of the New Testament deliberately lied about the historical record of women in the early church. They, for example, either played down or purged references to women in leadership positions, as Scott Bartchy argues in the case of Prisca (Bartchy 1999). In the absence of their ability to deny women their manifest sexual identities, patriarchal power strategies took the form of denying women recognition for playing what they saw as exclusively and essentially male-gendered roles, such as leadership. The classic expression of this misogynistic ideology is, of course, Paul's assertion that women should "obey their husbands" and thus be submissive to them (Ephesians 5:22; Colossians 3:18).

Intriguing and intuitively plausible as Schüssler-Fiorenza's thesis may be, we have some methodological lessons to learn about her feminist approach by posing some questions of the method ourselves. Why, for example, does she "think she is right" in advancing it? Why should we be suspicious of what the New Testament says about women as a kind of patriarchal ideological projection upon them, rather than an honest reflection of sex and gender conventions or culturally given roles in the Jesus movement? Why should we believe Schüssler-Fiorenza when she says that the Bible actively plays down the roles women had in the early church – *actively*? Maybe women were in fact willingly subordinate in the early church, and the Bible just witnesses to that fact? Why is Schüssler-Fiorenza's feminist critique of the biblical narrative any more than an ingenious effort to show how an alternative view of the Christian past *might have been* plausible? She readily admits that she cannot produce decisive historical evidence to support her new feminist "take," and even less her radical revision of the Christian past. Where, then, does this leave her thesis? What gives her the warrant to "think she is right"?

Of course, just in terms of good propaganda for feminist activism in the church, Schüssler-Fiorenza does not really need decisive evidence at the present time. It is enough that she has planted the "worm of doubt" into the minds of Christians. And enough historical evidence exists to make the case plausible. A look at the method Schüssler-Fiorenza uses might also offer feminists in the study of religion a model they might use in their own work.

Schüssler-Fiorenza believes we can get beyond propaganda and avail ourselves of a powerful interpretive technique. All this method requires is that we shift our perspective, or turn the argument around. Why, for example, should we assume women did little in the early church, or that they accepted subordination to men, and an ideology of sex and gender dualism? Once we question the assumption of essential inequality, the many statements of Jesus and Paul celebrating Christian sexual equality and human unity would begin to weigh in more heavily. Romans 16:1–3 mentions women like Phoebe, the deaconess in the church of Cenchreae, as well as "fellow-workers" of Paul, Aquilla, and Prisca (DeLashmutt 2010). We would also give new prominence to the ideal of an *ekklesia* that was democratic, not hierarchic or monarchic, as patriarchal "kyrocentric" ideology would have it (Schüssler-Fiorenza 1983, p. xxxi). Shifting perspective would cause us to reconsider the significance of why and how Jesus kept company with so many women, even prostitutes. What as well should we conclude about the role of women from the fact that one of them, Mary Magdalene, was the first to see the risen Christ? And why does Jesus warn us not to call any man "father," but does not warn against calling any woman "mother"?

This evidence, circumstantial, fragmentary and sparse though it may be, suffices to cast doubt upon an uncritical reading of the New Testament. There is evidence that the "good book," then, is

well "cooked." And that is good enough to encourage the feminist line of critical inquiry. To Schüssler-Fiorenza, the curiosities she has assembled suffice to shift the burden of proof to those who would declare patriarchy – Schüssler-Fiorenza's "hierarchy" – the fundamental spirit and law of early Christianity. She turns the tables on her critics. She thus believes her suspicions about the imposition of kyriarchy are at the very least plausible, given the harsh misogynist views of New Testament documents. Consider Pauline reproaches to women to remain silent in church assemblies, that they should submit to their husbands, and so on. We may reasonably presume, in other words, that the New Testament is a loaded document – loaded in favor of patriarchy or, as Schüssler-Fiorenza puts it, "kyriarchy." And raising such doubts, Schüssler-Fiorenza invites further historical investigation – indeed, precisely the sort of feminist history of early Christianity that flourishes, thanks to her work.

Earlier I mentioned the activist liberationist aspirations of some of the feminist scholars in this chapter. Schüssler-Fiorenza embraces this role enthusiastically in her seeking to undo the ideological constructions of what she calls "the kyrocentric text" (Schüssler-Fiorenza 1983, p. xxv). This is primarily a job done for the sake of forming the church's "common mind" in a new way. Imagine how this might work if we recall our earlier discussions of religion conceived in terms of the acknowledgment of a male "lord," built according to the rules established in the feudal order of society imposed on western Europe since the early Middle Ages. It takes little imagination to see how Schüssler-Fiorenza's attack on "kyriarchy" would challenge the Christian nature of the entire notion of hierarchy and subordination. How in the democratic, egalitarian, non-sexist spirit revealed by her research into early Christianity can present-day Christians countenance "kyriarchy" – which among other things enjoins the subordination of women to men? Schüssler-Fiorenza's speculative retrieval and revision of the nature of early Christian history thus holds great reconstructive potential for making a "new" Christianity. In ferreting out evidence for the participation of women in early Christianity, she brings out their "overlooked" leadership roles in early church history. And on the basis of such ingenious research one can imagine building a future renovated Christianity that recaptured the spirit of the Jesus movement's sex and gender egalitarianism.

Marija, the Great Mother Goddess, and the Two Christs

From what we have seen thus far, we could conclude that feminist religious studies has often taken its impetus from restrictions Christianity has imposed upon women. Feminist religious studies scholars have gone off in many directions in reaction to the felt hurts resulting from these limitations upon their religious liberty. Among the main exceptions is historian of religion Caroline Walker Bynum. She does not seem motivated at all by any particular personal and existential attitude toward Christianity. Indeed, I know nothing of the religious affiliations (or none) of Bynum. Neither would I liken her work to that of Schüssler-Fiorenza. Bynum is not about to launch some act of revolutionary praxis aimed at overthrowing dominant Christian modes of regarding the relation of the sexes to one another within the church. Indeed, as I have noted, Bynum couldn't care less about the contemporary relevance of her work. More radical than all her contemporaries in positioning herself in relation to Christianity is, however, Karen McCarthy Brown. Led by a woman "priestess" to embrace non-Christian deities, Brown's work establishes her feminist *bone fides* while counter-positioning herself toward Christianity. Even though she is a professor teaching at a Methodist divinity school, Brown seems, then, to have long since given up working "within the fold" even as a radical thinker, in the way that Schüssler-Fiorenza does. Her conversion to pre- or post-Christian Haitian Vodou says it all. What is lacking in *Mama Lola* is any explicit reflection by Brown about her own alienation from Christianity, even though the book and the experiences it records may speak for themselves. In the concluding pages of this chapter, I want to report on feminist theorists of religion who explicitly record their disillusionment with Christianity as a factor in their thinking and living. They both study the "goddess" and, like Brown, convert to her worship. This is to discuss the movement from "theology" to "thealogy" – the shift to religious theorizing,

thought, and practice free of the taint of what is known as "patriarchy."

Carol P. Christ represents an original, pioneering, and influential figure here. She not only seeks to read – and thus to study – religious literature for the presence of female deities or even to re-imagine existing religious traditions along strictly feminist lines. She, like Karen McCarthy Brown, whom she cites with admiration, has actually actively participated in and created (or re-instituted) – elements of a goddess religion in our own time (Christ 1987, p. 62). Christ reveals that she has taken a radical route in part out of admiration for Elisabeth Schüssler-Fiorenza. Nevertheless, she declined to take the path of Schüssler-Fiorenza, whose reformism remained allied with Christianity (Christ 1987, p. 66). Christ explains that, despite their religious differences, Schüssler-Fiorenza offered her a "model of historical reconstruction of the experience of early Christian women" and provided "an interpretative model and methodological justification for the kind of historical work feminists like myself are doing on the prehistoric goddesses" (Christ 1987, p. 63). But these were not enough for Christ to follow even Schüssler-Fiorenza's radical neo-Christian footsteps. Schüssler-Fiorenza's interpretive model urged readers to be suspicious of texts as potentially "androcentric," and therefore as not being "trustworthy evidence of human history, culture, and religion" (Christ 1987, p. 64). Carol Christ took Schüssler-Fiorenza's advice to heart, but far more radically than her teacher may have wished.

For Carol Christ, reforming Christianity seemed futile, given entrenched opposition to feminist reforms. Revolutionizing Christianity seemed downright impossible. Christianity was essentially patriarchal in her mind, and thus sexism would always remain part of its immutable essence. In a painful personal disclosure, Christ recalls a growing feeling of alienation from Christianity because of its essential elevation of the male principle over the female:

> My initiation into the symbols and rituals of the Goddesses began a number of years ago when my own experiences of the silencing of the voice of my experience and perception within patriarchal religious and academic structures led me to desire female God-language which would validate me.

The push of Christian sexism and the pull of goddess images eventually led Carol Christ to act.

> In the early 1970s this longing became so powerful that I could no longer participate in the Christian worship of Father and Son that had sustained me through much of my life. Whenever I set foot in church, I would find myself developing headaches, neck and shoulder aches, and stomachaches, as the enormity of the power of my exclusion from Christian worship sunk deeply into my bones. (Christ 1987, p. 58)

Christ's answer was to ditch Christianity and to replace it wholesale with devotion to "the Goddess" – someone who figured so prominently, as we have seen, in the writings of J.G. Frazer and Michael Carroll. For her, Christianity is incorrigibly sexist, and thus not reformable: "women's experiences have not founded the sacred stories of the biblical tradition," says Christ (1979a, p. 230). If, despite Schüssler-Fiorenza's revolutionary interpretive efforts, the experiences of women are not reflected in the founding documents of Christianity, how can women ever get proper spiritual nurture from Christianity? Further, given the nature of its commanding imagery of God the Father (and the Son), the Christian tradition should, then, be abandoned entirely in favor of the something else which better suited the spiritual needs of women. To be fair, Carol Christ realized that it is not only Christianity that suffers the disability of failing to reflect women's experiences. All the theisms for which we have historical documents reflect dominant male conceptions, imagery, or symbolism. Religions centered on the worship of a male God create "moods" and "motivations" that keep women in a state of psychological dependence on men and male authority, while at the same legitimating the political and social authority of fathers and sons in the institutions of society (Christ 1979b, p. 275). For Christ, religion needs to shed its patriarchal structure altogether if it is to speak to women. Women simply need their own kind of religion.

First, why does Christ "think she is right" to make her new feminist reading of Western history? After all, a critic might charge that, perhaps, it is just in the divine or "natural order of things" – in our biological makeup – that men rule in religion, as they do in other domains of life. But thanks to another senior scholar, Carol Christ came to think otherwise. This inspiration came from Lithuanian archeologist and Indo-Europeanist Marija Gimbutas, famous for her theories postulating the existence of a matriarchal culture of what has been called "old Europe." Gimbutas firmly rejected biological deterministic interpretations of sex and gender domination, based upon her controversial studies of these ancient traditions of "old Europe" (Banks 1975; Diamant 1976). In Gimbutas' view, sex and gender relations are neither God-given in our humanity nor hard-wired into our brains or genes. Which sex dominates or which gender properties are most valued is contingent upon social and historical conditions, not upon immutable nature or the eternal will of God. Gimbutas envisioned a distant, pre-patriarchal period of European civilization, "a culture matrifocal, and probably matrilineal, agricultural and sedentary, egalitarian and peaceful" (Gimbutas 1982, p. 9). Patriarchy came later, notes Gimbutas, with the invasion of Europe of such peoples as the Aryans. These would be the same "Aryans" to whom we have learned that Max Müller devoted decades of scholarly labor.

These later migrants differed fundamentally from the woman-dominated societies already in place in old Europe. Unlike the settled, matrilineal, and matrilocal peoples of old Europe, Gimbutas asserted, this newly arrived Aryans brought a religion and language that were "stratified, pastoral, mobile," and, perhaps most important of all, "war-oriented." As we know from Max Müller's discussions of Aryan gods like Indra and such, the Vedas exalted military, male power as supreme. God was moreover imagined as resident high in the heavens as Father (Dyaus-Pitr), pointedly not as Mother, or Mother Earth, for example. To this sort of linguistic evidence for the dominance of patriarchal values, then, available to Max Müller in the mid-nineteenth century, Gimbutas added the latest twentieth-century archeological discoveries. Troves of images of what seemed like a Great Goddess, Great Mother (Magna Mater), such as those discussed by Carroll in ancient Roman cults of Cybele, were discovered. They had no place, and found no mention, in Indo-European texts, such as the Vedas, Zend-Avesta, and others. Taken together, both linguistic and archeological evidence thus gave Gimbutas reasons the "think she was right" about her theory of old Europe and its demise. She therefore "thought she was right" to assert that patriarchy came to Europe with a historical invasion from the east, overwhelming the resident matriarchal culture. Patriarchy was thus not in the nature of things. It was violently "superimposed on all Europe, except the southern and western fringes ... between 4500 and 2500 BC" (Gimbutas 1982, p. 9).

Carol Christ and others then drew a practical conclusion of religious reform and revolution from Gimbutas' work. Because patriarchy came about by way of contingent historical causes, it does not have to be in charge forever! Patriarchy is instead a contingent historical state of affairs – and, thus, one that might not have been, and might not need to be in the future. But how to spur the prospects of goddess-religion? Christ reasoned that if we could recover traces of the old goddess religion of old Europe, women of today could reconnect with a spirituality in tune with their inner beings as women.

Thus, Carol Christ absorbed the lessons of Gimbutas' results eagerly. In this, she was in the company of other radical feminists, such as theologians like Rosemary Radford Ruether. Both drew the same conclusions that the present-day masculine gendering of God is the product of a historical accident. Since patriarchy was not always dominant, it need not be forever. It came about through specific historical causes. And it could change just as easily because of new historical movements. In religion especially, the advent of "patriarchy" and its hegemony are not something essential to conceiving the deity (Ruether 1993). Women might reinstate the goddess, as Ruether has proposed!

Carol Christ did her own exploring for concrete evidence for the goddess in southern Europe, specifically Greece. There, Gimbutas had argued, the patriarchal invasions never quite reached their greatest penetration into the culture. Christ, then, concentrated first on retrieving further evidence of the pre-patriarchal conceptions of the godhead to bolster the work

of scholars like Marija Gimbutas. Following the lead of the great Lithuanian archeologist, Christ became convinced that before the advent of patriarchy, goddesses ruled instead of gods. As Gimbutas notes, during "and after this [patriarchal] period the female deities, or accurately the Goddess Creatrix in her many aspects, was largely replaced by the predominantly male divinities of the Indo-Europeans" (Gimbutas 1982). When women held primary roles in religion, images of goddesses flourished. Gimbutas notes that for the Neolithic period (roughly 10000 BCE), we have over 100,000 artifacts of all kinds – masks, figurines, tools, jewelry, items of clothing, not to mention images on the walls of caves. These images "spoke" to Gimbutas of an old female religion of the Neolithic, focused on the "wheel of life and its cyclical turning ... [on] birth, nurturing, growth, death and regeneration, as well as crop cultivation and the raising of animals" (Gimbutas 2001, p. 3). The images of the Neolithic period – especially the figurines depicting women in stylized form – point unambiguously to a symbolism of the goddess (Gimbutas 2001, p. 4). To Christ, these images also "spoke" clearly of a religious sensibility declaring the reality of "female power" (Christ 2001, p. 572).

Inevitably perhaps, as with Karen Brown, Christ's intellectual engagement in the goddess took her beyond any sort of retrieval effort to seek active spiritual union. In Christ's view the approach to union could involve many steps – steps that she actually laid out for those seeking to walk in the way of the goddess. One begins by doing intellectual work as a "thealogian." This serves as an excellent preparation. Next, one affirms that the female body brings the goddess into one's life; finally, a celebration of what Christ calls "will," affirms the goddess in her fullness (Christ 1979b, pp. 279–280).

There remains only one more step for those who seek union with the goddess, and that is the kind of merging of beings described by Karen Brown in her marriage ceremony with Ogou. For those who are ready for total commitment, Christ lays out an ultimate and radical way to affirm the goddess. This is direct worship and direct, existential identification with the goddess – much like what Rudolf Otto described as an encounter with the numinous sacred – the experience of the *mysterium tremendum et fascinans*. For Christ, just such a moment of embrace of the goddess occurred unexpectedly. It happened on an academic trip to Greece that she undertook only reluctantly. Christ's diffidence toward the Greek goddesses stemmed from the feeling that far too much had been said about them, and not enough about those of her own American and northern European ethnic traditions. Yet Christ was taken by surprise – literally, as it happened. As she relates it, she did not choose the Greek goddess, "the Greek Goddesses have chosen me." Christ gives an account of this spiritual journey as one that first started with an academic interest, then slowly moved through a phase of empathetic understanding, but then veered away from any sort of modernist ideal of "objective" scholarship to total ecstatic union of subject and object. Instead of sitting at her word processor pounding out text, or poring over books in a library, we find Christ recounting incidents of her dancing in circles with other women hand in hand among the ruins of Eleusis, and feeling "an enormous surging of energy" reminiscent of Rudolf Otto's description of primary religious experience (Christ 1987, p. 59). Like Karen Brown, Carol Christ too, cuts her ties with modernity and enters another space. Parenthetically, we might ask ourselves here why it should not be called an existential state made conceivable by the way post-modernism relaxes restraints around what we call "knowledge"? If we dispose of the object/subject opposition in epistemology, why not abandon it when it comes to existential experience?

On one such occasion of experiencing the "enormous surging energy" of the goddess, Christ and a companion had visited the isle of Lesbos. There, they sought to step deeper into what they imagined devotion to the goddess would entail. "I would go to Aphrodite's temple in white symbolizing my desire to be initiated into her mysteries," the determined Christ tells us. Thus, bedecked in flowing white dresses and golden shawls, Carol Christ and her companion decide to celebrate their sexuality in the temple of Aphrodite with their own ritual of joyous embrace of womanhood. Setting the scene, Christ observes that the

"temple is at the far end of a farm road. No sign marks it. It is deserted." Worse than that, it is derelict and abandoned, and one might also think, vacant of its spiritual powers, as well. But no. "The temple is small," Christ observes, but traces of its power remain: "though none of its columns still stand, its grey stone floor is clearly exposed, and fragments of columns are strewn about the site." The adventurous Christ and her companion then "scrambled over a barbed-wire fence and found [themselves] ... standing amidst thorns in what must have been the temple's forecourt." Once inside, they could do what they had come to do: worship Aphrodite. "We filled our pitcher with red wine and the bowl with water. Ready to enter the temple, we were excited and apprehensive. As we paused at the threshold, I poured out the water and wine." What followed for Christ was not an experience of a place sapped of its sacredness, but an encounter with Aphrodite coming to life in her own special way. "All of a sudden," Christ interjects, "I heard what I can only describe as the laughter of Aphrodite." Like Brown in her Vodou ecstasies, Christ voyages out of the mundane world:

> The sound was clear and vivid. I heard Aphrodite saying through her golden laughter. "Whoever told you you could know sexual ecstasy without pain?" And then she began to laugh again saying, "What can you do but laugh?" I laughed with her. When I looked at my friend, I knew that she had heard the laughter too.

When Christ and her friend moved about the temple, however, no longer did they see a sad wreck of a ruin, but traces of the goddess instead. "We saw her everywhere," says Christ. They had entered the domain of Aphrodite's presence. They "found womblike spirals and vaginal roses carved in stone." Making an altar on one of the broken columns, their devotions commenced. For Christ, her love of Aphrodite took an original and personal form: "I opened my body to the midday sun. I anointed myself with milk and honey and poured milk and honey into my shells. The sun warmed and transformed my body. Alone with the Goddess in her sacred space, I felt myself opening, becoming whole" (Christ 1987, p. 60). And finally, in this revived sacred place, Christ finds resolution: "I became Aphrodite" (Christ 1987, pp. 60–61).

Thus, for Christ, as for Karen McCarthy Brown, the tasks of retrieval and reconsideration of women's religion pass into personal involvement in creating goddess religion anew along the lines developed out of their scholarship. *Studying* religion as an "object" – even an object with which one deeply empathizes – passes, by mysterious and perhaps deeply personal processes, into *becoming* a religious "subject" oneself. Brown and Christ *make* and *do* religion as well as studying it.

A New Women's History: Prelude to Liberation and Prophecy?

I wish to steer this chapter to a conclusion that reaffirms the difference between the academic study of religion over against the theologizing (thealogizing), activism, and personal commitment we have sampled in these latest examples. This is to say that while retrieval operations define a *study* of religion, what Brown and Christ in particular achieve is not some new and better way of studying religion, but the creation of religion itself. I do not disparage the creative work that results in such constructions of religion, but we should not confuse it with the *study of* religion. Indeed, I think the academic study of religion should study such constructions as a Carol Christ, a Mary Daly, a Rosemary Radford Ruether, or an Elisabeth Schüssler-Fiorenza produce. They might well be considered among other new religious movements. We should study them precisely because they *are* religion – or at the very least efforts to make a new religious consciousness! But making or doing religion is not the job of the university, any more than making or doing politics is.

In the previous chapter, I urged that we recognize the same distinction between a liberationist theology informed by Black political imperatives over against a study of religion that made race and Black religious experiences part of its canon. For many of the same reasons, a similar division separates the feminist thinkers met in this chapter into academic and theological camps, even though a given author may start by pursuing academic aims but end in prophecy. Thus, Elisabeth Schüssler-Fiorenza's ambitions to remake Christianity are clearly about leading a movement of religious reform with specific goals. In this way, her work represents an effort to help women achieve the "positive liberty" of liberationist thinkers, rather than the "negative liberty" of liberals. Her goal is not just to free women *from* impediments to their fulfillment, but to specify in *positive* terms in what that fulfillment consists. Feminist theologian Rosemary Radford Ruether concurs explicitly in this embrace of the prophetic tradition. "Feminist theology," she says, "is not asserting unprecedented ideas; rather it is rediscovering the prophetic context and content of Biblical faith itself when it defines the prophetic-liberating tradition as the norm" (Ruether 1993, p. 31).

In other cases, it is often harder to tease apart the ambitions both to retrieve and rethink over against the liberationist or prophetic role inherent in making religion anew. Sorting out the academic from the liberationist and prophetic also must be done with care for Karen Brown and her book *Mama Lola* – albeit in a different way. Here, retrieval passes into active construction, but rather subtly. Brown's fieldwork, analysis, understanding, and explaining of Haitian Vodou certainly do retrieve and make present the role of women in this tradition. As such, *Mama Lola*, in part, represents *studying* religion. But the central place given to featuring Brown's own commitment and conversion counts as something other than studying Vodou. It is a window into the religion of Vodou itself – at least as the non-Haitian Brown lives it and comprehends it. Here, Brown declares her own religious identification and, in doing so, affirms the worth of Haitian Vodou. As such, this aspect of Brown's book may be treated as a living example of what happens in religion, and in Vodou especially as Brown experiences it. But it is not the same as *studying* Vodou – even if one suggests, as does Brown, that in order to understand and explain Vodou, one must *become* its devotee – as she has done. It is precisely this methodological claim of Brown's that the study of religion in fact seeks to *study*, affirm or query, evaluate, celebrate, or criticize.

References

Banks, E.C. 1975. Review of Gimbutas, *The Goddesses and Gods of Old Europe*. *American Journal of Archaeology* 79(2): 156–157.

Bartchy, S.S. 1999. "Undermining Ancient Patriarchy: Paul's Vision of a Society of Siblings." *Biblical Theology Bulletin* 29: 68–78.

Brown, K.M. 1991. *Mama Lola*. Berkeley: University of California Press.

Brown, K.M. 1992. "Writing about the 'Other.'" *Chronicle for Higher Education*. Washington, DC.

Bynum, C.W. 1986. "Introduction: The Complexity of Symbols." In C.W. Bynum, S. Harrell, and P. Richman (eds.), *Gender and Religion*. Boston: Beacon Press.

Bynum, C.W. 1987. *Holy Feast and Holy Fast: The Religious Significance of Food to Medieval Women*. Berkeley: University of California Press.

Bynum, C.W. 1995. *The Resurrection of the Body in Western Christianity, 200–1336*. New York: Columbia University Press.

Castelli, E.A. 1995. "Heteroglossia, Hermeneutics, and History: A Review Essay of Recent Feminist Studies of Early Christianity." *Journal of Feminist Studies in Religion* 10(2): 73–98.

Christ, C.P. 1979a. "Spiritual Quest and Women's Experience ". In C.P. Christ and J. Plaskow (eds.), *Womanspirit Rising: A Feminist Reader in Religion*. San Francisco: Harper San Francisco.

Christ, C.P. 1979b. "Why Women Need the Goddess." In C.P. Christ and J. Plaskow (eds.), *Womanspirit Rising: A Feminist Reader in Religion*. San Francisco: Harper San Francisco.

Christ, C.P. 1987. "Reflections on the Initiation of an American Woman Scholar into the Symbols and Rituals of the Ancient Goddesses." *Journal of Feminist Studies in Religion* 3(1): 57–66.

Christ, C.P. 2001. "Mircea Eliade and the Feminist Paradigm Shift." In D.M. Juschka (ed.), *Feminism in the Study of Religion*. New York: Continuum.

Daly, M. 1973. *Beyond God the Father: Toward a Philosophy of Women's Liberation*. Boston: Beacon Press.

DeLashmutt, G. 2010. "Romans 16: 1–16: Paul's View of Women." *Xenos Christian Fellowship*. http://www.xenos.org/teachings/?teaching=534. Accessed June 13, 2014.

Delphy, C. 2001. "Rethinking Sex and Gender." In D.M. Juschka (ed.), *Feminism in the Study of Religion*. New York: Continuum.

Diamant, S. 1976. Review of Gimbutas, The Goddesses and Gods of Old Europe. *The Classical World* 70(1): 48–49.

Donadio, R. 2010. "Vatican Revises Abuse Process, but Causes Stir." *New York Times*, July 15.

Doniger, W. 1982. *Women, Androgynes and Other Mythical Beings*. Chicago: University of Chicago Press.

Doniger, W. 1995. *In Memory of Her: A Feminist Theological Reconstruction of Christian Origins*. New York: Crossroad.

Doniger, W. 2006. *The Woman Who Pretended To Be Who She Was*. New York: Oxford University Press.

Doniger, W. 2007. *"The Lady of the Jeweled Necklace" and "The Lady Who Shows Her Love"*. New York: New York University Press.

Gimbutas, M. 1982. *The Goddesses and Gods of Old Europe 6500–3500 B.C.: Myths, Legends, and Cult Images*. Berkeley: University of California Press.

Gimbutas, M. 2001. *The Living Goddesses*. Berkeley: University of California Press.

Juschka, D.M. (ed.). 2001a. *Feminism in the Study of Religion*. New York: Continuum,

Juschka, D.M. 2001b. "Introduction to Part One." In D.M. Juschka (ed.), *Feminism in the Study of Religion*. New York: Continuum.

Juschka, D.M. 2001c. "Introduction to Part Three." In D.M. Juschka (ed.), *Feminism in the Study of Religion*. New York: Continuum.

Keller, E.F. 1989. "Just What Is So Difficult about the Concept of Gender as a Social Category? (Response to Richards and Schuster)." *Social Studies of Science* 19: 721–724.

Kristensen, W.B. 1960. *The Meaning of Religion: Lectures in the Phenomenology of Religion*, trans. J.B. Carman. The Hague: Martinus Nijhoff.

Maynard, M. 2001. "Beyond the 'Big Three': The Development of Feminist Theory into the 1990s." In D.M. Juschka (ed.), *Feminism in the Study of Religion*. New York: Continuum.

McLaughlin, E.L. 1979. "The Christian Past: Does It Hold a Future for Women?" In C.P. Christ and J. Plaskow (eds.), *Womanspirit Rising: A Feminist Reader in Religion*. San Francisco: HarperCollins.

Mead, M. 1935. *Sex and Temperament in Three Primitive Societies*. New York: William Morrow.

Plaskow, J. 1992. "The Coming of Lilith: Toward a Feminist Theology." In C.P. Christ and J. Plaskow (eds.), *Womanspirit Rising: A Feminist Reader in Religion*. San Francisco: Harper San Francisco.

Ruether, R.R. 1993. *Sexism and God-Talk: Toward a Feminist Theology*. Boston: Beacon Press.

Schüssler-Fiorenza, E.S. 1983. *In Memory of Her: A Feminist Theological Reconstruction of Christian Origins*. New York: Crossroad.

Schüssler-Fiorenza, E.S. 1984. *But She Said: Feminist Practices of Biblical Interpretation*. Boston: Beacon Press.

Simmons, K.M. 2010. "Placing Theory. Thinking and Teaching: 'Women and Religion'." *JAAR* 78(2) (June): 542–563.

Taves, A. 2010. "A Conversation with the President." *Religious Studies News*.

Walters, M. 2005. *Feminism: A Very Short Introduction*. Oxford: Oxford University Press.

Warne, R.R. 2000. "Making the Gender-Critical Turn." In T. Jensen and M. Rothstein (eds.), *Secular Theories on Religion: Current Perspectives*. Copenhagen: Museum Tusculanum Press.

Further Reading

Butler, J. 1999. *Gender Trouble: Feminism and the Subversion of Identity*. New York: Routledge.

Mikaelsson, L. 2008. "Gendering the History of Religions." In P. Antes, A.W. Geertz, and R.R. Warne (eds.), *New Approaches to the Study of Religion,1: Regional, Critical and Historical Approaches*. Berlin: Walter De Gruyter.

Pritchard, E. 2007. "Religions That Matter." Review of Ellen T. Armour and Susan M. St. Ville (eds.), *Bodily Citations: Religion and Judith Butler. H-Net* (April).

Wayne, H. 1985. "Bronislaw Malinowski: The Influence of Various Women on His Life and Works." *American Ethnologist* 12(3) (August): 529–540.

17

Another "Otherness": Post-Colonial Theories of Religion

Said, Asad, Spivak, and Lincoln

In the previous two chapters I selected theorists and theoretical issues that give us keys to understanding recent studies of religion in race and gender. In the chapter on race, I suggested a powerful angle on theoretical approaches to religion and race was whether and how to contest the notion of "Black religion." This embroiled us in the issue of engagement versus detached or neutral scholarship. In the chapter on feminism and gender, I took as my main probe the theoretical claim that all studies of religion are necessarily "sexed" and/or "gendered," and thus that none can be universal. Now, in this chapter on post-colonialism, I focus on how religion figures in the historical residue of the global inequities defining relationships between former colonial rulers and the ruled. How, further, do the persisting effects of these inequities dictate how we think about the religion of formerly colonized folk? This puts contemporaries, such as Edward Said and Talal Asad, at the center of our discussions. But I will also consider a few thinkers who are indebted to, or critical of, Said or Asad, such as Gayatri Spivak, David Chidester, and Bruce Lincoln.

Post-colonial thinking thus has a flavor all its own. But, at the same time, it tastes surprisingly familiar. While race and gender theories took their departure from the fact of their peculiar sources of "otherness," post-colonial thinking raises attention to another kind of "otherness." Colonizers and the colonized lived in domains with differential distributions of collective economic, material, and cultural power. Post-colonial theory suggests these material conditions linger in our thinking about the colonized other. Perhaps Robert J.C. Young is right that post-colonial thinking has generated something less than a full-blown "theory" (Young 2001). Instead, post-colonial thinking is really a "set of critical concepts, and oppositional political identities and objectives" (Young 2001, p. 69). Post-colonial *thinking*, thus, begins from the need to gain the perspective of marginalized peoples, identified as members of human groups who in the past, and also in the present, can be regarded as colonized, or subject to imperial rule. Remote from centers of cultural, economic, and political power, but ruled from the imperial centers, these peoples find expression in post-colonial thinking's efforts to de-center our perspectives on the world. Here, the history of colonialism and empire, rather than of just racial or gender difference, informs the grievances giving rise to post-colonial thinking. Post-colonial thinking asks us to stretch our imaginations beyond empathy and sympathy. Post-colonial thinkers urge us to become aware

Understanding Theories of Religion: An Introduction, Second Edition. Ivan Strenski.
© 2015 Ivan Strenski. Published 2015 by John Wiley & Sons, Ltd.

of how colonial influences persist long after formal colonial status ends. This is why post-colonial thinkers claim that political independence conceals colonialism's dominance through a continuing range of kinds of dependence, the economic being only one. Post-colonial critique extends "the pursuit of liberation after the achievement of political independence" (Young 2001, p. 11).

Hindus Discover America:
A Post-Colonial Thought Experiment

Just to give an idea of how post-colonial perspectives bear on religious studies directly, let us do a thought experiment. A leading journal in the study of religion not long ago published a debate consisting of articles by Western and non-Western scholars on the theme "Who Speaks for Hinduism?" (Smith and Caldwell 2000). This showed special concern for the sensibilities and perspectives of religions studied by Western scholars. What happens when scholars come forth from those religious traditions to challenge perspectives thought to be neutral or universal as incorrigibly corrupted by the privileged positions of Western scholars as members of former imperial or colonial powers? One hotly contested cross-cultural term in the study of religion targeted for its Western bias is "religion'" itself. Post-colonial critique tries to change "those who were formerly the objects of history into history's new subjects" in part by challenging the right of the West to dictate terms of inquiry, like "religion" (Young 2001, p. 10). Why is the word "religion" an adequate word to apply in non-Western societies? After all, it is "our" word, and not necessarily "theirs." It derives from Latin and comes to us with its own Western history. A post-colonial alternative would pose the question: Why couldn't we be students of *dharma* or *sāsana* instead? Why don't we organize our field in terms of notions original to other – non-Western – cultures? After all, we already do so in terms of fields such as algebra and chemistry, where we borrow words taken first from Arab culture (*al jabr* and *al-kim-iya*, respectively). Why wouldn't it make sense, then, to refer to what we call "religious studies" as "dharmatology," for example? We would then see what we call "religion" against the template of the

Hindu notion of *dharma*, instead of reading *dharma* against the template of "religion." Post-colonial theorists would describe this situation as one in which non-Western civilizations, not the West, would be the "subject." Instead of non-Western civilizations being the "object," the West would be the "object." So, conceiving "religion" as *dharma* suggests a lived and experienced way of life, transcendence, sacrality, moral structures, ritual order, social institutions, and so on. But notably *dharma* would not put a "belief in god" at the top of the list defining religious studies as "dharmatology." It would reorient the study of religion's conception of "religion" by taking a post-colonial perspective on it.

The history of empire and world colonization by the West might have turned out differently than it did. Had South Asians set out in ships to find an alternative to the land trade routes to the Mediterranean, perhaps the Hindus – the real "Indians" – might have blown off course and landed in the "Americas," – or whatever our lost Indian navigators chose to call it. And who knows, thinking all the time they had arrived in Italy, our Indian navigators might well have recorded their first uneasy meetings with Native Americans as encounters with "Italians." Aren't Native Americans still called "Indians" for the same mistaken reasons? This fictional Hindu "discovery of America," and, perhaps, their subsequent colonization of it, would have produced a very different world history than the one in high school textbooks. Native ideas of superhuman beings, gods, might have seemed like odd versions of Shiva or Vishnu to them. But they would have been puzzled about whether (Aztec) human sacrifice could be comprehended within their category of (sacrifice) *yajña* or *hotra*, and that within *dharma*.

Later, when Hindu navigators eventually found their way to Italy, they found problems with both actual as well as sacramental forms of sacrifice. Yes, traces of human sacrifice were to be found in ancient Indian scriptures. But our later Hindu mariners saw only cannibalism in Italian Roman Catholic theological conceptions, embedded in the holy "sacrifice" of the Mass. Was this affection for "sacrifice" among, at least, Roman Catholic Europeans why were they so bloodthirsty and intolerant of people following other dharmas than their own? Yes, the *dharma* of some, like the *kšatriyas*, called for the career of murderous violence. But why did killing other humans seem at times a divine obligation laid upon all Europeans? Whatever this strange thing called "religion" was, it could not neatly be mapped onto *dharma*. They were just too different.

The moral to take from this thought experiment is that our naive assumption about the universality of the main categories of the study of religion might be badly in error. Maybe our categories, such as "religion," do not best comprehend the thought worlds of others. Maybe they fail to map onto other ways of looking on the world in a one-for-one correspondence. How do we *really* know other peoples have "religion" when that is *our* word not theirs? The debatable fit of a notion like "religion" to cover a world governed by *dharma* suggests as much. Post-colonial perspectives suggest that assuming that terms like "religion" or "magic" cover the world universally may, finally, just be Western ethnocentrism.

In its nastier form, our tendency to universalize our own concepts lies behind such self-confident arrogance as E.B. Tylor's casual reference to native folk as "savages." Tylor had no doubt that he possessed a set of universal categories for understanding all cultures. To him, it was just obvious that the "primitive" "they" were lower sorts of being – "savages" – while "we" were higher – "civilized." Recall as well how confidently evolutionist thinkers, like James George Frazer, refer to the way that "primitives" were supposed to have "evolved" from a belief in "magic" onto a higher level of development to an embrace of "religion." Frazer not only "knew" certainly what magic and religion were, he "knew" as well that all peoples had them – exactly in the form he himself thought about them.

We should take one additional thing from this little thought experiment: the hurt caused by our thinking. These characterizations of others might not only distort who they are, but they could also be deeply offensive. One implication behind them is the denial of full adult humanity and dignity to the others. Thus, saying that traditional folk practiced "magic" might imply that only "we" have real "religion," while other poor souls outside a certain charmed circle only have "magic" or "superstition," and so on. In doing so, we write about them like the conquerors – colonialists – that we are or once were.

But colonial attitudes were also deployed about religion within our own culture as well. Recall the prejudices against Mexican Roman Catholics in Tylor's *Anahuac*. This prejudice came from Tylor's belief that European and other rural peoples were frozen in time, like some sort of fossil trace of very ancient forms of human life. "History" was being made in the changing world of the urban centers of Western life, in its centers of artistic endeavor, or in its parliaments, factories, universities, seminaries, and such. By contrast, rural populations lived "outside of history," in what Eliade called "timeless time." Peasants and such, then, may be treated as the evolutionary equivalents of the "primitive" peoples now under the sway of Western colonial expansion.

Robert Orsi's work represents a systematic reaction against this kind of evolutionist thinking. Orsi does not deny that the religion of Italian American immigrants is the same as that of the cultural elites. But he defends its integrity and dignity, in the same way Karen McCarthy Brown (an interlocutor of Orsi's) also implicitly raises up Haitian Vodou for admiration. For Orsi and Brown, neither Italian immigrant Roman Catholicism nor Haitian Vodou are "lower" forms of religion. Different, yes; inferior, no. As Orsi tells us, the religion of his Italian immigrants offered "opportunities to form deep ties with saints, ancestors, demons, gods, ghosts and other special beings in whose company humans work on the world and themselves" (Orsi 2005, p. 2). Orsi objects to seeing such a traditional religion of "presence" as "primitive," simply because it is not a religion of abstract philosophy and theology – of beliefs, ethical principles, and doctrines. We "moderns" tend to think that the "modern" religious style emphasizing beliefs, ethics and such is superior to that of such a religion of "presence" described by Orsi. But is it? It is from such perceptions of moral offense against other people *en gros* that post-colonial discourse draws much of its impetus.

Post-Colonial Discourse: "Varied Genealogies"

Robert J. C. Young, a leading interpreter of post-colonial thinking, argues that rather than issuing from the mind of any one single thinker, post-colonial discourse traces its roots along the course of many "varied genealogies" (Young 2001, p. 69). Taking Young's words to heart, let me marshal both the main thinkers and concepts that define post-colonial discourse. Of seminal thinkers, Michel Foucault and Edward Said stand out, although many others are identified (and self-identified) as post-colonial theorists, in particular South Asian writers such as Gayatri Spivak, Homi Bhabha, Ashish Nandy, and even Mahatma Gandhi. In the study of religion, the better-known post-colonial thinkers are Talal Asad, Bruce Lincoln, and David Chidester. Of major concepts, the list includes colonialism, neo-colonialism, empire, imperialism, hegemony, exploitation, resistance, Eurocentrism, hybridity, orientalism, and the subaltern.

In this light, we ought to note that post-colonial thinkers tend, like prophetic Black thinkers and our radical feminists, to be "liberationist." Post-colonial liberationists advocate richly articulated programs of activist positive liberty – "freedom to." Gayatri Spivak and Edward Said, for example, have been quite vocal in advancing the cause of Palestinian liberation (Spivak 2005, pp. 521, 531). Thus, post-colonial thinkers set themselves off from primarily negative programs of liberation such as "liberal" thinkers advocate. The "emancipatory politics" of post-colonial liberationist thinkers strives for more than the content-poor, neutral ideal of negative liberty – freedom from. Post-colonial liberationists know precisely what their emancipatory politics calls for – equal access to resources of all kinds, ceaseless contestation of all forms of domination, and articulation of collective forms of cultural identity (Young 2001, p. 11).

The "liberationists" divide again into two sets: secular or religious. First, secular post-colonial liberationists can be identified with the commanding figure of Karl Marx, and with correspondingly Marxist revolutionary visions of the good society and classic methods of attaining it. They affirm the value of "resistance," and articulate their vision in terms of classic Marxist economic analysis. As to social change, they may embrace violent methods of social change where necessary to "enable successful resistance to, and transformation of, the degradation and material injustice to which disempowered peoples and societies remain subjected" (Young 2001, p. 69).

One salient feature of secular liberationism is antipathy to religion. Secular post-colonial thinking is "distinguished by its unmediated secularism, opposed to and consistently excluding the religions that have taken on the political identity of providing alternative value-systems to those of the west" (Young 2001, p. 338). Given either their dismissal of religion or their attempts to eliminate it from post-colonial thinking, thinkers such as Edward Said and Talal Asad fall into this category. Gayatri Spivak goes so far as to say that "religion is in fact always leaning towards varieties of totalitarianism" (Najmabadi and Spivak 1991, p. 125).

Second, we have post-colonial religious "liberationists." While remaining equally committed to activism, they reject the methods and vision of human nature advocated by their Marxist revolutionary brethren. The leading figure here is Mohandas K. Gandhi (1869–1948). In contrast to the historical materialism of the secularists, Gandhi argued for the "spiritualization of politics." To him, this meant that "the spiritual diffuses all aspects of everyday life, including the political and should form the basis of the way humans live" (Young 2001, p. 337). Thus, while Gandhi was likewise an advocate of a revolutionary positive program for forming a liberated India into a model of a new society, his revolutionary methods abjured violence. For this reason, and because of the hybrid Buddhist–Christian–Hindu rhetoric of the Gandhian movement, Gandhi's vision of post-colonial society can be said to be identifiably religious.

The Secular Post-Colonial Marx

That Marxism is "paramount as the fundamental framework of post-colonial thinking" tells us at least three things. First, a strong moral sense drives post-colonial discourse; second, post-colonial discourse is unapologetically activist – prophetic; third, consideration of the "objective material conditions" of life will figure in any analysis of religion, along with a more recent appreciation of the varied realities of "culture" (Young 2001, p. 6f). Asad, Said, and Spivak, for example, all freely identify with Marx. The basis of Marx's exposure of these "objective material conditions" of social life lay in his massive historical researches. Karl Marx was a polymath German social critic, historian, economist, philosopher, pamphleteer, and social activist. His often dense, but nonetheless passionate and informed, writing has inspired the socialist and communist movements of our own time. Particularly potent was his theory of how the new capitalist order worked to keep the entire class of laboring men and women in virtual bondage.

Many read Marx's great critical studies of modern capitalism narrowly as attempts at an objective scientific theory of political economy. Permit me to suggest that it is Marx's pervasive sense of moral outrage over the industrial order of his day that wins the hearts of his followers, post-colonial theorists among them. Appeals to science just don't make people lay down their lives for others. Marx argued that as an entire social class, employers were effectively stealing the fruits of the labor of ordinary workers from them in a number of ways. Workers were not being justly compensated by their employers. As a class, they were not only underpaid, but they were also estranged from the labor their own economic need required them to perform. Humans were being made into machines, their labor into something that could heartlessly be bought and sold. Capitalism was a rigorous system of the exploitation of those without power to resist such abuses. It was a moral evil. Worse still, the exploiting class would never willingly surrender its position of privilege, or indeed even share it to some acceptable degree. This left the working class with only one alternative to relieve their conditions – revolution. The entire class structure created by capitalism had to be overturned. Once the revolution had succeeded, the benefits of the new economy currently accruing only to the small group that owned and managed industry would be equitably distributed, especially to those who actually had created them.

Significantly for post-colonial theory, Marx did not limit his indictment of the capitalist order to the internal conditions of the industrializing West. He alone in his time indicted *imperialism* "for many of the wrongs, if not crimes, against humanity" that he saw as a "product of economic dominance of the north over the south" (Young 2001, p. 6). Vladimir

Lenin (1870–1924) developed the logic of Marx's analysis of colonialism and imperialism. Inspired by Marx, Lenin went on to make Russia the first socialist state in 1917 by leading the overthrow of the social democratic provisional government of Alexander Kerensky. Lenin's achievement did, however, produce difficulties for Marxist theory – but with no discernible effect on revolutionary practice – since Lenin reversed Marx's priorities. While Marx claimed that historical conditions had to ripen, and that revolutionary change would come as a natural unfolding of the logic of history, Lenin acted otherwise. He believed that a determined, even small, minority of militants, led by a radicalized intelligentsia, could set the spark that would ignite a full-blown revolution. In October 1917, Lenin realized his revision of Marx in practice: the Soviet Union was born, and the course of history was changed thereby.

As well as being a hands-on revolutionary, Lenin thought deeply about imperialism as well. His *Imperialism: The Highest Stage of Capitalism* (1916) argued that world wars were driven by economic motivations, not by their declared political purposes. International world wars, such as World War I, were inevitable because capitalists needed to gain advantage over their competitors for control of foreign markets. This pitted one nation against another. But beneath the political rhetoric was brute economic competition. Securing their international markets in the colonies, for example, would increase the profitability of international capitalist forces, which at the time was lessening in the developed world. Post-colonial theorists have picked up this moral theme in Marx's thought, and have adapted it to the relation between "have" and "have not" nations – between one-time colonial powers and their colonies – in the post-colonial age. In the study of religion we will see how aspects of the Marxist perspective inform the moral critiques of colonial and post-colonial exploitation, as in Bruce Lincoln's analyses of "resistance" or Talal Asad's and David Chidester's respective critiques of the "religion" concept. In the study of religion, I would argue, however, that Foucault's cultural critique tends to eclipse Marxian economic analyses, even when Marx's moral and politico-economic vision continues to play in the background.

Cultural Critiques, Not Marxist Ones

Thus, the novelty of post-colonial thinking in religious studies consists in its claiming descent from both Marx's critique of the "objective material conditions" of capitalism *and* Foucault's "culturalist" approach. But to accommodate both Marx and Foucault, post-colonial religious studies thinkers make some noteworthy adjustments. For example, as we will see, post-colonial thinking, like post-modern theory, departs from classical Marxism by stressing the power of the "subjective effects" of those objective conditions of capitalism. Post-colonial thinking engages in a "cultural politics" in seeking to work for the cultural integrity of colonized societies. It encourages "respect for local knowledge and practices of indigenous men and women" (Young 2001, p. 7). Here is where Asad, Chidester, Lincoln, and others make their mark in post-colonial studies of religion.

Most susceptible to the critiques of post-colonial thinkers are the nineteenth-century evolutionist theorists, such as Frazer, Robertson Smith, or Tylor. They wrote in the heyday of Western imperialism, and show it. Their writings are laced with arrogant and offensive expressions of superiority over peoples subject to the dominion of their own countries. A sense of classic British "effortless superiority," for example, encompassed both the peoples of the colonized "south" – Africa, Asia, Central and South America – but also those of the Latin West. As we have noted, Tylor thought about traditional religions, even Roman Catholicism, as "superstitious", "primitive," or "savage." Since both traditional religion and Roman Catholicism deployed elaborate imagery and pageantry, devoted to the "gods" and ancestors or the saints respectively, Tylor, and others of his ilk, felt that these religions were intellectually deficient. Only science told the truth about the world. Rituals and beliefs in spirits were definitely marks of inferior mental development. Or think as well how William Robertson Smith in effect lumped the religion of the tribes of Saudi Arabia with that of the early Hebrews in condemning them for their lack of "a natural capacity for spiritual religion." Even the prophets of the Bible charged the ancient Hebrews with being "peculiarly inaccessible to spiritual truths," Smith says. In its deficiency, ancient Hebrew religion was no better than the "paganism" of the traditional societies then being overwhelmed by the power of the British Empire. Says Robertson Smith, the ancient religion of the Jews was, therefore, "not one whit less degrading than those of the most savage nations … the lowest level of heathenism" (Smith 1912, pp. 482–483). Seeing the views of these thinkers in the light of post-colonial sensibility gives them an entirely new meaning. They exemplify an entire worldview typical of the imperial age of colonialism – a viewpoint that has left indelible marks not only on the people thus relegated to inferior status, but on the study of religion that fostered such points of view.

Foucault and Culturalist Post-Colonial Thought

Although post-colonial culturalist critics trace varied genealogies, the majority are "greatly indebted to" the work of historian and philosopher Michel Foucault (Said 1978, p. 23). Although many key post-colonial concepts can be traced to Foucault, none matters more than "power." Like the Italian Marxist thinker Antonio Gramsci, Foucault brings out the subtle ways that culture exerts a certain *hegemonic* power to shape the world through knowledge. Foucault insists that the power of culture begins with an appreciation of the reality of "discourse" as agent in the world – a key theoretical notion for Bruce Lincoln, as we will see. Recall how I stressed Foucault's vision of power as ubiquitous, even in places unseen by the naked eye, and felt like the bite of the lash. Our schemes of classification – the basic framework of our knowledge – form "discourses." Our taken-for-granted talk of "types," such as "us" versus "them," White versus Black, male versus female, primitive versus modern, Orient versus Occident, and so on form their own discourses as well (Said 1978, p. 119). These "forms of discourse" reveal an "impulse to classify nature and man" by establishing authoritative ways of thinking, talking, and writing (Said 1978, p. 119). By targeting classification, Foucault singles out discourse purporting to be "scientific," such as criminology, psychiatry, medicine, and so on. Since the regimes of knowledge established by these "sciences" classify and categorize things, they exert tremendous power by shaping the way we act (Foucault 1980, p. 84). Classifying someone as "schizophrenic," for example, rather than just "unhappy," "troubled," or even as "possessed" or "demonic," permits the wheeling in of the entire apparatus of control, confinement, institutionalization, and medication that constitutes our mental health system. Likewise, let us not forget what we learned in previous chapters about how racial and sexual classification similarly governs our behavior toward those so classified. Imperceptibly, but inevitably, then, these abstract classification "discourses" structure the way we act, because they shape what we take our world to be. We live in a world that is often strictly structured by a discourse featuring "Black" folks and "White" folks or "real men" and "real women," for example, rather than, say, one in which we mark categories like intelligence, beauty, strength, courage, compassion, and so on, of people instead of color or gender stereotypes. Not surprisingly, Edward Said explicitly credits Foucault with his idea of "Orientalism as a discourse" (Said 1978, p. 3). Gayatri Spivak, in turn, credits Said with urging her to go further with Foucault. And Asad lavishes praise upon Foucault for, among other notions, his own thinking about ascetic discipline (Asad 1993, pp. 106–109).

In bringing out the way we conceive of things, the way we presume that things are, the way we prefer to construct the world of our acquaintance, Foucault shows how a subtle form of power works. This is power as a "hegemonic" structure. It imperiously rules over the way we see various worlds – such as the Orient of Said's study. Thus, rather than being focused solely on the state, power is much more widely and subtly deployed: it is "a dynamic energy that infuses a social system" (Chidester 1988, p. 8). Whether this is, in the long run, the best way to think about power ought to be debated (Strenski 2010). Nonetheless, this broad notion of power, deployed through the many aspects of culture, has produced a vast output of post-colonial scholarship.

Consider only the new literature about colonialism, race, and other post-colonial themes. Foucault may have avoided discussing colonialism or race, but post-colonial thinkers have taken enthusiastically to him nonetheless. They are drawn to Foucault's "emphasis on forms of authority and exclusion ... his analysis of the operations of the technologies of power, of the apparatuses of surveillance, or of governing mentality." Some of Foucault's literary imagery, such as the expulsion of the insane, dumped as cargo onto a "ship of fools," for example, has inspired post-colonial thinkers to imagine the "forced migration" of subject peoples (Young 2001, p. 395). As far as post-colonial thinking goes, then, if, as Foucault says, knowledge is power, then his analyses lend themselves to exposing the many hidden ways disciplines touting their "scientific" credentials, such as oriental studies or religious studies, also establish regimes of power – discourses of and about power. Similarly, while Foucault avoids discussions of religion, religious studies scholars have not been similarly deterred. One well-known scholar in the study of religion who has exploited Foucault's work is student of religion in southern Africa, David Chidester.

Breast-Beating around the South African Bush: Chidester and Foucault

David Chidester's *Savage Systems* offers an excellent example of how one might adapt Foucault's insight to the study of religion (Chidester 1996). Chidester's target, like that of Foucault, is the putatively "scientific" work done on religion in southern Africa. How has the conceptualization of "religion" been implicated in regimes of power? How has this conception set in place or authorized certain hegemonic" structures that over time produced social consequences in southern Africa? Chidester finds a rich source of examples of the working out of the Foucauldian themes in the history of studies of religion in southern Africa. He believes that Foucault's critique of "particular sciences," such as criminology or psychiatry, can be applied to the "science" of the comparative study of religion.

Among others, Chidester brings his Foucauldian indictment of the "science" of the comparative study of religion to bear on two eighteenth-century German travelers to southern Africa, Peter Kolb and Otto Friedrich Mentzel. Kolb was a tireless fieldworker and interviewer of Hottentot folk, even attempting a method of "self-conscious" comparative study (Chidester 1996, p. 50). As secretary of the *landdrost* of Stellenbosch for about eight years, Kolb also wrote an influential book on life in the southern Cape (Chidester 1996, p. 48). Even though Kolb, the amateur, did not approach the dedication to a "science of religion" that we have seen in a Tiele or a Max Müller, Chidester thinks Kolb's studies of religion work with Foucault's theory. For example, Kolb's book exemplifies Foucault's knowledge/power dynamic. Kolb organized people under certain categories, thus making it easier for administrators to exert power over them. In fact, Chidester charges Kolb with contributing in this way to "the dispossession and displacement of Khoisan people in the Cape." By classifying certain Hottentot institutions as "religion," in particular, it made it all too easy for the native folk to be manipulated by colonial powers (Chidester 1996, pp. 71–72).

By defining the Hottentot according to certain Western notions, like "religion," religion has been defined as a strategic instrument. This leads Chidester to conclude that "the study of religion was entangled in the power relations of frontier conflict, military conquest and resistance, and imperial expansion... . It arises out of a violent history of colonial conquest and domination" (Chidester 1996, p. xii). And we can only expect those struggles to continue, believes Chidester (1996, p. 254). The moral of Chidester's story lies close to the surface: Foucault found malignancies in the unintended barbarities of otherwise avowedly enlightened programs, such as prison or asylum reforms. Perhaps students of religion should be alert to the way that other apparently innocent practices, like definition and classification, conceal deeper malignancies. Thus, Chidester's inquiry into the causes of these and other sorts of human domination originating with Foucault could – and arguably should – give rise to a host of academic enterprises in the humanities, mostly focused on the local exercise of power in human relations. On this view, religions become "the most finely tuned examples of power structures, patterns of force which control human lives and dictate how they are to be conducted. Make no mistake about it: religions are about power, about the power to be given you and about the power which controls you" (Lease 1994, p. 474).

All very well and good – as far as an amateur like Kolb goes. But what about the study of religion closer to more contemporary realities, such

as apartheid? Chidester again shows how Foucault's critiques of "particular science" work in southern Africa. Referring to anthropologist Louis Leakey, Chidester first notes how Leakey categorized the Mau Mau as a "religion" where, up to that point, he had classified them as a "political" group. In Foucauldian terms, Leakey alters our "knowledge" of the Kikuyu in the same way that classifying certain inmates of eighteenth-century asylums as "insane" did. Now, what consequences regarding power flow from this, according to Foucault's theory? Chidester makes his case by noting that Leakey's "pigeon-holing" our "knowledge" about the Kikuyu – once "political" now "religious" – occurred at the same time that the Kenyan colonial government was actually confining thousands of Kikuyus during the Mau Mau rebellion. The Kenyan colonial government thus exerted its power by making adjustments in the realm of knowledge – thanks, moreover, to one "scientist" in particular – Leakey!

Chidester draws a classically Foucauldian conclusion from these facts. The shift in "knowledge" of the Kikuyu corresponds to a shift in their relation to the power of a coercive force. "In the midst of a war zone ... Louis Leakey tried to reinforce a colonial conceptual closure around the Mau Mau movement by designating it as a religion." And, more or less in line with Foucauldian orthodoxy, Chidester sees Leakey's exertion of classificatory agency as equivalent to the imposition of hardcore coercive political power. Thus, Chidester says, "This conceptual containment coincided with the literal containment of tens of thousands of Kikuyu in prisons and 'rehabilitation' camps" (Chidester 1996, p. 256).

Before leaving Chidester, it might be noted how his attack on the frontier comparison of religion falls into the pattern of post-colonial thinkers' tendency to be hostile to religion. Chidester, in effect, argues that classifying the Kikuyu as "religious" is especially pernicious. No other classifications of the Kikuyu were responsible for their oppression. Only religious classification did this. But if we follow Foucault faithfully, would not *any* classification of the Kikuyu presumably "contain" them cognitively as well? And would that containment by classification not just as plausibly lead to their physical containment too? Why is being classified as "religious" more confining than classifying the Kikuyu as a "political" group, for example? Post-colonial theorists seem especially bent on discrediting religion, even to the extent of virtually eliminating or ignoring it. Indeed, Edward W. Said famously falls into this stereotype by ignoring religion in his pioneering work of post-colonial theorizing, *Orientalism*.

Edward Said and "Orientalism"

By general acclaim, former Columbia Professor of Literature Edward W. Said personified post-colonial theory. Along with Foucault, post-colonial theory is, in a way, a subset of Said's theoretical thinking. I do not exaggerate when I say that one book alone, Said's *Orientalism* (1978), could be said to sketch most of the key ideas in post-colonial theorizing. Said claims that the hegemony of Western writing over conceptions of the "oriental" Other distorted formerly colonized peoples in ways that became "conventional wisdom" for generations of thinkers. Said's exposure of the systematic manner in which these alleged distortions have been maintained by political realities in the West remains a continuing feature of post-colonial thought (Asad 1980; Manzalaoui 1980). For this reason, the theoretical proposals of Said's *Orientalism* will receive the lion's share of attention.

Born of Protestant Palestinian Arab parents in Jerusalem, Said tells us that disorienting experiences of exile, emigration, and ethnic and religious difference shaped his mind. He lived in two worlds. "Edward," reflected his Anglican father's affiliations, while "Said" bound him to his family's Arab ancestry. Said's early years in elite English schooling in Jerusalem, Cairo, and the United States afforded him a westward-looking and Protestant identity. He maintained this occidental orientation throughout his education in modern American and European literature at Columbia University. Arabic literature was relatively unknown to him. On the other hand, Said was a "wanderer," doomed to a life of alienation "that can never be rectified" (Said 1998). The pain of the dislocation of exile from Mandate Palestine as a Palestinian Arab in the West marked his second life. Massachusetts prep school life dealt Said the "preppie" schoolboy hurts of "the hostile attentions of Anglo-Saxons

whose language was not mine, and who made no bones about my belonging to an inferior, or somehow disapproved race" (Said 1998, p. 6). This bifurcated identity raised many questions for Said, but perhaps none more acutely than the gaps between what people around him said over against what he knew from personal experience. "Always feeling myself standing in the wrong corner," is how Said put it. Radicalized by the 1967 Arab–Israeli War, Said became a public intellectual. The conspicuous lack of recognition for his Palestinian identity in Western representations of the war took the form of an aching absence. In that conflict, it was as if Palestinians did not exist; only the triumphant Israelis did. In response, Said sought to "articulate a history of loss and dispossession" for Palestinians. He struggled constantly to win recognition for Palestinian national aims.

Edward Said: "Can the Canaanites Now Speak?"

An instructive example of this difficulty battling the "suppression of [Palestinian] history" was Said's exchange with historian Michael Walzer. Walzer's interpretation of the representation of the biblical book of Exodus in political struggles caught Said's attention (Said and Walzer 1986; Walzer and Said 1985–86). The ensuing debate was published in *Grand Street*, a New York City quarterly that featured some of the leading intellectuals of the late twentieth century. In New York City style, the intense exchange often got rough. Neither party played entirely fairly with the other. Few minds were changed, and many central issues were left unresolved. Still, we can benefit a good deal by seeing how Said played the role of a post-colonial theorist as he engaged Walzer.

In his *Exodus and Revolution*, Michael Walzer argued that the ancient biblical story of the Hebrew flight from Egyptian captivity and occupation of the Promised Land served as a powerful foundational myth for modern struggles of political liberation the world over. Inspirational Black spirituals, such as "Go Down, Moses," echoed with the Exodus liberation theme that pharaoh should "Let my people go!" The Boers of the eastern Cape of South Africa, gathered from the slums and impoverished countryside of the

Netherlands, saw their escape from poverty as a kind of Exodus liberation. Their subsequent taking of the land from its African inhabitants, similarly, echoed the Hebrew struggles to wrest the Promised Land from its Canaanite owners. The American Pilgrim Fathers, too, saw their departure from Europe as a freeing exodus, and their foundation of colonies in New England as setting up a "promised" holy land. Towns and cities with names like Canaan, New Canaan, New Haven, Bethel, Bethany, or Hebron tell the tale to this day. Jamaican reggae, likewise, celebrates struggles for Black liberation explicitly in terms of the biblical exodus: "Exodus, Movement of the People."

But for Said, this story of Exodus, as Walzer tells it, deserves a broader, more conflicted reading, one with troubling coded significances. Said's review article of Walzer's book bears the telling title, "Michael Walzer's 'Exodus and Revolution': A Canaanite Reading." There, Said counters Walzer by telling what he feels is the "other side" of the Exodus story. We all know the Hebrew side as Walzer tells it. But what of the Canaanite side? Making obvious implicit reference to the conflict between Jews and Arabs in Israel/Palestine, Said asserts that we know nothing of how the Canaanite felt about Hebrew incursions into their territory. All we have in the Bible is the Hebrew case – only the story of "Exodus insiders" (Said 1986, p. 104). Similarly, in the West, all Said felt one heard of the Jewish–Arab conflict in Israel/Palestine was the Israeli story. Predictably, the argument heats up in part because Said thinks Walzer "indifferent" to the fate of the Canaanites (read, Palestinians). He simply doesn't want to know the other side of the Exodus story, or of the many similar stories of dispossession it generates (Said 1998, p. 89). So Said proposes as well to tell the extermination story of the Hottentots, not the Exodus liberation myth of the Boers, the massacre accounts of Native Americans, not only the story of the Puritan Promised Land of New England, but also the tragedy of "the other less fortunate people, strange, displaced and outside moral concern" – Said's own Palestinian people, not the story of Israel's victories on the battlefield (Said 1998, p. 105). Thus, in the end, what rankles with Said most deeply is not the ancient history of the Hebrew settlement of Palestine, but how the

Exodus myth of Hebrew conquest gives modern Israel justification for policies dealing with his own Palestinian kith and kin. "Exodus does categorically enjoin victorious Jews to deal unforgivingly with their enemies, the prior native inhabitants of the Promised Land" (Said 1998, p. 93).

So, in the end, while liberation movements rouse the emotions, Said feels that Walzer only tells the winner's story. Half of the human story never gets told – only the story of conquest of the Philistines or Canaanites. The Bible says not a word about how the inhabitants of the Promised Land felt about their conquest and subjugation. And the Bible's insensitivity, moreover, has obvious consequences for the Jewish–Arab conflict in the Middle East. Like the biblical Canaanites, today's Palestinians just don't count. Walzer's telling of Exodus as a liberation story justifies claims against Palestine. In its most extreme form, Said's nightmare envisions the conquest of Canaan, and subsequent extermination of the Canaanite nation, as a metaphor for the elimination of a Palestinian nation and people. Readers will note that this theme catches the attention of our friend, the Black theorist of religion Bill Hart, for predictable reasons (Hart 2000, pp. 1–8). In response to the 1967 Arab–Israeli War, Said summarily notes:

> What I experienced, however, was the suppression of a history as everyone around me celebrated Israel's victory, its terrible swift sword, as Barbara Tuchman grandly put it, at the expense of the original inhabitants of Palestine, who now found themselves forced over and over again to prove that they had once existed. "There are no Palestinians," said Golda Meir in 1969, and that set me, and many others, the slightly preposterous challenge of disproving her, of beginning to articulate a history of loss and dispossession that had to be extricated, minute by minute, word by word, inch by inch, from the very real history of Israel's establishment, existence and achievements. (Said 1998)

Readers may now understand why I warned that the Said–Walzer confrontation would be a hot one. Deeply felt and deeply contested issues infuse this exchange with some of the most profound emotions humans can feel. The assertion of identity or the possibility of that identity's erasure can generate intense feelings. Putting aside the emotion-laden nature of this exchange for the moment, let me note, then, that Walzer broadly rejects Said's charges. For instance, Walzer denies that biblical precedents significantly guide modern Jews (Said and Walzer 1986, p. 249). Said's assumption that the Bible serves this function for modern Jews, then, amounts to a kind of projection of the literary imagination. Modern Jews do not necessarily see themselves in light of the religion of ancient Israel. Modern Judaism is the creation of rabbinical exegesis, not lock-step adherence to the literal words of the Hebrew Bible. Consider alone the dismissal of ritual sacrifice in Judaism, so central to Hebrew religion before the destruction of the Second Temple. Nor do the notorious commands of the book of Deuteronomy inform modern Jewish life. Today's Jews and Judaism are part of one thing; the religion and culture of ancient Israel belong to another time and place. Said's assumptions that modern Jews are attempting to recapitulate ancient Hebrew experience may reveal that Said remains under the influence of Christian super-sessionist theology. In the eyes of supersessionist Christian apologetics, Christianity "supersedes" Judaism, much as the New Testament "super-sedes" the Old. For supersessionists, modern Jews thus belong to the past, to the Jewish religion of ancient Israel and the Old Testament. They are not really "modern," then, but "primitive," as some of the evolutionist thinkers, like Robertson Smith, argued.

Without going much further into details about this debate, Walzer answers Said on other points too (Said and Walzer 1986). Walzer, for example, fully favors the existence of a Palestinian state alongside Israel, even though he feels loyal to the idea of a Jewish state. Everyone feels an unde-niable, even visceral, allegiance to a primary group. Such loyalties will always mean relegating other groups to lower levels of concern. Ironically, ethnic loyalties also have Said in their grip. What is missing from Said's thought, however, is engagement in this aching dilemma of conflicting loyalties. Walzer notes that Said says nothing about the Jews who were marginalized in, and thus compelled to leave, majority Muslim states. Said seems full of moral rage about Palestinians similarly pushed out of Israel upon its foundation, but not about Jews similarly treated. Neither situation can be called desirable. But both sets

of circumstances show how precarious are the positions of marginal groups in the present system of nation-states. Both situations also show how tortured a subject this can be for people who seek to be thoughtful about such vexed moral issues. Other critics have scored Said for ignoring the way scholars who represent marginalized peoples can distort their former colonial masters as well (Manzalaoui 1980, p. 839). These criti-cisms notwithstanding, we can understand that Said's anguish over the negation of Palestinian national or ethnic identity lies at the root of his post-colonial theorizing. This combination of general theorizing about "orientalism" and championing of the Palestinian cause establishes Said's *bona fides* as a classic post-colonial theorist. Said's example suggests that similar profound feel-ings may also drive other post-colonial theorists, especially those hailing from former colonies.

Post-Colonial Thinkers Don't Like Religion or "Religion"

The Said–Walzer exchange also reveals two ways in which Said eliminates religion from his theory. In doing so, he conforms to the general pattern of post-colonial theory's dismissal of religion as either a constructive or significant force in society. First, religion is not a *constructive* force in society because it is profoundly immoral. By "religion," it should be noted, Said means to indict the monotheism of the Hebrew Bible, modern Judaism and Christianity, but, oddly, not Islam! Why Said never gets round to condemning Islam as a religion is interesting, to say the least. This point emerges, second, when Said declares that some religions, notably Islam, are not *significant* forces in society. Said "thinks he is right" to think such an odd thing because Islam is not really a religion! It is some sort of "cultural" reality. Let me try to make sense of these frankly tortured views.

First, Said attacks religion as morally unhealthy. Religion (read, "monotheism," excluding Islam) is a form of "monism," and monism leads to fanati-cism. Since, by definition, monism pursues a pure, single vision of the world, it inevitably even-tuates in a single-minded, inflexible approach to life. Monistic worldviews disallow ambiguities and subtleties, such as those concerning sexual relations. Men are men, and women are women, and "never the twain shall meet," so to speak. So, at bottom, our Lake Woebegone sex/gender worldview of the previous chapter, where "all the men are strong, all the women good-looking" is founded in Hebrew Bible monotheism. Anthropologist Mary Douglas argued as much in her classic discussion of the abominations of Leviticus in *Purity and Danger* (Douglas 1970). The fixation upon everything having its place and every place being fixed is why homosexuality creates ambiguities, at least for the inhabitants of that idyllic Minnesota farming community. Homosexuality blurs the categories of "man" and "woman," and thus offends the single-minded monist view. Said sees the monotheisms behind Exodus, the Inquisition, the Crusades, the Wars of Religion, and so on, as examples of how seeing the world through a single uncompromising lens leads to intolerant elimination of its perceived enemies. It is the "mono" of monotheism, then, that causes greatest harm.

While Said uses his objections to monism against "religion," he does not limit his condemnation to "religion." Besides the single-mindedness of the patriarchs and prophets of the Hebrew Bible, Said also includes modern totalitarianisms under the fanatic's umbrella. Modern totalitarian political movements have simply appropriated monotheism's singular, intolerant vision of what is right, and applied it to public affairs. Thus, the "revolutionary fervor" that Walzer traces to Exodus commits all the same sins of the unforgiving, triumphant Hebrews who exterminated their enemies, ordered as they were by the command of the "merciless ferocity of Jahweh" (Said 1986, pp. 91–92). For good measure, I should note that Said is in the excellent company of political theorists like Sir Isaiah Berlin in being apprehensive of monism (Berlin 1979).

But why then, given his distaste for monism, does Said not also condemn Islam (Manzalaoui 1980, p. 839; Said 1978, p. 350n137; Sivan 1985)? One answer is Said's bizarre insistence on the view that Islam is not a religion. (But that doesn't mean it could not be a *monistic* "cultural" formation.) So it is hard to see how Said can free Islam from the same condemnations he has made of Judaism and Christianity. Said's view is so tortured that one is tempted to retort that Islam may be the *paradigm* of monism, and thus that Said is guilty of bad faith. Islam lacks the central

doctrines diluting Christian monotheism, such as the doctrine of the Trinity. Indeed, Jews and Muslims have traditionally charged Christianity with compromising with polytheism. Not only do doctrines such as those of the Trinity and the Incarnation, and the cult of the saints, muddle Christianity's monotheistic purity, Islamic monotheism took its rise historically in protest at Christianity's alleged failure to live up to the monistic standard re-established by Muhammad's reforms. So what could possibly be Said's rationale for his eccentric view of Islam? Why does he "think he is right"?

I suggest that perhaps Said's view has to do with polemics. The generation of Western scholars whom Said indicts as "orientalists" tended to see the Middle East only in terms of Islam. Said singles out Sir Hamilton Gibb, the flower of British orientalism, in this regard. Gibb declares that Islam, as a religion, has "an ultimate precedence and domination over all life in the Islamic Orient" (Said 1978, p. 279). Islam explains everything, in the minds of these orientalists. So Said reacts by saying that, as a religion, it explains *nothing*. Similarly, Said notes how another orientalist simply labeled the Palestinian resistance as "the return of Islam." Islam explains everything! So Said again flips the polemic framework and denies that Islam explains *anything* (Said 1978, p. 107).

However, if we delve somewhat more deeply into Said's systematic denigration of religion, we can learn something vital about Foucault's influence upon post-colonialism's theoretical thrust. While Said plays down religion, he believes that the orientalists had *political* reasons for defining the Middle East solely in terms of the pervasive agency and religious nature of Islam. Foucault declared the theoretical principle that everything is political. So Said is simply applying Foucauldian principles to the orientalist engagement with Islam. Behind religion lurks the reality of power and politics. The orientalists needed an excuse to construct the Arab world as an inferior "other," so they could aid in its imperial manipulation and exploitation. They needed to hold up a mirror image of the enlightened and scientific Western world to the backward and religious Islamic world in order to justify colonial occupation. "We" are democratic, scientific, and rational; "you," the Arabs, are autocratic, emotional, and benighted because of your religion – Islam (Said

1978, p. 122). But our colonial effort will fix all that. In reaction to what Said sees as orientalist prejudices, he then deliberately purged religion, Islam in this case, from being a major factor in his thinking about Arab and "Muslim" societies.

Said's practice of writing off religion has become standard among post-colonial thinkers. Some, like Talal Asad, dismiss the term "religion" as fatally infected with hidden Christian suppositions, and hence useless for cross-cultural comparison. "Religion" is a term that should "stay at home" in the Christian West. Others, like David Chidester, level moral critiques against colonial powers who use the concept and word "religion" to aid and abet imperial ideology. On the other hand, I shall argue that the subject and concept of religion are unavoidable. We need not fear using it, even if earlier generations of scholars overemphasized religion. I "think I am right" to take this position because all words originate in some particular place, and "religion" is no exception. The origin of the word, "religion" in the West no more disqualifies it from broad, cross-cultural application than the Arabic origin of the word "algebra" makes it useless across cultures. What is distinctly odd in post-colonial thinking then is that the writing off of religion has become a mark of post-colonial thinking about religion – even by some who associate themselves with religious studies!

Given post-colonial theory's aversion to religion it is odd how religious studies thinkers have nonetheless latched on to it. Said has been very much in vogue in the study of religion. Yet this affinity seems easy to explain. Students and scholars of religions are prime candidates for sharing natural sympathies with liberationism, whether that be with post-colonial liberationism, like Said's, or with Cornel West's liberationist thinking about race, and so on. Perhaps those of us in religious studies are especially prone to liberal moral feelings? We want to do the right thing, and to speak out against injustice. All well and good. Nonetheless, students of religion should take note that along with his noble moral ambitions, Said and other postmodernists bring a complex bias against religion. As an academic discipline, students of religion should try to be as fair as they can be about the objects of their study – religion included. We do not want to mirror the biases of Said or Gayatri

Spivak that religion is "bad" with an equally dogmatic and unempirical bias toward religion as always "good." Neither stance belongs in the university.

Orienting Minds

The most influential work to emerge from the activist post-colonial phase of Said's intellectual life is his *Orientalism* (1978). Because of its vast and profound influence on post-colonial thinking, it demands the dedicated treatment I shall give it in the pages to follow.

Said sheds light on how he was inspired to write what might be considered the first major work on post-colonial theorizing. The shock of the Arab–Israeli war got Said thinking along the following lines:

> What concerned me now was how a subject was constituted, how a language could be formed – writing as a construction of realities that served one or another purpose instrumentally. This was the world of power and re-presentations, a world that came into being as a series of decisions made by writers, politicians, philosophers to suggest or adumbrate one reality and at the same time efface another. (Said 1998, p. 10)

What do Said's words mean for the study of religion? Two answers suggest themselves. First, Said's *Orientalism* focuses specifically on the way the *Arab* and *Muslim* worlds have been conceived by those Said calls by the pejorative term "orientalists." Said criticizes how orientalists conceive or "construct" Arabs or Muslims according to the dictates of their occidental minds. That is to say that Said thinks that the orientalist imaginary is necessarily shaped by the superior power position of orientalist scholars over those they study. This is superiority resulting from the orientalists' being ensconced within the privileged world of colonial or imperial power. For example, Said notes how "orientalist intellectuals" fabricated an image of Muhammad as "imposter" (Said 1978, p. 49). In thus conceiving or "constructing" Muhammad as "imposter," orientalists failed to act as neutral observers participating in an objective study. Instead, they reflected their location as members of the West's colonial-imperialist hegemony over the Muslim world. In conquering and colonizing Egypt, Napoleon thus not only exercised *military* power, but also enabled imperialist *intellectual* power to be exerted over upon Egypt. The scholars he empowered, in fact, actually sponsored and created the Arab or Muslim "orient" according to their own colonialist or imperialist ideological design (Said 1978, pp. 86–87). "My contention," says Said, "is that Orientalism is fundamentally a political doctrine willed over the Orient because the Orient was weaker than the West" (Said 1978, p. 204). Like Foucault, Said feels that power and knowledge are intertwined. For that reason alone, he "thinks he is right" to suspect the allegedly scholarly work about the colonized "Other" that was produced under the conditions of colonial and imperial rule. The orientalist's "Orient is not the Orient as it is, but the Orient as it has been Orientalized" (read, intellectually colonized or conquered) (Said, 1978, p. 104). "It is therefore correct that every European, in what he could say about the Orient," says Said, "was consequently a racist, an imperialist, and almost totally ethnocentric" (Said 1978, p. 204). A harsh judgment indeed. But when we reflect on Tylor's references to certain colonized folk as "savages," we can better understand Said's strong words. Being able to be a racist or imperialist means that those using such language are garbed in the purple robes of power.

Said has larger ambitions than exposing "orientalism" in Western scholarship about Arabs or Muslims. And this brings me to my second point. Said's specialized work can be, and has been, generalized to cover any and all treatments of the world's "Others" by scholars from regimes of hegemonic domination. Said's pejorative term "orientalist" thus applies to that kind of Western scholarship which constructs *any* and all "Others" – not only Arab or Muslim, but also Jewish, African, Hindu, Chinese, etc. – according to Western imperialist prejudices. In this way, Said offers students of the world's religions a "hermeneutic of suspicion," a way to reflect skeptically on their own scholarship and that of their forebears. To wit, are these other fields – Indology, Sinology, Buddhology, Judaic studies – subject to the same criticism Said levels against the classic "orientalist" scholarship of Arab or Muslim worlds? If so, we today are morally responsible for exposing these constructions of the world's "Others." In

doing so, we would be fulfilling part of our moral obligation to act as liberators. We would be setting free the world's "Others" from harmful misconceptions about them.

If readers see Foucault's hand in Said's great work, I agree entirely. Said absorbs Foucault's association of knowledge and power into his analyses of how Western writers "created" the orientalist's Orient. Further, the power location of Western writers determined what they chose to "know" about the Orient. Their decision to highlight some things and to suppress others was a function of their relation to power. Orientalists constructed Arabs or Muslims as "subjects" of "knowledge" considering them as "others." But they constructed them as mirror images of "ourselves." In every case, "power" explains to Said (and Foucault) why things have turned out as they have. The orientalist knowledge industry constitutes "an exercise of cultural strength" (Said 1978, p. 40). It is "itself a product of certain political forces and activities" (Said 1978, p. 203).

In summary, we can list Said's major theses about the assumptions made by "orientalist" scholars (Manzalaoui 1980, p. 838).

1   Orientalists have exaggerated the differences between "East" and "West." This has resulted in different populations' alienation from one another. The distinction posited by the evolutionists between "modern" and "primitive" would be an example of such an alienating difference (Said 1978, p. 300).

2   At the same time, orientalists have exaggerated the seemingly menacing, weird, or "eccentric" elements of the "East," and passed over aspects of these cultures that are more typical of them. Is the "Orient" then something to be feared *en bloc* like the "Yellow Peril, the Mongol hordes"? Are the provisions of Muslim law calling for the extreme punishment of crimes, say, the cutting off of hands for theft, any more *typical* of Islam than Leviticus' many applications of the death penalty for what to us would be either misdemeanors or not crimes at all (Said 1978, p. 301)?

3   Orientalists have also "homogenized" the cultures of the "East," thus ignoring their great internal diversity. They see the Orient as "eternal, uniform, and incapable of defining itself" (Said 1978, p. 301). Thus, all Hindus are

really "mystics." All Japanese, even Japanese Buddhists, practice Zen. All Muslim women wear the veil, and so on.

4   Orientalists assume that "the Orient has a synchronic culture, not subject to social and temporal fluxes." The "East" is thus somehow "outside history," and dwells in a timeless, unchanging world. Robertson Smith reflected this kind of attitude when he approached the religion of the then Arabian peninsula. He assumed that going to Muslim Saudi Arabia was something like time travel. Among the tribes of the Arabian peninsula, one witnessed religious life such as it must have been back in the age of the patriarchs of the Hebrew Bible. The Muslim Arabian tribes were thus stuck in a kind of historical "deep freeze" while he, and his Western cultural kin, paved a hot path of progressive change.

5   Homogeneity and difference also inform the orientalist belief that "the inhabitants of various parts share common opinions with little individual differentiation" (Manzalaoui 1980, p. 838). "We," again, are cast as the exceptional individualists with our unique and original views about the world. "They," on the other hand, are sunk in dull conformity, sharing the same stereotyped views about the way things are among each other.

6   Finally, the oriental "they" are spiritual and religious, while the Western "we" are scientific-technical materialists. Readers might recall something of this sort of view informing Eliade's contrast of "archaic man" as essentially religious, while "we" secular Westerners are lost in a world of materialist meaninglessness.

From Said's point of view, then, many of the classic thinkers in the study of religion might well be classified as "orientalist." The study of religion would then need a major overhaul of its methods and theoretical ground rules to root out "orientalist" assumptions and constructions. Now, although Said himself does not undertake the task of updating religious studies to reflect his critique of orientalism, many thinkers in religious studies have done so. David Chidester's critique of "frontier" comparative studies of religion in southern Africa would qualify as one example. As we will see shortly, anthropologist Talal Asad perhaps launches the most potent critique of "orientalist" scholarship since Said's *Orientalism*.

Gayatri Spivak Speaks Up for the "Subaltern"

I have already mentioned Gayatri Spivak several times in this chapter, and for good reason. Born into a high-caste, cultured, bourgeois Bengali family, Gayatri Chakravorty took the familiar route of education in elite English schools. Although she describes her family as in a four-generation line of intimate association with the Sri Ramakrishna Mission, she seems personally to have been charmed by anglophone Bengali Enlightenment rationalism, and thus, eventually, by modern French theory, especially Jacques Derrida's deconstructionism. Nonetheless, in later years Spivak has reclaimed some of the Hindu piety that suffused her domestic scene. She speaks affectionately of being "born and raised in the verbality of the praise of Kali," the formidable goddess worshiped prominently in Bengal, and, significantly, by Sri Ramakrishna (Spivak 2001, p. 143). Fitted out by her social class and anglophile education in Bengal for the wider international anglophone scene, Spivak took degrees from universities in the United States, Canada, and the United Kingdom. She has been the recipient of many academic honors and is the author of a score of books. While her first publication dealt with the poetry of W.B. Yeats, she quickly picked up with French literary theory. Her English translation of Derrida's seminal *Of Grammatology* (1976) early on contributed to the introduction and dissemination of French literary theory to the English-speaking world. She was an active member of the Subaltern Studies group, and now teaches in Columbia University's Department of Comparative Literature, where Edward W. Said, as well, taught until his death in 2003. Lately, she has turned to Indian subjects in her books, both original and translations, such as her *Song for Kali: A Cycle* (2000), *Chotti Munda and His Arrow* (2002), and *Other Asias* (2005). Her main arguments about the "subaltern" appeared in article form in the mid to late 1980s – "Subaltern Studies: Deconstructing Historiography" (1985) and "Can the Subaltern Speak?" (1988).

Spivak, along with fellow New Yorkers Edward Said, and Talal Asad, worked along their own paths to create an identifiable nexus of post-colonial theorizing. Their common dedication to the work of Foucault, as well as the personal friendships they enjoyed with one another, have only deepened the intellectual affinity one finds in their thinking. This includes a strongly principled liberationist motivation, sensitivity to the role of language and ideas in authorizing certain behaviors and institutions, and attention to those marginalized by the distribution of power, especially peoples under the domination of imperial Western centers.

Despite their unity of outlook, Said, Spivak, and Asad all play their own variations on the common themes binding them to one another. For example, students of religion have found Gayatri Spivak's notion of the subaltern an engaging aspect of her work. While no one agrees about the origin or precise meaning of "subaltern," some cite Marxist theorist Antonio Gramsci as its author. He purportedly gave "subaltern" a meaning roughly equivalent to the idea of "proletarian," naming any subject or systematically subordinated person or class. Others call attention to the prominence of the term in the post-colonial critiques by South Asian scholars, like Spivak herself, and also Homi Bhabha. Here, "subaltern" refers more specifically to those of the lower ranks occupied by native Indian junior officers and recruits in the British imperial military forces. Or it may more generally refer to any non-elite agent, subject therefore to the hegemonic control of imperial power. But whatever the real origins or intended meaning of the term, the accepted meaning of "subaltern" has coalesced around the idea of a systematically oppressed agent, dominated by specifically hegemonic power structures of control. Given its place in the Foucauldian discourse of power, it is thus a natural term to form a central notion in the theoretical vocabulary of post-colonial thinking.

The term "Hinduism" shows how Spivak's idea of the subaltern can generate debate. Presuming first that the word "Hinduism" itself is acceptable as an analytic term, and second, that "religion" is a true category, this debate posed the question, "Who Speaks for Hinduism?" (Balagangadhara 1994; Smith and Caldwell 2000). Echoing these sentiments, Spivak says, "when I hear someone putting up one Indian voice as representing India, I feel like I should say: look there is more" (Najmabadi and Spivak 1991, p. 126). That is to say, no single authoritative point of view affords one a privileged place from which to represent Hinduism. But this perspectival aspect of the study of Hinduism, say, has been obscured by Western assumptions of the scientific neutrality – the rule of the myth of objectivity – accorded Western scholarship.

Since the study of the religion(s) of India has generally and historically been the preserve of Western scholars, in the West it is easily assumed that this scholarship is objective. It does not represent any particular point of view, and especially not one rooted in or shaped by the position of Western scholars in the centers of imperial power. Like Said's call for a "Canaanite" reading of Exodus, Spivak challenges the *objectivist* presumptions of Western scholarship about India, and calls for Indians – the subalterns, here –to find their voices and speak from their point of view. She derides romantic European visions of India, such as that connected with Hermann Hesse that make "'India' ... a stable symbol of the promise of mystical liberation" (Spivak 2001). But is Spivak right, even if we suspect we know why she thinks she is right?

Brian K. Smith and Sarah Caldwell, for example, have outlined a series of questions, occasioned by Spivak's theoretical ideas (Smith and Caldwell 2000). Can only "insiders" represent their own traditions? And which "insider" counts the most? The hyper-nationalist, *Hindutva* theorists claim that only they can speak with authority about Hinduism. But outcaste Indians, Dalits, reject the pretensions of the nationalists to do so, pointing out that they only reflect their own privileged position in the Indian social order. Then again, our globalized world spawns hybrids of West and East – the white Hindu as well as the Indian Enlightenment rationalist. Which of these speaks with greater authority about Hinduism? No matter, however, what position we may adopt regarding these questions, I want readers to see how Spivak's idea of the subaltern finally speaking up has and can generate interesting debates in our field. Perhaps all that one should really ask of a theory is that it stimulates thinking, rather than putting an end to it. In this respect, Spivak's theorizing has served a healthy purpose.

Talal Asad: "Religion" Reformer and Eliminator

Spivak, Said, and Talal Asad make a cozy three-some when it comes to the nostrums of post-colonial theory. Asad and Said, in particular, line up in agreement on a whole list of convictions. Asad came early, writing one the first reviews to celebrate Said's *Orientalism* for its radical thrust. Conventional reviews saw *Orientalism* as little more than a "catalogue of Western prejudices about and misrepresentations of Arabs and Muslims" (Asad 1980, p. 648). Not so, Asad. He shrewdly noted that Said had launched a massive attack against those deep authorizing structures that made "orientalist" prejudices possible. Said had identified the pervasive, yet often obscure, power relationships between imperialist colo-nizer and subordinated peoples, and he had exposed them. Foucault too represents another common touchstone of their thought. Just when and how Asad fell under Foucault's spell is hard to know, but Asad and Said share the same appre-ciation for Foucault's classic knowledge/power dynamic. Both commit to a systematic repairing of the ways the injustices perpetuate themselves by the workings of scholarship. And, finally, both also exemplify post-colonial theory's two-pronged minimizing of the importance of reli-gion: first, religion is either implicitly or explicitly of no importance in human affairs; or, second, the category "religion" should be eliminated from our analytic vocabulary, because it is incorrigibly compromised by its tethering to the intellectual framework of the West. Asad's eliminationist project for religion and "religion" informs his books, *Genealogies of Religion: Discipline and Reasons of Power in Christianity and Islam* (1993) and *Formations of the Secular: Christianity, Islam, Modernity* (2003). Talal Asad is held in consid-erable esteem by post-colonial theorists in the study of religion.

Asad's treatment of "religion" must take top priority in discussing him as a theorist because it has had such great impact in our field. I must alert readers, though, that the next few pages may require some extra patience from them. Asad is a deeply confused theorist. He cannot seem to decide whether to *reform* religion and "religion," or to *eliminate* them. This makes understanding him a little more difficult than normal.

Nevertheless, he has some constructive proposals for improving the study of religion, along with other ideas that seem to undermine these improve-ments. In effect, Asad goes to war against himself!

On the side of *reform*, Asad tries to make us aware of the Western origins of the term "reli-gion." This realization entails wanting to *repair* our concept of religion by *expanding* it to reflect a broader, more inclusive notion. We need a con-cept of religion that reflects the realities of the lives of the colonized "Others," and not just those of the history of religion in the West. For Asad, this means that religion will then "involve the cul-tivation of certain bodily attitudes (including emotions), the disciplined cultivation of habits, aspirations, desires," and so on, rather than the creeds, high-powered theologies, or doctrines typical of Western religion (Asad 1996, p. 11).

But on the other side, Asad seems compelled to march along with Said and Spivak and insist upon *eliminating* "religion" from the vocabulary of cross-cultural comparison. His reasons for this are complex. Part of why Asad "thinks he is right" to eliminate "religion" can be attributed to the ethnocentric origins of the term, but another part of his reasoning has deeper existential sources, as I shall argue.

Let's go into these different theoretical projects a little more deeply.

Asad, Reformer of "Religion"

First, as a reformer of the concept of "religion," Asad objects to the idea of religion as being constituted by having certain *beliefs*, such as belief in the existence of God. Readers of the present book should readily agree that Asad has correctly identified the definition as prevalent as it has developed in the West. We have seen throughout how Protestant or post-Reformation thinking dominated the study of religion for many years. It is no surprise that it has left its mark on the very idea of religion. Asad should be looked on as a critic of what I should call "cogni-tivism" – the idea that religion is essentially about beliefs, doctrines, dogmas, theologies, and such. Asad wants to *reform* this way of looking at reli-gion by expanding the notion beyond the domain of Western civilization. This is one reason, I believe, that we should welcome post-colonial theory.

Asad seeks, then, to what amounts to expanding the concept of religion to include the central place of emotions, body, and power. Asad's call for an expansion of our idea of religion falls right into line with the traditions of thinking and theorizing religion from the sixteenth century. What else were the Natural Religion theorists like Bodin and Herbert of Cherbury doing but proposing to broaden the understanding of religion beyond the narrow sectarian concepts that prevailed in the sixteenth century? What else was Durkheim achieving by including Buddhism within his definition of religion than expanding the prevailing theistic definition of religion used among the liberal Protestant theologians and historians of religion of his day? So Asad's expansion of "religion" to include a new "kind of religiosity" is good news. Post-colonial theory would then help religious studies break out of its own ethnocentric, historical biases (Asad 1996, p. 11). Post-colonial theory here offers an exciting reformist program for expanding the conceptual range of "religion." Here are some examples.

As an exercise in post-colonial theorizing, Asad shows how suspicions about Western ethnocentrism can improve the way we think about and understand religion. Asad's thrust is then to show up the narrowness of a Western ethnocentric study of religion. What would the study of medieval Christianity be without attention to the prominent place of the ascetic practices, especially in light of the work of feminist theorists, considered in the previous chapter, like Caroline Walker Bynum? Asad's post-colonial approach urges studies of religion focusing on non-cognitive, visceral, or corporeal modes of being, such as "disciplinary practices." Alert readers will immediately pick up Asad's appeal to the studies Foucault began in *Discipline and Punish* and continued in his work on the way religious "selves" are constructed by means of the exercise of power (Asad 1993, p. 125). Seeing medieval Christian "religion" only in terms of beliefs would give us a poor picture, when compared with that which we can have by including the study of the disciplinary and humiliation practices prominent in medieval Christian "religion." Similarly, the great late twelfth/early thirteenth-century reformer, St. Francis of Assisi, told his disciples that "It is no use walking anywhere to preach unless our walking is our preaching." Here Francis gives voice to a different kind of religion than, say, we met with in our nineteenth-century evolutionists, given as they were to seeing religion as belief. Francis says that his friars must "walk the talk," and put the "talk" aside. How would Tylor and his animist theory of religion deal with that? Putting Francis' disdain for cognitivist conceptions of religion even more forcefully, he abjures his disciples to "Preach the Gospel at all times and when necessary use words." Again words, beliefs, doctrines, cognitive elements are secondary, if not insignificant for Francis. But unlike Robertson Smith, Francis is *celebrating* religion as a practical affair, not disdaining it as "primitive." Asad wants students of religion to understand Francis' religion in terms of bodily practices, not doctrines or teachings – mostly because that is the way Francis saw his religion in the first place! So, the study of religion has much to gain by joining Asad's overthrow of the disembodied, over-intellectualized conception of religion as "belief" that I have called "cognitivism."

Asad's Other Side: Eliminating "Religion"

At the same time as he advances this reformist project of expanding the idea of "religion," Asad undercuts it by calling for the use of "religion" to be discontinued altogether. To state the matter baldly, Asad seeks, in effect, to eliminate the reality of religion and the term "religion" altogether from our attempts to understand and explain the world. He allies his eliminationist project with the "truly original" assertion of Harvard historian of religion Wilfrid Cantwell Smith, that religion lacks "any essence." Asad agrees with Smith that "religion" is a notion empty of any content or reference. If we used the word "religion" to *point out* something in the world, for example, we would either end up with no object at all or so many objects that we would be reduced to total confusion.

First, religion is not an empirical object (Asad 2001, p. 206). Religion is not a "thing," like a Honda; "religion" is not the name of something out there in the world, like "Honda." At most, "religion" is a vast basket like "art," "politics," "power," "culture," and such that we use to *organize* the brute data of the world of experience. And, as such, this basket is employed or not, depending upon the cultural facts on the ground. "Religion" is just a name we use to gather things into intellectual baskets. Some cultures have a basket like ours; others do not. Some cultures have similar contents in their baskets; other may not. In his book on the Calvinist origins of capitalism, Max Weber had a ready-made basket of "religions." He filled it with the usual suspects, Catholics, Lutherans, Baptists, Puritans, and so on. But when he went to fill the "capitalism" basket, he could not find agreement about what to put into it. Brigandage? Piracy? Merely being rich? Or when Durkheim went to fill his basket of religions, he found that his peers thought he should not include Buddhism in it. Durkheim dealt with this objection by saying that the "religion basket" was to be filled with *sacred* things, and all those activities in which the sacred was administered. Asad emphasizes that all such assignments are contestable. Even the idea of having a "religion basket" is debatable. So, we can well do without the "religion basket."

Asad's second reason for eliminating "religion" is that its definition names too many things to be called one thing. Is it believing in God or a god or goddess? If so, does not this leave out Buddhism or Daoism? Is religion what the nineteenth-century evolutionist theorists thought it to be, namely, morality tinged with feeling? But why not define religion as a sense of the sublime or transcendent? And so on. "Religion," thus, names no one "objective" thing in our world. So, how can we, then, use it to understand the world? Because there is nothing real to religion, we have no need for the concept "religion" – apparently in any form at all. It would be better just to talk of Buddhism, Christianity, or Daoism, and forget "religion." Because there is no one definition of "religion," Asad thinks we should abandon the word. "Religion" names no universal phenomenon of human life. Therefore, "we have to abandon the idea of religion as always and essentially the same" (Asad 2001, p. 220). Do Theravada Buddhists, Confucians, or Australian aborigines have "religion" in the same sense as Quakers or Southern Baptists? Many of the theorists we have already studied would not think so. If not, why try to stretch the term to cover such different things? Asad has argued in his classic of 1993, *Genealogies of Religion*, and repeatedly in other works, that "a transhistorical definition of religion is not viable" (Asad 1993, p. 30). As recently as 2003, Asad reinforced this dismissal of "religion" from any role in making sense of what people do cross-culturally because "there is nothing essentially religious, nor any universal essence that defines 'sacred' language or 'sacred' experience" (Asad 2003, p. 25). Because he holds these opinions, I believe it fair to say he wishes to *eliminate* "religion" from the vocabulary of understanding and explaining cultures.

Why Asad "Thinks He Is Right" to Eliminate "Religion"

Is there any way to make sense of the differences between Asad as reformer and radical eliminationist? As with other thinkers in this book, I am brought back to biography, to the way the life of an author is often reflected even in their abstract theoretical thinking. I think reflection upon Asad's biography and social context can help us perhaps resolve the dilemma he presents of seeming at once to retain but reform "religion," over against his will to eliminate it. No one would be surprised if a thinker might want to be rid of the idea of religion because of unhappy personal experiences at the hands of people who identify themselves with "religion." Asad's biography shows him to have been exposed to just this sort of arrogant Christian. Perhaps these missionaries had a hand in Asad's wanting to see "religion" eliminated totally from academic discourse or, more radically, to see all religious factors discounted in explaining how the world works? The evidence is compelling.

It would not be surprising to learn that some Western missionaries, staffing schools far from the Western world, represented their ways of being religious as the only, or most exalted, form of being so. In cases of this kind, one might expect the non-Christians in these Christian missionary schools to feel slighted and resentful. "Well, if *that* is what religion is, then I reject religion!" The Reverend Pat Robertson makes it pretty clear, for example, that Islam has no rights to membership in the category, "religion." "We have to recognize that Islam is not a religion," said Robertson in 2007. "It is a worldwide political movement bent on domination of the world" (Robertson 2007). Imagine the tender young Asad exposed to something like that. This teaching forces everyone into a kind of unitary straitjacket of their own fashioning: a religion like Islam cannot be a religion, because it is not like Reverend Robertson's Christianity. If one can empathize, and even perhaps sympathize, with the reactions to the sort of mission teaching that I have sketched, then one might have a picture, *mutatis mutandis*, of the background out of which Asad's eliminationist talk against religion and "religion" emerged.

As a matter of fact, Asad recounts just the kinds of humiliating experiences at the hands of Christian missionaries as those to which I have alluded (Scott 2006). Although I do not know the theological stripe of the missionary school teachers of Asad's childhood in Pakistan, at the very best their viewpoint might well have been "liberal Protestant" of the sort we met with in Robertson Smith. For Smith, we will recall that religion was fundamentally disembodied and "spiritual," consisting of beliefs and moral rules. The idea of religion that he assigns to anthropologist Clifford Geertz, and which is the specific target of his eliminationist project, conforms, on the whole, to Smith's (Asad 1993, p. 48). In an account of his schooling by Christian missionaries in Pakistan, Asad makes a special point of recalling the humiliating experiences he had as schoolboy at the hands of Christian missionaries. One can only imagine how a young Muslim boy of tender disposition would react to a view of "religion" that made little of his own Muslim religious life. In cases like these, justifiable resentment is sure to follow. Although treading on psychological territory can be treacherous, in Asad's case we are, in effect, invited in.

Thus, in concluding this discussion of Asad, I suggest that we can solve the dilemma of his conflicting approaches to religion if we allow that he only means to reject "religion" in the sense of its being equated with its liberal Protestant use – as "belief" and/or only with exclusively cognitive ideas of religion. If so, then there are reasons to applaud Asad's post-colonial-inspired reformation of our ideas of religion. His assertion of religion as involving "embodied practices" seems both useful and elegant, as is his conception of religion as consisting in "networks of emotional connection" (Asad 1996; 2005, p. 12). In sum, then, studies of religion might be enriched by adopting some – but not all – of the lessons Asad has drawn from reflecting on his own experience among colonized peoples.

Bruce Lincoln and the Discourses of Resistance

In religious studies itself, perhaps the most accomplished advocate of the "culturalist" tendency in post-colonial theory is University of Chicago comparativist Bruce Lincoln. The exception proving the rule, Lincoln refuses to play the post-colonial theorists' game of running down religion or the use of the term, "religion" to understand and explain phenomena. While open to expanding the conceptual range of such terms as "religion" in order to engage the data, Lincoln does not feel constrained to either eliminate the term "religion" from his work nor to pledge allegiance to any one particular definition of it. What matters, as we will see, in Lincoln's work is "discourse."

Yet beneath this distinctive analytic approach, the wide reputation enjoyed by Lincoln derives from the passionate moral grounding of his vast erudition. How many learned studies of Nordic myth, Druids, Amazons, Pahlavi texts, Scythian royal burials, Nietzsche's "blond beast," Trotsky, the Swazi Ncwala, popular American wrestling, the St. Bartholomew's Day massacre, Indo-European philology, or eighteenth-century British colonial administrators like Sir William Jones conclude with meditations on their moral implications? All of Lincoln's do! Discourse plays a major role in the resistance struggles Lincoln studies. He focuses especially upon features of discourse commonly classified as "religious." Departing from materialist Marxism, Lincoln holds that society is more than its economy or its scheme of concrete social relations. Rather, our "sentiments" of affinity and estrangement mark the borders of the social entity we call our own. And these are called forth by discourse. Says Lincoln, discourse is the "chief instrument by which such sentiment may aroused, manipulated, and rendered dormant" (Lincoln 1989, p. 11). This is to say that aspects of the religious life such as myth, ritual, symbolism, imagery, ideology, beliefs, and graphic, plastic and performing arts and such "matter." In several books, for example, Lincoln has shown how "subaltern" classes resort to discursive entities, like myths and rituals, to enable their projects of liberation and resistance. For Lincoln, discursive resistance can take many subtle forms, such as "muttering and ... groans ... halfhearted applause, and even ... silence" (Lincoln 1994, p. 53). Indeed, Lincoln is so optimistic about the prospects of successful resistance to counter material forces by means of discursive acts that he even believes that "flagrant use of force" cannot "extinguish speech in any absolute sense" (Lincoln 1994, p. 68).

Running through the cases Lincoln presents is his moral commitment to the act of subaltern "resistance" to domination. Resistance is the "continued mobilization of powerful sentiments of affinity, solidarity and corporate identity" by means of which subalterns form for themselves a powerful sense of a collective "we" (Lincoln 1989, p. 73). But how does discourse, including religious discourse, do this? How do myths, rituals, images, language, and such contribute to resistance against regimes of domination, whether imperial, colonial, or post-colonial? How does the enlisting of the voice of God, the People, ancestors, or prophets further the job of liberation? How does laughter undermine domination? Are there such things as "corrosive discourses" – ones capable of eating away at the authority of tyrants (Lincoln 1994, ch. 5)? What, as well, of the effect of curses, invoking divine sanctions, dismemberings, beheadings, or disturbing official ceremonial occasions? In pursuit of answers to such questions, Lincoln founded the Program in Comparative Studies in Discourse and Society at the University of Minnesota, and has also authored several books exploring how religious discourse in its many forms – myth, ritual, practices, imagery, ideology, emblems, and so on – battles oppression (Lincoln 1989, 1991, 1994, 1999).

In one such case of religious discourse working in the interests of resistance to the British Raj, Lincoln showed how Hindu pundits used their own myths for just such an effort against British colonial rule. The Hindus devised their plan of resistance in two steps. To begin with, the pundits thwarted British attempts to monopolize public discourse. They first "succeeded in refusing the stories and relations their rulers hoped to impose." The British, for example, constantly regaled the Indians with their own self-aggrandizing mythology of the British conquest of India, or tales of their own national pride, such as appeals to national myths like the Magna Carta, Enlightenment "progress," or the "white man's burden." But the pundits simply refused to let the British set the terms of debate in this way. Taking the initiative, they engaged the British in an exchange that permitted an Indian myth to set the terms of debate. On its face, the Indian myth to which the pundits alluded was an innocent enough sketch of Hindu cosmology. Yet every learned Indian understood it as a slap at British pretensions. The cosmology spelt out the shape of the world in visual form by locating Indians at the center of a circle, and the British, quite accurately, on the Western fringes of the world. By all accounts, the British made no protest, and indeed, seeking to show that they respected local traditions and cultures, nodded in approval at this sketch of cultural and political geography. Unbeknownst to the British, however, the Hindu pundits were not just making a bland observation about a geographical truth. By locating the British on the Western borders of India, the pundits identified them to knowledgeable Indians as polluting outsiders. The British colonial attempts to insinuate themselves into the (Indian) center by their intrusion into the subcontinent was thus judged as polluting or "dirtying" the Indian center. The British were, mythologically speaking, "filth" – matter out of place. The myth was telling everyone that the British did not belong in India, indeed that they corrupted it. And the mythology "proved" it. Thus, as a piece of "cultural resistance," the pundits told the British as far back as the eighteenth century, through the coded language of myth, what the independence fighters would tell them explicitly in the twentieth century: "Quit India!" Thus, "by remembering an alternative account of the past," the pundits opened a struggle of resistance to the discursive domination that British hoped to achieve. The pundits "held open an alternative understanding of the present and helped to imagine an alternative future" – the very essence of positive liberty (Lincoln 1999, p. 207).

Thus, while Lincoln's moral motivations recall those of other liberationist post-colonial critics, he does not assume the role of prophet. He presents the facts of domination and injustice, and lets them speak for themselves. He is, therefore, no Gandhi or Cornel West, even if his moral sympathies are with the welfare of subalterns. Instead, Lincoln says virtually nothing about any particular activist program of resistance. This does not mean, however, that he lacks a vision of the good society – of a desirable regime of liberation – or even that he is shy about letting his moral preferences show. Lincoln legitimately belongs among those I have called "liberationists," rather than "liberals." As a liberationist, Lincoln is not merely satisfied to conceive liberty or human flourishing negatively, as "freedom from" oppression. Instead, he sees liberty in positive terms as "freedom to" bring about certain states of affairs. Thus, his moral compass is set firmly on certain positive values shared by post-colonial thinkers, such as freedom to achieve justice and equality for all peoples across the globe and to lament the loss of those freedoms in the past.

Conclusion: Post-Post-Colonial?

Some recent critics have suggested that the day of post-colonial theory has passed into one where "post-secular" thinking dominates high-level theoretical discourse. Then we might also keep up to date on the dreary history of the oppression of "man by man" that seems to develop apace without the assistance of colonialism. What can one say about the tenacious hold on power of Robert Mugabe, or of the ambitions of the Islamic Republic of Iran in the Gulf, or of conflicts in Syria, and South Asia? What of China's throttling of the murmurings of Uighers or Tibetans? Perhaps changes in today's world have moved things along, at least to take attention off the West? After all, a world in which the Iranian model of the modern state seems as viable to some as the secular nation-state is a different world than one aching under the burdens of colonial oppression. Nonetheless, given that the colonial age has only recently passed, it is more likely that for some time yet to come much of what happens in the world will reflect the former condition of being either a colonial master or subject. Post-colonial theory reminds us of the larger world-historical situation all citizens of the globe occupy, and thus of the possible influences upon our thinking about religion given this situation.

Thus, Said reminds us about the perils of scholarship originating in the Western world, where we occupy a generally privileged position of cultural and economic hegemony over most of the "other" world, and certainly over our former colonial dominions. Drawing upon Foucault, Said argues this differential of power cannot but shape what we consider to be "knowledge" of the Other. Our position higher on the scale of imperial or post-colonial power authorizes us to think in certain ways about the Others. Because of our location at the center of colonial power, we will take things for granted as true that those on the periphery will not. Consider alone the trivial, but nonetheless common and offensive, assumption – indeed sometimes to the extent of being considered a natural right – of Americans that English will be understood and spoken the world over. The task of the scholar who wishes to overcome the distortions to reality that this situation produces will have a significant task of self-discipline on their hands. This self-discipline is so difficult because it is not simply a matter of shedding a few egregious stereotypes of the Others. It is difficult because the realities of power work from very deep places in our thinking, and are very difficult to root out. In this, "orientalism" is like racism or misogyny. All operate from deeply unconscious levels of our thinking.

Spivak tells much the same story of the need to complicate our understanding of the Others whose voices have been ignored because of their "subaltern" position in the calculus of colonial power. Her feminist spin on the Other, along with her position as a woman hailing from the Third World, distinguish her contributions to post-colonial theorizing. That said, however, one might complain that Spivak gives the subalterns so much voice that she unrealistically levels out all participants in a culture. Of course, every human voice is of equal value in and for itself. But that may overlook the fact that some voices have had more of a say in the way a culture or civilization has taken shape than others. Spivak thus resists the view that cultures or civilizations contain dominant values or traits. Spivak's giving voice to the voiceless is an especially attractive moral aspect of her thinking. But the voiceless are such for reasons mostly having to do with the distribution of power in a society – a notion Foucault would well understand.

Asad, on the other hand, speaks more directly to the student of religion. At his best, he demands that we be critical of our analytic categories, above all, "religion." Is our notion of religion capacious enough to include those Others we study? Or do we need to reassess our own understanding of "religion," even as it applies to us? For many years studies of religion proceeded as if "religion" were simply "belief in God." Asad puts the question to us of why we should press this definition in situations in which it may not apply. Why, when the Others do not conform to our Eurocentric definition of religion, do we then brand them as practicing "magic" or "superstition" or "Satanism"? Here, I have found Asad's attention to aspects of the religious life, such as emotions, bodily practices, and such, that he draws from the Islamic and medieval Christian worlds, usefully turned round to bring out these overlooked aspects of current religious life.

Yet when Asad turns radical, as we have seen, he challenges us as to whether, given these cultural and historical differences between the colonized "them" and the colonizing "us," we should continue using such an ethnocentric term as "religion" at all. At that point, I think, students of religion need to tread carefully. We can agree that the term "religion" covers a good deal of territory overlapping with other disciplines. Its definition shifts as need requires. And some definitions of it will remain foreign to others. But if students of religion abandon the term "religion," they will need some *raison d'être* for carrying on studying this strange object, religion. Actually, the study of religion is not alone in holding to concepts and terminology that may fail Descartes' geometric test of being "clear and distinct." Does "culture," claimed by anthropology as its own turf, have such a model of clarity and distinctness? What of the history which declares itself dedicated to the study of the "past"? *All* of the past, everywhere, and under any aspect? Or what, finally, of philosophy,

a discipline that often claims as its mark of distinction that it "reflects upon" reality? "Reflects," really? Doesn't that make us all philosophers? And if so, therefore none of us? And what, finally, of the concept of "power," so central to Asad's entire project? Borrowed from Foucault, the use of power has been subject to the same logical and historical criticism as has religion or art or politics, or language, and so on. "Religion," thus, suffers the same disabilities in this regard as all the main categories of the humanities. Perhaps we should thank Asad and others for reminding us of that. But having a critical attitude about our categories, mixed with some humility and adaptability does not require us to commit what would be disciplinary suicide by eliminating the term, "religion," as Asad wants. Not being attached to religious studies, Asad risks nothing in urging us to declare our discipline empty of content. Let him first similarly eliminate what is for him a key, but highly conflicted and vague concept, like "power" before he asks us to eliminate "religion."

Perhaps then only Bruce Lincoln offers students of religion an active, rigorous, and durable style of post-colonial critique of religion. Lincoln, in his own way, constantly seems to be putting the question: "What discursive *religious* agent or agents are responsible for various forms of colonial, imperial and post-colonial oppression or liberation from it?" How are the many features of the vast world of religious representations playing their part in holding colonized peoples down, or indeed in lifting them up? Lincoln's theoretical vision outlines a research program that can generate a long series of intriguing problems typical of the post-colonial condition.

Appendix: Major Post-Colonial Religious Studies Thinkers and Concepts

Thinkers
   Talal Asad (b. 1932)
   David Chidester (b. 1953)
   Michel Foucault (1926–84)
   Bruce Lincoln (b. 1943)
   Karl Marx (1818–83)
   Edward Said (1935–2003)
   Gayatri Spivak (b. 1942)

Concepts

colony a cultural or economic entity dependent upon and controlled by a distant political power.

colonialism the belief in the legitimacy of the establishment of control over foreign territories, known as "colonies."

empire an encompassing political entity, ruled from an imperial center, that contains within it smaller political bodies, such as nations, peoples, tribes, colonies, kingdoms, etc., under its control.

Eurocentrism the belief that European thought and/or practices occupy a privileged position among those of all other cultural entities.

hegemony the condition of dominance or control over thought or deed.

imperialism the belief that empire is the most legitimate form of political organization.

neo-colonialism the attempt to exert colonial control over former colonies in the absence of direct and explicit control.

References

Asad, T. 1980. Review of Said's *Orientalism. The English Historical Review* 95(376) (July): 648–649.

Asad, T. 1993. *Genealogies of Religion: Discipline and Reasons of Power in Christianity and Islam*. Baltimore: Johns Hopkins University Press.

Asad, T. 1996. "Modern Power and the Reconfiguration of Religious Traditions: Interview with Saha Mahmood." *SEHR* 5(1): 1–15.

Asad, T. 2001. "Reading a Modern Classic: W.C. Smith's *The Meaning and End of Religion*." *History of Religions* 40(3): 205–222.

Asad, T. 2003. *Formations of the Secular: Christianity, Islam, Modernity*. Stanford: Stanford University Press.

Asad, T. 2005. "Reflections on Laïcité & the Public Sphere." *Items and Issues* 5(3).

Balagangadhara, S.N. 1994. "*The Heathen in His Blindness....*": *Asia, the West and the Dynamic of Religion*. Leiden: E.J. Brill.

Berlin, I. 1979. "The Originality of Machiavelli." In I. Berlin, *Against the Current*. London: Penguin.

Chidester, D. 1988. *Patterns of Power: Religion and Politics in American Culture*. Englewood Cliffs: Prentice Hall.

Chidester, D. 1996. *Savage Systems: Colonialism and Comparative Religion in Southern Africa*. Bloomington: Indiana University Press.

Douglas, M. 1970. *Purity and Danger*. London: Penguin.

Foucault, M. 1980. *Power/Knowledge: Selected Interviews and Other Writings, 1972–1977*. New York: Pantheon.

Hart, W.D. 2000. *Edward Said and the Religious Effects of Culture*. Cambridge: Cambridge University Press.

Lease, G. 1994. "The History of "Religious" Consciousness and the Diffusion of Cultural Strategies for Surviving Dissolution." *Historical Reflections/Refléxions historiques* 20: 453–479.

Lincoln, B. 1989. *Discourse and the Construction of Society: Comparative Studies of Myth, Ritual, and Classification*. New York: Oxford University Press.

Lincoln, B. 1991. *Death, War, and Sacrifice Studies in Ideology and Practice*. Chicago: University of Chicago Press.

Lincoln, B. 1994. *Authority: Construction and Corrosion*. Chicago: University of Chicago Press.

Lincoln, B. 1999. *Theorizing Myth*. Chicago: University of Chicago Press.

Manzalaoui, M. 1980. Review of Edward Said's *Orientalism. The Modern Language Review* 75(4) (October): 837–839.

Martin, D. 1997. *Does Christianity Cause War?* Oxford: Oxford University Press.

Najmabadi, A., and G.C. Spivak. 1991. Interview with Gayatri Spivak. *Social Text* 28: 122–134.

Orsi, R.A. 2005. *Between Heaven and Earth: The Religious Worlds People Make and the Scholars Who Study Them*. Princeton: Princeton University Press.

Robertson, P. 2007. Broadcast of 12 June. In *The 700 Club*. USA.

Said, E.W. 1978. *Orientalism*. New York: Pantheon.

Said, E.W. 1986. "Michael Walzer's "Exodus and Revolution': A Canaanite Reading." *Grand Street* 5(2) (Winter): 86–106.

Said, E.W. 1998. "Between Worlds." *London Review of Books* 20(9): 3–7.

Said, E.W., and M. Walzer 1986. "An Exchange: "Exodus and Revolution." *Grand Street* 5(4) (Summer): 246–259.

Scott, D. 2006. "Appendix. The Trouble of Thinking: An Interview with Talal Asad." In D. Scott and C. Hirschkind (eds.), *Powers of the Secular Modern: Talal Asad and His Interlocutors*. Stanford: Stanford University Press, pp. 243–303.

Sivan, E. 1985. "Edward Said and His Arab Reviewers." In *Interpretations of Islam: Past and Present*. Princeton: Darwin Press.

Smith, B.K., and S. Caldwell. 2000. "Introduction: Who Speaks for Hinduism?" *JAAR* 68(4): 705–710.

Smith, W.R. 1912. "Animal Worship and Animal Tribes among the Arabs and in the Old Testament." In J.S. Black and G. Chrystal (eds.), *Lectures and Essays of William Robertson Smith*. London: Adam and Charles Black.

Spivak, G.C. 1999. *A Critique of Postcolonial Reason: Toward a History of the Vanishing Present*. Cambridge, MA: Harvard University Press.

Spivak, G.C. 2001. "Moving Devi." *Cultural Critique* 47(Winter): 120–163.

Spivak, G.C. 2005. "Thinking about Edward Said: Pages from a Memoir." *Critical Inquiry* 31(2): 519–525.

Strenski, I. 2010. *Why Politics Can't Be Freed from Religion: Radical Interrogations of Religion, Power and Politics*. Oxford: Wiley-Blackwell.

Walzer, M., and E.W. Said. 1985–86. "An Exchange: Michael Walzer and Edward Said." *Grand Street* 5(4) (Summer): 246–259.

Young, R.J.C. 2001. *Postcolonialism: An Historical Introduction*. Oxford: Blackwell.

18

Conclusion: Being "Smart" about Bringing "Religion" Back In

Post-Modern Virtues

A prime virtue of post-modern theories of religion is devotion to the *critical* study of religion, and along with this, a *critical* attitude about the concept, "religion." Post-modern theorists would apply Socrates' adage that the "unexamined life is not worth living" to theories and concepts. As Socrates urged young Athenians to take responsibility for their lives by examining them, so post-modern theorists want religious studies scholars to take responsibility for their concepts – primarily, our concept of religion. In this vein, theorists of religion are expected to challenge, to *examine* – to be critical of – what passes as given or taken for granted about religion. Question everyday assumptions about the key terms we use in the study of religion. Post-modern theorists have, thus, tried to make us think about religion in new ways by being critical of our language about religion. In the new chapters in the second edition of this book, I have tried to how they sought to make us *understand* religion in ways that bring in newer perspectives, such as the experience of different sexes/genders, races, and so on.

But being critical about fundamentals does not come naturally. In everyday life, most people find talking about religion easy, perhaps too easy.

Everyone thinks they know what religion is. And can we blame them? The term "religion" is widely, and often unproblematically, used all the time. Surely everyone *knows* what religion is as readily as everyone *knows* what morality, art, society, music, magic, politics, and such are. Conventional wisdom tells us that we know how to name these things. However, this conventional confidence means that we have no reason to bother being critical of the term "religion." We have no reason to scrutinize it. As a result, we don't "take responsibility" for our concept of religion. We just don't feel we have to do so.

Indeed, one of greatest works in the study of religion, Max Weber's *The Protestant Ethic and the Spirit of Capitalism*, is totally devoid of any critical examination of "religion." In other works Weber did critically ponder differences between "church" and "sect." But, in the main, he wrote uncritically about the way religions – like Calvinism, for example – influenced the rise of our capitalist economic system. However, readers will search in vain for words about what "religion" is. In this sense, like ordinary folks, Weber took for granted the ordinary census-category, unexamined usage of "religion." He took the idea of religion from off the shelf, so to speak. Whatever passed in ordinary language as religion was good enough for Weber – Lutheranism, Roman

Understanding Theories of Religion: An Introduction, Second Edition. Ivan Strenski.
© 2015 Ivan Strenski. Published 2014 by John Wiley & Sons, Ltd.

Catholicism, Pietism, Methodism, and, finally, Calvinism. He simply accepted that "religion" was an uncontroversial name for an empirical phenomenon as easily identifiable as art or music or politics or society. He then appealed to these religions to explore the religious origins of capitalism. And he got away with it!

In his uncritical taking religion for granted, Weber was like a lot of us – both ordinary folk and social scientists. No one gave him any trouble for not being critical. Except in extreme cases, we too do not scrutinize critically what important general words like "religion" mean. We usually only get critical about such key terms when trouble happens. Remember my earlier mention of Terry Eagleton's image of the appearance of "theories" as indicating that "something is amiss," like those "dreaded small bumps on the neck," warning us that all is not well in the religious world (Eagleton 1990). Theories aim to fix these problems by explaining how and why they occur. We are all doubtless familiar with how religious trouble can erupt in the public square. An outbreak of prejudice, ill will, or violence typically gets our attention. One group refuses to recognize others as members of a religion. Indeed, they may accuse them in inflammatory language of being satanic, fanatic, cultists, sectarians, and so on. The trouble can further be described as a breakdown in our common mind about religion. We disagree, even violently, about whether or how we should use the label "religion."

Although being critical and taking responsibility for one's concepts may seem abstract recommendations remote from real life, we can easily imagine ourselves in a concrete situation which brings home these ideas. Indulge me as I outline another thought experiment. In the morning, for example, a pair of Jehovah's Witnesses come by your house, *Watchtower* in hand. In their actions, and in the message of *Watchtower*, they give the impression of belonging to a religion – like yours. But you balk at the thought. You don't like the way they look or behave. You want to say that they belong to a "sect," not to a *real* religion – like yours. You and the Jehovah's Witnesses are of "two minds" about whether they should be called a "religion." You share no common mind with your Witness visitors about what to call a religion. Next, you run across a story in the morning newspaper about a young Buddhist CO (conscientious objector) who has been refused non-combatant status because the judge refuses to admit Buddhism as a "religion." Religions, says the judge, focus on the belief in God. But Buddhists do not. Buddhism is just a "philosophy," or at best, a "cultural" phenomenon, not a "religion." Therefore, Buddhists have no right to CO status by virtue of their being members of a religion. If the lack of a common mind troubles you because of your differences with the Jehovah's Witnesses in the first example, the lack of a common mind about religion in the law troubles you even more.

Later that day, you tune into TV news reports on the so-called "ethnic" or "sectarian" violence in Lebanon, Iraq, Syria, the former Yugoslavia, and so on. But since you've taken a few religious studies courses, you are alert to the fact that what the media call "sectarian" or "ethnic" violence is *religious* warfare, sometimes, or not, mixed up with ethnicity, too. Alawites, Roman Catholics, Maronite and Greek Orthodox Christians, Sunni and Shia Muslims are killing one another. These are all names of religions. So you then wonder why the TV people don't just call these *religious* wars. What's the point of their not admitting what should be obvious – at least to you? Are they fearful of offending their middle-class viewers by insinuating that religion causes violence? You begin then to appreciate how big a problem forming a common mind about religion will be when even the powerful mass media fail so miserably in achieving one. One final example. Recall when Mitt Romney, a prominent Mormon, ran for the US presidency in 2012. I remember some of my Evangelical friends saying that they could not bring themselves to refer to Mormonism as a "religion," much less as "Christian." They warned me away from the candidate because they say that the Church of Jesus Christ of Latter-day Saints is a "cult," and "cults" cannot be trusted. With views like these so commonplace, we know we are far from having achieved a common mind about religion that enables it to enter public discourse in a fruitful way.

Among their other achievements, the thinkers in this book have all been dedicated to helping society form such a common mind about religion, giving us a way to talk openly and freely about it. A good theory of religion might, for example, persuade that reluctant judge to expand his notion of religion by appealing to public evidence acceptable to both sides. Yes, Buddhism lacks a god at the center, but it is the basis of a thriving, long-lived monastic community. Mere "philosophies" don't do that. Buddhists also meditate for the purpose of achieving some sort of communion with transcendent states. If Buddhism is a "culture," it is a peculiar one, indeed, since it aims to connect with realities outside the human realm. That is what theoretical argument in the study of religion is supposed to be – critical inquiry about the way to use language. It is a vehicle for people to come to a common mind about religion. Over and above any personal religious commitments they may or may not have, theories try to provide ways to agree on the terms of public discourse about religion.

Post-Modern Vices

But for all its virtues, post-modernism is guilty of vices, too. First, a significant number of prominent post-modernists are either committed to *eliminating* religion, or to abandoning the study of religion for the critical study of the *concept* of religion, in and for itself. Those who want to eliminate religion from analytic discourse are, of course, free to do so. But it would also be reasonable for them to leave the rest of us in religious studies to go about our work. Those who simply want to make a critical study of the category of religion need to face up to the irony inherent in their task. They never reap the benefits of their critical labors because they never apply critically reformed concepts of religion to an object outside the discourse of religion! They talk incessantly *about* religion, but seldom or never *with* it. I propose that religious studies is a "scientific" discipline, and as such is about working *with* concepts of religion, not just thinking *about* them.

The first parties guilty of the vice of eliminating religion typify our most celebrated post-colonial theorists – Said, Spivak, Asad, and their imitators in the study of religion, such as Russell McCutcheon or Tim Fitzgerald. They want to be so critical of religion that they seek utterly to *eliminate* it from their scientific vocabularies as well as from the world of cultural "things." Recall Said's reluctance to treat Islam as a religion in his orientalist critiques. McCutcheon falls right into line, saying: "I must be clear on one important point: there is no such thing as a specifically religious social formation" (McCutcheon 2001). Similarly, Asad and his followers refuse to allow that religion can be used in cross-cultural comparison at all. At best, for them, religion is a culture-bound term of discourse originating in the West, and not something that names a cultural fact outside the ambit of the West.

The second post-modern vice consists in making such a virtue of being *critical* of our concept of religion, that the perpetrators never get round to employing critical categories to study religion. The problem here is not whether or how to be critical of our categories. That is a good thing in which I have taken eager part. Thus, in his "'Religion' and the Citizen's Unrequited Desires: Chips from the Religion Industry's Workshop" (McCutcheon 2003, ch. 11), for example, McCutcheon forcefully proposes an agreeable *critical* program for at least part of the "future of the study of religion." This "lies in the direction of a thoroughly self-reflexive historicization of the very existence of this socio-cognitive category [of religion] regardless its definition." Fine. But scholars like McCutcheon go no further. McCutcheon makes criticism an end in itself. Thus, in *Manufacturing Religion*, he titles an entire chapter subsection, "The Study of Religion *Is* the Study of Theories and Methodologies" (McCutcheon 1997, p. 194). "Is"? Yes, McCutcheon means precisely what he says: criticism is an end in itself, and the appropriate end of religious studies.

To grasp what McCutcheon means, compare the idea of thinking *about* a concept – "religion" – with actually thinking *with* a concept of religion! McCutcheon seems so enamored of critical dissatisfaction with concepts of religion, notably Eliade's idea of religion as "autonomous" of all other aspects of culture, that he can see no further. If readers think I exaggerate, then they should look to see whether, after being critical of, say, Eliade's concept of religion, McCutcheon goes on to employ such a resultant reformed concept of religion. I do not overstate this point. Has McCutcheon written one thing on any religion – or on anything one could call a "religion" – under any *conceptual construction* whatsoever? Thus, I believe it is fair to observe that some of our post-modern theorists devote themselves to thinking about the concept of religion, but with no intention of ever putting any such concept to use in the world of things – the world of the "science of religion."

Now, some thinkers of this sort retort that the reason they never publish on anything conceivably called "religion" is that no such thing exists. I have Tim Fitzgerald in mind. If Fitzgerald argues that the particular Western historical origins of "religion" disqualify it from being a good cross-cultural comparative term, then he should tell us why terms he uses, such as "politics" or "power" or "culture," are not as well (Fitzgerald 1997, 2000). Why does religion "exist" any more or less than these analytic terms of his preference? If Fitzgerald's point is to eliminate "religion" as a cross-cultural comparative term, then he might tell us why these other terms he privileges somehow escape the same fate. The problem of appropriate cross-cultural comparative language is real, but not insoluble. It is no answer to say that because a term has a particular historical origin it is disqualified from serving as a good cross-cultural comparative term. After all, every term has some particular historical origins.

Unlike the post-modern eliminationists, some of us actually want to think *with* religion, rather than incessantly *about* it, or *without* it. We want to use the concept, which we have struggled so hard to revise and reform in order to free it from its historical particularities, to explore the world. We want to build – to "construct" – despite the fact that we know all our constructs are contestable. Readers will note that all the great theorists in this volume also thought *with* some concept of religion, however we might want to *revise* it, not just incessantly (critically) *about* the term "religion." They in effect took the risk of having their concept of religion become conceptually obsolete as time went on. But that didn't stop the long years of trial and error that have marked all scientific enterprises – the study of religion included. What I am saying is that we should appreciate the theoretical contingency and imperfection of all our constructs, but without giving up on construction. Think about the constructs of Isaac Newton, Darwin, or Galileo. Immortal? Eternal? Set in concrete? Hardly. But have not these constructs moved science along? Newton had a pretty good run, as far as I can tell. Darwin and Galileo haven't done so badly either. The same goes for our theories in religious studies and the work we do with such "imperfect" notions as *religion*.

How to Think *with* "Religion," and Not Just *about* It

It would clearly be unwise for scholars of religion to follow post-modern thinkers like Asad or Said down the path of eliminating the concept of religion. At the very least, to eliminate the term "religion," or to dismiss the category, from our attempts to make sense of the world would court disciplinary suicide. What could it mean to call oneself a student of "religion" and, at the same time, seek to eliminate the term? Are departments of religious studies needed if "religion" can be eliminated as an analytic concept, as a concept fit for cross-cultural comparison? What, similarly, is the point of programs in political science, if we think that the idea of "politics" is just some culturally relative concept that cannot be applied to non-Western contexts? This is not to refuse being critical or skeptical of our categories, "religion" included. We do need to take responsibility for them. And so we should always be ready to think *about* our concepts, critically and skeptically, and thus be open to their revision, even if it be radical – eliminationist – revision.

On top of these arguments, eliminating "religion" from academic discourse makes no sense whatever today. Especially in the world that has come to be after 1989, and the collapse of the Soviet Union and communist regimes of eastern Europe and Yugoslavia, the idea of religion has become more useful than ever. As we know, the disappearance of the world order known as the Cold War has given way to what some have called the New World *Dis*order. I would argue, however, that instead of the chaos that the term "disorder" indicates, new principles of order now rule. And although there may be many kinds of new principles of order, many cluster about what cries out to be called a "religious" order. Instead of nation-states, such as Yugoslavia, we now have states organized in fact around the traditional religious affiliations of their citizens. Orthodox Serbians, Roman Catholic Croatians, Muslim Bosnians and Kosovars have replaced what had been for decades the "socialist" Yugoslavia. Insofar as such traditional religious designations persist to anchor personal and collective identities, we can say that "religion" has replaced "politics" as the principal organizing idea in the former Yugoslavia. If some think I am mistaken in describing the new principles governing order as religious, then the burden of proof rests with them. What better term names the principles of identity in a greater part of the New World *Disorder* than "religion" or "religious"?

At the very least, because of such examples we need to better *understand* what it means to make something like religion the organizing principle of citizenship in a nation instead of various economic or political notions. What is that thing called religion that claims to provide the basis for national identity? If a religion is, as I sometimes suspect, nothing more than a special mode of social organization, what is special about that mode of organizing society? How does it change the way nations behave over against those that call themselves "secular," for instance? Many in the West think, for example, that because Iran is just such an explicitly religious nation – the *Islamic* Republic of Iran – Muslim beliefs and practices will dictate its behavior on the world stage. These same observers worry, in particular, that, because Iranian Shia Islam places high value of sacrifice and martyrdom, it may wage war in a more extreme fashion, say, than nations valuing the sanctity of the individual. Recall, for example, Durkheim's argument precisely for this idea of the human individual as sacred in "Individualism and the Intellectuals" (Durkheim 1898). Indeed, Iranian tactics of futile human wave attacks against Iraq in the 1980–88 war suggest a certain radical valuation of the Islamic Republic or nation-state above the individual. Extending this line of discussion beyond Iran, the phenomenon of so-called "suicide bombers" in the Middle East and Sri Lanka has strengthened the view that "religious" violence will be more extreme – "fanatical" – than the violence perpetrated by secular states. Is this the time, then, to eliminate religion from public discourse, and thus from academic discourse, as post-modern theorists like Talal Asad argue? Whatever one's bad feelings about Western missionaries, or whatever anger is felt because of the predations of Western imperialism aided and abetted by Christianity, eliminating the use of analytic terms like "religion" may hinder our understanding of the world.

Less still is to be gained by eliminating academic programs in the study of religion. The university cannot even live up to its name without embracing the universe of human experience, a sizable portion of which is religion. Understanding and explaining religion is as essential to the mission of the university as understanding and explaining art, politics, society, or the human psyche.

It's the "Religion," Stupid!

I want to conclude this book by urging us to consider rebalancing our thinking against present-day post-modern fashions toward the use of the analytic term, "religion." To be sure, the lessons of post-modern conceptual criticism must be retained. What I mean by such rebalancing may be put in terms of post-colonial studies of the religion of immigrants. Now, for example, that post-colonial researchers have brought to light the lives of Guatemalan immigrants to Los Angeles, let us say, what is their "religion"? What does it mean to call attention to their religion over and above just referring to their several beliefs and practices? Is there something coherent and/or systematic about the whole of their religious lives, as opposed, say, to their political or economic lives? How does their religion compare or contrast, for instance, with that of Karen Brown's Haitian immigrants in Brooklyn? Does such a comparison, and others as well, point toward new category of religion that we might call "immigrant religion," on the model of my comments about "slave religion" as such a new category? And how does that idea of religion compare with, say, so-called "world religions"? Notice that, unlike Eliade, I am not presuming any particular *a priori* concept of what a religion is. We would *discover* precisely what the religion, say of Guatemalan immigrants, was by exploring *a posteriori* the particulars of the religion of these immigrant communities first. Retaining the concept of "religion" need not, then, mean presuming some universal. It could well mean discovering the many ways people have of being religious.

Now, it is also understandable for faculty in an interdisciplinary field like religious studies to have loyalties to several different disciplinary foci – art, politics, economics, as well as race, sex, and post-colonial marginalization. That is not the problem. It is, rather, a source of our strength. It is, however, the lack of loyalty to the category of "religion" as an analytic tool that is the problem. What we lack is *attention* to how the "religious" perspective contributes to understanding and explaining things thought *not* to be religious. I tried to show how today's economic globalization owed a debt to religious legitimations in a recent article, "The Religion in Globalization" (Strenski 2004; see also Strenski 2003; Sutton 2006). There, I tried to identify how movements, ideas, and such that can be called "religious" laid the foundations of what we know today as economic globalization. In seeking the religious element in such a profoundly secular reality, I discovered that theories of natural law and the law of nations, articulated by early modern theologians in religious terms, did this work. Similarly, in my recent book, *Why Politics Can't Be Freed from Religion* (2010), I attempted an analogous effort but there deconstructing what we mean by politics led me to its religious legitimations in medieval European history. In departments of religious studies, and in religious studies scholarship, I think we need more such work showing the utility of the concept "religion" for understanding the world at large. That's what I mean by loyalty to the category "religion."

Foucault has made us think about "politics" in all sorts of overtly non-political contexts. Some Foucauldians even claim that "everything is political." "Freakonomics" has, in a way, tried to see economics in aspects of life far from the science that purports to explore the system by which goods and services are exchanged. So why not start thinking about the "religion" in everyday life, or the "religion" in areas of life heretofore thought far from religion as traditionally understood? In the religious studies profession, we need to balance off loyalty to the concept of "religion" against the loyalty we all have to other such fundamental categories as "culture" or "Asia" or "race" or "sex" or "ethnicity" or "the (post-colonial) Other."

Without at least as much loyalty to the category of "religion" as to our ancillary disciplinary categories, how can religious studies hang together as a department or discipline? The term "religious studies" would devolve into no more than an empty convenient label for "none of the above" or "other," more like majors in "liberal studies" or "interdisciplinary studies." In reality, a major like liberal studies differs little from the names we slap on teams in "flag football" or in "skins versus shirts." There, the team names have no meaning

other than "not the other guys." Majors such as these are egregious examples of the intellectual failure of nerve in today's university. Failure of nerve cannot be, and need not be, the fate of religious studies.

The array of interesting and consequential religion theorists we have met in this book should be evidence enough that the study of religion has a real and substantial history. As such religious studies can make a distinctive contribution to the humanities in the modern university, much as political science, art history, language, and literature departments do. One could hardly improve upon the following way a major American religious studies department makes the case for religious studies' contribution to the humanities:

> Much as Political Science constitutes study about the political process rather than the promotion and participation in specific party politics, descriptive and comparative study about religion as carried out in the publicly-funded university is therefore to be distinguished from religious (theological) forms of study ... Religious Studies is therefore a key component of the University's humanities curriculum. (University of Alabama 2004)

Religious studies should thus "bring 'religion' back in," if only to play its role in the cooperative venture that the modern university is at its best. Oddly enough, this clear affirmation of the utility of the term "religion" was penned by Russell McCutcheon some years after his eliminationist manifesto. One would like to know what has happened in the interval.

But what would that contribution be? The category "religion" cannot be an empty sign, if religious studies is to remain a viable discipline. Nor can we treat it as such without cost. Belonging to a department of religious studies should mean something. But that also means that the category "religion" needs compelling content. We need compelling reasons to take "religion" into consideration as we do our work. But what content would show how "religion" could be "brought back in"? In concluding this book, I wish to make explicit two answers to this question, which are already implicit in the theories and methods we have studied. First, we can "bring religion back in" by becoming more aware that in our specialized studies we are dealing with what I call "*problems of religion.*" As I shall show shortly, these questions transcend any specialized subject, and thus invite comparative study of religions. Second, we can also "bring religion back in" by paying attention to the ways religions cohere in distinctive unities. A religion is a "something," not a nothing: "religion" is not just a convenient label, but the name of an organic unity. First, then, to the way the problems of religion "bring religion back in," and thus show the distinctiveness of religious studies.

To Study Religion Is at Least to Study "Problems of Religion"

In the Introduction I listed a series of "problems of religion" that I argued constituted just such a common content. Some have argued that certain key terms or concepts unite our field. I disagree. Mere ideas or terms are not enough. What matters to the making of a discipline is a culture of discourse, discussion, and debate. What makes a discipline and distinguishes it from others is what people argue about. Those who count themselves as part of a community have puzzled about the same things – often for generations. Who, in particular, are they who quarrel over a common, but evolving, set of problems? Insofar as religion and the study of religion are concerned it is those thinkers who made up the first edition of this book – everyone from Jean Bodin in the sixteenth century to Mircea Eliade in the twentieth. Notably, it was not primarily their *answers* that made them part of the same team of religious studies ancestors. Disagreement was rampant among the thinkers who approached different problems. But that didn't matter to their being devoted to the study of religion. It was their pursuit of common *questions* or *problems* that incorporated them into a community we can call the *religious studies community*.

These religious studies folk argued common issues across the years, often referring back to earlier thinkers, either to oppose or agree with them. Max Müller opposed Tylor; Tylor recalled Hume, and opposed Herbert of Cherbury; Frazer took on both Tylor and Max Müller, as did Robertson Smith; the hermeneutics of biblical interpretation became the starting point for the phenomenological method of empathetic understanding and a part of the approach Max Weber took to understanding capitalism and religion; Eliade, Freud, and Durkheim looked back to Robertson Smith for guidance about such matters as purity and impurity, the sacred, totemism, and so on. And so on. Each generation influenced the next generation or provided foils against which to fashion new answers. Taken together, they literally constituted a *tradition* since, as the original Latin testifies, they "passed down" ideas from their generation to the next. Many asked questions such as, What was the original or first religion? Bodin, Cherbury, Max Müller, Frazer, Tylor, Durkheim, Eliade, and Freud all addressed it; and each gave a different answer, fully aware of what the others had said. Or some of our theorists puzzled about which things belonged in the class, "religion." We may also recall how in the early period of our discipline, Bodin and Cherbury wondered whether all religions were equally true, or perhaps only one was. And if only one was true, which was it? Was it the religion of one of Bodin's invited guests, or perhaps it was another religion altogether more fundamental than all these particular religions? It is not hard to see how the inquiry about Natural Religion arose in this way. Maybe *all* the religions were equally false? But, in another way, perhaps each was partially true at the same time, insofar as it approximated Natural Religion? If one were, for example, to stage a debate among adherents of the different "religions" in Bodin's time, whom should one invite? Could Buddhists have been invited to Bodin's famous sixteenth-century dialogue of religions – even if he knew of their existence? Little or nothing was known of the Buddhists then, and even if something had been known of them, wouldn't Buddhist disinterest in the existence of God disqualify them from inclusion in a dialogue about "religion"? Who else would we want to invite in our time? Nationalists? Stalinists? Fascists? Humanists? Later, the evolutionists launched an entirely new line of questioning by raising a matter overlooked by earlier religious thinkers – that of religious *change*. Did religions change, and if so, do they change according to any regular principles, such as stepwise evolution in the case of Tylor, Frazer, and Robertson Smith, or by a process of historical degeneration, such as Max Müller claimed. Freud and Durkheim broached the problems involved in seeking to know whether religion is essentially personal or instead essentially social. Durkheim's inclusion of Buddhism in the list of things under the category "religion" also introduced the additional problem of deciding whether all religions required a belief in God. Earlier thinkers had more or less neglected this issue, or simply assumed that all religions had a "god."

In the same spirit of questioning, we have seen in Part IV how the post-modern scholars brought their own new problems to the table. They too felt that earlier thinkers had neglected or overlooked particular matters they took seriously about religion – such as the special role played by race, sex/gender, and cultural otherness. But behind their specifically focused work, I want us to see general cross-cultural and comparative questions, my so-called "problems of religion," just waiting to be made more explicit. Why, as I asked in the beginning of chapter 16, do men seem to dominate in religion – *generally* across cultures, times, and places? How would Karen Brown's revelations about Mama Lola as a female leader for Haitians challenge that assumption? Are religions where the god is "male" *universally* more prone to violence than those where a female goddess rules? Do women really require the goddess – a sex-specific deity – as Carol Christ believes, or are her arguments just peculiar to her own personal discontents with Christianity? Or perhaps the rise of sexless and genderless religious foci, such as Atman-Brahman, Nirvana, the Dao, suggests that religions generally evolve beyond conceiving deities with sex and gender?

The attempt to address these and similar problems is the beginning of what we call *theories*. This is not to say that in the spotty history of human curiosity these questions never occurred to believers, or that they were only asked in the West. It is only to say that it was not until the recent invention of religious studies in the West that a systematic discipline addressed to approaching these questions came to be. It is also to observe that the study of religion did not arise *everywhere* in the West either. The Netherlands, Switzerland, France, and Germany led, while Spain, Portugal, Greece, Ireland, and others lagged well behind. Therefore, I am not making some sort of claim to Occidental civilizational superiority. I merely call

attention to the obvious fact that no non-Western civilization has created sustaining institutions or "schools" for the study of religion. Singular individuals, like the philosopher, Al-Ghazali, at the height of the Abbasid (Muslim) Empire in the eleventh to twelfth centuries, made a start with his remarkable personal experimentation with different religions. The publication of Al-Ghazali's account of these experiments might have set in motion more studies of the same kind. But it did not. In the late sixteenth century at about the same time that Jean Bodin was writing his famous dialogue of religions, Emperor Akbar of India sponsored inter-religious dialogue among the representatives of the many religions in his realm not unlike that recorded by Bodin. But these first efforts too failed to take root. Nor did any of the other great world civilizations support lasting cultural forms, lines of inquiry, or major syllabi of questions about religion, and place them at the center of attention in their universities. That happened only in the West.

In the same way, no Western country initiated the first schools of mathematics and the scientific study of language. These developed first in ancient India and the Arab world, and not in Latin, Frankish, or Celtic Europe. Thus, the fact that religious studies is a Western invention should never be a reason for cultural arrogance. It is only a bland historical fact that could well have been otherwise, just as the origins of algebra, chemistry, and such might have been elsewhere than in "the East." The study of religion came to be, as I have tried to illustrate throughout this book, because history made it possible that religion became the sustained object of general, cross-cultural, and comparative questions and problems. Historians of mathematics and science ask themselves similar questions about their Indian and Arabian origins. Why didn't algebra get "discovered" in Elizabethan England or Jean Bodin's Paris, but rather in the Middle East? We have much, then, to understand about how things we take for granted came to be. Why and how, then, did religious studies come to be? My answer has been to emphasize *understanding* theories and theorists historically. To answer the question "Why did they think they were right?" we need to know some facts about theorists and how the times in which they lived gave them confidence to address such problems as they did.

The *problems* of religion are the ultimate "stuff" with which religious studies concerns itself. As an agenda of issues, taken together they are what make religious studies a discipline among others. They show the distinctive set of defined interests that unite our field. By being aware of them we realize one way of "bringing religion back in." But another way to "bring religion back in" is to appreciate the unity of those things we call "religions." What makes something we identify as a religion such a thing? How do we know that a religion really constitutes something whole and unified? The classic phenomenologists, from Tiele to Otto to Van der Leeuw, addressed just such a question by trying to demonstrate how religion had a logic of its own – how its various parts fit together to make religious sense, how the parts fit together to form religious "wholes." Like students of language, they wanted to uncover the "grammar" of religion by laying out the constituent parts in some systematic unity. I would like to conclude by bringing classic phenomenology up to date in the work of one of the greatest contemporary religious studies scholars, Ninian Smart. His work, too, attempts to produce just such a "grammar" of religion, and one that nicely ties up many of the themes of this book by sketching the bigger picture of how we can begin to understand and explain the religious world. Smart thus shows us yet another way to "bring religion back in."

Ninian Smart's "Dialectical" Phenomenology "Brings Religion Back In"

Ninian Smart (1927–2001) was one of the most important theorists and practical promoters of the study of religion in the English-speaking world of the late twentieth century. In global reputation, he ranks with a Mircea Eliade or Wilfrid Cantwell Smith as someone who conceived a distinctive approach to the study of religion, related in a long list of publications over a fifty-year period. In the original edition of this book, I treated Smart among the classic phenomenologists of religion. I have chosen to separate his theoretical ideas out here in the Conclusion to argue that his work deserves to be seen as on the cutting edge of the study of religion. If anyone has given a sound theoretical basis for "bringing

religion back in," it is Smart. If any thinker shows how to negotiate the treacherous terrain of trying to come to a "common mind" about religion, Smart would have to be among them.

A good deal of the uniqueness of Smart's theorizing about religion can be traced to his philosophical education in post-war Oxford. Ordinary language philosophy under Smart's tutor, John Austin, was a dominant influence, as was the philosophy of the later Wittgenstein. Philosophy of religion and philosophical theology were also in style. But although the Oxford philosophers felt free to make all sorts of claims about religion, they in fact knew very little at all about it, and even less about the diversity of religions. Philosophy of religion was, then, not well informed about its subject-matter. This led Smart along two paths of inquiry. First, he attacked the smug ignorance of his philosopher colleagues, and argued that doing philosophy of religion required actual *knowledge of religion* – a somewhat revolutionary thing to say at the time! Any serious conceptual or theoretical thinking about religion, insisted Smart, must rest upon a solid basis of knowledge about the cross-cultural and comparative study of religion. At this time, Smart immersed himself in the scriptures of the great world religions as well as in the works of the few historians and phenomenologists of religion in print or writing at the time. An approach to religious studies well informed by factual and structural knowledge about the world's religions, then, became one of the marks of Smart's conception of religious studies. Smart's first book, *Reasons and Faiths*, showcased much of what he felt was needed to reform the philosophy of religion. Second, while he severely castigated his philosopher colleagues for their ignorance, the *rigor* of the kind of philosophy engendered by the Oxford style of linguistic analysis remained a mark of Smart's approach. Conceptual analysis and intellectual rigor became characteristic of his influence. Smart brought this kind of expertise to bear on several areas of the study of religion, but most significantly on the phenomenology of religion. There, he sought to inject both a dynamism absent from the work of the classic phenomenologists and as well a way of thinking about religions as systematically interrelated totalities.

Having set his theoretical bearings in these ways, Smart built major institutions to actualize his vision of religious studies. He founded the first department of religious studies in the United Kingdom at the University of Lancaster in the mid-1960s. From the mid-1970s, he shared his time with the religious studies department at the University of California, Santa Barbara, one of the leading American departments in the field. Smart's students can be found in university teaching positions the world over, continuing his example of cross-cultural and comparative studies of religion. Shortly after arriving in Lancaster, Smart founded what has been, and continues to be, one of the leading academic journals for the study of religion, *Religion*. In the course of his illustrious career, Smart did the usual number of distinguished lectures, and received numerous honors for his accomplishments.

Smart's revisions of the phenomenology of religion aimed at finding a way all the better to grasp religious totality or wholeness. I am appealing to Smart's work here, because if we can show that religions form coherent structures or unities, as he did, this would give us reasons for "bringing religion back into" areas where it has been discounted or overlooked. Smart also gives us tools with which to manage a discourse about religion that shows great promise as the stuff of a "common mind" about religion. For Smart, seeing religion as a whole does not differ from how we see "the economy." This is not because we can tangibly "handle" the economy, or literally "see" it, but because economists have shown that the "life" of the distribution of goods and services follows certain rules, conforms to certain structural demands, forms different kinds of totalities or wholes. Thus, we talk of "*demand* economies" or "*command* economies" because they name different *schemes* or *systems* of organizing the distribution of goods and services. They form "wholes" of different kinds according to the different rules by which they are put together. Command economies *direct* the production of goods and services, whole demand economies allow the market *freedom*. They also seek different goals. Most command economies seek to maximize equal distributions of wealth instead of allowing freedom to make wealth as one might wish, while demand economies accept, and perhaps even celebrate, inequality and instead maximize freedom to make wealth as one chooses. Smart wants to encourage our seeing religion in much the same way. On this

analogy, what would the rules be that govern different schemes of religious life? Is Buddhism, say, like a *demand* economy, while Islam would be rather like a *command* economy? Both could count, for example, as "economies" (that is, religions), but they would operate according to different sets of rules, and maybe even seek different results. For Buddhists, meditation occupies the spiritual methods of the monk, while Muslims insist upon prayer and action in the world. For Buddhists, the ultimate goal is not a divinity, as Allah is for Muslims, but a transcendental state, Nirvana. If our comparison holds, then, what rules govern these two in the methods by which they pursue their different ultimates, and why do they place different goals at the center of religious life? How do Buddhism and Islam, respectively, hang together and form wholes? It is that sort of strategy that Smart's updated, dynamic phenomenology pursues.

Readers may recall that the classic phenomenologists, like Van der Leeuw, aspired to show the same thing, but left the picture of religion rather static or incomplete. Otto, for example, identified numinous experience as a core religious fact, yet left it isolated from other parts of religion. It was, then, no wonder that Otto's work was often just regarded as a kind of *psychology* of religion, rather than a total picture of the way religion works. Also, Van der Leeuw tried to say more about religion than to affirm Otto's numinous experience, as he did. To his credit, he produced a kind of *anatomy* of religion that listed Otto's idea of the holy among other kinds of religious experiences. But Van der Leeuw's anatomy, like medical studies in anatomy, was more like a biopsy. It laid out the bits and pieces of religion – experiences, saviors, gods, powers, prophets, mystics, and such – as if they were items "etherized upon a table." It was also rather like seeing religion as a language – but without ever hearing it spoken. Religion took on a rather static form of items classified under their rubrics, or a language as represented in a dictionary or grammar book. This view of religion left it lacking life, even though it showed how its parts might be classified systematically.

Smart found this static approach of classic phenomenology unsatisfactory. He instead sought to further the work of the classic phenomenologists by infusing life into their anatomical analyses. For Smart, religion should be seen as a dynamically structured "whole." In his view, it would be made up of seven mutually interconnected or "dialectically" interactive "dimensions" such as myths, rituals, doctrines, ethics, social forms and organizations, emotions and experiences, and material or esthetic elements. Now, although each of these dimensions may exist independently or in other domains of human culture, when they are clustered into an interactive complex, Smart thinks we can speak usefully of a "religion." This is religion in organic form, alive. It is religion defined by its social institutions, but in organic relation to the architecture of the buildings and physical property housing them. This is also how religion lives through its clergy, say, as they teach a set of sharply defined beliefs, lead a community of devotees, or administer a program of prescribed rituals. Religion here is also constituted by a group of adherents, living an experiential and emotional life involving a world beyond the material one. Smart is not only concerned with the "parts" of religion, or even the "sum of the parts," but to the "whole" of religion, which – like all wholes – is always greater than the sum of its parts – and alive.

Some examples of religious wholes drawn from what we have already read earlier might help bring home these points. Weber's approach to understanding the rise of capitalism suggests it doesn't just stand alone, but rather is connected with religion in this case. But, on top of this, Weber also, in effect, taught that religious *beliefs* about the disposal of wealth fit together intricately with the new capitalist lifestyle. To take one example, those fundamental Calvinist beliefs married with certain attitudes to *ritual*. In particular, the new Calvinist doctrines of predestination and divine immediacy meant that rituals were unnecessary. Likewise, the spare and disciplined *moral life* of the typical Calvinist made sense once we presumed those basic beliefs and grew in a religion in which rituals of mediation or indulgence were simply denied. Much of this complex of *beliefs* and *morality* was then reflected tellingly in the spare, unadorned architecture of Calvinist churches. See how Calvinist religion then formed a consistent whole?

Another example of how we can "bring religion back in" by using Smart's dynamic phenomenology comes from our chapter on Freudian interpretations of religion. To see how Smart's

idea of religion forming an interconnected, organic whole works to support explanations and understandings of religion, we can put this example in the form of a question. To wit, why did a *movement* for priestly celibacy – a *ritual* obligation of church discipline – become popular in fourth- and fifth-century CE Rome? We know that priestly celibacy has not always been the rule for the Catholic clergy. Indeed, if we think of Jesus' apostles as the first priests, many were married. Also, in the Eastern traditions today, a married priesthood remains the custom. So it is not just something natural, something not requiring explanation. Priestly celibacy needs to be explained and the reasons for its existence need to be understood. How does Smart help?

Smart's dynamic phenomenological approach suggests we try to understand and explain the popularity of the ritual of priestly celibacy in terms of connections with other dimensions of religion. We should try to show how one aspect of religion reinforced others, and how, therefore, religion hangs together as an interconnected, organic "whole." Most obviously, we can begin by noting that such a ritual obligation is the product of a *movement*, and that movements are kinds of fluid *social organizations*. We can think, for example, of social "movements" like the Arab Spring that erupted in places like Egypt. Something similar seems to have been responsible for the increase in popularity of priestly celibacy in ancient Christian Rome. So, in this way, we can immediately connect the dimensions of *ritual* and *social organization*. Priestly celibacy, the claim goes, was driven by a movement. What next?

What else was current in the context of the time and place in question? Carroll claims, for example, that *artistic* images of the suffering Jesus on the cross first appeared then and there (Carroll 1992). Likewise, we also find increased *doctrinal* emphasis upon the theological interpretations of the Eucharist as reproducing Jesus' bloody "sacrificial" death. Adding yet another of Smart's dimensions to the mix, it would be interesting if the gospel stories – the *myths* – recounting these parts of Jesus' life also became more salient then as well. Smart might note from this that we could also observe that the *artistic/material* and *mythical* dimensions of Christianity in Rome of that time seemed to reinforce *doctrinal* beliefs, such as those having to do with the status of the Eucharist. Now, if we could find a connection between these *artistic/material*, *mythical*, and *doctrinal* facts and the religious *social* movement and *ritual* observance of celibacy, we would have powerful evidence that the religion of this time constituted a "whole." We would also see that celibacy was some sort of by-product of a larger set of cultural changes. We would have five different dimensions of religion – one of them the ritual practice of priestly celibacy – all reinforcing one another. Can we do this?

Remember that Carroll thinks he knows why we can. He reasoned as follows. If we see celibacy as a ritual of the inflicting of suffering upon the person denying themselves sexual pleasure, then we could see how that fit with the rise of *mythical* and *graphic* representations of Jesus, and in doctrine as him denying himself normal human pleasure and enduring suffering for religious reasons. These images of the renunciant, suffering, sacrificial Jesus might, in turn, model an ideal of self-denial for the new priests. What we might then want to understand is the origins of the social movement that seems to have given rise to this already closely interconnected complex. Why was there such a religious *social* movement then and there?

Here is where Carroll argues his Freudian, some would say "extreme," view that the psychological make-up of recruits for this social movement of renunciation and celibacy resulted from their father-ineffective rearing. Briefly, without a male model of maturity, these young boys relied on their mothers to model strength and maturity. Strong identification with a female predisposed them for worship of a female divinity, such as Mary, or earlier, Cybele. But identification with a female also produced conflicts of sexual identity as the boys became young men. Overt identification threatened these newly pubescent boys with embarrassment among their peers. And so these female-identified young men did two things. First, they exaggerated their maleness – hence the phenomenon of machismo in the Mediterranean. Second, they suppressed overt identification with their mothers, in classic Freudian style. Taken together, overt identification gave way to *spiritual* identification with a goddess, such as Cybele, or someone like Mary, who in many ways *functioned* as a goddess. In

their devotion to the Marian "goddess," Carroll finally argues that these young men adopted a renunciant style of ritual observance – to wit, *celibacy*. With suppression of overt identification came the *religious experience* of guilt which haunted their memories of that unnatural, even sinful, overt identification with someone of the opposite sex, their mothers.

And *that* is how someone might understand and explain the occurrence of ritual celibacy among the Roman Catholic priesthood: by appealing to the complex of relationships among dimensions of religion, and stimulated with Freudian theory. In this respect, Carroll's approach to understanding and explaining aspects of Marian devotion might also remind us of another earlier discussion of the religious "grammar," so to speak, of the notion of "lord" in Christian worship. There, for example, "lord" is related to "ritual" acts of "devotion," "prayer," "sacrifice," "meditation," "worship," and so on. And, depending upon what kind of "lord" was worshiped, other dimensions of religion would change as well. Was the "lord" human ("incarnate") like Attis, Jesus, or Krishna, or only spiritual or "heavenly," like the Amitabha Buddha or the Bodhisattva Avalokitesvara? Different from these, perhaps the "lord" was beyond all conception, and thus "transcendent," like Allah or Yahweh, and such? If so, how would these differences inform a religion's "mythology" or the style of religious "experience" and "emotion"? Can one imagine a corresponding frivolity and fun, attached to worship of *Lord* Krishna, as in the *Holi* festival of misrule and riotous revelry, in the celebration of Lord Jesus' resurrection? Both celebrate incarnate "lords" in positive ways, but do so in radically different ways. Why? Or consider the much greater difference when comparing the numinous dynamism of a radiant "lord" Krishna in the *Bhagavad Gita* with an experience of the transcendent tranquility of a lordly Buddha? Can we likewise expect that religions emphasizing the "lordly" qualities of their focus will express them in certain forms of materiality – in the architecture of their sacred buildings, or, as we have seen in the graphic arts brought into our discussion of Otto and the numinous, in the graphic and musical dimensions of religious life? Likewise, and in Smart's "dialectical" style, would not certain styles of ritual, myth, material representation, and so on induce a sense of "lordship," even to the inducing of certain experiences of numinous lordliness? This same series of questions can be submitted to any particular religious context in which lordliness figures, whether that be ancient Israel or comparatively – across contexts – such as ancient Israel compared to ancient India. Given that elemental religious categories might be quite numerous, the kinds of relationships open to questioning of this and other kinds are literally infinite.

I hope that at least one effect of these demonstrations might be to help readers see how Smart's ingenuity "brings religion back in." I am tempted to borrow E.M. Forster's famous epigraph: "Only connect!" There really are things out there rightly called "religions," waiting to be explored, waiting for understanding and explanation of how they are connected within themselves, and how they connect with the world. Far from being a "nothing," religion is very much a "something"! In a way, this entire book has been nothing else than a record of how, over the past 500 years, people we call "theorists" have plotted these connections, and in doing so have tried to understand and explain religion.

References

Carroll, M.P. 1992. *The Cult of the Virgin Mary: Psychological Origins*. Princeton: Princeton University Press.

Durkheim, É. 1898. "Individualism and the Intellectuals." In W.S.F. Pickering (ed.), *Durkheim on Religion*. London: Routledge & Kegan Paul.

Eagleton, T. 1990. *The Significance of Theory*. Oxford: Blackwell.

Fitzgerald, T. 1997. "A Critique of "Religion" as a Cross-Cultural Category." *Method and Theory in the Study of Religion* 9(2): 91–110.

Fitzgerald, T. 2000. *The Ideology of Religious Studies*. New York: Oxford University Press.

McCutcheon, R.T. 1997. *Manufacturing Religion: The Discourse on Sui Generis Religion and the Politics of Nostalgia*. New York: Oxford University Press.

McCutcheon, R.T. 2001. *Critics Not Caretakers: Redescribing the Public Study of Religion*. Albany: SUNY.

McCutcheon, R.T. 2003. *The Discipline of Religion: Structure, Meaning, Rhetoric*. London: Taylor & Francis.

Strenski, I. 2003. "Economic Globalization and Natural Law Theology." *Australian Religious Studies Review* 16(2): 115–124.

Strenski, I. 2004. "The Religion in Globalization." *Journal of the American Academy of Religion* 72(3): 631–652.

Strenski, I. 2010. *Why Politics Can't Be Freed from Religion: Radical Interrogations of Religion, Power and Politics*. Oxford: Wiley-Blackwell.

Sutton, J. 2006. ""Minimal Religion" and Mikail Epstein's Interpretation of Religion in Late-Soviet and Post-Soviet Russia." *Studies in East European Thought* 58: 107–135.

University of Alabama. 2004. http://rel.as.ua.edu/humansciences.html. Tuscaloosa: University of Alabama Department of Religious Studies.

Index

aboriginal Australians, 136, 137, 234
  Intichiuma ritual, 139
Abrahamic tradition, 2, 10, 14, 15–16, 39–40, 226
Ackerman, Robert, 111
African-American Religion archive, 177
African Americans, 172, 173, 177–8, 184
Age of Discovery, 14
Agni, Vedic god of fire, 39, 41, 46
agnosticism, 34, 41, 134
Alabama, University of, 246
American Academy of Religion, 206
ancient Greece, 107, 114, 159
  goddesses, 70, 72, 113, 116, 211–12
  languages, 36
  literature, 159
  myths, 112
  religion/culture, 9, 29, 36, 39, 59, 66, 210
ancient Hebrew religion, 42, 56, 58, 60, 61, 71, 221
  and Arabic peoples, 57, 58, 59
  and paganism, 221
  prophetic age, 59, 131
  scriptures, 37, 56, 57, 59, 226–7
ancient Rome, 69
  compared to other cultures, 39, 69
  early Christianity in, 251–2
  history, 40
  languages, 36
  literature, 159
  Marian cult, 114–16

  myths, 69–70
  religions, 36
Anglican Church
  opposition to Max Müller, 34
animals
  sacrifices, 111, 112, 139–40
  as totems, 111, 112, 132
  worship, 59
animism, 42, 45–53
  and Spiritualism, 47
L'Année Sociologique journal, 132
anthropology, 45, 51, 53
  of religion, 29, 53, 66, 200
  see also ethnography
anti-Semitism, 41, 108
  see also Dreyfus Affair
apartheid, 171, 223
Aphrodite, Greek goddess of love, 212–13
Aquinas, Thomas, 196
  continues Aristotle's view of women as incomplete
    men, 196
Arabia
  cultural influence, 217
  as primitive culture, 57, 230
Arab–Israeli War (1967), 225
  effect on Said, 224, 225, 228
architecture, religious, 251, 252
Aristotle, 196
  Generation of Animals, 196

Understanding Theories of Religion: An Introduction, Second Edition. Ivan Strenski.
© 2015 Ivan Strenski. Published 2015 by John Wiley & Sons, Ltd.

Arjuna, Hindu myth of, 87–8, 161
art
    cave, 49
    as cultural marker, 9
    as propaganda, 176
Aryanism, 40, 41
    patriarchy, 210
    and racism, 41–2
Asad, Talal, 219, 220, 222, 228, 230, 232–5, 237–8
    biography, 234, 235
    eliminating "religion," 232, 233–4, 243, 245
    and Geertz, 235
    influence of Foucault, 232, 238
    as reformer of religion, 232–3
    works: *Formations of the Secular*, 232; *Genealogies of Religion*, 232, 234
asceticism, 98, 117
    and civilization, 125
    religious, 97, 100, 101, 104, 106, 117, 199
    Roman cults, 116
    worldly, 94, 98, 99, 100, 101, 102, 103, 104, 117, 130
atheism, 36, 134, 135, 179
atheistic humanism, 120
Attis myth, 21, 70, 72–3, 113
Austin, John, 249
Australia *see* aboriginal Australians
autonomy of religion, 81–2, 83, 84, 86, 107, 147

Bacon, Francis, 17
Balder, Norse hero, 68–9, 70–1
Barkin, Kenneth, 175, 176
Bartchy, Scott, 192, 207
    feminist, 192
Bataille, Georges, 49, 139
bathhouses, San Francisco, 159
Baumgarten, Hermann, 95
Baur, Ferdinand Christian, 27, 94
behaviorism, 108, 125, 126, 127, 160, 166
Bell, Catherine, 167
Bellah, Robert, 142
Benavides, Gustavo, 167, 168
Bentham, Jeremy, 160
Berkeley, CA, 159, 178
Berlin, Sir Isaiah, 227
Bhabha, Homi, 231
Bhagavad Gita, 87, 252
Bible, the
    criticism *see* biblical criticism
    discrepancies, 25
    focus of religiosity, 55
    as historical document, 33, 55–6
    insensitivity to Israel's defeated enemies, 225, 227
    origins of, 25–6
    patriarchy in, 206–8
    and totalitarianism, 227

biblical criticism, 18–19, 23–4, 25
    and confessionalism, 20, 24
    and context, 24
    and factual truth, 26
    historical-critical, 20–1, 34
    literal interpretations, 21
    and invention of printing, 23
    see also Higher Criticism
biblical literalism, 35
Black church, critiques (William D. Hart), 183–4
Black emancipation, 179, 185, 225
    see also racism; slavery
Black religion, 172–3, 180–3
    agent of social control, 183
    archive *see* African-American Religion Archive
    conservatism, 177
    eschatology, 179, 185
    formative rituals, 182
    methodology, 173, 177
    as "slave religion," 180, 182, 184
    spirituals *see* Black spirituals
Black religious studies, 174, 176, 180, 185–6
Black spirituals, 175, 182, 185, 224
Bloch, Marc, 85
Bodin, Jean, 2, 10, 14–16, 19, 247
    and civil war, 15
    Colloquium of the Seven, 15, 16
    and French law, 15
    methodology, 16
Boers of South Africa, 224–5
Brixham cave, Torbay, 49
Brown, Dan, *The Da Vinci Code*, 26
Brown, Karen McCarthy, 172, 177, 190, 197, 199–204
    and Christianity, 209
    "conversion" to Vodou, 202–3, 209, 213
    and Haley's *Roots*, 177
    Mama Lola, 172, 197, 199–201, 202, 203, 204, 209, 213
    methodology, 200–3, 205, 213, 218
    and post-modernism, 202
    and the quotidian, 201
    spiritual "marriage" with god Ogou, 202–3, 211
Buddha, the, 10, 118, 189, 252
Buddhism, 45–6, 243
    meditation, 145, 243, 250
    mission, 3–4
    nature of, 234, 242, 243, 247–8, 250
    a religion?, 2, 233, 234
    religious experience, 118
    sacred spaces, 145
Burton, Sir Richard, 57
Butler, Judith, 168–9
    and *Bodily Citations* (Armour and St. Ville), 168
Bynum, Caroline Walker, 189, 197, 198–9, 209, 233
    and phenomenology, 198

Caldwell, Sarah, 231
"calling," divine *see* vocation
Calvin, Jean, 103
Calvinism, 56, 99–100, 103–4, 251
 Bodin, 15
 doctrines, 103, 251
 Frazer, 65
 and ritual, 251
 Robertson Smith, 56, 62
 and suicide, 130
 Tiele, 81
 Weber, 96, 100, 103, 104, 175–6
Canaan, biblical land of, 224, 225
Canaanites as modern Palestinians, 224–6
capitalism
 defining, 96–7
 enterprise, 98–9
 and traditionalism, 101–2
 values, 98, 99–100, 102, 220
 see also Marxism; Weber
Capps, Walter, 142
Carnegie, Andrew, 98
Carol II, King of Romania, 152
Carroll, Michael, 113–17, 251, 252
 Freudian analysis, 107, 113–17, 129, 252
 on Marian cult, 113–15, 116, 210, 252
 on priestly celibacy, 251–2
categories, taking responsibility for, 241
cave art, 49
Chidester, David, 219, 220, 222–3, 230
 imperialist religion, 228
 influence of Foucault, 222, 223
 Savage Systems, 222
Christ, Carol P., 140, 190, 191, 197
 alienation from Christianity, 209–10
 and goddess religion, 211–13
 influence of Gimbutas, 210–11
 religious experience, 212–13
Christianity
 African American *see* Black religion
 Eucharist *see* Eucharist, Christian
 exclusivism, 17, 66, 70, 71, 80–1
 hidden paganism, 70–2, 113, 116
 inter-denominational conflict, 242
 medieval *see* medieval Europe
 missionary, 3, 234
 and monotheism, 226, 227
 and myth, 21, 28, 71–2, 73
 "primitive," 56
 progressive, 26, 57
 radical feminist critique, 204–5
 sacred spaces, 145
 secessionism, 226
 sexism, 206, 209–10
 role of women, 195–6, 197, 198–9,
  208, 209

 see also Calvinism; Jesus of Nazareth; Protestant
  Reformation; Roman Catholicism
Christmas Carol (Dickens), 97
Christy, Henry, 45
Church of Jesus Christ of Latter-Day Saints *see*
  Mormonism
Cioran, Emil, 150, 152
clairvoyance, 162
classification
 Foucault's, 221–2, 223–4
 phenomenology of religion, 90–1,
  96, 250
 post-colonial, 221–2, 223–4
 scientific, 221–2
Codreanu, Corneliu, 151, 152
 and the *Garda Fer*, 151
Cold War, end of, 244
color, and theories of religion, 171–3
common mind, formation of, 9–10, 26
 about the Bible, 27, 29
 about capitalism, 97
 in the church, 208
 confessional, 19, 20
 about faith, 10
 methodology, 10
 non-confessional, 20, 21, 22, 24, 25, 27
 purpose of, 27
 and quest for Natural Religion, 10, 13
 about religion, 9–10, 13, 14–17, 19–20, 22, 27, 48,
  50–1, 59, 68, 142, 143, 205, 242
 about sacred texts, 23, 24, 27, 34
 about social nature of religion, 134
comparative studies
 of linguistics, 29, 38, 43
 methodology, 51, 55, 69
 of religion *see* comparative study of religion
 of texts, 29
comparative study of religion, 38
 Bodin, 10, 15
 Frazer, 70–1
 Higher Criticism, 29
 history of, 9, 10, 35, 38, 43, 56
 Max Müller, 35, 38, 42, 43
 Robertson Smith, 55
 Smart, 249, 252
 Tylor, 51
 Weber, 94–5
 Wellhausen, 59
Cone, James B., 179, 180
 A Black Theology of Liberation, 180
confessional theology, 17, 19, 35, 79, 166
 constraints, 20, 24, 26, 48, 59
 divisions, 15
 return of, 180
Confucianism, 94, 234
Conrad, Joseph, 119

conscientious objectors, 242
Cosmic Tree, the, 145
creation, 146–7
  myths, 146
  and sacred time, 146–7
Creationism, and Darwinian evolution, 5
Crisis magazine, 176
critical studies of religion, vii, 26, 182
  post-modern, 241, 243
  see also Higher Criticism
cross-cultural comparison, 15, 167, 234, 244, 248
  hermeneutics, 181
  religion, 29, 38, 66, 81, 87, 184–5, 186, 243, 244, 248, 249, 250
  terminology, 217, 228, 232, 234
crucifixion, of Jesus, 61, 72, 114, 251
  compared to Attis myth, 72
cults, 90, 242
  of Cybele *see* Cybele cult
  Marian *see* Virgin Mary, cult of
cultural evolutionists, 49–50
  see also progressive evolution
Cybele cult, 116, 210
  connection to Marian cult, 70, 72, 113, 116, 252

Daly, Mary, 116, 190, 193, 197, 203
  influence, 205–6
  "Metapatriarchal Adventures and Ecstatic Travels," 206
Darmesteter, James, 131
Darwin, Charles, 48–9
  On the Origin of Species, 48
Dasgupta, Surendranath, 142
death
  and afterlife, 124
  Eliade's work, 148, 149
  Malinowski's work, 123–4
  mourning rituals, 123–4
  mystery of, 46, 68, 69
  as penalty for crime, 26, 229
  and resurrection, 22, 28, 68–9, 70–1, 73, 113
  sacrificial, 68; *see also* crucifixion
  as social event, 123
  see also funeral rites; myths
deconstruction, 166, 167, 168
Deists, 12, 17, 19, 22, 23
Delphy, Christine, 195
depth psychology, 143–4, 148
Derrida, Jacques, 166, 168
  Of Grammatology, 230
Deuteronomy, 226
deviance, 160
dharma
  concept of, 217
  religion as, 217, 218
  in Vedic religion, 42

Dilthey, Wilhelm, 89, 96, 126
"doctor knows best" position, 164–6
  Eliade, 144, 150
  Freud, 144
  Kristensen, 83
  Malinowski, 166
  modernism, 158, 165
Doniger, Wendy, 181, 193
Douglas, Mary, 56
  Purity and Danger, 56, 227
dreams
  interpretation of, 201
  as symbols, 46
  world of, 147, 148
Dreyfus, Alfred, 130, 132, 133
Dreyfus Affair, 130, 132, 133–4
Du Bois, W.E.B., 173–4
  biography, 174, 175–6
  fiction writer, 176
  German influences, 173, 175
  racial identity, 174–5
  rejection of science, 176
  social activism, 174, 176–7
  social research, 175, 177
  and Weber, 175, 176–7
  works: *Negro Church, The*, 175; *Philadelphia Negro, The*, 175
Dumézil, Georges, 43
Durkheim, Émile, 6, 129–40, 234
  anthropology of religion, 29
  biography, 130–2
  empathy, 135
  ethnography, 130, 136
  evolutionism, 136–7
  French nationalism, 131, 132–4, 150
  and human rights, 130, 133
  Judaism, 131
  and Malinowski, 122
  phenomenology, 91, 131–2
  philosophical influences, 131
  and primitivism, 136, 138–40
  in public life, 130, 132, 133
  reductionism, 134
  on religion and morality, 86
  on religious groups, 129–30
  religious liberalism, 131
  and Robertson Smith, 137–8
  and science of religion, 165, 166
  sociological approach, 129–30, 134–6
  and Tylor, 135–6
  works: "Concerning the Definition of Religious Phenomena," 91; *Elementary Forms of the Religious Life*, 132, 134, 135, 137, 139–40; "Individualism and the Intellectuals," 245; *Suicide*, 130, 133, 137, 138, 175
Durkheimian scholars, 90–1, 119

Eagleton, Terry, 4, 242
Easter
    date of, 113
    pagan influences, 113, 116
    resurrection theology, 185
Eastern Rite Catholicism, 185
economies, as analogy for religion, 250
education
    French system, 130–1, 159
    Dutch, system, 79, 80, 89
    and science of religion, 80–1
ego, Freudian concept of, 110–11, 125, 144
Egypt
    Arab Spring, 251
    conquest by Napoleon, 229
Eliade, Mircea, 2, 82, 90, 142–53, 159, 161, 168, 230
    ahistorical approach, 143, 149, 152–3
    biography, 150, 152
    creative hermeneutics, 143, 144, 147
    on "doctor knows best," 144
    exile, 152
    and fascism, 151–2
    and Freudian ideas, 143–5
    Homo religiosus concept see Homo religiosus
    Indian spirituality, 142, 148
    intuition, 143, 144, 147, 151, 153
    methodology, 143–4
    novelist, 143, 148
    phenomenology of religion, 147
    psychology of religion, 143–4
    on religious experience, 145, 157
    on Romanian folk-spirit, 150
    on sex, 191
    on shamanism, 161
    on "timeless time," 146–7, 157, 218
    works: Autobiography, 151; Forbidden Forest,
        The, 148–9, 152; Mademoiselle Christina, 149;
        Salazar şi Revoluţia in Portugalia, 152;
        Serpent, The, 149
eliminationism, post-modern, 232–4,
    243, 244
Ellis, Henry Havelock, 125
empathy, 84, 85, 96, 126
    as methodology, 25, 89, 119, 120, 126, 135, 143, 198, 203
    and post-colonial thinking, 203, 216
    see also under phenomenology of religion
Encyclopedia Britannica, 59
Enlightenment
    French, 133, 151
    ideal of abstract humanity, 40
    and individualism, 133
    rationalism, 230
    social reformers, 183
    values of, 131, 133, 160, 236
environment, natural
    human control of, 66, 78

    nostalgia for, 35, 39
    and surpluses, 100
epistemology
    post-modern, 163, 202–3
    of the sacred, 147, 149, 202–3
epochē, practice of, 81, 89, 95
eternity, 146–7
    as haven, 149
ethnography, 23, 83
    as critical methodology, 55–6, 203
Eucharist, Christian, 251–2
    in early church, 251–2
    as "sacrifice," 61, 217, 251
eunuchs, 116–17
Europe
    Aryans, 210; see also Aryanism
    colonialism see Western colonialism
    communism, 159, 244; see also Marx, Karl; Marxism
    early modern, vii, 9–10, 12–14, 15, 20
    imperialism see imperialism
    languages, 36–7, 38, 40
    medieval, 85–6, 208, 246
    and the New World, 12, 13–14, 225
    nineteenth-century, 36–40, 46, 48, 51, 79
    paganism, 69, 72
    prehistoric, 6, 48, 49, 52, 210–11
    Protestant Reformation see Protestant Reformation
    religious wars, 14, 38
    South Pacific voyages, 100
evolutionism, 48, 50, 55, 171–2
    Darwin's theory see Darwin, Charles
    and phenomenology of religion, 78
    racist basis for, 171
    religious see religious evolutionism
    and Tylor, 48, 50–1, 65–6
Exodus liberation theme, 224–5, 227

fascism, 151–2
    of everyday life (Foucault), 161
feasting, sacrificial, 61–2, 67, 112–13, 138
    and totemism, 139
feminism, 38, 116, 181, 248
    complexity, 191–2
    and gendered language, 190, 197
    methodology, 201, 213
    moral basis for, 196
    and religious theorizing, 189–213
    see also goddess religion; thealogy
fieldwork see ethnography
Fisk University, Nashville, 174–5
Fiske, John, 42
Fitzgerald, Tim, 244
Ford, Henry, 97, 98
Ford Motors, 97, 98
Foucault, Michel, 158–64, 168
    academic career, 159

alienation, 159
and Black scholarship, 177
classification, 221–2, 223–4
culturalism, 221–2
eclipse of Marxism, 220, 221
fatalism, 163, 179
homosexuality, 159
imagery, 222
on the Panopticon, 160
on politics, 246
and post-colonial thinking, 219, 220, 221–2
on power, 159–61, 183, 205, 206, 221–2
and science, 221–2
secularism, 179
works: *Discipline and Punish*, 160; *History of
Sexuality, The*, 159; *Madness and Civilization*,
160
France, 132–3
Dreyfus Affair, 130, 132, 133–4
republican tradition, 133
Francis of Assisi, 233
Franklin, Benjamin, 97
Frazer, James, 59, 65–73, 111, 113, 210
biography, 65–6
Calvinism, 65
and Christian exclusivism, 70–3, 113
comparative study of religion, 70–1, 78
on goddess worship, 113, 116, 210
Golden Bough see *Golden Bough*
and Hume, 65
influence of Tylor, 65
on magic, 67, 218
methodology, 69, 70–1
and Robertson Smith, 65–6
on technology, 66–8
French Revolution, 131, 133, 138
Freud, Sigmund, 6, 83, 86, 106–17, 163, 165
as doctor, 157
influence of Frazer and Robertson
Smith, 111
Oedipus complex, 112
originality, 110, 113
psychoanalysis see psychoanalysis, Freudian
on religious experience, 107–8, 118
on repression, 109–10
on the self, 110–11
on sexual gratification, 106
on the unconscious, 109–10
on wish-fulfillment, 123
works: *Civilization and its Discontents*, 111; *Future
of an Illusion, The*, 135; *Interpretation of Dreams,
The*, 109; *Moses and Monotheism*, 111; *Totem and
Taboo*, 111, 125
Frodo to Jesus of Nazareth, 21
functionalism, Malinowski's, 119, 120, 122, 123
funeral rites, 108, 123

Galli priests, 116
Gandhi, Mohandas K. (Mahatma), 219
Geertz, Clifford, 96, 235
gender, *see* sex
Genesis, book of, 15–16, 22
and sex, 194
German Idealism, 37, 41
Germany
Aryanism, 40–1
Catholicism, 99, 100
colonialism, 66
development of biblical criticism, 29, 34
Indology, 40–1
liberal Protestantism, 56, 61
national identity, 40
Nazism, 151, 152
nineteenth-century, 23, 56, 99, 174
threat to France, 133, 137
Gibb, Sir Hamilton, 227
Gilligan, Carol, 192
Gimbutas, Marija, 38, 190, 210
and ancient matriarchy, 210–11
globalization, 231, 246
religion in, 246
victims, 2
Gnostic gospels, 25, 26
Goblet d'Alviella, Comte Eugène, 77, 78, 82
goddess religion, 38, 115–17, 140, 190, 196, 197,
209–10
and castration, 116–17
fertility/motherhood, 70, 72, 113, 115–16
Freudian analysis, 113
link with Marian cult, 72, 113–14, 115
in Old Europe, 210–11
Vedic, 39, 41
Golden Bough, The (Frazer), 65, 66, 67, 68, 87
Attis myth, 72–3, 113
Balder myth, 68–9
as encyclopedia, 68
popularity of, 68
purpose of, 70–1
Gospel of Matthew, 24, 28, 63
gospels, 72, 251
Gnostic, 25, 26, 41
inclusion in New Testament, 26
as myths, 251
non-canonical, 26
stories of Jesus, 21–2, 113, 251
and women, 26
see also Bible
Gramsci, Antonio, 221, 231
Grapard, Allan, 161–2, 163
Greek mythology, 21, 70, 72–3, 112, 113
see also ancient Greece
Green, Garrett, 166
Gross, Rita, 204

Haiti, 201
  see also Vodou, Haitian
Haley, Alex, 177
  Roots, 177
Hart, William D., 181, 183, 225
Harvey, Van A., 20
Hegel, Georg Wilhelm Friedrich, 27
Herbert of Cherbury, Edward, 1st Baron, 16–18, 19,
    23, 247
  "ambidextrous theory," 17
  and confessionalism, 17
  De Veritate, 17
  and English Civil Wars, 17
  and Francis Bacon, 17
  methodology, 17–18
  Natural Religion, 16–17, 18, 23
hermeneutics, 19, 24–5, 83
  and dreams, 109
  methodology, 24–5, 143
Higher Criticism, 18–29, 34, 191
  and the Black church, 177
  effect of, 26, 28–9, 34, 55
  feminist, 204
  methodology, 22, 24, 25–8, 33–4
  suppression of, 24, 56
Higher Education Act, 1876 (Holland), 79, 80, 89
Hinduism, 29, 231
  Bengali, 230
  concept of *dharma*, 217
  cosmology, 236
  Krishna *see* Krishna
  meditation, 145
  monism, 142
  and nature, 40
  resistance to colonialism, 236
  sacred spaces, 145
  scriptures, 87, 252
  see also Vedic religion
Hindutva theorists, 231
history
  and Black religion, 182, 184
  imaginary, 217
  of languages, 40–2
  and racism, 177–8
  as science, 21, 22, 61, 63, 151
  source of terror, 149, 152–3
  study of, 143
  of texts, 18–29
Homo religiosus
  Eliade's concept, 145
  feminist criticism, 167, 190–1, 196
homosexuality, vii–viii, 159, 227
  and HIV/AIDS, 159
Hook, Sidney, 95
Hottentot people *see* Khoisan of southern Africa
Hubert, Henri, 91, 132

human sacrifice, 14, 52, 69, 70, 111, 139, 217
human sciences, 51, 180
humanism, 14, 126
  atheistic, 120
  and Black religious studies, 180
  contrast with theology, 180
  Dilthey, 126
  empathetic, 120
  and Freud, 110
  and Malinowski, 125–6
  methods of study, 17, 21, 22, 24, 27, 29, 36, 59–60;
    see also biblical criticism
  religious, 28
Hume, David, 18, 22–3, 35
  Natural History of Religion, 22–3
Huntington, Henry, 98

iconography, 77, 151
immigrant religion, 245
immortality, 123
  aspiration, 82, 119, 124
  belief in, 123–4, 129
imperialism, 38, 61, 164, 220
  definition, 239
  language of, 229
  post-colonial critiques, 221, 227–8
  see also Western colonialism
India
  caste system, 231
  colonial, 231, 236
  religious texts, 29, 36
  spiritualization of politics, 219
  Western romantic ideas of, 231
  see also Aryanism; Hinduism; Vedic religion
individualism, 151, 159
  capitalist, 130
  defense of, 133–4, 137
  divisiveness, 133
  economic, 133
  as a religion, 134, 150, 245
  social, 133–4
  suppression of, 134, 137
  Western, 159, 230
Indo-European culture, 36–8, 40–3, 190, 210
  and Aryanism, 38, 40
  languages, 29, 36–7, 38, 40, 51, 143
  Max Müller's discoveries, 36–8, 41–2
  patriarchy, 37, 38, 210–11
  region of, 37
  religions, 36, 37
  ways of thought, 37–8
institutions, religious, 129, 251
Ionescu, Nae, 150, 151–2
  link with Nazis, 151
Iran, Islamic Republic of, 237, 245
  war with Iraq, 245

Isaiah, book of, 87, 108
Islam, 13, 226–8
    attitudes towards women, 197
    early, 5
    monotheism, 226–7
    as religion, 227–8, 234–5, 250
    Shia, 245
    see also Muslims; Quran

Japanese women shamans, 161–2
Jehovah's Witnesses, 242
Jesuits, 13
Jesus of Nazareth
    faith in, 21–2
    focus of biblical scholarship, 21, 26
    gendering, 195–6
    "historical," 21, 28
    incarnation, 71–2
    as "mother," 196
    pagan equivalents, 71–2
    resurrection, 252
    as sacrifice, 61
    self-denial, 252
    symbol of perfection, 61
    and women, 208
Jones, Robert Alun, 138
Jones, Sir William, 36
Josephus, Flavius, 21
Judaism, 16, 59, 226
    early, 197
    in modern Israel, 226
    "primitive," 58, 60, 62
    ritual sacrifice, 226
Jung, Carl Gustav, 143–4
Juschka, Darlene, 194

Kant, Immanuel, 132, 145
Kathedersozialisten, 173, 175, 179
Keller, Evelyn Fox, 121, 126–7, 195
Khoisan of southern Africa, 222
    colonial domination through religion, 223
Kikuyu of East Africa, 223
Kolb, Peter, 222–3
Krishna, 252
    as incarnate deity, 71–2, 87, 88, 161, 252
    lordship, 89–90
    Prince Arjuna's charioteer, 87–8
    worship, 252
Kristensen, William Brede, 81, 82–6, 107
    methodology, 82–4, 202
Kuenen, Abraham, 80
"kyriarchy," 207–8

labor
    and capitalism, 97
    Marxist view, 220

    servile, 185
    specialization, 97
    traditionalist, 101
    value of, 102
    Weber on, 97, 99
Lagarde, Paul, 29
Lake Woebegone dualism, 192, 195
    origin in Hebrew monism, 227
    as traditional sex template, 193, 194, 195, 196, 197, 198, 200
languages, 23
    comparison of, 36–7
    and cultural knowledge, 23
    history of, 36–7
    study of, 23
    translation of sacred scriptures, 23
laughter, 212, 236
Leakey, Louis, 223
Legion of the Archangel Michael, Romania, 151, 152
Lenin, Vladimir, 220
    Imperialism, 220
Lévi-Strauss, Claude, 159
Leviticus, book of, 227
liberal Protestantism, 56, 59, 61, 62
    concept of progress, 62
    and phenomenology of religion, 157
    see also theological liberalism
liberationism, 162–3, 186
    activism, 179, 186
    Black, 178, 179, 228
    feminist, 205, 208
    post-colonial, 219, 228, 237
    and post-modernism, 163, 164, 169, 205
    religious, 219
    secular, 219
    theories of, 161, 162, 163, 205
liberty, 162
    individual, 133, 151
    negative, 150, 162, 163–4, 178–9, 184, 237
    positive, 150, 162, 163–4, 176, 178–9, 197, 199, 204, 205, 213, 237
Lincoln, Bruce, 219, 220, 221, 235–7, 238
    on discourse, 235, 238
    liberationism, 237
    on subaltern resistance, 235–6
Lincoln, C. Eric, 178
linguistics, 29, 36–8, 40, 210–11, 249
Long, Charles H., 181, 182, 193
lordship, 84, 89, 208, 252–3
    see also "kyriarchy"
Luther, Martin, 103
Lutherans, 15, 58, 86, 94, 99, 103
Luxenberg, Christophe, 27
Lyell, Charles, 51
Lyotard, Jean-François, 168
    Postmodern Condition, The, 165

Malinowski, Bronislaw, 3, 66, 83, 108, 118–27, 129, 165
  behaviorism, 122, 124, 125, 126, 129, 135, 166
  biography, 119–20, 125
  "bipolarities," 119–20, 121, 125–6, 127
  and Durkheim, 122, 135
  ethnography, 119, 121, 123
  and Frazer, 119
  and Freud, 118–19, 122–3, 124–5
  methodology, 119, 126
  phenomenology, 119, 125–7
  pragmatic functionalism, 119, 120, 122, 123
  on religion as survival mechanism, 122–3
  Riddell Lectures (1931), 119, 124
  and women, 121–2
  works: Argonauts of the Western Pacific, 119, 126;
    Coral Gardens and Their Magic, 122; Sex and
    Repression in Savage Society, 125; Sexual Lives of
    Savages, The, 125
Marble, Manning, Blackwater, 178
Marett, R.R., 49
Marty, Martin, 166–7
martyrdom, 245
Marx, Karl, 95, 219–20
  on capitalism, 220
  on imperialism, 220
Marxism, 219–21
  Leninism, 220
  post-colonial critiques, 220
  and war, 220
masochistic spirituality, 198
Massachusetts, racism in, 173
Mau Mau rebellion, 223
Mauss, Marcel, 91, 132
  Gift, The, 119
Max Müller, Friedrich, 11, 29, 33, 34–43, 53
  agnosticism, 34, 41
  autobiography, 39
  comparative study of religion, 35, 43, 59
  on "families of religions," 43
  and Higher Criticism, 34
  on industrialization, 34–5, 38, 39
  liberal theology of, 34–5, 77
  linguistic study, 40–2, 51
  on mysticism, 33, 36
  on Natural Religion, 35–6, 42, 78
  opposition to, 35
  on revelation, 34, 36
  Sacred Books of the East, 34
  on Vedic religion, 40–2, 45, 210
McClennan, John F., 55
McClintock, Barbara, 126–7
McCutcheon, Russell, 157–8, 243, 246
  influence of Eliade, 243
  works: Manufacturing Religion, 243; "'Religion'
    and the Citizen's Unrequited Desires," 243
Mead, Margaret, 190, 200

medieval Europe, 85–6, 208, 246
  Christianity, 198–9, 233, 238
  women, 198–9
Meir, Golda, 225
Melanesia, 125
mental health, 160, 221–2
  asylums, 160
Mentzel, Otto Friedrich, 222
Mexico
  ethnographic studies in, 14, 45, 47, 53, 78, 120
  European conquest, 13
  pre-Contact religion, 12
Milbank, John, 166
Minnesota, University of, 236
miracles, 26, 28, 113, 114, 149
missionary religion, 3, 234–5
Mithraism, 71
Molendijk, Arie, 79
monasticism, 100, 101, 103
monism, 41, 42, 142, 226–7
morality, 18, 110
  Christian, 179
  different forms of, 9
  feminist, 196
  and manifest evil, 164
  origins of, 60
  religion as, 60, 62, 86, 88
  spiritual, 60
Mormonism, 242
Muhammad, founder of Islam, 16
Muslims
  Black, 178, 184
  conflict between Sunni and Shia, 242
  leadership of, 5
  and social action, 250
mysticism
  as escapism, 149
  Indian, 142
  and knowledge, 162
  Romantic, 39–40, 41, 42
  transcendental, 151
  as unifying religious force, 36, 41
myth, 21, 28
  creation, 146
  Freudian slant on, 112–13
  gospels as, 251
  of life and death, 68–70, 71, 113
  of parricide, 111, 112, 115
  as resistance, 236
  as survival tool, 119
  use in The Golden Bough, 68–71
  see also Norse myths

Nation of Islam, 178
nationalism, 40, 151
  as religious phenomenon, 131, 132

Native Americans, 225
  miscalled "Indians," 217
  religions, 12, 13–14, 59
Natural Religion, 6, 10–12, 35, 60, 71, 165, 247
  as response to events, 12, 15
  and revelation, 11, 17
  tenets of, 17, 71, 79
  as universal religion, 15, 17, 35–6, 42, 79
natural sciences, 10, 80
  methodology, 17
  and religion, 10, 81
  see also social sciences
nature, study of, 80
naturism, 11, 41
Nazi Party, 151, 152
Nemi, Italy, 65, 69, 87
  priest-kings, 70, 111
neo-colonialism, 239
Neolithic culture, 2, 211
neo-primitivism, 139
neutrality, scholarly, 163, 216
  on liberty, 219
  on religion, 17, 27, 89, 205, 217, 228
  on sex, 167, 190, 191
  teaching, 167
  on textual criticism, 24
new religious movements (NRMs), 96
New World, the
  competition for dominance, 13
  discovery of, 12–14, 217
  religions see under Native Americans
New World Disorder, post-Cold War, 244
  religious affiliations in, 244–5
New York City
  electric light in, 66
  intellectuals, 121, 227
  journals, 195, 227
New York Times, 195
Noel, James Anthony, 183
Norse myths, 68–70

Oedipus complex, 112, 115, 116
  criticism, 118, 125
Old Europe, 210–11
ordination, of women, 195–6
orientalism, 222, 224, 227, 228–30
  and imperialism, 227, 228–9
  and Islam, 227
  prejudice, 227–8
  see also "Otherness"; Said, Edward
Orsi, Robert, 164, 218
Orthodox Christianity, 113–14, 195, 251
"Otherness," 216, 229–30
  encounters with, 88, 200, 203
  and feminism, 237
  identification with, 200, 237

and imperialism, 229, 237
objectification, 12, 13
post-colonial, 169, 216, 218, 232, 237
religious, 14, 39, 200, 203, 237–8
stereotypes, 237
other-worldliness
  monastic, 97, 98, 117
  myths, 119
Otto, Rudolf, 86–8, 158, 250
  and autonomy of religion, 86
  Idea of the Holy, The, 86
  on numinous experience, 87, 103, 107, 211, 250
Oxford, UK, 36
  Anglican establishment, 35
  see also University of Oxford

paganism, 66
  in Christianity, 71
  as religious template, 58, 66
  see also "primitive" culture/religion
Pagels, Elaine, 26
Paine, Tom, 11, 12
Pakistan, 234, 235
Palestinian liberation, 219, 224, 225
  and Islam, 227
Panopticon, the, 160
pantheism, 41
Paradise, idea of, 15, 185
parenting, Freudian analysis of, 111–12,
  114–15
patriarchy, 37–8, 93, 204–5
  and battle of the sexes, 204
  effects of, 204–5
  and objectivism, 202
  in religion, 189, 190, 194–5, 196, 197, 209–10
  temporary nature proposed, 211
phenomenology of religion, 25, 77–91, 126, 147–8,
  157, 249–50
  classification, 90–1, 96, 250
  and Dutch university system, 79–80
  and dynamism, 90, 250–1
  empathetic approach, 83, 84, 96, 147, 203
  insider point of view, 83–4, 96, 107–8, 148, 166,
    202–3, 231
  modern, 249–50
  Natural Religion, 79
  opposition, 107
  and philology, 23, 41
philology, 20, 23, 41, 143
philosophy, 238
  Aryan, 42
  compared with religion, 84
  Durkheim, 130, 131, 132, 151
  Eliade, 150–1
  Frazer, 65
  German Idealist, 37

philosophy (*cont'd*)
  Indian, 41
  and linguistic analysis, 249
  Max Müller, 42
philosophy of history, 27
philosophy of religion, 218, 249
philosophy of science, 84, 120
Pietism, 102
Pilgrim Fathers, 13, 225
Pinn, Anthony, 172, 182
  Black religious essentialism, 183
  criticisms of, 183
  and Eliade, 181, 183
  religion of suffering, 182
  works: *Terror and Triumph*, 182; *Why Lord?*,
    182
Plaskow, Judith, 204, 206
polytheism, 23, 42, 78
  as first religion, 35, 41
Popper, Karl, 84
post-colonial thinking, 216–38
  aims, 216–17
  antipathy to religion, 223, 227–8
  and classification, 221–2, 223–4
  ethnography, 245
  influence of Foucault, 221–2, 227
  liberationist, 219, 228
  and Marxism, 220–1
  and modernism, 221
  origins, 219
post-modernism, viii, 157–69, 241–4, 248
  bias against religion, 228
  critical study of religion, viii, 2, 241, 243
  criticism of, 167, 168
  elimination of religion, 232–4, 243, 244
  as historical epoch, 165
  methodology, 166
  as mode of discourse, 165–6
  objectivity and subjectivity, 157, 163–4,
    165–6
  opposition to modernism, 167–8, 176–7
  relativism, 205
  theologizing, 166–7, 205
post-structuralism, 166
power, political, 160–1
  as dynamic energy, 161
  Foucault's theories *see under* Foucault
  of men over women, 206–7
  and race, 172
  and the state, 161
power, ubiquitous (Foucault), 221
prayer, 84–5
  Islamic, 250
  and lordship, 85, 252
  positions, 84–5

  styles, 85
  unanswered, 67
predestination, 103, 251
prehistoric cultures, 49, 51, 52
  see also Neolithic culture; "primitive" culture/
    religion
presence, religions of, 164–5, 218
priesthood, 70
  celibacy, 251–2
  and ritual, 59, 61, 70, 251
"primitive" culture/religion, 28–9, 45–6, 52, 78–9, 113,
    137, 233
  beliefs, 46
  distinction from "modern," 165, 168, 221, 226, 229
  Durkheimian views, 90–1
  and evolutionism, 113, 138, 165, 218
  Frazer's views, 78–9, 113
  living, 45, 51, 52, 83, 136–7
  nature of, 137
  prejudice against, 164
  racist discourse, 171
  ritual, 139
  Robertson Smith's views, 58, 62, 63
  social cohesion, 137
  Tylor's views *see under* Tylor
  see also racism; religious evolutionism
prison reform, 160, 223
progressive evolution, 2, 34, 48
  Protestant belief in, 49
  see also religious evolutionism
Protestant Reformation, 12, 62, 95
  and economics, 95
  and Wars of Religion, 14
  see also Calvinism; Lutherans; Quakers
psychoanalysis, Freudian, 108–16, 157
  father–son conflict, 111–12
  id and superego, 110, 115, 144
  origins of, 108–9
  projection, 115
  religion, 116
  and repression, 109–10, 112, 116
  as science, 108–9
  as therapy, 108
  unconscious, 109–10, 112, 113, 115, 116, 124,
    129, 144–5
psychology of religion, 107
  archetypes, 143–4
  behaviorist, 108
  mentalist, 107

Quakers, 47
quotidian activities, 9, 201
Quran, the, 16
  critical study of, 27, 55
  as revelation, 11, 38

Raboteau, Albert, 172, 180, 184, 185
  Black religion likened to Russian Orthodoxy, 172
  works: *Slave Religion*, 184, 185; *Sorrowful Joy*, 185
race, 186n1
  socio-cultural construct, 186n1
  and theories of religion, 171–86, 186n1
  see also color
racism, color-conscious, 171–7
  American, 173, 175, 176–7, 179
  language of, 229
  and myth, 177
  and primitivism, 171
  resistance to science, 176
  see also anti-Semitism
Rashke, Carl, 165
reductionism, 83, 84, 86, 107, 134, 147
religion, concept of, vii, 232–4, 243–7
religion, nature of, vii, viii, 18, 52, 165, 245, 249, 250
  and citizenship, 245
  dynamism, 90, 250–1
  as human universal, 172, 245
Religion journal, 250
religious evolutionism, 57–9, 62, 67, 71, 78–9
  as certainty, 77
  criticisms of, 78–9
  and phenomenology, 78–85
  reductionist, 78, 137
  Tylor, 49–51, 55
religious exceptionalism, 38–9
religious experience, 6, 82, 86–7
  autonomy of, 118
  as driver of theory, 36, 103
  and mystery, 87, 129–30, 211–12
  Ninian Smart, 90, 157, 249
  pagan, 212
  pragmatic critiques of, 119
  Rudolf Otto, 82, 86–8
  shamanic, 161
  shaped by power, 161
  social causality, 129, 134
  in time and space, 145
religious pluralism, 17
religious sites *see* sacred centers
religious studies, ix, 95, 111, 144, 158, 159, 243–7
  autonomy of religion, 157
  and biblical criticism, 22, 29, 55
  Black, 180, 181–2, 185–6
  community, 247–8
  and concepts, 239, 243–6
  differentiated from theology, 166, 169, 205, 246
  divisions, 204
  ethnocentrism, 230, 233
  feminist, 190, 191–2, 197, 199, 205, 209
  and Foucault, 222
  founders, 2, 10, 14, 15–16, 33, 77

  importance of, 244–6
  and liberal morality, 228
  liberationist, 161, 163; *see also* liberationism
  orientalism, 230
  post-colonial, 217, 221, 228
  post-modern, viii, 167, 205, 243–6
  prophetic voices, 198
  purpose of, 167, 206, 243
  scientific discipline, 222, 243
  teaching, 167
  theologizing, 166–7, 205
  thinkers, 192–3, 230, 235, 239
  women scholars *see under* women
  see also critical studies of religion; theories of
    religion
religious wars, 14, 242, 245
  miscalled "ethnic conflicts," 242
Remonstrants, 80, 81–2
Renaissance, 14
  and religion, 9–10
  skepticism, 9–10, 11, 19
  see also Bodin, Jean; Herbert of Cherbury
Renan, Ernest, 21, 24, 28
Renouvier, Charles, 132
revelation, 11, 24
  divine, 2, 10, 16, 27, 62, 161
  and Natural Religion, 11–12
  primordial, 82
  in sacred texts, 11, 34, 38, 57
  see also religious experience
ritual
  Christian, 59, 61
  essential feature of religion, 63, 138
  Jewish, 61, 62
  see also sacrifice
Robertson, Revd Pat, 234
Robertson Smith, William, 6, 20, 29, 55–63, 86,
    230, 235
  as Abdullah Effendi, 57
  biography, 56–9
  Calvinism, 56, 62
  ethnography, 58–61
  heresy charges, 57
  on Natural Religion, 60
  on religious evolution, 58, 60–2, 221
  ritual as original religion, 138
  on scripture, 21, 26, 56–7, 221
  and Wellhausen, 56, 59, 62
  works: *Kinship and Marriage in Early Arabia*, 58;
    Lectures on the Religion of Semites, 59–60, 137
Rolland, Romain, 107
Roman Catholicism
  accepts Aristotle's view of women as incomplete
    men, 196
  asceticism, 125

Roman Catholicism (*cont'd*)
   authoritarianism, 133
   and capitalism, 100
   celibacy for priests, 251
   collectivism, 133
   Eastern Rite *see* Eastern Rite Catholicism
   eucharistic "sacrifice," 61, 217, 251
   Italian American, 164
   Mexican, 47, 78
   priestly ritual, 59, 61, 251
   role of women, 5, 195–6
   and superstition, 164
   and traditionalism, 101
   Tylor's critique, 47, 78, 221
   see also Virgin Mary, cult of
Romania
   in Eliade's novels, 148, 149
   folk-spirit, 150–1
   Iron Guard, 151
   twentieth-century history, 149, 150–1, 152–3
Romanticism, 11, 39–40
   and German nationalism, 40
Rome *see* ancient Rome
Romney, Mitt, 242
Ruether, Rosemary Radford, 190, 197, 211, 213
Russian Empire, 172, 185
   as first socialist state *see* Soviet Union

sacred centers, 145–6
   nostalgia for, 146
sacred spaces, 145
   see also architecture, religious
sacrifice, 111, 112–13, 138–9
   animal, 61, 111, 112, 139–40
   as atonement, 61
   as bribe, 67
   Durkheim's discussion of, 138–40
   as evidence of the "primitive," 60, 61–2
   and feasting *see* feasting, sacrificial
   human *see* human sacrifice
   in Islam, 245
   and taboo, 111
   totemic, 139–40
Sahlins, Marshall, 100
Said, Edward, 224–30
   bias against religion, 228
   biography, 224
   Canaanites, 224–6
   chief post-colonial theorist, 219
   exile, 224
   on Exodus story, 225
   influence of Foucault, 222, 229, 232
   on monotheism, 226–7
   Orientalism, 224, 228–9, 232
   and "orientalists," 222, 224, 228–30, 237

   Palestinian heritage, 224–6
   and Walzer, 224–6, 227
Salazar, António de Oliveira, 152
Sanskrit, 36–7, 40
   see also Vedic religion
Schleiermacher, Friedrich, 24–5
Schmoller, Gustav von, 173, 175
Scholten, Jan Hendrik, 80, 81–2
Schüssler-Fiorenza, Elisabeth, 190, 205
   influence of, 209
   In Memory of Her, 206
   kyriarchy, 191
   methodology, 207
   and New Testament patriarchy, 206–7
   reform of Christianity, 209, 213
science, 51, 56, 80–1, 126–7
   historical *see under* history
   methodology, 221–2
   natural *see* natural sciences
   and sex and gender, 202
Science du Judaïsme, 131
"science of religion," 4, 35–6, 52, 79, 80, 186
   and evolutionism, 80
   methodology, 80
   and phenomenology of religion, 80
   post-modern rejection of, 166, 243–4
scriptures, religious, 11, 28–9
   critical study of, 18–29, 35–7, 55
   see also Bible; gospels: non-canonical; Higher
      Criticism; India: religious texts; Quran
secularism, 34–5, 179, 219
secularization, 142–3
self-mutilation, 116–17
Semites, 56, 57, 58
   ancient religion of, 55, 58, 59–60, 131,
      137, 138
   language, 43
   sacrificial feasts, 111, 138, 139
sex
   and academic careers, 120, 121–2, 166
   conflation with gender, 190, 193–4, 196–7, 207
   cosmologies, 93
   and dress, 116–17
   essentialism, 194
   ideology, 194, 201–2
   and religion, 2, 38, 113, 162, 167, 189–90
   and science, 126–7
   socialization, 127
   stereotyping, 194–5
   transsexuals, 116, 193
sexuality, viii, 116
   Foucault, 159
   Weber, 106
   see also homosexuality; transgendering; transsexuals
Shakers, 5

shared humanity, 171
Simon, Richard, 21, 24
skepticism, 9–10, 11, 19, 34
slave religion, 172, 174, 178, 182, 184–5
  compared with Russian "serf religion," 185
slavery, 172, 178
  racial terror, 182
  and religion *see* slave religion
  resistance, 178
  rituals, 182, 183
Smart, Ninian, 43, 90, 157, 249–53
  academic background, 249
  comparative study of religion, 249
  "dialectical phenomenology," 249
  influence of Wittgenstein, 249
  institutional development, 250
  Reasons and Faiths, 249
Smith, Brian K., 231
Smith, J.Z., 157
Smith, Wilfred Cantwell, 157, 233
social evolution *see* progressive evolution
social sciences, 20, 21, 96, 160
social values, 133, 134, 164
Socrates, 241
Sontag, Susan, 152
South Africa, Republic of, 171, 222–3, 224–5
  see also apartheid
southern Africa, 222–3
Soviet Union, 220
Sozzini, Fausto, 21
Spinoza, Baruch, 21, 24, 26–7
  influence on Higher Criticism, 27
Spivak, Gayatri, 219, 222, 228, 230–1
  bias against religion, 228
  biography, 230
  challenge to objectivism, 231
  feminism, 230–1, 237
  Hinduism, 230, 231
  influence of Derrida, 230
  influence of Foucault, 231
  subaltern, idea of, 230–1, 237
  works: "Can the Subaltern Speak?," 230; *Chotti Mundi and His Arrow*, 230; *Other Asias*, 230; *Song for Kali*, 230; "Subaltern Studies," 230
Stampp, Kenneth M., 172
  Peculiar Institution, The, 172, 177
Strauss, David Friedrich, 20, 28, 94
  Life of Jesus, 28
Strenski, Ivan
  "Religion in Globalization," 246
  Why Politics Can't Be Freed from Religion, 246
subaltern groups, 230–1, 235–6
suicide, 130, 133, 137, 138, 175
suicide bombers, 245
sun worship, 37

superstition, 108, 218, 238
  association with religion, 34, 164
  liberation from, 50, 164
surrealism, 144
symbols, 72, 109, 111, 112, 144, 145–6
  Balder myth, 68–9
  Christian, 21, 61
  Cosmic Tree, 145
  meaning of, 147

taboos, 56, 111
Taoism, 118, 234
Taves, Ann, 205–6
technology
  comparative, 52–3
  control of nature, 35, 67
  primitive, 49, 50, 52, 67, 88
  metaphor of progress, 50, 66
  negative aspects, 34–5
  superior status, 66, 67–8
  and Western exceptionalism, 38, 66
thealogy, 197–8, 209, 211
theological liberalism, 34–5, 79, 157
theories of religion, 157, 241–2, 247–8, 253
  Black, 180, 183
  contexts, 12, 23
  and culturalism, 234
  dialectic in, 2, 3, 23, 27
  dominance of Protestantism, 232
  Eurocentric, 4, 29, 229, 232, 233, 238, 239
  feminist, 194–213
  non-cognitive, 63, 138, 232, 233, 235, 238
  objectivity, 5, 157, 201
  and philosophy, 23, 37, 42, 217, 238, 249
  post-colonial, 216–41; *see also* post-colonial thinking
  post-secular, 237
  production of, 1–3, 247
  and race/color, 171–3, 183
  and sex, 190
  study of, 3, 5
  terminology, 233–4, 237–8, 241, 244
  themes, 2–3, 4–6
  see also individual theorists
Theravada Buddhism, 234
thought experiments, 217–18, 242
Tiele, Cornelius P., 78, 80
  Elements of the Science of Religion, 4, 81
  and evolutionism, 81
  History of the Egyptian Religion, 78
  and Natural Religion, 82
  religious morphology, 80, 81
  as Remonstrant, 81–2
time, 146–7
totemism, 111, 112, 138
transgendering, 194

transsexuals, 116, 194
Treitschke, Heinrich von, 173, 175
Troeltsch, Ernst, 20
Tübingen School, 24, 27–8
Tuchman, Barbara, 225
Tudor England, 14
Tweed, Tom, 161
Tylor, Edward Burnett, 2, 29, 36, 45–53
   and animism, 45–7, 233
   and anthropology, 45, 51, 53, 55
   attitude to primitive culture, 2, 45, 46, 47, 48, 49,
      50–1, 52, 66, 78, 218
   debt to Lyell, 51, 52
   on empiricism, 45–6
   and mainstream Christianity, 47–8, 49, 78, 221
   racist theorizing, 171
   reductionism, 84
   "theory of survivals," 48, 51, 77, 123
   works: *Anahuac*, 45, 47, 53, 218; *Anthropology*, 84;
      Religion in Primitive Culture, 45, 65

Union of Free Believers, 134, 135, 138
Union of Free Thinkers, 134, 135, 138
University of Lancaster, 250
University of Leiden, 80, 81
University of Oxford
   Max Müller, 29, 35, 36
   Smart, 249
   Tylor, 29, 45, 47

van der Leeuw, Gerardus, 81, 86, 88–90, 250
   anatomy of religion, 88–9, 90, 250
   methodology, 89
   Religion in Essence and Manifestation, 89
Vedic religion, 29, 37, 40–1, 45
   and Aryanism, 41, 210
   and Natural Religion, 39
Vernes, Maurice, 78
Virgin Mary, cult of, 72, 107, 113–14
   Freudian analysis, 114–17, 252
   and goddess Cybele, 113, 117
   origins, 114–16, 252
vitalism, 67, 73
vocation, 103
Vodou, Haitian, 197, 200–3, 213
   "marriage" to a god, 202–3

Wagner, Adolf, 173, 175
Walzer, Michael, 224–6, 227
   Exodus and Revolution, 224–5

Wayne, Helena, 121
Weber, Max, 86, 93–104, 110, 241, 251
   asceticism, 117
   biography, 93–4, 106–7
   Calvinism, 96, 100, 103, 104, 175–6,
      234, 242
   on capitalism, 93, 95, 96–101, 234
   comparative study of religion, 94–5
   and Lutherans, 94, 103
   methodology, 96
   Protestant Ethic and the Spirit of Capitalism, The, 94,
      95–6, 241
   on traditionalism, 100–1
   uncritical defining of religion, 96, 241
Wellhausen, Julius, 20, 29, 56, 59, 62
West, Cornel, 162, 163, 176–7, 178–81
   and Du Bois, 178, 179
   and Foucault, 179
   as "prophet," 178–9, 197
   works, 178, 180
Western colonialism, 38–9, 61, 66, 238
   continued dominance, 217
   political independence, 216–17
   repression, 223
   see also post-colonial thinking
Wiebe, Donald, 167
Wills, David W., 177
Wilmore, Gayraud S., 178, 180
   African-American Religious Studies, 178
Wimbush, Vincent L., 177
wish-fulfillment, 123, 124
Wolfart, Johannes, 167
women
   in academe, 163
   historical visibility, 199, 200
   male domination, 161, 201
   medieval, 198–9
   ordination, 195–6
   professional self-esteem, 121
   religious practitioners, 161–2, 172, 198–9,
      200–1, 207
   religious studies scholars, 189, 192–3, 197, 199,
      205, 209
   seen as incomplete men, 196
   sex stereotyping, resistance to, 198
   see also feminism; sex
work *see* labor

Young, Robert J.C., 216, 218–19
Yugoslavia, breakdown of, 244

CPSIA information can be obtained
at www.ICGtesting.com
Printed in the USA
LVHW100538020821
693975LV00007B/63

9 781444 330847